CHESS EVOLUTION

November 2011

By

Arkadij Naiditsch

Quality Chess
www.qualitychess.co.uk

First edition 2011 by Anuk.doo
with technical assistance from Quality Chess UK Ltd

CHESS EVOLUTION - November 2011

ISBN 978-1-907982-07-1

All sales or enquiries should be directed to Quality Chess UK Ltd,
20 Balvie Road, Milngavie, Glasgow G62 7TA, United Kingdom
Phone +44 141 333 9588
e-mail: info@qualitychess.co.uk
website: www.qualitychess.co.uk

Distributed in US and Canada by SCB Distributors, Gardena, California, US
www.scbdistributors.com

Distributed in Rest of the World by Quality Chess UK Ltd through
Sunrise Handicrafts, Smyczkowa 4/98, 20-844 Lublin, Poland

Responsible editor: Arkadij Naiditsch
Typeset by Keti Arakhamia-Grant
Proofreading by Colin McNab
Additional editing by Colin McNab, Andrew Greet & John Shaw
Cover design by Milos Sibinovic
Printed in Poland by Drukarnia Pionier, 31-983 Krakow, ul. Igolomska 12

CONTENTS

Key to symbols used

±   White is slightly better
∓   Black is slightly better
±   White is better
∓   Black is better
+−   White has a decisive advantage
−+   Black has a decisive advantage
=   equality
∞   with compensation
⇄   with counterplay
∞   unclear
↑   with initiative
→   with an attack
Δ   with the idea
□   only move

?   a weak move
??   a blunder
!   a good move
!!   an excellent move
!?   a move worth considering
?!   a move of doubtful value
mate

Editorial Preface

First, I would like to offer my apologies to readers for there being some delay to the November issue of Chess Evolution. The whole Chess Evolution team has been working as hard as possible, but the European Team Championship slowed down our work for a week, and we decided "better to have about a week of delay and still produce a 100% job".

I have tried to base the current issue on analyses from many different GMs. If this been a good idea, only our readers can judge. In the January issue we shall be going back to having fewer commentators involved.

New contributors for the November issue:
Paco Vallejo Pons – the Spanish number one.
Alexander Ipatov – a young Ukrainian-born GM, now representing Spain.
David Baramidze – a young German GM.
Yannick Gozzoli – the head of the French version of CE has finally decided to comment on some games himself. I was very positively surprised by his extremely high level of analysis!

Etienne Bacrot has written a very nice article mainly based on his own games. He has also provided great analysis of a typical rook endgame from the recent game J. Polgar – Vachier Lagrave, an ending which quite often occurs.

We have the usual puzzles section, again done by Jacob Aagaard. This time there are 24 puzzles included – in response to requests from our readers who liked the previous puzzles a lot and wanted a larger section.

As usual I hope that our readers receive a lot of new information from this issue of CE, and succeed in winning many games using the novelties given in this book!

Finally, I have to show off a little – the German Team became 2011 European Champions, with yours truly playing on board one, so reading CE brings results even at the very highest level! ☺

Arkadij Naiditsch
November 2011

Contributors

Etienne Bacrot: France, 28 years old, GM 2714, number 29 in the world. Became GM at the age of 14, a record at the time.
Six times French Champion starting from 1999.

Winner of many international events including: 2005: 1st place in Poikovsky, 3rd in Dortmund and 3rd of the World Cup in Khanty-Mansiysk. 2009: 1st in Aeroflot Open, second in Montreal and Antwerp. 2010: First equal in Gibraltar, 3rd in Nanjing and winner of Geneva Open. 2011: First equal in Basel, Geneva (rapid) and Rabat (blitz).

Yannick Gozzoli: France, 28 years old, GM 2549.

For the last few years Yannick was an extremely high-rated IM, and he recently completed the requirements for the Grandmaster title.

Sebastien Maze: France, 26 years old, GM 2577

Winner of 2008 Rabat blitz tournament, 1st equal in Marseille 2009 and Menton 2009.

Member of the French team in the Olympiad in Dresden 2008.

Was the second of Etienne Bacrot in FIDE Grand Prix Elista 2008, Dortmund 2009 and Nanjing 2010.

Kamil Miton: Poland, 27 years old, GM 2622.

World Junior U12 Champion in 1996. No 2 at the World Junior Champion (U 20).

Twice the winner (2002 and 2005) of one of the world's biggest tournaments, the World Open in Philadelphia, USA.

Arkadij Naiditsch: Germany, 26 years old, GM 2712, number 31 in the world. Became International Master at the age of 13, Grandmaster at 15.

Winner of 2005 Super-tournament in Dortmund and since 2006 the top-rated German player. In 2007 was German Champion and won the Baku Open. In 2010 Arkadij won a match against Efimenko in Mukachevo and was 1st equal in the European Rapid Championship in Warsaw.

Borki Predojevic: Bosnia and Herzegovina, 24 years old, GM 2642. Gained the GM title at the Calvia Olympiad in 2004 when he was 17. Best Elo was 2654 in September 2009. Joined the top 100 in 2007; highest place so far was 68th on the October 2007 list.

Winner of several international open tournaments including: Open Metalis in Bizovac, Croatia in 2006, Zagreb Open, Croatia in 2007, Hit Open in Nova Gorica, Slovenia in 2008, Acropolis Open in Greece 2009. in 2008, Acropolis Open in Greece 2009.

Paco Vallejo Pons: Spain, 29 years old, GM 2705, number 40 in the world.

Former child prodigy who became a grandmaster aged 16 and won the under-18 World Youth Championship in the year 2000. Has been competing at the highest levels for many years.

Ivan Sokolov: 43 years old, GM 2646 . Best world ranking on the FIDE list of 12th (several times).

Winner of many top GM events of which the most important are: Hastings, Sarajevo, Selfoss, Reykjavik, Hoogeveen, Lost Boys, Staunton Memorial. Yugoslav Champion in 1988 and Dutch Champion in 1995 and 1998. Won team gold with the Dutch team at the 2005 European Championship in Gothenburg.

A

GAME 1

▷ **P. Eljanov (2683)**
▶ **R. Ponomariov (2758)**
Governor's Cup, Saratov
Round 11, 19.10.2011 **[A13]**
Annotated by Yannick Gozzoli

This was quite a bizarre game. Eljanov went for the fashionable English/Catalan hybrid and chose the tricky 7.d3!?, which deserves serious attention. I don't know what happened in the players' minds as Ponomariov reacted with a known theoretical mistake in 7...b6?, which allows White to win material for insufficient compensation by force. But for some reason Eljanov rejected the critical 8.♘d4 in favour of the new 8.♘g5N, and a double-edged middlegame ensued. The game was balanced until Eljanov played the dubious 17.e5?! which weakened his position considerably. But Ponomariov was unable to take full advantage, and after a few inaccuracies on both sides the game ended in a draw.

Overall the game was not of great theoretical significance, apart from drawing attention to the 'refutation' of Black's play by 8.♘d4, as well as the revival of the 7.d3!? variation. Black's normal reply of 7...♗d6 has been analysed in the notes, along with the computer suggestion of 9...♘b8!?N, which seems quite interesting.

1.c4 ♘f6 2.♘f3 e6 3.g3 d5 4.♗g2 dxc4

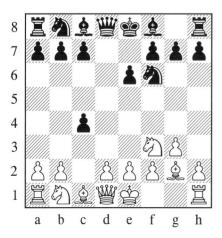

5.♕a4† ♘bd7 6.♕xc4 c5

6...a6 occurred in the game Fressinet – Bacrot, as analysed on page 292 of September's *Chess Evolution*.

7.d3!?

Quite a tricky move. White has a lot of other possibilities as well.

7.0–0

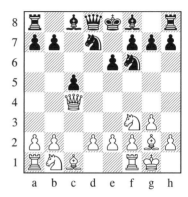

7...b6!

7...a6 is playable, but the text is the most attractive. Now, compared to the game, the queen on c4 is not protected which allows Black to get away with exposing himself on the long diagonal.

8.♘d4

8.b3 is not ambitious and Black easily gets a good position: 8...♗b7 9.♗b2 ♗e7 10.d3 a6 11.♘bd2 b5 12.♕c2 0–0= King – Korchnoi, Switzerland 1997.

8...♘e5 9.♘c6 ♘xc4 10.♘xd8

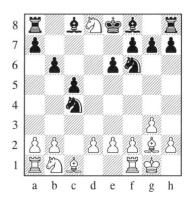

10...♘d5! 11.♘c3

White wants to use the strength of the bishop on the long diagonal.

11.d3?? ♘a5–+ leaves the knight trapped on d8.

11.♘c6?! ♗d7 12.d3 is not dangerous: 12...♗xc6 This equalizes easily. (Black can try for an advantage with 12...♘xb2!? although after 13.e4 or 13.♘e5 White's development advantage gives him decent compensation) 13.dxc4 ♘b4 14.♘c3 0–0–0 15.♗f4 ♗xg2 16.♔xg2 ♗e7= Black has no problems at all.

11...♔xd8 12.♘xd5 ♗b7 13.♘c3 ♗xg2 14.♔xg2 ♘e5

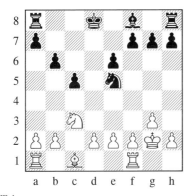

15.♖d1

Planning to open the centre in the hope of exploiting the temporary misplacement of the black king.

15.b3 ♘c6=

15...♘c6 16.d4 cxd4 17.e3 ♔c7 18.exd4 ♖d8 19.d5

19.♗e3 ♗b4=

19...exd5 20.♘xd5† ♔b7 21.♗g5 f6 22.♗e3 ♗d6

The position is equal.

7.♕b3!? ♖b8!

The safest path to equality.

7...♗d6 is less reliable. 8.0–0 0–0 Now Roiz mentions a strong idea for White: 9.a4! (9.♘c3 a6 10.a4 [10.d4!? b5 11.♘e5 cxd4 12.♗xa8 ♘xe5 13.♘e4 ♘xe4 14.♗xe4 ♘c5∞] 10...♕c7! 11.d3 b6 12.♘e5 ♗b7=

Black obtained a good game but went on to lose after pushing too hard for a win, Roiz – Naiditsch, Heidelberg 2010.)

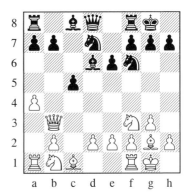

9...♖b8 Preparing ...b6, but White can thwart that idea. 10.♘a3! Threatening to go to b5. 10...a6 11.♘c4 ♗c7 12.a5± Black will have problems developing his light-squared bishop without damaging his pawn structure.

8.d3 ♗d6 9.♘c3

Compared with the note to Black's 7th move above, the plan of 9.♘a3?! is strongly countered by 9...b5! when the white knight looks stupid on the edge of the board, and 10.♘xb5?? is impossible due to 10...♕a5†–+.

9...a6 10.0–0

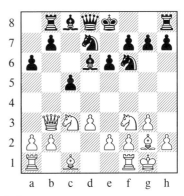

10...0–0

10...b6 11.♘d2 0–0 12.♘c4 ♗c7 13.a4 ♘e5 14.♖d1 ♗b7 15.♗xb7 ♖xb7 16.♗g5 ♘c6 17.♘d2 ♘a5 18.♕c2 h6 ½–½ Schlosser – Yusupov, Vienna 1998.

11.♗g5 b5 12.♘e4 ♗e7 13.♘xf6† ♗xf6
14.♗xf6 ♕xf6 15.♖fc1 ♗b7 16.♕c3 ♕e7
17.♘d2 ♗xg2 18.♔xg2±

Naiditsch – Efimenko, Rogaska Slatina
2011.

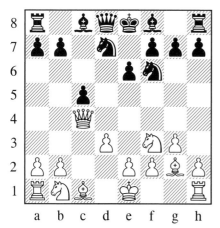

7...b6?

A really strange choice from Ponomariov,
who is known to be strong in openings (and
other areas too of course). Black's last move
has occurred in three previous games in my
database; on each occasion White has won
material in the same way, and gone on to win
the game.

Why would such a strong player make a
move which has been dismissed with a "??" by
some annotators? The first possibility is that
Ponomariov was unaware of the refutation or
mixed up his variations, but this is difficult to
believe. The alternative explanation is that he
analysed the position at home and concluded
that the critical line was okay for Black after he
gives up an exchange. However, after analysing
the variations myself I fail to see how Black
can justify the material sacrifice that his last
move entails, so Ponomariov's reasons remain
a mystery to me.

The main line is:
7...♗d6

Developing and avoiding any weakening
pawn moves for the moment.

8.a4

This has been White's highest-scoring reply.
8...0–0 9.♕b3

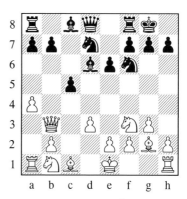

From this position a) 9...♘e5 is a solid move,
but the untested b) 9...♘b8!?N also deserves
serious attention.

a) 9...♘e5 10.♘xe5 ♗xe5 11.♘a3 ♖b8

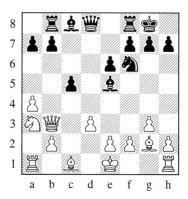

12.♘c4

12.0–0 ♘d5 13.♘c4 ♗c7 14.♘e3 ♘e7
(Black should be able to improve with
14...♘b4!? 15.♗d2 a5) 15.♕c3 b6 16.b4
gave White some initiative in Hauchard –
Kiselev, Bucharest 1993.
12...♗c7 13.♕a3 b6 14.b4 cxb4 15.♕xb4 e5
16.0–0 ♗g4

½–½ Lputian – Ivanchuk, Batumi 1999.

b) 9...♘b8!?N

This computer move is not as stupid as
it looks. The black knight will go to its

'rightful' home on c6 and then Black will play ...e5.

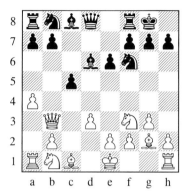

10.♘a3 ♘c6 11.♘c4 e5 12.0–0 ♖b8 13.♗e3
   13.a5   h6   14.♗e3   ♗e6   15.♕c2   ♘d5
   16.♘xd6 ♘xe3 17.fxe3 ♕xd6 18.♕c3 ♗d5=
   (18...e4!?)
13...b6 14.a5

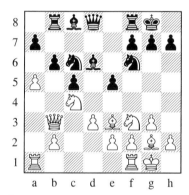

14...♗c7
   14...♘xa5!? 15.♘xa5 bxa5 16.♕a3 (16.♕c2
   ♗e6 looks fine for Black) 16...c4 17.♕xa5
   cxd3 18.exd3 ♕e7 is more or less equal.
   White should probably try 19.d4!? if he
   wants to search for some initiative.
15.axb6 axb6 16.♘a3 ♗e6 17.♕a4
   17.♕b5 ♘a5∓
17...♖a8
   17...♗d5 18.♘b5↑
18.♕h4 h6 19.♘d2 ♕d7!?
   A typical computer move! The whole idea
   is based on the bad position of the white
   queen.

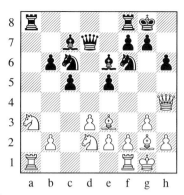

20.♗xh6
   20.♘b5 ♖xa1 21.♖xa1 ♘d4∓ is pleasant for
   Black.
20...♘d5 21.♗xd5
   21.♗g5 ♘d4!? gives Black promising play.
21...♗xd5 22.♗xg7=
The game will shortly end in perpetual check.

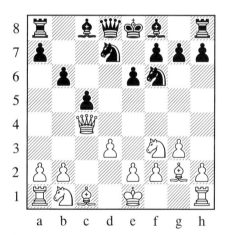

8.♘g5?!N
What a surprise from Eljanov! He decides
against 'refuting' Black's last move, and goes
for something that has never previously been
tested. His chosen move is not bad in itself,
but it fails to punish Black's last move in the
way it deserved.

8.♘d4!
This is the critical test, and I have not been
able to find a good reason for White not to play
it. Black can reply with a) 8...♘d5 or b) 8...♘e5.

a) 8...♘d5

This move is interesting, but the tactics work out in White's favour.

9.♗xd5 ♘e5 10.♕a4†

But not 10.♘c6?? exd5! 11.♘xd8 dxc4–+ and the knight is trapped.

10...♗d7

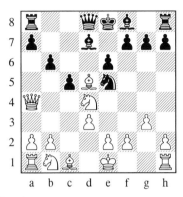

11.♘xe6!

This simple blow wins a pawn. Other moves turn out badly for White:

11.♗c6? ♘xc6 12.♘xc6 ♕c7∓

11.♕b3?! exd5 12.♕xd5 ♘xd3†! 13.exd3 cxd4 14.0–0 (14.♕xd4?! would be met by the simple 14...♗c6 15.♕xd8† ♖xd8 16.0–0 ♖xd3∓) 14...♗e7 15.♕xd4 0–0 16.♘c3 ♗h3 17.♕xd8 ♖axd8∓ is also slightly better for Black.

11...♗xa4

11...fxe6 12.♕e4! exd5 13.♕xe5†+–

12.♘xd8 ♖xd8 13.♗g2±

Black has no compensation whatsoever.

b) In all three of the games to have been played so far, Black played:

8...♘e5 9.♘c6 ♘xc6

The point of White's 7th move can be seen after 9...♘xc4? 10.♘xd8!+– when Black has both a rook and a knight under attack.

10.♗xc6† ♗d7 11.♗xa8 ♕xa8

Here we are. The last few moves were forced, and have led us to a position where White is a full exchange up for no clear

compensation. We will need to do some digging to understand or at least to guess why Ponomariov chose the 'losing' 7...b6 move.

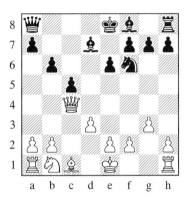

12.0–0

12.f3 has been played twice and is also good, but in my opinion there is no need to weaken the kingside structure. 12...h5!? Trying to create some counterplay, but it is not enough. (12...b5 13.♕c2 ♗e7 14.e4 0–0 15.♗e3 ♖c8 16.♘d2± Tregubov – Monin, St Petersburg 1993) 103.♘c3 h4 14.g4 ♕c6 15.a4 ♗d6

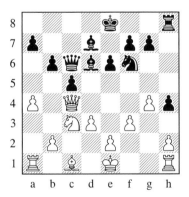

This was Sher – S. Polgar, Aarhus 1993, and now White could have played 16.♗f4!N with an almost winning position, for instance: 16...♘d5 17.♗xd6 ♕xd6 18.d4 0–0 (18...♘e3 19.dxc5 bxc5 [19...♕e5 20.♕d3 bxc5 21.♔f2+–] 20.♕e4+–) 19.♘e4 ♕f4 20.dxc5 bxc5 (20...♘e3 21.♕c1 intending ♖a3 wins) 21.♕c1±

12...h5!?

Trying to develop a kingside initiative. It is hard to suggest any other sensible plan for Black.

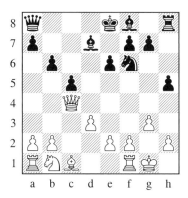

13.h4

13.♗g5!? followed by e4 and ♘d2 also gives White a clear advantage.

13...♗d6 14.♘c3±

White's moves have been good and logical. Black has no attack on the kingside and is simply an exchange down without serious compensation.

8...♖b8

Black will complete development by exchanging the strong bishop on g2, but he will still have to be careful as his queenside light squares could become weak.

9.♗f4

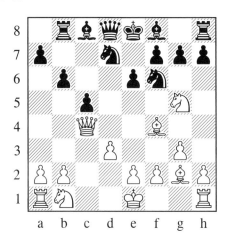

9...♗b7

Black can also consider expanding on the queenside.

9...b5!? 10.♕b3 ♖b6

Now the critical continuation is:

11.a4!?

Fighting for control of the c4-square.

11.0–0 ♗e7 12.♘f3 (12.a4?! is less effective if Black can play ...♘d5 with the bishop already on e7: 12...bxa4 [12...♘d5!?] 13.♕c2 ♘d5 14.♘h3 ♗b7 Black's position is comfortable.) 12...♘d5 13.♗d2 Black must be careful here, as White has a direct threat of ♗a5 and some positional threats such as a4 or e4. The active 13...c4∞ may be the best solution.

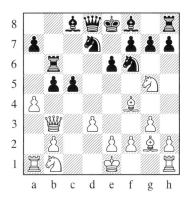

11...c4!?

11...bxa4 is less enterprising but still playable: 12.♕c2 (12.♕xa4? ♖a6 13.♕xa6 ♗xa6 14.♖xa6∓ White has active pieces and a solid structure, but a queen is still a queen!) 12...♘d5 (12...♗e7 13.♘f3 ♘d5 14.♗d2 transposes) 13.♗d2 ♗e7 14.♘f3 0–0 15.0–0 White's structure is better but Black has decent piece play and some pressure on the b-file. 15...♘b4 16.♕d1 ♗b7 17.♖xa4 White's position is preferable but Black should be able to hold.

After the text move White can choose between a) 12.dxc4 and b) 12.♕c2!?.

a) 12.dxc4

Taking the pawn is the most natural reaction.

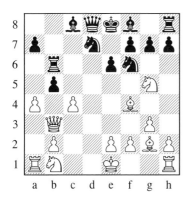

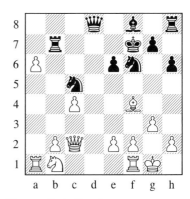

12...h6?

This is a bad move, but it was nevertheless interesting to analyse.

12...bxc4 13.♕xc4 h6∞

13.♘xf7!

This powerful sacrifice gives Black serious problems.

13.♘f3 bxc4 14.♕xc4 ♘d5 15.0–0 ♗e7 followed by ...0–0 gives Black some compensation for the pawn thanks to his pressure on the b-file.

13...♔xf7 14.axb5

White has three pawns for the piece and the a7-pawn is under attack. Moreover, Black is suffering from a serious lack of development and it is not easy to find good squares for his pieces.

14...♘c5?

This natural move only makes matters worse, as the white queen will move to a better position and the knight is not stable on c5.

14...♗b7 is the best chance although 15.0–0 ♗xg2 16.♔xg2 ♕a8† 17.f3 ♗c5 18.♕c3 still leaves White on top.

15.♕c2 a6

15...♗b7 16.♖xa7±

16.0–0 ♗b7

16...axb5 17.♖a7† ♖b7 (17...♗b7 18.b4 ♖a6 19.♖xa6 ♘xa6 20.♗xb7+–) 18.♖a8±

17.♗xb7 ♖xb7 18.bxa6!?

There is also 18.♖d1 ♕b6 19.b4± when White wins back the piece, keeping an extra pawn and a fine position.

18...♖a7 19.♘d2 ♖xa6

19...♘xa6 20.♘f3±

20.♘f3 ♖xa1 21.♘e5† ♔g8 22.♖xa1±

White's position is almost winning. However, we must not forget that Black could have avoided all this with 12...bxc4 instead of 12...h6?.

b) 12.♕c2!?

After this move Black will have to be careful in order to avoid an inferior endgame.

12...cxd3 13.♕xd3 h6 14.♘f3 bxa4 15.♘c3

White has to develop his pieces quickly if he is to have any chance of exploiting Black's temporary lack of piece coordination.

15.♖xa4 ♖xb2 gives Black a good position.

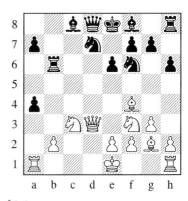

15...♗b4

Safest, although Black is still not ensured of equality.

15...♖xb2 is playable but slightly riskier: 16.♘xa4 ♖b4 (16...♕a5†? is bad: 17.♗d2

♖xd2 18.♘xd2 ♗b4 19.0–0! ♗xd2 [19...♗a6 20.♕c2 ♗xd2 21.♘b2 ♕c3 22.♖fc1!±] 20.♘b2 ♘c5 [20...♕c3 21.♕xc3 ♗xc3 22.♖ac1+–; 20...♕b4 21.♘c4 ♗g5 22.h4+–] 21.♕c2 ♕c7 [21...♕c3 22.♖fc1!+–] 22.♘d3+–) 17.0–0 ♗b7 18.♗d2 ♗e4 19.♕a6↑ White keeps some pressure due to Black's backward development.

16.0–0

16.♖xa4 can be met by 16...a5 followed by ...0–0 and ...♗b7 or ...♗a6 when Black is fine.

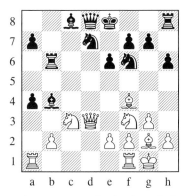

From here it is worth checking b1) 16...a5? and b2) 16...♗a6.

b1) 16...a5?

This move is a luxury that Black can ill-afford, and allows White to seize the advantage.

17.♘xa4

The point is that the rook is in some trouble.

17...♖a6

17...♗a6?! only makes things worse: 18.♕d1 ♖c6 19.♘d4! ♖c4 (19...♖c8 20.♘c6+–)

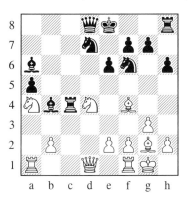

20.♘c6 ♕c8 (20...♖xc6 21.♗xc6 0–0 22.♖c1+–) 21.♘xb4 ♖xb4 (21...axb4 22.♕d6+– The black king is stuck in the centre and White plans ♖fc1 followed by b3, winning material.) 22.♖c1 ♕d8 (22...♖c4 is met by 23.♕d6+– followed by b3) 23.♗c7 ♕c8 24.♘b6 ♖xb6 25.♗xb6 ♖c4 (25...♕b8 26.♗c7 ♕c8 27.♕d6+–) 26.♖xc4 ♗xc4 27.♕d6 Threatening ♗b7. 27...♗d5 28.♖d1 It is all over, as 28...♗xg2 29.♗c5 is mating by force.

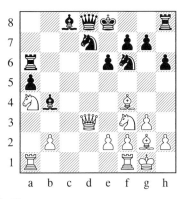

18.♘e5!

Black's position is critical. His pieces are suffering from a serious lack of coordination and he has several weak squares on the 6th rank.

18...g5!?

The only move to continue the fight.

18...♘xe5 19.♕xd8† ♔xd8 20.♗xe5± is highly unpleasant for Black. His king is unsafe, the rook on a6 can barely move, and White can easily improve his position by taking control over the c- and d-files.

19.♘xd7 ♘xd7

19...♕xd7 20.♗e5 ♖xd3 21.exd3 ♔e7 22.d4 ♖d8 23.♘c5 ♗xc5 24.dxc5± The passed c-pawn and the powerful bishop pair should decide the game in White's favour.

20.♗e3 ♖d6 21.♕b3 0–0 22.♘c3±

White keeps a clear plus due to his superior piece coordination and the opponent's numerous weaknesses.

b2) 16...♗a6

This is a much sounder move.

17.♕d4

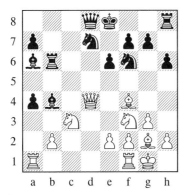

17...♗xc3

Black has some alternatives:

17...0–0? is weak and leads to a loss of material: 18.♘xa4 ♖b5 (Perhaps Black's best chance would be to give up the exchange with 18...♗xe2, but this is hardly an ideal solution either.) 19.♖fd1 Increasing the pressure on the d-file. 19...♕e7 (19...♘d5 is met by 20.e4 ♘xf4 21.gxf4 ♗c8 22.♘e5+– when Black is forced to give up the exchange on e5.) 20.♕xa7± White has an extra pawn and the better position.

17...♗c5 18.♕xa4 0–0 19.♖fd1 ♕e7 20.♘e5 ♘xe5 21.♗xe5±

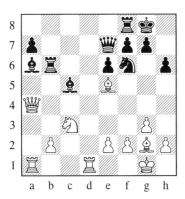

Black has chances to equalize, but White's pressure on the a- and d-files gives him a pleasant advantage.

18.bxc3

White has a passed pawn and strong pressure along the a-file and on the dark squares. But with precise play, Black should be able to equalize.

18...0–0

18...♗xe2?! is dangerous, for instance: 19.♖fe1 ♗xf3 20.♗xf3 0–0 21.♖xa4± The a7-pawn is weak, White's pieces control the board and Black has no counterplay.

19.♖xa4 ♕c8!

19...♗xe2 20.♖fe1 is analysed above.

The point of the text move is to restrain the c-pawn. The following line is not forced, but it looks logical to me.

20.c4 ♘c5 21.♖a2 ♘b3

21...♖d8!?

22.♕b2 ♘a5

After 22...♗xc4 23.♖xa7± White keeps a slight edge due to his pressure on the dark squares.

23.♕a1

A nice square for the queen, where it adds to the pressure on the a-file while keeping an eye on the a1-h8 diagonal.

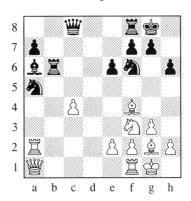

23...♘b3

23...♘xc4?! allows 24.♘e5! when White unleashes the power of his light-squared bishop: 24...♘d5 (24...♘xe5 25.♗xe5±) 25.♖c1 f6 26.♘xc4 ♗xc4 27.♖ac2 ♖c6 28.♕xa7± White is almost winning.

24.♕d1 ♗xc4

24...♕xc4?! allows White a good initiative: 25.♘e5 ♕c8 26.♘c6 ♖xc6 27.♗xc6 ♗c4 28.♗g2 a5± White has won material although converting his extra exchange will not be easy.

25.♖c2 ♕a6 26.♘e5 ♗d5 27.e4 ♗a8 28.♖e1

Black should be okay here, although White is the only one who can hope for an advantage.

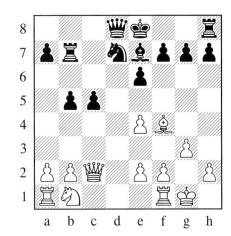

The position is more or less equal. White has a slight structural disadvantage, but he is slightly ahead in development and Black's queenside is a little loose. White can try to exploit the open d-file and the d6-square, while Black will try to advance his queenside pawns, especially with ...c4 which will free the c5-square for his pieces.

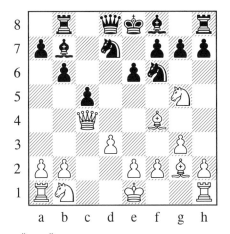

10.♘e4 ♘xe4

10...b5 11.♕c2 ♘xe4 12.♗xe4 transposes to the game. Via this move order White can also consider 12.♗xb8!? ♘xf2 13.♗xb7 (13.0–0 ♘xd3 14.♗xb7 ♕xb8 15.♗c6 ♘3e5 16.♗xd7† ♘xd7 is good for Black, as White's king is weak and his pawn structure is bad) 13...♕xb8 14.♔xf2 ♕xb7∞ although in this line Black's safer king and superior structure gives him good compensation.

11.♗xe4 b5

12...e5?! 13.♗e3 is not helping Black, whose light squares have been weakened.

Black could have considered 11...♗xe4 12.dxe4 and now 12...b5 transposing to the game. (But note that 12...♖c8? 13.♘c3± is bad for him as White has good control over the centre and light squares.)

12.♕c2 ♗xe4 13.dxe4 ♖b7 14.0–0 ♗e7

15.a4

Trying to create some weaknesses in the enemy queenside.

15...a6

15...b4? would be a huge positional mistake as it surrenders the c4-square and fixes Black's structure. After 16.♘d2± followed by ♘c4 and doubling rooks on the d-file, White has a considerable advantage.

16.♘c3 0–0 17.e5?!

This double-edged move is perhaps a bit too ambitious. White frees the e4-square for his pieces – especially his knight – and fixes an outpost on d6. On the other hand the e5-pawn could become weak and White has to watch out for the possibility of ...g5.

A sounder continuation would have been: 17.axb5 axb5 18.♖fd1

Now Black must decide where to put his

queen, as she is clearly not comfortable on the d-file.

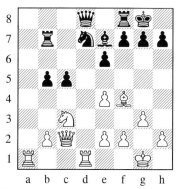

18...♕c8

18...c4? is bad: 19.♘xb5! ♖xb5 20.♖a7 ♗c5 21.♖dxd7 (21.♖axd7 ♕b6 22.e3 ♖xb2 23.♕xc4±) 21...♗xa7 (21...♕b6 22.♖ab7 ♕xb7 23.♖xb7 ♖xb7 24.♕xc4±) 22.♖xd8 ♖xd8 23.♕a4 ♗b7 24.♕a6± White will win the c4-pawn although the technical task of converting his material advantage will not be easy.

However, 18...♕b6 is playable; the queen controls the a5-square, but she is also a bit more exposed. 19.e5 Freeing the e4-square for the knight. 19...h6 Taking control over the g5-square. (19...c4!? is also possible.) 20.♘e4 c4 21.♘d6 ♖c7 22.h4 The position is close to equal, but I would take White if given the choice.

19.♖a5

Hoping to provoke the b-pawn into advancing, in order to obtain the c4-square for his knight.

19...b4?!

Not the best move, but we will analyse it to see how White's strategy might play out. Black's main problem is that he needs to involve the f8-rook in the support of his queenside pawns.

The right path is 19...♕c6! 20.♖da1 c4 21.♖a6 ♕c8 22.♖6a5 ♕c6 23.♖a6= with a draw by repetition.

20.♘b5!

20.♘b1? allows 20...e5 21.♗e3 ♕c7 22.♖a1 c4 when Black is better.

After the text move Black's position is tricky, for instance:

20...♕c6?!

This natural move gives White an opportunity to invade.

20...e5! is correct, when White's position is a bit easier to play, but objectively Black should be fine.

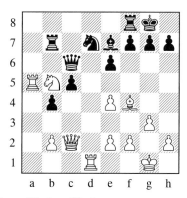

21.♘a7! ♕b6 22.♕a4

Black has no time to breath. He is threatened with ♖xd7 and ♖a6, so the choices are limited.

22...♘b8

The only chance.

22...♘f6?? 23.♖a6+− wins immediately.

After 22...e5 23.♘c6 ♗f6 24.♗e3± White obtains a fantastic position. His pieces are super-active while Black has no way to create counterplay.

23.♗xb8!

Now, a strong sequence of moves gives White an overwhelming position.

23...♖bxb8

23...♖fxb8 loses by force: 24.♖b5 ♕c7 25.♖xb7 ♖xb7 26.♕e8† ♗f8 27.♘c8 f6 28.♖d8 ♕f7 29.♕c6 ♖c7 30.♕d6 ♖b7 31.♘b6 Threatening to invade on d7. 31...♕e7 (31...♖e7 32.♕b8 followed by ♕c8 and ♘d7 wins.) 32.♕xe7 ♖xe7 33.♘d7 ♖f7 34.♘xc5+− White wins easily.

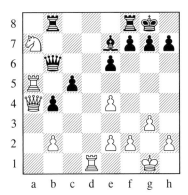

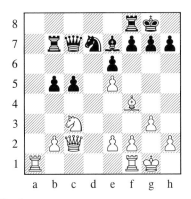

24.♘c6 ♖b7 25.♖a6 ♕c7 26.♘a5! ♖b6

26...♖a7? 27.♖xa7 ♕xa7 28.♖d7+−

27.♖xb6 ♕xb6 28.♖d7 ♗f6 29.♘c4±

With total domination.

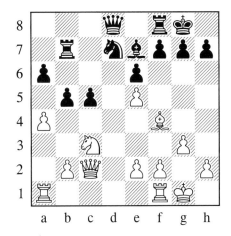

17...c4

A logical move, although it also looks tempting to attack the e5-pawn with:

17...♕c7 18.axb5

Opening the a-file for the rook while creating a weakness on b5.

Also possible is: 18.♖fd1 ♘xe5 19.♕e4 ♗f6 20.axb5 axb5 21.♖a6 c4 22.♕e3 Threatening ♘e4. 22...♘g4 (Black can try 22...b4 23.♘e4 c3 but the draw is not far away after 24.bxc3 bxc3 25.♖c1 c2 26.♘xf6† gxf6 27.♕e4 ♖b2 28.♗xe5 ♕xe5 29.♕xe5 fxe5 30.♖c6=) 23.♕f3 ♘e5 24.♕e3 ♘g4= A draw by repetition is the most likely outcome.

18...axb5

19.♘e4

19.♕e4?! c4∓ is awkward for White; the black knight is heading for the c5-square and the queenside pawns will soon get moving.

19.♖a6 b4 20.♘e4 ♘xe5 transposes to 19.♘e4.

19...♘xe5

Black is able to take this pawn as the pin does not hurt him too much. Now his pieces lack harmony, but he is not in any real trouble and a pawn is a pawn.

20.♖a6

Threatening ♕c3.

The immediate 20.♕c3 can be met by 20...♕c6! 21.♘xc5 (21.♗xe5?! ♕xe4 22.♗xg7 b4 23.♕e5 ♕xe5 24.♗xe5 f6 25.♗f4 c4∓ is clearly in Black's favour; 21.♕xe5 f6 22.♘xf6† ♗xf6 23.♕d6 ♕xd6 24.♗xd6 ♖c8∓ and Black has the upper hand.) 21...♕xc5 22.♕xc5 ♗xc5 23.♗xe5 with equality.

20...b4

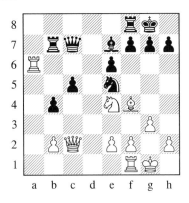

Black cannot move many pieces, so he stops the threat while preparing to create counterplay with his queenside pawns.

21.♖fa1

21.♖d1 is also possible, but after the forcing line 21...c4 22.♘d6 ♗xd6 23.♖dxd6 ♕c5 24.♕e4 ♘g4 25.♗e3 (In the event of 25.♕f3 c3 26.bxc3 b3 27.♖d1 b2 28.♖b1 ♕h5 29.h4 ♕f5 30.e4 ♕b5 31.♖a2 h5 32.c4 ♕xc4 33.♖axb2 ♖xb2 34.♖xb2 ♕d4= the position is roughly equal but only Black can play for a win.) 25...♘xe3 26.♖xb7 c3 27.bxc3 ♕xc3 28.fxe3 ♕e1† 29.♔g2 ♕xe2† the game ends up in perpetual check.

21...c4 22.♖6a5

22.♖1a5 f6 23.♘g5 fxg5 24.♗xe5 ♕c8=

22...f6 23.♗xe5 fxe5 24.♖a6 ♕c8 25.♔g2 ♖c7 26.f3=

It is hard for either side to improve their position, so a draw should be the logical outcome.

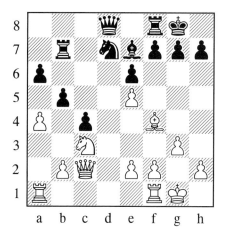

18.axb5 axb5 19.♘e4 ♕b6?!

I do not understand this move.

Better is 19...♕c7 20.♘d6 (20.♖fd1 ♘xe5 21.♖a6 b4 is analysed in the previous note) 20...♗xd6 21.exd6 ♕c6 when Black is fine; he can play ...f6 and ...e5 to cut off the support for the d6-pawn, while Black's own queenside pawns are ready to advance at any moment.

20.♖fd1 ♕c6

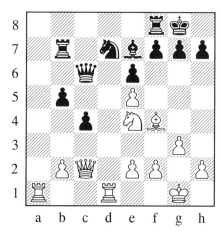

21.h4?!

This move secures the position of the bishop on f4 while preparing to put a piece on g5, but I think it is too slow.

21.♘d6

This seems like a more logical sequel to White's last few moves. Now Black can choose between taking the knight or moving the rook.

21...♖c7!

The best move in my opinion. Black does not need to exchange the knight, and indeed he can look to undermine it by striking at the e5-pawn, perhaps after having driven the bishop away from f4. From White's point of view the knight looks nice on d6, but what should he do with it?

21...♗xd6?! is a radical decision but not the best. 22.♖xd6 ♕c7 23.♖ad1 ♘b6 (23...♘c5 is not helping as the knight is going nowhere from this square.) 24.♗d2 Threatening ♗a5. 24...♕c5 25.♗e3 ♕c7 26.♗xb6 ♖xb6 27.♕e4 The position should be level, but at the same time it is Black who has to be more careful.

22.♖a5

The immediate 22.♕e4 is similar.

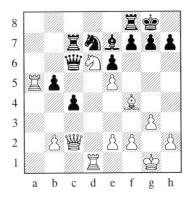

22...Rb8 23.We4 Wxe4 24.Nxe4 h6

In this position I see no reason for White to be better, and Black might soon be able to start thinking about seizing the initiative on the queenside.

25.Nd6

After the 'mechanical' 25.h4?! Black can seize the initiative: 25...Bb4 26.Ra2 Nc5 27.Nd6 (After 27.Nc3!? Bxc3 28.bxc3 Kh7 White should be able to survive although only Black can try to win.) 27...c3! 28.bxc3 Bxc3∓

25...g5 26.Nxb5

26.Be3 is also possible. 26...Nxe5 27.Nxb5 Nc6 (27...Bb4 28.Ra7 Rxa7 29.Nxa7 Ba5 30.Ra1 Bb6 31.Bxb6 Rxb6 Despite Black's superior position, a draw is the most likely outcome.) 28.Nxc7 Nxa5 29.Ra1 Nc6 30.Rc1 Rxb2 31.Rxc4 Ne5 32.Re4 Nd7 33.Kf1=∓ Black can play on for a while, but the position should of course be a draw.

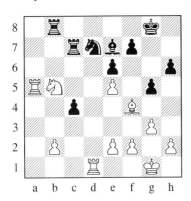

26...Rcb7

26...Rxb5? would be a mistake as after 27.Rxb5 gxf4 28.gxf4 White has a serious advantage. The c4-pawn is weak, the rook has to guard the 7th rank and the minor pieces have no good squares. On the other hand White can improve his king's position and then start to mobilize his central pawns while keeping pressure on the c4-pawn.

27.Bc1 Nxe5

27...Bb4 28.Ra4 Rxb5 29.Rxd7 Rxe5 30.Bd2 leads to an immediate draw after 30...Bxd2 31.Rxd2 Reb5 32.Rxc4 Rxb2 33.Rcc2 Rxc2 34.Rxc2=.

28.Nc3 Nc6 29.Ra4 Nb4=

Black has an active position but White can secure enough counterplay by attacking the c4-pawn, so the game should end in a draw.

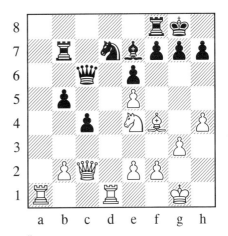

21...Nc5

Now Black has no problems and can look to make something of his queenside majority.

22.Ng5 g6

Avoiding exchanges for the moment.

After 22...Bxg5 23.hxg5 Nb3 24.Ra3 White will obtain counterplay with the help of the d6-square: 24...Rd7 25.Rd6 Wb7 (25...Rxd6 26.exd6 Nd4 27.Wd2 Wd5 28.Be3 e5 29.f4 f6 30.gxf6 gxf6 31.Ra6 leads to a draw, for

instance 31...♛b7 32.♖a3 ♛d5 33.♖a6=)
26.♖aa6 ♖xd6 27.♖xd6 g6 28.♗e3= White
intends f3, ♔g2 and ♛d1, with equal chances.

23.h5

Now White can start thinking about plans
such as f3, ♔g2 and putting some pieces on
the h-file. Black has to be careful and must try
to exchange rooks to remain with the better
minor pieces.

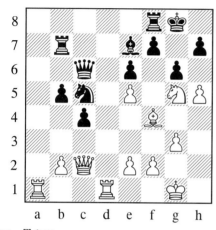

23...♖d7?!

The wrong rook!

23...♖d8

This would have been more accurate. One
of the main advantages of this move is that
White will not have time to bring his knight
to e4.

24.♖xd8† ♗xd8 25.f3

25.♖a8 ♖d7∓

25.♖d1 ♖d7 also suits Black well: 26.♖xd7
♛xd7 27.hxg6 (27.♘e4 ♘xe4 28.♛xe4
♛d1† 29.♔h2 ♛d5∓) 27...hxg6∓ Black has
an extra pawn on the queenside and the
better minor pieces. White will have to fight
hard for a draw.

25...♖d7 26.♔g2 ♘b3!

It is important to drive the rook away from
a1. From that square it has access to both the
h-file and the 8th rank, but now it will have to
choose one or the other.

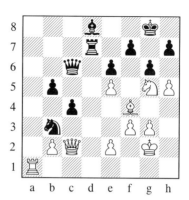

27.♖h1?!

Better is 27.♖a3 although after 27...♘d4
28.♛e4 h6 29.♛xc6 ♘xc6 30.♘e4 gxh5
31.♘d6 it is still Black who is fighting for
an advantage.

The text move is tempting but inaccurate.
Now Black can eliminate the dangerous
knight, as he no longer has to worry about
being mated on the back rank.

27...♘d4 28.♛e4 ♗xg5 29.♛xc6

After 29.♗xg5 ♛xe4 30.fxe4 ♘b3∓ Black
can improve his king and then prepare to
advance his c-pawn. Meanwhile the white
rook has no access to the open files.

29...♘xc6 30.♗xg5 gxh5!

It is important to give the king some fresh
air.

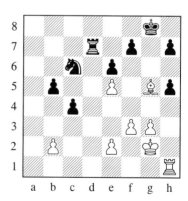

31.♖xh5

31.♗f6?! ♔f8! 32.♖xh5 ♖d2 shows why the
bishop should not lose sight of the second
rank.

Also after 31.♖a1 ♖a7 32.♖d1 ♔g7 the black king is safe and it will soon be time to advance the queenside pawns.

31...♖d5 32.♗f4 ♘e7

Black has excellent winning chances.

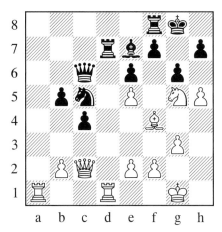

24.♖xd7 ♕xd7 25.♘e4

Exchanging the strong black knight.

25...♘xe4

I do not like this move, which draws the white queen to a better square.

Black could have kept a nice advantage with: 25...♕d5! 26.♘d6

Presumably this is what Ponomariov wanted to avoid.

26.♘xc5 is possible although compared with the game White's queen is less well placed. 26...g5 27.♖d1 ♕c6 28.♗e3

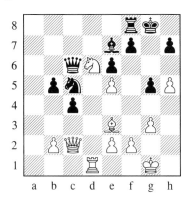

28...f6!

Undermining the knight.

29.♗d4

29.♕c3 ♖d8 is unpleasant for White.

29...♘b3 30.♗c3 fxe5 31.♕e4 ♕xe4

After 31...♕c5 32.♗xe5 ♕xf2† 33.♔h1 ♗xd6 34.♗xd6 ♕f5 35.♕c6⇄ White has some counterplay due to the weakened position of the black king and the passivity of the knight on b3.

32.♘xe4 b4 33.♗xe5 ♘c5 34.♘xc5 ♗xc5 35.e3 ♖f5 36.♗d6 g4

The game should end in a draw, but Black has some chances to press.

26.♕xe4

Now White's well-placed queen gives him chances for counterplay, but Black's position remains slightly preferable.

26...♖c8

After 26...♕d5 27.♕xd5 exd5 28.♖a7 White is out of danger.

27.♗e3 b4 28.♖a7 ♕e8

28...♖c7 29.♕a8† ♗f8 30.♖xc7 ♕xc7 31.♗h6 ♕c5 32.♗xf8 ♕xf8 33.♕c6=

29.h6 c3

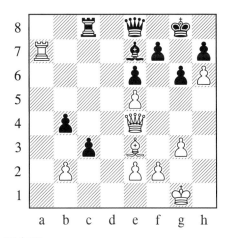

30.b3?!

There is no reason for White to offer his opponent a strong protected passed pawn.

30.bxc3 bxc3 31.♕b7

This would have been the right path to equality.

31...♗f8

After 31...♗f8 32.♔g2 neither side can improve their position. The finish might be 32...♖b8 (32...c2? would be a huge mistake due to 33.♗c1± followed by ♖a2 and ♕e4 when Black will lose the c-pawn) 33.♕c7 ♖c8 34.♕b7 ♖b8 35.♕c7= with a repetition of moves.

32.♕f3 c2 33.♗c1

Once again the game should be headed for a draw in the near future.

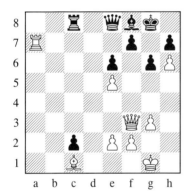

33...♗c5

Black can avoid the move repetition with 33...♗c5 34.♔g2 ♖xe5?! 35.♖c7, but only White can have winning chances here.

34.♕f6 ♗f8 35.♕f3=

30...c2 31.♗c1 ♗f8

Now White is in some trouble.

32.♔g2 ♕d8?!

In order to keep any winning chances alive, Black should have gone for a queen exchange on a different square.

32...♕c6! 33.♕xc6 ♖xc6

White should be able to draw from here, but

there are still some moves to make. Here is an illustrative line:

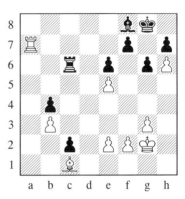

34.♔f3

34.g4!? is a possible improvement.

34...♖c3† 35.♔g4 ♖xb3 36.♖c7 ♖c3 37.♖xc3 bxc3

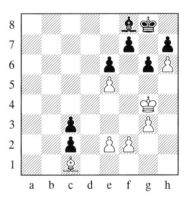

38.♔f3

38.e4? is well met by 38...g5! 39.♔xg5 ♗c5, intending to bring the bishop to d2 via f2 and e1. 40.g4 ♗xf2 41.♔f4 ♗h4 42.g5 ♗f2 43.♔f3 ♗d4 44.♔e2 ♗xe5 45.♔d3 f5 46.gxf6 ♔f7 47.♔xc2 ♗xf6 48.♗a3 ♔g6 49.♗f8 ♔h5 50.♔d1 (50.♔g7 ♗g5 51.♔d1 ♗xh6 52.♗xc3 ♔g4 53.♔e1 ♔f3 54.♔f1 ♗e3 55.♗e1 ♔xe4 56.♔g2 e5 57.♗c3 ♗d4 58.♗d2 ♔d3 59.♗c1 e4 60.♔g3 ♗c3–+) 50...♗g5 51.♗g7 ♗xh6 52.♗xc3 ♔g4 53.♗e2 ♔g3 54.♔f1 ♗e3 By now Black is winning easily. 55.♗e1† ♔f3 56.♗h4 ♔xe4 57.♔g2 ♔f5 58.♗e7 e5

59.♗h4 ♔g4 60.♗e1 e4 61.♗a5 h5 62.♔h1 ♗f4 63.♔g2 h4 64.♗b6 h3† 65.♔g1 ♗g3 66.♗d4 ♔f3–+

38...g5 39.♔e4 ♗xh6 40.♔d3 ♔g7 41.♔xc3

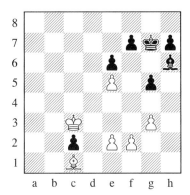

41...♔g6

41...g4 42.♗xh6† ♔xh6 43.♔xc2 is a simple draw. 43...♔g5 44.♔d3 h5 (44...♔f5 45.♔d4 h6 46.e4†=) 45.♔e3 h4 46.gxh4† ♔xh4 47.♔f4 ♔h3 (47...♔h5 48.f3=) 48.♔g5 g3 49.fxg3 ♔xg3 50.♔f6 ♔f4= 42.♔xc2 ♗g7 43.♔b2 h5 44.♔d3 ♔f5 45.f3 ♗xe5 46.g4† hxg4 47.fxg4† ♔f6 48.♗c1

Black can play on for a while, but White should not have too much trouble holding the endgame a pawn down.

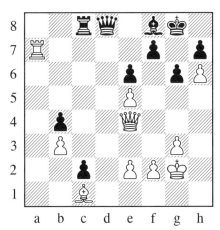

33.♕b7 ♕d5† 34.♕xd5 exd5 35.♖d7

Now White is out of danger, as there is no way for Black to force his c-pawn through.

35...g5 36.♖xd5 ♗xh6 37.g4

Ensuring that the black bishop will not be able to assist his passed pawn.

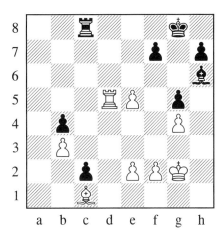

37...♗g7 38.♔f3 ♖c3† 39.♔e4 h6

Neither side can play for a win, so they repeat moves.

40.♖d3 ♖c5 41.♖d5 ♖c3 42.♖d3
½–½

GAME 2
▷ **Wang Hao (2733)**
▶ **S. Rublevsky (2681)**
European Club Cup, Rogaska Slatina
28.09.2011 **[A20]**
Annotated by Borki Predojevic

The following game leads us into an old line of the English Opening. White can reach the variation with 7.d4 only from the move order with 2.g3 when he "saves" the move ♘c3 for later. Wang Hao has played this line with White before and in this game he improved on his previous play with the dangerous idea 10.♘d2!?. Black played the natural 10...0–0 and after 11.♘b3! he replied 11...♕d6!?N which looks playable for Black. Very soon after Black quickly played 12...♕g6?! and next 13...f4? when White was clearly better after 15.♘a5± and he convincingly won the game.

The correct move was 12...♘b4!N when I was unable to find any advantage for White.

I also suggest that the readers consider the line with 11...♗d6 and 13...♗a6!N which also looks okay for Black. This variation is very rich in ideas so I am sure that there are also other ways to play it with White.

1.c4 e5 2.g3 ♘f6 3.♗g2 d5 4.cxd5 ♘xd5 5.♘f3

When White replies to 1...e5 with 2.g3 then this line is possible since White delays playing ♘c3. White is concentrating on playing a very fast d2-d4.

5...♘c6 6.0–0

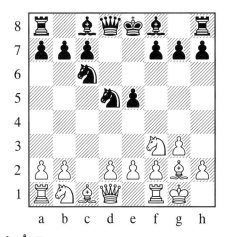

6...♗e7

Black can play 6...♘b6 in order to avoid the line which was played in this game. This move order also gives White the chance to play another set-up after 7.d3 ♗e7 8.a3 0–0 9.♘bd2 (premature is 9.b4?! ♗f6↑ and White has problems on the a1-h8 diagonal) 9...a5 10.b3 This was played recently at a high level in rapid games. This line is not related to the main line in the game, so we will not discuss it, at least not this time.

7.d4

This is a typical break in the Accelerated Dragon variation of the Sicilian. With reversed colours, when White is faced with this problem, he cannot get any advantage. The main reason White plays this line is the fact that he is a tempo up compared to the position with reversed colours, so he has chances to gain the advantage.

7...e4

The alternative is:

7...exd4 8.♘xd4 ♘xd4 9.♕xd4

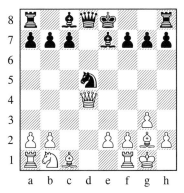

9...♘f6

On 9...♘b4? White can take the pawn with: 10.♕xg7! ♗f6 11.♕h6 ♘c2 12.♘c3

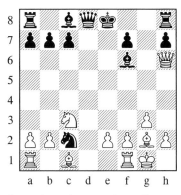

12...♘xa1 (12...♗xc3 13.bxc3 ♘xa1 14.♕g7 ♖f8 15.♗a3+–) 13.♖d1 Black's position is hopeless. A game continued: 13...♗d7 14.♘d5 ♗e7 15.♕g7 ♖f8 16.♗h6+– f6 17.♗f3 ♗f5 18.♗h5† ♗g6 19.♗xg6† hxg6 20.♕xg6† ♔d7 21.♘xf6† 1–0 Franco Ocampos – Needleman, Buenos Aires 2003.

After the text move the main reply is:

10.♕a4†

10.♕xd8† ♔xd8 11.♘c3 c6 12.b4± also looks better for White since his minority attack with a4 and b5 is very fast.

10...♕d7

10...c6 11.♖d1 ♕b6 12.♗e3 ♗c5 13.♗xc5 ♕xc5 14.b4 ♕b6 15.♘c3 0–0 16.b5± is better for White. His pieces are more active and Black is faced with an attack on his queenside pawns.

11.♕c2! c6 12.♖d1 ♕e6 13.♘c3 0–0 14.h3±

White is slightly better thanks to the possibility of quickly advancing his central pawns. Black's queen is on a bad square so he must lose some time solving this problem.

8.♘e5 f5 9.♘xc6 bxc6

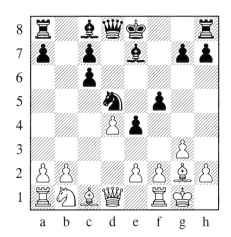

10.♘d2!?

Probably this was a surprise for Rublevsky. White usually plays 10.♘c3 or 10.♕a4.

A few months earlier Wang Hao played differently with:

10.♕c2

Now Black can react with:

10...♕d6!?

Also interesting looks 10...♕d7 11.♘c3 0–0 12.♘xd5 cxd5 13.♗f4 ♗a6! 14.♖fc1 ♖ac8 15.e3 c5 16.dxc5 ♗xc5 17.♕b3⇄ and

although Black lost this game, his position was okay at this point in Wang Hao – Karjakin, Ningbo 2011.

11.♘c3 ♗e6 12.♘xd5 ♗xd5 13.♗f4 ♕d7 14.f3 exf3 15.♗xf3 0–0

Black did not have any problems.

16.♗e5

16.♗xd5† ♕xd5 17.e3 c5 18.dxc5 g5! 19.♗xc7 ♖ac8 20.♖ad1 ♕e6 21.♗d6 ♗xd6 22.♖xd6 ♕xe3†= leads to an equal position.

16...♗d6 17.♗xd6 cxd6 18.e4 fxe4 19.♗xe4 ♗xe4 20.♕xe4 d5 21.♕d3 ♕g4 22.♔g2 h5=

A draw was agreed in Miroshnichenko – Eljanov, Ukraine (ch) 2011.

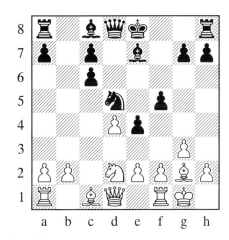

10...0–0

In Janssen – Van den Doel, Dieren (op) 2001, Black played: 10...c5 11.dxc5 ♗xc5? Now White replied 12.♕c2? missing a very nice tactical blow: 12.♘xe4! fxe4 13.♕a4† ♔f7 (13...♗d7 14.♕xe4†+–) 14.♕c6+– White regains the piece with a winning position.

A very aggressive but suspect try for Black is:

10...h5?!

Generally this kind of move should not be played in the opening phase, but compared to the positions from the Accelerated Dragon, Black is a tempo down, and the missing move is castling short. This is the reason Black can try this idea.

11.♕c2

After the passive 11.♘b3?! h4 12.♗d2 ♕d6⇄ Black had reasonable chances in C. Foisor – Minnebo, Liechtenstein 1996.
11.♘c4 h4 12.♕a4 ♗d7 13.♘e5 ♗d6±
11...♗d7 12.♘c4↑/±

White is faster with his attack in centre; his idea is to play ♘a5 or ♘e5. It is also possible to play f3.

After 10...e3 11.♘c4 exf2† 12.♖xf2 0–0 13.♕a4± White is better thanks to the weakness on c6. His next move will be ♘e5 and Black cannot defend against it.

10...a5!?N is a possible idea to fight against the plan with ♘b3-a5, but we will see that after 10...0–0 Black also has many options.

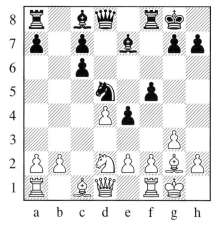

11.♘b3!

An alternative is 11.♘c4, but this doesn't look as strong as the game move. Black's best reply is: 11...♗a6! (after 11...c5 12.dxc5 ♗xc5 13.♗g5 ♘f6 14.♕c2 ♗e6 15.♖ac1↑ White was better in King – Joyce, Dublin 1995) 12.♘e5 ♕d6⇄ With the idea of playing ...♗f6 or ...c5. For example, 13.f3 exf3 14.♗xf3 ♖ad8 looks very comfortable for Black.

11.a3 looks slow as after 11...a5∞ White has made no progress.

11...♕d6!?N

Later in the same tournament Black played:
11...♗d6!?
White replied:
12.♗d2
The normal 12.♕c2 ♕e8 13.♘a5 is met by:
13...♘b4 14.♕b1 (14.♕a4 ♗a6 15.a3 ♗b5 16.♕b3† ♘d5⇄ Black intends ...♕h5.) 14...♗a6 15.a3 ♘d5 16.♕c2 ♕h5! This secures Black a good game.
12...♕e8 13.e3
The active 13.♘a5 can be met by 13...f4⇄.

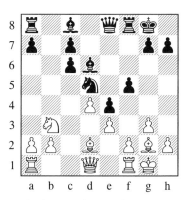

Here Black missed a good active move:
13...♗a6!N
After 13...♗e6 14.♖c1 ♘e7 15.♘a5 ♗d5 16.b3 ♖f6 17.♕e2 h5 18.h4! ♕g6 19.♘c4± White was better in Vitiugov – Motylev, Rogaska Slatina 2011.
14.♖e1 ♖b8 15.♖c1
15.♗f1 ♗b5 16.♕c2 ♖f6! 17.♘a5 ♖h6⇄ offers Black a good game.
15...♖f6!⇄
This position looks very good for Black. He can continue his kingside attack and if White tries to attack the c6-pawn then Black has the simple ...♗b5.

11...♗e6
This normal development does not look best since after ♘c5 the bishop on e6 will be attacked. White can continue with his plan:
12.♗d2 ♘b6

12...♖f6?! 13.♖c1 ♕e8 14.♗g5 ♖g6 15.♗xe7 ♘xe7 16.♘c5 leads to a clear positional advantage for White. 16...d5 17.♕d2 ♘c8 18.♕f4 ♘d6 19.f3!? ♕e7 (after 19...exf3 20.exf3!± White occupies the e-file) 20.fxe4 fxe4 21.♕e5 ♖e8 22.♕xe7 ♖xe7 23.b3± White was on top in Milos – Adla, Buenos Aires 1991.

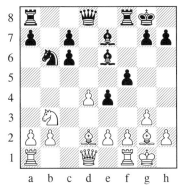

13.♘a5!N

The alternative 13.♕c2 ♘c4 14.e3 ♘xd2 15.♘xd2 ♗d5 16.♘c4 a5 looks slow, as in Matamoros Franco – Lapshun, Philadelphia 2011.

13...♕d5 14.♖c1 c5 15.dxc5 ♗xc5 16.♕c2 ♗d6 17.b3±

White has a nice positional advantage. At some point he can play e3 and activate the light-squared bishop by playing ♗f1.

The former World Champion Veselin Topalov played 11...a5?! but after: 12.♗d2 a4 13.♘a5 ♗d7 (13...c5!? 14.♘c6 ♕d7 15.♘xe7† ♕xe7 16.dxc5 ♕xc5 17.♖c1 ♕b5 18.♖c2±) 14.♕xa4 ♕e8 Now in D. Paunovic – Topalov, Villarrobledo 2008, White should have played the simple 15.♕c2!±/± when he is obviously better.

The attacking idea 11...f4?! looks premature. After 12.♗xe4 ♗h3 White can even play: 13.♕c2! (also after 13.♖e1 Black's compensation is questionable) 13...fxg3 14.hxg3 ♗xf1 15.♕xc6 ♘f6 16.♕xa8 ♗xe2

11...♗a6 12.♗d2 ♖b8 13.♖c1 ♕d7 14.♖e1 ♕e6 15.♕c2 ♘b4 16.♗xb4 ♗xb4 17.♖ed1 ♗d6 18.e3± is better for White.

12.♕c2

After 12.♘a5 c5 13.dxc5 ♕xc5 14.♗d2 ♕b6 15.♖c1 c5⇄ Black's position looks good. He has more space, which compensates for his worse pawn structure.

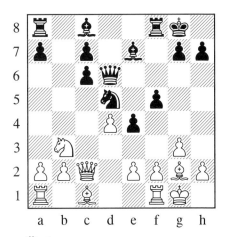

12...♕g6?!

Black dreams about counterplay with the break ...f4, but with his last move he loses his way.

Black's best reaction was:
12...♘b4! 13.♕c3 ♘d5

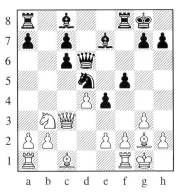

And if White wants to play for the advantage he is obliged to play:

14.♕a5

14.♕c4 is met by 14...a5! and White's queen on c4 is exposed to a new threat: ♗a6.

14.♕c2 ♘b4=

Probably in most positions this manoeuvre to a5 would be useful for White, but not here. From a5 the queen does not create pressure on the c6-pawn and also the a5-square is not free for White's knight. These facts help Black, so now it is time for the plan he tried in the game:

14...♕g6!

Black prepares his attack with ...f4, while White's pieces are not as coordinated as in the game. For example:

15.♘c5 ♗xc5

15...h5 16.♗d2 h4 also looks good.

16.♕xc5 ♗a6 17.♖e1

Or 17.♕c2 ♖ae8⇄ and next ...f4.

17...f4!

Black has a very good game.

13.♗d2±

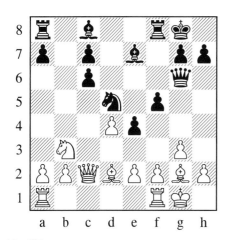

13...f4?

The plan with 12...♕g6 and 13...f4? looks too aggressive and it will be punished very quickly.

More consistent was 13...♖f6. After 14.♘a5 ♗a6 (14...f4?? 15.♗xe4 ♗f5 16.♗xf5 ♖xf5

17.♕xc6+–) 15.♖fe1± it is very hard to believe that Black's kingside attack will be successful while White will increase his pressure on the queenside by playing ♖ac1 and then a3 and b4.

14.♖fc1! ♖f6

After 14...fxg3 15.fxg3± Black loses his attacking chances and there is no doubt that White is clearly better.

15.♘a5±

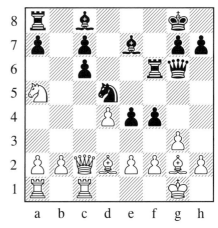

Strong and concrete. White is not afraid of ghosts, so he doesn't play any defensive moves on the kingside. It is remarkable how Wang Hao achieved a clearly better position just by playing a few natural moves. It seems that Black always needed one more tempo – the extra move which White usually has in the Sicilian Defence.

15...f3

15...♗d7 16.♕xe4 ♗f5 17.♕f3+–

In reply to 15...fxg3 16.hxg3 ♗f5 White has: 17.♘xc6 ♗d6 (17...e3 18.♕b3 exf2† 19.♔f1+–) 18.♘e5 ♗xe5 19.dxe5 ♖e6 (19...e3 20.♗xd5† ♔h8 21.♕xc7+–) 20.♕b3 c6 21.♖c5± White is on top. Still this was Black's best option since after 15...f3 as in the game, he ends up in a worse endgame without any counter-chances.

16.exf3 exf3 17.♕xg6 hxg6 18.♗f1 ♗d7

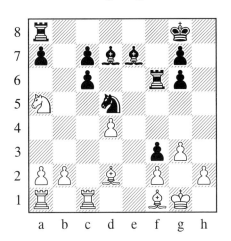

19.a3!

With this move White increases his advantage on the queenside by preparing to fix Black's doubled pawns with b2-b4.

19...♖e8 20.b4 ♗f8 21.♗g5 ♖f5 22.h4!?

Another option was 22.♗h3 ♖f7 23.♗xd7 ♖xd7 24.♘xc6±/+− but White has no need to hurry with taking material, as Black cannot save the pawn on c6.

22...♘e7

A better option for Black was: 22...♗e7 23.♗h3 (23.♗xe7 ♘xe7±) 23...♗xg5 24.hxg5 ♖f7 25.♗xd7 ♖xd7 26.♘xc6±/+− Even so, White has a near decisive advantage.

23.♘c4

White had plenty of options here. For example 23.♗c4† ♘d5 24.♗d3+− wins the exchange.

23...♖d5 24.♘e5 ♖xd4 25.♗e3 ♖d5 26.♗c4+−

Finally White decides to convert his huge positional advantage into a decisive material advantage. Some players would have resigned here, but this is not today's fashion. Black continued to fight with:

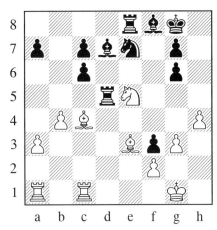

26...♗e6 27.♗xd5 ♗xd5 28.♗xa7 ♘f5 29.♘xg6 ♗d6 30.♗c5 ♔h7 31.h5 ♗xc5 32.♖xc5 ♘d4 33.♖d1 ♘e2† 34.♔h2 ♔h6 35.g4 ♖e4 36.♔h3 ♘d4 37.♗g3 ♔g5 38.♖xd4 ♖xd4 39.♘e5 ♔f6 40.♘xc6 ♖d3 41.b5

And after passing the first time control, Black resigned.

1–0

GAME 3
▷ **T. Radjabov (2744)**
▶ **V. Ivanchuk (2768)**
FIDE World Cup 2011, Khanty-Mansiysk
Round 5, Game 2, 10.09.2011 **[A37]**
Annotated by Borki Predojevic

In the Ivanchuk – Radjabov match in the 2011 World Cup, the first game resulted in a win for Ivanchuk. Radjabov had to find a way to win the second game in order to stay in the match. The English Opening was his choice in the following game. He employed a very nice idea in the variation with 5...e6 and 6...♘ge7. His novelty 9.h5N was connected with the quite shocking 10.♘xg5!. Ivanchuk became confused and he already made a little mistake on the 11th move. Radjabov obtained the advantage, and it was converted into a win very quickly, thanks to a lot of help from Ivanchuk. My conclusion about the 10.♘xg5!

sacrifice is that Black should be able to hold the position, but the line deserves attention and further analysis.

1.♘f3 c5 2.g3 g6 3.c4 ♗g7 4.♗g2 ♘c6 5.♘c3 e6 6.d3 ♘ge7 7.h4!?

This idea was analysed in the July issue of Chess Evolution but from another move order, first 6.h4 and then 7.d3. The main idea is to get an extra tempo compared to the line 7.♗g5 h6 8.♗d2. White threatens h4-h5, and so the most logical reply is:

7...h6

After 7...b6 8.h5↑ White would achieve his goal.

8.♗d2 b6

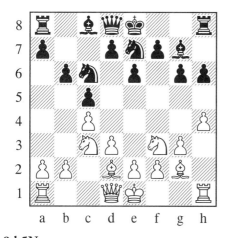

9.h5N

This novelty is connected with White's next move, which to say the least is surprising.

9...g5

A more concrete approach is 9...d5!?. After 10.hxg6 fxg6, White can continue with the typical idea: 11.a3 (11.♕a4 g5 12.0-0-0 ♗d7 13.♔b1↑ is another plan for White, but I don't think it is any better) 11...g5 12.♖b1 (The original 12.♘h2!? preparing f2-f4 and ♘g4 also deserves attention.) Here Black has two options:

a) 12...0-0 13.b4 dxc4

With this move order, White has the intermediate move:

14.b5! ♘a5

14...♘d4 looks more active, but the lines I analysed turn out slightly better for White: 15.♘xg5 ♗d7 16.e3! (16.♘ge4 cxd3 17.exd3 ♘ef5 18.a4↑ is also pleasant for White) 16...♘b3 17.♘ge4 ♘xd2 18.♕xd2 cxd3 19.♕xd3 a6! (19...♕c7 20.♕c4 ♖ad8 21.♗h3±) 20.♕c4 axb5 21.♘xb5 ♘d5 22.♘ed6 ♕e7 23.0-0 ♖ad8 24.♖bd1± with a solid plus for White.

15.♘xg5! ♖b8 16.♘ge4 ♗b7

16...♘f5 17.♘a4! cxd3 18.♗xa5 bxa5 19.exd3 ♘d6 20.♘axc5±

16...cxd3 17.♗xh6±

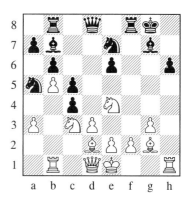

17.♖xh6! ♗xh6

I think that this is more or less forced.

17...cxd3 18.♖xe6 ♘f5 19.♖g6 dxe2 20.♕xe2 ♕e8 21.♕g4!±

18.♗xh6 ♖f5 19.♗h3 ♘g6!
  19...cxd3? 20.exd3+– opens the way for the white queen to come to g4.
20.dxc4
  20.♗xf5 exf5 21.♗g5 ♘e7 22.♘f6† ♔f7 23.dxc4 ♕d4± is another possibility for White.
20...♖e5
  20...♘xc4 21.♗xf5 exf5 22.♕b3 fxe4 23.♕xc4† ♔h7 24.♗e3±/+–
21.♕xd8†
  21.♘g5?! ♕f6!⇄
21...♖xd8 22.♘g5 ♘f8 23.f4 ♖e3 24.♖c1 ♖xg3 25.♔f2 ♖xg5 26.♗xg5 ♖d4 27.♗h6 ♘xc4

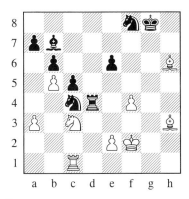

28.e4!
  I think White is better after this. The best defence is:
28...♖d2† 29.♘e2 ♗xe4 30.♖g1† ♔f7 31.♖g7† ♔f6 32.♖xa7 ♘d7 33.f5 ♖a2!
  Worse is 33...♖d3 34.fxe6 ♖f3† 35.♔g1 ♘de5 36.♗g7† ♔g5 37.♗xe5 ♖xh3 38.e7 ♖h1† 39.♔f2 ♗g6 40.♗c7, and the pawn on e7 gives a decisive advantage to White.
34.♖xd7
  Another option is the long line 34.fxe6 ♘de5 35.♗g7† ♔g5 36.♗xe5 ♘xe5 37.♖g7† ♔h6 38.♖g3 ♗d3 39.♖e3 ♖xe2† 40.♖xe2 ♗xe2 41.♔xe2 ♔g6 42.a4 ♔f6 43.♔e3 ♔e7 44.♔e4 ♘c4 45.♗g4±, but I am not sure if White is able to win this ending.
34...♗xf5 35.♗xf5 ♔xf5 36.♗c1±
  White has a clear advantage.

b) 12...dxc4!
  This is the best idea for Black.
13.dxc4 ♗b7 14.♘e4!?
  14.b4 cxb4 15.axb4 0–0⇄
14...0–0 15.♗c3 ♕xd1†
  Black seems to be able to hold the ensuing endgame.
  After 15...♘d4 16.♘fd2± White can continue with e2-e3.
16.♖xd1 ♖ad8 17.♖d6

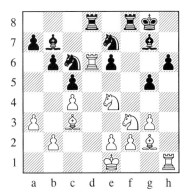

17...♘d4! 18.♗xd4 ♗xd4 19.♖xe6
  19.♖xd8 ♖xd8 20.♘xd4 ♗xe4□ 21.♖xe4 ♖xd4 22.♗d3 ♔g7 23.♔d2 ♘c6 24.e3 ♖d8 25.♔c3 ♘e5 26.♗e2 g4! 27.♖h5 ♘d7 28.♖h4 ♘f6 should be equal.
19...♗xe4
  19...♘f5 20.g4 ♗xe4 21.gxf5 ♗xb2 22.♖g6† ♗g7 23.♖hxh6 ♗xf5 24.♖xg5±
20.♖xe4 ♗xb2 21.♖xe7 ♗c3† 22.♘d2 ♖xd2
  22...♖xd2† 23.♔d1!±

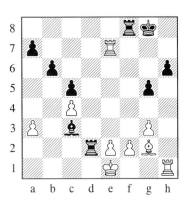

23.0–0 ♖f6±/=

White may have slightly more practical chances, but objectively the position is equal.

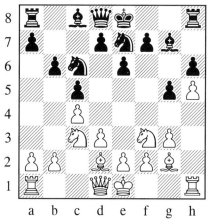

10.♘xg5!

This was probably a big shock for Ivanchuk, but it looks to be the only consistent follow-up to 9.h5. Otherwise Black would play a quick ...d5, giving him the better prospects.

10...hxg5 11.♗xg5 ♗xc3†?!

This is not a good decision. The dark squares become very weak, which White is able to use immediately. As further analysis confirms, this was the critical moment in the game, with Black having two playable options:

a) 11...f6 12.♗f4 (The forced line after 12.h6 fxg5 13.hxg7 ♖xh1† 14.♗xh1 ♘g8 15.♗xc6 dxc6 16.♔d2 ♔f7 17.♕h1 ♗d7 18.♘e4 ♔xg7 19.♕h5 ♗e8 20.♕xg5† ♕xg5† 21.♘xg5 ♗d7∓ is in Black's favour.) There is now another split:

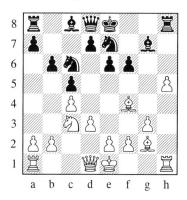

a1) 12...e5 13.h6 exf4

On 13...♗f8 White has 14.e3! ♕c7 (14...d6? is met by 15.♕h5† ♔d7 16.♕f7! exf4 17.♕xf6 ♗xh6 18.♘b5 and suddenly Black is lost) 15.♕h5† ♔d8 16.♘b5 ♕b8 17.♗g5! fxg5 18.♕xg5.

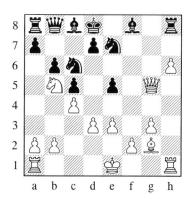

White is better, despite being two pieces down! Black can defend against the threat of ♕f6 only with: 18...e4 19.♗xe4 d5 (19...♕e5 20.♕xe5 ♘xe5 is objectively better. However, after 21.♗xa8 ♘xd3† 22.♔e2 ♘xb2 23.♘d6± White keeps a huge advantage.) 20.♗xd5 ♗d7 21.f4!+– Stopping ...♕e5, and preparing ♕f6 with a decisive advantage to White.

14.hxg7 ♖xh1† 15.♗xh1 ♘f7

15...fxg3 is met by the nice 16.♕d2! and White will protect the pawn on g7. For example: 16...♔f7 17.♕h6 ♖b8 18.♗f3 g2 19.♗d2 ♘e5 20.♗xg2+– looks very bad for Black.

16.gxf4 ♕g8 17.♗d5†! ♘xd5 18.cxd5 ♘e7

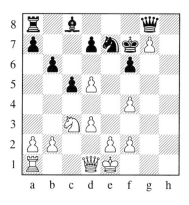

19.♔d2! ♕h7!

19...♕xg7 loses after 20.d6 ♘c6 (20...♗b7 21.dxe7 ♔xe7 22.♕g1±) 21.♕h1 ♗b7 22.♖g1 ♕h8 23.♕d5† ♔f8 24.♕f5! and White's attack is too strong. On 24...♘b8 25.♘e4 ♗xe4 26.♕xe4 ♘c6 27.♖h1 ♕g8 (27...♕g7 28.♖h7+–) 28.♖h6 ♕g7 29.♖h7+– Black can't defend against all the threats.

20.d6 ♘c6 21.♕b3† ♔xg7 22.♖g1† ♔f8 23.♕d5 ♗b7 24.♘e4 ♘a5 25.♘xf6 ♗xd5 26.♘xh7† ♔f7 27.♘g5† ♔f8 28.b3

28.♘h7†=

28...♗g8 29.f5 ♘c6 30.f4⩱

White has excellent compensation.

a2) 12...♘f5

This looks most critical.

13.g4

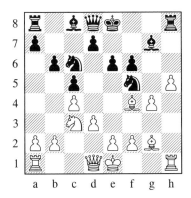

13...♗h6!

13...♗h6 would give White very good compensation after 14.♘b5 e5 (14...♔f7 15.♗e4⩱) 15.♗xh6 ♗xh6 16.♘d6† ♔e7 17.♘f5† ♔f8 18.♘xh6 ♖xh6 19.♕d2 ♖h8 20.0–0–0⩱ and White's next moves, such as f4 or g5, will open up the black king.

14.gxf5 ♗xf4 15.e3 ♗e5 16.♕g4 ♕e7 17.fxe6 ♗b7 18.exd7† ♔xd7 19.♕xd7† ♔xd7 20.♗d2

White has three pawns for the piece, but that is only enough for an unclear game and equality.

b) 11...♗b7!

This is logical, putting the onus on White to demonstrate his compensation.

12.♕d2

12.♘e4 ♕c7 13.♘f6† ♗xf6 14.♗xf6 ♖h6! 15.♗g5 ♖h7 16.♕d2 ♘d4∓ is better for Black.

12...f6

An interesting idea for Black is: 12...♕c7!? 13.♘b5 (13.h6 ♗xc3 14.bxc3 ♖h7∞/∓) 13...♕b8 14.h6 ♗e5 (14...♗d4 15.e3 a6 16.♘xd4 cxd4 17.0–0–0⩱ gives White good compensation) 15.f4 ♗d4 16.e3 f6 17.♗h4

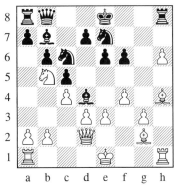

17...♗xe3! 18.♕xe3 ♖xh6 19.♕f2 a6 20.♘c3 ♘f5∞ Black has given the piece back, but in return White no longer has any pressure.

13.h6 fxg5 14.hxg7 ♖xh1† 15.♗xh1 ♔f7 16.♕xg5

After 16.♘e4 ♔xg7 (16...♘c8 17.♘xg5† ♔xg7 18.♕f4 ♕e7 19.♘e4⩱) 17.♘d6 ♗a6 18.♕xg5† ♔g6□ 19.♕d2 ♕e7 20.♗xc6 dxc6 21.♕c3† ♔g8 22.♘e4 e5∓/∓ Black has successfully defended the position and holds the advantage.

16...♘g8

The alternative is 16...♘f5 17.♕f4 ♔xg7 18.♗e4 ♕e7 (18...♘h6 19.0–0–0 ♕e7∞ is a transposition to the line after 16...♘g8) 19.♗xf5 exf5 20.♕xf5 ♖h8 21.0–0–0 ♖h6∞ with a complicated position.

17.♕f4† ♔xg7 18.0–0–0 ♕e7 19.♗e4 ♘h6

19...♕f7 20.♕c7 d5 21.♕xf7† ♔xf7 22.cxd5 exd5 23.♘xd5⇄

20.♖h1 ♖h8 21.♘b5 e5

The endgame after 21...♘f7 22.♖xh8 ♔xh8 23.♘xa7 ♕g5 24.♕xg5 ♘xg5 25.♘xc6 ♗xc6 26.♗xc6 dxc6 can be dangerous for Black.

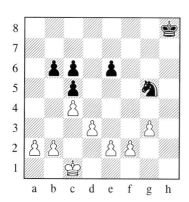

27.a4! e5! (On 27...♘f7 White can try 28.d4! cxd4 29.c5! bxc5 30.a5 ♘d6 31.a6 ♘b5? [the correct defence is 31...♘c8! 32.b3 e5 33.f3 ♔g7 34.♔d2 ♔f7 35.♔d3 ♔e7 36.g4 ♔e6= with a drawish position] 32.b3! e5 33.f3 ♔g7 34.♔c2 ♔f6 35.♔d3 ♔e6 36.g4!± and Black has problems. His knight is tied to the a-pawn, while the white king is free to invade his position via e4 or c4.) 28.b4 cxb4 29.c5 bxc5 30.a5 ♘e6 31.a6 ♘c7 32.a7 ♘a8 33.♔b2 ♔g7 34.♔b3 ♔f6 35.g4 ♘b6 36.e3 ♔g5 37.f3 ♔f6 38.f4 exf4 39.exf4 ♘a8= The game should finish as a draw.

22.♕e3 d6

22...a6 23.♘c7 ♘f7 24.♖xh8 ♔xh8 25.♘d5 ♕d8 26.♗g6 ♘g5 27.f4⩱

22...♘a5 23.♘xa7∞

23.♖h5 ♘f7 24.♖xh8 ♔xh8 25.♗d5 ♘cd8 26.♗xb7 ♕xb7 27.♘xd6 ♕h1† 28.♔c2 ♔g7∞

The final position is similar to some of the above lines. White has managed to capture one more pawn and obtain material equality. On other hand, Black shouldn't be worse here.

12.bxc3 ♗b7 13.♕d2 ♕c7 14.♗f6

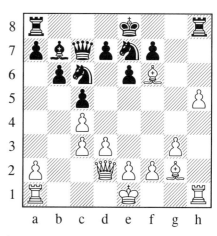

14...0–0–0

On 14...♖h7 White has 15.♗e4! ♘g8 16.♕g5 and Black can't avoid the loss of material: 16...♘xf6 17.♕xf6 ♕d8 (17...♘e5 18.♗xh7 ♗xh1 19.f4! looks winning for White) 18.♕xd8† ♘xd8 19.♗xh7 ♗xh1 20.f3 f5 21.♔f2 ♗xf3 22.exf3 ♔f7 23.g4 ♔g7 24.♗g6± and White is a pawn up in the endgame.

15.0–0–0

White doesn't hurry to take the exchange. The reason is very simple – his bishop on f6 is much stronger than either of Black's rooks.

15...♖hg8?

A better option was:

15...♖he8

I reckon Ivanchuk didn't want to play this because his rook on d8 would be left without any squares.

16.f4!?

This has the idea of stopping the ...♘e5-g6 manoeuvre.

16.h6 ♘e5 17.♗xb7† (17.e4 ♘g4⇄) 17...♔xb7 18.♕f4 (18.h7 ♘5g6 19.e4 d5±) 18...d6 19.h7 ♘5g6 20.♕f3† ♔b8 21.♖h6↑ is also better for White.

16...♘b8

16...♖g8 would lead to a position similar to that which could arise in the game: 17.♗xc6 ♗xc6 18.♗xe7 ♖de8 19.♗h4 ♗xh1

20.♖xh1 ♕c6 21.e4 e5 (21...f5 22.♖e1↑) 22.f5 ♖g7 23.f6 ♖h7 24.g4 ♖g8 25.♕e2 b5 26.g5 bxc4 27.dxc4± and White is superior. 17.♗xb7† ♔xb7 18.h6 ♖c8 19.h7 ♘g6 20.e4 d6 21.♖h6 ♘d7 22.♗g7 ♕c6 23.g4±

White is better. The main problem for Black is the lack of counterplay; all his pieces are passive.

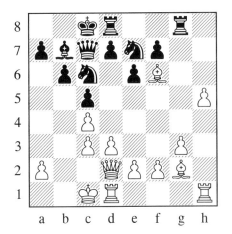

16.♗xc6! dxc6?

This loses immediately.

16...♘xc6 17.h6 ♖g6 18.♗xd8 ♕xd8 19.h7 ♕h8 20.♔c2 ♘e5 21.f3± looks very good for White, the pawn on h7 paralysing the black pieces.

Most resistance was offered by: 16...♗xc6 17.♗xe7 ♖de8 18.♗g5 ♗xh1 19.♖xh1 f6 20.♗f4 e5 21.♗e3 ♕c6 22.♖h4±/± White has the better position, but Black still has reasonable chances to survive.

17.h6+–

Now everything is clear. Black cannot stop the pawn coming to h7.

17...♖g6 18.h7 ♖xf6 19.h8=♕ ♖xh8 20.♖xh8† ♔d7 21.d4!

This is most precise. White opens the centre and the black king is left without any shield.

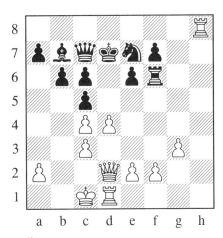

21...♕d6

21...♖xf2 22.dxc5† ♘d5 23.♕e3 ♖f5 24.cxb6 axb6 25.♖hh1!?+– was a better defence, although Black is still lost.

22.♕g5 ♖f5

After 22...♖g6 23.♕h4 ♔c7 24.dxc5 ♕xc5 25.♖e8+– it is time to resign.

23.♕h4 cxd4 24.♖xd4 ♖d5

A last desperate try.

25.cxd5 ♕a3† 26.♔b1 cxd5 27.♖h7 ♕xc3 28.♖xf7

1–0

GAME 4
▷ **B. Gelfand (2746)**
▶ **B. Jobava (2712)**
European Club Cup, Rogaska Slatina
27.09.2011 **[A61]**
Annotated by Kamil Miton

The Benoni family of defences are rarely seen at the highest level, with the major exception of Vugar Gashimov who uses the Modern Benoni regularly. The present game sees Badur Jobava, one of the most combative players around, playing the aggressive 9...b5!? against White's ♗f4/♕a4 set-up. Unfortunately for the Georgian grandmaster he soon went wrong in a known position with the weak 13...♘a6? and quickly lost the game. The critical continuation is 13...b4 14.♘b1 ♖c8!? as analysed in the notes.

1.d4 ♘f6 2.c4 e6 3.♘f3 c5 4.d5 exd5 5.cxd5 g6 6.♘c3 ♗g7

Benoni positions tend to lead to unbalanced play and murky complications, so the opening is often employed by aggressive players, especially when playing for a win against a weaker opponent – not that the last description in any way applies to Boris Gelfand.

7.♗f4 d6 8.♕a4† ♗d7 9.♕b3

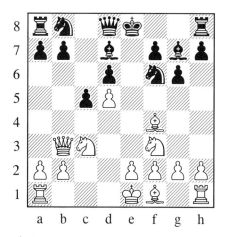

9...b5!?

Apart from this aggressive move Black has some quieter options.

9...♗c8!? appears to be a tempo loss but is not such a bad move, as the white queen is not ideally placed on b3.

9...♕c7 10.e4

10.♗xd6?? is of course disastrous due to 10...♕xd6 11.♕xb7 ♕b6 12. ♕xa8 ♕xb2–+. However, White can consider a quieter set-up involving 10.e3!? intending h3 (securing a retreat square on h2 for the bishop) followed by ♗e2 and ♘d2-c4.

10...0–0

White has a space advantage in the centre and his main plan will be to break through in the centre with e4-e5. Meanwhile Black will either look to seize space on the queenside with ...b5, or strive for the initiative on the kingside with ...f5.

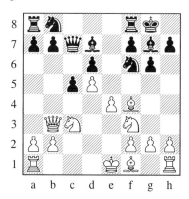

White can try a few ideas from this position.

a) 11.♗d3?!

In my opinion this move is inaccurate and enables Black to generate the kind of dynamic counterplay that is so typical for the Modern Benoni.

11...♖e8 12.♘d2

12.0–0 can be met by the thematic 12...c4! 13.♕xc4 ♕xc4 14.♗xc4 ♘xe4 15.♖fe1 ♘xc3 16.♖xe8† ♗xe8 17.bxc3 ♘d7 with equality.

12...♘h5 13.♗e3

F. Mueller – D. Richter, Nordhausen 2009.

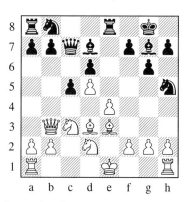

13...f5!N 14.exf5

14.f3?! weakens the dark squares. 14...♗d4!
15.♗xd4 cxd4 16.♘e2 (16.♘b5 ♕b6 17.a4
♘a6 18.♘c4 ♕d8↑) 16...♘a6 17.♗xa6 bxa6
18.♘xd4 ♘f4↑

14.g3 fxe4 15.♘dxe4 ♗f5 16.♘b5 ♕a5†
17.♘d2 ♗xd3 18.♕xd3 ♗xb2 19.♘xd6
♗xa1 20.♘xe8 ♘d7 21.♘d6∞

14...♘f4

14...gxf5 15.0–0 f4 16.♕d1 fxe3 (16...♖e5
17.♘c4 ♖g5 18.♘e4 ♖xd5 19.♘cxd6±)
17.♗xh7† ♔xh7 18.♕xh5† ♔g8 19.fxe3
♕d8 20.♘de4→

15.♗f1

15.♗e4 ♖xe4 16.♘dxe4 ♘xg2† 17.♔e2
♘xe3 18.fxe3 ♗xf5⹊

15...gxf5 16.g3 ♘g6 17.♗e2 ♘a6 18.0–0 f4
19.gxf4 ♖f8 20.♔h1 ♘xf4 21.♖g1

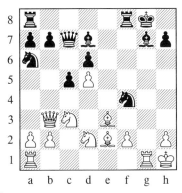

21...♗e8!∞

Better than 21...♘xe2 22.♖xg7† ♔xg7
23.♘xe2 ♗f5 24.♖g1† ♔g6 25.♘f4 ♕e7
26.♘e6† ♔g8 27.♗g5 when White has an
attack.

b) 11.♗e2 b5!?

The e4-pawn is not well defended and the
white king has not yet castled, which is
enough to justify Black's activity on the
queenside.

12.e5

12.♘xb5 ♗xb5 13.♕xb5 ♘xe4 14.0–0
♘d7!? 15.♕c6 ♕d8 16.♗d3 ♖c8 17.♕a6
f5∞

12.♗xb5 ♘xe4 13.♘xe4 ♕a5† 14.♗d2
♕xb5 15.♗xb5 ♗xb5 16.♘xd6 ♗d3∞

12...♘h5 13.♗e3 c4 14.♕b4 ♖c8!? 15.♖c1
After 15.exd6 ♕b7 the white queen is
awkwardly placed.
15...♘a6 16.♕xd6 ♕xd6 17.exd6 ♘c5 18.0–0
b4 19.♘d1 ♘d3∞

c) 11.♘d2

A typical manoeuvre. The knight is heading
for c4, where it attacks the pawn on d6 while
supporting the future advance of the e-pawn.

11...♘h5

Aiming for ...f5, although one should not
forget that the move ...b5 could appear at an
appropriate moment.

12.♗e3 f5 13.exf5

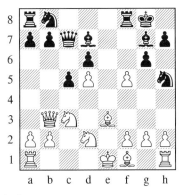

13...♗xf5

Also possible is: 13...gxf5 14.♗e2 f4N
(14...♗e8?! Black's pieces are uncoordinated
and ...f4 is still not a real threat. 15.0–0 a6
[15...f4 16.♗xc5±] 16.♕d1 ♘f6 17.♘f3
b5 18.♘g5 ♗f7 19.♗d3 ♕c8 20.♕f3
♗g6 21.♘e6 ♘bd7 22.♗f4± Inarkiev –
Gashimov, Baku 2008.) 15.♗xc5 ♕xc5
Thanks to the strong bishop on g7, Black has
some compensation for the pawn. 16.♘de4
(16.♗xh5 a5 17.0–0 a4 18.♕d1 a3 19.♘de4
♕d4 20.b3 ♕xd1 21.♖axd1 ♘a6⹊) 16...♕b6
17.♗xh5 ♕xb3 18.axb3 ♗e5 19.0–0 ♘a6⹊

14.♗e2

14.♘b5?! ♕d8 15.♘c4 a6 16.♘bxd6 b5
17.♘xf5 gxf5↑

14.h3 ♕e7!⇄ The threat of ...♘g3 is unpleasant for White.

14...♘f6 15.0–0 a6

15...♘bd7? 16.♘b5 ♕b8 17.♗f4 ♘e8 18.♘c4±

15...♘a6 16.a3 ♕f7 17.♘c4 ♖ad8 18.♖ad1±

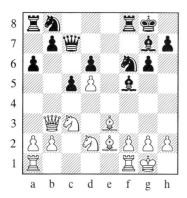

In this position I analysed two continuations for White:

c1) 16.a4

In most types of Benoni this move is virtually an automatic reaction to ...a6. In the present case it is playable, but not the best.

16...♘bd7 17.h3 ♘e5

17...♖ae8?! 18.g4 ♘e4 19.gxf5 ♘xd2 20.♗xd2 ♗xc3 21.♕xc3 ♖xe2 22.♗h6 (22.♖ae1 ♖xd2 23.♕xd2 ♖xf5∞) 22...♖f7 23.♖ae1↑ The black king is vulnerable.

After the text move Black has managed to get organized and his position is quite all right, for instance:

18.f4

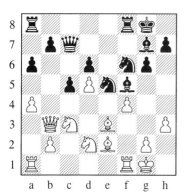

18...♘d3! 19.g4

White is playing a risky game as his pieces are a long way from the kingside. Nevertheless the position remains in balance.

19...♕e7! 20.♘d1

20.♖f3 ♗xg4 21.hxg4 ♘xg4 22.♗xd3 ♘xe3 23.♘e2 ♗d4 24.♘xd4 cxd4→

20.♘c4 b5!? 21.axb5 axb5 22.♘xb5 (22.♕xb5 ♖xa1 23.♖xa1 ♘h5! [23...♘xg4=] 24.gxf5 ♘hxf4 25.♗f1 ♗d4 26.♗xd4 cxd4 27.f6 ♖xf6→) 22...♖xa1 23.♖xa1 ♘xf4 24.♗xf4 (24.♗f1 ♖xh3† 25.♗xh3 ♘xg4→) 24...♖xe2 25.gxf5 ♘e4 26.♖f1 ♖xf5 27.♘e3 ♖f8→

20...♘xg4 21.hxg4 ♕h4 22.♖f2 ♘xf2 23.♗xf2 ♕e7 24.♕e3 ♕xe3 25.♘xe3 ♗d7∞

c2) 16.h3!

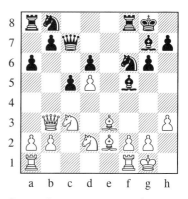

In fact White can ignore his opponent's queenside play and accelerate his own plans.

16...b5 17.g4 ♗c8

17...c4 18.♕b4 ♗d3 19.♗xd3 cxd3 20.a4± The d3-pawn is weak.

18.a4!

A thematic move to seize control over the c4-square.

18...b4 19.♘ce4±

White controls the c4-square and Black's queenside play is blocked. Additionally, White is better developed and has the promising plan of ♘g5-e6.

10.♗xd6

10.♘xb5?! has been played in several games, but after 10...♗xb5 11.♕xb5† ♘bd7 12.♗xd6 ♘e4 13.♗e5 0–0 14.♗xg7 ♔xg7 White's king remains in the centre and Black may develop a strong attack using the b-file and a5-e1 diagonal.

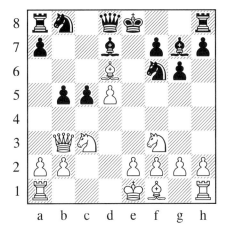

10...♕b6

10...♘a6?!

This move is inaccurate, but it is important for White to know how to react.

11.♘xb5

11.a4 ♕b6 12.♘xb5 ♘e4 13.♗e5 0–0 14.♕c4 ♖fe8 15.♕xe4 ♘b4↑

11.e3 c4 12.♕d1 ♗g4 13.♗e5 0–0∞

11...♘e4

11...♕a5† 12.♘c3 ♘e4 13.♗e5±

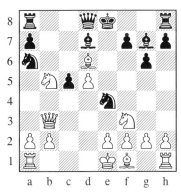

12.♘d2!

12.♕a4 ♘b4 13.♗xc5 ♘xc5 14.♘d6† ♔f8

15.♕xb4 ♕e7 16.♕xc5 ♗xb2 17.♖b1 ♖c8 18.♕xa7 ♗c3† 19.♘d2 ♕xd6 20.e4 ♔g7∞

12...♕a5 13.0–0–0 ♗xb5

13...♘xd2 14.♕e3† ♔d8 15.♗e7† ♔c8 16.♘d6† ♔c7 17.♖xd2 ♕xa2 18.♕a3±

14.♘xe4 ♔d7

14...0–0–0 15.♗e7±

15.e3 ♖ab8 16.♗xb8 ♖xb8 17.♗xb5† ♖xb5 18.♕c4 ♗xb2† 19.♔c2 f5 20.a4 ♖b6 21.♖b1 fxe4 22.♖xb2 ♘b4† 23.♔d1 ♕xa4† 24.♔e2±

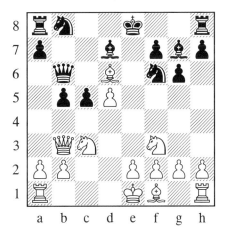

11.♗e5

Aiming to neutralize the g7-bishop.

11.e4? is worse: 11...♕xd6 12.e5 c4 13.♘xb5 ♕xe5† (13...♕b6 14.♗xc4 ♘e4∓) 14.♘xe5 cxb3 15.♘c7† ♔e7 16.f4 ♖c8 17.♘xa8 ♘xd5 18.axb3 ♗xe5 19.fxe5 ♘c6 20.♗a6 ♖xa8 21.♗b7 ♖b8 22.♗xc6 ♗xc6 23.♖xa7† ♔e6 24.0–0 ♗e8∓

11...0–0 12.e3

White has an extra pawn but he still requires two tempos to complete his development. In that time Black will strive for counterplay by advancing on the queenside and attacking the d5-pawn.

12...c4

Improving over a previous game where Gelfand had the white pieces.

12...b4?!

Weakening the c4-square does not make a good impression. Now even if Black regains the d5-pawn (which is far from guaranteed) White is still likely to maintain a slight positional advantage based on a strong piece outpost on c4.

13.♘b1

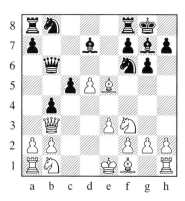

13...a5

13...♗b5 14.♗xb5 ♕xb5 15.♗xf6 ♗xf6 16.♘a3 ♕b7 17.♘c4 ♕xd5 18.♘b6±

13...♗f5 14.♘bd2 ♘bd7 15.♘c4 ♕d8 16.♖d1 (16.♗e2 ♘xe5 17.♘cxe5 ♗e4 18.0–0 ♗xd5 19.♗c4± 16.d6±) 16...♘xe5 17.♘fxe5 ♗xd5 18.♗e2 ♕c7 19.♖xd5 ♗e6 20.♘xg6 hxg6 21.♖d1±

14.a4 ♗g4

14...♗f5!? 15.♘bd2 ♘bd7 16.♗d3 ♘xe5 17.♘xe5 ♗xd3 18.♕xd3 ♖ad8 19.♘ec4 ♖xd5 20.♘xb6 ♖xd3 21.♘bc4±

15.♘bd2 ♘bd7 16.♗b5 ♖fd8 17.♗g3 ♗xf3 18.gxf3 ♕a7

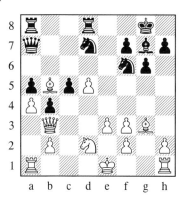

19.0–0?

19.d6!N±

19...♘xd5! 20.♗c6 c4 21.♘xc4 ♘c5 22.♕c2 ♖ac8⇄

Gelfand – Gashimov, Linares 2010.

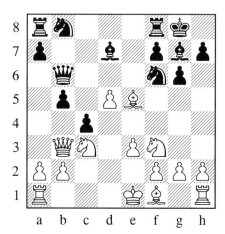

13.♕d1

This position has been reached in several games. Black's next move must have been either a bad decision at the board or faulty preparation.

13...♘a6?

A weak move.

The right path is:
13...b4!

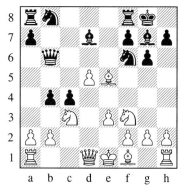

This move can lead to all kinds of complicated variations. We will check the various possibilities, one by one.

a) 14.♘a4?! ♛a5 15.♛d4 (15.b3 ♝xa4 16.bxa4 ♘bd7∓) 15...♝xa4 16.♝xf6 ♝xf6 17.♛xf6 ♘d7 18.♛d4 c3 19.♝e2 cxb2 20.♛xb2 ♖fc8 21.♘d4 ♘f6 22.0–0 ♘xd5=

b) 14.♘e2

Temporarily blocking White's development, but the idea is to put the knight on f4 to help protect the d5-pawn.

14...♝b5 15.♘f4

15.♝d4 ♛b7 16.♖c1 ♖c8∞ The d5-pawn is weak.

15.♘ed4 ♘bd7 16.♝xf6 (16.♘xb5 ♛xb5 17.♝d4 ♛xd5 18.♝e2 ♖fc8 19.0–0 c3∞) 16...♘xf6 17.♖c1 ♖ac8 18.♘xb5 ♛xb5 19.♖xc4 ♖xc4 20.b3 ♛xd5 21.♝xc4 ♛xd1† 22.♔xd1 ♘e4=

15...♘bd7 16.♝d4 ♛b7

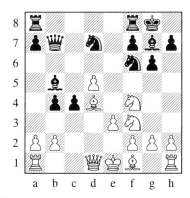

17.♝e2

17.d6 ♝h6 18.♝e2 ♖fe8 19.0–0 g5⇄

17.♖c1!? ♝h6 18.♝xc4 (18.♝xf6 ♘xf6 19.♛d4 ♝xf4 20.♛xf6 ♝h6⊜) 18...♝xf4 19.exf4 ♖ac8 20.b3 ♘xd5 21.0–0 ♝xc4 22.bxc4 ♘xf4 23.♛d2 ♘e6 24.♝a1 Black has some problems to solve, due to the potential threats on the long diagonal.

17...♘xd5 18.♘xd5

18.♝xg7 ♘xf4 19.♝xf8 ♘xe2 20.♝xb4 c3 21.♝xc3 ♘c5 22.♛d6 ♘e4↑

18...♛xd5 19.♝xg7 ♛xd1† 20.♖xd1 ♔xg7 21.♘d4 ♝a6

21...a6 22.♘xb5 axb5 23.♖xd7 ♖xa2 24.♖d2

♖fa8 25.0–0 c3 26.♖c2 cxb2 27.♖b1 b3 28.♖cxb2 ♖xb2 29.♖xb2 ♖a2 30.♖xb3 ♖xe2 31.g4±

22.♘c2 ♝b5 23.♘xb4 ♖ab8 24.0–0 ♘f6 25.♖d4 ♝d7 26.a3 a5 27.♘d5 ♘xd5 28.♖xd5 ♖xb2 29.♝xc4 ♝e6 30.♖b5 ♖b8=

c) 14.♘b1

Probably the most challenging move.

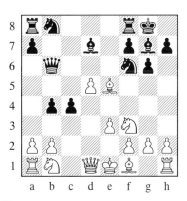

14...♖c8!

Supporting a future advance of the c-pawn. Other moves do not equalize:

14...♛c5 15.♘bd2 c3 16.bxc3 bxc3 17.♘b3 ♛xd5 18.♝xc3±

14...♝b5 has been the usual move, but so far no one has found the best reaction: 15.a3!N Weakening Black's queenside structure and securing the c3-square for the knight. Even if Black regains the d5-pawn, White should maintain a positional advantage. 15...♘bd7 16.♝d4 ♛a5 17.♘bd2 ♖ac8 18.axb4 ♛xb4 19.♝c3±

After 14...♖c8! White has four main candidates.

c1) 15.♝d4 ♛b7 16.♘bd2 ♝b5 17.a4 ♝a6 (17...bxa3?! weakens Black's structure and eliminates the possibility of pushing the c-pawn. 18.♖xa3 ♛xd5 19.♝e2 ♘c6 20.♝c3±) 18.♖c1 ♛xd5 19.♝e2 ♘c6 20.0–0 (20.♝xf6 ♝xf6 21.♝xc4 ♖xc4 22.♘xc4 ♝c3† 23.bxc3 ♛xc4 24.cxb4 ♛xb4† 25.♛d2 ♛xa4=)

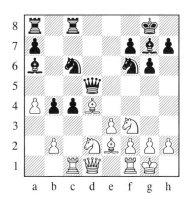

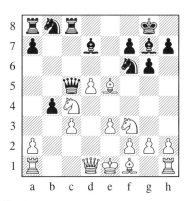

20...♘xd4 21.♘xd4 ♖ab8 22.b3 ♕d7 23.♗xc4 ♗b7∞ Black has compensation thanks to his strong pair of bishops and the possibility of transferring the knight to c3.

c2) 15.♘bd2 c3 16.♘c4

16.bxc3 bxc3 17.♘c4 ♕a6 18.♘d6 (18.♖c1 ♗a4 19.♘d6 ♕xd6 20.♕xa4 [20.♗xd6 ♗xd1 21.♖xd1 c2 22.♖c1 ♘xd5 23.♗d3 ♘c6⇄] 20...♕xd5 21.♖xc3 ♘bd7 22.♗a6 ♘xe5 23.♖xc8† ♖xc8 24.♗xc8 ♘e4 25.0–0 ♘xf3† 26.gxf3 ♘d2=) 18...c2 19.♕d2 ♕a3

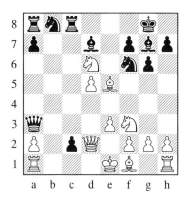

20.♖c1 (20.♘xc8 ♘e4 21.♕xc2 ♗e5 22.♘xe5 ♕a5† 23.♔e2 ♘c3† 24.♔f3 ♕xd5† 25.e4 ♕xe5 26.♖c1 ♘c6 27.♕xc3 ♘d4† 28.♔e3 ♖xc8 29.♕d2 ♘f5† 30.♔f3 ♘d4†=) 20...♗f8 21.♖xc2 ♗xd6 22.♖xc8† ♗xc8 23.♗b2 ♕xa2 24.♗xf6 ♕b1† 25.♕d1 ♗b4† 26.♘d2 ♕a2 27.♕c1 ♘d7 28.♗c3 ♗xc3 29.♕xc3 ♗a6↑

16...♕c5 17.bxc3

17...♘xd5

17...bxc3 18.♗xc3 ♗b5 19.♗d4 ♕b4† 20.♕d2 ♖xc4 21.♗xc4 ♕xc4 22.♖c1 ♕a4 23.♖c8† ♘e8 24.♗xg7 ♔xg7 25.♕d4† ♕xd4 26.♘xd4 ♗d7 27.♖c5± In this instance White's rook and two pawns are better than Black's two pieces because White has a strong centre and he may easily strengthen his position with moves like ♔d2, e4, ♖hc1, ♖a5, ♔e3 and so on.

18.♗xg7 ♔xg7 19.cxb4

19.♕d4† f6 20.♕xc5 ♖xc5 21.cxb4 ♘xb4 22.♖b1 ♘xa2=

19...♕xb4† 20.♘fd2 ♗a4 21.♕c1 ♘a6∞ 22.a3 ♕e7 23.♗e2 ♘c5 24.♕b2† f6 25.0–0 ♖ab8 26.♕d4 ♖d8

Black's activity provides ongoing compensation.

c3) 15.a3 ♕a5

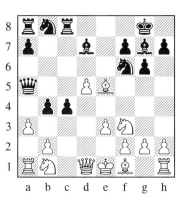

16.♘bd2

16.♕d4 c3 17.bxc3 bxc3 18.♘xc3 ♘e4
19.♕xe4 (19.♗xg7 ♖xc3 20.♘d2 ♖c2
21.♕b4 ♕xb4 22.axb4 ♖xd2 23.♗d3 ♖c8
24.♗xd2 ♔xg7 25.b5⩲) 19...♖xe5 20.♕xe5
♖xc3 21.♘d2 ♗e6 22.♗e2 ♘c6 23.♕f4
♗xd5 24.0–0 ♖c2 25.♘e4 ♖xe2 26.♖ac1
♗xe4 27.♕xe4 ♕xa3 28.♖xc6=

16...c3

Highlighting the main advantage of
14...♖c8! over the more common 14...♗b5.

17.bxc3

17.♘c4 ♕xd5 18.axb4 cxb2 19.♗xb2 ♕b7⩲

17...bxc3 18.♘c4 ♕xd5

18...♕a6 is met by 19.♘d6 when the queen
does not have the a3-square available.
19...c2 20.♕d2 ♕xd6 21.♗xd6 ♘e4 22.♗e5
♘xd2 23.♔xd2 ♖c5 24.♗xg7 ♔xg7 25.♗d3
♖xd5 26.♔e2±

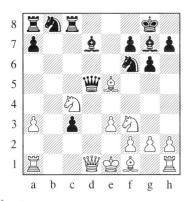

19.♗xc3

19.♘d6 ♖c6 20.♗c4 ♕xd1† 21.♖xd1 ♘g4
22.♗g3 ♗e6∞

19...♗e6 20.♕xd5 ♗xd5 21.♘fd2 ♘bd7
22.♗d4

White still has some problems with
development as ♗e2 will allow ...♗xg2.
Meanwhile Black will develop counterplay
along the b- and c-files, and against the
vulnerable a3-pawn.

22...♘b6

22...♖c7!? is another idea.

23.♗xb6 ♗xc4 24.♗xc4

24.♘xc4 axb6 25.♘xb6 ♘e4 26.♘xc8 ♗c3†

27.♔e2 ♗xa1=
24...axb6 25.0–0 ♘e8 26.♖a2 ♘d6 27.♗b3
b5⩲

c4) 15.♗e2

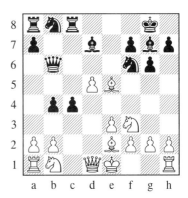

15...♗f5

15...♕c5!? 16.0–0 ♕xd5 17.♖xd5 ♘xd5
18.♗xg7 ♔xg7 19.♖c1 ♗b5 20.♘d4 c3
21.bxc3 ♗xe2 22.♘xe2 ♘a6⩲

16.♘bd2

Maybe White should consider: 16.0–0
♘bd7 17.♗d4 ♕a5 18.♘h4!? (18.a3 c3↑;
18.♘bd2 c3 19.♘c4 ♕xd5 20.bxc3 bxc3
21.♗xc3 ♕xd1 22.♖fxd1 ♗e6 23.♗xf6
[23.♘fd2 ♘b6 24.♘xb6 axb6 25.♗d4
♘d5⩲] 23...♗xf6 24.♖ac1 ♘b6 25.♘xb6
axb6 26.♖xc8† ♖xc8 27.a4 ♗b3 28.♖b1
♗xa4 29.♖xb6 ♖c1† 30.♗f1 ♔g7=) 18...♗e4
19.♘d2 ♗xd5 20.a3!±

**16...c3 17.♘c4 ♕d8 18.bxc3 ♘bd7 19.cxb4
♘xe5**

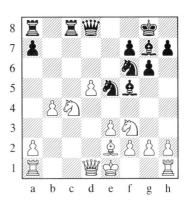

20.♘cxe5

20.♘fxe5!? ♘xd5 21.0–0 ♗e6 leaves White's knights unstable, while the strong g7-bishop and weakness of the c3-square seem to give Black promising counterplay. Nevertheless after 22.♕d2 (22.♖c1 ♘xb4 23.♕xd8† ♖xd8 24.a3 ♘a2 25.♖c2 ♖ac8 26.f4 ♖c5⇄) 22...♕c7 23.f4 ♖d8 24.♕e1 f6 25.♘f3 ♘xf4 26.exf4 ♗xc4 27.♗xc4† ♕xc4 28.f5± White's position is a bit easier.

20...♘xd5 21.0–0

21.♕d4 ♗e6⯈

21...♗e4 22.♖c1

22.♗c4 ♖xc4 23.♘xc4 ♗xa1 24.♕xa1 ♗xf3 25.gxf3 ♕g5† 26.♔h1 ♕f5 27.♘d2 ♘xb4 28.♕d4 a5 29.a3 ♘c2 30.♕d6 ♘xa3 31.♕xa3 ♖d8 32.♖b1 ♕c2 33.♕xa5 ♕xd2 34.♕xd2 ♖xd2 35.♔g2±

22...♖xc1 23.♕xc1 ♖c8

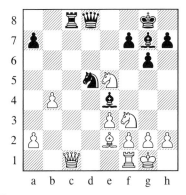

24.♕d2

24.♘c6 ♕e8 25.b5 ♘c3⇄

24...♕e7

24...♗xe5 25.♘xe5 ♗xg2 26.♗g4±

25.♗d3 ♗xf3 26.♘xf3 ♕xb4 27.♖c1 ♘c3

The strong knight makes it hard for the white rook to join in the game, making it difficult for White to make much use of his extra pawn. The a2-pawn is also vulnerable, and ...a5-a4-a3 may feature in Black's plans.

To summarize, 13...b4 14.♘b1 ♖c8! was the critical continuation for this line, and would

have given Black much better chances than the game continuation. We examined a jungle of variations. In a few of them White maintained somewhat better chances, it is hard to say if this would be enough for serious winning chances at a high level.

Let us now return to the game after 13...♘a6?, after which White quickly obtained a large advantage.

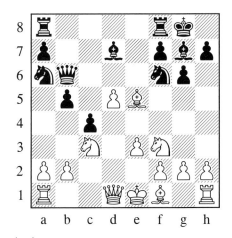

14.a4!±

White's idea is the same as after a2-a3 against a black pawn on b4: to destroy the enemy queenside structure.

14...♘b4

14...b4 15.♘b5±

15.axb5

15.♗e2 bxa4 16.0–0± is also tempting.

15...♗f5 16.♗xc4

Simplest, although White could also have considered: 16.♖c1!? ♘d3† (16...♖ac8 17.♕d4 ♘c2† 18.♖xc2 ♗xc2 19.d6 ♕xd4 20.♘xd4 ♗b3 21.♘c6↑) 17.♗xd3 ♗xd3 18.b3 (18.♗d4 ♕d6 19.♘e5 ♘xd5 20.♘xc4 ♗xc4 21.♗xg7 ♖fd8 22.♘xd5 ♗xd5 23.♗c3 ♗xg2 24.♕xd6 ♖xd6 25.♖g1 ♗e4) 18...♖fe8 19.♗d4 ♕d6 20.bxc4 ♗xc4 21.♘d2 ♗xd5 22.0–0±

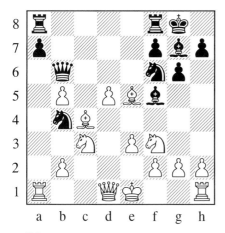

16...♖fc8

16...♘c2† 17.♔e2 (17.♔f1 ♘g4 18.♖a6 ♘gxe3† 19.fxe3 ♘xe3† 20.♔g1 ♘xd1† 21.♖xb6 axb6 22.♘xd1 ♗xe5 23.♘xe5 ♖fe8 24.♘f3 ♖a1 25.♔f2 ♘c2 26.♗e2±) 17...♘xa1 18.♕xa1 ♘e4 19.♗xg7 ♔xg7 20.b3± White has a great position: three pawns for the exchange, numerous stable outposts for his pieces in the centre, and weaknesses in the enemy king position on the dark squares.

17.b3 ♘g4 18.♗xg7

18.♘a4 was also winning.

18...♘c2†

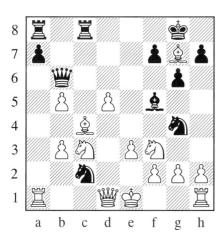

19.♕xc2!!

19.♔e2 was also winning, but Gelfand's queen sacrifice makes a lovely aesthetic impression.

19...♗xc2 20.♗d4 ♕d8 21.0–0+–

The material balance is approximately even, with White having two pieces and three pawns for the queen. But White's pieces are perfectly coordinated in the centre, and his position is so strong that it practically wins by itself, with no effort from the player.

21...♕e7 22.♖fc1 ♗f5 23.e4! ♗d7 24.h3 ♘f6 25.d6 ♕d8 26.e5 ♘h5 27.♘d5

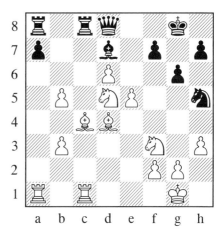

The board reveals a beautiful picture of total domination by the white pieces.

27...♔f8 28.♗e3 ♘g7 29.♗g5 1–0

B

GAME 5

▷ **F. Caruana (2712)**
▶ **P. Eljanov (2683)**
European Club Cup, Rogaska Slatina
01.10.2011**[B12]**
Annotated by Borki Predojevic

The Caro-Kann is one of the most popular openings at the top level today, so we frequently see interesting new ideas in this line. In the 4.♘d2 line of the Advance Variation, Eljanov chose the rare line 6...c5!? and it seems this is playable for Black. Eljanov then played the novelty 11...♗g6N, but the previously played 11...0–0 also looks fine for Black. After the opening Black had no problems and when White let him achieve a break with ...b4 it was clear that only Black could win the game. After a period of waiting moves from both sides, White made the fatal mistake 52.f4?? and soon resigned.

It is worth mentioning that I also cover new games in the more popular 6...a6!? line. Both 6...c5 and 6...a6!? are currently giving Black good results, so now it is up to White to find a new way to fight for an advantage.

1.e4 c6 2.d4 d5 3.e5 ♗f5 4.♘d2 e6 5.♘b3 ♘d7 6.♘f3

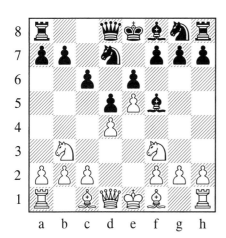

6...c5!?

In the European Club Cup my team-mates GM Berkes and GM Ragger played instead the popular:

6...a6!?

Black wants to push ...c6-c5 without allowing ♗b5†. Now there are two options: a) 7.♗e3 and the main move b) 7.♗e2.

a) **7.♗e3**

White is trying to stop ...c5 but Black can plays the normal:

7...♖c8

Once again ...c5 is coming.

8.c3 c5 9.dxc5

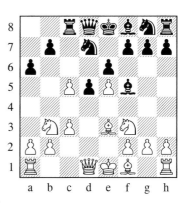

9...♗xc5!

Black is okay.

Worse is 9...♘xc5 10.♘fd4! ♗g6 11.♗e2 ♘h6 12.h4± and White is clearly better. In Jakovenko – Eljanov, Odessa 2010, the game continued 12...♘xb3 13.axb3 ♗c5 and after 14.h5 ♗f5 15.♗xh6 gxh6 16.g4 ♗xd4 17.♕xd4 ♗c2 18.♖a3 ♕g5 19.♕d2+− Black lost a piece.

Normal now is:

10.♘xc5 ♘xc5 11.♗e2 ♘e7

White can chose a plan with:

12.♘h4

But after:

12...h6 13.♘xf5 ♘xf5 14.♗xc5 ♖xc5=

Black had no problems. Now White made an error:

15.♗d3?

  15.0–0 0–0=

15...d4! 16.♕a4† b5 17.♕xa6 ♖xe5†∓

Black was clearly better in Navara – Grischuk, Khanty-Mansiysk 2011.

b) 7.♗e2 c5 8.dxc5 ♗xc5!

As we have already seen, this is Black's main idea.

9.0–0 ♘e7 10.♘xc5 ♘xc5

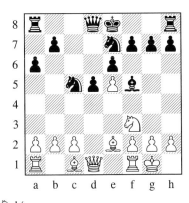

11.♘d4

After 11.♗e3 ♖c8 12.c4 0–0 13.♖c1 ♘d7 14.♗g5 the best reaction is: 14...h6!N (worse is 14...♗e4 15.♘d2 ♗f5 16.♘f3 ♗e4 17.♘d2 ♗f5 18.cxd5 ♖xc1 19.♕xc1 ♘xe5 20.dxe6 ♗xe6 21.♖d1± Van Kampen – Turov, Haarlem 2011) 15.♗xe7 ♕xe7 16.cxd5 ♖xc1 17.♕xc1 exd5 18.♕c7 ♕b4⇄ Black has nothing to worry about.

11.♘h4 ♗e4 12.f3 ♗g6 leads to a good game for Black. After 13.♗e3 ♖c8 14.c3 b5! 15.♖e1 ♘a4 16.♕d2 ♘c6 17.♘xg6 hxg6 18.f4 ♘a5 19.♗d4 ♘c4 20.♗xc4 dxc4⇄ Black had a nice position in Z. Almasi – Grischuk, Ningbo 2011.

11...0–0 12.a4

With this move White stops ...b5.

12...♖c8 13.♗e3 ♘d7

After the games from the European Club Cup we also saw fights in this line in the Poikovsky 2011 super-tournament. In one of these games Black played the interesting

13...♕c7!? and White replied: 14.f4 ♗e4 15.a5 ♘f5 16.♗f2 f6! 17.exf6 ♖xf6 18.g3 ♘d7 19.♗a3 ♘xd4 20.♗xd4 ♕f8 21.♗d3 ♗xd3 22.cxd3

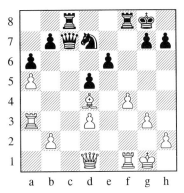

22...♘b8! 23.♕g4 ♕d7 24.♖e1 ♘c6 25.♗c5 ♖f6 26.d4 h6 This was Caruana – Motylev, Poikovsky 2011, which you can find analysed in detail in Game 6, starting on page 60.

14.f4 ♗e4 15.c3 ♘c6 16.♘xc6 ♖xc6 17.♗d4 Inaccurate is 17.a5. Black continues with his plan: 17...f6 18.exf6 ♕xf6 19.♖f2 ♕g6!⇄ And now after 20.♗h5 ♕h6 21.♗e2 ♕g6 22.♕b3 ♖c7 23.♖e1 ♘e5!= 24.♕d1 a draw was agreed in Grischuk – Ragger, ECC 2011. Black has no problems and 24...♘c4 would lead to easy equality.

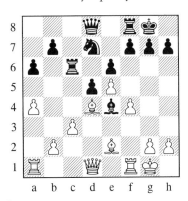

17...f6

A typical idea in this set-up. Many players will compare this position with those which arise from the French Defence.

18.♕d2

18.exf6 ♘xf6 19.♕d2 ♘e8! 20.♖ae1 ♘d6
21.b3 ♘f5 22.♗f3 ♗xf3 23.♖xf3 ♕a5 ½–½
Rublevsky – Laznicka, Poikovsky 2011.
18...♘c5! 19.♖a3 fxe5 20.♗xe5 ♘d7 21.♗d4

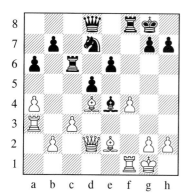

21...e5?!

Too optimistic. As Ferenc told me after
the game, he saw 21...♘b6 22.♕e3 ♕c7
(22...♘c4?! 23.♗xc4 ♖xc4 would be met
by 24.♗c5 ♖f6 25.b3 ♖xc5 26.♕xc5± with
a clear advantage for White) 23.♖a2 ♘c4
24.♗xc4 ♖xc4= which leads to a more or less
equal position, but he thought that the move
in the game was better.
22.fxe5 ♖g6 23.♖xf8† ♘xf8 24.♗f1 ♘e6
25.♗e3 h5 26.♖b3 h4 27.h3 ♕c7 28.c4

28.a5!?± would keep some pressure.

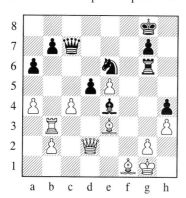

28...d4! 29.♗xd4 ♕d8 30.♗e3 ♕xd2 31.♗xd2
♘d4 32.♖e3 ♘f3† 33.♖xf3 ♗xf3 34.♗e1 ♗c6
35.♗xh4 ♖xa4 36.♗e1 ♗b3
½–½ Svidler – Berkes, ECC 2011.
7.dxc5 ♗xc5 8.♘xc5 ♘xc5

The idea of ...c6-c5 and ...♗xc5 is logical
since White has played ♘b1-d2-b3 just to take
Black's bishop. Positionally, Black has made a
correct decision since he gained plenty of time
to develop his pieces.

9.♘d4 ♘e7 10.♗b5† ♘d7 11.♗g5

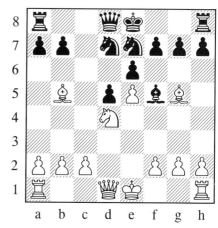

11...♗g6N

This is a novelty. Previously Black had
played:

11...0–0

This is also very interesting. Logical in reply
is:
12.♘xf5 exf5 13.♗xe7

After 13.0–0 ♘xe5 14.♖e1 f6 15.♗e3 a6
16.♗a4 ♖c8⇄ Black is okay.
13...♕xe7 14.♗xd7 ♕xd7 15.0–0

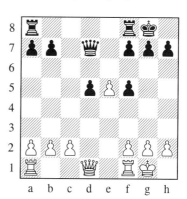

This position is very interesting. Black has a weakness on d5, but this is not so important, as he can create pressure on the c- and e-files.

15...♖ac8!N

This looks more precise than the alternative below since now ♕d4 is not possible (c2 would be hanging).

15...♖fd8 16.♕d4 ♖ac8 17.♖ac1 ♖c4 18.♕xa7 ♖a4 (18...d4!? 19.♕a3 ♕b5±/= was more acceptable for Black) 19.♕b6 ♖xa2 20.♖a1 ♖xa1 21.♖xa1 ♖c8 22.c3± White was better in T. Antal – Magyar, Hungary 2011.

16.c3 ♖c4 17.♖e1 ♖e8 18.♕d3 ♖e4! 19.♖xe4 fxe4 20.♕d4 ♕b5 21.b3 ♕d3 22.♕xd3 exd3 23.♖d1 (23.f4 ♖c8!) 23...♖xe5 24.g3 ♖e2 25.♖xd3 ♖xa2 26.♖xd5 g6=

The position is equal. This line shows that 11...0–0 should be tested more in the future.

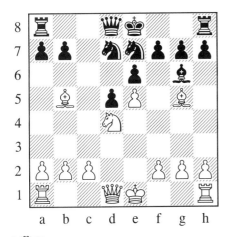

12.♕d2

After this game White tried to find an advantage by playing:

12.h4!? h6 13.♗xe7 ♕xe7 14.h5 ♗h7 15.♕g4 But now Black doesn't have to play ...a6.

15...0–0 16.♗xd7 ♕xd7 17.0–0 ♖ac8

We have reached a position which is important for us, as in the main game we will see a similar fight between bishop and knight.

18.c3 b5 19.a3 a5 20.♖fe1 b4 21.axb4 axb4

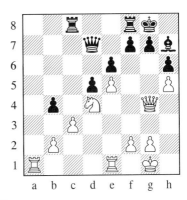

22.♖e3

More promising was 22.cxb4!? ♖c4 23.b5 since I don't see a better move than 23...♕xb5. After 24.♕xg7† ♔xg7 25.♘xb5 ♖b4 26.♘d6 ♖xb2 27.♖e3 ♗g8 28.♖a7↑ White is better but the question is whether he can convert it into a win.

22...bxc3 23.bxc3 ♔h8 24.♖g3 ♖g8=

De la Riva Aguado – Peralta, Barcelona 2011, was equal.

12...a6

This is not the only reaction, but Eljanov doesn't want to castle before his opponent.

One alternative was: 12...0–0 13.♗xe7 (13.♕b4 ♖e8 14.0–0 a6 15.♗xd7 ♕xd7⇄ gives Black a better version than in the game) 13...♕xe7 14.♗xd7 ♕xd7 Now I do not see anything better than the normal 15.0–0 (15.h4 h6=) when after 15...♖ac8 16.c3 b5⇄ Black has counterplay.

13.♗xe7 ♕xe7 14.♗xd7† ♕xd7 15.h4 h5!?

A very interesting moment; many players would not consider this unusual reaction at all, since Black puts one more pawn on a white square. A more solid reaction was 15...h6 16.h5 ♗h7, but then White can play 17.♖h3∞ and place his king on f1.

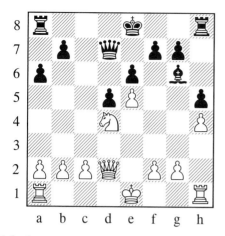

16.c3

On 16.a4 Black has time for 16...♕c7!?. After 17.0–0 (17.♕g5 ♕b6 18.♕d2 ♕c7=) 17...♕xe5 (another move is 17...0–0⇄) 18.f4 ♕f6 19.f5 exf5 20.♖ae1† ♔f8 21.♘f3∞ White has enough compensation, but no more than that.

16...b5

Both players are trying to save castling for later. If Black castles short then very quickly there would be a possibility of White playing g2-g4.

17.♕g5 a5 18.a3 ♖c8 19.0–0 0–0 20.♖fe1

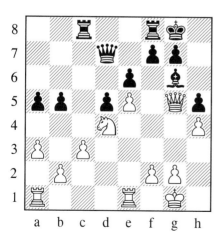

20...♖c4 21.♖e3?!

This does not look best as now Black will play ...b4.

More logical was 21.♖ad1!. Now Black has to prepare ...b4 with 21...♖b8 (21...b4? 22.cxb4 axb4 23.b3 ♖c3 24.axb4± is simply better for White. He will play next b4-b5 and the bishop on g6 is out of the game, having no influence on the queenside). After the aggressive 22.g4 ♕d8! 23.♕xd8† ♖xd8 24.gxh5 ♗xh5 25.f3∞ White would have better chances than in the game, but even so Black has no real problems here.

21...b4 22.axb4 axb4 23.g4 bxc3 24.bxc3 ♕d8!

This nice defensive move slowly leads to a slightly better position for Black.

25.gxh5 ♕xg5† 26.hxg5 ♗xh5

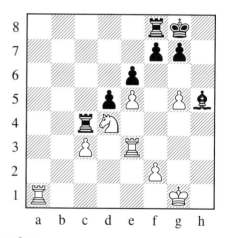

27.f3?!

There was no reason for this move, but probably Caruana missed Black's positional plan. More precise was 27.♖h3 ♗g6 (27...g6 28.♔g2 ♖fc8 29.♘b5 ♖b8 30.♘d4=) 28.♔g2 ♖fc8 29.♖ah1 ♔f8 30.♖a1!= with an equal position.

27...♖fc8 28.♘e2 ♖b8

Black could start his main plan immediately

with 28...♔h7!∓ and probably this was better than the waiting moves chosen in the game.

29.♔f2 ♗g6 30.♔g3 ♖c7 31.♘d4 ♖bc8 32.♖a3 ♖c5 33.♖b3 ♔h7!

Finally Black prepares to transfer the king to g6. I guess both players were in time trouble, as this would explain why during this stage of the game both sides were playing neutral moves.

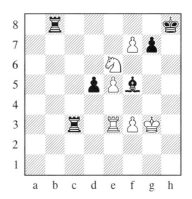

Now White can steer the game to a draw with: 52.♖e1! ♔h7 53.♘g5† ♔g6 54.e6! ♗xe6 55.♖xe6† ♔xg5 56.♖e8 ♖cc8 57.f8=♕ ♖xe8 58.♕f4† ♔g6 59.♕d6† ♔h7 60.♕xd5=

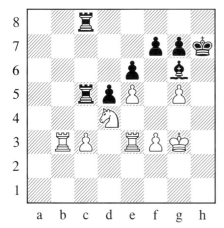

34.♘e2 ♖5c7 35.♘d4 ♖a7 36.♔f4 ♖a1 37.♖b2 ♖c1 38.♘e2 ♖c4† 39.♔g3 ♖e1 40.♖d2 ♖a4∓

In the last few moves Black activated his pieces, while White was obliged to wait. It is clear that White will have a hard job defending this position.

41.♖d4 ♖a2 42.♖h4† ♔g8 43.♔f2 ♖b1!

Now Black controls the a- and b-files. With every move Black improves one of his pieces, but the big question is if he can win this position.

44.♔g3 ♖a3 45.♔f2 ♖b2 46.♔g3 ♖c2

After 46...♗d3 47.♘d4 ♖xc3 48.g6!= White would gain counterplay which would be enough for a draw. For example: 48...♖b1 49.♖h8† ♔xh8 50.gxf7 ♖b8 51.♘xe6 ♗f5

47.♖b4 ♖a1 48.♖h4 ♖e1 49.♔f2 ♖d1!

Black's main threat is ...♗d3.

50.♖d4

On 50.♔g3 ♗d3 51.♖h2 (51.♖d4 ♖xe2 52.♖dxd3 ♖g1† 53.♔h3 ♖h1† 54.♔g3 ♖eh2!∓) 51...♗c4 Black's bishop would be on a much better post. After 52.g6 fxg6 53.♘f4 ♖g1† 54.♖g2 ♖cxg2† 55.♘xg2 g5∓ /–+ Black is, technically speaking, winning.

50...♖h1!

This is a key move; Black prepares a king invasion on the h-file.

51.♔g3 ♖h5

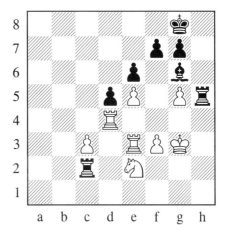

52.f4??

This is a game-ending mistake. Much stronger was 52.♖g4!∓/∓ when Black would be faced with technical problems.

52...♗f5–+

Now all the black pieces will be activated and White can't do anything about it.

53.♔f3 ♖h2 54.♖b4 ♔h7!

In the end even the black king joins the attack.

55.♖a4 ♔g6 56.♖b4 ♔h5

White resigned since he can't defend against all the threats. For example, 57.♖b8 ♗g4† 58.♔g3 ♖h3† 59.♔f2 ♖xe3–+ wins a piece.

0–1

GAME 6
▷ **F. Caruana (2712)**
▶ **A. Motylev (2690)**
12th Karpov International, Poikovsky
Round 8, 12.10.2011 **[B12]**
Annotated by Yannick Gozzoli

In this game Motylev chose the solid Caro-Kann and Caruana responded with the Advance Variation with 4.♘d2 instead of the fashionable 4.♘f3. Motylev's 6...a6!, intending to play a 'safe' ...c6-c5, is interesting and gives Black a decent and solid position, although Black has some playable alternatives as well. The critical position seems to occur around the 10th move, where White has to decide how to activate his pieces. Perhaps a plan involving c4 is most ambitious, although it has the potential to backfire due to the holes on the queenside and weakness of the e5-pawn.

The game turned into a complicated positional battle where Black chose the dubious 16...f6?!. White obtained some advantage, but failed to make the most of it and the game ended in a draw. I can only conclude by saying that these positions require a deep understanding of pawn structures and piece play, as any positional imprecision could have severe consequences.

1.e4 c6 2.d4 d5 3.e5 ♗f5 4.♘d2!?

The Advance Variation of the Caro-Kann is rather fashionable these days, as Black has had some problems equalizing. Of particular significance is the so-called "Short System" with 4.♘f3 e6 5.♗e2, which is considered the main line nowadays thanks in particular to the efforts of Karjakin amongst others. You can find several relevant games in the previous issues of *Chess Evolution*.

Of course there are a number of other possibilities, each with their own subtleties. The text move is also quite popular, and has been championed by Sergei Rublevsky.

4...e6 5.♘b3

White's main idea is to impede Black's thematic counterplay with ...c6-c5. In some cases the knight may even play a role in a queenside offensive, for instance by jumping to a5 or c5. The knight's position also has some drawbacks; it blocks the b-pawn, which takes away some options on the queenside such as developing the bishop on b2.

5...♘d7

Despite White's last move, Black can still go ahead with:

5...c5!?

However, it is a bit risky as Black must exchange an important bishop and expose his queen.

6.dxc5 ♗xc5 7.♘xc5 ♕a5† 8.c3 ♕xc5

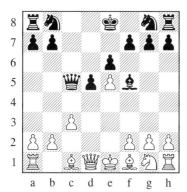

9.♕a4†!

White is searching for a concrete way to put pressure on the enemy position using the bishop pair.

9.♗e3 ♕c7 10.f4 was the latest try of Rublevsky. Undoubtedly he has his own ideas about it, but personally I do not like the idea of restricting the scope of the dark-squared bishop and weakening the e4-square. 10...♘e7 11.♘f3 ♘bc6 12.♗e2 0–0 13.0–0 ♗e4 14.♘d2 ♗g6 15.♘b3 ♖fd8 This was Rublevsky – Laznicka, Valjevo 2011. Black's position is super-solid; it is not easy for White to find a clear plan and the game was eventually drawn.

9...♘d7

9...♘c6 10.♗e3 ♕a5 11.♕xa5 ♘xa5 12.♘f3± gives White a slight edge thanks to his bishop pair.

10.♗b5 ♕c7 11.♘f3 ♘e7

11...a6!? is a possible improvement: 12.0–0 ♖c8 13.♗e2 ♘e7 14.♗g5 ♘c6 (14...♘g6?! 15.♘d4! 0–0 16.g4↑; 14...♗e4!?) 15.♘d4!? White's position seems pleasant, but the situation is not that clear. 15...0–0 (15...♕xe5?! 16.♕a3!→) 16.♘xf5 exf5∞

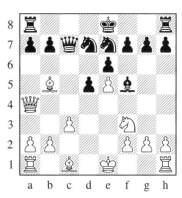

12.0–0 a6 13.♗g5 ♘g6?!

13...♘c6 14.♘d4 is also unpleasant for Black.

13...♕d8 was the best chance although White's position remains preferable.

14.♘d4!↑

Vachier Lagrave – Mchedlishvili, Mulheim 2010.

6.♘f3

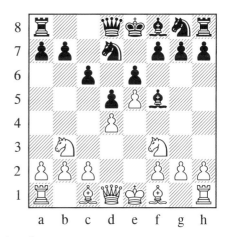

6...a6!

I like this prophylactic move. The main idea is to prepare ...c5 and meet dxc5 with ...♘xc5 without fearing a troublesome check on b5.

Black has several other options available. Here is a brief summary based on the latest games:

6...♗g6 7.♗e2 ♘h6 8.0–0 ♗e7 9.a4 0–0

10.a5 b5 11.♘e1 a6 12.♘d3± Areshchenko – Sundararajan, Chennai 2011.

6...f6 7.♗e2 ♘e7 8.0–0 fxe5 9.♘xe5 ♘xe5 10.dxe5 ♕c7

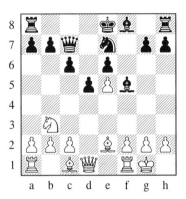

11.♖e1!?N An interesting improvement. (11.c4?! 0–0–0 12.♕e1 d4 was excellent for Black in Svidler – Ponomariov, Moscow 2008) Now if Black tries 11...0–0–0?! as in the aforementioned game, then 12.♘d4! ♕xe5 13.♗g5↑ is highly unpleasant for Black.

6...c5!? can also be played immediately: 7.dxc5 (7.c4!? is interesting and deserves further investigations) 7...♗xc5 8.♘xc5 ♘xc5 9.♘d4

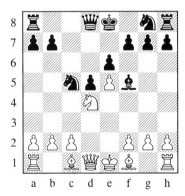

9...♘e7 10.♗b5† ♘d7 11.♗g5 ♗g6 12.♕d2 a6 13.♗xe7 ♕xe7 14.♗xd7† ♕xd7 15.h4 h5 16.c3 b5 17.♕g5 a5 18.a3 ♖c8 19.0–0 0–0= Caruana – Eljanov, Rogaska Slatina 2011.

6...♘e7

This is a solid option. Black gives priority to the development of his pieces rather than pushing the c-pawn.
7.♗e2

From here Black must decide where to put the e7-knight before developing the dark-squared bishop. His choices are a) 7...♘c8 and b) 7...♗g6 preparing ...♘f5.

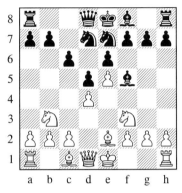

a) 7...♘c8 8.0–0 ♗e7 9.♘e1

The knight is heading for the d3-square, where it helps to control c5.
9.a4!? is an idea of Rublevsky. White plans to push the a-pawn as far as possible to create a weakness in Black's queenside. 9...0–0 10.a5 a6 11.c4 dxc4 12.♗xc4 ♘a7 Highlighting one of the advantages of the knight on c8. 13.♗e3 ♘b5 14.♕e2 ♘c7 15.♘e1 ♘d5 16.♘d3±

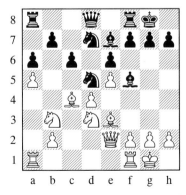

White has a pleasant position. He has a lot of space to manoeuvre his pieces, and the c5-square could make a nice outpost. On the other hand Black's position is extremely solid and he was able to draw it in Rublevsky – Doettling, Baden Baden 2011.

9...♘cb6 10.♗g4 ♗g6 11.♘d3

With the 'threat' of ♘f4 to secure the advantage of the bishop pair.

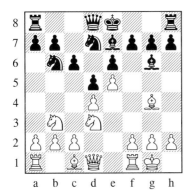

11...♗xd3?

A bad decision, after which White has a great position. Why should Black give up this bishop so readily?

12.cxd3 c5?!

Consistent, but illogical. Black only succeeds in opening the position for White's bishops. **13.dxc5 ♗xc5 14.♘xc5 ♘xc5 15.b3 ♘cd7 16.d4 0–0 17.♗a3 ♖e8 18.♖c1±**

J. Polgar – Prohaszka, Eretria 2011.

b) 7...♗g6 8.0–0 ♘f5

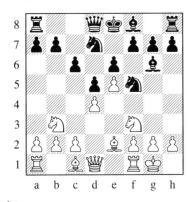

9.♗d2

9.c3 ♖c8 10.♗f4 c5?! (10...♗e7 was probably better) **11.dxc5 ♗xc5 12.♘xc5 ♘xc5 13.♗b5† ♘d7 14.♗g5 ♕c7 15.c4 a6 16.cxd5 axb5 17.♖c1 ♕b8 18.dxe6 fxe6 19.♕b3⯑** White had a strong initiative for the piece in J. Polgar – Iordachescu, Aix-les-Bains 2011.

9...♗e7

9...♖c8 10.♖c1 ♗e7 11.♗a5 b6 12.♗d2 0–0 13.c4 ♗h5 14.♖e1± Rublevsky – Hovhannisyan, Aix-les-Bains 2011.

10.g4 ♘h4 11.♘xh4 ♗xh4 12.f4

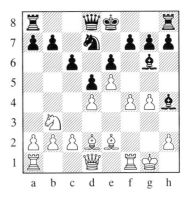

12...f5

12...♗e4 13.♗f3 ♗xf3 14.♕xf3 ♗e7 15.f5 0–0 16.♖ae1 c5 17.c3 c4 18.♘c1 ♗g5 19.♗xg5 ♕xg5 20.♘e2 exf5 21.♕xf5 ♕e7 22.♘f4 ♘b6 23.♘h5 ♕e6 24.♕g5 ♕g6 25.♕h4 ♖ae8 26.♖f5± Rublevsky – Vuckovic, Aix-les-Bains 2011.

13.exf6 ♗xf6 14.g5 ♗e7 15.♗g4 ♘f5 16.♖e1 0–0 17.♖xe6! ♗xe6 18.♗xe6† ♔h8 19.♕h5 g6 20.♕h6⯑

White eventually lost in Efimenko – Parligras, Delmenhorst 2011, but at this stage he has an excellent position with fine compensation for the small material investment.

7.♗e2!?

7.♗e3 ♖c8 8.c3 c5 9.dxc5 ♗xc5! (Improving over 9...♘xc5 10.♘fd4 ♗g6 11.♗e2 ♘h6?! 12.h4!± Jakovenko – Eljanov, Odessa 2010) **10.♘xc5 ♘xc5 11.♗e2 ♘e7 12.♘h4 h6**

13.♘xf5 ♘xf5 14.♗xc5 ♖xc5= Black position was fully satisfactory in Navara – Grischuk, Khanty-Mansiysk 2011.

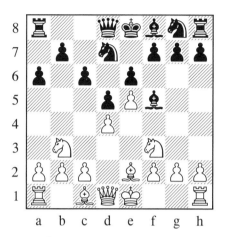

7...c5 8.dxc5

The attempt to attack in the centre with 8.c4?! is strongly met by 8...dxc4 9.♗xc4 b5∓.

8...♗xc5

8...♘xc5?! 9.♘fd4± resembles the aforementioned Jakovenko – Eljanov game, and is better for White.

9.♘xc5 ♘xc5

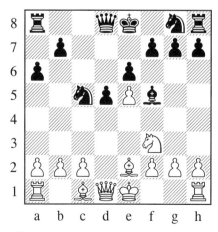

10.♘d4

White has two other ideas which deserve attention.

10.0–0 ♘e7 11.♘h4 ♗e4 (11...h6!? is possible; Grischuk actually used the same type of idea against Navara a month later in a similar position.) 12.f3 ♗g6 13.♗e3 ♖c8 14.c3 b5

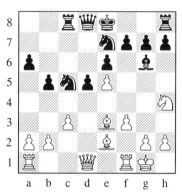

Once again White's position looks like it should be somewhat better, but Black remains as solid as ever and it is not easy for White to make progress. In the game Almasi – Grischuk, Ningbo 2011, White failed to find a convincing plan and later he got into trouble and lost.

Another interesting line is:
10.♗e3 ♖c8 11.0–0 ♘e7 12.c4!?

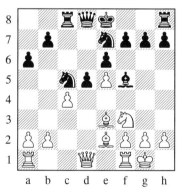

With the intention of opening the centre in order to make full use of the bishop pair. Black can try a) 12...dxc4 or b) 12...0–0.

a) 12...dxc4 13.♕xd8† ♔xd8 14.♗xc4 ♘a4 15.b3 ♘b2 16.♗e2 ♘d5 17.♘e1
In this odd-looking position Black has some

problems with his knight on b2 and his king is not safe. On the other hand White is uncoordinated and it will take some time to reorganize his pieces.

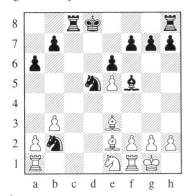

17...♔c7

17...♘c3 18.♗f3±

It is worth pointing out that 17...♘xe3? is a serious mistake, as after 18.fxe3± White is already threatening ♖xf5 followed by ♖b1 winning the knight. Black has a hard time avoiding this, as 18...♗g6 is met by 19.e4! ♗xe4 20.♗f3 ♗xf3 (20...♗g6 21.♖f2+−) 21.♖xf3+− when the knight is doomed.

18.♗h5 ♖hd8!

18...g6 19.♗f3 ♘d3 20.♗d4 (20.♗xd5 wins a pawn but after 20...♘xe1 21.♗xe6 [21.♗xb7 ♔xb7 22.♖fxe1 ♖hd8± is similar] 21...♘f3† 22.gxf3 ♗xe6± Black has good chances to hold the position a pawn down, thanks to his active pieces and the opposite-coloured bishops.) 20...♖hd8 21.♘xd3 ♗xd3± White has a slight edge but the black position is solid enough.

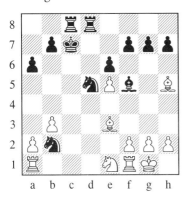

19.♗xf7 ♔b8

19...♘xe3 20.fxe3 ♔b6 21.♖f4±

20.♗g5 ♖d7 21.♗h5

White is a pawn up but his lack of coordination gives Black some counterplay.

b) 12...0–0

This seems like the safer option.

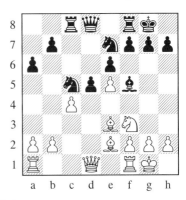

13.♖c1

Threatening to take on d5.

13...♘d7!∞

13...dxc4 14.♖xc4 is a bit more pleasant for White. After the text move White's position is optically better, but Black has a healthier pawn structure and good squares for his knights.

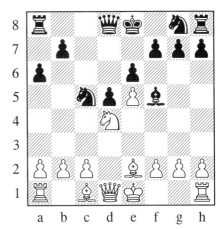

10...♘e7 11.0–0 0–0 12.♗e3 ♖c8 13.a4 ♕c7=

Black has equalized. He has some counterplay

on the c-file and against the e5-pawn. If White tries to solve the latter problem by putting his pawn on f4, the black pieces will get a nice square on e4.

At the same time it is not easy for Black to generate much activity. The only way to break White's position is to strike at the centre with ...f6, but this can create weaknesses as we will see in the game.

Black has also achieved solid results with 13...♘d7 in three recent games: 14.f4 ♗e4 15.c3 ♘c6 16.♘xc6 ♖xc6

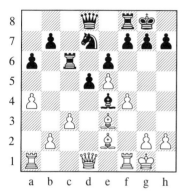

17.♗d4 (17.a5 f6 18.exf6 ♕xf6 19.♖f2 ♕g6 20.♗h5 ♕h6 21.♗e2 ♕g6 22.♕b3 ♖c7 23.♖e1 ♘e5 24.♕d1 ½–½ Grischuk – Ragger, Rogaska Slatina 2011) 17...f6 18.♕d2 (18.exf6 ♘xf6 19.♕d2 ♘e8 20.♖ae1 ♘d6 21.b3 ♘f5 22.♗f3 ♗xf3 23.♖xf3 ♖a5 ½–½ Rublevsky – Laznicka, Poikovsky 2011) 18...♘c5 19.♖a3 fxe5 20.♗xe5 ♘d7 21.♗d4 e5 22.fxe5 ♖g6 23.♖xf8† ♔xf8 24.♗f1 ♘e6 25.♗e3 h5= Svidler – F. Berkes, Rogaska Slatina 2011.

14.f4 ♗e4

Vacating the f5-square for the knight.

15.a5

Fixing the b7-pawn and giving the rook the option of joining the action along the a-file at some point.

15...♘f5 16.♗f2

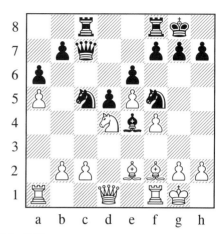

16...f6?!

Black must have been hoping to take advantage of the passivity of White's pieces. However it looks too risky to weaken the e6-pawn and the dark squares.

16...♘xd4 17.♗xd4 ♗g6 was more solid. In that case Black's position would remain fully sound, although it would be difficult for him to play for more than a win.

17.exf6

Natural, but too slow.

The strongest move was:
17.b4!
Leading to a forcing line where White has good chances to exploit his bishop pair and the weakness of the e6-pawn and the dark squares.
17...♘xd4 18.♗xd4 ♘d7 19.exf6

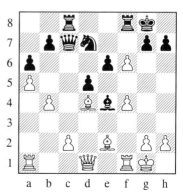

19...gxf6?!

19...♖xf6 is safer although after 20.♗d3± White has a pleasant edge.

20.♗d3 ♗xd3 21.cxd3 ♕d6

21...e5 22.♕g4† ♔h8 23.♗f2± reaches a position where Black's king is unsafe and his central pawns are rather shaky.

22.♕d2±

White is better. His bishop is shining on the board, the e6-pawn is weak and the black king is vulnerable.

17...♖xf6 18.g3

18.b4?! is not as effective in this situation, as after 18...♘d7 Black has an improved version of the above note. His rook can go to g6, and the pawns on c2 and f4 are both vulnerable. Furthermore, his knight might go to d6 and later c4 or e4.

18...♘d7 19.♖a3

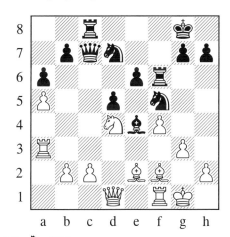

19...♖xd4?!

This move just activates the enemy bishop for no good reason. Better was: 19...♘d6 20.♗d3 (maybe White should try 20.♖c3!? ♕xa5 21.♖xc8† ♘xc8 22.♗g4 ♘f8 23.♘b3 ♕c7 24.♘c5 ♘d6 25.♗d4∞) 20...♖cf8 (or 20...e5!? immediately) intending ...e5 with a good game for Black.

20.♗xd4 ♖ff8

20...♕xc2 is strongly met by: 21.♖b3! (21.♗xf6 ♘xf6∞) 21...e5 (21...♖f7 22.♖xb7±) 22.fxe5 ♖xf1† 23.♔xf1±

21.♗d3 ♗xd3 22.cxd3±

White has emerged with a pleasant edge.

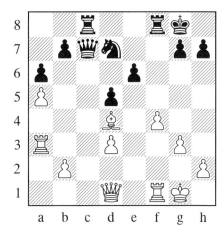

22...♘b8!

Improving the position of the worst piece.

23.♕g4 ♕d7 24.♖e1 ♘c6 25.♗c5 ♖f6 26.d4

Black's position is solid and it will not be easy for White to break through. On the other hand it is clear that Black is playing for no more than a draw.

26...h6 27.♖ae3?!

A strange decision. White could and should have calmly improved his position with 27.b4±. This secures the queenside and sets up the possibility of breaking with b5 at some moment in the future. Black has no active ideas and can only sit and wait.

27...♔h7?!

Believing the opponent's bluff. It is hard to see why Black rejected 27...♘xa5 28.♖xe6 ♖xe6 29.♕xe6† (or 29.♖xe6 ♘b3= and there is no way for White to avoid mass exchanges) 29...♕xe6 30.♖xe6 ♘b3 31.♖b6 ♘xc5 32.dxc5 ♖xc5 33.♖xb7 with a drawn endgame.

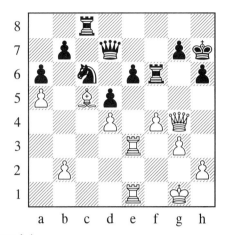

28.b4

Now Black is on the defensive again.

28...♖e8 29.♕h5 ♔g8 30.♕e2

White's advantage may not be enough to win, but he should certainly be able to play for a win without any risk. But for some reason Caruana felt differently and decided to repeat the position.

30...♕f7 31.♕d3 ♕d7 32.♕e2 ♕f7 33.♕d3 ♕d7 34.♕e2

½–½

GAME 7
▷ **S. Karjakin (2772)**
▶ **V. Laznicka (2701)**

12th Karpov International, Poikovsky
Round 3, 06.10.2011 **[B12]**
Annotated by Kamil Miton

The Czech grandmaster Laznicka decided to play one of the most complex lines of the Advance Variation of the Caro-Kann Defence. It seems that during his preparation he did not anticipate the strong move 13.♗d1!N employed by Karjakin. This novelty means that 11...♗b4?! should be considered imprecise. Although Black was not immediately losing after 18...♕xc2, his position seemed to be very difficult. On the eleventh move I feel that 11...♖b8!? is worthy of attention.

1.e4 c6 2.d4 d5 3.e5 ♗f5 4.♘f3 e6 5.♗e2 c5 6.♗e3 ♕b6 7.♘c3 ♘c6 8.0–0

After 8.♘a4 ♕a5† the knight is poorly placed on a4.

8.♗b5 is also an interesting idea, and has been employed twice by Naiditsch.

8...♕xb2 9.♕e1 c4

9...cxd4 10.♗xd4 ♘xd4 11.♘xd4 ♗b4 12.♖b1 ♗xc3 13.♖xb2 ♗xe1 14.♖xe1 b6 15.♗b5† ♔f8 16.♘xf5 exf5 17.♖b3 ♘e7 18.♖c3 has been played in a couple of games, and it is clear that White has the initiative.

10.♖b1 ♕xc2 11.♖xb7

11.♗d1 ♕xb1 12.♘xb1 ♗xb1 13.♗a4 ♗g6 14.♕a5 ♔d7 15.♗c1 b6 16.♕b5 ♖c8 17.♕a6 ♖c7 18.♗b5 ♘ge7 19.♗a3 ♘c8 20.♗c1 ♗e7∞

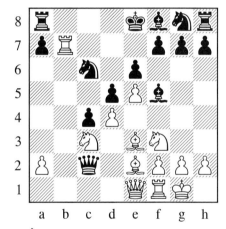

11...♗b4?!

The alternative is:
11...♖b8!? 12.♖xb8†
12.♗d1 ♖xb7 13.♗xc2 ♗xc2 14.♕c1 ♗d3 15.♖d1 In exchange for his queen, Black has rook, bishop and a very strong pawn on c4, but most important of all, his king is safe. That is why I think his position should not be any worse, although he needs to be wary of tricks of the ♖xd3 and ♘xd5 variety. 15...♘ge7 16.♖d2 (16.♕a3 ♖b6 17.♕a4 ♖b4 18.♕a3 ♖b6=) 16...♖b6 (16...♘f5 17.♖xd3

cxd3 18.♘xd5 ♔d7 19.g4→) 17.♖b2 ♘c8
18.♘a4 ♗a3 19.♘xb6 ♘xb6 20.♖xb6 ♗xc1
21.♖xc6 ♗xe3 22.♖c8† ♔d7 23.♖xh8 ♗c1∞
12...♘xb8

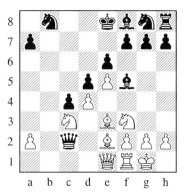

The character of the position is very complicated and the following analysis features typical computer variations. However, we may notice some more general ideas and plans which apply in several lines. White's aims include the fastest possible activation of his pieces (for example, ♕a1, ♖b1, ♗d1-a4, ♘b5, ♗c1-a3 and ♘g5), in order to attack the black king. Whereas Black aims to develop his kingside as quickly as possible, to defend his king and to seek simplification.

We look at two options here:

a) 13.♕a1 ♗b4 14.♖b1 ♗xc3
14...♕xc3 15.♕xc3 ♗xc3 16.♖xb8† ♔d7
17.♘g5 ♗g6 18.♖b7† ♔c6 19.♖xf7 ♘h6
20.♖xa7 ♘f5 21.♘xe6

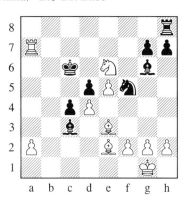

21...♖b8 (21...♔b6 22.♖d7 ♔c6 23.♖c7†
♔b6 24.♗f3 ♗xd4 25.♗xd4† ♘xd4 26.♗xd5
♘xe6 27.♖c6† ♔b5 28.a4† ♔xa4 29.♗xe6
♔b5 30.♖c7 ♗d3 31.f4±) 22.♗d1 ♔b6
(22...♖b1 23.♘d8†±) 23.♖d7 ♗e8 24.♖xd5
♗f7 25.♘f4 ♗a6 26.♗c2 ♗xd5 27.♗xf5±
15.♖xb8† ♔d7
15...♔e7!? 16.♕f1 h6∞
16.♕d1
16.♕f1 ♔c7 17.♖f8 (17.♖a8 ♕xa2∞)
17...♗b4 18.♖xf7† ♘e7 One of Black's main tasks is solving the problems of being tied up along the back rank. At the price of the f7-pawn, Black may introduce his pieces into the game, an idea appears in several variations. 19.♗g5 ♔d7 20.♖xg7 ♖b8∞
16.♕c1 ♔c7 17.♖a8 ♗b7 18.♖f8 ♕xc1†
19.♗xc1 ♗g6∞ C. Balogh – Michalik, Aix-les-Bains 2011.
16...♕xa2
16...h6!?

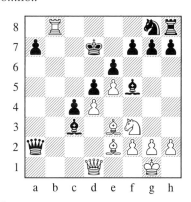

17.♘g5
17.♕c1!? ♔c7 Getting rid of the rook from the back rank is a top priority. 18.♕xc3 (18.♖f8 ♗b4! 19.♖xf7† ♘e7∓; 18.♖b5 ♗a5∞)
18...♕xb8 19.♕b4† ♔c7 20.♕d6† ♔b7
21.♕d7† ♔b6 22. ♘d2! with advantage to White.
17...♔c7
17...♗g6 18.♘xf7 (18.♗f1 ♕a1 19.♕f3 ♘h6
20.♖xh8 ♗d3 21.h3 ♕xf1† 22.♔h2 ♗b4∞)
18...♗xf7 19.♖b7† ♔c6 (19...♔e8 20.♗f1±

It's hard to believe, but it appears that Black cannot defend here.) 20.♖xf7 ♘h6 21.♗xh6 gxh6 22.♗f1∞

18.♖a8

18.♖f8 ♗b4 19.♖xf7† ♘e7 20.g4 ♗c2 21.♕f1 ♔d7∓

18...♗g6

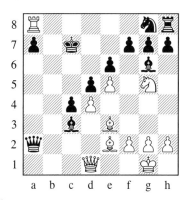

19.♗f1

Played in order to improve the queen's position, which will enable White to create threats against the f7- and e6-pawns.

19.h4 h6 (after 19...h5 White can continue as in the main line with 20.♗f1, when the interjection of the h-pawns' moves favours White) 20.♗xc4 ♕a1 21.♕xa1 ♗xa1 22.♘xf7 ♗xf7 23.♗xd5 exd5 24.♖xa7† ♔d8 25.♖xf7∞

19...♕b3

Since our main line does not turn out well for Black, it might be worth trying the murky: 19...♗b4 20.♗xc4 (20.♕f3!?) 20...♕xc4 21.♖a4 a6 22.♕e8 ♔b6 23.♘xf7 (23.♖c8 ♘e7 24.♖b8† ♔a5 25.♕xh8 ♘c6∞) 23...♘e7 24.♕xh8 ♗xf7 25.♕d8† ♔b5∞

19...h6? 20.♘xf7 ♗xf7 21.♕f3+−

20.♕f3 ♕b7 21.♖f8

21.♘xe6† ♔b6 22.♗xc4 ♕xa8 23.♗xd5 ♗h5 24.♕xh5 ♕xd5 25.♕xf7 ♘h6 26.♕xg7 ♖c8 27.♕xh6 ♖c6 28.g3 ♗xd4 29.♕f4 (after 29.♗xd4† ♕xd4 30.♘xd4 ♖xh6 the black a-pawn is very strong) 29...♖xe6 30.♗xd4† ♔b5∞

21...♕b4

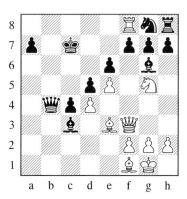

22.g3!

22.♖xf7† ♗xf7 23.♘xf7 ♕f8 24.♘xh8 ♕xf3 25.gxf3 a5↑

22.h4 ♘e7 23.♖xc4 ♗h5 24.g4 ♗xg4 25.♕xf7 ♖xf7 26.♖xf7† ♔c6 27.♗d3 h6 28.♘h7 a5∞

22...a5 23.♖a8 ♔b7

23...♕b7 24.♖xe6† fxe6 25.♕f8+−
24.♖e8 ♕b1 25.♘xf7 ♗d3 26.♘d6† ♔c6 27.h3 ♕xf1† 28.♔h2+−

b) 13.♗d1 ♕b2 14.♗a4†

Black has two sensible ways to react to the check:

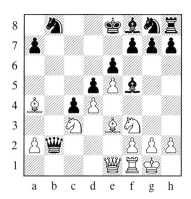

b1) 14...♘d7 15.♘b5

15.♕d1 ♕b7∓

15...♗b4

15...a6 16.♕a5+− is a disaster for Black.

15...♕b4 16.♕d1 and now:

i) 16...♘b6 At the cost of the h8-rook, Black aims to simplify the position, hoping that the strong c4-pawn will give him some initiative. 17.♘d6† ♔d8 18.♘g5 ♕xa4 19.♘gxf7† ♔d7 20.♕xa4† ♘xa4 21.♘xf5 exf5 22.♖b1 ♘b6 23.♘xh8 ♔e6 24.a4 ♘e7 25.a5 ♘d7 26.♖b7±

ii) 16...♕a5 17.♗d2 White activates another piece. 17...♕d8 18.♕e1 ♗e7 19.♗a5 ♘b6 20.♘xa7† ♔f8 21.♗d2 ♕b8 22.♘c6 ♕a8 23.♗b5 ♘c8 24.♗b4 ♕b7 25.a4±

iii) 16...c3 17.♘xa7 ♘h6 18.♕b3 ♕xb3 19.axb3 ♗a3 20.♘b5 ♗b2 21.♘xc3±

16.♗c1

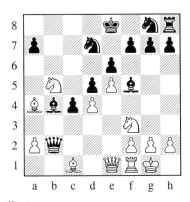

16...♕b1

16...♗xe1 17.♘d6† ♔f8 18.♗xb2 ♘b6 19.♗a3 ♘e7 20.♖xe1 ♘xa4 21.♘c8±

17.♘d6† ♗xd6 18.exd6 ♘gf6 19.♘e5 h6

19...♕b7 20.g4 ♗xg4 21.♗xd7† ♘xd7 22.♘xg4±

20.♕a5 ♕b6 21.♘c5 ♕xc5 22.dxc5 ♗c2 23.♗xc2 ♘xe5 24.♗a4†±

b2) 14...♔d8 15.♗g5†

White's other attempts seem less dangerous:
15.♘xd5 exd5 16.♕a5† ♔c8 17.♕xd5 ♗e6 18.♕e4 ♕b7 19.♕c2⩲⩲

15.♗c1 ♕b6∞

15.♘b5 ♗b4 16.♕d1 (16.♗d2 ♗xd2 17.♘xd2 ♕b4 18.♕d1 ♘e7 19.♘d6 ♗g6†) 16...♗d3 17.♘g5 ♘h6 (17...♗xf1 18.♗xf7† ♔e7 19.♗g5† ♔f8 20.♘c7 ♗e2 21.♘xe6†

♔xf7 22.♘d8† ♔f8 23.♘e6†=) 18.♕h5 ♖f8!? 19.♘d6 ♗xd6 20.exd6 ♔c8 21.♘xh7 ♗xf1 22.♘xf8 (22.d7† ♘xd7 23.♗xd7† ♔b7! 24.♗xe6 ♖d8 25.♗xd5† ♔a6 26.♗xf1 ♕b1† 27.♔e2 ♕c2† 28.♔e1 ♖b8−+) 22...♕b1 23.♕d1 ♖xd1 24.♗xd1 ♗d3 25.♗a4 ♘f5 26.♗f4 ♘xd4 27.d7† ♘xd7 28.♗xd7† ♔d8∓

15...♘e7

Black could try: 15...♔c8 16.♘b5 ♕b4 17.♕d1∞

16.♘b5 ♘bc6

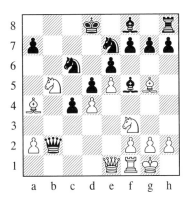

17.♗c1

17.♘xa7 ♘xa7 18.♕a5† ♔c8 19.♕xa7 ♕b7 20.♕c5† ♔b8 21.♕d6† ♕c7=

17.♘d6 ♔c7 18.♘xf5 (18.♘xf7 ♖g8∓) 18...♘xf5 19.♗xc6 ♔xc6 20.♕a5 ♕b6 21.♕a4† ♕b5 22.♕xa7 ♕b7 23.♕a4† ♕b5= 24.♕c2?! ♗a3 25.♖b1 ♕a6∓

17...♕b4 18.♕d1 ♘c8

18...♗d3?! 19.♖e1 ♘c8 (19...h6!?) 20.a3 ♕e7 21.♗g5 f6 22.exf6 gxf6 23.♗h4±

19.♗d2

19.a3 ♕a5 20.♘d6 ♗xd6 21.exd6 ♕a6 22.♗xc6 ♕xc6 23.♘e5 ♕b7 24.d7 ♘d6 25.♗d2 f6 26.♗a5† ♔e7 27.♕h5 fxe5 28.d8=♕† ♖xd8 29.♕g5† ♔f7 30.♕xd8 ♘b5 31.dxe5 h6∓

19...♕e7 20.♗g5

20.♘d6 ♗xd6 21.♗xc6 ♘c8 22.♕a4 ♕c7 23.♘g5

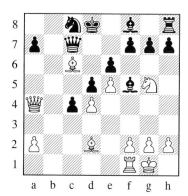

23...♘b6! (23...♗g6 24.♖b1! ♘b6 25.♖xb6
axb6 26.♗e8 ♕b7 27.♗xf7 b5 28.♕a5†
♔d7 29.♗xg6 ♗e7 30.♗f7 ♖a8 31.♗xe6†
♔e8 32.♕c3 ♖xa2 33.h4→) 24.♘xf7† ♔xf7
25.♗g5† ♔c8 26.♕a6† ♔b8 27.♗d8 ♗b4
28.♗xb6 ♖c8 29.♗d8 ♖xd8 30.♕b5† ♔c8
31.♕a6†=

20...f6 21.♗h4→ a6

21...♖g8!?

22.♘c3

22.exf6 gxf6 23.♘e5 ♘xe5 24.dxe5 axb5
25.♗xf6 bxa4 26.♕xa4 ♕xf6 27.exf6 ♗d6∞
22...♘b4 23.a3 ♘d3 24.exf6 gxf6 25.♘e5
♔c7 26.♗c2

26.♘xc4 dxc4 27.♕f3 ♘b2 28.♕c6† ♔b8
29.♗g3† e5 30.♕xa6 ♘xa4 31.♘xa4 ♕d6
32.♕b5† ♔a7∞

26...♕xa3 27.♗xf6 ♖g8 28.♘b1±

12.♖xb4 ♘xb4

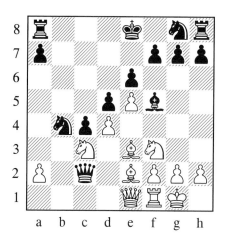

13.♗d1!N

A very strong new move.

13.♕a1 ♘xa2 14.♘xa2 ♕a4 (14...♕xe2?
15.♘c3 ♕c2 16.♖b1 ♘e7 and now rather
than winning the queen with 17.♘e1 ♕xc3
18.♕xc3 ♗xb1 19.♕b4 ♗g6 20.♗g5 ♘c6
21.♕b7 0–0 22.♕xc6 a5∞, White should
prefer 17.♖b7!±) 15.♘c3 ♕xa1 16.♖xa1 ♘e7
17.♗c1 ♖b8 18.♗d1 0–0 19.♗a3 ♖b7 20.♗a4
a6 21.h3 ½–½ Motylev – Alsina Leal, Moscow
2011.

13...♕d3

13...♕b2 14.♗c1 ♘d3 15.♗a4† ♔f8
16.♗xb2 ♘xe1 17.♖xe1±

14.♗a4†

14.♘b5 c3 15.♘c7† ♔d7 16.♘xa8 ♘c2
17.♗xc2 ♕xc2 18.♕c1 ♕xc1 19.♖xc1 ♘e7
20.♖xc3 ♖xa8=

14...♔f8 15.♕a1

This is more precise than 15.♕c1 ♘c2∞.

15...♗g4

Now 15...♘c2 can be met by 16.♗xc2 ♕xc2
17.♖c1 ♕d3 18.♘e1+–.

15...♗g6 16.h3+– leaves the queen in trouble
on d3.

16.♕b2

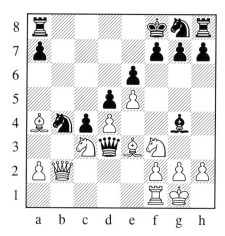

16...♖b8

16...a5 17.♘e1 ♛g6 18.a3 ♖b8 19.axb4 axb4 20.f3 ♗f5 21.♘b5±

17.♖b1 ♗xf3

Or 17...f6 18.♘e1 ♛g6 19.♛xb4† ♖xb4 20.♖xb4→, and once again Black fails to get h8-rook out.

18.♗c2 ♗e2?

18...♛xc2 19.♛xc2 ♘xc2 20.♖xb8† ♔e7 21.gxf3

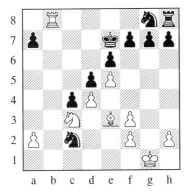

We can compare this to the variation with 11...♖b8, where similar positions with a pin along the 8th rank occurred. There Black could chase away the white rook, either with ...♔c7 and ...♗b4 or by bringing back his queen, but here he does not have that possibility. Thus Black is forced to play without two pieces, and his extra pawn is not enough to make up for this. White can slowly strengthen his position by bringing his king to the centre with ♔f1-e2-d2, and then he may play ♘b5 at the right moment. 21...♔d7 (21...f6 22.♖b7† ♔d8 23.♘b5 ♔e7 24.♖xa7 ♘xe3 25.fxe3 fxe5 26.dxe5±; 21...a6 22.♔f1±) 22.♘b5 (22.♔f1 f6 23.f4±) 22...a6 23.♘d6 ♘xe3 24.fxe3 c3 (24...♘e7 25.♖xh8 c3 26.♘b7+−) 25.♖b7† ♔c6 26.♖b3 ♘h6 27.♖xc3† ♔d7 28.♖b3 ♘f5 29.♘xf5 exf5 30.♖b7† ♔e6 31.♖b6† ♔e7 32.♖xa6 ♖c8 33.♔f2 ♖c2† 34.♔g3 ♖e2 35.♔f4±

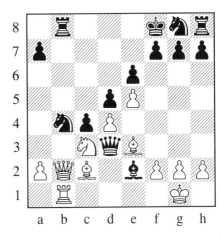

19.♗xd3 ♗xd3 20.a3 ♗xb1 21.axb4+− ♗g6
The lack of development of the kingside makes Black's position hopeless.

22.♛a3 ♖b7 23.b5† ♔e7 24.♗f4 h6 25.h4 ♖h7 26.♛a6 ♗f5 27.♗c1 f6 28.♗a3 fxe5 29.♛c8† ♔f7 30.♘xd5
1–0

GAME 8
▷ **L. Dominguez (2719)**
▶ **J. Polgar (2699)**
FIDE World Cup 2011, Khanty-Mansiysk
Round 4, Game 2, 07.09.2011 **[B33]**
Annotated by Alexander Ipatov

This game features the Grivas Sicilian, which is a rare guest at the highest level, although it is quite popular with players up to 2600. Nevertheless, even elite players sometimes choose it in critical games, for example, Gelfand recently played it against Kamsky in their Candidates match in Kazan 2011, in a game that Gelfand had to win with Black in order to equalize the score.

In this game Dominguez played 7.♗g5 and introduced a novelty on the very next move! I believe that 8.♛f3!?N is very strong because White is able to create concrete threats on the kingside. Nevertheless, I think that with

7...♗e7 (instead of Polgar's 7...a6) Black would avoid any big problems.

1.e4 c5 2.♘f3 ♘c6 3.d4 cxd4 4.♘xd4 ♛b6

This is the starting point of the Grivas Sicilian, the variation being named after the Greek grandmaster Efstratios Grivas, who analysed it in detail and has been successfully defending his analyses for more than twenty years.

5.♘b3 ♘f6

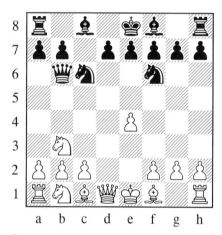

6.♘c3

After knocking out Dominguez, Polgar played the Grivas Sicilian once again in the next round and easily equalized against the eventual World Cup winner, Peter Svidler:

6.♗d3

I doubt whether this move can be better than the normal 6. ♘c3.

6...e6

The Dragon style of development can be applied in the Grivas Sicilian as well: 6...g6!? 7.0–0 ♗g7 8.♗e3 ♛c7 9.♘c3 0–0 10.h3 d6 11.f4 a6∞ B. Pavlovic – Kurajica, Bor 1983.

7.0–0 ♗e7

According to Grivas, an immediate 7...d5?! doesn't work well: 8.♘c3! dxe4 (8...d4 9.♘e2 e5 10.c3! and the opening of centre is good for White as he's ahead in development) 9.♘xe4

♗e7 (9...♘xe4?! 10.♗xe4 ♗e7 11.♗e3 ♛c7 12.♛h5± Nilsson – V. Schneider, Marianske Lazne 2008) 10.♘xf6† ♗xf6 11.♛h5 and White has some initiative.

8.c4 d5!

Both players are playing in a principled way.

9.cxd5 exd5 10.♘c3 ♗e6

10...dxe4!? is possible too: 11.♘xe4 0–0 12.♛e2 ♘d4 13.♘xd4 ♛xd4∞ Timoshenko – Epishin, Tbilisi 1989

11.exd5 ♘xd5 12.♘xd5 ♗xd5

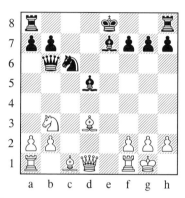

13.♖e1!N

White develops a piece, taking advantage of the fact that Black can't yet castle. White may then choose whether to develop his bishop to e3 or g5.

13.♗e3?! ♛b4 14.♛c2? This allows a forced draw. (14.♖e1! is useful in all circumstances, so why not make it now? 14...0–0–0 The best reply, Black doesn't want to defend passively, preferring to look for counterplay. 15.♛c2 ♔b8! 16.♗d2 ♛g4 17.♗e4∞) 14...♛xg2! 15.♔xg2 ♛g4† 16.♔h1 ♛f3† 17.♔g1 ♛g4† ½–½ Svidler – J. Polgar, FIDE World Cup (5.1), Khanty-Mansiysk 2011.

13...♖d8

A sensible move.

13...0–0? 14.♗xh7† ♔xh7 15.♛xd5±

14.♗g5 ♗e6

White can keep an advantage after 14...h6!? as well, but that may be the more practical choice for Black as more material is exchanged. White has:

a) 15.♗h4?! g5 (15...♗e6?? 16.♖xe6! fxe6 17.♗g6† ♔f8 18.♕f3†+−) 16.♗g3 ♗c4 17.♗xc4 (17.♖e3? ♕b5!∓) 17...♖xd1 18.♖axd1⯹

b) 15.♗xe7 ♘xe7 16.♕g4!

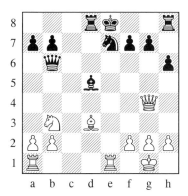

White endeavours to exploit his initiative. 16...0–0 17.♖xe7 ♗xb3 18.♕e4! f5 19.♕xb7 (An alternative is 19.♗c4† ♗xc4 20.♕xc4† ♔h7 21.♕c3 ♔f6 [21...♖d4? 22.♖xb7 ♕xb7 23.♕xd4±] 22.♖ae1 ♖df8! 23.a3 ♖8f7 24.h4± and White is still better due to activity of his pieces, but if Black defends correctly the game should be drawn.) 19...♕xb7 20.♖xb7 ♖xd3 21.axb3 ♖f7! 22.♖xf7 ♔xf7 23.♖xa7† ♔f6 24.♖a6† ♔f7 25.g3 ♖xb3 26.♖a2± White is a pawn up but it seems that Black can hold the position thanks to the activity of his rook.

15.♗e3!

The exchange of bishops gives nothing: 15.♗xe7?! ♘xe7 16.♕c2 ♖c8 17.♕d2 ♖d8!= (but not 17...0–0 18.♘d4!)

15...♕b4 16.♕c2!

Black is prevented from castling again.

16...h6 17.♘c5↑

Black will have to defend very precisely.

6...e6 7.♗g5

This is known as the "Poseidon" subvariation of the Grivas Sicilian. It has some ideas in common with the Rauzer Attack.

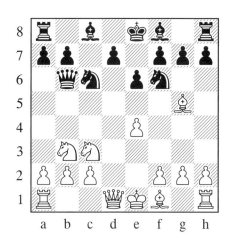

7...a6

A fair alternative is:

7...♗e7!? 8.♕d2 0–0 9.0–0–0 ♖d8

Black wants to break in the centre with ...d5.

10.♕e1 d5!

10...d6 is possible, but less principled.

11.e5

11.exd5 doesn't bring any problems for Black: 11...♘xd5 12.♗xe7 (12.♖xd5 ♖xd5 13.♘xd5 ♗xg5† 14.f4 ♕d8 15.fxg5 exd5=) 12...♘cxe7= (12...♘dxe7!? 13.♖xd8† ♕xd8 14.♗d3 e5!∞ is also possible, and Black can continue with ...♕b6, ...♗e6, etc.)

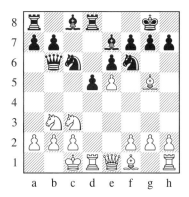

11...♘xe5!!

An unexpected move, after which it is not an easy task for White to find the route to equality.

In his book Grivas suggests the weaker 11...♘g4?! 12.♗xe7 ♘xe7 13.♘d4 ♘c6

14.♘xc6 bxc6 15.h3 ♘h6= (15...♘xf2??
16.♘a4+–), but even here the position is
okay for Black.
12.♕xe5 ♘g4 13.♕f4 e5 14.♕d2 ♗xg5
15.♕xg5 ♘xf2 16.♗d3!

16.♖xd5 ♗e6 17.♖xd8† (17.♖b5 ♕d6!
Threatening mate in two. 18.♗e2 [18.♖g1??
♕d1† 19.♘xd1 ♖xd1#] 18...♘xh1∓ Black
is an exchange up and White can't obtain
enough compensation as his rook is a bit
ridiculous on b5.) 17...♖xd8 18.♖g1 The
only move. 18...f6 19.♕h4 (after 19.♕g3
♘d3† 20.♗xd3 ♕xg1†∓ Black has an easy
game while it is not clear where White
should put his pieces) 19...♘d3† 20.♗xd3
♕xg1† 21.♘d1 ♕xg2 22.♖xh7†♔f7∓ Once
the queens are exchanged, the h2-pawn will
be extremely weak.
16.♘xd5 ♗e6!

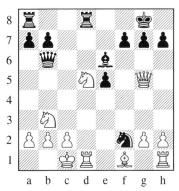

17.♗c4 (17.♘f6† ♔h8 18.♗d3 ♘xd3†
19.♖xd3 ♖xd3 20.cxd3 ♗xb3 21.axb3 gxf6∓;
17.♘xb6?? ♖xd1#) 17...♗xd5 18.♗xd5
♘xh1 19.♕xe5 ♘f2 20.♖d4 White wants
to prevent the return home of the black
knight. (20.♖f1 ♘g4 21.♗xf7† ♔h8 22.♕e2
♕e3† 23.♕xe3 ♘xe3∓) 20...♕h6† 21.♔b1
♖e8 22.♕f4 (22.♗xf7†? ♔xf7 23.♕f5†
[23.♕d5† ♕e6–+] 23...♕f6–+) 22...♖e1†
23.♘c1 ♕xf4 24.♖xf4 ♖d8 25.♗xf7† ♔h8
26.♖xf2 (26.♗d5 g5!∓) 26...♖dd1 27.b4
♖xc1† 28.♔b2 ♖f1 29.♖d2 ♖cd1 30.♖e2
♖fe1 31.♖f2 g6∓ White has quite good
chances for a draw, but it's clear that only
Black can play for a victory.
16...♘xh1 17.♖xh1 ♕f6!
Black should exchange queens to minimize
White's active play; after this exchange
Black's centre will be strong rather than
weak.
17...e4 gives away control over the d4-
square. 18.♗e2 ♗e6 19.♖d1 ♖ac8 20.♘d4
a6 21.♕e5!∞
17...♕d6 18.♖d1!
18.♕xf6 gxf6 19.♖f1 ♔g7=
The position is about equal, but Black has
the easier play.

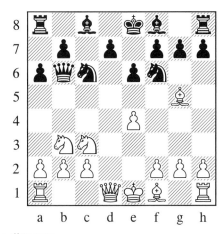

8.♕f3!?N

Quite a strong novelty, in my opinion. White
wants to transfer his queen to g3, and then
perhaps to h4, in order to disturb the black
king. In a blitz game later in the same match
Dominguez varied, but was convincingly
beaten:
8.♕d2 ♕c7N 9.0–0–0 b5 10.f3
White secures his e4-pawn and will go for an
attack with g2-g4.
10...♗e7 11.♔b1 0–0
I believe that Black has emerged from the
opening with no real problems.
12.g4?!
This move weakens the f3-pawn and the
h1-a8 diagonal.

Attacking with 12.h4!? was probably better.

12...♞e5! 13.♗f4

After 13.♗e2 ♗b7 14.♗f4 d5! 15.♕d4 ♗d6 16.a3 ♖fd8! Black has an ideal position.

13...b4

Black seizes the initiative.

14.♞e2

I reckon Dominguez did not want to put his knight on the edge of the board as it would be out of play. After 14.♞a4 ♖b8! Black defends the b4-pawn, and intends ...d6 and ...♗d7 to attack the knight on a4.

14...♖d8

The idea of this move is very clear: to support the advance ...d5.

14...a5!? 15.♞bd4 a4→ was also worthy of consideration.

15.♞ed4 ♗b7

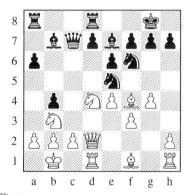

16.♕e1

White wishes to avoid the confrontation with the black rook on the d-file, meanwhile keeping an eye on the e4-square.

16...♖ac8

Black brings the last piece into the play. Everything is ready for the break in the centre with ...d5.

17.h4

White is too late with his attack on the kingside.

17...d5!

Finally! In response to White's attack on the flank, Black counters in the centre – one of the principal axioms in chess!

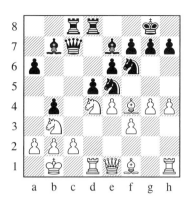

18.exd5?!

Now the f3-pawn becomes even weaker. The opening of centre is favourable for Black as she has the much better coordinated pieces. An improvement was 18.g5 ♞h5 19.♗h2 g6 20.♗e2 dxe4 21.fxe4 ♗d6∓, although with ...a5-a4 coming and the e4-pawn hanging, Black is doing well. 22.♗xh5?! gxh5 23.♖f1 a5!∓

18...♖xd5 19.h5 ♞xf3! 20.♕g3

20.♗xc7 doesn't hold the position either: 20...♞xe1 21.♖xe1 ♖xc7–+

20...e5–+ 21.♗g2 exf4 22.♕xf3 ♖xd4 23.♞xd4 ♗xf3 24.♗xf3 ♞d7 25.♖he1 ♗f6 26.♞c6 ♞e5 27.♞xe5 ♕xc2† 28.♔a1 ♗xe5 29.♖b1 f6 30.♗e4 ♕d2 31.♗f5 ♗xb2†!

0–1 Dominguez – J. Polgar, FIDE World Cup (4.8 – blitz), Khanty-Mansiysk 2011.

8...♗e7 9.♕g3 d6 10.0–0–0 0–0

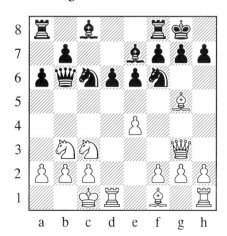

Everything has been quite logical up to this point. Now White has a couple of ways to go.

11.♔b1

Taking the d6-pawn seems to be risky for White: 11.♗xf6?! ♗xf6 12.♖xd6 ♕c7! 13.♖d1 ♗e5 14.♕f3 b5 with powerful compensation.

11.h4!?

This has the pretty simple idea of pushing the pawn to h6. Nevertheless, I couldn't find even a tiny advantage for White here.

11...♔h8!

A necessary prophylactic move, so that ...h6 can be played in order to stop the white h-pawn.

11...♖d8?! is too reckless, as after 12.h5! Black can't stop h5-h6, which will seriously weaken his kingside pawn structure.

12.h5 h6

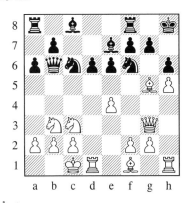

13.♗e3

13.♗f4 can be met by: 13...e5! 14.♗e3 ♕c7 15.f3 b5 16.♕f2 ♖b8 17.g4 b4 18.♘d5 (18.♘a4? blunders a pawn to 18...♗xg4! 19.♘b6 [of course not 19.fxg4?? ♘xg4 20.♕f3 ♘xe3 21.♕xe3 ♗g5–+] 19...♗e6∓) 18...♘xd5 19.exd5 ♘a5 20.♘xa5 ♕xa5 21.♔b1 f5!⇄

13...♕c7 14.f3 b5 15.♕f2 ♘e5 16.♗b6
16.g4? ♘fxg4–+

16...♕b7 17.♘a5 ♕b8

White's pieces will soon be kicked away from their advanced positions.

18.a3

18.f4? ♘fg4 19.♕d4 ♘d7 20.♘c6 ♕xb6 21.♕xb6 ♘xb6 22.♘xe7 ♘f2 23.♖xd6 ♘xh1 24.♖xb6 ♗d7∓

18...♘fd7 19.♗e3 b4 20.axb4 ♕xb4 21.♘b3 ♘c5!→

11...♖d8

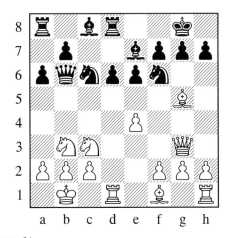

12.f4

White had another interesting way to continue his attack on the kingside:

12.♗e2!? ♕c7 13.♗h6 ♘e8

Black will defend without creating pawn weaknesses in front of his king.

After 13...g6?! 14.h4! White has a target to attack!

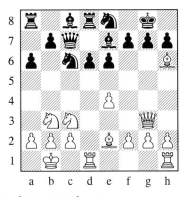

14.h4! ♗f6 15.h5 ♗xc3!

Spoiling White's pawn structure.

16.bxc3 ♔h8 17.♗e3
  17.♗g5 f6 18.♗e3 h6!
17...h6!
  Preventing h5-h6 by White.
18.f4
  White has to react quickly in order to compensate for the weakness on c3.
18...♘f6 19.♗f3 e5
  After 19...a5 20.♕f2± both ♗e3-b6 and g2-g4-g5 are threatened; White is faster with his attack.
20.♕f2 ♘g4!
  20...♘d7 is too passive, as 21.g4! gives White a strong attack.
21.♗xg4 ♗xg4 22.♗b6 ♕e7 23.♗xd8 ♖xd8
24.♖d3 exf4 25.♕xf4 ♘e5⩲

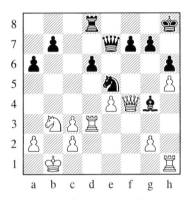

Despite White being an exchange up, Black has very good compensation for the following reasons:

1) White has many pawn weaknesses across the whole board.

2) Black has good chances to attack on the queenside due to the damaged pawn structure next to white king.

3) Black's pieces are perfectly coordinated.

12...♕c7 13.♗d3

A very aggressive set-up by White; his target is the h7-pawn.

13...b5

Black must look for counterplay.

14.♕h4!

White prepares to sacrifice.

14...h6

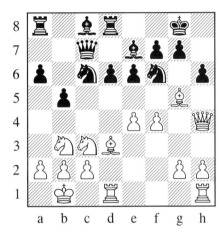

Black accepts the challenge. The game now develops into a very complicated struggle.

15.♗xh6 gxh6

15...♘xe4?! does not seem to be a good option for Black: 16.♗g5 ♗xg5 (16...♘xc3†
17.bxc3 f5 18.g4→) 17.fxg5 ♘xc3† 18.bxc3 g6 19.♕f2→ Freeing the way for h-pawn. I believe White has the better chances here. (If instead 19.♘d2 then 19...d5! prevents the invasion ♘d2-e4-f6.)

16.♕xh6 ♘e8

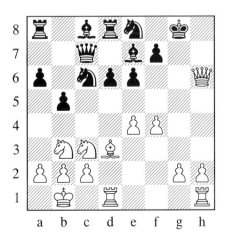

17.e5

The main alternative was 17.♘d5!? exd5 18.exd5 ♗f6 19.♗h7† ♔h8 20.dxc6 ♗g7 21.♕h4 (21.♕h5?? ♘f6–+) 21...♘f6 22.♗f5† ♔g8 23.♘d4 ♔f8∞. The position remains very unclear, but I believe that Black can hold it.

17...f5

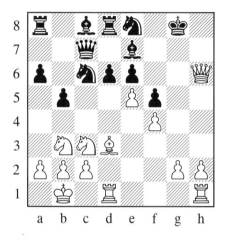

18.♗xf5?

White missed a good opportunity:
18.♕g6†! ♘g7
After 18...♔f8? 19.g4+– the opening of the g-file decides the game.
19.h4 b4!
I believe this is the only chance for Black to hold the position!
19...♘d7? 20.g4! ♗e8 21.♕h6+– and Black can't prevent the opening of the kingside.
19...dxe5?! 20.h5 ♗f8 21.h6 ♖a7 (21...♘e7 22.♕g5 exf4 23.♖h3!± followed by doubling rooks on the h-file) 22.♘e4! fxe4 23.♗xe4± and Black is in trouble.
19...♗f8?? 20.♗xf5 ♘e7 (20...exf5 21.♘d5+–) 21.♕h7† ♔f7 22.♗g4+–
20.h5!?
20.♘e2!? ♗f8 21.h5 dxe5 (21...♘e7 22.♕g5!→ and h5-h6 is coming) 22.h6 exf4 23.hxg7 ♗xg7 (23...♕xg7 24.♗xf5! ♕xg6 25.♗xg6 e5 26.♗h7† ♔f7 27.♘e4±) 24.♗c4 ♖xd1† 25.♖xd1 ♕f7 26.♕g5 ♘e5 27.♕d8†

(27.♖d8† ♔h7 28.♕xf4 ♕f6! and Black will hold the position) 27...♕f8 28.♕c7 and White retains an unpleasant initiative.
20.♘a4!? is also worthy of consideration.

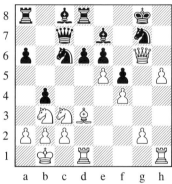

20...bxc3 21.h6 ♗f8 22.g4!
Opening more files and diagonals!
22...♘e7
22...♕f7?? 23.h7†+–
23.♕g5 ♗b7 24.hxg7 ♗xg7 25.♖h6 dxe5 26.♖xe6⩲
White has excellent compensation.

18...exf5 19.♘d5

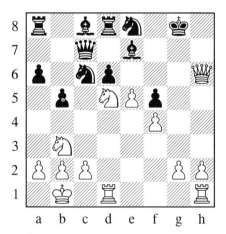

19...♗f8!

This move forces White to exchange queens, after which his attack comes to an end.

20.♘xc7 ♗xh6 21.♘xa8 ♗xf4 22.exd6 ♗xd6

Quite a forced line has resulted from 19...♗f8. Let's evaluate the position. White has a rook and two pawns for two bishops, and the position is close to being dynamically equal. Nevertheless, I would prefer to play Black in this position as the black pieces have more potential.

23.♘b6 ♗e6 24.♘d5 ♔f7

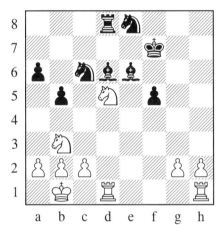

25.♘e3?!

This is the wrong direction. White should have tried to force the exchange of the kingside pawns by playing 25.h3! with the idea of g2-g4.

25...♘f6

Black's pieces have become significantly more active over the last few moves.

26.g3 ♘g4 27.♘xg4 fxg4

Now it is clear that Black is doing well. It seems likely that the following moves were made in time trouble.

28.♘d4 ♘xd4 29.♖xd4 ♗c7 30.♖f1† ♔e7 31.♖e4 ♖g8 32.a4 ♗d6 33.axb5 axb5 34.♖f5 b4 35.♖h5 ♖g6 36.h3 gxh3 37.♖xh3 ♔d7 38.♖h7† ♔c6 39.b3 ♗d5 40.♖e3 ♗xg3–+

In the time trouble White has lost a valuable pawn, and he now has to conduct a passive defence as Black's rook and pair of bishops make up a considerable force. Probably White's position is already lost...

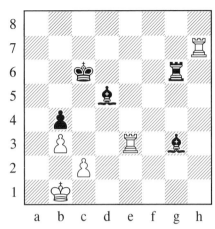

41.♖a7 ♖g4 42.♖a4 ♗f4 43.♖e1 ♗d2 44.♖d1 ♗c3 45.♖a6† ♔b7 46.♖a5 ♗e4 47.♖a4 ♖g2 48.♖a2 ♔b6 49.♖d6† ♔b5 50.♖d1 ♗f3 51.♖f1 ♔c5 52.♖a7 ♗e4 53.♖c1 ♔b6 54.♖a2 ♖g3 55.♖f1 ♗g7 56.♔c1 ♖g2 57.♔b1 ♖d2 58.♔c1 ♖h2 59.♔b1 ♗c3 60.♖d1 ♗f3 61.♖f1 ♔c5 62.♖a7 ♗e4 63.♖c1 ♔d4 64.♖d7† ♔e3 65.♖e7 ♖h6 66.♖a7 ♗d2 67.♖g1 ♔f2 68.♖d1 ♔e2 69.♖g1 ♗e3 70.♖e7 ♖h4 71.♖g8 ♗d4 72.♔a2 ♔d2 73.♖d7 ♗xc2 74.♖h8

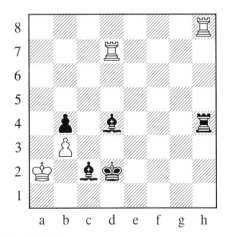

74...♖xh8??

74...♔c1! would have won the game immediately: 75.♖xh4 (75.♖c7 ♗c3! 76.♖xc3 ♖xh8–+) 75...♗b1#

75.♖xd4† ♗d3 76.♖xb4 ♔c3 77.♖a4 ♖h2† 78.♔a3 ♖b2 79.♖g4

White's best defence was 79.♖b4! ♖b1 80.♔a2! and now Black can't take the rook due to stalemate! 80...♖h1 81.♖b7 and White keeps chances to draw.

79...♖xb3† 80.♔a4 ♖b1 81.♔a5 ♖b5† 82.♔a4 ♖f5 83.♖g3 ♖f4† 84.♔a3 ♖f1 85.♖g2 ♖h1 86.♖b2 ♖a1† 87.♖a2 ♖b1 88.♖g2 ♖b3† 89.♔a4 ♖b4† 90.♔a3 ♖b6 91.♖g4 ♖a6† 92.♖a4 ♖b6 93.♖g4 ♖b7 94.♖h4 ♖b1 95.♖h2 ♖b6 96.♖h4 ♗f1 97.♖g4 ♖b5 98.♖g3† ♗d3 99.♖g4 ♖b1 100.♖g2 ♖b3† 101.♔a4 ♖b5 102.♖g4 ♖f5 103.♔a3 ♖f1 104.♖g2 ♖b1 105.♖h2 ♗f5 106.♖g2 ♗d3 107.♖h2 ♗f1 108.♖f2 ♗c4 109.♖f3† ♗d3 110.♖f2 ♖b3† 111.♔a2 ♖b6 112.♔a1 ♖g6
0–1

GAME 9
▷ **A. Motylev (2690)**
▶ **V. Laznicka (2701)**
12th Karpov International, Poikovsky
Round 7, 11.10.2011 **[B48]**
Annotated by Alexander Ipatov

White won the opening battle due to his deeper preparation, and then one mistake by Black was enough to lose the game. On the 19th move Motylev employed a logical novelty, which is the first choice of Houdini, and obtained a powerful attack. Black made a serious mistake on the 21st move, after which his position became hopeless. But even if Black had played all the best moves, that would only have been enough to reach an inferior endgame. I believe Black had some improvements earlier in the game, such as 12...♘xd4 or 18...g6, with a perfectly playable position.

1.e4 c5 2.♘f3 e6 3.d4 cxd4 4.♘xd4 ♘c6 5.♘c3 ♕c7 6.♗e3 a6 7.♕d2

This main alternative is 7.♗e2 ♘f6 8.0–0, transposing to Rublevsky – Bruzon, Poikovsky 2011, which is analysed on page 86.

7...♘f6 8.0–0–0 ♗e7

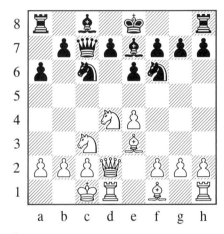

9.f3

White has a more aggressive weapon at his disposal: 9.f4!? b5 10.e5 The principled move. (10.♗d3 is less ambitious. 10...b4 11.♘a4 ♖b8 12.♔b1 d6 13.b3 0–0 14.♘xc6 ♕xc6 15.♖he1 ♕c7 16.♕e2 ♗d7 17.♘b2 ♗b5 18.♗d4 ♕c6 19.♕f3 ♖fc8 and Black was fine in Gashimov – Movsesian, Reggio Emilia 2010.) 10...b4 11.exf6 bxc3 12.♕xc3 ♗xf6

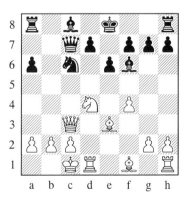

13.g4 h6 14.h4 ♗b7 15.♖h2 ♖c8 16.♕d2 ♗xd4 17.♗xd4 ♘xd4 18.♕xd4 0–0 19.g5 h5

20.♖f2 ♕a5 21.a3 ♖c7∞ Inarkiev – Movsesian, Olginka 2011.

9...0–0

Black can stop g2-g4, although he could then have some problems with castling short:
9...h5!?

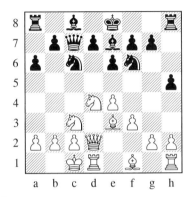

10.♘xc6

10.♔b1!? b5 11.♕f2 d6 12.h3 ♗b7 13.♗d3 h4 14.♘xc6 ♗xc6 15.♖he1 b4 16.♘e2 e5 17.♘b6 ♕b7 18.♘c1 ♘d7 19.♗a5 0–0 20.♗c4 ♖fc8 21.♘d3± Y. Yu – Movsesian, Khanty-Mansiysk 2009.

10.♘b3 d6 11.♗g5 ♖b8 12.f4 b5 13.♗xf6 gxf6 14.♗d3 b4 15.♘e2 a5 16.♔b1 a4→ Abergel – Negi, St Petersburg 2009.

10...bxc6 11.♗f4 e5 12.♗g5 d6 13.♗c4 ♗e6 14.♗b3 ♖d8 15.♕e2

15.h3 ♗xb3 16.axb3 h4 17.♔b1 ♘h5! 18.♗xe7 ♕xe7= Guerra Mendez – Iturrizaga Bonelli, Collado Villalba 2010.

15...a5 16.♔b1 0–0 17.h3 ♕b7 18.g4 d5 19.exd5 ♘xd5 20.♗xd5 cxd5 21.♗xe7 (21.♕xe5!?) 21...♕xe7 22.gxh5 d4 23.♘e4 f5 24.♘d2 ♗f7=

Negi – Vachier Lagrave, Biel 2010.

10.g4 b5 11.g5 ♘h5

The other possible knight move has been successfully played several times by Morozevich:
11...♘e8!? 12.♘xc6

12.♗f4 ♘e5 13.♗xe5?! concedes the bishop pair: 13...♕xe5 14.f4 ♕c7 15.e5 d6 16.♗g2 ♗b7 17.♖he1 b4 18.♘e4 ♔h8 19.♘f3 ♖d8! 20.♕e2 ♘d5 21.♔b1 a5↑ Motylev – Morozevich, Lugo 2007.

12.h4 ♗b7 (12...♘e5!?) 13.h5 ♘xd4 14.♗xd4 ♖c8 and now:

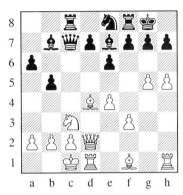

a) 15.g6? b4 16.gxh7† ♔h8 17.h6 (17.♘e2 ♗g5! 18.f4 ♗xe4–+) 17...e5 18.hxg7† ♔xg7 19.♗d3 exd4∓

b) 15.♔b1 b4 16.♘a4 ♗xg5! 17.♕g2 h6∓ Gelfand – Karpov, Tallinn 2005.

c) 15.♗e3 b4⇄

12...dxc6

12...♕xc6!?

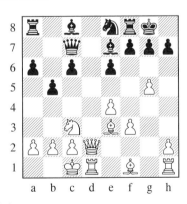

13.h4

13.f4 ♘d6 14.♕d4 ♘b7 15.♕b6 ♕xb6 16.♗xb6 e5! 17.♗e3 exf4 18.♗xf4 ♘c5 19.♖g1 ♗b7= and Black had no problems in Gashimov – Morozevich, Dagomys 2008.

13...e5 14.♕f2 ♗e6 15.♗h3 ♗xh3 16.♖xh3 ♘d6=

The knight is heading to c4, Leko – Morozevich, Moscow 2008.

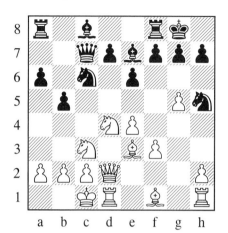

12.♔b1

White can also consider:

12.♘ce2 ♖d8!

Preparing the typical ...d5 break; Black has no real problems.

13.♘g3

13.f4 ♗b7 14.♗g2 g6 15.♘b3 ♖ac8 16.♔b1 d5 17.e5 d4!? 18.♘exd4 ♘xd4 19.♘xd4 ♗c5 20.♗xb7 ♕xb7 21.♕f2 ♕e4∞ Solodovnichenko – Fier, Sabadell 2009.

13...♘xd4 14.♕xd4

14.♗xd4 ♘f4 15.h4 ♗b7 16.♔b1 (16.♗b6? is very bad, as it weakens the dark squares and gives the bishop pair to Black. 16...♕xb6 17.♕xf4 d5∓ Flores Rios – Leitao, Sao Paulo 2009.) 16...♖ac8⇄

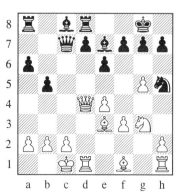

14...♘f4 15.h4

15.♔b1 ♘g6!? Preventing h2-h4, as the knight on g3 would be hanging. (15...♗b7?! 16.♗xf4! ♕xf4 17.♘h5 e5 18.♕f2 ♗c5! [18...♕xg5? 19.♘xg7!±] 19.♕xc5 ♕xf3 20.♘f6† gxf6 21.♗d3 and White had a strong attack in Quesada Perez – Fier, Sabadell 2010.) 16.♕b6 (16.♘h5 ♗f8!) 16...♕xb6 17.♗xb6 ♖e8 18.h4 d5! 19.exd5 exd5 20.♘h5 ♗d6 21.♗d4 ♗e5 22.♗xe5 ♘xe5 23.♗e2 ♘c4 24.♖xd5 ♗b7↑ Huschenbeth – Fier, Moscow 2011.

15...♗b7 16.♕b6

16.♔b1 ♖ac8 17.♕d2 ♘g6 18.h5 ♘e5 19.f4 (19.♕f2 ♗c5 20.♗xc5 ♕xc5 21.♖xc5 ♖xc5 22.♗e2 d5!) 19...♘g4 20.♗d3 d5!↑ Bok – Gharamian, Biel 2011.

16...♕b8 17.♔b1 d5!

This leads by force to a repetition of moves.

18.♗xf4 ♕xf4 19.♕xb7 ♗c5

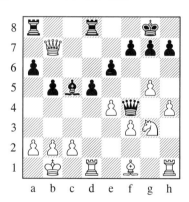

20.exd5

20.♖h3 ♖db8 21.♕c6 ♖c8 22.♕b7= Neumann – Bern, e-mail 2008.

20.♘e2 ♕d6!

20...♕xg3 21.♗d3 ♖db8 22.♕c6 ♖c8 23.♕b7 ♖cb8 24.♕c6=

Salgado Lopez – Movsesian, Moscow 2011.

12...♘e5

The plan of preparing ...d5 doesn't work properly here: 12...♖d8 13.♕f2! b4 14.♘a4 (14.♘ce2!?) 14...d5 15.exd5 exd5 16.♘xc6

♕xc6 17.♘b6 ♖b8 18.♘xc8 ♖bxc8 19.♗h3!
♖c7 20.♗g4 g6 21.♗xh5 gxh5 22.♖he1±

Worthy of Black's consideration is:
12...♘xd4!? 13.♗xd4 ♗b7 14.♘e2 ♖ac8N
  This is an improvement on: 14...e5?! 15.♗c3
♖ac8 16.a3 d5 17.♗a5 ♕d7 18.h4!± and
White's bishop is going to h3, Amonatov –
J. Geller, Izhevsk 2010.
15.♗h3
  Threatening ♗g4 and forcing Black's reply.

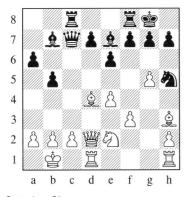

15...f5! 16.gxf6
  16.exf5 ♗xf3 and now:
  a) 17.f6 gxf6 18.♖hg1 (18.gxf6 ♗xf6
19.♖hg1† ♔h8∓ and White has no real
compensation for the pawn) 18...fxg5
19.♖xg5† ♗xg5 20.♕xg5† ♔f7 21.♖d2 In
order to defend the c2-pawn. 21...♕d6!∞

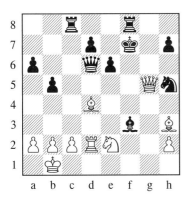

At first glance White might appear to have a
mating attack, but that is not the case. Black

can hold this position and even think about
more than a half point.
  b) 17.fxe6 d5! and White has to sacrifice the
exchange on h1, as otherwise Black would
get a crushing position after 18.♖hf1?!
♕xh2!∓.
16...♗xf6 17.♗xf6 ♘xf6 18.♘d4 ♖ce8∞
  The position remains unclear. White has
a simple plan of pressing on the g-file, while
Black has some prospects on the f-file. I believe
that overall Black is doing fine.

13.f4!
  The most ambitious.

After 13.♗e2?! ♗b7 14.f4 (14.♖hf1 ♖ac8 15.a3
b4!→) 14...♘c4 15.♗xc4 ♕xc4, the initiative is
clearly on Black's side.

13...♘g4
  13...♘c4 14.♗xc4 bxc4? (Black should
certainly play 14...♕xc4, although after 15.f5
White keeps some initiative) 15.♘f5!

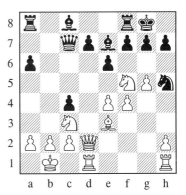

15...♗c5 (15...exf5 16.♘d5 ♕d6 [16...♕d8
17.♗b6+–] 17.♕e2! g6 18.♘f6† ♘xf6 19.♖xd6
♘xe4 20.♖dd1 c3 21.b3+–) 16.♗xc5 ♕xc5
17.♘g3 ♘xg3 18.hxg3 and White obtained
a decisive attack on the h-file in Kurmann –
Brunello, Merlimont 2011.

14.e5
  This move leads to quite a forced line.

14.♘ce2 ♗b7 15.♗h3 ♗b4 16.♕d3 ♘xe3 17.♕xe3 f5!⇄ Ozolin – J. Geller, Izhevsk 2010.

14...♗b7 15.♖g1 ♘xe3 16.♕xe3 b4 17.♘e4 ♗xe4 18.♕xe4

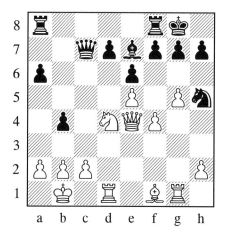

18...d5

This move was first played by Movsesian against Inarkiev two weeks before the current game.

Black should give serious consideration to: 18...g6!? 19.♖d3 (19.♗e2 ♘g7 20.h4 ♗c5 21.♗g4 d6! 22.h5 dxe5 23.fxe5 ♖fd8 24.hxg6 hxg6 25.♖h1 ♖ac8 26.♘f3 ♖xd1† 27.♖xd1 a5= and Black had no problems in Erdogdu – Miladinovic, Skopje 2002) 19...♖ac8 20.♗e2 ♘g7 21.♖gd1

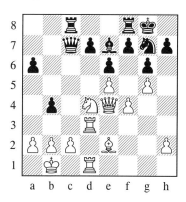

21...d5! 22.exd6 ♗xd6 23.♖f3 e5 24.fxe5 ♗xe5 25.♗xa6 ♖cd8 26.♖fd3 ♗xd4 27.♖xd4 ♘e6 28.♖4d2 ♖xd2 29.♖xd2 ♘c5 30.♕e2 ♕f4∞ with excellent compensation for the pawn in Florea – Heinke, e-mail 2009.

19.exd6N

A very logical novelty. According to Houdini this is the only move to keep an advantage.

In that earlier game Inarkiev didn't react properly and found himself in an inferior position: 19.♕e3?! g6 20.♗e2 ♘g7 21.h4 ♗c5 22.♗g4 ♖fc8 23.♖d2

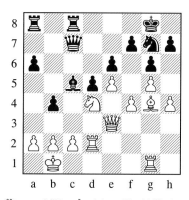

23...♕a7! 24.♖h1 ♗xd4 25.♖xd4 ♖c4 26.♖hd1 a5∓ Inarkiev – Movsesian, Rogaska Slatina 2011.

19...♗xd6 20.f5! exf5 21.♘xf5 ♖fe8 22.♕f3

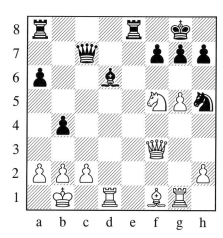

22...♗c5?

The only move was:

22...♗xh2!

This is a really difficult move to make over the board, especially if it appears that your opponent is still following his preparation.

23.♖h1 ♘g3

23...g6!?

24.♘xg3 ♗xg3 25.♕h5 h6 26.♗d3

26.gxh6 g6!

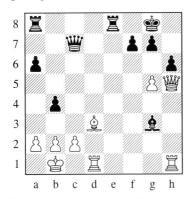

26...♕e5! 27.♗c4 ♖a7! 28.♖df1 ♖ee7!

Black has to keep making only moves in order to defend.

29.gxh6

29.g6 ♕xh5 30.♖xh5 ♔f8 31.♗xf7 ♗e5!∞ and the bishop moves to a fine defensive post on f6.

29...♕xh5 30.♖xh5 gxh6 31.♖xh6

31.♖g1?! ♖e1†! 32.♖xe1 ♗xe1=

31...♔g7 32.♖xa6 ♖xa6 33.♗xa6 ♖e1† 34.♖xe1 ♗xe1 35.♔c1 ♔f6 36.♔d1 ♗f2 37.♔d2 ♗d4!

Black should hold the endgame.

23.♖g4!

The rook joins the attack.

23...♖ad8 24.♗d3

White's pieces are perfectly coordinated and have a simple target to attack.

24...g6 25.♘h6† ♔f8

After 25...♔g7 26.♖h4 ♖e6 27.♖f1!+− White's threats are too powerful.

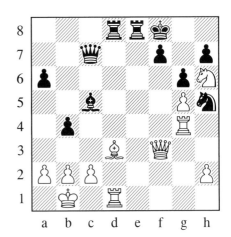

26.♖f1 f6

26...♖e7 27.♖e4! ♖dd7 28.♖xe7 ♖xe7 29.♕a8† ♖e8 30.♕xa6+− and White is a pawn up while retaining a powerful attack.

27.gxf6 ♖e3 28.♕h1 ♗d4 29.♗xg6!

Demolishing the pawn structure in front of Black's king.

29...hxg6 30.♖xg6 ♕h7

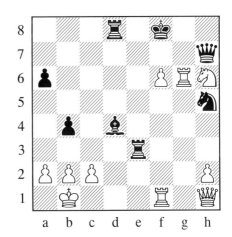

31.♕b7!

A very nice move!

31...♕xg6 32.♕xb4† ♔e8 33.f7†
1–0

GAME 10

▷ **S. Rublevsky (2681)**
▶ **L. Bruzon (2682)**

12th Karpov International, Poikovsky
Round 9, 13.10.2011 **[B85]**
Annotated by Alexander Ipatov

In a well-known variation Black showed good opening preparation and employed the interesting novelty 18...h6!?, after which Black experienced no problems equalizing. White then drifted into an inferior position without making any big mistakes, which demonstrates the real strength of Black's novelty. I think White will have to look for new ways to get an opening advantage.

1.e4 c5 2.♘f3 e6 3.d4 cxd4 4.♘xd4 a6 5.♗e2 ♘f6 6.♘c3 ♕c7 7.0–0 ♘c6 8.♗e3

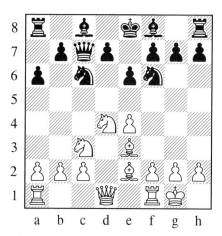

8...♗e7

A fair alternative is:

8...♗b4

This has been played many times by Anand, Karpov and other top players. The idea is quite simple: Black wants to organize immediate pressure on White's centre, and especially the e4-pawn.

9.♘a4!

The only move to fight for an opening advantage.

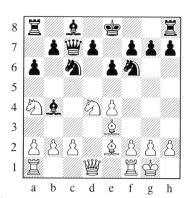

9...♗e7

Black has tried several other moves:

a) 9...♗d6!? is quite playable.

b) 9...♘xe4? 10.♘xc6 ♕xc6□ (10...dxc6?? 11.♕d4+–) 11.♘b6 ♖b8 12.♕d4 ♗e7 (12...♗f8 13.c4±) 13.♗f3 d5 14.c4↑

c) 9...b5?! does not seem good for Black: 10.♘xc6 dxc6 11.♗c5! bxa4 (11...♗xc5 12.♘xc5±) 12.♗xb4 c5 13.♗a3 ♘xe4 14.♗f3↑

d) 9...d5?! 10.♘xc6 bxc6 11.♘b6 ♖b8 12.♘xc8 ♖xc8 (12...♕xc8 13.exd5 cxd5 [13...♘xd5 14.♗d4 0–0 15.♗e5 ♖a8 16.c4 ♘e7 17.♕a4±] 14.c3 ♗e7 15.♕a4†± After the exchange of queens, White will have a simple plan based on pushing his queenside pawns with the support of the bishop pair.) 13.exd5 ♘xd5 14.♗xa6 ♘xe3 15.fxe3 ♖d8 16.♕f3± White is a pawn up and Black's compensation is probably not enough.

10.♘xc6

10.c4 ♘xe4 11.c5!⯐ is the main alternative. A lot of games have been played from this position and they have shown that White has good compensation for the pawn.

10...bxc6 11.♘b6 ♖b8 12.♘xc8 ♕xc8 13.♗d4 0–0 14.e5 ♘d5 15.c4±

White is slightly better due to his bishop pair and space advantage. Nevertheless, we shouldn't underestimate Black's chances, and his results in practice have not been too bad.

9.f4 d6 10.a4

Preventing the possibility of ...b5 by Black.

10.♕e1

This is another popular continuation, but it doesn't offer White much. We shall take a look at some of Ivanchuk's games which confirm that Black is doing fine.

10...0–0 11.♕g3 ♘xd4 12.♗xd4 b5 13.a3 ♗b7 14.♖ae1

Quite a forced line.

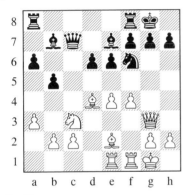

14...♖ad8

Black continues to centralize, developing the rooks to d8 and e8 in order to break in the centre with ...e5 or ...d5 later.

The other main plan is to construct a queen and bishop battery on the a8-h1 diagonal: 14...♗c6!? 15.♔h1 ♕b7 16.♗d3 b4 17.axb4 ♕xb4 18.♘e2 ♕b7 19.e5 ♘h5 20.♕h3 g6= Shirov – Ivanchuk, Linares 1993.

15.♗d3 ♖fe8 16.♔h1 ♘d7 17.♘d1

17.f5 e5 18.♗e3 ♔h8 19.♗g5 ♘h5 20.♕h4 ♗xg5 21.♕xg5 ♘f6 22.♖f3 ♕c5! 23.♖g3

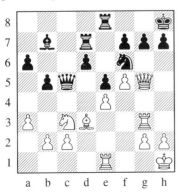

23...♖g8∓

White's attack has ground to a halt, while Black still has many strong ideas such as ...b4 or ...d5. Black went on to win convincingly in Anand – Ivanchuk, Leon (rapid – 1) 2008.

17...g6 18.♗c3 ♘h5 19.♕h3 ♗f6 20.e5 dxe5 21.fxe5 ♗g5?!

It is better to retreat the bishop: 21...♗e7 22.♘e3 ♖xa3! 23.♗e2 ♔h8 24.♗xh5 gxh5 25.♕xh5 ♖g8⇄

22.♕g4 ♕d8 23.♘f2 ♗h4 24.♖e2 ♕g5 25.♕xg5 ♗xg5 26.♘e4 ♗xe4 27.♖xe4±

Anand – Ivanchuk, Leon (rapid – 3) 2008.

10...0–0 11.♔h1 ♖e8 12.♗f3

12.♘b3 b6 13.♕e1 ♘b4⇄ Ermenkov – Jansa, Cienfuegos 1975.

Here too White can play 12.♕e1, but after 12...♘xd4 13.♗xd4 Black has the typical break 13...e5! to obtain counterplay in the centre. I believe that Black has no problems provided he knows what he is doing. White has a couple of options:

a) 14.♗e3 exf4 15.♗xf4 ♗e6 16.a5!?

White fixes the pawn structure on the queenside, aiming for a strategic battle.

16.♕g3 is met by 16...♘d7! and the knight heads for the e5-square, where it will be perfectly placed:

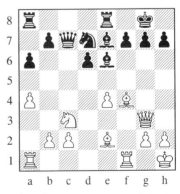

i) 17.♗e3 ♗f8 18.♖f2 g6 19.♗d4 ♘e5 20.a5

♗g7 21.♗b6 ♕e7 22.♖d1 ♖ac8= Klovans – Magerramov, Moscow 1979.

ii) 17.♗g4 ♘e5 18.♗xe6 fxe6 19.♖ad1 ♗f6 20.♗g5 ♗xg5 21.♕xg5 ♖ac8∓ Lukashuk – Najer, Polanica Zdroj 1999.

iii) 17.♗d3 ♘e5 18.♘d5 ♗xd5 19.exd5 ♘xd3 20.♕xd3 ♗f6 21.c3 ♗e5= Iskov – Ftacnik, Berlin 1984.

16...♘d7!

The idea for improving the knight that we have already seen.

17.♕g3 ♘e5 18.♗e3 ♗f8 19.♗b6 ♕c6 20.♗d3 g6 21.♘e2! ♗g7 22.♘d4 ♕d7 23.♖ad1 ♖ac8=

As compensation for the weakness on d6, Black has a strong knight on e5, an active rook on the c-file and other well-coordinated pieces, Kamsky – Van Wely, Wijk aan Zee 2006.

b) 14.fxe5 dxe5 15.♕g3

15.♗e3 ♗e6 16.♕g3 ♔h8 17.a5 ♗c5 18.♗g5 ♗e7 19.♗e3 ♗b4 20.♕h4 ♗e7= Chandler – Psakhis, Sochi 1982.

15...♗d8!

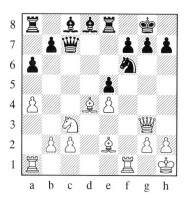

16.♗e3

16.♗g1 ♗e6 17.a5 ♔h8 18.♖fd1 ♖c8 19.♖d2 ♕b8 20.♗d3 b5! 21.axb6 ♗xb6↑ Draoui – David, Coubertin 2009.

16...♔h8! 17.♗g5 ♗e6 18.♖ad1 ♗e7 19.♗xf6 ♗xf6 20.♗g4 ♖ad8=

Padevsky – Ermenkov, Varna 1973.

12...♘xd4

A popular alternative is 12...♗f8 and now:

a) 13.g4 ♘xd4 14.♗xd4 e5 15.♗g1 exf4 16.g5 ♘d7 17.♘d5 ♕d8 18.♕d2

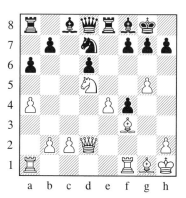

18...♕xg5!?N

18...h6? 19.gxh6 g5 20.♕g2 ♔h7 21.♗h5± David – Berend, Germany 1998.

19.♘c7 ♘e5 20.♗g2

20.♘xa8 ♘xf3 21.♖xf3 ♗g4 22.♖ff1 (22.♖xf4?? ♗f3† 23.♖xf3 ♕xd2–+) 22...♖xa8 23.♕xf4 ♕xf4 (23...♕h5!?) 24.♖xf4 ♗d7 25.♗d4 ♗c6∞

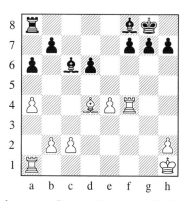

20...♗d7 21.♘xa8 ♖xa8 22.♕xf4 ♕xf4 23.♖xf4 ♘g6 24.♖f2 ♘h4!∞

b) 13.♘b3!

This has the simple idea of blocking Black's queenside by a4-a5 and avoiding any exchange on d4. Black seems unable to achieve full equality.

13...b6

13...♘a5 14.♘xa5 ♕xa5 15.♔d2±

14.a5! bxa5

14...b5?! 15.e5±

14...♘d7 15.axb6 ♘xb6 16.♕e2 ♗b7 17.♘a4±

15.e5 dxe5 16.fxe5 ♖d8 17.♘d4 ♘xd4

The sacrifice of the exchange doesn't give enough compensation: 17...♘xe5?! 18.♗xa8 ♘eg4 19.♗g1 e5 20.♘ce2 exd4 21.♘xd4 ♗d7 22.♗f3 a4 23.♕e2±

18.♗xd4 ♘d5 19.♘xd5 exd5 20.♕d2±

13.♕xd4 e5!

A typical break.

14.♕d2 exf4 15.♗xf4 ♗e6 16.♖fd1

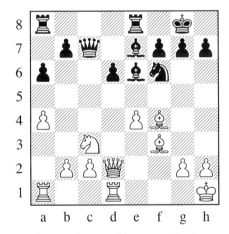

Black now faces a dilemma: whether to put his rooks on d8 and e8, or on d8 and c8. Both set-ups have been tried many times in practice.

16...♖ed8

16...♖ad8 17.h3! White prevents the transfer of the knight to e5. Now it will only be possible via the d7-square, but that would cost the d6-pawn. (17.a5?! ♘g4! 18.♗xg4 Otherwise the knight comes to e5. 18...♗xg4 19.♘d5 ♕d7 20.♖e1 ♗e6 21.♘b6 ♕b5 22.b3 ♗f6 23.♖ab1 ♗e5= and Black was fine in Glek – Andersson, Berlin 1996.) 17...♕c8 18.♕f2±

Hodzic – Erdeljan, corr. 1980. White has prevented both the knight transfer to e5 and the liberating move ...d5, and he stands better.

17.a5

17.h3 has the idea of preventing ...♘g4-e5. 17...♖ac8 Compared with the previous note, the rook is more active on c8 than on e8. 18.a5 ♘d7!N Black temporarily sacrifices a pawn in order to activate his pieces. 19.♗xd6 ♗xd6 20.♕xd6 ♕xd6 21.♖xd6 ♘e5

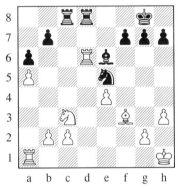

Black's pieces are wonderfully coordinated. 22.♖xd8† (22.♖b6?! ♖c7! 23.♔g1 ♔f8 24.♖d1 Otherwise ...♖d2 will give Black good play. 24...♖xd1† 25.♗xd1 ♘c4 26.♖b4 ♘xa5∓) 22...♖xd8 23.♖d1 ♖xd1† 24.♗xd1 ♘c6 25.♔g1 ♘xa5=

17...♖ac8 18.♖a4

18.h3 ♘d7! transposes to the previous note.

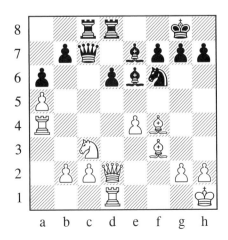

18...h6!?N

This novelty has two points. Firstly, Black makes a bolt-hole for the king so that he no longer needs to worry about the weakness of the back rank, and secondly he will have the possibility of expanding on the kingside with ...g5.

18...♘d7?! is an idea we have already seen, but here it doesn't work so well: 19.♗xd6 ♗xd6 20.♕xd6 ♕xd6 21.♖xd6 ♘e5 22.♖xd8† ♖xd8 23.♘d5 ♗xd5 24.♖d4!± White is a pawn up for little compensation, and he went on to win in Galkin – Gashimov, Batumi 2002.

19.♖b4

19.♗g3 ♘d7! 20.♗xd6 ♕xd6 21.♕xd6 ♗xd6 22.♖xd6 ♘e5 23.♖xd8† ♖xd8 24.♖b4 (24.♘d5? ♗xd5 25.♖d4 ♖c8 26.♖xd5 ♖xc2∓ and compared with Galkin – Gashimov above, there is no mate on d8 thanks to 18...h6) 24...♖d2 25.♖xb7 ♖xc2 26.♔g1 ♘c4=

19.♖d4

Increasing the pressure on the d6-pawn.
19...♔h7!

Black need not fear the capture on d6.
20.♗xd6 ♗xd6 21.♖xd6 ♖xd6 22.♕xd6 ♕xa5 23.e5 ♘g4□ 24.♖e1

24.♕d4 ♖c4 25.♕d3† g6 26.♗xg4 ♖xg4 27.♘d5 ♗xd5 28.♕xd5 ♕xd5 29.♖xd5 ♖e4 30.♔g1 ♖e2=

24...g6!

A strong move, with the idea of avoiding any checks on the b1-h7 diagonal.
25.♗xb7

25.♗xg4 ♗xg4 26.♕e7 (26.♘e4?? ♕xe1#) 26...♕c7 27.♕xc7 ♖xc7 28.♘d5 ♖c4 29.b3 ♖d4 30.♘f6† ♔g7 31.♘xg4 (31.c3? ♖d1 32.♖xd1 ♗xd1 33.b4 ♔f8 34.♘e4 ♔e7 35.♘c5 b6 36.♘xa6 ♔e6∓ and the more active king along with a bishop in an open position promises Black a clear advantage) 31...♖xg4 32.e6=

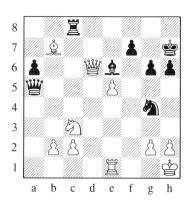

25...♖xc3!

This leads by force to perpetual check.
26.bxc3 ♕xc3 27.♖b1 ♘f2† 28.♔g1 ♕e3 29.♕b6□ ♘h3† 30.♔h1 ♘f2†=

19...♘d7 20.♘a4 g5!

Otherwise White would just put his knight on b6 with pleasant play.

21.♗xg5□

White has to sacrifice the bishop.

After 21.♗e3? d5!∓ the rook on b4 is under attack.

21.♗g3? ♕xc2 22.♕xc2 ♖xc2 23.♘b6 ♖dc7† and Black is just a pawn up.

21...hxg5 22.♕xg5† ♔h8 23.♘b6 ♘h7 24.♕d2 ♗g5 25.♕e1 ♖e7 26.♘xc8 ♗xc8∞

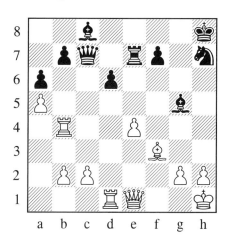

White has rook and two pawns for bishop and knight, and it seems to me that the position is dynamically equal. Black has the weaker king, but on the other hand he controls the important e5-square. I believe that the position is easier to play with Black, as his plan is very simple: to coordinate his pieces and start pressing on the kingside. It is not so easy for White to determine the correct set-up for his pieces.

27.♕g3 ♖e5!

The control over the e5-square plays a key role.

28.♖b3 ♗e6 29.♖c3 ♕xa5 30.♖xd6 ♗f6 31.h4?! ♘f8 32.♖cd3 ♘g6∓

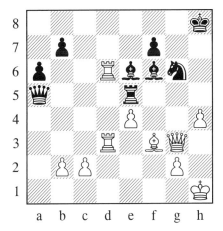

Black's pieces have become a lot more active over the last few moves. His position is now much superior as White has seriously weakened his kingside.

33.h5?

White is playing on the side where he is much inferior, giving Black more and more control over important squares.

33...♖g5 34.♕f2 ♘f4!

Black launches a final attack on the white king.

35.♖d1 ♕e5 36.c3 ♔h7 37.♕d4?

A decisive blunder.

**37...♖xh5† 38.♔g1 ♘e2† 39.♗xe2 ♕h2†
40.♔f2 ♗xd4†**

0–1

A quality game by Black!

GAME 11

▷ **A. Motylev (2690)**
▶ **R. Wojtaszek (2704)**

European Club Cup, Rogaska Slatina
Round 3, 27.09.2011 **[B90]**
Annotated by Sebastien Maze

In Game 15 of July's *Chess Evolution*, I analysed a crazy game between Kamsky and Gelfand from the 2011 Candidates matches in Kazan, which featured a rare anti-Najdorf line with h3 and ♕f3. In my opinion it is not so easy for Black to find a good antidote. My recommendation would be to play 9...a5!?N instead of the natural 9...♘bd7. In the game Wojtaszek tried a new idea with 10...♘b6 in order to look for activity on the c-file, while leaving the h-pawn on h7 instead of h6 in order to avoid giving White a target on the kingside.

Later Motylev went wrong with the passive 17.♖c1?, when the superior 17.a3 would have offered him a pleasant position. After that the Polish player built a serious advantage step by step, but he missed several good opportunities and White eventually succeeded in drawing a difficult endgame.

**1.e4 c5 2.♘f3 d6 3.d4 cxd4 4.♘xd4 ♘f6
5.♘c3 a6**

Wojtaszek is one of Anand's seconds, so he is extremely well prepared and likes to play sharp openings such as the Najdorf.

6.♗e3 e5 7.♘b3 ♗e7 8.h3!? ♗e6 9.♕f3!?

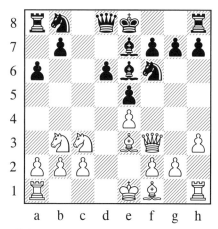

9...♘bd7

There is not much established theory from this position. Here are a few other possibilities:

9...0–0 is playable although it is not to everyone's taste to commit the king so early.

9...h5 is a typical move to restrain the white g-pawn. 10.0–0–0 ♘bd7 11.♔b1 ♕c7 (11...♘b6 12.g4 hxg4 13.hxg4 ♖xh1 14.♕xh1 ♗xg4 15.f3 ♗h5 16.♕g1 ♘fd7 17.♕xg7±) 12.♘d5 ♗xd5 13.exd5

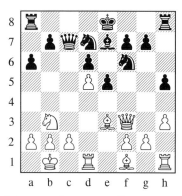

13...♘b6 (13...♖c8 14.c3 ♘b6 15.g4 ♘bxd5 16.g5 ♘xe3 17.fxe3 ♘d7 18.g6↑ gives White good attacking chances) 14.c3 h4 15.g4 hxg3 16.fxg3±

9...a5!?N

This interesting move was the proposition of Arkadij Naiditsch. The weakening of the b5-pawn is of course an issue, but Black has enough active play to justify it.

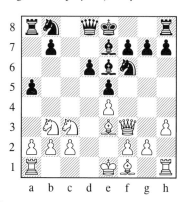

10.♗b5†

10.0–0–0 ♘bd7 11.a4?! (11.♗b5 0–0 12.g4 ♘e8 13.♕e2 ♘c7 14.♗a4 b5 15.♘xb5 ♘xb5 16.♕xb5 ♕c7 17.♕c6 ♕b8 18.♕b5 ♕c7=) 11...♖c8 12.g4

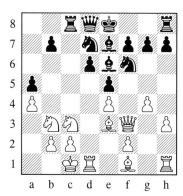

12...♖xc3! (12...h6?! 13.♗b5 0–0 14.♔b1 ♘b6 15.g5 hxg5 16.♗xg5±) 13.bxc3 ♕c7 14.♔b2 0–0 15.g5 ♖c8 16.♗d2 ♘e8 Black has excellent compensation. All of his pieces are headed for the queenside and at some point ...b7-b5 will be strong.

10...♘bd7 11.a4

11.0–0–0 0–0 12.♔b1 (12.g4 ♘e8 13.♘a4 ♘c7 14.♗xd7 ♗xd7 15.♘b6 a4 16.♘c5 [16.♘xa8? axb3 17.♘b6 bxa2∓] 16...♗c6 17.♘d3 a3 18.b3 ♘b5∞ Black has a promising initiative) 12...♘e8! This is the key to Black's plan.

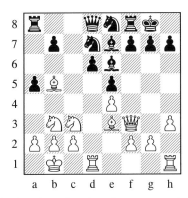

The knight is heading for c7, in order to hit the bishop and prepare ...b5 when the time is right. 13.♕e2 ♘c7 14.♗a4 b5! (14...♕b8?! 15.f4 b5 16.♘xb5 ♘b6 17.♗xb6 ♕xb6 18.fxe5 dxe5 19.♘c3±) 15.♘xb5 ♘xb5 16.♕xb5 ♕c7 17.c3 ♖fc8 18.f3 ♖ab8 19.♕xa5 ♕c4∞

11...0–0 12.0–0 ♘b6

It is not easy to find a convincing plan for White now.

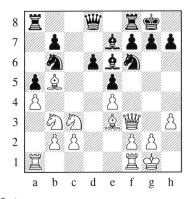

13.♘d2

13.♖fd1 ♘c4 14.♗xc4 ♗xc4 15.♘d2 ♗e6=
13...♖fd7 14.♕e2 ♖c8 15.♖fd1 ♘c5

Black should keep his other knight on b6 in order to prevent ♗c4.

15...h6 16.♘f1 ♘c4 17.♗c1 ♗g5 (17...f5 18.♘g3 fxe4 19.♘gxe4 ♘f6 20.♗xf6† ♖xf6 21.♘e4 ♖f8 22.b3±) 18.♗xd7 ♕xd7 19.b3 ♗xc1 20.♖dxc1 ♘b6 21.♘b5 d5 22.exd5 ♕xd5 23.♖d1±

16.♘f3

16...♘bd7

16...♗f6 17.♖d2 ♕e7 18.♖ad1 ♖fd8 19.♘h2±

16...♕c7 17.♘g5 ♗d7 (17...♗xg5 18.♗xg5 f6 19.♗e3 ♖fd8 20.♖d2 ♕f7 21.b3±) 18.♗xc5 ♕xc5 19.♗xd7 ♘xd7 20.♖d5 ♕b6 21.♖b5 ♕c6 22.♘f3±

17.♖d2

Now that the knight has moved from d2, White cannot play 17.♗c4? due to 17...♘xe4∓.

17...♘f6 18.♘g5 ♗d7 19.♗xd7 ♕xd7

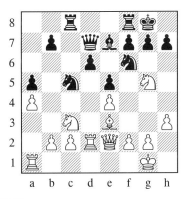

20.♖dd1

After 20.♕b5 ♕xb5 21.axb5 b6 22.♖e2 ♘cd7 Black should be able to hold the position.

20...h6 21.♗xc5 ♖xc5 22.♘f3 ♖fc8 23.♘d2 b6 24.♘b3 ♖c4=

White does not have enough coordination to force a favourable 'good knight versus bad bishop' position, so the chances are level.

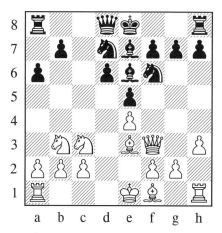

10.g4 ♘b6

Varying from 10...h6 11.0–0–0 ♖c8 12.♘d5 ♗xd5 13.exd5 ♘b6 14.h4∞ as in Kamsky – Gelfand, Kazan 2011, which was analysed in Game 15 of the July *Chess Evolution*.

The text move is not technically a novelty, but according to my database it was just played once in an amateur game, and Motylev deviates on the next turn. Wojtaszek's idea is to transfer the king's knight to d7 and prepare some counterplay on the queenside.

11.g5N ♘fd7 12.h4

12.0–0–0 ♗xg5 13.♖xd6 ♗xe3† 14.♕xe3 ♕c7 15.♖d2 0–0 16.♖g1 ♖fd8 17.h4 ♘f8 should be okay for Black.

12...♖c8

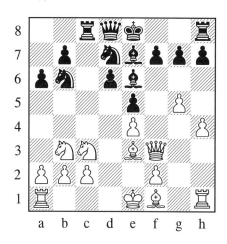

13.♖g1!

Motylev does not want to castle before Black plays ...♘c4, so he plays a waiting move. Of course the rook move has some useful aspects, such as supporting a future kingside attack and even swinging to the centre via g3.

The following line shows why White should not be in a hurry to castle: 13.0–0–0?! ♖xc3! (13...♘c4?! 14.♘d5 0–0 15.♔b1 ♘db6 16.♗d3±) 14.bxc3 ♘a4 15.♗d2 (15.c4 ♕c8 16.♗d2 ♘db6∞) 15...♘db6 16.♔b1 (16.♗h3 ♗xh3 17.♖xh3 ♘c4 18.♕d3∓) 16...0–0 17.♗h3 ♕c8 18.h5 d5! Black has excellent compensation.

13...♘c4 14.0–0–0

Now it is safe to castle.

14...♕c7

14...♘xe3 15.♕xe3 (15.fxe3 ♖xc3! 16.bxc3 ♘b6↑ gives Black a strong initiative against the poor white king) 15...b5 16.f4 (16.♘d5 ♗xd5 17.♖xd5 ♕b6 18.♕xb6 ♘xb6 19.♖d3 g6=) 16...♕c7 17.♖g2 exf4 18.♕xf4 ♘e5 19.♘d4± is pleasant for White, whose knights will find excellent homes on d5 and f5.

15.♗xc4 ♕xc4 16.♔b1 b5

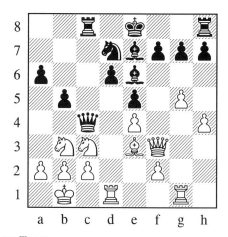

17.♖c1?!

I cannot understand the thinking behind this move. The rook was shining on d1, where it supported a future knight jump to d5. Now that it has gone to c1 Black will have no trouble on the d-file.

The right continuation was:
17.a3!
Safeguarding the future of the knight on c3.
17...0–0 18.♕g2!
The idea of this move is to play f4 and use the queen to defend c2.

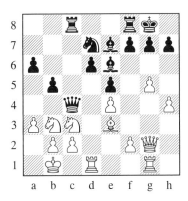

18...♖b8
18...b4?! is strongly met by 19.♘a5! ♕c7 20.axb4 ♕b8 21.♘d5±.
18...♖fe8 19.h5 ♕c6 20.f4 gives White a strong attack.
19.♘d5 ♗xd5 20.♖xd5 ♖fc8 21.f4 b4 22.a4 exf4 23.♗xf4 ♘b6 24.♖a5!
White has a good advantage.

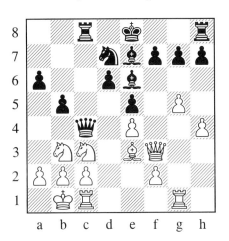

17...0–0 18.♘d2 ♕c7 19.♘d5 ♗xd5 20.exd5 f5!
Opening the f-file for the rook while giving some fresh air to Black's other pieces.

21.gxf6 ♘xf6 22.♕g2 ♖f7 23.f4
Motylev is trying to find some play against the enemy castle.

23...exf4

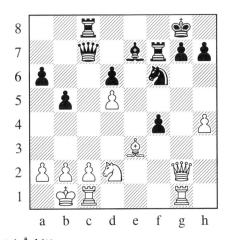

24.♗d4?!
Too optimistic. White should have accepted that he had nothing and played for equality. Now he is just a pawn down.

Correct was 24.♗xf4 ♕b7 25.♗h6 ♗f8 (25...♖xd5 can be met by 26.♕xg7†! ♖xg7 27.♖xg7† ♔h8 28.♖xe7 ♖g8 29.♖f1 when White has enough activity to compensate for the missing queen) 26.♘e4 ♘xe4 27.♖xe4 ♕e7 28.♕h1 ♖c4 when Black's position remains a bit easier, but White should be able to survive.

24...♕b7 25.♕h3 ♖e8 26.♘f3 ♕d7 27.♕g2?!
27.♕xd7 ♘xd7 28.♖ce1 h6 29.c3 was the best chance to hold the position.

27...♘h5 28.♖ce1 ♗f6 29.♗xf6 ♖xf6 30.♖xe8† ♕xe8 31.♕g4

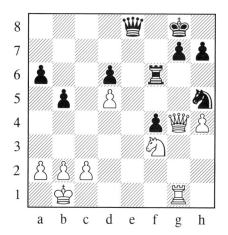

31...h6?

31...罝g6 was winning comfortably: 32.包g5
包f6 33.豐d1 豐e5 34.罝e1 豐f5 Black intends
...h6 next, and the passed f-pawn should secure
Black's victory.

**32.罝e1 豐g6 33.豐c8† 罝f8 34.豐xa6 豐g3
35.豐a3 包f6 36.豐d3 包g4 37.豐e4 包e5
38.包xe5 罝e8 39.豐h1 dxe5 40.罝g1 豐f2
41.罝f1 豐c5 42.豐e4 豐c4 43.豐g2??**

Overlooking a simple draw with: 43.罝xf4!
exf4 44.豐xe8† 含h7 45.a4 豐xd5 46.axb5 f3
47.豐f8 豐d1† 48.含a2 豐e2 49.豐f5† 含g8
50.豐c8†=

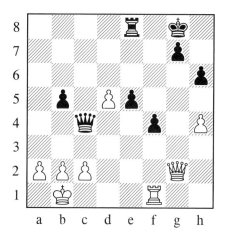

43...e4?

There is no need to give up the strong

f-pawn. The simple 43...罝f8 44.d6 e4 45.罝g1
豐d4–+ was winning easily.

44.罝xf4 豐xd5

Despite missing two clear wins Black is still
better, and the strong passed e-pawn is a real
pain for White.

**45.罝f1 豐h5 46.罝g1 罝e7 47.豐d2 含h7
48.豐b4 罝e5 49.罝e1 e3 50.罝e2 罝f7
51.豐e1 罝f3**

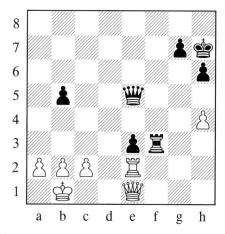

52.a3??

Under pressure, White commits what should
have been a losing blunder. Of course, when
you are defending such a position it is hard to
maintain full concentration for every move.

White should have played 52.豐d1! 豐d5!
53.含c1! 豐xa2 54.豐d3† g6 55.罝xe3 罝xe3
56.豐xe3 豐a1† 57.含d2 豐xb2 58.豐e7†
豐g7 59.豐c5 with good chances to hold the
position.

52...豐f4?

Black could have won with 52...豐f5!,
the difference being that this controls the
d5-square. 53.含a2 (53.豐c3 罝f1† 54.含a2
豐d5† 55.b3 豐d1–+) 53...罝f1 54.豐b4
豐d5† 55.b3 豐e5 56.罝e1 e2 57.豐d2 罝xe1
58.豐xe1 豐e4–+

53.♕c3 ♕e4 54.b3 ♖h3 55.h5 ♖xh5 56.♖xe3 ♕d5 57.♖d3

Now the position should be drawn.

57...♕e5

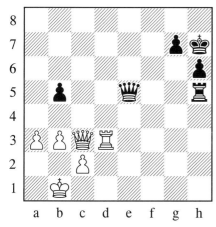

58.♕xe5?

It was better to play 58.♔b2, activating the king for the rook endgame.

58...♖xe5

Despite the reduced material White is in some danger, as the black pawns are more nimble.

59.c4?

I dislike this move, as split pawns are slower than connected ones. White could have drawn relatively easily with the help of a pawn sacrifice: 59.b4 g5 60.a4! bxa4 61.c4 Now the pawns are united and the draw is inevitable. 61...♖e4 62.♖c3 g4 63.b5 g3 64.b6 g2 65.♖g3 ♖xc4 66.♖xg2 a3 67.♖a2 ♖c3 68.b7 ♖b3† 69.♔c2 ♖xb7 70.♖xa3 ♔g6 71.♔d2 ♔g5 72.♔e2 ♔g4 73.♔f2=

59...bxc4 60.bxc4 g5 61.♖c3 g4?

61...♖c5! was a much stronger move, blocking the dangerous c-pawn. 62.♔c2 g4

63.♔d3 h5 64.♔e3 (64.♔d4?? ♖g5 65.c5 g3 wins immediately) 64...h4 65.♔f4 g3 66.♖c1 g2 67.♔f3 h3

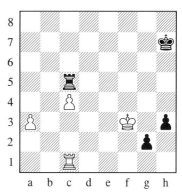

68.♔f2 (68.♔g3? ♖f5! 69.♖g1 ♖f1 70.♔h2 ♔g6 71.a4 ♔f5 72.a5 ♔f4 73.a6 ♖xg1 74.♔xg1 ♔g3 75.a7 h2#) 68...♔g6 The black king is heading for the queenside and it is not clear if White can hold the position.

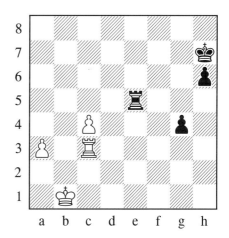

62.c5

Now the black rook will be forced into a passive position and it will be easy for White to stop the kingside pawns.

62...h5 63.c6 ♖e8 64.♔c2 ♔g6 65.c7 ♖c8 66.♔d2 ♔f5 67.♔e3 ♔e5 68.♖c5†
½–½

GAME 12

▷ **A. Grischuk (2746)**
▶ **A. Morozevich (2694)**
FIDE World Cup, Khanty-Mansiysk
Round 3, Game 1, 03.09.2011 **[C02]**
Annotated by Kamil Miton

In the 3.e5 variation of the French Defence, Grischuk chose the interesting 6.♗d3 which he had previously employed in his practice. The critical moment in the opening was 10...a6 which is too slow and after which, in my opinion, White gains a considerable advantage. The alternative for Black was 10...♘c6, which results in unclear positions which require very detailed examination. If it turns out that White also has the advantage there, then Black would need to give up on the move 7...♗c5 altogether.

1.e4 e6 2.d4 d5 3.e5 c5 4.c3 ♗d7 5.♘f3 ♛b6 6.♗d3 cxd4

6...♘c6 is an option.

7.♘xd4

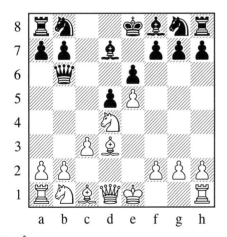

7...♗c5

I shall also mention Black's important alternatives:

7...♘e7 8.♘d2 ♘bc6 9.♘xc6 ♘xc6 10.♘f3

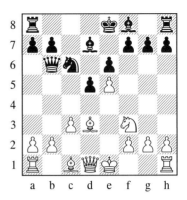

10...h6

10...♛c7 11.♛e2 ♗e7 12.0–0 0–0 13.♗f4± White's position is more pleasing. White's set-up with ♗f4-♛e2-♖e1, which is typical for this structure, strengthens the crucial e5-point. Thanks to this, it will be more difficult for Black to fight for the centre with ...f6, which is a typical move in the French Defence. That is why Black's plan should be to try to open one of the b-, c- or d-files with ...b5-b4 or ...d5-d4. Meanwhile White will focus mainly on the kingside, where he can play h4-h5 in order to weaken the black king or attempt to transfer one of his heavy pieces into the attack, for example the queen to g4. I will add that usually the exchange of light-squared bishops is advantageous for Black, and of the dark-squared ones for White.

11.0–0

11.h4 ♗c5 (11...d4 12.♛e2 dxc3 13.bxc3±) 12.♛e2 a5 13.♗f4±

11...g5 12.♖e1 ♗g7 13.h3 0–0–0 14.b4 ♛c7 14...♔b8 15.b5 ♘a5 16.♗e3 ♛c7 17.b6 axb6 18.♖b1 ♘c4 19.♗xc4 ♛xc4 20.♖xb6→ 15.♛e2 f6 16.exf6 ♗xf6 17.♗b2 h5 18.b5 ♘a5 19.c4↑

7...♘c6 8.♘xc6 bxc6

8...♗xc6 9.♛e2 (9.a4!?) 9...d4 (9...♘e7 10.♘d2 ♘g6 11.♘f3 ♗e7 12.0–0 ♛c7 13.♗d2±) 10.0–0 ♖d8 11.♘d2 dxc3 12.♘c4 ♛c7 (12...♛d4 13.♖d1 ♛d5 14.f3 ♗c5† 15.♔h1±) 13.bxc3 b5 14.♘d6† ♗xd6

15.exd6 ♕xd6 16.♗xb5 ♘e7 17.a4±
9.0–0 ♘e7 10.♘d2 ♘g6 11.♘f3 ♗e7 12.♕e2
0–0 13.h4! h6 14.h5 ♘h8 15.♗f4 f5 16.exf6
♗xf6 17.♗d6 ♖fe8 18.♘e5 ♗xe5 19.♗xe5
♘f7 20.♖ae1 ♘xe5 21.♕xe5 ♕b8 22.f4 c5
23.♖f2±

Brynell – Akesson, Gothenburg 2006.

8.0–0

Another line starts 8.♕g4 ♘e7.

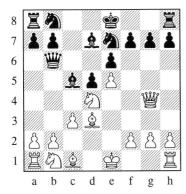

Now White has two main options:

a) 9.0–0 ♘g6 10.♘b3

10.♘d2 ♗xd4 (10...♘c6 11.♘xc6 ♗xc6
12.h4 h5 13.♕g3 ♗b5 14.c4 dxc4 15.♗xg6
c3 16.bxc3 ♗xf1 17.♔xf1 fxg6 18.♕xg6†
♔f8 19.♖b1↑) 11.cxd4 ♗b5 12.♗xb5†
♕xb5 13.h4 ♘c6 14.h5 ♘ge7 15.♕xg7 ♖g8
16.♕xh7 ♘xd4 17.♖e1 ♖c8∓

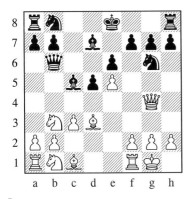

10...♘c6

10...♗b5 11.♘xc5 ♕xc5 12.♗e3 ♘c6 13.c4
♗xc4 14.♖c1 ♕a6 15.♗xc4 dxc4 16.♘d2
0–0 17.♘xc4 ♘c6=

10...0–0 11.♘xc5 ♕xc5 12.♗e3 ♕c7 13.f4±

11.♗xg6

11.♘xc5 ♕xc5 12.♗e3 ♘cxe5 13.♗xg6
♘xg4 14.♗xf7† ♔xf7 15.♗xc5=

11...hxg6

11...fxg6 12.♘xc5 ♕xc5 13.b3 ♘xe5
14.♕g3 ♘c6 15.♗a3 ♕a5 16.♗d6 ♘e7∞

12.♘xc5 ♕xc5 13.♖e1 ♖h5 14.♕g3 ♘e7
15.♘d2 ♕h4=

b) 9.♕xg7 ♖g8

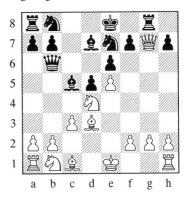

10.♕f6!?

10.♕xh7?! ♘bc6 (10...♖xg2 11.♔f1 ♖g8
12.♖g1 ♖xg1† 13.♔xg1 ♔d8 14.♘d2
♗xd4 15.cxd4 ♕xd4 16.h3 ♕xe5 17.♘f3
♕f6 18.♗g2↑; 10...♗xd4 11.cxd4 ♕xd4
12.0–0 ♖xg2† 13.♔xg2 ♕g4†=) 11.0–0
♘xe5 12.♗e2 0–0–0∞

10...♖xg2

10...♘bc6 11.♗xh7 ♖xg2 12.♕h8† ♖g8
13.♗xg8 0–0–0⩲

11.♗xh7 ♗xd4 12.cxd4 ♕xd4 13.♘c3 ♕g4
14.h4 ♕h5 15.♔f1 ♖xf2† 16.♔xf2 ♕xh7
17.♗g5 ♘bc6 18.♖ac1±

Volokitin – Volkov, Dresden 2007.

8...♗xd4 9.cxd4 ♕xd4 10.♘c3

By sacrificing the pawn, White gained better
piece development and weakened the dark
squares around the black king.

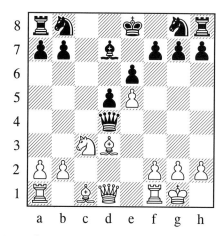

10...a6

In this way, Black neutralizes the threat of ♘b5. However, one needs to bear in mind that the position is dynamic and Black should try to develop his pieces and consolidate his position as soon as possible. Another interesting possibility would be:

10...♘c6!?∞

From a practical point of view, choosing this move is a very difficult decision, because grabbing another pawn with Black is connected with the very dynamic introduction of White's pieces into the game. As the variations demonstrate, although White has a strong initiative, a definite advantage is difficult to prove.

11.♘b5

11.♖e1?! ♘xe5 12.♖e3 ♘f6 (12...♘xd3 13.♖xd3 ♕h4∓) 13.♘e2 ♕h4 14.♖xe5 ♘g4 15.♗f4 ♕xf2† 16.♔h1 ♕b6 17.♗g3 ♘xe5 18.♗xe5 f6∞

11.♗e3 ♕xe5 12.♖e1 ♘ge7 13.♗xa7 ♕f6 14.♗c5 0–0∞

11...♕xe5 12.♕g4

12.♕a4 ♕b8 13.♕a3 ♘ge7 14.♘d6† ♔f8∓

12.♖e1 ♕b8 13.♕g4 (13.b3 ♘ge7 14.♗a3 0–0 15.♗d6 ♕d8) 13...♔f8 14.♗f4 (14.♗e3 ♘f6 15.♗c5† ♔g8 16.♕h4 a6 17.♘d6 b6 18.♗a3 a5 19.♖e3 ♘b4) 14...e5 15.♕xd7 ♘f6 16.♗xe5 ♘xd7 17.♗xb8 ♖xb8

18.♖ad1⩲

12.f4 ♕b8 13.f5 e5 14.♕g4 ♘f8 15.♗e3 ♘f6 16.♕h4 h6∓

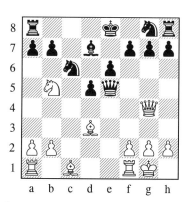

12...♔f8

12...♘f6 13.♕xg7 ♖g8 14.♕h6 ♘g4 15.♕h4

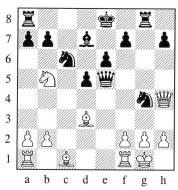

15...♘b4 (15...a6 16.f4 ♕b8 17.♗xh7 ♖g7 18.h3 axb5 19.hxg4∞; 15...♘e7 16.f3∞) 16.♗xh7 ♗xb5 (16...♗g7 17.f4 ♕b8 18.♗f5 ♖g8 19.a4⩲) 17.♗xg8 ♕g7 (17...♗xf1 18.♕xg4 ♗c4 19.♗f4 ♕xb2 20.♗xf7†+−) 18.♖e1 ♕xg8 19.♗g5 ♘xf2 20.♕xb4 ♘h3† 21.♔h1 ♘f2† 22.♔g1 ♘h3†= 23.gxh3 ♕xg5† 24.♕g4 ♕h6∞

12...♘h6 13.♗xh6 gxh6 14.♖fe1 ♕g5 15.♘c7† ♔e7 16.♕xg5† hxg5 17.♘xa8 ♖xa8 18.♗xh7∞

13.♗f4 h5

13...♘f6 14.♕g3 ♕h5 15.♖fe1 ♕g4 16.♕e3↑

14.♕h4 ♕f6 15.♗g5 ♕xb2 16.♖ab1 ♕e5
17.♗f4 ♕f6 18.♗g5 ♕e5= 19.♖fe1 ♕b8∞

11.♖e1

11.♗e3 ♕xe5 12.♖e1 ♗c6∞

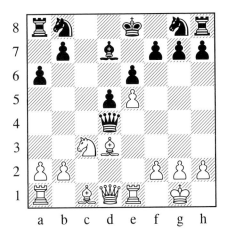

11...♗c6

The plan of ...a6 and ...♗c6 turns out to be too slow. White can now improve his pieces, taking advantage of the bad position of the black queen. Therefore the alternatives are especially important:

11...♘e7 12.♗e3 ♕xe5 13.♗c5 ♕g5 14.♗xe7 ♕xe7 15.♘xd5

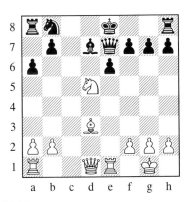

15...♕d6

15...♕d8 16.♕b3 b5 (16...♘c6 17.♘b6 ♖b8 18.♖ad1±; 16...0–0 17.♘b6 ♖a7 18.♖ad1 ♕c7 19.♗b1 g6 20.♕e3±) 17.♗e4

♗c6 18.♖ad1 0–0 19.♘b4 ♕e8 20.♘xc6
♘xc6 21.♕a3±

16.♗e4

White's pieces are very active and it will be difficult for Black to defend against all the threats.

16.♕h5 ♔f8 17.♘c3 ♘c6 18.♖ad1 ♕e7∞

16...♗c6

16...exd5 17.♗xd5† ♗e6 18.♕b3 0–0
19.♗xe6 ♘c6 20.♗d5 ♖ad8 21.♖ad1±

17.♘b6 ♕xd1 18.♖axd1 ♖a7 19.♘c8 ♖a8
20.♖c1 ♔f8=

11...♘c6 12.♗e3

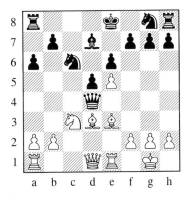

12...♕b4

12...♕xe5 13.♗c5+−

12...♕h4 13.♗c5 ♘ge7 14.♘a4 ♘xe5
(14...0–0 15.♖e3 h6 16.♗d6±) 15.♘b6
♘xd3 16.♕xd3 ♗b5 17.♕c3 ♖d8 18.♕xg7
♖g8 19.♗xe7 ♔xe7 20.♘xd5† ♖xd5
21.♕xg8 ♖g5 22.♖e4 ♕h5 23.♕b8 ♗c6
24.♕c7† ♔e8 25.♕b8†=

13.a3

13.♘a4 ♘xe5 14.♘b6 ♖d8 15.♘xd5 ♕d6
16.♗f4 ♕xd5 17.♖xe5 ♕d4∞

13...♕xb2 14.♘a4 ♕xe5 15.♘b6 ♖d8 16.♗c5
♕g5 17.f4 ♕h6 18.♘xd5 ♘ge7 19.♘c7† ♔f8
20.f5 e5 21.♕b3↑

12.♘e2 ♕g4

On the kingside the queen will be a target of attack for the white pieces, however other options are much worse for Black. For example, 12...♕b6 13.♗e3 ♕c7 14.♗c5± or 12...♖xe5 13.♘g3 ♕f6 14.♘h5±.

13.h3 ♕h5

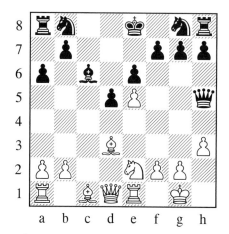

14.♗f4

A logical and correct move, although one could also position the bishop on e3, where it would be more flexible, as it would be active not only along the c1-h6 diagonal but also along g1-a7. Let's see some lines:

14.♗e3!?

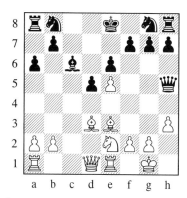

14...♘d7

14...♖xe5? 15.♗d4 ♕g5 16.f4 ♕h6 17.♘g3+−

14...♘b5 15.♕b3 ♘e7 16.♗c5±

15.♕d2 ♘e7

15...♘xe5 16.♘g3 ♕h4 17.♘f5 exf5

18.♗g5 ♕d4 19.♖xe5† ♕xe5 20.♖e1 ♕e4 21.f3 ♕xe1† 22.♕xe1† ♔f8 23.♕b4† ♔e8 24.♗xf5→

16.♘g3

16.♗g5 f6 17.exf6 gxf6 18.♘d4 ♕xg5 19.f4 ♕h5 20.♖xe6 ♘c5 21.♖xe7† ♔xe7 22.♕b4 ♔f7 23.♕xc5 ♖he8∞

16...♕h4

16...♕xe5 17.♗f4 ♕d4 18.♖xe6 fxe6 19.♗g6† ♘xg6 20.♕xd4 e5 21.♗xe5 ♘gxe5 22.f4±

17.♗g5 ♕d4 18.♘h5

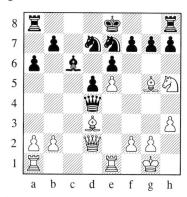

18...♘xe5

18...♖g8 19.♗xe7 ♔xe7 20.♕g5† f6 21.exf6† gxf6 22.♕f5 ♘e5 23.♕xf6† ♔d6 24.♗xh7 ♖gf8∞

19.♖xe5 ♕xe5 20.♖e1 ♕d4

20...♕d6 21.♘xg7† ♔d7 22.♗f4 ♕c5 23.♘xe6 fxe6 24.♕e2→

21.g4!↑

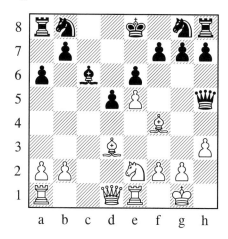

14...♗b5

In principle, a legitimate decision. Although now Black loses two pawns, thanks to the exchange of the light-squared bishop the black queen will not be in danger and White's pressure on the kingside will not be as strong.

After the natural 14...♘e7 White gains a strong attack, as the following lines show:

Following 14...♘e7 15.♕d2 h6

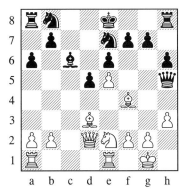

We must consider two options:

a) 16.♘d4 ♗b5 17.♗c2
   17.♘xb5 axb5 18.♗xb5† ♘bc6 19.♗e3 0–0 20.f4 ♖fc8∞
   17.♗xb5† axb5 18.♘xb5 0–0 19.♘d6 ♘bc6 20.♘xb7 ♖fb8 21.♘d6 ♘g6 22.♗g3 ♘gxe5 23.a4∞
17...♘g6
   17...♘bc6 18.♘f3 d4 19.♖ac1 a5 (19...d3 20.♗d1±) 20.♗e4 0–0 21.♔h2 f5 22.exf6 ♖xf6 23.♘d6 ♕f7 24.♖c5↑
18.♗xg6
   18.♘xe6 fxe6 19.g4 ♘h4 20.gxh5 ♘f3† 21.♔g2 ♘xd2 22.♗xd2 0–0=
18...♕xg6 19.♖e3 ♘c6 20.♖g3 ♕h7 21.♘xc6 ♗xc6 22.♗e3⩲

b) 16.♔h2 ♘g6 17.g4 ♕h4 18.♗g3 ♕e7 19.♘d4

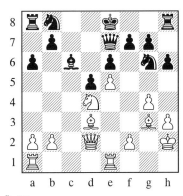

19...♘d7
   19...h5 20.♘xe6 h4 21.♘xg7† (21.♗f4 ♕xe6 22.♗f5 ♘xf4 23.♗xe6 ♘xe6 24.f4∞) 21...♔f8 22.♘f5 hxg3† 23.♔xg3 ♕c7 24.♖ac1↑
   19...♗d7 20.f4 ♘c6 21.♘xc6 ♗xc6 22.f5 ♘f8 23.f6 gxf6 24.exf6 ♕d8 25.♕f4±
20.f4 0–0
   20...♘c5 21.f5 ♘xd3 22.♕xd3 ♘f8 23.f6 gxf6 24.♘f5 ♕b4 25.♘d6† ♔d7 26.exf6 ♕xb2† 27.♔g1 d4 28.♘e4 ♔e8 29.♖ab1 ♕xa2 30.♖xb7+−
21.f5 ♘gxe5

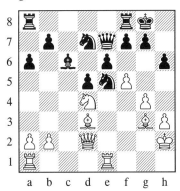

22.fxe6
   22.♖xe5 ♘xe5 23.♗xe5 f6 24.♗g3 e5 25.♘xc6 bxc6 26.♖c1∞
22...♘xd3 23.♕xd3 ♘f6 24.♘f5 ♕b4 25.e7
   25.exf7† ♖xf7 26.♘xh6† gxh6 27.♕g6† ♖g7 28.♕xf6 ♖f8 29.♕e6† ♔h7∞
25...♕xb2† 26.♔g1 ♖fc8 27.♗e5 d4 28.♕f1 ♘e8 29.♘xg7 ♗b5 30.♘xe8 ♗xf1 31.♘f6† ♔g7 32.♖xf1 ♔g6∞

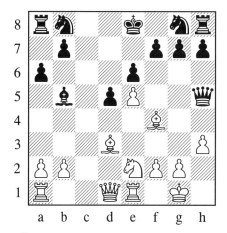

15.♕b3

White overlooked a quite complicated opportunity of gaining a big advantage:

15.♕c1! ♘c6

15...♘d7 16.♗xb5 axb5 17.♘d4 ♘e7
18.♕c7 ♖d8 (18...♕h4 19.g3 ♕xh3
20.♘xb5 ♘f5 21.♘d6† ♘xd6 22.♕xd6
♖a6 23.♕c7 ♖a8 24.♖ac1 ♖d8 25.♗d2
0–0 26.♗b4 ♖fe8 27.♗e7+–) 19.♕xb7 0–0
20.♗g3±

16.♘g3 ♕h4

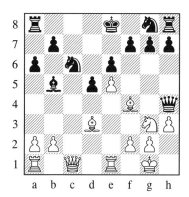

17.♗e4

Now Black has problems with his queen and bishop.

17...♕d8

17...h6 18.♗xd5 ♘ge7 (18...exd5 19.♘f5
♕d8 20.♕c3±) 19.♗f3 0–0 20.♘e4 ♘f5
(20...♘d4 21.♗g4 ♘g6 22.♘f6† gxf6 23.g3

♘f3† 24.♔h1) 21.a4 ♗d3 22.♘d6 (22.♘c5
♘cd4 23.♘xd3 ♘xf3† 24.gxf3 ♕xh3
25.♗g3 ♘xg3 26.fxg3 ♕xg3† 27.♔f1 ♕xf3†
28.♘f2∞) 22...♘fd4 23.♗xc6 ♘xc6 24.♕d2
♗g6 25.♖ac1±

17...♘e7 18.♗xd5±

18.a4 ♗c4 19.♘h5 ♔f8

19...g6 20.♗g5 ♕c7 21.♘f6† ♘xf6 22.♗xf6
♖f8 23.♗f3±

20.♗g5

20.♗b1 a5 21.♖a3↑

20...♕d7

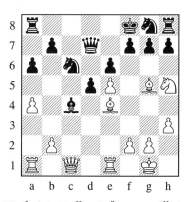

21.b3!? ♗xb3 22.♕a3† ♘ge7 23.♕xb3 dxe4
24.♖ad1 ♕c7

24...♘d5 25.♘xg7+–

25.♖xe4↑

**15...♘e7 16.♗xb5† axb5 17.♕xb5† ♘bc6
18.♕xb7**

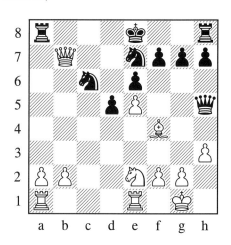

18...0–0

The character of the position has changed dramatically. Black has solved all his problems and although it may be hard to believe, he has compensation for the pawn in the form of pressure on the a-, b- and c-files. In addition, after the possible move ...♘g6 the e5-pawn is endangered, and the black queen, which had been weak earlier, after the exchange of light-squared bishops can become very active on the weakened squares of the b1-h7 diagonal.

Another option was: 18...♖b8!? 19.♕a6 0–0 (19...♖xb2 20.♘d4+–) 20.♕a3 ♕f5∞

19.♕b3 ♖ab8

Black unnecessarily helps White improve his pieces. Instead I would suggest 19...♖fc8!?.

20.♕c3 ♖fc8 21.♘d2±

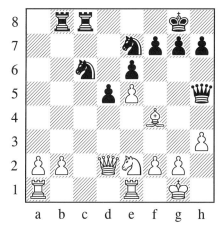

White has managed to consolidate his position. Morozevich once again played too slowly and did not take advantage of the time available to play more actively and scare the opponent with some specific threats.

21...h6 22.♖ac1 ♕h4 23.b3

23.♖c3 was also possible.

23...♘f5 24.g4

If 24.♖c2 then 24...g5 in order to force the bishop to h2, where it would occupy a very passive position and be difficult to improve. For example: 25.♗h2 ♘cd4 26.♘xd4 ♕xd4 27.♕xd4 ♘xd4 28.♖d2 ♘c2 29.♖ee2 ♘b4∞

24...♘fe7 25.♔g2 ♖a8 26.♖c5 f5

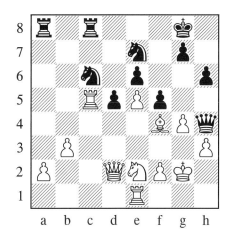

27.gxf5?

From a strategic point of view, much better was capturing on f6, which solves two problems for White straight away: he eliminates the e5-pawn, which in many variations may be attacked, and at the same time he activates the bishop. After the move in the game, the white king's position is weakened, the bishop remains passive and Black gains the fine square f5 for his knight. Thanks to this defective move, very good chances for black counterplay suddenly materialize.

The correct path was 27.exf6 ♕xf6 28.♗g3±.

27...♘xf5 28.♖ec1 ♘ce7 29.♖xc8† ♘xc8∞

The position is rather unclear and at first sight it is not easy to spot that Black may very quickly and efficiently organize strong counterplay against the white king, via the weakened light squares.

30.♖c6

30...♕e7

A key alternative was:

30...♕d8

In comparison to the game move, in addition to the plan of ...♕e8-g6, Black also prepares ...d5-d4 and ...♕d5.

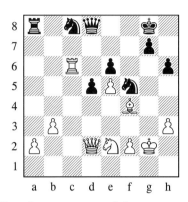

White has various possibilities:

a) 31.♘d4 ♕d7 32.♖c2 ♘xd4 33.♕xd4 ♘e7 34.a4 ♘f5 35.♕d3 ♘h4† 36.♔g1 ♖f8↑

b) 31.♕c2 d4 32.♕e4 (32.♕c4 ♘ce7 33.♕xe6† ♔h7 34.♖d6 ♕c7∓) 32...♖xa2 33.♘c1 ♖b2 34.♖xe6 ♕d7 35.♕xf5 ♘e7 36.♕g4 ♕d5† 37.♔g1 h5 38.♕xh5 ♕xe6 39.♕e8† ♔h7 40.♕h5†=

c) 31.♖xe6 d4 32.♔f1 (32.♔h2 ♘h4↑) 32...♕h4 33.♕d3 ♘e3† 34.♔e1 ♕xh3 35.♖e8† ♔f7 36.e6† ♔xe8 37.♕g6† ♔d8 38.fxe3 ♕h1† 39.♔f2 ♕h4† 40.♔f3 ♕h1†=

d) 31.a4 d4↑

e) 31.♗g3 d4↑

31.♕c2 ♕e8 32.a4

32.♗g3 ♖xa2 33.♖xc8 ♖xc2 34.♖xe8† ♔f7∓

32...♕g6†

Maybe more precise was:

32...♘ce7!?

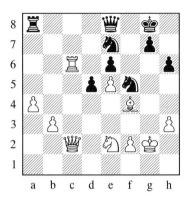

Because capturing the e6-pawn brings White nothing:

33.♖c7

33.♖xe6 ♘h4† 34.♔f1 ♕d7 35.♘d4 ♘ef5 36.♘xf5 (36.♕d3 ♘xd4 37.♖d6 ♕a7 38.♖xd5∞; 36.♕c6 ♕xc6 37.♘xc6 ♗f7 38.♖d6 ♘xd6 39.exd6 ♔e6∞) 36...♕xe6 37.♘xh4 ♕xh3† 38.♔g1 ♕xh4 39.♕c6 ♖d8∓

33...d4 34.♕e4 ♘d5 35.♖c4 ♗f7 36.♘xd4 ♘h4† 37.♔g3 ♖f8 38.♗e3 g5 39.b4

39.a5 ♘xe3 40.♕xe3 ♕b7 41.♖c6 ♖f3† 42.♕xf3 ♘xf3 43.♔xf3 ♕b4∞

39...♘xe3 40.♕xe3 ♕b7 41.f3 ♕d5↑

33.♗g3 ♘ce7 34.♘f4

34.♖c7!?

34...♕f7 35.♖c7 g5 36.♘e2 ♖f8 37.a5

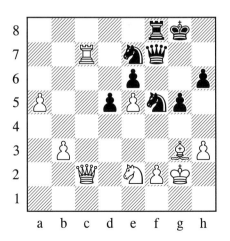

37...h5?

The decisive mistake. Morozevich is famous for his complex games and great ability to calculate variations, but he was not at his best during this game and once again he overlooked a tactical possibility which could have resulted in a draw:

37...d4

With the idea of ...♘e3†.

38.♕d3

38.a6 ♘e3† 39.fxe3 ♕f1† 40.♔h2 d3 41.♕xd3 ♖f2†=

38.♔g1 ♕h5 39.♕c4 ♕f3 40.♘xd4 ♕d1† 41.♔g2 ♘xd4 42.♖xe7 ♕f3† 43.♔h2 ♕d1 44.♔g2=

38.♖d7 ♕e8 with the idea of attacking on the a8-h1 diagonal.

38...h5 39.♘xd4

39.♕d2 ♘e3† 40.fxe3 ♕f1† 41.♔h2 ♘d5 42.♖c1 ♖f2† 43.♗xf2 ♕xf2† 44.♔h1 ♘xe3 45.♖g1 ♕f3† 46.♔h2 ♕f2†=

39...♘xd4 40.♕xd4 ♕f3† 41.♔g1 ♘d5 42.♖d7 h4 43.♗h2 ♕xb3 44.a6 ♕b1† 45.♔g2 ♕b5 46.♖d6 ♕e2=

38.♕d2+–

Now the game is over as a contest.

38...♕g6 39.a6 h4 40.♗h2 g4 41.♘f4 ♕g5 42.♕e2 ♘h6 43.♖xe7 gxh3† 44.♔xh3 ♕xe7 45.♘g6 ♕b4 46.♘xf8 ♔xf8 47.a7 ♕a5 48.♗f4 ♘f5 49.♕h5

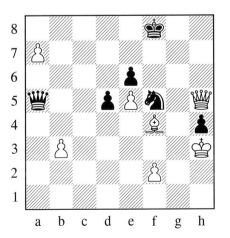

49...♔g7 50.♕g5† ♔h7 51.♕h5† ♔g7 52.♗g5 ♕c3† 53.♔g2 h3† 54.♕xh3 ♕c6 55.♗f6† ♔g6 56.♕g4†

1–0

GAME 13

▷ **D. Navara (2705)**
▶ **B. Grachev (2682)**
Croatian Team Championship, Sibenik
12.10.2011 **[C03]**
Annotated by Paco Vallejo Pons

Navara tried a rare line in the French Defence by playing 6.c4!? and managed to create a very unclear situation which was a little better for White. But after good play from Black the position gradually became equal, and then soon ended in a draw by repetition.

1.e4 e6 2.d4 d5 3.♘d2 a6

The idea of this move is normally twofold, to surprise your opponent and to avoid a check on b5 in lines where you get an isolated pawn.

4.♘gf3

The main alternative is 4.♗d3 c5 5.dxc5 (otherwise ...c4 will come) 5...♗xc5 and we arrive at a position with plenty of theory.

4.e5

Trying to take advantage of the not-so-useful ...a6 move, but White's move ♘d2 will also prove to be somewhat unnecessary.

4...c5 5.c3 ♘c6 6.♘gf3

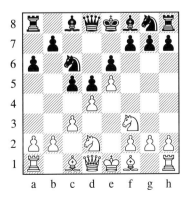

6...cxd4!?

    6...♘h6? 7.♘b3±

    6...♘ge7!? 7.♗d3 (7.dxc5 ♘g6) 7...♘f5
8.♗xf5 exf5 9.0–0 (9.dxc5 ♗xc5 10.♘b3
♗a7 with a very solid position) 9...b6!?∞

7.cxd4 ♕b6

The knight on d2 is misplaced, while the
knight on g8 is better placed than it would be
on d7.

4...c5 5.exd5 exd5

6.c4!?

    At first sight this may just look like a
simplifying move, but as it is coming from
Navara, who is a great fighter and well
prepared, this is an indication that the line
contains some poisonous ideas. Moreover
he has been happy to repeat the line a few
times.

6...cxd4

The alternative is:

6...♘f6 7.♗e2

    7.cxd5 ♘xd5 (7...cxd4 is just a transposition
to the main game) 8.♗c4 b5 9.♗xd5 ♕xd5
10.0–0 ♗e6N (10...♘c6 11.dxc5 ♗xc5
12.♘e4 ♕xd1 13.♖xd1 ♗e7 14.♘d6†
♗xd6 15.♖xd6 ♘d8 16.♗e3 0–0 17.♘d4
♖e8 18.♖c1 h6 19.h3 ♘e6 20.♘c6 ♘g5
21.♘a7 ♘e4 22.♘xc8 ♖axc8 23.♖xc8 ♘xd6

24.♖xe8† ♘xe8 and White has no advantage
at all Navara – Volkov, Dagomys 2008)

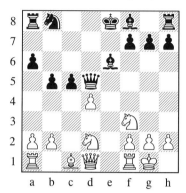

11.dxc5 (11.♘b1!? b4 12.♗e3 ♘d7=)
11...♗xc5 12.♘b3 ♗e7 13.♘fd4 0–0
14.♘xe6 ♕xe6 15.♖e1 ♕f6=

7...♘c6 8.0–0 cxd4 9.cxd5 ♕xd5 10.♗c4 ♕h5
11.♖e1† ♗e7

Black is doing okay.

7.cxd5

    It is difficult to believe that 7.♗e2 can create
any problems for Black; both 7...♘c6!? and
7...♘f6!? should equalize.

7...♘f6

    7...♕e7† 8.♕e2 ♘f6 9.♘xd4 ♘xd5 10.♘e4
♘c6 11.♘xc6 bxc6 12.♘d6† ♔d7 13.♘xc8
♔xc8 14.♗d2 with a comfortable position for
White.

7...♗c5?! is a bad square for the bishop.
Although it is desirable to protect the d4-
pawn, the bishop is too easily attacked. 8.♗d3
♘f6 9.0–0 0–0 10.♘e4±

8.♗c4 b5

Black can first play:
8...♕e7†!? 9.♔f1

The ambitious move.

    9.♕e2!? aims for a pleasant endgame:
9...♕xe2† 10.♗xe2 ♘xd5 11.♘xd4 and
White's slight lead in development gives him
a microscopic advantage.

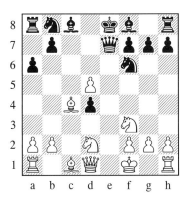

9...b5!?N

This is an improvement on 9...♕d6? and now:

a) 10.♗b3 b5? 11.a4?! (11.♕c2!N is very strong, almost winning. 11...♘bd7 [11...♕c5 12.♕d3+–] 12.♘e4 ♘xe4 13.♕xe4† ♗e7 14.♗f4 ♕g6 15.♕e2±) 11...♗e7 12.axb5 0–0 13.♘d4 ♕c5 14.♖a4 ♗b7 15.♘f5 axb5 16.♘e4 ♘xe4 17.♖xe4 ♗f6 18.♗e3 ♕c7 19.h4 ♕d7 20.g4 ♘c6 21.♗g5 ♘e5 22.♗xf6 gxf6 23.♕c1 1–0 Navara – Delchev, Bled (ol) 2002.

b) 10.♕c2!?N is probably even better than Navara's move. 10...♗e7 11.♘e4 ♘xe4 12.♕xe4 0–0 13.♗f4! ♕b4 14.♖c1 The white pieces are all coordinating well. 14...♗f6 15.h4!? (15.♗d2!?±) 15...g6 16.♗h6 ♗f5 17.♗xf8! ♕xc4† 18.♖xc4 ♗xe4 19.♖c8 ♗f5 20.♗e7† ♔xc8 21.♗xf6±

10.♗b3

We have transposed back into the main game.

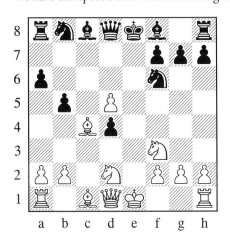

9.♗b3

9.♗d3N aims to take advantage of the weak black queenside, but with precise play Black is able to hold the balance: 9...♗e7! 10.a4 (10.♘b3 ♕xd5) 10...♗b7 11.axb5 0–0! An important and beautiful move. 12.0–0 (12.bxa6?! ♘xa6↑ and ...♘b4 is coming) 12...axb5 13.♖xa8 ♗xa8 14.♗xb5 (14.♘xd4 ♕xd5=) 14...♕xd5 15.♗c4 ♕d7=

9.♕e2†N avoids the white king being displaced: 9...♗e7! (9...♕e7 10.♗d3! ♕xe2† 11.♗xe2 ♗b7 12.0–0 ♗xd5 13.a4± with a better endgame) 10.♗b3 0–0 11.0–0 ♖e8! 12.♘xd4 ♗c5! 13.♕d3 ♗xd4! Conceding the bishop pair, just for a while. 14.♕xd4 ♘c6! 15.♕c5 ♘a5⇄

9...♕e7†

9...♗c5?! 10.♕e2†! ♕e7 11.♕xe7† ♔xe7 12.0–0 ♖d8 13.♘g5!↑

10.♔f1

With the bishop having retreated from the c4-square, 10.♕e2 is now even less interesting: 10...♕xe2† 11.♔xe2 ♗c5⇄

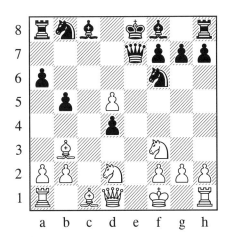

10...♗b7?!

Black can try using his d-pawn to help paralyse the white pieces:
10...d3!?N 11.♘b1!

A wonderful idea. White immediately attacks the d3-pawn, while aiming to reorganize his pieces with ♘c3, ♗f4, ♕d2 and ♖e1.

11.a4 ♗b7 12.axb5 ♘xd5 13.bxa6 ♘xa6 14.♗a4† (14.g3?! tries to get the h1-rook into play, but will put the king on a very dangerous diagonal. 14...♘c5 15.♖xa8† ♗xa8 16.♔g2 ♕d7 17.♘c4 ♗e7!↑) 14...♔d8∞ and it's very difficult to assess what is happening here.

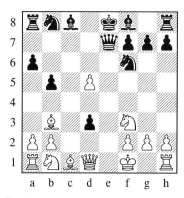

11...♕c7!

11...♗f5?! 12.♘c3 b4 13.♘a4 ♘bd7 14.♗f4!↑

11...♘bd7 12.♘c3 ♘c5 13.♗f4 b4 14.d6 ♕b7 15.♘a4→

12.♗g5 ♗e7 13.♕xd3 0–0 14.♘c3 ♘bd7

Black has decent compensation for the pawn thanks to the misplaced king on f1.

10...g6? is a good idea... but it is too slow! 11.♘g5! ♗g7 12.d6+–

10...♘bd7? 11.♘g5±

11.♘xd4

11.g3 ♕d7! (11...♗xd5?! 12.♗xd5 ♘xd5 13.♔g2 ♕b7 14.♘b3!↑) 12.♔g2 ♗e7 13.♘e5 ♗xd5† 14.♘df3 ♕b7 15.♗xd5 ♘xd5! (15...♕xd5 16.♕xd4±) 16.♕xd4 0–0=

11...g6

11...♘xd5 12.♘2f3↑

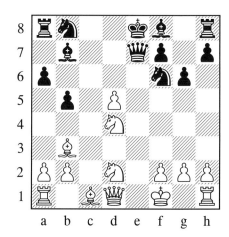

12.h4

12.♘2f3!N It was necessary to bring the bishop into play to fight for the advantage! 12...♗g7 13.♗f4! ♘xd5 (13...0–0 14.d6±) 14.♘f5! gxf5 15.♗xd5 ♘c6□ 16.♕d2 0–0 17.♗d6!±

12...♗g7 13.h5 0–0 14.hxg6 hxg6 15.♘2f3 ♗xd5

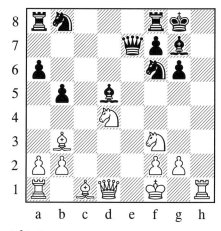

16.♗h6

16.♗xd5!? was maybe the last try: 16...♘xd5 17.♔g1±

16...♗xh6 17.♖xh6 ♖d8 18.♕d2 ♘e4 19.♕f4 ♕f6!=

Black has finally achieved a safe position, the rest is just very drawish.

20.♕e3 ♗xb3 21.axb3 ♖e8 22.♔g1 ♘d6
23.♕d2 ♘e4 24.♕e3 ♘d6 25.♕d2 ♘e4
26.♕e3
½–½

GAME 14
▷ **L. Dominguez (2710)**
▶ **Le Quang Liem (2717)**
5th SPICE Cup, Lubbock
Round 5, 19.10.2011 **[C11]**
Annotated by David Baramidze

In a topical line of the French Defence,
Dominguez tried the interesting 12.dxc5!?,
instead of the more popular 12.♘d1, and
obtained a small but pleasant edge. Le Quang
Liem played some inexact moves and White
obtained a serious strategic advantage. He
missed a clear win with 39.♔b5, but still kept
the upper hand and eventually won after Black
failed to defend in the most precise way.

**1.e4 e6 2.d4 d5 3.♘c3 ♘f6 4.e5 ♘fd7 5.f4
c5 6.♘f3 ♘c6 7.♗e3 ♗e7 8.♕d2 0–0 9.♗e2**
    White must avoid 9.0–0–0? c4! when he will
be massacred on the queenside.

The main alternative to the text move is 9.dxc5
♗xc5 10.0–0–0 ♕a5 11.♗xc5 ♘xc5 12.h4
with complex play.

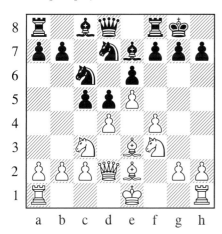

9...a6

9...b6!? leads to a different type of position.
Black intends to follow up with ...f5, meeting
exf6 with ...♘xf6 when the pawn c5 will be
protected.

10.0–0 b5 11.a3
    11.♘d1 is less popular, and after 11...b4
12.♘f2 a5 Black will obtain a decent position
after exchanging his bad bishop with ...♗a6.

11.♔h1!?
    This interesting move has been tested by
some strong players. White makes a useful
move and waits to see what Black is going
to do.

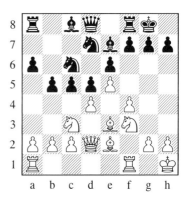

11...♕b6
    Several other moves are possible:
    11...b4 can be met by 12.♘a4! cxd4
13.♘xd4 ♘xd4 14.♗xd4 ♗b7 15.b3!?N
(15.f5 is slightly premature: 15...exf5
16.♖xf5 ♗c6 17.b3 ♗xa4 18.bxa4 ♘c5∞
Nijboer – Gurevich, Amsterdam 2000)
15...♗c6 16.♘b2 White brings the knight
out of harm's way and intends to play f5 in
the near future.
    After 11...♗b7 White should play 12.♘d1!.
Now Black's typical response would be
12...b4 13.♘f2 a5 intending ...♗a6, but this
would now entail the loss of a tempo since
Black has already played ...♗b7.
    11...♕c7!? is a flexible reply. 12.a3 (12.♘d1
is met by 12...b4 when 13.c4 is not so strong,

since 13...dxc4 14.d5? exd5 15.♕xd5 ♘b6† does not work for White.) 12...♗b7 13.♖ad1 ♖ac8 14.♕e1 cxd4 15.♘xd4 ♘xd4 16.♗xd4 ♗c5

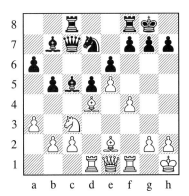

Black had no problems in Karjakin – Carlsen, Wijk aan Zee 2010.

12.♘d1

12.a3 ♗b7 13.♖ad1 ♖ac8 14.♕e1 cxd4 15.♘xd4 ♘xd4 16.♗xd4 ♗c5=

12...b4 13.c4

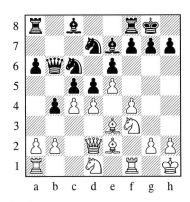

13...dxc4

13...cxd4 does not equalize: 14.♘xd4 ♘xd4 15.♗xd4 ♗c5 16.♗xc5 ♘xc5 17.cxd5 exd5 18.♕d4± Potkin – Wang Hao, Ningbo 2010.

14.d5!?

Leading to a sharp and unbalanced position.

14...exd5 15.♕xd5 ♘a5 16.♗g1!

Freeing the e3-square for the knight.

16...♕c7 17.♘e3 ♘b6 18.♕e4 ♗b7 19.♕c2

The position is complex and offers chances to both sides. White is a pawn down but he can win it back if he so desires. Alternatively he might just go for a kingside attack with f5.

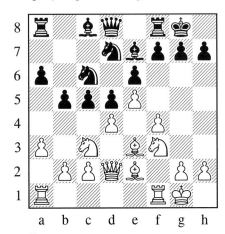

11...♕c7

Naturally Black has some other playable options.

11...♗b7 12.♘d1 (12.♖ad1 ♖c8 13.♔h1 cxd4 14.♘xd4 ♘xd4 15.♗xd4 ♗c5) 12...♕c7 13.c3 (13.♘f2 cxd4 14.♘xd4 ♖ac8) 13...♘a5 14.♕e1 ♘c4 15.♗d3 was unclear in Alekseev – Rakhmanov, Irkutsk 2010.

11...♕b6 12.♘d1 a5 13.c3

Preventing the plan of ...b4 and ...♗a6.

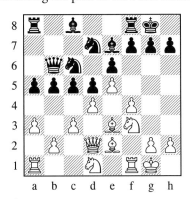

13...a4

Black hopes to exploit the light-square weaknesses on the queenside.

After 13...b4? 14.axb4 cxb4 the change in the pawn structure favours White, as his solid centre provides the foundation for a kingside attack. 15.f5!?↑ looks like the most energetic continuation.

13...♗a6?! is also unsatisfactory, as 14.dxc5 ♗xc5 15.b4 ♗xe3† 16.♘xe3 f6 17.♘d4 gives White a nice bind on the dark squares. 14.♗d3

14.♘f2 ♘a5 15.♖ad1 ♗b7?! (better is 15...♘c4! 16.♕c1 ♘xe3 17.♕xe3 b4⇄) 16.♗d3 ♘c4 17.♕e2 ♘xe3 18.♕xe3 b4 19.f5 gave White a promising attack in Karjakin – Rodriguez Vila, Khanty-Mansiysk 2009.

14...♘a5

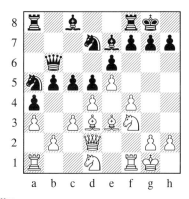

15.♕f2!?

15.♕e2 ♘c4 16.♗f2 f5∞ led to unclear play in several other games.

15...f5

15...♘c4 allows 16.f5↑.

16.exf6 ♘xf6 17.dxc5 ♕c7 18.♘d4 ♗d7 19.c6 ♘xc6

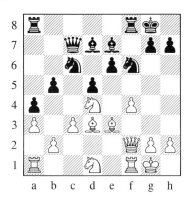

Xu Yuhua – X. Zhang, Jiangsu Wuxi 2008. Here White's best chance for an advantage would have been:

20.♘xb5!?N

The game continued: 20.♘xc6 ♕xc6?! (20...♗xc6 21.♗d4 ♘e4=) 21.♗d4 ♗d6 22.♘e3±

20...♕b7 21.♘d4 ♘g4 22.♕g3 ♘xe3 23.♘xc6 ♗xc6 24.♘xe3

White keeps an extra pawn but converting it will not be easy.

24...♗b5

24...♕xb2? 25.♕h3+–

25.♘c2 ♗c5† 26.♔h1

26.♘d4 ♗xd3 27.♕xd3 ♖a6 28.♔h1 ♖b6⇄

26...♖f6⯑

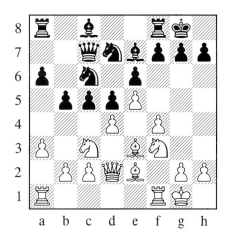

12.dxc5!?

It is not clear if White is getting anywhere after the more popular 12.♘d1 f6 (also possible is 12...♗b7 13.c3 ♘a5) 13.c3 ♘a5⇄, so Dominguez tries a different idea.

12...♗xc5N

In the one previous game, Black preferred 12...♘xc5

which seems sensible enough. Play continued:

13.♘d4 ♗b7 14.♘xc6 ♕xc6 15.♗d4 ♖ac8

15...f5!?N looks better to me, and after 16.exf6 ♗xf6 17.♗xf6 ♖xf6 18.♕d4 ♖af8

19.♗d3 ♘e4 20.♘e2 ♕c7 the position is unclear.

16.♕e3 ♖fd8

16...♘e4 17.♘xe4 dxe4 18.c3 ♗c5 (18...♖fd8 19.b4±) 19.♗xc5 ♕xc5 20.♕xc5 ♖xc5 21.g3± White will put his king on e3 with a good position. (The immediate 21.♔f2?! would allow 21...e3†⇄.)

We have been following the game Voronov – Dmitrenko, Alushta 2008. At this point White could have obtained some advantage with:

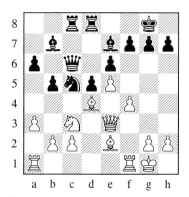

17.b4!N

17.♗d3 was played in the game.

17...♘e4 18.♘xe4 dxe4 19.c3±
The bishop on d4 is excellent.

13.♗xc5 ♘xc5

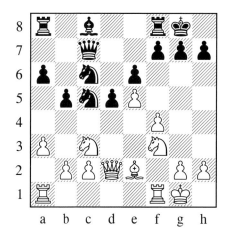

14.♖ad1

14.b4?!
It is too early for this ambitious move.

14...♘e4!

14...♘d7 15.a4 ♘xb4 16.axb5 ♗b7 17.♘d4 gives White a slight advantage.

15.♘xe4 dxe4 16.♘g5 ♖d8 17.♕e3 ♘d4

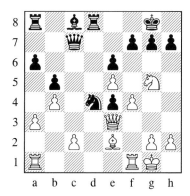

18.♖ad1

18.♕xe4?! is too greedy in view of 18...g6, threatening ...♗b7 with fine compensation. 19.♕xa8?! only makes matters worse for White: 19...♘xe2† 20.♔f2 ♗b7 21.♕a7 ♖d2 22.♖ad1 ♖xc2 23.♕e3 ♘xf4† 24.♖d2 ♘xg2 25.♕d3 ♕xe5 26.♖xc2 ♕xg5 with great play for Black.

18...♘xe2† 19.♕xe2 ♗b7 20.♘xe4 ♗xe4 21.♕xe4 g6=

Black has sufficient compensation and is likely to regain his pawn in the near future.

14...♗b7 15.♕e3

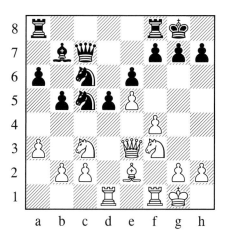

15...♘d7

An interesting alternative was:

15...♘e7!?

Intending to play ...♘e4 and/or ...♘f5.

16.♗d3

16.♘d4 ♘e4 17.♘a2 (17.♘xe4 dxe4 is equal, for instance: 18.♖c1 ♖fd8 19.c4 bxc4 20.♗xc4 ♕d7 21.♖fd1 ♖ac8= Black will establish a piece on d5.) 17...♘c6 (17...♘f5 18.♘xf5 exf5 19.♘b4 ♖fd8 20.c3±) 18.♘xc6 ♕xc6 19.♘b4 ♕c5 20.♕xc5 ♘xc5= Black is okay as the knight is misplaced on b4.

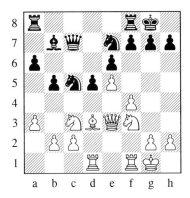

16...♖fd8

16...♘xd3 17.cxd3 ♘f5 18.♕f2 ♖ac8 (18...♕e7 19.♘e2 b4 20.g4 ♘h6 21.h3 bxa3 22.bxa3 ♕xa3 23.f5→; 18...d4 19.♘xd4 ♘xd4 20.♕xd4±) 19.♘e2±

16...♖ac8 17.♘e2 (17.♗xh7† ♔xh7 18.♘g5† ♔g8 19.♕h3 ♖fe8 20.♕h7† ♔f8 21.♕h8† ♔g8 22.♘h7† ♔e7 23.♕xg7 ♖d8 24.♘g5 ♘e7 25.♘xf7† ♔d7 is okay for Black) 17...♖fd8 18.♘ed4±

17.♘e2

White maintains a slight plus, for instance:

17...♘a4

17...♖ac8 18.♘ed4±

18.b3 ♘b2

18...♕c5?! 19.♘ed4±

19.♖c1 ♖ac8 20.♘g5 ♘xd3 21.cxd3 ♕a5 22.♕a7 ♖xc1 23.♖xc1 ♖c8 24.♔f2 ♖xc1 25.♘xc1 ♕c7 26.♘e2±

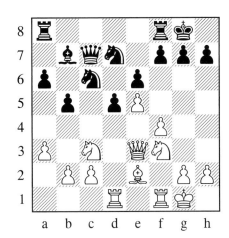

16.♗d3 ♕b6

The queen exchange does not equalize for Black, but if he does not take the opportunity then his king will be in danger.

17.♕xb6 ♘xb6 18.♘e2 ♖ac8

18...♘a4 19.b3 ♘c5 20.♘ed4± is also possible.

19.b3 f6

Of course Black has no intention of waiting to see how White improves his position. 19...♘d7 20.♘ed4 ♘c5 21.g4↑ is unpleasant for him.

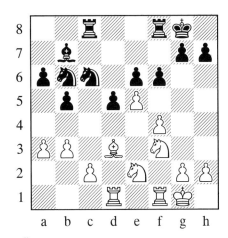

20.♘ed4

After 20.exf6 gxf6 21.♖de1 ♖ce8 22.♘ed4

♘xd4 23.♘xd4 e5 24.fxe5 fxe5 25.♖xf8†
♔xf8 26.♖f1† ♔e7 27.♘f5† ♔d7 Black has
no problems.

**20...♘xd4 21.♘xd4 fxe5 22.fxe5 ♖xf1†
23.♖xf1 ♖e8?!**

Black should have preferred 23...♘d7
24.♘xe6 g6 (24...♘xe5 25.♗f5 g6 26.♗h3)
25.♘d4 ♘xe5 when his position remains
worse, but overall his chances of defending are
higher than in the game.

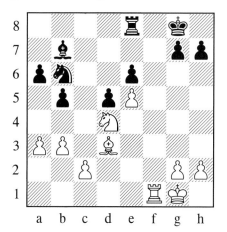

24.♗e2!

A good manoeuvre. White improves the
position of the bishop and ties another enemy
piece to the defence of the e6-pawn.

24...♘d7 25.♗g4 ♘f8

25...♘xe5?! 26.♗xe6† ♔h8 27.♖f5 ♘c6
28.♖xd5 sees White emerge with an extra
pawn.

26.♖f3

Planning to take over the c-file.

26...♖e7 27.g3 ♗c8

Black would like to put his rook on c7, but
of course White will not allow that.

**28.♖c3 ♗b7 29.♖f3 ♗c8 30.♖c3 ♗b7 31.h4
♔f7 32.♔f2 ♔e8 33.♔e2 ♔d7 34.♔d2**

Planning to walk the king to a5.

An interesting alternative is: 34.a4!? b4
(34...bxa4 35.bxa4 leaves the a6-pawn
seriously weak, and White has good winning
chances.) 35.♖f3 ♘g6 36.♖e3 ♘f8 37.c3 bxc3
38.♖xc3 ♖e8 39.b4±

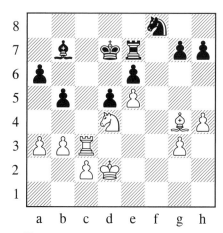

34...♖e8?

34...♖f7 was a better defence, and after
35.♔e2 ♖e7 White has to find another way to
improve his position. (See the note to White's
34th move for the right idea.)

35.♖f3 ♔e7 36.♔c3 ♖a8

36...a5 prevents the king invasion but
weakens the queenside pawns: 37.♖f2 ♖c8†
38.♔b2 ♗c6 (38...b4 39.axb4 axb4 40.♘b5+–)
39.♗h5 g6 40.♗e2+–

37.♖e3!

Very solid. 37.♔b4 is also winning, but
White has no need to hurry with this move
as Black cannot prevent it. In any case the
next few moves might be 37...♘d7 (37...♗c8
38.♔a5+–) 38.♖e3 a5† 39.♔xb5 ♗a6†
40.♔a4 winning.

37...♗c8 38.♔b4 a5†!

The only chance to create some counterplay.

38...♗d7 is too passive. After 39.♔a5+– Black
is almost paralysed and White will win at his
leisure by playing ♖c3, ♗e2 and later ♔b6.

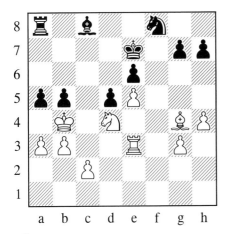

39.♔c3?

Maybe White miscalculated something in time trouble, as he could simply have taken the pawn: 39.♔xb5 a4 (39...♗a6† 40.♔a4 ♘d7 41.♖c3 ♘xe5 42.♗xe6 ♔d6 43.♗h3+−) 40.b4

40...♘d7 (40...♗a6† 41.♔c6 ♘d7 42.♘xe6 d4 43.♖e1+−) 41.♔c6!? (41.♘c6† ♔f7 42.♘a5+−) 41...♖a7 42.♘b5 ♗b7 43.♘d6 ♘b8† 44.♔c5 ♖c7† 45.♔b5 ♗d7† 46.♔a5 ♖xc2 47.b5+− The knight on b8 is out of play and White threatens ♖f3. Black's position is hopeless.

39...♘d7 40.♗e2 b4† 41.axb4 ♖c8† 42.♔d2

42.♔b2 axb4 43.♔d3 ♗e8 44.♖e1 ♖a8 45.g4±

42...axb4 43.♗d3 ♗e8 44.♖e1 ♘d7?

This move allows White to obtain a serious advantage.

The right path was 44...♖a8 45.g4 h6 (45...♖a7 46.g5 ♖a8 47.♖f1 ♖a7 48.h5 ♖a8 49.h6 g6 50.c3±) 46.h5± although Black still faces a difficult defence here. White's plan is to play c3 and push the b-pawn. (But note that 46.g5 hxg5 47.hxg5 ♘g6!?⇄ is not so clear.)

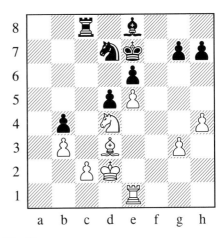

45.g4?

White could have got away with grabbing the h-pawn: 45.♗xh7! g6 46.♗g8 ♘c5 47.♔e3 ♗d7 48.♗h7 ♔f7 (48...♗e8 49.♖a1+−) 49.h5 gxh5 50.♖h1 ♔g7 (50...♖h8 51.♖xh5 ♔g7 52.♗g6+−) 51.♖xh5 ♗e8 52.♖h1 ♗g6 53.♗xg6 ♔xg6 White is just a pawn up and should win this position.

45...h6 46.g5

Another idea was 46.♗b5 ♘c5 47.♖xe8 ♔xe8 48.♖a1 when Black is under pressure.

46...hxg5 47.hxg5 ♖c7

The most precise defence was 47...♖c3! when 48.♗b5 is met by 48...♘c5= and 48.♘b5 by 48...♖c5=. With those two ideas not working, it will be difficult for White to improve his position.

48.♗b5 ♘c5?

The wrong direction. It was essential to play 48...♘f8 to control the g6-square, and after 49.♗xe8 ♔xe8 50.♖a1 ♖b7 Black has good chances to hold the position. For example: 51.♖a6 ♔f7 52.♔e3 ♔g6 53.♘xe6 ♘xe6 54.♖xe6† ♔xg5 55.♔d4 ♖c7 56.♔xd5 ♖xc2 57.♖b6 ♔f5 58.♖xb4 ♖e2= Drawing by one tempo.

49.♗xe8 ♔xe8 50.g6!

This keeps the black king caged while preventing the rook from going to the f-file.

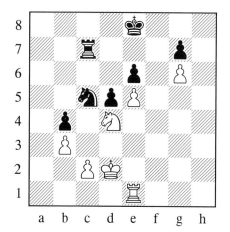

50...♘e4†?!

50...♔e7 would have offered more resistance. Play then continues: 51.♖a1 (51.♖f1 ♘e4† 52.♔d1 ♖d7 defends) 51...♖c8 (51...♘d7 52.♖a6 ♘f8 53.♘c6† ♔e8 54.♘xb4 ♘xg6 55.♖xe6† ♔f7 56.♖a6 ♘xe5 57.♘xd5+–) 52.♖a7† ♘d7 53.♖a6 ♘c5 54.♖b6 ♖h8 55.♘c6† ♔d7 56.♘xb4 ♖h6 57.♖d6† ♔e8 58.♖c6 ♘e4† 59.♔e3 White should be winning.

51.♔e3 ♔e7

51...♔d7 does not change anything after 52.♖a1+–.

52.♖a1 ♘g3

52...♘c5 loses to 53.♖f1 followed by ♘b5.

52...♖c3† 53.♔f4 ♘c5 54.♘c6† ♔d7 55.♘xb4 is also hopeless for Black.

53.♔f4 ♘f5 54.♘xf5† exf5 55.♔xf5

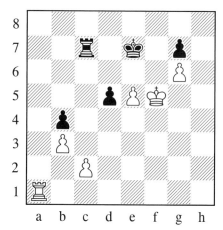

55...d4 56.♖a2 ♔d7 57.♔e4 ♖c6

57...♔e6 58.♖a6† ♔e7 59.♔d5+–

58.♔d5 ♖xg6 59.e6†
1–0

GAME 15
▷ **A. Morozevich (2737)**
▶ **N. Vitiugov (2726)**
Governor's Cup, Saratov
Round 2, 09.10.2011 **[C11]**
Annotated by Yannick Gozzoli

Morozevich chose the modern 8.a3!?, as played in Ivanchuk – Carlsen, Bilbao 2011. This move was very fashionable during the Saratov tournament and will probably be the topic of many games in the future. The reply 8...♕b6 is an interesting alternative to the game and deserves further investigation. Black's major mistake was the premature 10...f5?, after which Morozevich conducted the game energetically and won in impressive style. Instead, Black should probably follow what Morozevich himself played a few rounds later, the interesting 10...a6!?, waiting for White to show his intentions.

1.e4 e6 2.d4 d5 3.♘c3 ♘f6 4.e5 ♘fd7 5.f4 c5 6.♘f3 ♘c6 7.♗e3 ♗e7 8.a3!?

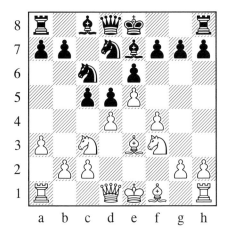

This move had totally disappeared from practice until Ivanchuk used it against Carlsen in Bilbao 2011, since when it has become highly fashionable, appearing no less than three times during the strong Saratov tournament. The main lines are 8.♕d2 and 8.♗e2.

8...b6

This move has two ideas: Black gives a square to his queen's bishop, and also prevents White's idea of taking on c5 followed by using the d4-square for his knights. Black's plan will now involve the ...f6 push, as the d7-knight has nowhere to go. Black has others options:

8...0–0

This was Carlsen's choice against Ivanchuk. 9.♕d2

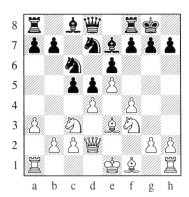

9...b6

9...a6 10.♗e2 b5 11.0–0 is also possible, with a transposition to Dominguez – Le Quang Liem, Lubbock 2011 (see page 113).

10.g3!?

A new idea. White wants to hinder the ...f6 break by putting the bishop on h3.

10.♗d3 is the other move.

10...♔h8 11.h4 f6 12.exf6 ♘xf6

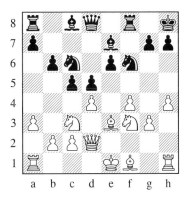

13.0–0–0!?

This gives a double-edged position with castling on opposite sides. In my opinion White has the better chances because of the weakness of the e6-pawn, and also his attack seems to be a little bit faster.

13.♗h3   ♗d7   (13...♘h5!?)   14.♖d1 (14.0–0–0 was probably best, but not as good as on the previous move. 14...a5∞) 14...cxd4! 15.♘xd4 e5! and Black seized the initiative in Ivanchuk – Carlsen, Bilbao 2011.

13...♖b8 14.♔b1 b5!?

This is the speediest way to develop an initiative.

15.♗xb5

15.dxc5 ♕a5!? is also possible.

15...cxd4 16.♘xd4 ♘xd4 17.♗xd4

After 17.♕xd4 ♘g4 the position is not clear, but it looks more pleasant for Black:

a) 18.f5 ♘xe3 19.♕xe3 a6 (19...♕a5!?∞; 19...♖xf5?! 20.♕xa7 ♖b7 21.♕e3± followed by a3-a4 is better for White) 20.fxe6 axb5 21.♘xd5 ♗b7∞

b) 18.♗d2 a6 (18...♕b6 19.♕xb6 ♖xb6 20.♗e1 ♘e3∞) 19.♗e2 ♗xa3 20.♗c1 (20.♘b5 ♗xb2 21.♗xb2 ♘f6 22.♗b4 ♗d7 23.♗xf8 ♕xf8⯑ and Black has enough compensations for the exchange) 20...♘h6∞ The position is double-edged and it is not yet clear who will gain the upper hand.

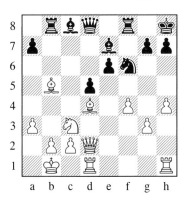

17...a6

After 17...♗xa3?! 18.h5! the d4-bishop becomes very powerful:

a) 18...a6 19.h6 g6 20.bxa3 and:

a1) 20...axb5 21.♗e5! ♖b7 22.♘e4+−

a2) 20...♔g8 21.f5 ♘e4 (21...exf5 22.♖he1+−) 22.♘xe4 dxe4 23.a4+−

a3) 20...♗d7 21.♔c1 axb5 (21...♗xb5 22.♕e3+−) 22.♗e5 ♖b7 23.♘xd5! exd5 24.♕xd5+−

b) 18...h6 19.g4→

c) 18...♗d7 19.h6 g6 20.♕e3 a6 (20...♗xb5 21.♘xb5 ♖xb5 [21...♗xb2 22.♗xb2 ♖xb5 23.♕xa7+−] 22.♕xa3 ♔g8 23.♕xa7±) 21.♘xd5!? ♗xb2 22.♗xb2 exd5 23.♗xd7 ♕xd7 24.♔c1±

18.♗e2 ♗xa3 19.b3↑

This is clearly in White's favour. His attack will develop easily and naturally with h5 and g4-g5, whereas it is not obvious how Black should continue his attack.

8...♕b6 was played two rounds later by Vitiugov against Shirov.

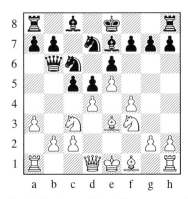

a) 9.♘a4 ♕a5† 10.♗d2 ♕c7 11.dxc5 ♘xc5 12.♘xc5 ♗xc5 13.b4

13.♗d3 ♕b6?! (13...a5= was the right way to go. White can no longer play b2-b4 and Black can try to seize the initiative on the queenside with ...♕b6, ...♗d7, ...a4 and ...♘a5.) 14.b4 ♗e3 15.♖b1?! (After 15.♕e2!± Black has no time to exchange knights with ...♘d4, and will remain with a passive bishop on d7 and the knight lacking a good outpost.) 15...♗d7 16.♕e2 ♗xd2† 17.♕xd2 ♘d4 18.♘xd4 ♕xd4 19.c3 ♕b6 20.♕f2 0–0 21.♕d4 f6?! (21...♖fc8!⯑ gives Black a fine position) 22.exf6 gxf6 23.♔d2± White had secured a pleasant plus in Wen Yang – Volkov, Moscow 2009.

13...♗b6 14.c4 dxc4 15.♖c1 ♕d8

15...a5!? 16.b5 ♘e7 is interesting.

16.♖xc4 h6=

Shirov – Vitiugov, Saratov 2011. The black position is very solid and if White does not quickly find a way to develop an initiative, he will stand worse because of his pawn structure.

b) 9.♗e2 aims to follow the "normal" plan, and has to be considered:

b1) 9...cxd4 10.♘xd4 ♘xd4

10...♗c5 11.♘a4 ♕a5† 12.c3 ♗xd4 (12...♘xd4?! 13.b4 ♕d8 14.cxd4±) 13.♗xd4 (13.b4?! is not accurate. Black can react strongly with 13...♕xa4! 14.♕xa4 ♗xc3† 15.♔f2 d4⯑ and Black wins material.)

13...♘xd4 14.b4 (14.♕xd4 b6!= intending ...♗a6 and/or ...♘c5) 14...♘f3† (14...♕d8 15.cxd4± is better for White) 15.♗xf3 ♕c7 16.♕d4 0–0 17.0–0 b5 18.♘b2 a5⇄

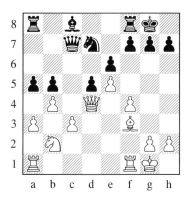

The position is slightly better for White, but Black has good counterplay on the queenside.

11.♗xd4 ♗c5 12.♗xc5 ♘xc5

12...♕xc5 is also possible.

13.b4 ♘d7

13...♘e4 14.♘xe4 dxe4 15.c4±

14.♘b5 0–0 15.♕d4 ♕xd4 16.♘xd4 ♘b6=

Followed by ...♗d7, and Black will have good counterplay against the weakened white queenside.

b2) 9...0–0 10.0–0 ♘xd4 11.♘xd4 cxd4 12.♗xd4 ♗c5

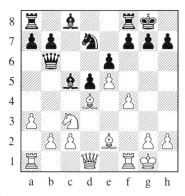

13.♘a4

13.♗xc5 ♕xc5† 14.♔h1 f6 15.exf6 ♘xf6

16.♗d3 ♗d7⇄ and the position is balanced.

13...♗xd4† 14.♔h1 ♕c7 15.♕xd4 a6

After 15...♘b6 16.♘xb6 axb6, only White can play for an advantage.

Taking the pawn is possible, but looks risky:

15...♕xc2!? 16.♗d3 ♕c7∞

15...f6 16.exf6 ♘xf6 17.c4±

15...b6!?

16.♘c3 b6 17.♖ae1 ♗b7 18.♗d3 f6⇄

9.♗d3 0–0 10.0–0

The point of White's move order is that he has kept his queen on d1, and so it can reach the h-file quite easily after moving his knight, thereby creating threats against the black king.

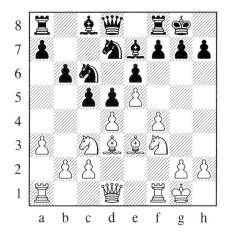

10...f5?

A logical move, but a mistake which gives White a very strong initiative. In the sixth round, Morozevich played this position as Black against Shirov and continued with:

10...a6!?

Black delays pushing the f-pawn. He wants White to declare his intention in order to react suitably.

11.♘e2?!

A tactical mistake. 11.♕e1!? is a possible improvement.

11...c4

The following sequence of moves is forced.

12.♗xh7† ♔xh7 13.♘g5† ♗xg5 14.fxg5

White has obtained an interesting position from a practical point of view, as it's not easy for Black to organize his defence, but objectively it doesn't look convincing.

14...♖h8?!

14...♘e7!?

15.♖xf7 ♔g8 16.g6 ♘f8?

16...♕e8! with the idea of ...♘d8 is better.

17.♘f4⊞

Shirov – Morozevich, Saratov 2011, ended in a draw after a long struggle.

11.exf6 ♘xf6

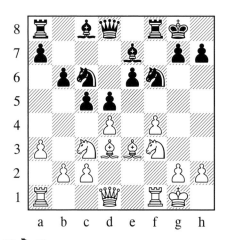

12.♘e5!

White can install his knight on a strong square in the centre and will develop his attack on the kingside.

12...♗b7 13.♕f3

The queen is heading for the superb h3-square, from where it will attack the h7- and e6-pawns.

13...♗d6?!

Another inaccuracy that Morozevich will exploit in great dynamic style.

Better was 13...cxd4 14.♘xc6 ♗xc6 15.♗xd4 ♗c5 16.♘e2± although White has a pleasant advantage.

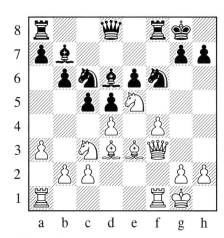

14.♘b5! ♗e7?!

14...cxd4 15.♘xd4 ♗xe5 (15...♘xd4 16.♗xd4±) 16.♘xc6 ♗xc6 17.fxe5 ♘e4 18.♕g4± was a better defence, but it is still hard to play for Black.

14...♖b8 15.dxc5 ♗xe5? (15...♘xe5 16.fxe5 ♗xe5 17.♕h3 ♕e7 18.cxb6 [18.♖ae1!?] 18...axb6 19.♘d4±) 16.fxe5 ♘xe5 17.♕g3 ♘xd3 18.cxd3 ♕d7 19.♘d6 ♗a6 20.♗d4± Oparin – Rychagov, St Petersburg 2011.

15.♕h3 ♕c8

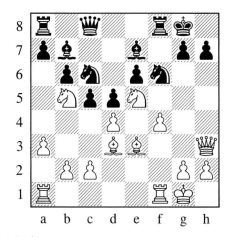

16.c4!

Also possible is: 16.♖ad1!? c4 (16...a6? 17.♘c7! c4 [17...♕xc7? 18.♗xh7†! ♘xh7

19.♕xe6†]   18.♘xa8   cxd3   19.♘xb6+–)
17.♗e2± with total control of the board.

But 16.♘c7?! is wrong: 16...c4! 17.♘xa8 cxd3
18.♘xb6 axb6 19.cxd3 ♗d6 and Black is still
in the game.

16...♘e4?

After this mistake, White obtains a winning
endgame by force.

The lesser evil was 16...dxc4 17.♘xc4 ♖d8
18.♖ac1± although White retains a huge
advantage.

17.dxc5! ♘xe5

17...bxc5 18.♖ad1+–

18.fxe5 ♗xc5 19.♖xf8† ♕xf8 20.♗xe4 dxe4 21.b4

Forcing the exchange of Black's good bishop.

Inaccurate is 21.♕xe6†?! which allows Black
some counterplay against the e-pawn after
21...♔h8 followed by ...♖e8. White's position
remains better, but Black is still alive.

21...♗xe3† 22.♕xe3+–

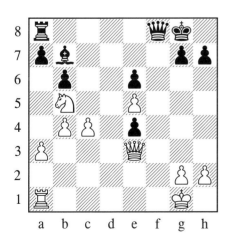

White's position is winning. He has a
potential passed pawn on the c-file, Black has

a lot of weaknesses (especially the doubled
e-pawns), and above all White has a fantastic
outpost for his knight on d6 which will obstruct
the d-file and dominate the bad bishop. The
final part of the game doesn't need any analysis,
as it is just a matter of technique for White to
convert his huge positional advantage.

22...♕f5 23.♕g3 ♕h5 24.♘d6 ♗c6 25.b5

After removing the bishop from the long
diagonal, White can quietly take the e4-pawn.

25...♗e8 26.♘xe4 ♗g6 27.♘d6 ♕e2

After 27...♖f8 with the idea of creating some
counterplay with ...♕e2, White has the simple
28.♕e3! controlling all the entry squares in his
position. Then he can continue with ideas such
as a4-a5.

28.♕f3

Black cannot avoid the exchange of queens
and White is easily winning.

28...♕xf3 29.gxf3

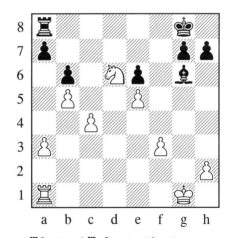

29...♖f8 30.a4 ♖xf3 31.a5 bxa5

31...♖f8 32.axb6 axb6 33.c5! bxc5 34.b6
♗h5 35.b7 ♗f3 36.♖c1+–

32.♖xa5 h5 33.♖xa7 ♖b3 34.c5

1–0

GAME 16

▷ **Ni Hua (2670)**
▶ **A. Shirov (2713)**
Governor's Cup, Saratov
Round 8, 16.10.2011 **[C45]**
Annotated by Kamil Miton

In one of the main lines of the Scotch Game, Shirov eschewed the normal 10...♕b4† in favour of the slightly unusual 10...♗g7!? and obtained a good position without difficulty. The answer to the question of where White may strengthen his game remains uncertain, but in my view the endgame following 13.♗xd2 is the critical direction. Later Shirov managed to seize the initiative in a complex ending, but Ni Hua narrowly held on for a draw.

1.e4 e5 2.♘f3 ♘c6 3.d4 exd4 4.♘xd4 ♘f6 5.♘xc6 bxc6 6.e5 ♕e7 7.♕e2 ♘d5 8.c4 ♗a6 9.♘d2 g6 10.♘f3

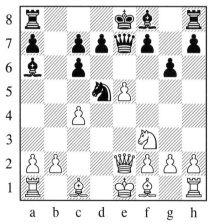

10...♗g7!?

This was the first time an elite grandmaster has tried this move.

The usual continuation has been:
10...♕b4† 11.♔d1

It is not uncommon for White to forfeit the right to castle in this opening, as Black's pieces are not well placed to exploit it. At this point the path divides between a) 11...♖b8 and b) 11...♘b6.

a) 11...♖b8 12.♕c2
    12.e6 ♗g7↑
12...♘e7

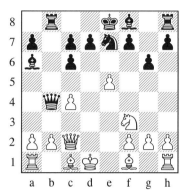

And here White can choose between a1) 13.b3 and a2) 13.♕b3.

a1) 13.b3 ♗g7 14.♗d2 ♕b6
    14...♕a3!?   15.b4   (15.♗d3!?;   15.♕c3
    0–0 16.♕a5 ♕xa5 17.♗xa5 ♖bc8)
    15...c5 (15...♖xb4 16.♗xb4 ♕xb4 17.♖b1
    ♕c5 18.♖b8† ♗c8 19.♘d3 0–0 20.♖e1±;
    15...♗c8!?∞) 16.b5 ♗b7 17.♕b3 ♕xb3†
    18.axb3 ♖a8 19.♘d3 f6 20.exf6 ♗xf6 21.♖a5
    a6 22.bxa6 ♖xa6 23.♖xa6 ♗xa6=
15.c5 ♕b7 16.♗xa6 ♕xa6 17.♖e1
This was Svidler's attempt to improve on a game between Ponomariov and Leko. White is trying to discourage ...d6 and ...f6.
17...0–0 18.♕c4
Here Black should be able to equalize with the help of the following improvement:

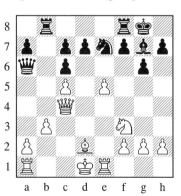

18...♕xc4!N

In the game Black failed to equalize: 18...♕b7?! 19.♖c1 ♘d5 20.♗e2 ♖fe8 21.♔f1 ♕b5 22.g3 a5 23.♕xb5 ♖xb5 24.♗e4 ♖a8 25.♘e1!± A typical manoeuvre. From d3 the knight will support the pawns on c5 and e5 while making way for a kingside advance. White went on to win in Svidler – Hracek, Aix-les-Bains 2011.

19.bxc4 d5!

19...♖b2 20.♖f1 f6 21.♗c3 ♖bb8 22.exf6 ♗xf6 23.♔c2 ♗xc3 24.♔xc3±

19...f6!? 20.e6 dxe6 21.♖xe6 ♔f7 22.♖e3 ♘f5!? 23.♖a3 ♖fd8 24.♖xa7 ♖d7 25.♔c2 ♗f8 26.♖a5 g5⇄ 27.♗xg5 fxg5 28.♘e5† ♔e6 29.♘xd7 ♔xd7∞

20.cxd6

20.exd6 cxd6 21.♖xe7 ♗xa1 22.cxd6 ♗f6 23.♖xa7 ♖a8 24.♖c7 ♖fc8∞ 25.♖xc8† ♖xc8 26.c5 ♖a8∓

20...cxd6 21.♗c3 d5 22.♔c2 dxc4 23.♖e4 ♘d5 24.♖xc4 ♘xc3 25.♖xc3 f6=

a2) 13.♕b3

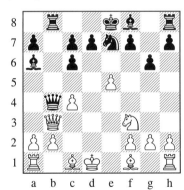

13...c5 14.♕xb4 cxb4 15.♗d3

15.♗e3?! ♘f5 16.♗xa7 ♖a8 17.♗e3 ♘xe3† 18.fxe3 ♗c5=

15...♗g7

15...♘f5 16.♖e1 ♗c5 17.♗xf5 gxf5 18.♗e3 ♗xe3 19.♖xe3 ♗xc4 20.♖c1↑

16.♖e1

16.♗e3 ♘c6 17.♗c5 f6 18.exf6 ♗xf6 19.♔c2 ♔f7=

16...0–0 17.♔c2 ♘c6 18.b3

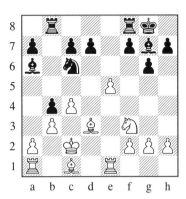

18...d5!

Black must act quickly, otherwise White will complete his development with a great position.

19.cxd5 ♗xd3† 20.♔xd3 ♖fd8 21.♗f4 ♖xd5† 22.♔e4 ♖a5 23.♖ac1 ♘d8

23...♘e7!?N∞ deserves attention. The white king is not safe as a lot of pieces remain on the board.

24.♖xc7 ♘e6 25.♖c2 ♖d8 26.h4 h5 27.g3 ♗f8

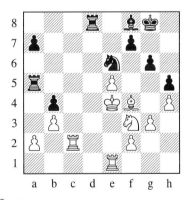

28.♘g5?

28.♗e3±

28...f5†!∓

Howell – Adams, Sheffield 2011.

b) The other option is:

11...♘b6 12.b3 ♗g7 13.♕d2

And here Black can choose between b1) 13...♕xd2† and b2) 13...♕e7.

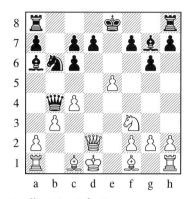

b1) 13...♛xd2† 14.♗xd2

14.♔xd2!? has not been tested but might be an option.

14...0–0

14...c5 15.♔c2 ♗b7 16.♖d1 0–0 17.♗e3 ♖fe8 18.♗xc5 ♗xf3 19.gxf3 ♖xe5 20.♗e3 d6 21.f4±

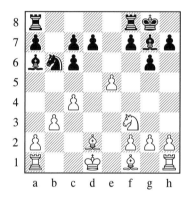

15.c5!

15.♖c1 is met by 15...c5 16.♗d3 ♗b7 17.♖e1 ♖fe8 18.♗f4 d6 19.exd6 cxd6 20.♔c2 d5 (or 20...♗f8) when Black is okay.

15.♔c2 d5 leads to interesting play: 16.c5 (After 16.cxd5 ♗xf1 17.♖hxf1 cxd5 the position of the king on c2 prevents White from organizing any pressure on the c-file, and Black will obtain a good game with ...c5 coming next.) 16...♗xf1 17.♖axf1 ♘d7 18.♘d4 ♘xe5 19.f4 ♘d7 20.♘xc6 ♖fe8 21.♖e1 ♘xc5 22.♘e7† ♔h8 23.♘xd5 reaches an interesting situation.

It looks as though White should have some advantage due to his better structure and more active king, but computers evaluate the position after 23...♖ed8 as equal. Indeed White is not yet fully coordinated and Black's pieces are active, so the second player should be okay.

15...♗xf1 16.♖xf1 ♘d5 17.♖c1 f6

17...♖fb8 18.♖c4 ♗f8 19.♘e1!± is pleasant for White.

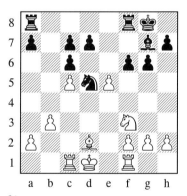

18.exf6

White can also consider 18.e6 dxe6 19.♘d4 e5 20.♘xc6 f5 21.♔e2 with a slight edge.

18...♗xf6 19.♖c4±

The situation is rather unorthodox. Black's pieces are quite active but they do not create specific problems for White. On the other hand White has a kingside pawn majority which he should eventually be able to put to good use. Moreover, the strong rook on c4 is well placed to attack any of Black's queenside pawns should they become vulnerable.

b2) 13...♕e7

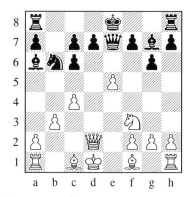

14.♗b2 0–0 15.♔c2 c5

In such positions Black's standard plan is to eliminate the strong e5-pawn with ...d6 or ...f6, as well as dropping his bishop back to b7. However, in the following game Peter Svidler came up with a different idea.

16.h4

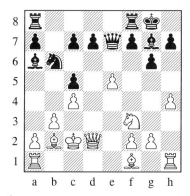

16...d5!?

A dynamic solution, but it does not fully solve Black's problems.

Also after 16...♗b7 17.♖e1 a5 (17...h5 18.♘g5±) 18.a4 d5 19.exd6 ♕xd6 20.♗xg7 ♔xg7 21.♗d3± White is slightly better as Black's queenside pawns are weak.

17.exd6 ♕xd6 18.♗xg7 ♕xd2† 19.♔xd2 ♔xg7 20.♘e4 ♘d7 21.♖d1 ♗b7 22.♘c3 ♘f6 23.f3 ♖fe8 24.♗d3±

Black has no real compensation for his awful queenside structure and White converts his advantage efficiently.

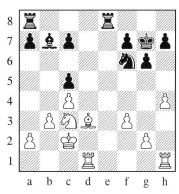

24...a5 25.♖he1 ♗c6 26.♘b5 ♖xe1 27.♖xe1 ♖e8 28.♖xe8 ♘xe8 29.♔b2

With the simple plan of using the king to gobble the a-pawn.

29...♔h6 30.♗e2 ♘g7 31.♔a3 ♘f5 32.♔a4 ♘xh4 33.♗f1 ♘f5 34.♔xa5 ♘e3 35.♘xc7! ♘xf1 36.♔b6 ♗d7 37.♘d5 ♔g7 38.a4 ♗c8 39.♘e7 1–0 Nepomniachtchi – Svidler, Moscow 2010.

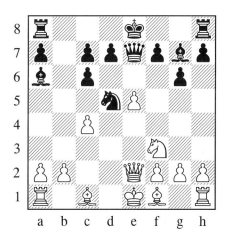

11.♗g5

11.♕e4 ♘b6 is decent enough for Black.

More interesting, but still harmless is:
11.♕c2!? ♘b4

11...♘xe5!? leads to intense complications: 12.cxd5 (12.♗e2 ♘f4) 12...♗xb2† 13.♗e3 ♕b4† 14.♔d1 (14.♗d2 ♕e7† 15.♔d1 ♗xa1 16.♗xa6 0–0 17.dxc6 dxc6 18.♕xc6 ♖ab8∞) 14...♗xf1 15.♗c5 ♕b5 16.♖b1 ♖b8 17.♗d4

♗d3 18.♖e1† ♔f8 19.♕xb2 ♕a4† 20.♔d2 ♖xb2† 21.♖xb2 f6 22.♔xd3∞

11...♘b6 is not particularly promising: 12.c5 (12.♗e2 0–0 13.0–0 f6 14.exf6 ♕xf6 15.♖b1 ♖ae8 16.b3 c5) 12...♗xf1 13.♔xf1 ♘d5 14.♗g5 ♕e6 15.♖e1 0–0 (15...♘b4 16.♕e4 ♘xa2 17.♗f6 0–0 18.♗xg7 ♔xg7 19.h4) 16.h4 ♘b4 (16...h6 17.♘d4 [17.♗d2!±] 17...♘b4 18.♘xe6 ♘xc2 19.♘xf8 ♘xe1 20.♘xd7 hxg5 21.♔xe1 ♗xe5=) 17.♕d2 ♖ab8 18.h5 ♕d5 19.h6 ♗h8 20.♖h4 ♕xd2 21.♗xd2 ♘d3 22.♖e3 ♘xb2 23.♔e2↑

12.♕a4

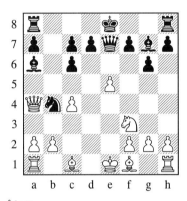

12...♗b7!

Not the only move, but it leads to a good position without excessive complications.

12...♗xe5!? 13.♗e2 (13.♔d1 ♕d6† 14.♗d2 c5 15.a3 [15.♘xe5 ♕xe5 16.♗xb4 cxb4 17.♕xa6 ♕xb2 18.♖c1 0–0∞] 15...♘c6 16.♕xa6 ♗xb2 17.♖b1 ♗c3 18.♗d3 0–0 19.♗e4 ♖ab8⇄) 13...♗xc4 (13...♗g7 14.0–0 0–0 15.♖e1 ♗b7 16.♗f1 ♕d6 17.♖d1 ♕e7 18.♗g5 f6 19.♖e1 ♕f7 20.♗e3 a5 21.a3 ♘a6 22.c5±) 14.♗xc4 ♗xb2† 15.♗e3 ♗xa1 16.0–0↑

13.a3

13.♗e2 0–0 14.0–0 c5 enables Black to find good homes for his knight and light-squared bishop. This usually ensures him of a good game in such positions, and the present case is no exception.

13...♘a6 14.♗e3 0–0 15.c5

15.♗e2 d6 16.0–0 c5 17.exd6 cxd6=
15...♘xc5 16.♕b4 d6 17.♗xc5 dxc5 18.♕xb7 ♗xe5→

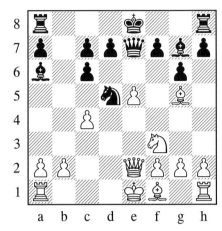

11...♕b4†

Black can also go for a different type of endgame with:

11...f6 12.exf6 ♕xe2† 13.♗xe2 ♘xf6 14.0–0–0

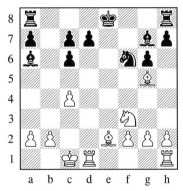

Commenting on this position, GM Postny remarked that "White is slightly better and can play for a win without any risk thanks to his superior pawn structure." In regards to the structure, I agree completely. However, I believe that if Black can achieve the desired set-up with ...d6, ...c5 and ...♗b7, then the position should be equal.

14...0–0–0

Three other moves deserve some attention.

14...d6 15.♘d4 (15.♖he1!? 0–0 16.c5 ♗xe2 17.♖xe2 ♘d5 18.♘d4 ♗xd4 19.♖xd4 ♖ae8 20.♖xe8 ♖xe8 21.♔d1±) 15...0–0 16.f3 (16.♘xc6? ♘e4∓) 16...♖fe8 (16...c5 17.♘b5 ♘e8 18.h4±) 17.♖he1 ♗b7 18.c5!? ♘d5 19.♘b3 ♖e5 20.♗d2 ♖ae8 21.♗c4±

14...c5 15.♖he1 (15.♘e5 ♘e4 16.♗f3 [16.♖xd7?! 0–0∓] 16...♘xg5 17.♗xa8 ♗xe5 18.♖he1 d6 19.f4 ♔d7 20.♖xe5 ♘f7 21.♗d5 dxe5 22.♗xf7† ♔e7 23.♗d5 exf4 24.♖e1† ♔d7=) 15...0–0 (15...d6 16.♗d3† ♔f7 [16...♔d7 17.♗c2±] 17.♗d2 White can exploit the temporary weakness of the e6-square. 17...♖he8 18.♘g5† ♔g8 19.♘e6±) 16.♗xf6 ♖xf6 17.♖xd7 ♖e8 18.♖xc7 ♖fe6 19.♔d1 ♖d6† 20.♔c2 ♖de6 21.♘g1± ♗e5?! 22.♗g4±

The above two moves do not quite equalize, but 14...♖b8!? looks better: 15.♖he1 0–0 16.♗e3 (16.♗d3 d5 17.♘e5 [17.cxd5 ♗xd3 18.♖xd3 ♘xd5 19.♖e2 h6 20.♗e3 ♖fe8∞; 17.b3!?] 17...♘e4 18.♗xe4 ♗xe5 19.♗xd5† cxd5 20.♖xe5 ♖xf2=)

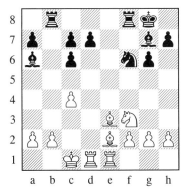

16...♘g4! (16...♘e4 17.♖xd7 ♗xb2† 18.♔c2 ♗f6 (18...♗c3 19.♖b1 ♖xb1 20.♔xb1 ♗a5 21.♗d4→) 19.♗d4 ♗xd4 20.♖xd4±) 17.♗d4 ♗xd4 18.♖xd4 ♘f6 Black has the simple plan of ...d6 and ...c5. For me the position looks equal.

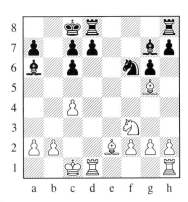

15.♘d2

15.♗e3 should be met by 15...♖de8 intending ...d6 and ...c5, rather than 15...♘g4? 16.♗xa7 ♗b7 17.♗c5 d6 18.h3±.
15...c5 16.♖he1 ♗b7 17.♗f3 ♖de8 18.♗xb7† ♔xb7 19.♔c2 d6 20.f3

White has a mostly symbolic advantage thanks to his kingside majority and control over the light squares, but Black should not have any serious problems.

12.♕d2

So far no one has tested 12.♔d1!?N h6 (12...0–0? 13.♕c2 ♘b6 14.a3 ♕a4 15.b3 ♕a5 16.♗d2+–) 13.♗c1 with a murky position.

12...♕xd2† 13.♗xd2?!

This is harmless.
If White wishes to fight for an advantage then he should try:
13.♗xd2 ♘b6

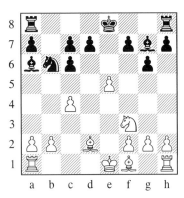

In this position the restrained a) 14.b3 and the more energetic b) 14.c5!? both deserve attention.

a) 14.b3 d6

14...d5?! 15.cxd5 ♗xf1 16.♔xf1 cxd5 17.♖c1 ♖c8 18.♖c5±

14...c5 15.0–0–0 ♗b7 16.♗e3 ♗xf3 17.gxf3 ♗xe5 18.♗xc5 ♗f4† 19.♔c2 d6 20.♗d4 0–0 21.♗d3±

15.0–0–0

15.♗c3 ♘d7 16.0–0–0 c5∞

15.c5!? ♗xf1 16.♔xf1

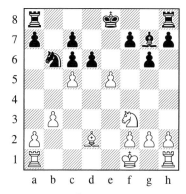

16...dxc5 (16...♘d7 17.cxd6 cxd6 18.♖c1 dxe5 19.♖xc6 0–0 20.♔e2 e4 21.♘g5 h6!∞) 17.♖c1 ♘d7 18.♗e3 0–0–0∞ (18...♘xe5?! 19.♘xe5 ♗xe5 20.♖xc5 ♗d6 21.♖xc6 a5 22.a4 ♖b8 23.♖c3 0–0 24.♔e2 ♖b4 25.♖d1 ♖fb8 26.♔c2 ♗e5 27.♖d3 c5 28.♗d2±)

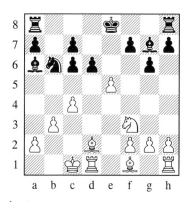

15...dxe5

15...0–0 16.♗f4 d5 17.c5 ♗xf1 18.♖hxf1 ♘d7 19.♘d4 ♗xe5 20.♗xe5 (20.♗h6 ♖fe8 21.♘xc6 ♘xc5 22.♖xd5 ♗d6) 20...♘xe5 21.♖fe1 ♖fe8 22.♖e3↑

16.♘xe5 ♗xe5 17.♖e1 ♘d7 18.f4 f6 19.fxe5 ♘xe5 20.♗c3

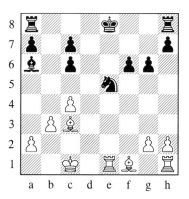

20...0–0–0!

The king should go to the queenside to help defend the pawn weaknesses.

20...0–0 21.♗e2!? (21.♗xe5 fxe5 22.♖xe5 ♖f2⇄) 21...♖fe8 (21...c5 22.♗xe5 fxe5 23.♗f3 ♖ae8 24.♖e2↑) 22.♗xe5 ♖xe5 23.♗f3 ♗b7 (23...♖ae8 24.♖xe5 ♖xe5 25.♖d1 ♔f7 26.♖xc6 ♗c8 27.♖d8±) 24.♖xe5 fxe5 25.♖d1 ♖f8 26.♔c2±

21.♗xe5 fxe5 22.♖xe5 ♖he8 23.♖xe8 ♖xe8 24.♔d2 c5

Black is okay, with ...♗b7 coming next.

b) 14.c5!? ♗xf1 15.♖xf1

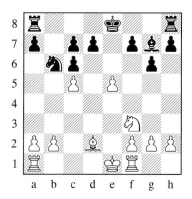

15...♘d5

15...♘a4 16.♖c1 ♘xb2 17.♔e2 ♖b8 (17...d5 18.cxd6 cxd6 19.♖c2 dxe5 20.♖xb2 e4 21.♖b7 exf3† 22.♔xf3 0–0 23.♗e3↑) 18.♖c2 ♘a4 19.♖fc1! 0–0 20.♖c4 ♘b2 21.♖d4±

16.♖c1

16.0–0–0 ♗f8 17.b4 a5⇄

16.f6 17.exf6 ♗xf6 18.b3 ♔f7 19.♖c4

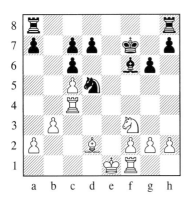

19...a5! 20.♔d1 a4 21.♖xa4

21.b4!? may be a better way to fight for an advantage.

21...♖xa4 22.bxa4 ♖b8⇄

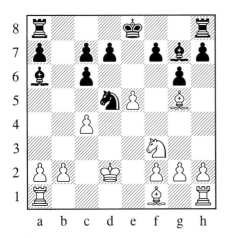

13...h6!

Exposing the downside of White's last move. Now retreating to h4 would leave the bishop on a worse diagonal, so White is more or less forced to go for the following sequence.

14.cxd5 ♗xf1 15.♖axf1 hxg5

Having exchanged off his two problem minor pieces, Black has equalized.

16.♘xg5

16.dxc6 g4 17.♘e1 ♗xe5 18.♘d3 ♗d6 19.cxd7† ♔xd7=

16...♖b8 17.b3 cxd5

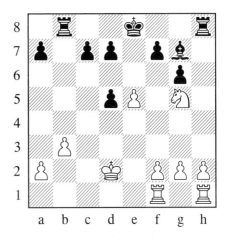

An interesting endgame has arisen with a most unusual pawn structure. Black's plan will involve ...a5-a4 to break up the enemy queenside and open some lines for his rooks. The bishop's future is less certain, but the undermining ...d6 or ...f6 may play a role.

18.f4 a5 19.h4 a4 20.♖f3 ♖b4 21.g3 0–0

21...♔e7 22.f5 ♗xe5 (22...♖h6 23.f6† ♔e8 24.♖f4 leaves the rook on h8 misplaced) 23.fxg6 fxg6 24.♖e1 d6 25.♖f7† ♔d8 26.♘e6† ♔c8 27.♘xc7 axb3 28.axb3 ♗xg3 29.♖c1 ♖bxh4 30.♘xd5† ♔b8 31.♖cc7 ♖d4† 32.♔c3 ♖xd5 33.♖b7†=

22.♖d3 c6 23.♘f3

23.♖b1 ♖a8↑

23...axb3 24.axb3 ♖a8 25.h5 ♖a2† 26.♔c3 ♖e4

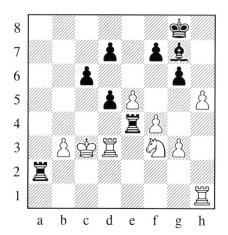

27.♖d2

27.♘g5 ♖ee2 (27...♖xe5!? 28.fxe5 ♗xe5†
29.♔b4 ♗d6†=; 27...d4† 28.♖xd4 ♖xd4
29.♔xd4 f6 30.h6 fxg5 31.hxg7 gxf4 32.gxf4
♔xg7=) 28.h6 ♗h8 29.♔b4 ♖ec2! Threatening
...♖a8! followed by ...c5† with a mating net,
but White can defend. 30.♖c3! ♖xc3 31.♔xc3
f6 32.h7† ♔f8 33.exf6 ♗xf6† 34.♔d3 ♗h8=

27...♖a3

27...♖xd2 28.♔xd2 gxh5 29.♖xh5 f6
30.exf6 ♗xf6=

27...♖e3† 28.♔d4 ♖xd2† 29.♔xe3 ♖b2
30.h6 (30.♘d2 ♔f8) 30...♖xb3† 31.♔e2 ♗h8
32.♘g5 ♖b8=

28.♔b2 ♖a8 29.h6 ♗h8

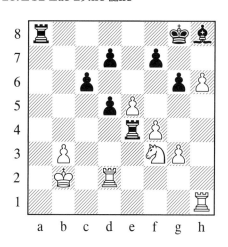

30.♖e1?

Exchanging this rook will leave the h-pawn
weak.

Correct was: 30.h7† ♔f8 31.♔c2 d6 (31...♖e3
32.♖d3 ♖a2† 33.♔c3 ♖xd3†?! 34.♔xd3 ♖g2
35.♖a1→) 32.exd6 ♖e3 33.♘e5 ♖a2† 34.♔b1
♖xd2 35.d7 ♔e7 36.♘xf7 ♔xd7 37.♘xh8
♖xb3† 38.♔c1 ♖db2 39.♖h4 ♖b1†=

**30...♖xe1 31.♘xe1 f6 32.exf6 ♗xf6† 33.♔c2
♔h7 34.g4 g5 35.♘f3**

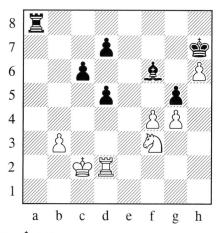

35...♔xh6

Worse is 35...gxf4?! 36.g5 ♗h8 37.♖e2
♖a2† 38.♔d3 ♖xe2 39.♔xe2 ♔g6 40.♔d3 c5
41.♔e2 d6 42.♔d3 ♗e5 43.♔e2= when Black
is unable to improve his position, as ...c4 can
always be met by b4.

36.fxg5† ♗xg5 37.♖h2† ♔g7 38.♖h5 ♗f4

38...♗f6 was also possible.

39.♖f5 ♖f8?!

In my opinion it was too early to exchange
the rooks.

39...♗d6!?

This would have kept better winning chances.
From d6 the bishop prevents b4-b5, while
the rook can head for the g2-square.

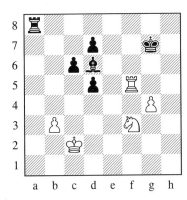

40.♔d3

40.♘e5 ♗xe5 41.♖xe5 ♔f6 42.♖e1 (42.♖f5†
♔e6 43.♖h5 ♖a2† 44.♔d3 ♖g2∓) 42...♖a2†
43.♔c3 ♖g2 44.♔b4 ♖xg4† 45.♔c5 ♖e4
46.♖h1 ♔e7–+

40.♖g5† ♔f6 41.♖f5† ♔e7 42.g5 (42.♖h5
♖a2† 43.♔d3 ♖g2 44.♖h7† ♔d8 45.♖g7
♗f4↑) 42...♖f8 (42...♖a2† 43.♔d3 ♖g2∓)
43.♖xf8 ♔xf8 44.♔c3 c5 45.♔d3 ♔f7
46.♘h4 ♗f4 47.g6† ♔f6 48.♘f5 ♗g5 49.g7
♔f7∓ 50.♔c2?! ♗f6 51.♘e3 d4–+

40...♖b8 41.♔c3

41.♘d4 ♔g6∓

41...♖e8

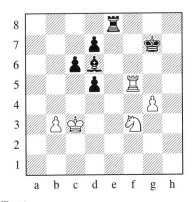

42.♖g5†

42.♔d3 ♖e4 43.♘g5 ♖b4 44.♖f7† ♔g6
45.♖xd7 ♔xg5 46.♖xd6 ♖xb3† 47.♔d2
(47.♔d4 is met by 47...♖b4† and ...♖c4
next) 47...♖b6 48.♔c3 ♔xg4 49.♖h6 ♔f5–+
Black has an easy winning plan of ...♔e5,
...♖a6 and ...d4.

42...♔f6 43.♖f5† ♔e7

It is hard to give a definite evaluation, but
Black certainly keeps some winning chances.

40.♖xf8 ♔xf8

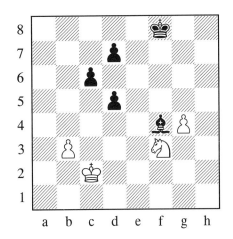

41.b4!

With this move White intends either to
simplify or to create another passed pawn.

41...♗c7

White seems to be drawing everywhere, as
shown by the following analysis.

41...♔f7 42.b5

The following line is even simpler: 42.♔b3
♔f6 43.b5 ♗e3 44.g5† ♔f5 45.bxc6 dxc6
46.g6=

42...♗c7 43.♘d4!

43.bxc6 dxc6∓

43...c5 44.♘f3 d4

44...♔f6 45.♔d3 ♔e6 46.♔c3 d4†
(46...♗d8 47.g5 d6 48.♔d3 ♔f5 49.♘d4†
cxd4 50.♔xd4 ♔e6–+) 47.♔c4 ♗b6
48.♘g5† ♔e5 49.♘f3† ♔e4 50.♘d2† ♔f4
51.♔d5⇄

45.♔d3 d5 46.g5 ♗b6

46...♔e6 47.g6 ♔f6 48.♘xd4 ♔xg6 49.♘e6
♗d6 50.b6 ♔f6 51.♘c7 ♔e5 52.♘a6 c4†
53.♔d2 d4 54.b7 ♔e4 55.b8=♕ ♗xb8
56.♘xb8=

47.♘e5† ♔g7 48.♘c6 c4† 49.♔d2

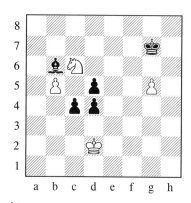

49...d3

49...&c5 50.♘d8=

50.♘e7 &a5† 51.♔c1 d4 52.♘f5† ♔g6 53.♘xd4 ♔xg5 54.♘c6 &c7 55.b6 &f4† 56.♔b2 ♔g4 57.b7 ♔f3 58.♔c3 d2 59.b8=♕ d1=♕ 60.♘d4†=

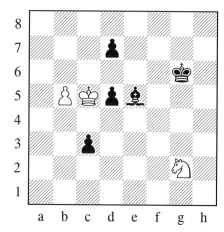

52.♘e1 d4 53.♔c4 ♔f5 54.♔d3 ♔e6 55.♔c2 ♔d5 56.♘d3 &g3 57.♔b3 &d6 58.♔c2 ♔c4 59.b6 ♔b5 60.b7 ♔b6 61.♔b3 ♔xb7 62.♔c2 ♔c6

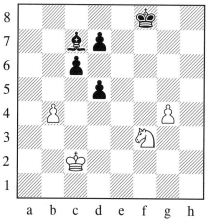

42.♔b3 ♔e7 43.b5 c5 44.g5 ♔e6 45.g6 ♔f6 46.♘h4 c4†

46...&d8 47.♘f5 ♔xg6 48.♘e3 d4 49.♘d5 ♔f5 50.b6=

47.♔b4 &d6† 48.♔c3 &g3 49.♘g2 &e5† 50.♔b4 ♔xg6 51.♔c5 c3

Forced, but now White can arrange a permanent blockade on the light squares.

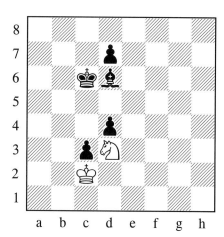

Black is unable to make use of his three(!) extra pawns. The only way would be to arrange a zugzwang, but from d3 the knight has eight squares available, and Black is unable to control all of them.

63.♔b3 ♔d5 64.♔c2 ♔e4 65.♘f2† ♔e3 66.♘d3

½–½

GAME 17

▷ T. Radjabov (2752)

▶ R. Ponomariov (2758)

European Club Cup, Rogaska Slatina

30.09.2011 **[C65]**

Annotated by Borki Predojevic

In the following game we will see one of White's most popular side lines against the Berlin Defence. 4.d3 has recently been played by many top-level grandmasters and it seems that White has chances to fight for the advantage in this line. Ponomariov, who has had a few games in this line, chose his favourite set-up with 4...♗c5 and after that 7...h6 and 8...♗b6. Radjabov was well prepared and by playing the precise moves 10.d4! and 11.♗d3 he secured a promising position with White. After the premature reaction 13...c5?! Ponomariov was slightly worse. Radjabov then played a very good technical game. It should be mentioned that Ponomariov played a few imprecise moves (probably he was exhausted after his long fights in the World Cup) which helped Radjabov to convert his advantage into a fairly easy win.

1.e4 e5 2.♘f3 ♘c6 3.♗b5 ♘f6 4.d3 ♗c5 5.0–0

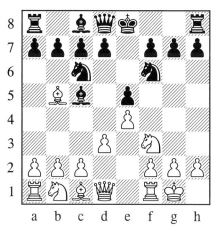

An interesting move order. White has usually preferred 5.c3 which stops Black's idea of ...♘d4. However, Black gains other options against 5.c3. For example, he can play 5...0–0 6.0–0 (6.♗xc6 bxc6 7.♘xe5 d5 is another very sharp line) 6...♖e8!? omitting the move ...d7-d6 for the moment, and perhaps later he will achieve ...d7-d5 in one move.

5...d6

A logical decision from Ponomariov. Recently in the World Cup he did not have any problems in holding this set-up with the black pieces.

Another popular line is 5...♘d4 6.♘xd4 ♗xd4 with a complicated game. It is worth mentioning that Ponomariov has played against this line with the white pieces.

Note that 5...0–0? is bad, as after 6.♗xc6 bxc6 7.♘xe5± White simply wins a pawn.

6.c3

A few rounds earlier I had the same position against Movsesian, and here he decided to play a rare move:

6.d4!?

The game continued:

6...exd4 7.♘xd4 ♗d7 8.♗xc6 bxc6 9.♘c3

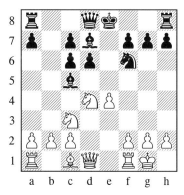

I played "safe" with:

9...h6

During the game I had the feeling that

9...0–0 10.♗g5 h6 11.♗h4 is better for White, since I cannot bring back my bishop to e7 to defend the kingside; maybe this was not a good evaluation. After 11...♖e8 12.♖e1 ♖b8 13.♘b3 ♗b6 14.h3 ♖e6!⇄ Black will play ...♕e7 or ...♕e8 with a good game.

Movsesian answered with the direct:

10.♗f4 0–0 11.e5 dxe5 12.♗xe5 ♖e8 13.♘f3

But after:

13...♗f5 14.♕xd8 ♖axd8 15.♗xc7 ♖d7 16.♗g3 ♗xc2 17.♖fc1 ♗e4!⇄

I did not have any real problems in holding equality in Movsesian – Predojevic, Rogaska Slatina 2011.

6...0–0 7.♘bd2 h6

This is always a useful move for Black; it also delays making a decision about which set-up Black will choose.

The favourite line of GM Arman Pashikian is: 7...a6

Ponomariov has also played this line.

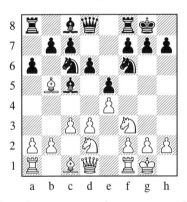

Now there are two lines to consider: A) 8.♗xc6 and B) 8.♗a4.

A) 8.♗xc6 bxc6 9.d4 exd4 10.cxd4 ♗b6

This does not look dangerous for Black. Ponomariov has had this position with the black pieces twice and these games are good examples of how to play this set-up as Black. 11.♕c2 ♖e8 12.♖e1 ♗d7 13.b3 c5! 14.♗b2

On 14.d5 Black has 14...c6 15.dxc6 ♗xc6 16.♗b2 ♗a5! 17.♖ad1 h6 18.♘e3 ♖e6⇄. Ivanchuk continued: 19.♘c4 ♗c7 20.e5 ♘d5 21.♖ee1 ♘f4 And here he blundered: 22.♕f5? (Best was 22.exd6 ♗xf3 23.dxc7:

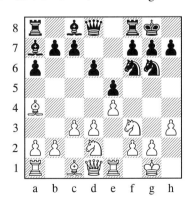

23...♘h3†! 24.♔f1 ♗xg2† 25.♔xg2 ♕g5†= This leads to a draw by perpetual check.) After the simple 22...♗xf3 23.gxf3 ♕h4 24.♖e4 dxe5 25.♖d7 ♖g6† 26.♔f1 ♖g2 White resigned in Ivanchuk – Ponomariov, Russia 2011.

14...cxd4 15.♗xd4 ♗xd4 16.♘xd4 a5= 17.♖ad1 ♕b8 18.♘4f3

½–½ Areshchenko – Ponomariov, Ukraine (ch) 2011.

B) White's best answer is:
8.♗a4 ♗a7 9.h3 ♘e7 10.♖e1 ♘g6

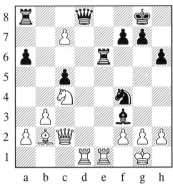

11.♘f1

A typical manoeuvre.

White has also tried a more direct approach with 11.d4, but this premature reaction in the centre gives Black the opportunity to play actively: 11...b5 12.♗c2 (12.♗b3 c5⇄) 12...c5 13.♘f1 cxd4 14.cxd4 exd4 15.♘xd4 ♗b7⇄ Black had no problems in Efimenko – Pashikian, Rogaska Slatina 2011.

11...c6

Now the idea with 11...b5 is not so effective as before, as White can keep a stable centre since he has not pushed d3-d4. For example, 12.♗b3 ♗b7 13.♘g3 h6 14.♘h2!∞/± with the typical plan of ♘g4 and ♕f3. The position remains complicated and unclear, but I prefer White.

12.♘g3 d5

12...♖e8 13.d4 h6 14.♗c2 leads to a similar type of position as in the main game.

13.exd5 ♘xd5 14.♗b3 ♖e8

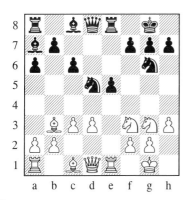

15.♗g5

15.d4! exd4 16.♖xe8† ♕xe8 17.♗xd5 cxd5 18.♘xd4±/= was another idea for White. In my opinion this was the right way to fight for the advantage.

15...f6 16.♗e3 ♗xe3 17.fxe3 ♗e6 18.♕d2 ♕c7 19.♖ad1 ♖ad8=

Radjabov – Kramnik, Kazan (m/9) 2011.

8.h3 ♗b6

The main idea of the set-up with ...♗b6 is to avoid losing time with ...a6 and ...♗a7; Black prepares ...♘e7 and ...c6. As we shall see,

White has to play precise moves here to fight for the advantage.

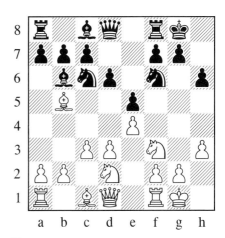

9.♖e1

Another plan is:

9.♘c4

I do not find this idea dangerous for Black and again it is enough to follow Ponomariov's games to gain equality.

9...♘e7 10.♗a4 ♘g6 11.♗c2 ♗e6 12.a4

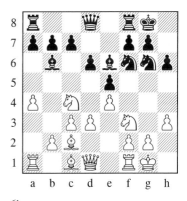

12...c6!

In a few games Black tried 12...♗xc4 13.dxc4 a5, but this is in White's favour since after 14.g3± and next ♔g2, Black lacks real counterplay while White slowly improves his position.

13.♘xb6

The only logical move, as otherwise Black would play ...♗c7.

13...axb6

Black's main idea is to push ...d5 or ...b5, and it seems that White cannot avoid this.

14.♗e3

14.♖e1 b5 15.♗e3 bxa4 16.♗xa4 ♕c7 17.♗c2 c5= and next ...d5 looks nice for Black.

14.♗d2 d5 15.exd5 ♗xd5=

14...d5! 15.d4

15.exd5 ♗xd5 16.♖e1 ♖e8⇄

15...exd4 16.♘xd4 ♗d7 17.exd5 ♘xd5 18.♗d2 ♕f6 19.♕f3 ♘df4 20.♗xf4

Black had no problems and a draw was agreed in Svidler – Ponomariov, World Cup (m/1) 2011.

9...♘e7

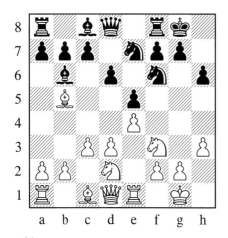

10.d4!

The best reaction. With his last two moves Black prepared ...c6, but the main drawback of this plan is that Black lost control over the d4-square. This gives White the opportunity to push d3-d4, which immediately frees a square for White's light-squared bishop on the c2-h7 diagonal. Otherwise White would lose more time with the manoeuvre ♗a4-c2.

After 10.♘f1 c6 11.♗a4 ♘g6 12.♘g3 ♖e8 Black will quickly play ...d5. Here we can see a better version of the position reached

in the game Radjabov – Kramnik, Kazan (m/9) 2011, which was given in the line after 7...a6. 13.♘h2 d5! 14.♕f3 ♘h4 15.♔e2 ♗e6 16.♗c2 ♕d7 is good for Black, E. Berg – P. H. Nielsen, Oslo 2009.

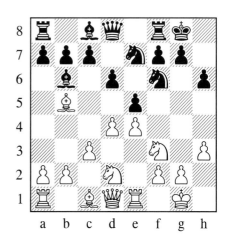

10...c6

Black could try to save the move ...c6 for later and choose instead:

10...♘g6

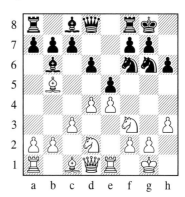

We shall consider two replies: A) 11.♘f1 and B) 11.♗d3.

A) 11.♘f1

The normal move allows Black's idea with:

11...♗d7!?

11...c6 12.♗d3 leads to the same position as in the game.

12.♗d3

38.♖xe5 b5 39.♘f5 ♗xf5 40.♖xf5+−

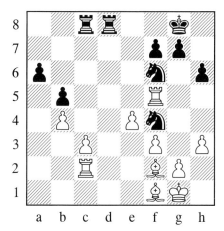

40...♘d3 41.♗b6

41.♗xd3 ♖xd3 42.♖c5±/+− was another alternative.

**41...♖d6 42.♗a5 ♘d7 43.♖d5! ♖xd5
44.exd5 ♘3e5 45.d6**

White plans ♗c7.

45...♖c6

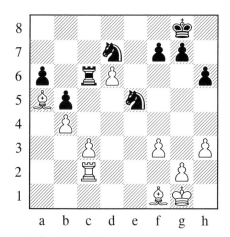

46.f4! ♘g6 47.c4!

Radjabov temporarily sacrifices the f4-pawn; after this break Black has no chance, as White's activity on the queenside is decisive.

47...bxc4

After 47...♘xf4 White wins with 48.g3 ♘e6 49.c5+−.

**48.♗c7 ♘xf4 49.♖xc4 ♖xc4 50.♗xc4 ♔f8
51.♗xa6 ♔e8 52.b5 ♘e6 53.b6 ♘xb6
54.♗xb6+−**

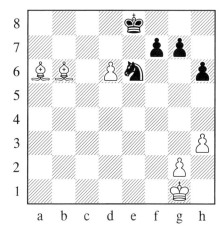

White has had a winning position for a long time and now he is a clear piece up. The rest of game doesn't deserve any comments!

**54...♔d7 55.♗c4 ♔xd6 56.♗xe6 ♔xe6
57.♔f2 ♔f5 58.♔f3 f6 59.♗d4 ♔g5
60.♗e3† ♔f5 61.♗d2 h5 62.g3 ♔e5
63.♗c3† ♔f5 64.♗b2 ♔g5 65.♔e4 ♔g6
66.♔f4 ♔f7 67.♔f5 g6† 68.♔e4 ♔e6
69.♗c3 ♔f7 70.♔d5 ♔e7 71.♗d4 ♔f7
72.♔d6 g5 73.g4**
1–0

GAME 18
▷ **D. Andreikin (2705)**
▶ **A. Morozevich (2737)**
Governor's Cup, Saratov
Round 8, 16.10.2011 [C69]
Annotated by Ivan Sokolov

In this game Morozevich opted for a rarely played line of the Spanish Exchange variation with 7...cxd4 8.exd4 ♕d7. In a sharp game Black seemed to obtain enough compensation for the sacrificed pawn. Also critical for the evaluation of this line is the old Fischer move 9.h3, and it would be interesting to know what Moro had in mind there.

1.e4 e5 2.♘f3 ♘c6 3.♗b5 a6 4.♗xc6 dxc6 5.0–0 f6 6.d4 ♗g4 7.c3 exd4 8.cxd4 ♕d7

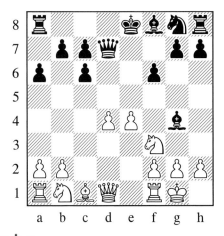

9.♗e3

The other logical choice for White here is the old Fischer move 9.h3. Black has many different options at his disposal, though the road to equality is not easy to find:

a) 9...♗h5 10.♘e5 ♗xd1
  10...♕xh3 11.gxh3 ♗xd1 12.♖xd1 fxe5 13.dxe5 ♗c5 14.♔g2 ♘e7 15.f4 ♘g6 (15...0–0 16.f5 [16.e6 and 16.♘c3 ♘g6 17.♔g3 are also possible] 16...♘xf5 17.exf5 ♖xf5 18.♖f1 ♖xe5 19.♘c3 with a plus for

White) 16.e6 0–0 17.f5 ♘e5 18.♘c3± g6 19.♗h6 ♖f6 20.♗g5 ♖ff8 21.f6+– Mozes – Krantz, Harrachov 1967.
11.♘xd7 ♔xd7 12.♖xd1 ♖e8

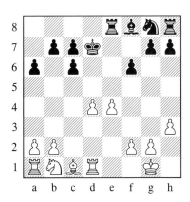

13.f3

White may be able to get some advantage with 13.♘c3, since ideas with ...f5 appear to work less well here: 13...♗b4 14.f3 f5 (14...♘e7 15.♘a4 ♔c8 16.a3 ♗d6 17.b4±) 15.exf5 ♘e7 16.g4 ♗xc3 17.bxc3 g6 (17...♘d5 18.c4 ♘e3 19.♗xe3 ♖xe3 20.♔f2±) 18.♗d2 (After 18.f6 Black has a promising exchange sacrifice: 18...♘d5 19.♗h6 ♘xc3 20.f7 ♖b8! An important nuance. [The "logical" 20...♖ef8? fails to 21.♖d3 ♘d5 22.♗g7!.] 21.♖d3 ♘d5 22.♖e1 ♖hf8 23.♗xf8 ♖xf8∞) 18...gxf5 19.♔f2±

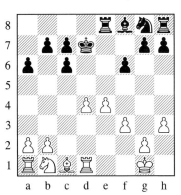

13...♘e7

Black's play can be improved here with 13...f5!=. Should White try to be "clever",

he can easily get into trouble, for example:
14.exf5?! ♘e7 15.g4 g6 16.f6 (16.fxg6 hxg6
17.♔g2 ♘d5∓) 16...♘d5 17.g5 h6 18.h4
hxg5 19.♗xg5 ♗b4 20.♘d2 ♗xd2 21.♖xd2
♖hf8∓

14.♘c3 ♔c8 15.♗e3 f5 16.♖ac1 fxe4 17.fxe4
g6 18.♗f4 ♗g7 19.d5 ♖d8 20.♘a4 ♖hf8
21.g3±

Fischer – Jimenez Zerquera, Havana (ol)
1966.

b) 9...♗xf3 10.♕xf3

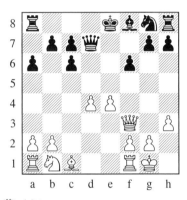

10...♕xd4?!

This early pawn collecting is not going to
bring Black anything good.

Perhaps Moro investigated in the direction
of: 10...0–0–0 11.♘c3 ♘e7 12.♗f4 ♘g6
13.♗g3 ♗d6 14.♖fd1 ♗xg3 15.fxg3 This
move may have been inspired by Fischer's
decision in a similar position to recapture on
g3 with his f-pawn – see his game against
Gligoric below. (However, 15.♕xg3 looks
more logical for White here.) 15...♔b8
16.♖ac1 ♖he8 17.♕h5 ♘f8 18.♕a5 ♕c8
19.b4 ♖d6 with a sharp game in Tatai –
Donner, Palma de Mallorca 1967.

11.♖d1 ♕c4 12.♗f4 ♗d6 13.♗xd6 cxd6
14.♖xd6

White has regained the pawn and still has a
lead in development.

14...♘h6 15.♘a3 ♕b4 16.♖ad1 0–0 17.♖1d2
♘f7 18.♖6d4 ♕c5 19.♘c4 ♖ad8 20.♕d1

♖xd4 21.♖xd4 ♕e7 22.♘a5 ♖d8 23.b4

The black queenside pawn majority cannot
move and is actually a target here, while White
was able to advance his kingside pawn majority
and went on to win in Timman – Beliavsky,
Linares 1988.

c) 9...♗e6 10.♘c3 0–0–0

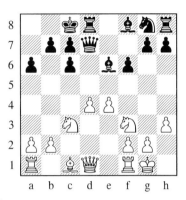

11.♗f4

White may also consider 11.♗e3. The white
bishop is perhaps not as actively placed
as on the h2-b8 diagonal, however the
...g5 pawn push now does not come with
tempo: 11...g5 12.♖c1 h5? 13.d5! cxd5
14.exd5 (14.♕d4! with ♕a7 to follow looks
extremely strong) 14...♗xd5 15.♘xd5 ♕xd5
16.♕c2 ♕f7 17.♘d4 ♗d6 18.b4 ♘e7 19.b5
axb5 20.♘xb5 ♘d5 21.♕a4+– Rozentalis –
Sosnicki, Lubniewice 1998.

11...g5!

Immediate kingside play is probably Black's
best here.

11...♘e7 was played in an old classic, but
it looks too slow: 12.♖c1 ♘g6 13.♗g3 ♗d6
14.♘a4! ♗xg3 15.fxg3 ♔b8 16.♘c5 ♕d6
17.♕a4 ♔a7?? A terrible blunder losing on
the spot, though Black's situation is in any
case far from ideal. (After 17...♗c8 18.♖c3
White has a strong attack.) 18.♘xa6 ♗xh3
19.e5+– Fischer – Gligoric, Havana (ol)
1966.

12.♗g3

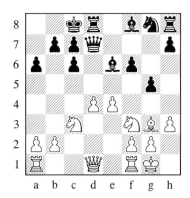

12...g4

Perhaps Black should focus his research efforts along the lines of: 12...h5!? 13.d5 h4 14.♘h2 (14.dxe6?! ♕e8 15.♕b3 hxg3 16.fxg3 g4→) 14...cxd5 15.♖c1 ♗d6∞

13.d5! cxd5

13...gxf3 14.dxe6 ♕xe6 15.♕xf3 gives White the advantage.

14.exd5 ♗xd5 15.♘xd5 ♕xd5 16.hxg4 ♕xd1 17.♖fxd1 ♖xd1† 18.♖xd1 ♘h6 19.g5 ♘f5 20.gxf6 ♘xg3 21.fxg3 ♗c5† 22.♔h2 ♖f8 23.♖d5 ♗d6 24.♖f5 ♔d7 25.♔h3?

After 25.♘g5! h6 26.♘e4± White remains a sound pawn up and should likely win the ending.

25...♔e6

½–½ Petrushin – Yudasin, Soviet Union 1981.

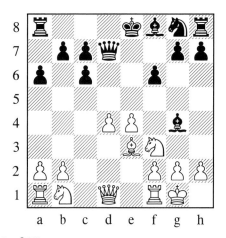

9...f5N

This is a positionally sound concept for Black in this pawn structure. However, the black king is still in the centre and White can try to take advantage of that. Previously Black has played:

9...0–0–0 10.♘bd2 ♘e7

Black should also consider 10...f5!? here.

11.b4 ♘g6 12.♕b3 ♕e7 13.♕c2 ♖e8!

An interesting concept, the threat of ...♗xf3 is now unpleasant and White has to act on the queenside.

14.a4?

White pushes the wrong pawn. He had to play 14.b5! cxb5 (14...axb5 15.a4 b4 16.a5→) 15.♖fc1 ♕d7 16.a4 b4 17.♘e1! with ♘d3 to follow, with strong compensation for the sacrificed pawn.

14...♗xf3 15.gxf3 ♕e6 16.♔h1 ♗xb4 17.♖g1 ♘h4∓

Magem Badals – Lin Weiguo, Beijing 1998.

10.♕b3 ♗xf3 11.♕xb7 ♖d8 12.gxf3 fxe4

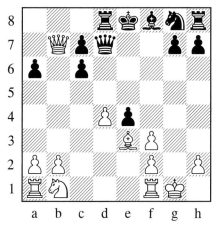

13.♖c1!

Putting immediate pressure on the weakness on c6 is probably White's best here.

13.♖e1 should not worry Black: 13...♗d6! (13...exf3 leads to an advantage for White after 14.♗f4† ♗e7 15.♘d2 ♘f6 [or 15...♘h6 16.♕xc7 ♕xc7 17.♗xc7 ♖d7 18.♗e5 0–0

19.♘b3±] 16.♗g3± 0–0 17.♘xf3 ♖b8
18.♘e5!) 14.fxe4 (14.♘c3? exf3 15.♗f4†
♘e7∓) 14...♕g4† 15.♔f1 ♘e7 16.e5 ♗xe5
17.dxe5 ♕c4† 18.♔g2 ♕g4†= with perpetual
check.

13...exf3

White is better in the event of 13...♘e7
14.♘d2! exf3 15.♔h1, as Black has problems
completing his development.

14.♕xc6 ♗d6

It is essential for Black to first develop his
bishop to d6 before placing his knight on e7.

15.♘d2

White is now going to be a pawn up.

15...♕xc6 16.♖xc6 ♘e7 17.♖xa6 0–0

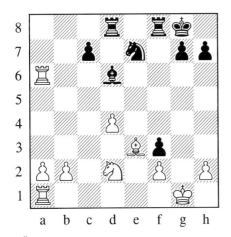

18.♘e4

More testing was:
18.♘c4! ♖f5!
This seems to generate enough kingside
counterplay for a draw.
Less convincing for Black is 18...♘d5, since
after 19.♗g5 ♖d7 20.♘xd6 cxd6 21.♖a5!
♘f4 22.♗xf4 ♖xf4 23.♖c1! Black's situation
is not easy: 23...♖e7 (or 23...♖xd4 24.♖c8†
♔f7 25.♖f5† ♔e6 26.♖xf3±) 24.h3±
19.♘xd6 cxd6 20.b4

The white rooks are passive and Black
appears to be just in time.
20...♖f6! 21.b5 ♖g6† 22.♔h1 ♖g2 23.a4
Or 23.b6 ♘xe3 24.fxe3 ♖b2=.
23...♖e8 24.♖g1 ♘xe3 25.fxe3 ♖b2
25...♖a2 is also possible.
26.♖a7 ♖xe3 27.♖axg7† ♔f8
With a likely draw.

18...♗f4! 19.♖e6 ♘d5

Black has strong compensation and White
must be careful.

20.♘c3 ♖f5

Black had a winning attempt in: 20...♗xe3!
21.fxe3 (21.♘xd5?! ♗xd4) 21...f2† 22.♔f1
♖d6 23.♖xd6 (23.♖e4?? runs into mate after
23...♘xc3 24.bxc3 ♖g6 25.♔e2 f1=♕†!
26.♖xf1 ♖g2† 27.♔e1 ♖b8) 23...♘xe3†
24.♔e2 cxd6 25.♔xe3 f1=♕ 26.♖xf1 ♖xf1 In
this unusual position Black is favourite, but is
it enough to win? It is not easy to say.

21.♘xd5 ♖dxd5

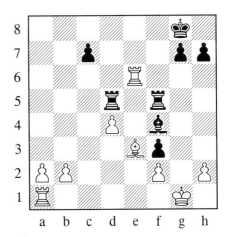

22.♗xf4

This forces a draw.

White's last winning attempt was 22.a4!. Then
Black should avoid: 22...♗xe3 23.♖e8†! It is
important that the f3-pawn would hang with

check. 23...♔f7 24.♖xe3 ♖xd4 25.a5 and Black is in bad shape.

Instead 22...♗d6! is probably the only move here, offering Black counterplay on the kingside. Andreikin obviously did not like this and therefore settled for a draw. However, the white a-pawn is very dangerous and White would retain some winning chances.

22...♖xf4 23.♖e3 ♖g5† 24.♔h1 ♖h5!

A strong and precise move!

25.♖ae1 ♖fh4 26.♖e8† ♔f7 27.♖8e7† ♔f8 28.♖e8† ♔f7 29.♖8e7†
½–½

GAME 19
▷ **A. Volokitin (2686)**
▶ **V. Iordachescu (2646)**
Romanian League, Brasov
08.10.2011 **[C70]**
Annotated by Alexander Ipatov and Kamil Miton

In this game White implemented an interesting novelty with 10.♘d2!?, which proved a success as Black was unable to solve his opening problems. Our analysis indicates that Black could have maintained the balance with 10...♘xb3 followed by some strong computer moves, although it must be said that the position would be rather unpleasant for an unprepared player. In the game White could have improved by playing 11.♗c3 with a small but pleasant advantage. Later he got a big advantage anyway following Black's error on move 13, but failed to convert it and the game finally ended in a draw.

1.e4 e5 2.♘f3 ♘c6 3.♗b5 a6 4.♗a4 ♘ge7

The delayed Cozio set-up is slightly unusual, but has been tested by a number of strong players in recent years.

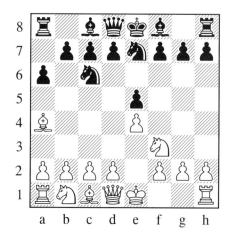

5.c3

The most logical set-up, planning to construct a strong pawn centre. Recent practice has also seen:

5.d4 exd4 6.♗b3 ♘a5 7.♕xd4 ♘xb3 8.axb3 ♘c6 9.♕d3 d6= Vallejo Pons – Turov, Nakhchivan 2011.

5.♘c3 d6 6.0–0 ♗d7 7.a3 g6 8.d4 ♗g7 9.dxe5 ♘xe5 10.♘xe5 ♗xe5 11.♗b3 ♗e6 12.♘d5 ♘xd5 13.♗xd5 ♗xd5 14.exd5 0–0= Smeets – Grischuk, Wijk aan Zee 2011.

5.0–0 g6 6.c3 (6.d4 exd4 7.♘xd4 ♗g7 8.c3 0–0 9.♗g5 ♘xd4 10.cxd4 h6 11.♗h4 g5 12.♗g3 f5!⇄ Frolyanov – Svidler, Olginka 2011) 6...♗g7 7.d4 exd4 8.cxd4 0–0 9.d5 b5 10.♗c2 ♘a5

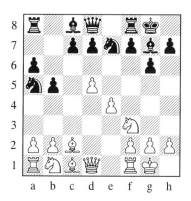

11.♗d2! A similar idea to the one we will encounter later in the game. 11...c5 (11...♗xb2 12.♗xa5 ♗xa1 13.♘c3 ♗xc3 [13...♗b2 14.d6 ♘c6 15.♗xc7 ♕e8 16.♘d5∞] 14.♗xc3 d6 15.♗f6!∞) 12.d6 ♘ec6 13.♘c3 ♘c4 14.♗g5 ♘xb2 15.♕c1 f6 16.♗e3 ♘c4 17.♗xc5± Zherebukh – Zvjaginsev, Aix-les-Bains 2011.

5...g6 6.d4

6.0–0 transposes to 5.0–0 above, which also seems quite promising for White.

6...exd4 7.cxd4 b5 8.♗b3

8.♗c2

This move brings no advantage if Black reacts correctly.

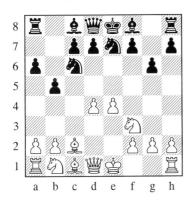

8...d5!

Without this White would have the better chances.

8...♗g7 9.d5 ♘a5 10.0–0 0–0 11.♗d2! transposes to Zherebukh – Zvjaginsev as referenced above.

9.e5

9.exd5 ♘b4! (9...♘xd5?! 10.0–0 ♗g7 11.♗g5 ♕d6 [11...f6 12.♖e1† ♘ce7 13.♗d2 0–0 14.♘c3±] 12.♖e1† ♗e6 13.♘c3 ♘xc3 14.bxc3 0–0 15.♘d2!±) 10.♗b3 ♗g7 11.0–0 ♘bxd5=

9...♗g7 10.♘bd2 0–0 11.h3 f6! 12.exf6 ♖xf6 13.0–0 ♕f8 14.♖e1 h6

Black obtained equal chances in Karjakin – Aronian, Monaco (rapid) 2011.

8...♗g7 9.d5

The most challenging move.

9.♘c3 ♘a5 10.♗e3

10.♗c2 d6 does not even bring White the slightest advantage, for instance: 11.h3 0–0 12.0–0 ♗b7 13.♖b1 ♘c4 14.b3 ♘b6 Black has easy play, and soon took over the initiative in a recent game: 15.♘e2 ♕d7 16.♘h2?! ♖ae8 17.♗f4 f5!↑ Delchev – Demuth, Mulhouse 2011.

10...d6 11.♕d2

Hoping to exchange the dark-squared bishops and start an attack, but Black is ready with a good reply.

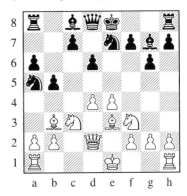

11...f5!

Creating immediate counterplay.

12.d5 ♘xb3 13.axb3 b4 14.♘e2 fxe4 15.♘fd4 0–0∓ Bobras – Chuchelov, Germany 2011.

9...♘a5

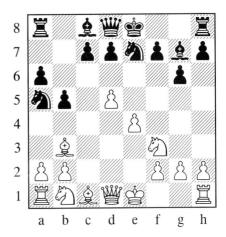

10.♗d2!?N

An interesting novelty. White aims for quick development and activation of pieces instead of keeping the bishop pair. However, it looks like Black can equalize by playing a few strong moves in a row.

The usual 10.♗c2 does not give White much, for instance: 10...0–0 11.0–0 d6 12.♘c3 (12.h3 c6! 13.dxc6 ♘exc6 14.♘c3 ♗e6 15.♘d5 ♘c4⇆ Djukic – Khalifman, Aix-les-Bains 2011) 12...♗b7 13.♖b1 b4 14.♘a4 c6! This typical idea works fine here as well. 15.dxc6 ♗xc6= N. Kosintseva – I. Sokolov, Sarajevo 2010.

10...c5

This is a reasonable move which avoids serious complications. However, White could have obtained an edge with an improvement on the next move, so it is possible that Black should look to improve here. We checked three alternatives, of which the last is clearly critical.

10...♘b7? is too passive and gives White easy play: 11.♗c3! The exchange of dark-squared bishops robs the black position of much of its dynamism. 11...♗xc3† 12.♘xc3 d6 13.♕d2 0–0 14.0–0 ♗g4 15.♘d4±

10...♗xb2?

Iordachescu was right to avoid this move, which may already be losing by force.
11.♗xa5 ♗xa1 12.♘c3 ♗xc3†
12...♗b2 13.♕c2 ♗a3 14.♘b1 ♗d6 15.e5+–
13.♗xc3
In return for the exchange White has a vicious attack.
13...f6
13...0–0? loses by force: 14.♕d2! d6 15.♕h6 f6 16.♘g5! ♖f7 (16...fxg5 17.♗g7#) 17.♘xf7 ♕f8 18.♕xf8† ♔xf8 19.♘d8+–
13...♖f8 14.0–0 f6 (14...d6 15.♘g5±) 15.e5! fxe5 16.♘xe5 with a decisive attack.

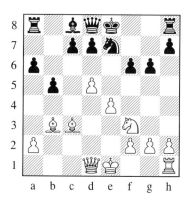

14.d6! cxd6
14...♘c6 15.♘g5!+–
15.♗xf6 ♖f8 16.♗g7 ♘c6 17.♗xf8 ♔xf8 18.♕a1! ♕a5† 19.♔e2±
Black's survival chances are minimal.

10...♘xb3

This is the most challenging reply. Now there is a major division between a) 11.♕xb3 and b) 11.axb3.

a) 11.♕xb3 c5!
11...f5? is completely unjustified: 12.♗c3! ♗xc3† (12...0–0?? 13.d6†+–) 13.♘xc3 d6 14.0–0±
11...d6?! 12.♗c3! 0–0 13.♗xg7 ♔xg7 14.0–0± White is better thanks to his strong central position and Black's weak dark squares.

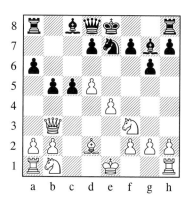

In this position it is worth considering a1) 12.d6, a2) 12.♗c3, a3) 12.dxc6 and a4) 12.a4.

a1) 12.d6 seems a little premature and after 12...♘c6, intending ...c4 and ...0–0, Black has a decent game.

a2) 12.♗c3 f6!

Without this move Black would be worse.
13.0–0

13.d6!? leads to messy complications: 13...♘c6 14.♕d5 (14.♘g5 c4 15.♕d1 0–0 16.♕d5† ♔h8 17.♘f7† ♖xf7 18.♕xf7 b4⇄; 14.0–0 c4 15.♕c2 0–0 [15...♗b7!? 16.♘bd2 ♖c8 17.a3 a5] 16.b3 cxb3 17.♕xb3† ♔h8 18.♘bd2) 14...b4 15.♘g5 (15.♗d2 ♗b7 16.♕xc5 [16.0–0 ♕b6 17.♗e3 ♘d4 18.♕c4 ♕b5] 16...f5 17.e5 ♖c8 18.♕e3 0–0∞) 15...♖f8 16.♘xh7 bxc3 17.♘xf8 c2 18.0–0 ♔xf8 (18...cxb1=♕ 19.♘xg6+–) 19.♘a3 ♕b6∞

13...d6

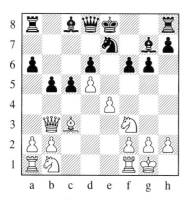

Black has excellent prospects, with a pair of bishops and a solid position. In the future he can either play for ...f5, or look to advance his position on the queenside first. Meanwhile White's coordination is not great.
14.a3

14.♘g5?! b4 15.♘e6 ♗xe6 16.dxe6 bxc3 17.♕a4† ♔f8 18.♘xc3 f5∓

14...0–0 15.♖e1 ♗b7 16.♘bd2 ♕d7 17.♕c2 h6

17...f5 can be met by 18.♗xg7 ♔xg7 19.♘g5.

But 17...a5!? is interesting.

18.b4 cxb4 19.axb4 ♖ac8 20.♕b2 ♖xc3 21.♕xc3 f5!∓

a3) 12.dxc6

With this move White obtains a better pawn structure, but he risks opening the position for the enemy bishop pair. It is worth considering both **a31)** 12...dxc6?! and the superior **a32)** 12...♘xc6!.

a31) 12...dxc6?! 13.♗c3

Compared with line 'a2' above, Black is worse off as he can hardly contemplate the reply ...f7-f6.

13...♗e6 14.♕b4 0–0 15.♗xg7 ♔xg7 16.♘bd2!

The knight is better here than on c3, as it does not block the c-file and also has the option of manoeuvring to c5 via b3 at some point. If Black were able to play ...c5 then he would have no problems, but this is easier said than done.

16...♖c8

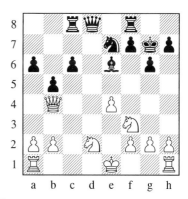

17.♕c3†!

A very important check! By forcing the king back to g8, White prevents the plan of ...♘g8 followed by exchanging queens.

The immediate 17.♕c5 allows Black to execute that very idea: 17...♘g8! 18.0–0 ♕e7 (18...♘f6!? is possible too) 19.♘b3 (19.♕b6 ♕c7 20.♕d4† ♘f6 21.e5 ♘d7∞; 19.♖fc1 ♕xc5 20.♖xc5 ♖fd8= The activity of Black's pieces fully compensates for the weakness on c6.) 19...♗xb3 Otherwise White takes on e7 and puts the knight on c5. 20.♕xe7 ♘xe7 21.axb3 ♖a8 22.♖fd1 ♖fd8 23.♔f1 ♖xd1† 24.♖xd1 ♖a7! It is important to defend the 7th rank. 25.♔e2 a5=

17...♔g8

17...f6 18.♕c5±

18.♕c5±

The c6-pawn is firmly blocked and Black has little chance of freeing himself. White has a pleasant, long-term advantage.

a32) 12...♘xc6!

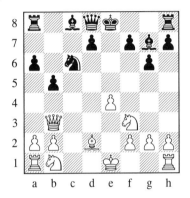

This is the better way: Black puts the welfare of his pieces above that of his pawn structure.

13.♗c3

13.0–0 0–0 14.♘c3 ♘a5 (14...♗b7 15.♗g5 ♘d4) 15.♕b4 ♘c4 16.♗g5 ♕a5 17.♕xa5 ♘xa5 18.♘d5 ♗xb2 19.e5 ♗xa1 20.♘e7† ♔g7 21.♗f6† ♔h6 22.♖xa1→

13...f6!

A resolute move. Black wants to keep his dark-squared bishop on the board, but he must be sure that White will neither be able to break open the centre to attack his king, nor bring his knight to d5 quickly. Meanwhile Black intends to bring his queen to e7 and e6 (or f7) to facilitate castling.

13...0–0?! 14.♗xg7 ♔xg7 15.0–0 gives White an obvious advantage thanks to his safer king, better pawn structure and better piece coordination.

14.0–0 ♕e7

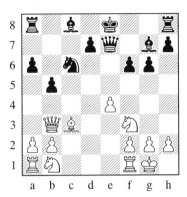

15.♖d1

15.♗d2 frees the c3-square for the knight, but it costs time and after 15...♗b7 16.♘c3 ♘a5! 17.♕d1 ♘c4 18.♘d5 ♗xd5 19.exd5 0–0= Black is fine.

15...♕e6! 16.♘bd2 0–0=

Black has no problems as White's knights are a long way from d5.

a4) Finally, another challenging idea is:
12.a4

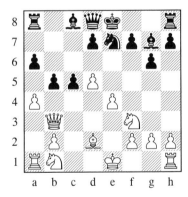

12...b4!

It is worth giving up the c4-square in order to keep the queenside pawn chain intact, while also preventing the enemy pieces from using the c3-square.

12...c4? is worse: 13.♕a3 ♗b7 14.0–0 0–0 15.♘c3 ♖e8 (15...f5 16.♗g5!±) 16.axb5 axb5 17.♕b4± Black's queenside pawns are seriously weak.

13.♗f4

Improving the bishop while making way for the knight.

13...0–0

This seems like the safest route for Black.

13...a5?! is slightly inaccurate: 14.♘bd2 ♗a6 15.♗e5! (15.♘c4? ♗xc4 16.♕xc4 ♗b2 17.♖a2 ♗c3†∓) 15...♗xe5 (15...f6 16.♗d6 ♕b6 17.♗xe7 ♔xe7 18.♘c4 ♗xc4 19.♕xc4 ♖he8 20.0–0±) 16.♘xe5 d6 17.♘ec4±

13...d6 is also a bit risky: 14.♘bd2 0–0 15.0–0 f5 (15...a5 16.♘c4 ♗a6 17.♗xd6! ♗xf1 18.♖xf1 gives White powerful compensation)

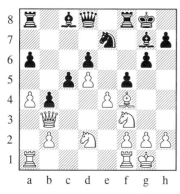

16.e5! Of course! 16...♗b7□ 17.♗g5 ♕d7 (The best practical chance may be 17...♗xd5!? 18.♗xe7 ♗xb3 19.♗xd8 ♖fxd8 20.♘xb3 dxe5 21.♘xc5 e4 22.♘g5 ♖dc8∞ when objectively Black's compensation is not quite sufficient, but White will have to play extremely precisely to prove it.) 18.exd6 (18.e6?! ♕e8 19.♗xe7 ♕xe7 20.♖ad1 f4!⇄) 18...♘c8 Hoping to use the knight to blockade on d6. (18...♗xd5 19.♘c4↑) 19.♖fe1! Forcing Black to take with the queen instead of the knight. 19...♕xd6 20.♘c4 ♗xd5 21.♖ad1 ♕c6□ 22.♘fe5!∞ White has a powerful initiative.

14.♘bd2 a5!

14...d6 transposes to 13...d6 above.

15.0–0

15.♗e5 ♗xe5 16.♘xe5 d6 17.♘ec4 is well

met by 17...f5! 18.0–0 fxe4 19.♘xe4 ♘f5 20.♖fe1 ♗a6 and Black seizes the initiative.

15.♘c4 ♗a6 16.♘fd2 also gives White nothing special after 16...♘c8! intending ...♘b6.

15...♗a6

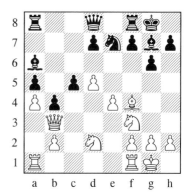

16.♘c4

16.♗d6 ♗xf1 17.♖xf1 ♖e8 18.♘c4 ♘c8 is okay for Black.

16.♖fe1 d6 17.♖ab1 ♕d7 18.♘c4 ♗xc4 19.♕xc4 ♘c8!∞

16...♘c8!

This typical manoeuvre works well here too.

17.♖fc1

White has to keep control over the c4-square.

17.♖fe1? allows Black to grab a pawn with 17...♗xc4 18.♕xc4 ♗b2 19.♖a2 ♗c3∓ when the b- and c-pawns are powerful.

After 17.e5?! ♘b6 18.♘xb6 ♕xb6∓ Black is better thanks to the bishop pair and the strong plan of ...c5-c4.

17...d6

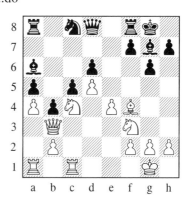

18.♖c2

18.e5 is well met by 18...♗xc4 19.♕xc4 ♘b6 20.♕b5 ♕b8!⇄ when White has serious problems keeping his pawn centre together. 18...♗xc4 19.♕xc4 ♕d7! 20.♕b3 ♘b6 21.♘d2 f5!↑

Overall Black seems to be holding his own after 11.♕xb3 c5, but we must also pay attention to the more dynamic pawn capture.

b) 11.axb3!? ♗xb2

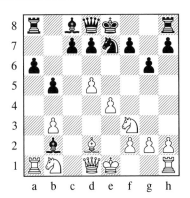

Now White can choose between b1) 12.♖a2, b2) 12.♘c3!? and finally the most dangerous b3) 12.♗c3!.

b1) 12.♖a2

This move is too slow, but we should consider it anyway.

12...♗g7 13.♗c3

13.d6 ♘c6 14.♗g5 f6 15.♗f4 ♘e5! 16.0–0 cxd6 17.♘c3 ♗b7 18.♕xd6 ♘f7! 19.♕d3 0–0 is more than okay for Black.

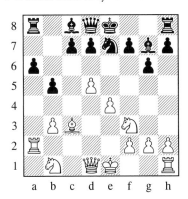

13...f6!

Black should avoid the bishop exchange in order to keep his dark squares safe.

14.0–0

14.d6?! ♘c6 15.0–0 cxd6 16.♖d2 0–0 17.♖xd6 ♕e7∓

14.♗a5 d6 15.♖c2 ♖a7! 16.♕c1 0–0 17.♗xc7 ♖xc7! 18.♖xc7 f5⯑ gives Black perfect compensation.

14...0–0

White obviously has some compensation for the pawn, but Black has the bishop pair and no real weaknesses, so he should be okay.

15.♗a5 d6 16.♖c2 ♖a7 17.♖e1

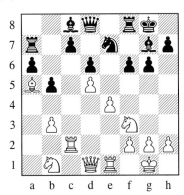

17...f5 18.e5

18.♘c3 should be met by 18...♖b7.

18...dxe5 19.♘xe5 ♕d6 20.♕d4 ♖b7 20...♖xd5 21.♕xa7 ♗xe5∞

21.♗b4 ♕xd5 22.♕xd5† ♘xd5 23.♗xf8 ♗xf8 24.♖d2 ♘b6∞

b2) 12.♘c3!?

Having already sacrificed a pawn, White forces his opponent to take an exchange as well.

12...♗xa1

It makes no sense to improve the white knight with: 12...b4?! 13.♘e2 ♗xa1 (13...c5!?) 14.♕xa1 0–0 15.♗g5 White should be doing well here, for instance 15...a5 16.♘f4 ♕e8 17.0–0 f6 18.♗xf6 h6 19.h4! with an attack. (19.♖c1 g5 20.♗h8 ♕f7 21.♘h5 a4! is not so clear.)

13.♕xa1 0–0

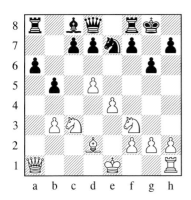

14.0–0

14.♗h6 f6 15.♗xf8 (15.♘xb5 ♗b7 16.♘a3 ♖f7 17.0–0 a5∞) 15...♖xf8 16.♘xb5 (16.♕a5 ♗b7 17.♕xc7 ♕c8 18.♕a5 f5 19.0–0 fxe4 20.♘xe4 ♘xd5∞) 16...♗b7 17.♘xc7 ♖c8 18.d6 (18.0–0 ♖xc7 19.d6 ♖c8 20.dxe7 ♕xe7 21.♖e1∞) 18...♗xe4 19.♕xa6 ♘f5 20.♕c4† ♔g7 21.♕xe4 ♘xd6 22.♕c2 ♕d8=

14...♗b7

14...f6 15.♘xb5 ♗b7 16.♘a3↑

15.♗h6 f6 16.♘d1!?

16.♗xf8 ♕xf8 17.♖e1⯶

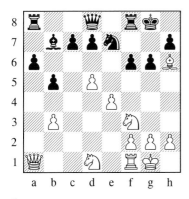

16...c6

Getting the bishop into the game.

16...♖f7 is playable but riskier: 17.♘e3 g5 18.♘g4 ♘g6 19.h4! (19.e5 ♘xe5 20.♘fxe5 fxe5 21.f4 ♕e7 22.♗xg5 ♕c5† 23.♖f2 ♕d4∞)

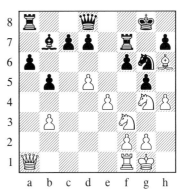

19...gxh4 (19...♘xh4 20.♘xg5 fxg5 21.f4 ♕e8 22.♗xg5 h5 23.♘h6† ♔h7 24.♘xf7 ♕xf7 25.♗xh4±) 20.♖e1 (20.e5?! fxe5 21.♘fxe5 ♘xe5 22.♕xe5 ♕e7 23.♕d4 ♕d6 24.♗g5 h5 25.♘h6† ♔h7 26.♘xf7 ♕xd5 27.♕xd5 ♗xd5 28.♘e5 d6⯥) 20...d6 21.♗d2 ♗c8 22.♘h6† ♔f8 23.♘d4↑

The other option is 16...♘c8 when our main line leads to a draw: 17.♘e3 ♘d6 18.e5 (18.♗xf8 ♕xf8 19.♖c1 ♖c8 20.♕d4 c5 21.dxc6 ♗xc6=) 18...♘e4 (18...fxe5 19.♘xe5 ♕e7 20.♖e1 ♖ae8 21.♘3g4→)

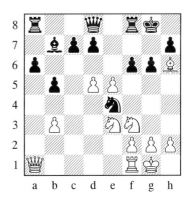

19.♘g4 (19.♕d4 f5 20.g4 c5⇄) 19...f5 20.e6 ♕e7 21.d6 cxd6 22.♗g5 ♕g7 23.♘h6† ♔h8 24.e7 ♕xa1 25.exf8=♕† ♖xf8 26.♖xa1 ♘xg5 27.♘xg5 ♗d5 28.♖xa6 ♔g7 29.♖xd6 ♗xb3 30.♘xf5† ♖xf5 31.♖xd7†=

17.d6

17.♘e3 cxd5 18.♗xf8 (18.e5 d4) 18...♕xf8 19.♘g4 dxe4 20.♘xf6† ♔h8 21.♘h5† ♔g8 22.♘f6† ♔h8= 23.♘g5 ♕g7 24.♘gxh7∞

17...♘c8 18.e5

18.♕d4? c5∓

18.♘e3 ♘xd6 19.e5 ♘f7 20.♗xf8 ♕xf8 21.e6 (21.♘g4 ♘xe5 22.♘fxe5 fxe5 23.♕xe5 d6∓) 21...♘h6 22.exd7 ♖d8 23.♖d1 ♕e7 Black is fine.

18...c5 19.♘e3 ♗xf3 20.gxf3 ♖e8

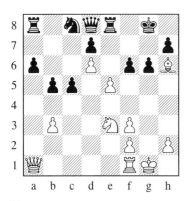

21.exf6

21.♘g4 fxe5 22.♖e1 ♘xd6 23.♖xe5 ♖xe5 24.♕xe5 ♘f5 25.♕d5† ♔h8 26.♗c1 ♕f8 27.♘h6 ♘d4 28.♘f7† ♔g8 29.♘e5† ♔g7 30.♕xd7† ♔g8 31.♗h6 ♕xh6 32.♕d5† ♔g7 33.♕b7† ♔g8=

21.f4!? ♖e6 22.♘d5 fxe5 23.fxe5 ♕h4 24.♗f4∞

21...♔f7 22.♘g4 ♘xd6 23.♘e5† ♖xe5

23...♔g8? 24.f7† ♘xf7 25.♘xf7 ♔xf7 26.♕g7† ♔e6 27.♖d1+−

24.♕xe5 ♘f5 25.♕d5† ♔xf6 26.♗c1∞

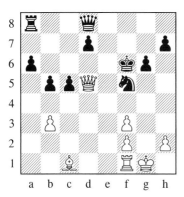

The position is messy, but the powerful

knight on f5 should be enough to hold Black's position together. 12.♘c3 leads to rich play with many dangers for both sides, but overall the situation seems roughly balanced.

b3) 12.♗c3!

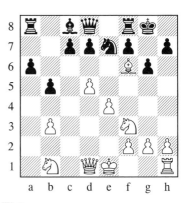

This seems to be White's most dangerous option. Now it is worth considering b31) 12...♗xa1?! and b32) 12...♗xc3†.

b31) 12...♗xa1?!

This looks extremely risky.

13.♗xa1 0–0

The best chance, but it is not good enough.

14.♗f6

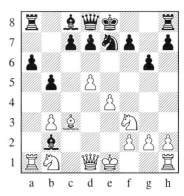

14...♖b8

Hoping to defend via b6.

14...♕e8 15.♕d2 ♘f5 16.0–0! ♕xe4 17.♖e1 ♕g4 18.♘c3 a5 19.♘e4 ♖a6 20.♕c3±

If Black has a way to make this line playable

then 14...a5!? 15.d6 cxd6 might be the way to do it. Compared with the main line, Black will be able to put his bishop on b7 without blocking the rook's path to the third rank.

15.d6!

15.♘c3? ♖b6∓

15.♘e5? ♖b6 16.♘g4 h5∓

15.♕c1   ♖b6   16.♗d4   ♘xd5   (16...f6 17.♕h6) 17.exd5 (17.♕h6 ♘f6 18.♘g5 ♖e8) 17...♖e8† 18.♔d1 ♖d6 19.♘c3 ♗b7 20.♕h6 f6 21.♘g5 ♕e7 22.♔c2 ♗xd5 23.♘xd5 ♖xd5 24.♖e1 ♖xd4 25.♖xe7 ♖xe7 26.♘f3∞

15...cxd6 16.0–0!

16.♘c3 ♗b7 17.♕xd6 ♖e8 18.0–0! b4 19.♕f4 bxc3 20.♕h6 ♘f5 defends.

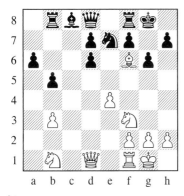

16...♗b7

16...♖e8 17.♕d2 ♗b7 18.♖e1 transposes to 16...♗b7.

16...d5 17.exd5 d6 18.♕d2 looks totally lost for Black, for instance: 18...♕d7 19.♘c3 ♘f5 20.♘e4 ♖e8 (20...♗b7 21.g4+−) 21.♗e5+−

17.♕d2

17.♕xd6 ♖e8 18.♕f4 (18.♘g5 h6 19.♕f4 ♕b6 20.♘xf7 ♘f5 21.♗a1 ♔xf7 22.exf5 g5; 18.♘e5 ♘c8 19.♕xb8 ♕xf6 20.♕xb7 ♕xe5=) 18...♗xe4 19.♕xe4 ♘d5 20.♕xd5 ♕xf6 21.♘bd2 is possible, but the text is stronger.

17...♖e8

17...♗xe4 18.♖e1±

18.♖e1 d5

18...♖c8 19.♘h4 ♖c5 20.♘f5 ♖xf5 21.exf5 ♗xg2 22.fxg6 fxg6 23.♔xg2 ♕a8† 24.f3±

19.♘e5 d6 20.♘g4 ♕c8 21.♕f4 dxe4 22.♗a1 ♘f5 23.♘f6† ♔f8 24.g4+−

b32) 12...♗xc3†

Definitely the safer option.

13.♘xc3

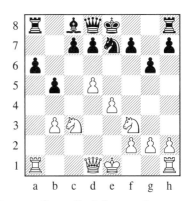

Now we face a final division between b321) 13...0–0 and b322) 13...♗b7!.

b321) 13...0–0

This move is playable, but White will keep some advantage after regaining his pawn.

14.♘xb5 a5

14...c6 15.♘d6 cxd5 16.e5±

14...f5 15.e5 (15.d6 cxd6 16.♘xd6 fxe4 17.♘e5 e3 18.0–0 exf2† 19.♔h1 ♕b6 20.♘xc8 ♖fxc8 21.♘xd7 ♕c6 22.♖xf2=) 15...d6 16.exd6 cxd6 17.0–0 ♗b7 18.♘c3 ♖c8 19.♕d2 ♕b6 20.♖fe1± White is better thanks to the vulnerability of the black kingside and especially the e6-square.

15.♘c3

15.0–0 ♗a6 16.♘xc7 ♕xc7 17.d6 ♕d8 18.dxe7 ♕xe7 19.♖e1 ♗b7 20.♕d2±

15...♗a6 16.h4!

16.♖xa5 c6 17.♕a1 ♕b6 18.♘e5 ♘xd5 19.♘xd7 ♕d4 20.♘xd5 ♕xe4† 21.♔d2 ♕d3† 22.♔c1 cxd5 23.♘f6† ♔h8→

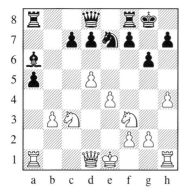

16...f5 17.e5

17.h5 fxe4 18.♘xe4 looks totally unclear.

17...♛b8 18.h5 ♛b4 19.♘d2

White keeps some initiative.

b322) 13...♝b7!

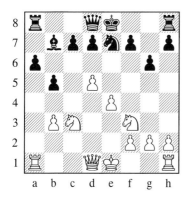

14.0–0

14.♕d4 0–0 15.0–0 f5 16.e5 b4 17.♕xb4 ♝xd5 18.♘xd5 ♘xd5 19.♕c4 c6 20.♖xa6 ♖xa6 21.♕xa6 ♕b6=

14...0–0 15.♕d2

15.b4 ♘c8∞

15...f5 16.♕h6 ♖f7 17.♘e5 ♖g7 18.f3 d6 19.♘d3 c6 20.♘f4 ♕b6† 21.♔h1∞

Summing up, according to our analysis 11...♘xb3 should enable Black to maintain the balance. Nevertheless from a practical perspective his task will not be easy, as White has several interesting options, all of which require accurate handling.

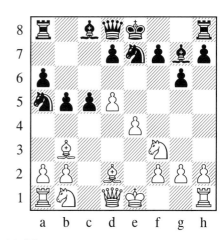

11.d6

The most ambitious, but not the strongest move. White grabs a space advantage, but on the other hand he enables the e7-knight to get better prospects.

11.♝c3!

This would have given White a stable positional edge. The key is to keep the knight passive on e7.

11...0–0

11...f6? does not work here due to 12.d6 ♘ec6 13.♝d5±.

12.♝xg7 ♔xg7 13.0–0

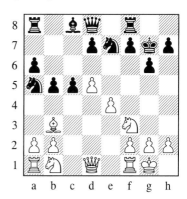

13...d6

The alternative is: 13...♘xb3 14.♕xb3 d6 15.♘bd2 ♘g8! Improving the bad knight. 16.♖fe1 ♖e8 17.♕c3† ♘f6 18.b4! c4 19.a4 ♝d7 20.h3± White has a space advantage and can combine his play in the centre and on the queenside.

14.♗c2 ♘c4 15.♘bd2!

A strong temporary pawn sacrifice.

15...♘xb2 16.♕c1 ♘c4 17.♘xc4 bxc4 18.♘d2 a5 19.♘xc4 ♗a6 20.♗d3±

Black still has some problems to solve, the biggest one being the bad knight on e7.

11...♘ec6

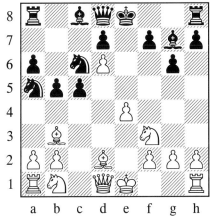

12.♗g5

12.♗c3!? is an interesting alternative: 12...0–0 13.♗d5 ♗b7 14.0–0 ♕b6 (14...♕b8?! 15.♕d2! b4 16.♗xg7 ♔xg7 17.a3! ♕xd6 18.axb4 cxb4 19.b3⯹ White has compensation as the a5-knight is out of play.) 15.♖e1 ♖ae8∞ The position remains sharp, and practical testing will be required for a more precise evaluation.

12...♗f6

12...♕b6?! is met by 13.♘c3 when White seizes the initiative.

13.h4!?

A consistent and interesting move, but it should not be too dangerous for Black.

13...c4?

A positional error: Black keeps his bad knight on the edge of the board, instead of exchanging

it for the enemy bishop. Furthermore, Black deprives his other knight of a potentially useful square on c4.

13...♘xb3!

This natural move would have led to a complex game where Black is doing fine.

14.axb3

14.♕xb3 ♗b7 15.e5 ♗xg5! 16.hxg5 (16.♘xg5? ♘xe5 17.0–0 0–0∓) 16...♘d4! 17.♘xd4 cxd4 18.♕g3 The g5-pawn was hanging. 18...♖c8 19.♘d2 ♖c2⇄

14...♗b7 15.♕d5 0–0 16.♕xc5 ♖e8

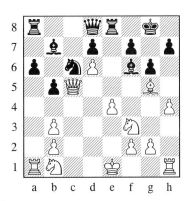

17.♘c3

17.♘bd2 ♖c8⯹

17...♗xc3† 18.bxc3 ♖xe4† 19.♔f1

19.♗e3 ♖c8↑

19...f6∞

14.♗c2 h6 15.♗xf6 ♕xf6 16.♘c3±

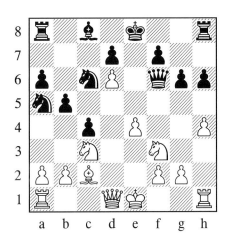

Thanks to Black's mistake on move 13, White has a clear advantage. Black is weak on the kingside and on the dark squares generally, while the knight on a5 is clearly misplaced. Meanwhile White is well coordinated and can easily complete his development and improve his position.

16...♗b7 17.♕d2

Keeping an eye on the h6-pawn to prevent castling.

17...♘b4 18.♗b1!

White has a space advantage so of course he avoids unnecessary exchanges.

18...♔f8

Black is unable to castle by normal means, so he attempts a 'custom-made' solution.

The idea of sacrificing a pawn for some activity fails to solve Black's problems: 18...♘d3†?! 19.♗xd3 cxd3 20.♕xd3 ♖c8 21.0–0 0–0 22.♘d5 ♕d6 23.♕d2! A double attack on a5 and h6. 23...♗xd5 24.exd5 ♘c4 25.♕xh6± White is a clear pawn up.

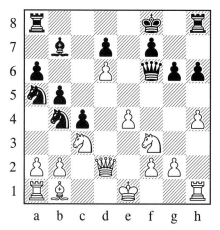

19.e5?!

A better alternative was:
19.0–0!

In order to prevent the ...♕e6-g4 manoeuvre which happened in the game.

19...♔g7 20.e5 ♕e6 21.♘e4 ♗xe4

Now 21...♕g4?? just loses a piece after 22.♕xb4 ♗xe4 23.♗xe4 ♕xe4 24.♕xa5+–.

22.♗xe4 ♘ac6 23.a3 ♘d3 24.♗xd3 cxd3 25.♖fe1 f6

25...♖d5 26.♖e3±

26.exf6† ♕xf6 27.♕xd3

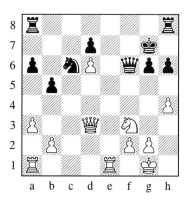

27...♕xb2

27...♖ae8 28.♕d2±

28.h5! ♕f6

28...g5?? 29.♕g6† ♔f8 30.♕f5†+–
28...gxh5 29.♘h4±

29.♘h4! ♖hf8

29...♕xh4?? 30.♕xg6† ♔f8 31.♕f5† ♔g8 32.♖e3+–

30.♕xg6† ♕xg6 31.♘xg6±

19...♕e6 20.♘e4 ♕g4!

Suddenly Black's pieces have become active.

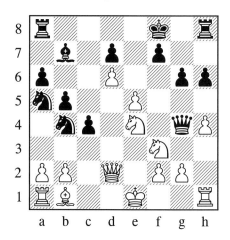

21.0–0

21.♘g3? keeps more pieces on the board but leads to a good position for Black after: 21...c3! 22.♕xc3 (22.bxc3 ♘c4 23.♕d4 ♕xd4 24.cxd4 [after 24.♘xd4 ♘d5⇄ both the c3- and e5-pawns are under attack] 24...♘a3 25.♔d2 ♖c8⯑ Black's active pieces compensate for the missing pawn.) 22...♖c8 23.♕d2□ (23.♕e3? ♘d5 24.♕d2 ♘f4–+) 23...♖e8↑

21...♗xe4 22.♗xe4 ♕xe4 23.♕xb4 ♘c6 24.♕c3±

White is still better, but his advantage is smaller than it would have been after 19.0–0!.

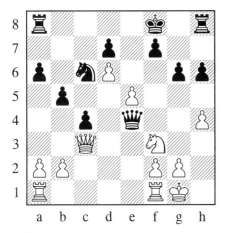

24...♖g8?!

A better defensive try was 24...b4, kicking White's queen away from its active square.

25.♖fe1 ♕f5 26.a4!

Enlarging the battlefield.

26...♖e8 27.axb5 axb5 28.♘d4 ♘xd4 29.♕xd4 g5!

Black has to go for immediate counterplay, otherwise he will be lost.

30.♖a5

White could also have considered 30.h5!? g4 31.♖e4! which sets a nasty trap. 31...♕xh5?

(Instead Black should prefer 31...♕e6 although 32.♖a5± still leaves him in trouble.)

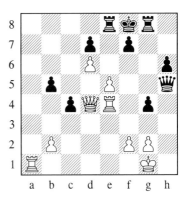

32.e6!! dxe6 (32...fxe6 33.♖f4†+–; 32...♖xe6 33.♖a8†+–) 33.d7 ♖d8 34.♖xe6! fxe6 (34...♕f5 35.♖e8† ♖xe8 36.dxe8=♕† ♔xe8 37.♖a8† ♔e7 38.♖xg8+–) 35.♕f6† ♕f7 36.♕xd8† ♔g7 37.♕c7+–

30...♖b8 31.♖a7 ♕e6 32.♖e4 ♖e8

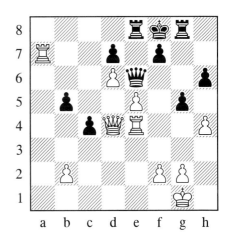

33.♖b7?

Correct was 33.h5! when White keeps a clear plus.

33...gxh4!

Liberating the rook and forcing simplifications.

34.♖xh4 ♕xe5 35.♖xd7 ♖g6 36.♕f4 ♖f6

37.♕xe5 ♖xe5

With the queens off the board and the d-pawn about to drop, White's advantage has almost evaporated.

38.♖d4 ♖ee6 39.♖d5 ♔e8 40.♖c7 ♖xd6 41.♖xb5 ♖b6 42.♖xb6 ♖xb6 43.♖xc4 ♖xb2 44.♖c6 ♔f8 45.♖xh6 ♔g7=

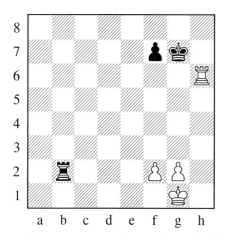

Volokitin carries on playing for a while, but the position is an easy draw.

46.♖d6 ♖a2 47.g3 ♖b2 48.♔g2 ♖a2 49.g4 f6 50.♔g3 ♖a3† 51.♔f4 ♔g6 52.♖d4 ♖a5 53.f3 ♖b5 54.♖d3 ♖a5 55.♔g3 ♖a1 56.f4 ♖g1† 57.♔h3 f5 58.♖d6† ♔g7 59.gxf5 ♔f7 60.♖a6 ♔g8 61.♔h4 ♖g1 62.♔h5 ♖g2 63.♖g6 ♖h2† 64.♔g4 ♖g2† 65.♔f3 ♖xg6 66.fxg6† ♔xg6 67.♔e4 ♔f6 68.f5
½–½

▷ **A. Grischuk (2757)**
▶ **A. Shirov (2713)**

European Club Cup, Rogaska Slatina
Round 7, 01.10.2011 **[C78]**
Annotated by Sebastien Maze

In a fashionable line of the Ruy Lopez, Shirov deviates from theory with the interesting novelty 13...♖e8. He obtained a decent position but soon went wrong with 17...♖xe5? instead of the much more solid 17...dxe5. Grischuk got a big advantage but then misplayed it and allowed his opponent to equalize. But then Shirov made a terrible blunder in time trouble with 39...♖e8?? and gifted Grischuk a winning endgame, which he converted easily.

1.e4 e5 2.♘f3 ♘c6 3.♗b5 a6 4.♗a4 ♘f6 5.0–0 b5 6.♗b3 ♗c5 7.c3 d6 8.a4

8.d4 ♗b6 9.h3 is another possibility, but the text is the main line.

8...♖b8 9.d4 ♗b6

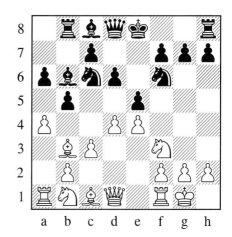

10.a5!?

An interesting idea. White gains space on the queenside instead of opening the a-file and going after the b5-pawn.

The usual continuation is 10.axb5 axb5. Now

11.♘a3 is the main line although 11.♗e3 has also been tried, for instance by Kamsky against Svidler at the 2011 World Cup.

10...♗a7

10...♘xa5? is extremely risky when Black has not yet castled: 11.♖xa5! ♗xa5 12.dxe5 ♘g4 13.♗g5 f6 14.exf6 gxf6 15.♗h4 White has a splendid attacking position.

11.h3 0–0 12.♗e3 ♖a8

Black has to lose a tempo with the rook in order to protect the bishop on a7, as dxe5 was a significant threat.

12...exd4?! avoids this loss of time, but brings other drawbacks. 13.cxd4 ♘xe4 14.♕c2 ♕e8 15.♘c3 ♘f6 16.♖fe1 White has a pleasant position with promising compensation for the pawn, Timofeev – Halklias, Dresden 2007.

13.♘bd2

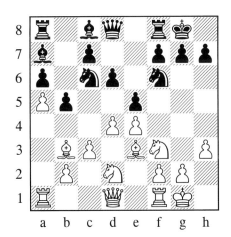

13...♖e8N

In 2010 Shirov tried 13...♗b7 against Anand. After 14.♖e1 ♖e8 15.♘g5 ♖e7 the position was unclear, with just a slight plus for White. Shirov eventually lost the game, so perhaps he wanted to avoid the unpleasant memories.

14.♖e1 h6

Compared to the above game with Anand, the Spanish player decided to avoid any potential trouble after ♘g5. A good decision!

15.♕c2 ♗b7 16.dxe5 ♘xe5 17.♘xe5 ♖xe5?

A surprising choice from Shirov. Maybe he wanted to exert pressure along the e-file, but underestimated the simple plan of f4 and e5 which gave White an excellent position.

The right choice was of course:
17...dxe5
White will have a hard time proving an advantage in the position with a symmetrical pawn structure.
18.♗xa7 ♖xa7
Now Black's ideas include ...c5 and possibly ...♗c8-e6, neutralizing White's strongest piece and also opening a path for the rook to join the game along the 7th rank.

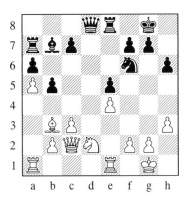

19.c4
19.♘f1 c5 20.c4 ♕c7 is fine for Black.
19.♖ad1 is met by 19...♕e7= with ...c5 coming next.
19...♕e7 20.♖ac1 ♖c8!
20...c6 does not quite equalize: 21.c5 ♖aa8 22.♘f3 ♖ad8 23.♖ed1 ♗c8 24.♗a2 ♗e6 25.♗xe6 ♕xe6 26.♖d6 ♖xd6 27.cxd6 ♕xd6 28.♕xc6 Black has some problems in the endgame as his queenside is weak. 28...♖e6 29.♕xd6 ♖xd6 30.♘xe5 ♘xe4

31.♖c8† ♔h7 32.♘xf7 ♖d1† 33.♔h2 ♗xf2
34.♖c6 ♖h1† 35.♔g3 ♘e4† 36.♔f4 ♘f6
37.♔e5±

21.c5

21.♘f3 c5 22.♕c3 b4 23.♕xe5 ♗xe4 24.♗a4
♕xe5 25.♘xe5 ♖e7=

21...♗c6 22.♘f3 ♖aa8 23.♗a2 ♖d8

The position is very close to equal, although
if I had to pick a side I would slightly prefer
White.

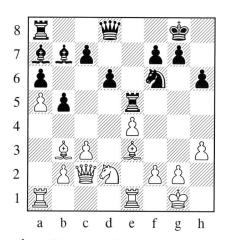

18.♗xa7 ♖xa7 19.f4 ♖e7 20.e5±

Black has only made a single error on move
17, but his position is already difficult. Note
the misplaced rook on a7, which will require
several moves to find a sensible square.

20...♕e8

The immediate 20...dxe5 also fails to solve
Black's problems: 21.fxe5 ♘d7 22.e6 fxe6
23.♖xe6 ♔h8 24.♕d3!? To apply some
pressure on the d-file. (24.♖ae1 ♖xe6 25.♗xe6
♖a8 26.♘b3 ♕h4 27.♖f1±) 24...♖xe6 25.♗xe6
♕g5 (25...♗c6 26.♖d1 ♕e7 27.♗xd7 ♗xd7
28.♘e4±) 26.♘f3 ♕c5† (26...♗xf3 27.♕xf3
♕c5† 28.♔h1±) 27.♔h1 ♘f8 28.♖e1
White is clearly better, as Black's pieces are
uncoordinated and his king is weak.

21.♘f3 dxe5

21...♗xf3? loses to 22.♕f2!.

Also 21...♘d7? 22.♘d4 dxe5 23.♘f5 e4
24.♕f2± is nasty for Black.

22.fxe5

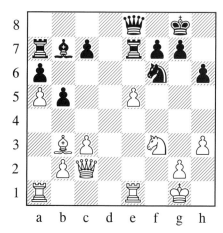

22...♘d7?

A bad choice.

22...♘h7 was the lesser evil: 23.♘d4 (After
23.♕f2 ♖a8 24.♘h4 ♘g5! the knight finds
an excellent square where it defends f7 and
prepares to go to e6 at any moment. 25.♘f5
♖xe5 26.h4 ♘e4 27.♕f4 The position is
unclear.) 23...♘g5 24.h4 ♘e6 25.♖ad1 ♖a8
26.♗a2! Intending to drop the bishop back
to b1 at a suitable moment. White keeps the
better chances, but his advantage is smaller
than in the game.

23.e6?!

Too soon.

It was better to improve White's strongest
piece before taking any direct action: 23.♕f2!
Hitting both the rook on a7 and the pawn on
f7. 23...c5 (23...♖a8 24.♘h4 ♘xe5 25.♘f5
♔h8 26.♘xe7 ♕xe7 27.♖ad1±) 24.♘h4!
♘xe5 (24...♖xe5 25.♖xe5 ♘xe5 26.♖e1+−)
25.♘f5 ♗c8 26.♘xe7† ♖xe7 27.♖ad1±

23...fxe6

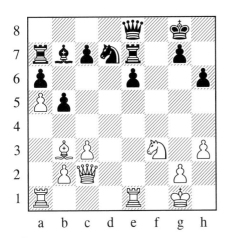

24.♕f5?!

24.♘d4 looks stronger, as the knight could become dangerous on e6. 24...♔h8 (24...♘f8 25.♖e5 ♗c8 26.♖ae1 gives White a strong initiative) 25.♘xe6 ♘c5 26.♖e5 ♘xe6 27.♖ae1 ♗c8 28.♕e4 c5 29.♗xe6 ♗xe6 30.♖xe6 ♖xe6 31.♕xe6 ♕xe6 32.♖xe6 White has a pleasant endgame advantage due to the passive rook on a7.

24...♔h8 25.♖xe6 ♖xe6 26.♗xe6 ♘f6

After some inaccurate moves, Grischuk has almost lost his advantage.

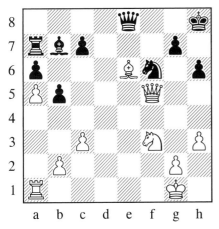

27.♘d4 ♗e4 28.♕e5 ♕g6 29.g4 ♖a8

Black needs to bring his rook back into the game; the fate of the c7-pawn is irrelevant.

30.♖f1 ♖e8

After 30...c6 31.♗f7 ♕xf7 32.♖xe4 ♖c8 33.♕e5 White is slightly better.

31.♕xc7 ♕g5 32.♕f4 ♕c5

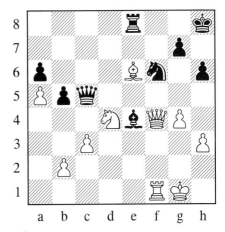

33.♔h2?!

33.♗f7!? would have given more chances for an advantage: 33...♖f8 34.♗b3 b4 35.♕e3 bxc3 36.♕xc3 (after 36.bxc3 ♗a8 Black has good compensation for the pawn) 36...♕a7 37.♕e3 ♕c5 38.h4 ♗h7 39.♘f5 ♕c7 40.♕e7 ♕xe7 41.♘xe7 ♖b8 42.♗c4 ♖xb2 43.♖f4 The position is close to equal, but Black still needs to take great care due to his vulnerable king.

33...b4!

A good move, simplifying the position and weakening White's queenside structure. By now Black is almost out of the woods.

34.♗f7 ♖c8 35.♘e6 ♕e7 36.g5 ♕xf7 37.♕xe4 ♘xe4?!

Not the best move. Objectively Black is still okay, but he will have to be more careful now.

Best was: 37...hxg5 38.cxb4 (38.♘xg5 ♘xe4 39.♘xf7† ♔g8 40.♖f4 bxc3 41.bxc3 ♖xc3 42.♖xe4 ♔xf7=) 38...♕e7 39.♕e5 ♖e8 40.♖e1 ♕xb4

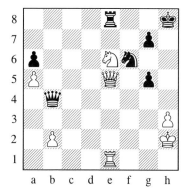

Black still has some weakness, but nevertheless it should be easy for him to make a draw.

38.罝xf7 ⊘xg5 39.罝c7!

A strong move just before the time control! Now Black has to make an important decision with little time remaining.

39.罝e7 bxc3 40.bxc3 ⊘xe6 41.罝xe6 罝xc3 42.罝xa6 罝a3= is a simple draw.

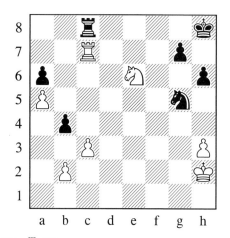

39...罝e8??

A terrible blunder from Shirov, who was presumably in zeitnot. The ensuing rook endgame is a fairly easy win for White.

Black has to go for the knight endgame if he is to survive: 39...罝xc7 40.⊘xc7 ⊘f3† 41.當g3 bxc3 42.bxc3 ⊘d2 43.⊘xa6 ⊘b3! It is crucial

that Black eliminates the a-pawn and leaves the c-pawn, which will be easier for him to stop. 44.當f4 ⊘xa5 45.當e5 當h7 46.⊘c5 當g6 Black has excellent chances to draw this endgame.

40.⊘xg5 hxg5 41.cxb4 罝e2† 42.當g3 罝xb2 43.罝b7+−

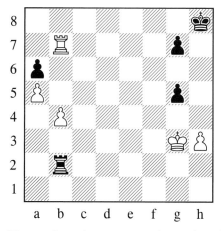

This rook endgame is just lost. The white king will arrive on the queenside, the rook will take the a6-pawn, and the connected passed pawns will be unstoppable.

43...當h7 44.當g4 當h6 45.當f5 罝f2†

45...罝b3 46.罝b8 罝f3† 47.當e4 罝b3 48.當d5 當g6 49.罝b6† 當f5 50.當c4 罝xh3 51.罝xa6 g4 52.罝d6

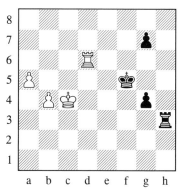

52...罝a3 53.a6 g3 54.當b5 g2 55.罝d1 當g4

56.♔b6 ♔g3 57.a7 ♔f2 58.♔b7 g1=♕ 59.♖xg1 ♔xg1 60.a8=♕ ♖xa8 61.♔xa8 g5 62.b5 g4 63.b6 g3 64.b7 g2 65.b8=♕+− The endgame with queen against a pawn on the knight's file is a trivial win.

46.♔e5 ♖f4 47.♔d5

The king continues his 'walk' to the queenside.

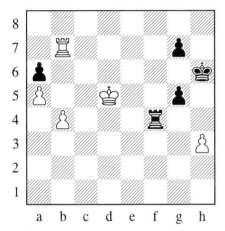

47...♔h5

47...♖h4 also fails to save the game: 48.♔c5 ♖xh3 49.♖b6† ♔h5 50.♖xa6 ♖c3† 51.♔b5 g4 52.♖a7 g6 53.♖h7† ♔g5 54.a6 g3 55.♖h1 ♔f4 56.a7 ♖c8 57.♔a6 g5 58.b5+−

48.♔c5 ♔h4 49.♖xg7 ♖f5† 50.♔b6 ♖f6† 51.♔a7

1–0

Black resigned as he has no defence against ♖b7 and ♖b6, winning easily.

GAME 21

▷ **F. Caruana (2712)**
▶ **D. Jakovenko (2716)**
12th Karpov International, Poikovsky
Round 1, 04.10.2011 **[C84]**
Annotated by Borki Predojevic

The early 6.d3 is an interesting way to start a fight in the Ruy Lopez. In the following game Black chose the line with 8...♗d7, which is a very solid answer. White decided to play a typical plan with the manoeuvre ♘b1-d2-f1-e3 to fight for the d5-square. Black's novelty was 16...b4N but I don't like it. The simple 16...♗e6 is the main line and should be okay for Black.

Caruana found a very nice line for White and after 22.♗c4! he had the advantage. In mutual time trouble both players made inaccuracies, but the final mistake was 44...♖b3?. Just two moves later, Black resigned.

1.e4 e5 2.♘f3 ♘c6 3.♗b5 a6 4.♗a4 ♘f6 5.0–0 ♗e7

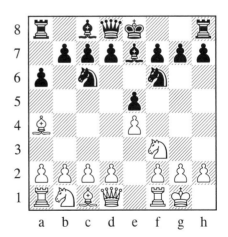

6.d3!?

This is a very dangerous side line in the Ruy Lopez. All the main analysts of *Chess Evolution* who play 1.e4 have successfully played this line with the white pieces.

6...b5 7.♗b3 d6 8.a4 ♗d7

After 8...♗g4 9.c3 0–0 10.h3 ♗d7 11.♘bd2 ♘a5 12.♗c2 c5 13.♖e1 ♖e8 14.♘f1 White would have a tempo more and the possibility of playing ♘h2 faster than in the game, so this line should be good for White.

8...b4 is another possibility for Black which was recently played by Aronian.

9.c3

The main alternative is:
9.♗d2

This was a problem for Black a few years ago, but then a strong reply was found:
9...b4!

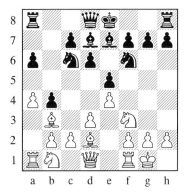

Still, the position is complicated and here we will see some fresh examples:
10.a5

In my opinion, this move is obligatory.
If White tries to omit a4-a5 by playing 10.c3 0–0 11.♖e1 ♖b8 12.♗c4 ♕c8, after 13.d4 Black has a strong answer: 13...♘a5! 14.♗f1 c5! 15.cxb4 (15.dxe5 dxe5 16.♘xe5 ♗e6⊟) 15...cxb4 16.♗g5 h6 17.♗h4 exd4 18.♘bd2 g5 19.e5 gxh4 20.exf6 ♗xf6 21.♘e4 ♗g7 22.♘xh4 ♕d8∓ Navara – Aronian, Khanty-Mansiysk (ol) 2010.
10...0–0 11.c3 ♖b8 12.h3
12.♗c4 ♕c8 13.♖e1 ♗e6 14.♕a4 ♗xc4 15.dxc4 ♕b7= Saltaev – Michalczak, Dortmund 2011.

12...♕c8 13.♖e1

In the following game White gained an advantage, but Black could have played better:

13...bxc3 14.bxc3 ♗e6 15.♗xe6 ♕xe6 16.♕a4 d5 17.exd5

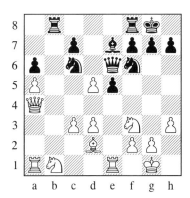

17...♕xd5
17...♘xd5∞
18.c4 ♕d6 19.♘c3 ♘b4
19...♖fe8!?⇄
20.c5 ♕xc5 21.♖xe5 ♕d6 22.♖ae1 ♗d8 23.d4 ♘d3 24.♖1e3 ♖b4 25.♕a1! ♘xe5 26.dxe5 ♕c6 27.exf6 ♗xf6 28.♕e1±
Naiditsch – Sanikidze, France 2011.

9...0–0

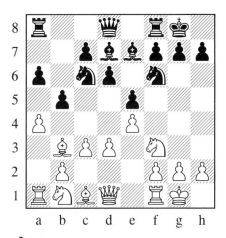

10.♘bd2

In the recent European Club Cup White

tried an idea with 10.♗a2, but after 10...h6 11.h3 ♖e8 12.♖e1 ♗f8 13.♘bd2 ♘e7 14.♘f1 ♘g6 15.♘3h2 ♗e6! 16.♗xe6 ♖xe6 17.♘g4 d5 18.♘xf6† ♖xf6 19.exd5= Black was okay and a draw was agreed in Svidler – Adams, ECC 2011.

10...♘a5 11.♗c2 c5 12.♖e1 ♖e8

On 12...♕c7 White can continue with the normal 13.♘f1↑ with the same plan as in the game. Usually Black plays ...♕c7 to support the e5-pawn if it is under attack, but this move would not make so much sense now.

13.♘f1 h6

13...♗f8 would give White the chance for 14.♗g5± which is a typical idea in the Ruy Lopez with d2-d3: the main idea is to fight for the d5-square.

14.♘e3 ♗f8

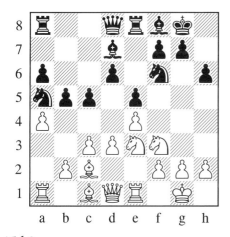

15.h3

Less strong is 15.♗d2. After 15...♕b6 (15...♘c6 16.axb5 axb5 17.♖xa8 ♕xa8 18.♘h4 ♕d8 19.♕f3 ♗e6 20.♘d5 ♘h7 21.♘f5 ♘e7 22.♖a1 ♘xd5 23.exd5 ♗xf5 24.♕xf5± Arakhamia-Grant – Qin Kanying, New Delhi 2000) 16.b4 cxb4 17.cxb4 ♘c6 18.♗b3= a draw was agreed in Nunn – Lein, Hastings 1979.

White can play ♗d2 at any point if required, and the move played in the game is more to the point; White prepares the typical manoeuvre ♘f3-h2-g4.

15...♘c6

Black can immediately play 15...g6!? which is an important alternative. After the normal 16.♘h2 ♗e6 17.axb5 axb5 18.♘hg4 h5 19.♘xf6† ♕xf6 20.♗d2 ♘c6 21.♖xa8 ♖xa8= the position was equal in P. Jaracz – Ibragimov, Biel 1997.

15...♗c6?! is certainly dubious. After 16.b4 ♘b7 17.♗b3 ♖c8 18.♗d2 g6 19.axb5 axb5 20.♖a6± White was clearly better in Xu Tong – Shen Yang, Beijing 2008.

16.♘h2

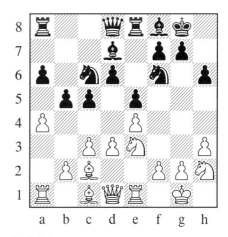

16...b4N

This is a novelty, but I prefer the old move as 16...b4 is premature. It would be very interesting to see what Caruana had prepared in the main line:

16...♗e6

Now White has two main options: A) 17.♘hg4 and B) 17.♕f3.

A) 17.♘hg4 ♘xg4

On 17...♘d7 White can play: 18.♘d5!?N
(18.axb5 axb5 19.♖xa8 ♕xa8 20.♘d5 ♕b7
[20...♗xd5? 21.exd5 ♘e7 22.♘xh6† gxh6
23.♕g4† ♘g6 24.♕xd7+– Dutreeuw –
P. Nikolic, Belgium 2009] 21.♘ge3 ♖a8⇄)
With the idea: 18...♘b6 19.♗xh6! ♗xd5
(19...gxh6 20.♘gf6† ♔h8 21.♘xe8 ♗xd5
22.exd5 ♗xd5 23.axb5+–) 20.exd5 ♗xd5
21.d4!↑ With the better prospects for White.
18.hxg4

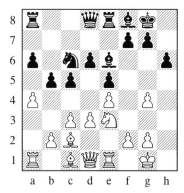

18...♗e7!
    It is also very hard to claim any advantage
after 18...b4. We shall see more of this
position below in the note to Black's 18th
move of the game.
19.♘d5 b4 20.a5 bxc3 21.bxc3 ♘xa5 22.♗a4
♖f8 23.c4 ♗g5 24.♗d2 ♗xd2 25.♕xd2 ♖c8
26.♖eb1 ♘c6 27.♗xc6 ♖xc6 28.♖b7=
    Zhao Jun – Peng Xiaomin, HeiBei 2001.

B) 17.♕f3
    This looks more interesting than the
17.♘hg4 line above.

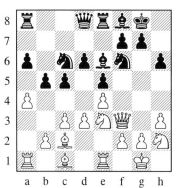

Now there are four moves to consider:
B1) 17...♔h7, B2) 17...♕a5, B3) 17...b4 and
B4) 17...♘e7.

B1) 17...♔h7 is not a natural move. After
18.♘d5 ♖c8 19.♘xf6† ♖xf6 20.♕xf6 gxf6
21.♘g4 ♗g7 22.axb5 axb5 23.♖a6 f5 24.exf5
♗xf5 25.♘e3 ♗g6 26.♖b6 ♘d4 27.♗d1 ♖c6
28.♖b7 ♘e6 29.♗f3 ♖cc8 30.♗e4± White was
dominating in Ryskin – Aleksandrov, Minsk
1987.

B2) The computer moves 17...♕a5 18.♖e2
b4 should lead to a slightly worse position for
Black after 19.♗d2±. The benefits of 17...♕a5
compared to 17...b4 are invisible.

B3) 17...b4

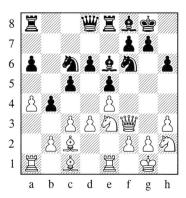

White can now play the typical move:
18.♘d5!?N
    18.g4?! looks suspicious: 18...d5 19.♘f5
And now in Wang – Kashlinskaya, Moscow
2010, Black missed a strong idea: 19...c4!
20.dxc4 dxe4 21.♗xe4 ♘xe4 22.♖xe4 bxc3
23.♕xc3 (23.bxc3 ♕c7∓) 23...♕d1† 24.♖e1
♕d7↑
    18.♘hg4 ♘xg4 19.hxg4 ♗e7= Of course
Black plans ...♗g5.
18...♗xd5 19.exd5 ♘e7 20.♗xh6
    The computer suggests 20.c4!? which is also
very interesting. White has two main threats:
♗xh6 and a4-a5 with the idea ♗a4. The

best answer is 20...♘d7! and after 21.a5 g6 22.♗a4 ♘f5⇄ Black's position is acceptable.

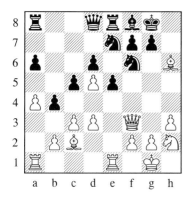

20...bxc3 21.bxc3 ♖b8

21...gxh6 22.♕xf6 ♘d5 23.♕f3 ♘f4 24.d4 cxd4 25.cxd4↑ must be worse for Black.

22.♗g5 ♘exd5 23.♘g4 ♗e7

23...♖b2 24.♗b1↑

24.♘xf6† ♗xf6 25.♕xd5 ♗xg5 26.♗b3 ♖e7 27.♖e2 ♖eb7 28.♗c4±

B4) 17...♘e7

In my opinion this is Black's most logical answer.

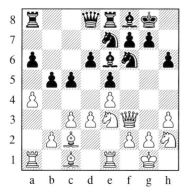

In reply the natural move is:
18.♘hg4N

18.h4 has been tested: 18...♕d7 19.♗d2 d5 20.exd5 ♘exd5 21.♘ef1 ♗d6 22.axb5 axb5 23.♖xa8 ♖xa8 24.c4 bxc4 25.dxc4 ♘b6 26.b3∞ Black was okay in Ye Jiangchuan – L.B. Hansen, Moscow (ol) 1994.

18.♗d2 ♕d7 19.♖a3!?∞ looks interesting.
18...♘xg4

18...♘d7 19.♘f5 ♘g6 20.♗d2± with possible ideas of g3 and h4.

19.hxg4 ♕d7 20.♕g3 ♘g6∞

The position is unclear.

My conclusion is that 16...♗e6 at least gives Black an easier position to play than in the main game.

17.♘hg4 ♘xg4 18.hxg4

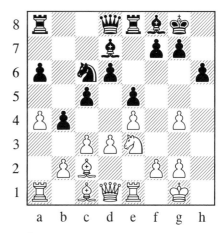

18...♗e7

Jakovenko is planning ...♗g5.

More natural was:
18...♗e6

This transposes to a sub-line of line A of the 16...♗e6 variation.

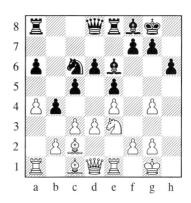

We can study this position more:

19.♗b3

19.♕f3 ♖b8 20.♗d2 ♗e7 The bishop comes
to g5 with good counterplay for Black. For
example: 21.g3 ♗g5 22.♕e2 bxc3 23.bxc3
♘a5 24.♖eb1 ♗b3 25.♕d1 ♗xe3 26.♗xe3
♗xc2 27.♕xc2 ♕d7 28.♖xb8 ♖xb8 29.♖b1
♖xb1† 30.♕xb1 ♕b7 31.♕xb7 ♘xb7= The
endgame was equal in N. Kosintseva – Shen
Yang, Nalchik 2008.

19...♘a5

19...bxc3 20.bxc3 ♘a5 21.♗d5 ♖b8 22.♗d2
♕d7 23.♕c2 ♗e7 24.♖ab1 g6 25.c4
♕c7 26.g3 ♘c6 27.♗xc6 ♕xc6 28.♗g2
♕d7 29.f3 ♗g5⇄ Emms – L.B. Hansen,
Copenhagen 1995.

Another alternative for Black is 19...♖b8
20.♗d5 ♕d7, when White has the interesting
idea 21.♗xc6!? ♕xc6 22.c4∞ and next ♘f5.
The final position should not be better for
White, but in practice Black will have more
problems finding a good plan.

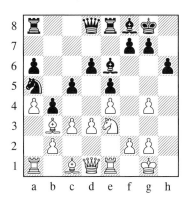

20.♗xe6!N fxe6 21.cxb4 cxb4 22.♘c4 ♘c6
22...♘xc4 23.dxc4±

23.a5 ♖b8

And now the best chance of fighting for an
advantage is:

24.g5!

24.♗e3 ♖b5 25.♕a4 d5 26.♖ec1 ♗c5
27.♗xc5 dxc4 28.♖xc4 ♖xa5 29.♕d1 ♖xa1
30.♕xa1 ♕xd3 31.♕xa6=

Now there is a forced line:

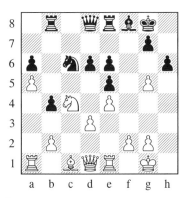

24...d5!

24...hxg5 25.♕g4 ♘d4 26.♗xg5 ♕c7
27.♖ad1 ♘b3 28.♖e3→

25.exd5 exd5 26.♘b6 ♘xa5 27.♖xa5 ♖xb6
28.gxh6 ♖xh6 29.♗xh6 ♕xa5 30.♗f4 ♕b6
31.♗xe5±↑

White retains the better chances since he
is dominating the centre, while Black has
problems with his king.

19.♗b3 ♗e6 20.♗d5 ♖c8

If 20...♗xd5 then White can play directly:
21.exd5! ♘a5 22.cxb4 cxb4 23.♘f5±↑ With
very good chances of building a serious
advantage. Possible plans include attacking the
b4-pawn with ♗d2 or breaking in the centre
with d3-d4.

21.♘f5 ♗g5

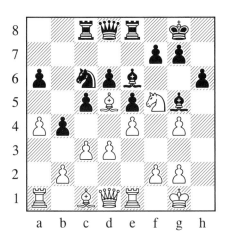

22.&c4!±

A very deep idea by Caruana. He doesn't want to exchange bishops on e6 or g5. Black is more or less obliged to take on c4, but then White has pressure on d6. Instead after 22.&xg5 hxg5⇄ Black could use the h-file for his heavy pieces.

22...&xc4 23.dxc4 &e6 24.&xg5 ♛xg5 25.♖e3!

A useful move; by putting the rook on the third rank White prepares to increase the pressure with ♖d3 or possibly create an attack with ♖h3.

25...♖d8 26.♖d3 &h7?!

An imprecise move. 26...♖g6 was stronger, but of course Black is still struggling. White replies 27.♛d2! and the endgame after 27...♛xd2 28.♖xd2 bxc3 29.bxc3 ♖xg4 (29...♘a5 30.♘e7†±) 30.♖xd6 ♖xd6 31.♘xd6 ♘a5 32.♖b1↑ is better for White.

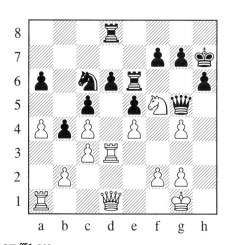

27.♖h3?!

Too positional. I do not understand why Caruana didn't take pawn with 27.♘xd6!. After 27...♖f6 28.f3 h5 29.gxh5 ♛xh5 30.♘f5± White is clearly on top.

27...♖b8 28.♛e2 ♖g6 29.♘e3 ♘e7 30.♖d1±

Even without taking the d6-pawn, White

is still better. Black has to be very careful and patient in order to hold this position.

30...a5 31.♖h5 ♛f6 32.♘f5! bxc3 33.bxc3 ♖b6 34.g3 &g8

34...♖g5 35.♖h1↑

35.&g2

Suddenly, Black has problems with his pieces on the kingside. His g6-rook is out of play, while White's rook on h5 can always go back to h1 and prepare to attack on the queenside. Positionally, this is an unpleasant situation for Black.

35...♛e6

Again 35...♖g5 is met by 36.♖hh1↑ and Black's problems are similar to the game.

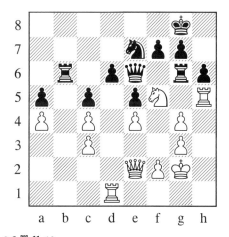

36.♖dh1?

Better was 36.♖hh1! and then ♖b1 will gain a big advantage. For example, 36...♛d7 37.♖b1 ♖xb1 38.♖xb1 &h7 39.♖b5 ♘c6 40.f3± looks very nice for White.

36...♖b3

Now Black could try 36...♛d7 with the idea of bringing the g6-rook back into the game. Breaking with 37.g5? does not work, as Black has 37...♘xf5 38.exf5 ♖xg5 39.♖xg5 hxg5 40.♛h5 ♛c6†!∓.

37.♕f3 ♖g5 38.♖5h2

38.♖xg5 hxg5 39.♕d3 ♘xf5 40.gxf5 ♕e7 41.♖b1 ♖xb1 42.♕xb1 ♔h7 43.♕b6 is not dangerous for Black. He can play 43...g4! when White cannot improve his position since 44.♕xa5 is met by 44...♕b7!=.

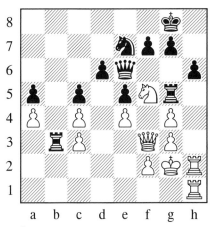

38...♘xf5?!

This was certainly not forced and was not Black's best choice. After 38...♖b2⇄ it would be very hard to improve White's position.

39.exf5 e4

39...♕c8 40.♖d1 ♕b8 41.♖hh1↑ would give White decent chances since the rook on g5 is still out of the game.

40.♕f4 ♕e7 41.♖e1

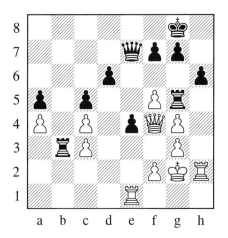

41...♖xc3

41...♔h7 42.♖xe4 ♕b7 43.♔h3 ♖xc3 44.♖e3 ♖c2⇄ was another option for Black.

42.♖xe4 ♕b7 43.♔h3 f6 44.♖e3 ♖b3??

The final mistake. After Black had survived all the unpleasant pressure, he made a huge blunder. The only move was 44...h5!

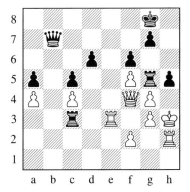

when after 45.f3 ♖xe3 46.♕xe3 hxg4† 47.fxg4 g6! White cannot improve his position. After 48.♕e6† ♔g7 49.♖b2 ♕xb2 50.♕e7†= the game would end in a draw.

45.♖xb3 ♕xb3 46.♕e4!

Black resigned since he cannot avoid f2-f4. For example: 46...h5 47.♕e8† ♔h7 48.f4+–

1–0

D

GAME 22

▷ **S. Mamedyarov (2746)**

▶ **E. Inarkiev (2692)**

European Club Cup, Rogaska Slatina

30.09.2011 **[D11]**

Annotated by Sebastian Maze

In the fashionable 4.♕c2 line of the Slav, Inarkiev played an interesting novelty with 13...♖fe8N which gave Black an equal position. After some logical moves the Russian player chose the wrong plan with 21...♖d6; the simple 21...♘e6 would have led to a solid position. Later Black blundered with 27...♕a5 allowing Mamedyarov to increase his advantage with a beautiful punch. Finally, he won easily in a rook endgame.

1.d4 d5 2.c4 c6 3.♘f3 ♘f6 4.♕c2

Mamedyarov is the world's leading expert on this line, having played it almost twenty times just in the last two years! In fact, this move is now frequently played at a high level because there is not a lot of theory and it can lead to many interesting positions.

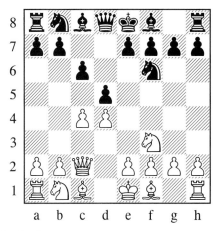

4...dxc4

4...g6 is also a popular line.

5.♕xc4 ♗g4

5...♗f5 is the main line of this variation.

6.♘c3

6...♘bd2 is an alternative with the idea of avoiding a bad pawn structure after ...♗xf3.

6...♘bd7 7.e4 ♗xf3 8.gxf3

White has a big centre and his plan is quite simple: hide his king by castling long and create pressure along the g-file with his rooks.

8...e5 9.♗e3 exd4 10.♗xd4 ♗d6 11.0–0–0 ♕c7 12.♘e2 0–0 13.♕c2

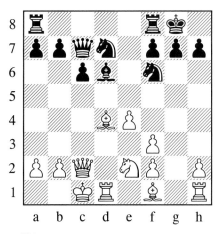

13...♖fe8N

Gelfand tried 13...b5?! against Ponomariov in 2009. As Black I would prefer not to touch anything on the queenside, because now the c6-pawn will be weak and later if Black plays ...c5 then the d5-square will be excellent for White. 14.♔b1 ♖fe8 15.♗h3 c5 16.♗e3 and White is slightly better; the pair of bishops are strong and in fact all White's pieces are well placed.

13...♖ad8 is a playable alternative. For example, Khismatullin – Potkin, Moscow 2010, continued: 14.♔b1 ♖fe8 15.♗h3 ♘h5 16.♘g3 ♘df6 17.♗g4 ♗e5∞

14.h4

A logical move with the idea of developing the f1-bishop on h3. Instead after 14.♘g3?! c5

15.♗c3 ♖ad8 16.♘f5 ♗f4† 17.♔b1 g6 18.♘e3 ♘e5 Black has no problems.

14...♘h5 15.♗h3 ♖ad8 16.♔b1 ♘f8

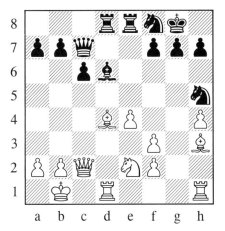

17.♗e3

A couple of other moves are worth a look:

17.♗g4 ♘f4 18.♘xf4 ♗xf4 19.h5 h6 20.♖hg1 ♗h2 21.♖ge1 ♗e5 22.♗e3 ♘e6=

17.♕c3?! c5 18.♗e3 ♘g6 19.♗f5 b6 and ...♗e5 is coming, giving Black a pleasant position.

17...♗e5= 18.♖dg1

Since the novelty on move 13, all the moves from both sides have looked normal.

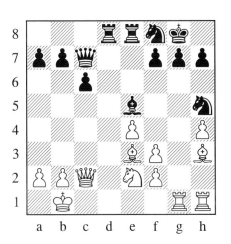

18...♘f4

18...♘g6 was also reasonable. Honestly, the position looks equal to me, and it's difficult to see how an attack against the black king could be possible. For example: 19.♗g5 ♗f6 20.♗f5 ♕e5 21.♗xf6 ♘xf6 22.h5 ♘e7 23.♖g5 ♘xf5 24.♖xf5 ♕d6 25.♖g1 ♗e5 26.♖xe5 ♕xe5 27.h6 g6 28.♖d1 ♖d6=

19.♘xf4 ♗xf4 20.h5 ♕e5

20...♗xe3 was also playable. 21.fxe3 ♕d6 22.♕g2 g6 23.hxg6 fxg6 24.♕f2

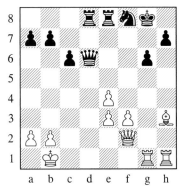

24...a5 (24...♕d2? 25.♖h4 ♕xe3 26.♗e6† ♘xe6 27.♕xh7† ♔f8 28.♕xg6 and Black is in trouble!) 25.♗f5 a4 26.a3 ♖e7∞ With a complicated position, but White has no real threats and all the black pieces are well placed.

21.♗f5 ♖d6?

This move looks logical, with the idea of doubling rooks on the d-file, but the reality is different. In my opinion, it's a strategic mistake because after the next few forced moves White will create strong pressure on the g-file and Black has no time to create play with his rooks.

21...♘e6
It was better to activate the knight.
22.♖g4 ♗xe3 23.fxe3 ♕c5 24.♔b3 ♕b5

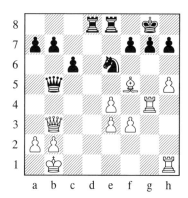

25.♕xb5

25.♗xe6 fxe6 26.♕xb5 cxb5 27.♖c1 ♖d7 28.e5 ♖f8 29.f4 ♖d3=

25...cxb5 26.f4 ♘c5 27.e5 ♖d2 28.♖hg1 g6 29.hxg6 hxg6 30.♗c2

30.♗xg6 fxg6 31.♖xg6† ♔f7 32.♖f6† ♔e7 and Black is fine.

30...♔f8 31.♖h4 a5 32.♖h8† ♔e7 33.♖h7 ♔f8 34.♖c1 b6=

22.♖g4 ♗xe3 23.fxe3 ♖ed8 24.f4±

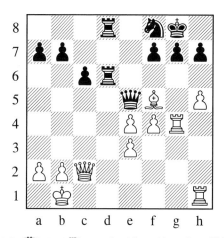

24...♕b5 25.♖hg1 g6 26.hxg6 hxg6 27.♖4g2 ♕a5?

What a weird choice by Inarkiev. When a player like Mamedyarov is attacking you, I think the best choice is to exchange queens: 27...♕d3 was the only move! 28.e5 ♕d1† 29.♖xd1 ♖xd1† 30.♕xd1 ♖xd1† 31.♔c2 Generally, the combination of rook and

bishop is better than rook and knight. And in this endgame, it is true, the position is open (good for the bishop) and many black pawns, such as b7 and f7, could become targets.

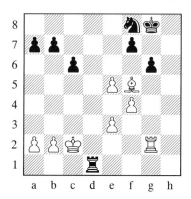

31...♖e1 32.♔d3 ♖d1† 33.♔e4 ♖d8 But with accurate defence, I would say that Black has good chances to hold the draw.

28.e5± ♖d2

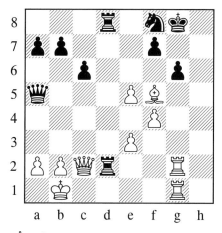

29.♗xg6!

A strong sacrifice which destroys the black king's defences. Inarkiev missed this idea when he played 27...♕a5.

29...♘xg6

Of course we must see what happens if Black takes the queen:
29...♖xc2 30.♗h7†!!

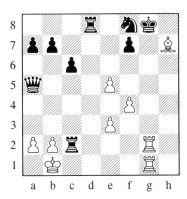

The point.

30...♔h8

30...♔xh7?? 31.♖h1# is a beautiful checkmate.

31.♗xc2

White's queen is gone, but the activity of the rooks and the weak king on h8 gives huge compensation.

31...♘g6 32.e6 ♖d2

32...fxe6 33.♖xg6 ♕h5 34.♖6g5 ♕f3 (or 34...♕h3 35.♗e4+– winning the queen) 35.a3 a5 36.♖g7 ♕h5 37.♖xb7+–

33.♖g5 ♕b4 34.exf7 ♖xc2

34...♔g7 35.a3 ♕b6 36.♖f5 ♖d8 37.♖h5 ♔xf7 38.♖xg6 ♖d2 39.♖h7† ♔f8 40.♖f6† ♔g8 41.♖ff7+–

35.♔xc2 ♔g7 36.♖xg6† ♔xf7 37.♖6g5 ♕e4† 38.♔d2 ♕b4† 39.♔c1 ♕c4† 40.♔b1 ♕d3† 41.♔a1±

30.♖xg6† ♔f8 31.♖g8† ♔e7 32.♕b3

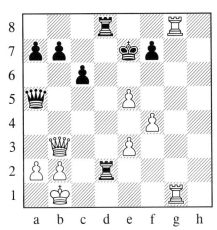

32...♖8d7?

32...♕d5 was the last chance to stay alive. 33.♕a3† c5 34.♖xd8 ♔xd8 35.♔c1 An important move, controlling the d1-square and also the king is safe now. 35...♔e7 36.♕a4 ♖d3 37.♔d1 ♔f8 38.♕c2 ♖xd1† 39.♕xd1 ♕c4† 40.♕c2 ♕f1† 41.♔d2 ♕f2† 42.♔d3 ♕f1† 43.♔c3± White is a pawn up in this queen endgame.

33.e4!

This move ends the fight because now the d5- and f5-squares are controlled by the white pawn and e5-e6 is coming. Of course the immediate 33.e6? was premature: 33...♕f5† 34.♔c1 ♕xe6=

33...♕c5

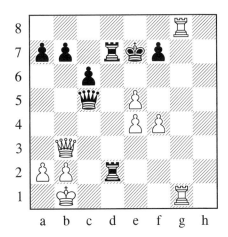

34.e6! ♖7d3

Of course not 34...fxe6?? 35.♖1g7† ♔d6 36.♖xd7† ♔xd7 37.♕xb7† ♔d6 38.♖d8#.

35.♕xb7† ♖d7 36.♕b3

In time trouble, it is always a good idea to repeat moves when you are winning. It helps avoid lines such as: 36.exd7?? ♕c2† 37.♔a1 ♕d1† 38.♖xd1 ♖xd1#

36...♖7d3 37.exf7 ♕xg1† 38.♖xg1 ♖xb3 39.axb3+–

After some exchanges, Mamedyarov reaches a rook endgame with two extra pawns.

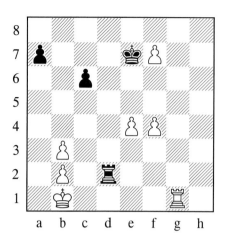

39...♖d4 40.♖g6 ♔xf7

Or 40...♖xe4 41.♖xc6 ♔xf7 (41...♖xf4 42.♖c7† ♔f8 43.♖xa7 is winning easily) 42.♖c4 and it is the same endgame as in the game.

41.♖xc6 ♖xe4 42.♖c4

This endgame is completely winning for White, as he is two pawns up and the black king is cut off. The plan for White is very simple – activate his king on the queenside!

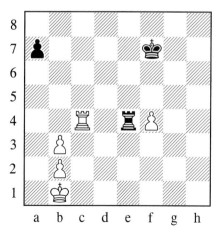

42...♖e1† 43.♔c2 ♔f6 44.b4 ♔e6 45.b5 ♖e3 46.b3 ♖f3 47.♔b2 ♔f5 48.♔a3 ♖xf4

49.♖xf4† ♔xf4 50.♔b4 ♔e4 51.♔c4 ♔e3 52.b4 ♔d2 53.b6

A nice finesse after which the Azeri player forces resignation.

53...axb6 54.b5
1–0

GAME 23
▷ **Le Quang Liem (2717)**
▶ **L. Dominguez (2710)**
5th SPICE Cup, Lubbock
Round 10, 25.10.2011 **[D16]**
Annotated by David Baramidze

This game was played in the last round of the SPICE Cup. Dominguez was leading and Le Quang Liem needed to win to finish ahead of him. In a sharp line of the Slav White surprised his opponent with 16.♖fd1N!?. After the weak 17....♘e4?! Le Quang missed a chance to obtain the advantage with 18.♘d5!. Black was better, but he missed the strong 21...♖f8! and the position became equal. Then Dominguez made a terrible blunder with 26....♗f5? which allowed Le Quang Liem to win the game, and with it the tournament.

1.d4 d5 2.♘f3 ♘f6 3.c4 c6 4.♘c3 dxc4 5.a4 e6 6.e4!?

Needing to win, White chooses an aggressive option. The normal move is 6.e3, when 6...c5 7.♗xc4 ♘c6 reaches a Queen's Gambit Accepted in which the move a2-a4 has been played 'for free', which brings certain advantages for both sides.

6...♗b4 7.♗g5 ♕a5

The main alternative is 7...♗xc3† 8.bxc3 ♕a5 9.e5 ♘e4 10.♗d2 ♕d5.

8.♗d2

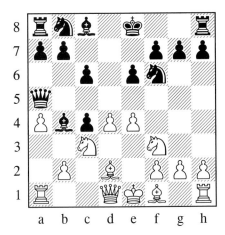

8...c5

This is the most logical move. Black wants to destroy his opponent's strong centre.

8...♘bd7?!

This is too passive.

9.♗xc4 0–0 10.e5

10.0–0?! allows Black to free himself with 10...e5!.

10...♘d5

From here White has more than one route to a better position.

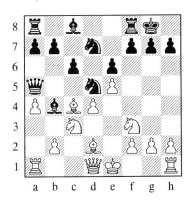

11.♖c1

11.0–0!? ♘xc3 12.bxc3 ♗xc3 13.♗xc3 ♕xc3 14.♗d3± gives White fine compensation for the pawn. Black is underdeveloped and his bishop is a particular problem. White will try to prevent ...c5 for as long as possible, and will also look to bring his knight to a

more threatening position.

11.♕c2 is also promising: 11...c5 12.0–0 ♘5b6 (12...♘e7?! 13.d5 exd5 14.♗xd5 ♘xd5 15.♘xd5 ♗xd2 16.♖fd1!↑) 13.♗d3 h6 (13...cxd4? 14.♗xh7† ♔h8 15.♕e4+–)

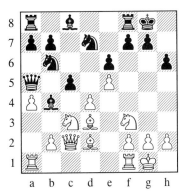

14.♘b5! (After 14.♘e4 ♘d5 [14...♗xd2 15.♘exd2 cxd4 16.♘b3 ♕b4 17.♖fd1±] 15.dxc5 ♗xd2 16.♘fxd2 ♘xe5 17.♘c4 ♘xc4 18.♕xc4 b6 Black can breathe again and should be able to equalize.) 14...♗xd2 15.♘xd2 cxd4 16.♖fe1±

11...♘e7

11...f6 12.exf6 ♘7xf6 13.0–0±

11...c5 12.♘xd5 exd5 13.♗xd5 cxd4 14.♗xb4 ♕xb4† 15.♕d2 ♕xa4? Too risky. (Black should settle for a slight disadvantage with 15...♕xd2† 16.♔xd2±) 16.0–0 ♘b6 17.♗e4

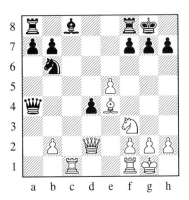

Black has problems, for instance: 17...♗g4 18.♘g5 h6 19.♘h7 ♘c4 (19...♖fc8 20.♘f6†

gxf6 21.exf6 ♖xc1 22.♖xc1 ♖c8 23.♖e1+–)
20.♘f6† ♔h8 (20...gxf6 21.♖xc4 ♕xc4
22.exf6+–) 21.♖xc4 ♕xc4 22.♘xg4+–

12.♗d3

12.0–0 c5 13.dxc5 (13.d5 exd5 14.♘xd5
♘xd5 15.♗xd5 ♗xd2 16.♘xd2 ♘xe5=)
13...♘xc5 14.♗g5 ♘g6 15.♘a2 h6 16.♗e3
♖d8 17.♕c2 ♗d7 18.♗xb4 ♕xb4 19.♗xc5
♕xc5 20.♕xg6 fxg6 21.♗xe6† ♗xe6 22.♖xc5
♖ac8⩲

12...h6

12...c5? 13.♗xh7† ♔xh7 14.♘g5† ♔g6
15.♕g4 f6 16.♘xe6† ♔f7 17.0–0+–

13.0–0 c5 14.♘b5

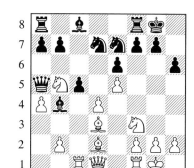

14...a6

14...♗xd2?! 15.♘xd2 cxd4 (15...a6 16.♘b3
♕xa4 17.♘d6±) 16.♘b3 ♕xa4 (16...♕d8
17.♕e2±) 17.♘c7 ♖b8 18.♗b5 ♕a2 19.♕c2
♘c6 20.♖a1 ♘b4 21.♕c4 ♕xb2 22.♕xb4±
15.♘d6 ♗xd2

15...cxd4 16.♘c4 ♕c5 17.♖e1↑

16.♘xd2 cxd4 17.♘2c4 ♕b4 18.♗e4↑ White
is better, thanks to the powerful knight.

9.♗xc4

In another recent game White preferred:
9.dxc5 ♘c6
After 9...♕xc5 10.e5 ♗xc3 11.♗xc3 ♘e4
12.♕d4 ♕xd4 13.♗xd4 ♘c6 (13...c3
14.♗d3↑) 14.♗xc4 ♘xd4 15.♘xd4 ♗d7
16.♔e2 ♔e7 17.♖hc1 ♖hc8 18.♗e3 ♘c5
19.a5 White has a pleasant position.

10.♗xc4 ♕xc5 11.♕e2 e5

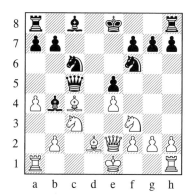

Now it is worth considering a) 12.♗e3 and
b) 12.0–0N.

a) 12.♗e3

This was White's choice in Pelletier – Shirov,
Biel 2011.

12...♘d4!N

This is a more convincing equalizer than
Shirov's 12...♕e7.

13.♗b5†

13.♖c1?! ♗e6 14.♗b5† (14.♗xe6? ♘xe2∓)
14...♕xb5↑

13.♕d3 ♘c2† 14.♕xc2 ♕xc4=

13.♔f1 0–0 (13...♘xe2 14.♗xc5 ♗xc5
15.♔xe2 ♗g4=) 14.♕d3 ♗e6 15.♗xe6 fxe6
16.♘xd4 exd4 17.♗xd4 ♕e7 18.f3 ♖ad8↑

13...♕xb5 14.axb5 ♘xe2 15.♔xe2 ♗xc3
16.bxc3 ♘xe4 17.c4 ♗e6 18.♖hc1 f6=

White can regain his pawn but he has no
advantage.

b) 12.0–0N

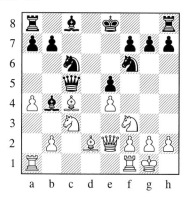

This is a better try, but Black can still maintain the balance.

12...♗g4 13.♖ac1

13.♗e3 ♗xf3 14.gxf3 ♕e7=

13...♕e7

Also possible is 13...♘d4 14.♗b5† ♕xb5 (14...♔f8 15.♕d1 ♗xf3 16.gxf3 ♕e7 17.♗e3∞) 15.♕xb5† ♕xb5 16.♘xb5 ♗xd2 17.♘xd2 ♖d8 18.♘c4 ♗e2 19.♘cd6† ♔e7 20.♖c7† ♖d7 21.♖fc1 ♗xb5 22.♘f5† ♔e6 23.♘xg7† ♔d6 24.♘f5† ♔e6 25.axb5 ♖xc7 26.♖xc7 ♘xe4 and Black is okay.

14.♗g5 ♗xc3 15.♖xc3

15.bxc3 h6 16.♗h4 0–0 is nothing much for White.

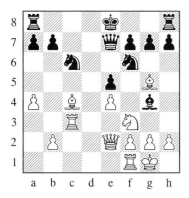

15...h6

Also possible is: 15...0–0 16.♕e3 ♖ad8 (16...h6? 17.♗xh6± gxh6 18.♕xh6 ♘xe4 19.♕g6† ♔h8 20.♕xg4+−) 17.h3 ♗xf3 18.♕xf3 ♖d6 19.♕g3 ♕d8 (19...♕d7 20.♖e1 h6 21.♗xh6 ♘h5 22.♕g4 ♕xg4 23.hxg4 ♖xh6 24.gxh5 ♖xh5 25.♗d5↑) 20.♕e3 (20.♖e1 h6 21.♗xh6 [21.♗xf6 ♕xf6=] 21...♘h5 22.♗g5 ♘xg3 23.♗xd8 ♘xe4=) 20...h6 21.♗xf6 ♕xf6 22.♗d5=

16.♗xf6

16.♗h4 0–0 17.♕e3 ♖ad8 18.h3 ♗xf3 19.♕xf3 ♖d6=

16...♕xf6 17.♗b5 0–0 18.♗xc6 bxc6 19.♖fc1 ♖ab8 20.♖xc6 ♗xf3 21.gxf3

21.♕xf3 ♕xf3 22.gxf3 ♖xb2=

21...♕g5† 22.♔h1 ♖fd8=

White has virtually no chance of converting his extra pawn, as his kingside has been compromised and Black's pieces are active enough.

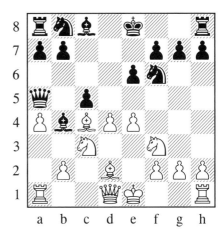

9...cxd4

Black can also wait for his opponent to make the exchange of pawns:

9...0–0 10.dxc5 ♕xc5

This is certainly playable, although the queen is a bit exposed on c5 so White has chances to develop some initiative.

11.♕e2 e5

11...♘c6 12.0–0 ♘e5 13.♘xe5 ♕xe5 14.f4↑

12.0–0

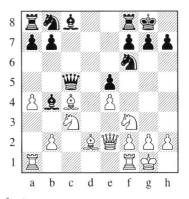

12...♗g4

12...♗xc3 is well met by 13.♖ac1!↑.

12...♘c6 does not quite equalize: 13.♗e3 ♕e7 14.♘d5 ♘xd5 15.exd5 ♘a5 16.♗a2

♗f5 17.♗d2!?± (17.♖fc1)

13.♖ac1 ♗xf3

13...♘c6 14.♘d5 ♘xd5 15.♗xd5 ♕e7 16.♗e3 ♖ac8 17.h3 ♗d7 (after 17...♗h5 18.g4! ♗g6 19.♖c4↑ Black's bishop is out of play.) 18.♖fd1 h6 19.♘h2!? White keeps some pressure; the plan is ♕h5.

14.♕xf3!N

White can afford to leave the bishop on c4 hanging.

After 14.gxf3 ♘c6 15.♘a2 ♕e7 16.♘xb4 ♘xb4 17.f4 ♘c6 18.f3 ♖ad8 19.♔h1 ♘h5 White achieved no advantage in the game Rapport – Laznicka, Aix-les-Bains 2011.

14...♘c6

14...♕xc4? 15.♘d5 is the justification for White's last move.

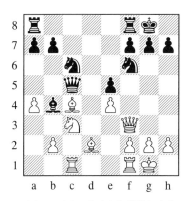

From this position I think White's best try is: 15.♘a2!?

Threatening to win the queen.

15.♘b5 is another idea: 15...♕e7 (15...♕b6 16.♗g5 ♗e7 17.♗e3 ♕a5 18.♘c3 ♖ac8 Now 19.b3 ♗a3 20.♖c2 ♗c5 gives Black counterplay, but 19.♕f5!?↑ looks promising.) 16.♗g5 ♖ac8 17.♗d5 a6 18.♗xc6 ♖xc6 19.♖xc6 bxc6 20.♗xf6 ♕xf6 21.♕xf6 gxf6 22.♘a7 ♗c5 23.♘xc6 ♖c8

Black's active pieces should enable him to equalize from here: 24.♘a5 ♗b4 (24...♗b6!? 25.♘b7 ♖c4 26.a5 ♖c7 27.♘d6 ♗xa5 28.h4 ♗b4 29.♘f5 ♖c2∞) 25.♘b3 ♖c2 26.♖b1 ♖e2!? 27.f3 ♖e3 28.♘a1 ♖e2 29.♔f1 ♖d2=

15.♘d5 is also interesting: 15...♗xd2 16.♘xf6† ♔h8 17.♕f5 gxf6 18.♕xf6† ♔g8 19.♗xf7† ♖xf7 20.♕xf7† ♔xf7 21.♖xc5 ♔e6 22.g3 ♖g8 23.♔h1 White's position is slightly easier, but I think Black should be okay.

15...♕d6

15...♕e7 16.♘xb4 ♘xb4 17.♖fd1 ♘c6 18.♗e3±

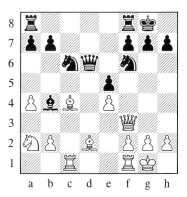

16.♗e3

16.♘xb4 ♕xd2 17.♘d5 ♘xd5 18.exd5 ♘d4 (18...♘a5 19.b3) 19.♕e3 ♕xb2 20.♖b1 ♕c2 21.♖fc1 ♕xa4 22.♕xe5 b5 23.♕xd4 bxc4 24.♖xc4 ♕d7 25.d6 ♖ac8=

16...♖fd8 17.♖fd1 ♕e7 18.♗d5 ♗a5 19.♘c3 ♗b6 20.♗g5 ♘d4 21.♕g3↑

10.♘xd4

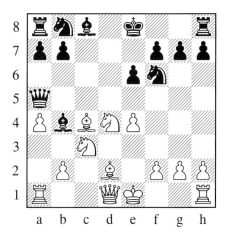

10...0–0

After 10...♕c5 White plays 11.♗b5†± followed by ♘b3.

11.♕e2

11.♘c2!?

This interesting move deserves attention. I think the best response is:

11...♘c6

11...♕c7 is imprecise: 12.♕e2 ♗e7 13.e5 ♘fd7 14.f4 ♘c6 15.0–0± Potkin – Shirov, Khanty-Mansiysk 2011.

Also after 11...♗xc3 12.♗xc3 ♕g5 13.♕f3 (13.♕e2 ♕xg2) 13...♘c6 14.h4 ♕g6 15.♗xf6 ♕xf6 16.♕xf6 gxf6 17.0–0–0 White has a small advantage.

12.♘xb4 ♕xb4 13.b3 ♖d8 14.0–0 ♕e7=

Black will complete development by playing ...b6 and ...♗b7.

11...♘c6

11...♘bd7 is unlikely to have independent significance, for instance 12.0–0 (12.♘c2 ♘e5) 12...♘e5 13.♗a2 ♖d8 14.♘c2 and we have transposed to the game.

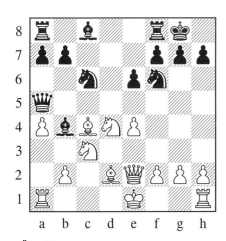

12.♘c2N

The first new move of the game, but not the last.

White gets no advantage with: 12.♘xc6 bxc6

13.0–0 ♘d7!?N Intending ...♘e5. (13...e5 14.♗g5 ♗e7 is also reasonable; Black fixes the centre and puts his rooks on the open b- and d-files.) 14.f4 (14.♖fd1 is not dangerous: 14...♘e5 15.♗f4 ♘xc4 16.♕xc4 ♗a6 17.♕xc6 ♖ac8 18.♘d7 ♗c5 19.♕d2 [19.♘b5 ♕b6 20.♕d2 ♗xb5=] 19...♖fd8 20.♕c2 ♗d4=) 14...♖d8 Black intends ...♘b6 and ...♗b7 with good counterplay. (14...e5 is also possible, but there is no need to play it immediately.)

12...♘e5

12...e5 is less good: 13.♘xb4 ♕xb4 14.♘d5 ♕d6 15.♗c3 ♘xd5 16.♗xd5 ♘e7 17.♗b3 ♗e6 18.♖d1 ♕c6 19.♗xe6 ♕xe6 20.♕b5 ♘c6 21.0–0 ♕e7 22.♖d5↑

An interesting attempt is:

12...♖d8!?

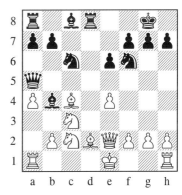

13.0–0

13.f3 ♘d4 14.♘xd4 ♖xd4 15.♖c1 ♖d8 16.0–0 ♗d7=

13.♘xb4 ♕xb4 14.b3 ♘d4 15.♕d1 ♕d6 16.0–0 e5 17.♗g5 ♗e6=

13...♘xe4

13...♘d4!? 14.♘xd4 ♖xd4 15.♖fd1 e5 16.h3 ♗e6 17.♗xe6 fxe6∞ Black has doubled pawns but his pieces are excellent.

14.♕xe4

This is White's only chance to fight for an advantage.

14.♘xe4?! ♗xd2 15.♖ad1 ♗h6∓

14.♘xb4 ♘xd2 15.♘xc6 bxc6 16.♖fd1
♘xc4 17.b4 ♕b6 18.♖xd8† ♕xd8 19.♕xc4
♕e7=

14...♖xd2

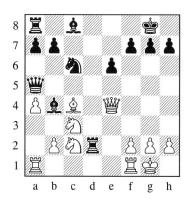

15.♗d3 g6

15...f5!? 16.♕e3 ♗xc3 17.bxc3 ♕xc3 18.♖a3
♕a5 19.♖b1 ♘e5 20.♕e1 ♗d7 21.♘b4
♖xd3 22.♘xd3 ♕xe1† 23.♘xe1 ♖b8 I think
Black should be able to hold.

16.♘b1 ♖xc2 17.♗xc2 e5

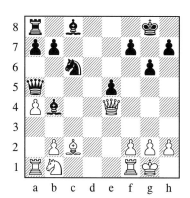

Black has good compensation for the
exchange, for example:

18.♗d3

18.♘a3 ♗f5 19.♕f3 (or 19.♕e3 ♗e6↑
followed by ...♗c5) 19...♗e6 20.♗d3 ♘d4
21.♕xb7 ♗d5 22.♕d7 ♗e6 23.♕b7 ♗d5=

18.♗b3 ♗f5 19.♕d5 ♕c7 20.♕c4 ♖d8
21.♖d1 ♖xd1† 22.♗xd1 ♕d6 23.♘c3 ♕d2
24.♕e2 ♗xc3 25.bxc3 ♕xc3 26.♖a2=

18...♗f5

18...♗e6 19.♗b5 ♖c8 20.♘c3 (20.♖c1 a6
21.♗xc6 ♗c5 22.♕e2 ♖xc6 23.♘d2 ♗d5∞)
20...♗c5 21.♖ac1 ♗d4∞

19.♕f3 ♗e6

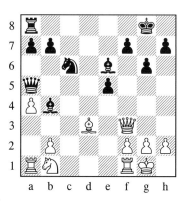

20.♗b5

20.♘c3 should be met by 20...♖b8!?∞
intending ...♘d4, rather than 20...♗xc3?!
21.bxc3 ♕xc3 22.♗e4±.

20...♘d4 21.♕xb7 ♕d8! 22.♘a3

22.♕e4?! ♗f5↑ 23.♕xe5? ♗d6–+

22.♘c3?! a6 23.♗xa6 (23.♗c6 ♖b8 24.♕xa6
♖b6 25.♕a8 ♘xc6∓) 23...♗xc3 24.bxc3
♗d5 25.♕b4 (25.♕b2? ♘f3†–+) 25...♘f3†
26.♔h1 (26.gxf3 ♗xf3 27.h4 ♖xa6∓)
26...♖xa6 27.♖fd1 ♕a8∓

22...♗xa3 23.♖xa3 a6 24.♗c6

24.♗d3? ♗d5 25.♕b4 ♕g5 26.f3 ♘xf3†
27.♖xf3 ♗xf3 28.♗f1 ♗d5∓

24...♖b8 25.♕xa6 ♖b6 26.♕a8 ♖b8=

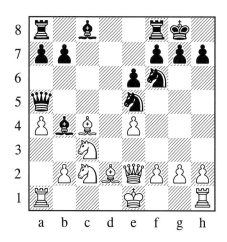

13.♗a2N

This is White's second novelty of the game, as the same position previously arose via a different move order. Three other moves deserve attention.

13.♘xb4 ♕xb4 14.b3 ♕c5 (14...♘xc4 15.bxc4 b6 16.0–0 ♗b7 17.♘d5 ♕b2 18.♖ab1 ♕e5 19.♘xf6† ♕xf6 20.a5 ♕d4=) 15.0–0 ♗d7=

13.f4?! ♘xc4 14.♕xc4
Ding – Yu, Danzhou 2010.

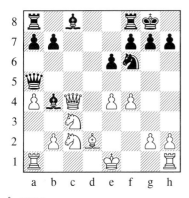

14...♗e7!?N

This seems even better than the game continuation of 14...♗xc3 15.♗xc3 ♕a6 16.♕xa6 bxa6 17.♗xf6 gxf6=.
15.e5 ♘d5
   15...♘g4!?
16.♘xd5 exd5 17.♕d3 ♕b6 Black is fine.

13.♗b5!? a6
   13...♖d8 14.0–0 ♗d7 15.f4↑
14.♘xb4

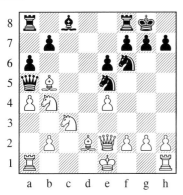

Now Black must choose which piece to take. We will consider a) 14...axb5 and the riskier b) 14...♕xb4!?.

a) 14... axb5 15.♘xb5 ♗d7 16.♘c6 ♕b6 17.♘cd4 ♖fc8 18.b3
   18.0–0 ♖c4=
18...♘c6 19.♘f3 ♘a5
   19...♘e5 20.0–0 ♘xf3† 21.gxf3 e5 22.♖ac1±
   19...♘b4 20.0–0 ♘c2 21.♖ad1 White is better.
20.♗e3 ♕c6 21.0–0 ♕xe4 22.♘d6 ♕c2
Black seems to be okay.

b) 14...♕xb4!? 15.f4 ♘g6!
   15...♘ed7 16.♗c4 e5 17.f5±
   15...♘c6 16.♗xc6 bxc6 17.e5↑
   15...axb5 16.fxe5 ♘d7 17.♕xb5 ♕xb5 18.♘xb5 ♘xe5 19.♘c7 ♖a7 20.♗c3 ♘c6 21.♘b5 ♖a8 22.b4↑
16.♗d3 e5

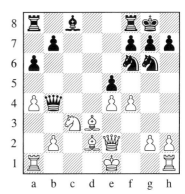

17.♘d5

17.f5 ♘f4 18.♗xf4 exf4 19.0–0 ♖e8 20.♖xf4 ♗d7 21.g4 ♕d4† (21...♗c6!? 22.g5 ♘d5 23.♘xd5 ♗xd5∞) 22.♔h1 ♗c6 23.g5 ♘d5 24.♘xd5 ♗xd5 25.♖af1 ♗b3 26.♖h4 ♖ac8∞ (26...♗xa4? 27.g6±)
17...♕xb2 18.♖b1 ♕d4 19.♗e3 ♕xa4 20.♘xf6† gxf6 21.f5 ♘f4 22.♗xf4 exf4 23.0–0 ♕d4† 24.♔h1 b5 25.♖xf4 ♔h8 26.♖d1 ♕b6 27.♕h5 ♖g8 28.♗e2 ♖g7 29.♖g4 ♗b7 30.♖xg7 ♔xg7 31.♖d7 ♖f8 32.♕g4† ♔h8 33.♕h4 ♔g7 34.♕g4†=

13...罝d8

13...b6 is less reliable, and after 14.包xb4 豐xb4 15.f4 包g6 16.e5 包d5 17.包xd5 豐xb2 18.0–0 exd5 19.豐e1 豐d4† 20.鸢e3 豐e4 21.豐f2 White has the better chances.

14.0–0

14.包xb4 豐xb4 15.0–0 b6 transposes to the game.

14...b6

14...鸢d7 is worse, due to the following line: 15.包xb4 豐xb4 16.f4 包c6

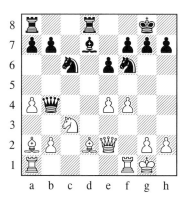

17.鸢e1!N (after 17.e5 包d4 Black obtained good counterplay in Edouard – Inarkiev, Barcelona 2010) 17...包d4 (17...鸢h8 18.e5 包d4 19.豐d1 鸢c6 20.exf6 包f3† 21.豐xf3 鸢xf3 22.fxg7† 鸢xg7 23.罝xf3±) 18.豐d1 豐c5 (18...鸢c6 19.包d5 豐c5 20.鸢f2↑) 19.鸢f2 鸢c6 20.包d5 exd5 21.鸢xd4↑

14...包c6?
This is almost losing by force.
15.包xb4 豐xb4 16.包d5 豐xb2 17.罝fb1 豐e5 17...豐c2? 18.鸢b3 豐c5 19.罝c1 豐f8 (19...豐d6 20.包xf6† gxf6 21.鸢h6 鸢h8 22.豐h5+–) 20.包xf6† gxf6 21.罝c3 鸢h8 (21...包e5 22.罝h3 鸢h8 23.豐h5 豐g7 24.罝d1+–) 22.鸢c1!+– Black has no good defence against the plan of 豐h5 followed by 鸢a3.
18.鸢c3 豐g5

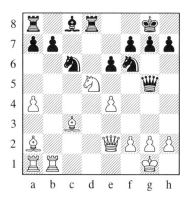

19.f4!N
More accurate than 19.包xf6† gxf6 20.罝b3 e5 21.鸢b2 鸢g4 22.豐f1 (22.豐b5!?) 22...鸢h8 (22...豐d2!⇄ 23.罝xb7?! 包a5 24.罝xf7 豐xb2 25.罝b7† 豐xa2 26.罝xa2 包xb7) 23.罝xb7 罝ab8?! (23...鸢e6±) 24.f4! exf4? 25.豐b5!+– Vitiugov – Chadaev, Taganrog 2011.
19...包xd5 20.fxg5 包xc3 21.豐f2 包xb1 22.罝xb1±
Material is roughly level, but White has the strong plan of pushing his h-pawn up the board.

15.包xb4 豐xb4

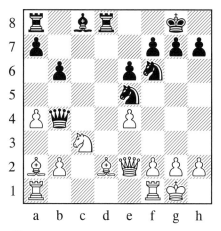

16.罝fd1N

The third novelty of the game!

16.鸢g5 promises no advantage. 16...a5 (16...鸢b7?! 17.f4 包d3 18.f5↑) 17.罝ad1 罝xd1

18.♖xd1 ♗a6 19.♕c2 At this point the players agreed a draw in Shulman – Potkin, Khanty-Mansiysk 2011. The position is indeed level, for instance: 19...♖c8 20.h3 h6 21.♗e3 ♘d3 22.♖xd3 ♗xd3 23.♕xd3 ♕xb2 24.♗d4 ♖xc3 25.♗xc3 ♕xa2 26.♕d8† ♔h7 27.♗xf6 gxf6 28.♕xf6 ♔g8=

16...♗b7 17.♖e1

17.♗g5? ♖xd1† 18.♖xd1 ♘xe4 19.♘xe4 ♗xe4 20.♖e1 ♘d3 21.♗d2 ♕c5∓

17...♘xe4?

A mistake, as the tactics do not quite work for Black.

Correct was 17...♖xd1! 18.♖xd1 and only now 18...♘xe4, when the absence of a white rook from a1 helps Black. (See the note to White's 18th move below for the explanation.)

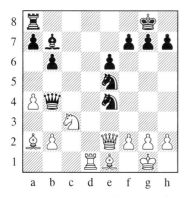

Play continues 19.f3 ♕c5† 20.♔h1 ♘xc3 21.♗xc3 when White has some initiative for the sacrificed pawn, but no objective advantage if Black defends correctly. 21...♘c6 22.♕e1 (22.♖d7 ♗c8 23.♖d2 ♗b7=) 22...♕e7 23.b4 ♖d8 24.b5 ♘b8 (24...♘a5) 25.♖xd8† ♕xd8 26.♗xe6 fxe6 27.♕xe6† ♔h8 28.♕e5 ♕d1† 29.♗e1 ♕d8 30.♗c3=

18.♘b5?

Missing a chance to get a clear advantage. After this poor move White will not even be able to claim equality. He had to play:

18.♘d5!

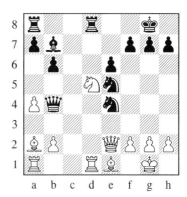

18...♕xa4

18...♕d6 19.♘f6† gxf6 20.♖xd6 ♖xd6 21.a5±

19.♘e7† ♔h8 20.♗d5!

This move shows White Black should have exchanged rooks on move 17, to draw the white rook away from a1.

20...♕xd1

20...♕xa1 21.♖xa1 exd5 22.f3 ♖e8 23.♗b4 a5 24.fxe4 axb4 25.♖xa8 ♗xa8 26.♘xd5±

21.♖xd1 exd5 22.f3 ♖e8 23.♗b4 a5

23...♘c6 24.♘xc6 ♘c3 25.♕d2 ♘xd1 26.♘e7 a5 27.♗a3 b5 28.♗c5 ♘xb2 29.♕xb2 b4 30.♘f5 f6 31.♕d4±

24.fxe4 axb4 25.♘xd5±

Black has problems as he will not be able to protect the weak pawns on b4 and b6.

18...♖xd1 19.♖xd1 ♕xa4 20.b3 ♕a6 21.♗b1

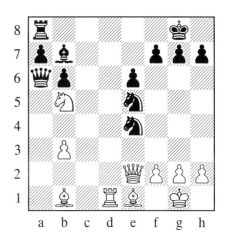

21...f5?!

This squanders Black's advantage, although in the resulting position he is not worse.

Stronger was:

21...♖f8!

Defending the e4-knight indirectly. Now White faces an uphill battle to draw.

22.♖d4

22.f3?! ♗c6∓

22.♗xe4 ♗xe4 23.♗c3 f6 24.♗xe5 fxe5 25.♕xe4 ♕xb5†

22.♗b4 ♖c8 23.f3 (23.♗xe4 ♗xe4 24.♗c3 ♘g6 25.♖d7 ♗b7 26.h3 e5 27.♕d3 ♗e4! 28.♕xe4 ♕xb5 29.♖xa7 ♕xb3∓) 23...♗c6 24.♖c1 ♗xb5 25.♖xc8† ♕xc8 26.♕xe4 ♘g6†

22...♗c6 23.♖xe4 ♗xb5

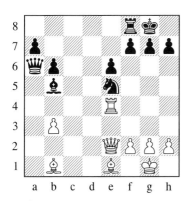

24.♖h4! ♘d3

24...♘g6 25.♕h5 h6 26.♗xg6 ♕a1!? 27.♖e4 ♗e8 28.♗xf7† ♗xf7 29.♕e5 ♕xe5 30.♖xe5 ♖c8∓

25.♖a4!

White's inventive rook manoeuvres are enough to keep him in the game, but he is still clearly worse.

25...♘xe1 26.♗xh7† ♗xh7 27.♕e4† f5 28.♕h4† ♗g8 29.♖xa6 ♗xa6 30.♕e7 ♘d3

Clearly Black will be the one pushing for a win in this endgame. The continuation might be:

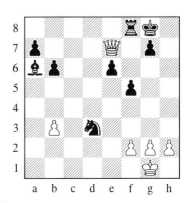

31.♕xa7

31.♕xe6† ♗h7 32.♕d7 ♖f6 33.♕xa7 ♗b5∓

31...♖c8 32.♕xb6 ♘f4 33.b4 ♘d5 34.♕d6 ♗f7 35.b5 ♖e8 36.h3 ♖e7 37.♕d8 ♗b7 38.f3 e5∓

Black intends to push the e-pawn.

22.f3 ♗c6 23.fxe4 ♗xb5 24.♕b2 ♘d3

24...♘g6 25.exf5 exf5 26.♗xf5 ♕b7 is equal too.

25.♗xd3 ♗xd3 26.exf5

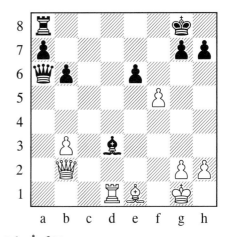

26...♗xf5??

Losing instantly.

26...exf5?? 27.♕c3 is winning for White, as bishop moves allow the white rook to come to d7 and 27...♖d8 is no good due to 28.♕c7.

However, after the correct 26...♕b5 27.fxe6 ♕c5† 28.♗f2 ♕c2 the position is equal, for instance:

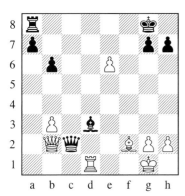

29.♕a1   (29.♕xc2   ♗xc2   30.♖d7   ♗xb3 31.♗d4 [31.e7   ♖e8   32.♖xa7   ♔f7=] 31...g6 32.♖g7† ♔f8 33.♖f7† ♔g8 34.♖g7† ♔f8 35.e7† ♔e8 36.♖xh7 ♔g8 37.♖g7 ♗f7 38.♗f6 ♖c8=) 29...♖f8 30.♗e3 ♗e4 31.♖d2 ♕xb3 32.♗d4 ♕xe6 33.♗xg7 ♖e8 34.♗h6 ♕e7 35.h3 ♗g6 36.♖e2 ♕d7=

27.♖d7 e5 28.♕xe5! ♗xd7 29.♗c3 1–0

Black resigned in view of 29...♔f7 30.♕xg7† ♔e6 (30...♔e8 31.♕h8† ♔e7 32.♕f6† is the same) 31.♕e5† ♔f7 32.♕f6† ♔e8 33.♗b4 with mate to follow.

GAME 24
▷ **I. Nepomniachtchi (2718)**
▶ **D. Pavasovic (2561)**
European Club Cup, Rogaska Slatina
27.09.2011 **[D31]**
Annotated by Borki Predojevic

This game features the interesting 8.♘e2!? in Marshall's 'other' gambit in the Semi-Slav. The first critical moment came on move 11 when Black opted for 11...♘c2†, a move which did not have the best reputation in the past. Pavasovic unveiled a new idea in 15...♗e6!N which is an important improvement for Black.

After a series of more or less forced moves Black made a mistake with 22...♘e1?, instead of the correct 22...♘f4! which would have brought him a reasonable position and a probable draw. After missing this chance he never recovered and Nepomniachtchi won pretty convincingly.

1.d4 d5 2.c4 e6 3.♘c3 c6 4.e4 dxe4 5.♘xe4 ♗b4† 6.♗d2 ♕xd4 7.♗xb4 ♕xe4† 8.♘e2!?

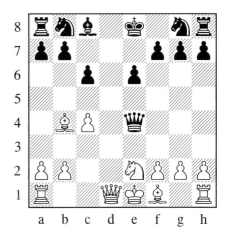

This move has become a modern way to fight for the advantage. Of course it is not a new move, but merely one which was 'forgotten', having been considered harmless for many years.

The other main move is of course 8.♗e2.

8...♘a6
The main line, although some other moves have been tested. Here is a quick summary of them.

8...♘e7 9.♕d2 ♘d7 (9...c5 10.♗xc5 ♘bc6 11.♖d1 0–0 12.♕f4 ♕xf4 13.♘xf4±) 10.f3 ♕h4† 11.g3 ♕f6 12.♗g2 0–0 13.0–0≅ with good compensation.

8...e5?!
This looks rather suspicious.
9.♕d6

9.♕d2 ♘a6 10.♗f8 ♘e7 11.♗xg7 ♖g8 12.♗f6 ♗e6⇄

9...♘d7

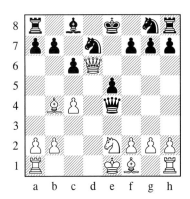

10.♖d1

White can also try 10.0–0–0!?N c5 11.♘g3 ♕c6 12.♘xc6 bxc6 13.♗c3⯑ with good compensation.

10...h5!N

10...c5? 11.♗xc5 ♕xc4 12.♗a3±

10...♕xc4?! 11.♘d4! ♕d5 12.♕xd5 cxd5 13.♘b5 ♔d8 14.♘d6 ♘h6 15.♖xd5± Black is not able to defend his position.

10...b6 11.f3 ♕g6 12.♕c7 c5 13.♗c3 ♘h6 14.♘g3 0–0 15.♗d3± was excellent for White in Wells – Haba, Crailsheim 1996.

11.h4

This 'copied' move is a good answer.

11...♖h6 12.♕d2 ♕xc4 13.♘g3 ♕d4 14.♕xd4 exd4 15.♘f5↑

White has the better chances.

8...♘d7!?

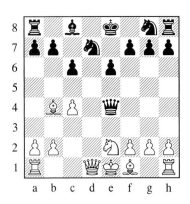

This is a reasonable move, although White keeps a typical initiative on the dark squares.

9.♕d6 c5

9...a5 10.♗a3↑

10.♗c3 ♘e7

10...♘gf6 11.0–0–0 ♕c6 12.♕g3 ♖g8 13.f3↑ looks good for White.

11.0–0–0 ♘f5 12.♕c7

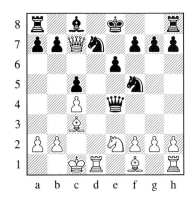

Black seems to have some problems in this line, for instance:

12...♕h4

12...♕c6 13.♕xc6 bxc6 14.g4 ♘h4 15.♘g3 ♔e7 16.♗xg7 ♖g8 17.♘h5± Baumegger – Braun, Olbia 2008. 12...0–0 13.♘g3 ♕c6 14.♕xc6 bxc6 15.♘xf5 exf5 16.♗e2⯑

13.g4!

This aggressive move is better than 13.♘g3 ♘d4⇄.

13...♕xg4 14.♖g1 ♕h4 15.♘g3 ♘d4 16.♗xd4 cxd4 17.♘f5! exf5□ 18.♖e1† ♘e5 19.♕xe5† ♗e6

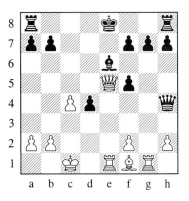

20.罝xg7!N

White got nowhere in the following game: 20.豐b5† 曲f8 21.豐c5†? 曲g8 22.盒d3 g6 23.豐c7 b6–+ Bronowicki – Tikkanen, Ceska Trebova 2008.

20...豐h6†

20...0–0–0 21.豐c5! is awkward, as 21...曲b8? allows 22.罝xe6+–.

21.曲c2 0–0–0 22.盒d3±

Black's extra pawn is virtually meaningless and he faces a difficult defence.

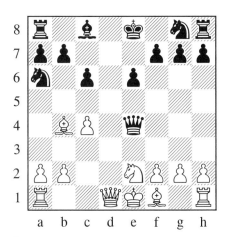

9.盒f8

This funny-looking move is a typical attacking device.

9...ᵒe7

Worse is 9...e5? 10.豐d6! 豐g6 (10...盒f5?? 11.盒xg7 ᵒe7 12.盒f6 ᵒg6 13.罝d1 1–0 Arencibia – Zepeda, Havana 2010) 11.豐xg6 hxg6 12.盒xg7 罝h4 13.盒xe5 ᵒb4 14.曲d2 with a clear advantage for White.

9...豐e5 10.豐d2 豐f6 is well met by 11.盒d6! (On 11.盒a3 Black can play 11...c5! [but not 11...ᵒe7? 12.0–0–0 0–0 13.豐d8! 豐h6† 14.f4 ᵒg6 15.盒xf8 as in Richter – Y. Meister, Berlin 2008] 12.罝d1 ᵒh6 13.ᵒg3 0–0 with an unclear game.) 11...ᵒh6 12.0–0–0 ᵒf5 13.盒e5 豐e7 14.ᵒg3± when Black has problems.

9...g6N is playable but 10.盒d6⩱ gives White full compensation.

10.盒xg7 ᵒb4

The best reply to 10...罝g8 is 11.豐d4! (11.盒c3 also gives him a modest advantage) 11...豐xd4 12.盒xd4 when White will have better chances thanks to his bishop pair. This evaluation was confirmed in the following recent game: 12...c5 13.盒f6 罝g6 14.盒c3 ᵒb4

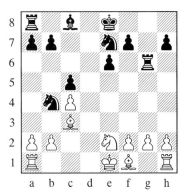

15.ᵒf4! (Worse is 15.盒d2 e5!↑ Tunik – Sveshnikov, St Petersburg 1994) 15...罝g5 16.h4 罝f5 17.ᵒd3 ᵒc2† 18.曲d2 ᵒxa1 19.g4 罝f3 20.盒e2 罝xd3† 21.盒xd3 e5 22.f3 f5 23.g5± Timofeev – Frolyanov, Taganrog 2011.

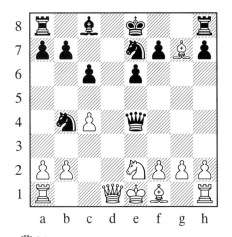

11.豐d6!

The most precise.

11.♗xh8

This alternative takes away Black's option of 11...♘d3†, but it brings other disadvantages for White.

11...e5

11...♘d3†? is inadvisable. 12.♔d2 ♘xf2 13.♕c2 ♕xc2† 14.♔xc2 ♘xh1 15.♗d4 The position of the knight on h1 gives Black serious problems, for example: 15...♘f5 (Also 15...e5 16.♗xe5 ♗f5† 17.♔c3 c5 18.♗d6 b6 [18...0–0–0 19.♗xc5+–] 19.g4! ♗e4 20.♘f4 gives White a huge advantage.) 16.♗g1 e5 17.g3 ♘d6 18.♘c3 ♗f5† 19.♔b3 The knight will soon be trapped. 19...♗e6 20.♗c5 0–0–0 21.♗e2+–

12.♕d6!?

12.♖c1?! ♘d3† 13.♔d2 ♗f5→ Conquest – Korneev, Mondariz 2002.

12.♕b3 ♘c2† 13.♔d2 ♘xa1 14.♕d3 ♕h4 15.♗xe5 ♗f5 16.♗g3 ♕f6 17.♕c3 0–0–0† 18.♔c1 ♗c2! 19.b3 ♖d1† 20.♔b2 ♖b1† 21.♔a3 ♗xb3 22.axb3 ♖xb3† 23.♕xb3 ♘xb3 24.♔xb3 ♕a1!↑ was also good for Black in T. Fodor – K. Szabo, Budapest 2009.

12...♘c2† 13.♔d2

Now Black can virtually force a draw with the accurate:

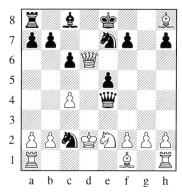

13...♗f5!

13...♘xa1 14.f3! transposes to the main game.

14.♘g3 ♕f4† 15.♔c3□ ♘d5†

15...♘xa1!? 16.♕d2 ♕xd2† 17.♔xd2 0–0–0† 18.♔c3 ♖xh8 19.♘xf5 ♘xf5 20.♗d3 ♘h4 21.g3 ♘f3 22.♖xa1 ♔c7∞

16.cxd5 ♕d4† 17.♔b3 ♘xa1† 18.♔a3 ♘c2† 19.♔b3 ♘a1†=

With perpetual check.

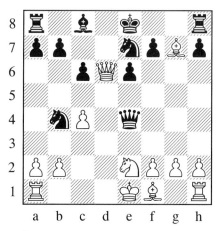

11...♘c2†!?

One of the critical moments of the game. Pavasovic chooses the most direct and forcing line, whereas the following alternative would have led to a slightly worse but nonetheless tenable endgame:

11...♘d3† 12.♔d2 ♘f5 13.♕xd3 ♕xd3† 14.♔xd3 ♘xg7 15.♔c3 ♗e7

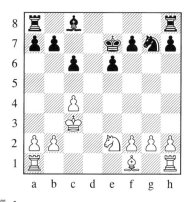

16.♖e1

16.♘g3 c5 17.♗d3 b6 18.♗e4 ♖b8 19.♖he1 ♗b7 20.♖ad1 ♗xe4 21.♖xe4 f5 22.♖ee1 (22.♖h4±) 22...♖bd8 23.b4 ♖xd1 24.♖xd1

♖c8 25.b5 ♘e8 26.♘h5 ♖d8 27.♖xd8
♔xd8= Kharlov – Galkin, Batumi 2002.

16...♗d7 17.g3 ♖ad8 18.♗g2

White has a pleasant edge, but in the following game Black was able to neutralize it.

18...f6 19.f4

19.♘d4!?±

19...h5 20.♘c1 ♗e8 21.b4 ♗g6 22.a4 h4
23.♗f3 ♘f5 24.g4 ♘d4 25.♗d1 ♔f7 26.♖e3
♖d7 27.c5 ♖hd8=

Aleksandrov – S. Zhigalko, Minsk 2010.

12.♔d2 ♘xa1

12...♘f5? 13.♕e5 ♕xe5 14.♗xe5 f6 15.♗xf6
♖f8 16.♔xc2± Pruess – Strugatsky, Reno 2005.

13.♗xh8 e5

The alternative is:

13...♕c2† 14.♔e1 ♕xc4

This seems rather risky. More reliable is
14...e5 when 15.f3! transposes to the main
game.

15.♘c3! ♕b4

At this point White has to play a novelty to
obtain the upper hand.

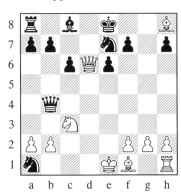

16.♕d1!N

After 16.♕d2 e5! 17.♕c1 ♗g4! Black
has good chances. For example: 18.f3
(18.h3 ♗h5 19.♗xe5 0–0–0 20.g4 ♘d5!⇄
is complicated) 18...♗xf3 19.♗f6 (19.♗xe5
♗h5 20.♕xa1 0–0–0∓ gives Black a strong
attack; 19.gxf3 ♕h4† 20.♔e2 ♘g6 21.♕xa1
0–0–0 22.♘e4 ♘f4† 23.♔e3 ♖xh8→ is also

dangerous for White.) 19...♘d5 20.♗xe5
♕e7! Black is already better, and after
21.gxf3 ♕xe5† 22.♔f2 ♕d4† 23.♔g3 ♘e3
24.♗h3 (24.♕xa1 ♘f5† 25.♔g2 0–0–0–+)
24...♘ac2–+ he soon won in Christiansen –
Robson, Saint Louis 2009.

16...♕xb2

The only answer, but White gets a good
game with simple development.

17.♗d3 ♘g6 18.♗f6 e5 19.♕d2! ♕b4

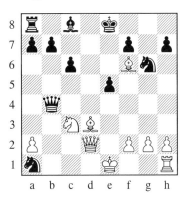

20.g3!

After this precise move Black's position is
critical. 20.♗xg6 does not lead to mate as
20...fxg6 clears the f7-square.

Also we mustn't forget that 20.0–0 is
impossible since White has already moved
his king!

20...♗g4 21.f4! exf4 22.♘e4±

Black has a tough position and the knight on
a1 is in trouble.

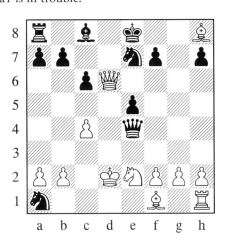

14.f3 ♕c2†

Wrong is 14...♕xc4? 15.♗f6 ♕e6 16.♗xe7 ♕xe7 17.♕xe7† ♔xe7 18.♘g3+– and Black will lose the knight on a1.

15.♔e1

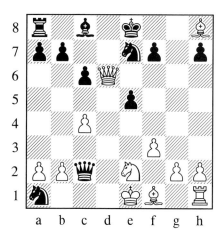

15...♗e6!N

The first new move, and a clear improvement. Now the play becomes very concrete, and we will see that the next few moves are more or less forced.

15...♕b1†? led to an easy win for White after 16.♔f2 ♘c2? 17.♗f6 ♕e1† 18.♔g1 ♕b4 19.♗xe7 1–0 Wojtaszek – K. Szabo, Rilton Cup 2007.

In the above game Black could have offered more resistance with 16...♗e6N 17.♗f6 ♘g6, but even this can be refuted by White's elegant reply:

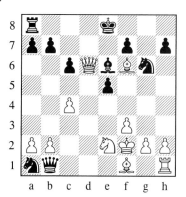

18.♘f4!! exf4 (18...♕xb2† 19.♔e2 ♕d4† 20.♕xd4 exd4 21.♘xe6 fxe6 22.♖xa1 leaves Black a piece down) 19.♗d3! ♕xh1 20.♗xg6+– and Black is about to be mated.

16.♗f6 ♘g6 17.h4!

With the deadly threat of h5.

17...♕f5!

After 17...h5? 18.♘g3+– it is hard to suggest anything against the threats of ♗d3 and ♘xh5.

18.♗g5 h6!

Again this is only move to keep Black in the game.

18...f6?! 19.♘g3! ♕b1† 20.♔f2 ♕xb2† 21.♗e2 ♕d4† 22.♕xd4 exd4 23.h5! ♘f8 (23...fxg5 24.hxg6+–) 24.♗xf6 ♘c2 25.♘e4± is depressing for him.

19.♗xh6 ♖d8

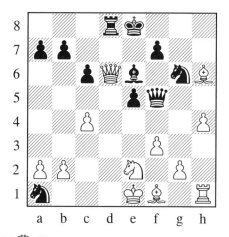

20.♕c5!?

This seems to be the most accurate.

20.♕c7 is less challenging: 20...♘c2† 21.♔f2 e4 22.♕xb7 ♕c5† 23.♔g3 exf3 24.gxf3 ♕e5† 25.♔f2 (25.♔g2?? ♘e1† 26.♔f2 ♘d3† 27.♔g2 ♕c5–+) 25...♕c5†=

20...♕b1†

After 20...♘e7 21.♔f2± White consolidates his position and Black's outlook is bleak.

21.♔f2 ♘c2

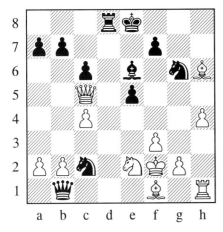

22.h5

22.♗g5

This move is reasonable, but if Black reacts correctly he should be fine.

22...f6!

Leading to a balanced endgame.

23.h5

After 23.♗xf6 ♖d2! 24.♔g3 ♖xe2 25.♗xe2 ♕xh1 26.♗d3 ♕e1† 27.♔h2 ♔f7 28.♗g5 ♘d4 29.♗xg6† ♔xg6 30.♕f8 ♘f5 31.♕f6† ♔h7 32.♕xe6 ♕g3† 33.♔h1 ♕e1† the game ends in perpetual check.

23...♕e1† 24.♔g1 ♖d1 25.♕f2 ♗xc4 26.♘g3 ♘f4 27.♕xe1 ♖xe1 28.♔f2 fxg5 29.♗xc4 ♖xh1 30.♘xh1

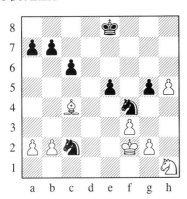

30...e4!

30...♘xh5?? 31.♗d3+–

31.h6

31.fxe4 ♘xh5=

31.♘g3 e3† 32.♔f1 b5⇄ cannot be worse for Black.

31...e3† 32.♔f1 ♔f8 33.g3 ♘d5 34.♗xd5 cxd5 35.♔e2 d4 36.g4 ♔f7 37.♘g3 ♔g6 38.♘f5 ♔h7=

The ending is drawn.

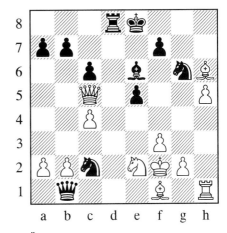

22...♘e1?

The right path was 22...♘f4! 23.♘xf4 ♕e1† 24.♔g1 ♘d4! when suddenly it is White who must find only moves to maintain the balance:

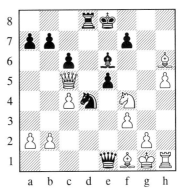

25.♕f8†□ ♔d7 26.♕a3! ♗xc4 27.♕c3 ♕xf1† 28.♔h2 ♕f2 29.♘h3 ♕e2!⇄ The position remains complex, but it should be a draw if both sides play accurately.

23.♔g1! ♘d3 24.♕e3+‒

Thanks to his opponent's error, White has a comfortably winning position. The h-pawn is too strong and Black has little counterplay.

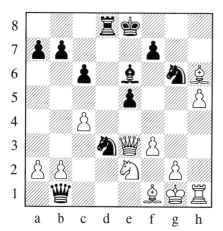

24...♘e7 25.♘g3?!

Imprecise, but still good enough to win.

The most accurate move was 25.♗g5 when Black has nothing against h6-h7.

25...f5

25...♗xc4 26.♗g5!+‒

26.♕g5 ♘f4 27.♔h2 ♕xb2 28.♗g7 ♖d2 29.♖g1 ♗xc4 30.h6

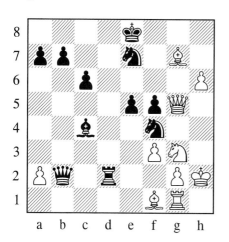

30...♗d5?

Accelerating the end. Black could have offered sterner resistance with 30...♗xf1 31.♘xf1 ♖e2 32.h7 ♘eg6 33.h8=♕† ♘xh8 34.♗xh8 b5!?± when White should be winning, but he will still have to work for a while to prove it.

31.h7 ♘eg6 32.♘xf5
1‒0

GAME 25
▷ **P. Eljanov (2683)**
▶ **A. Moiseenko (2726)**
Governor's Cup, Saratov
Round 4, 11.10.2011 **[D38]**
Annotated by Kamil Miton

In this game Eljanov had to fight against a weapon which he also uses when playing Black. Moiseenko tried a new idea, just taking the pawn with 12...♕xa2, which probably surprised Eljanov. Analysis shows that the idea is very risky for Black and after correct play, either 13.♗e2 or 14.c6!, White would get a strong initiative. Eventually, in an inferior endgame Eljanov found a nice trick and after a forced line he achieved an equal position.

1.d4 ♘f6 2.c4 e6 3.♘f3 d5 4.♘c3 ♗b4 5.cxd5 exd5 6.♗g5 ♘bd7 7.e3 c5 8.dxc5 ♕a5 9.♖c1

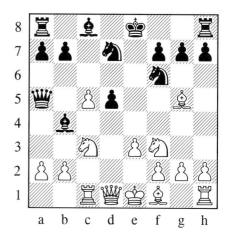

9...♗xc3†

Black can play two other lines:

a) 9...♘e4

Some games by Kramnik suggest that White can obtain a better position here.

10.♕xd5 ♘xc3 11.bxc3 ♗xc3† 12.♔d1 0–0 13.♗c4

13.♗e7 ♖e8 14.♗d6 ♘f6 15.♕b3 ♘e4 16.♗c4 ♗e6 17.♔e2 ♗xc4† 18.♕xc4 b5 19.♕d5 b4 20.♖hd1 ♕a6† 21.♖d3 ♖ad8 22.♘g5 ♘xg5 23.♕xg5 ♕xa2† 24.♔f3 a5∓ D. Gurevich – Gareev, Irvine 2010.

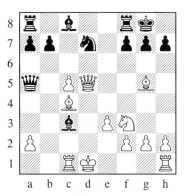

There is now a split:

a1) 13...♘xc5 14.♗e7 ♗b4

14...♗e6 15.♕xc5 ♕a4† 16.♗b3 ♗xb3† 17.axb3 ♕xb3† 18.♔e2 ♕b2† (18...♖fc8 19.♕f5+–) 19.♔d3 ♖fc8 20.♕d5 ♗a5 21.♖xc8† (21.♕e5 ♕b3† 22.♔e4 ♗c3 23.♕d5 ♕a4† 24.♘d4 ♕e8 25.♔e5 ♖c6 26.♖xc3 ♖xc3∞) 21...♖xc8 22.♔e4 ♗b6 23.♕d7 ♕c2† 24.♔f4 h6 25.♔g3 The white king escapes, and Black does not have enough compensation for the piece. 25...♖c6 26.♘h4 ♗c7† 27.f4 (27.♔h3 ♕xf2 28.♘f5↑) 27...♖e6 28.♕e8† ♔h7 29.♕xf7 ♖xe3† 30.♘f3 ♖e2 31.♖g1 ♗xf4† 32.♕xf4 ♖xe7 33.♖c1±

15.♗xf8 ♗e6 16.♕d4 ♖xf8 17.♗xe6

17.♔e2!? ♗a3 18.♗xe6 ♗xc1 19.♗c4 ♗a3 20.♘g5 b5 21.♗xf7† ♖xf7 22.♘xf7 ♔xf7 23.♖d1↑

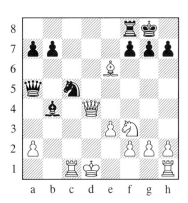

17...♖d8

17...♘xe6 18.♕c4 b5 19.♕c2 ♗a3 20.♖b1 ♘c5 21.♔e2 ♘a4 22.♖b3 b4 23.♖a1 ♘c5 24.♔f1 ♘xb3 25.axb3± and the bishop is badly placed on a3.

17...fxe6 18.♕c4 b5 19.♕c2 ♗a3 20.♔e2 ♕a6 21.♘g5 ♖f5 22.f4 ♗xc1 23.♖xc1 h6 24.g4 b4† 25.♔f3 ♕b7† 26.♔f2 ♖xg5 27.fxg5 ♘e4† 28.♔g1 ♘c3 29.g6±

18.♗d5 ♗e6 19.♕e4 ♖xd5† 20.♔e2 ♕xa2† 21.♕c2 ♕a6† 22.♕c4±

a2) 13...♗b4 14.♗e7 ♘b6

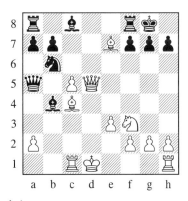

15.cxb6

15.♕d3?! ♘xc4 16.♖xc4 ♗e6 (16...♖e8 17.♘g5 g6 18.♗d6 ♗d7 19.♕d5 ♖e6↑) 17.♘g5 ♖fd8 18.♗xd8 ♖xd8 19.♖d4 ♖xd4 20.exd4 ♕xa2 (20...♗d7!?) 21.♖xh7† ♔f8 22.♘xe6† fxe6 23.♕c2 ♕a1† 24.♕c1 ♕xd4† 25.♔e2 ♗xc5 26.♕e3 ♕b2† 27.♕d2 ♕e5†=

15...♕xd5† 16.♗xd5 ♗xe7 17.♔e2
  17.bxa7 ♖d8∓

17...axb6 18.♖hd1 ♖d8 19.♖c7 ♔f8 20.♗b3
♖xd1 21.♔xd1 ♔e8 22.♘d4 ♖d8 23.♖c2±

The better structure gives White a stable
advantage.

a3) 13...♘f6 14.♗xf6 ♗xf6 15.♔e2 b5
  15...♗e6 16.♕e4 ♖ae8 17.♖hd1 ♗h3
  18.♕xb7 ♗xg2 19.♕a6 ♕c7 20.♕d6±

16.cxb6
  16.c6 ♗a6 17.♕f5 ♕a3 18.♗d3 ♖fd8
  19.c7 ♕xa2† 20.♘d2 ♖xd3 21.♕xd3 b4
  22.♔f3 ♗b7† 23.♔g3 h5 24.h3 ♕a5 25.f4±
  Kramnik – Ponomariov, Moscow 2009.
  16...♕xd5 17.♗xd5 ♗a6† 18.♗c4 axb6 19.a4
  ♗b2 20.♖c2 ♖fc8 21.♘d2 b5 22.axb5 ♗xb5
  23.♖b1 ♗xc4† 24.♖xc4±
  Kramnik – Mamedyarov, Dortmund 2010.

b) 9...0–0 and now:

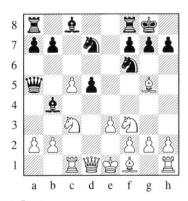

b1) 10.♘d2
  The idea of this move, which I recently
  played myself, is to avoid ...♘e4.
10...b6 11.c6 d4 12.cxd7 dxc3 13.bxc3 ♗xc3
14.♗xf6 gxf6 15.dxc8=♕ ♖axc8 16.♗c4
♖fd8!N
  16...♖xc4 17.0–0±
  16...♖cd8 17.♕g4† ♔h8 18.0–0 ♗xd2
  19.♖c2 ♗b4 20.♗b3 ♗d6 21.♖c4 ♖g8
  22.♕h3 ♖g7 23.g3± Miton – Battaglini,
  Mulhouse 2011.

17.0–0 ♗xd2 18.♖c2 ♗xe3 19.♕f3
  19.♕g4† ♕g5 20.♕h3 ♗xf2† 21.♖fxf2
  ♖d1† 22.♗f1 ♖xf1† 23.♔xf1 ♕b5† 24.♖fe2
  ♖xc2 25.♕g3† ♔f8 26.♕d6†=
19...♗d4 20.♗xf7† ♔h8 21.♖xc8 ♖xc8 22.g3±
  White can get this position by force, and
  has the advantage in view of the exposed black
  king. The question is whether White can create
  enough pressure against the black king, or if
  Black will manage to exchange queens and
  then draw easily.

b2) 10.a3 ♗xc3† 11.♖xc3 ♘e4 12.b4 ♘xc3
13.♕a1 ♕a4 14.♕xc3
  For the exchange, White has a pawn along
  with control over the dark squares.
14...h6
  14...a5 15.b5 ♖e8 16.♗e2 ♘f8 17.♘d4 ♘e6
  18.♘xe6 ♗xe6 19.0–0 ♖ac8 20.♖c1±
15.♗f4
  15.♗h4 a5 16.b5 ♘xc5 The bishop being
  more exposed on h4 makes this sacrifice
  playable. 17.♕xc5 ♗f5 18.♕d4 ♕xa3
  19.♗e2∞ Aronian – Kramnik, Moscow
  2010.
15...a5 16.b5
  Black now has two options:

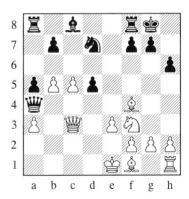

b21) 16...♖e8
  The idea is to transfer the knight to e6 in
  order to fight for the important d4-square.
17.♘d4
  17.♗e2 ♘f8 18.0–0 ♗g4 19.♕b2 ♘e6

20.♗d6 ♗xf3 21.♗xf3 ♖ad8 22.b6 ♖c8
23.♖c1 ♖ed8 24.♗e2 ♕e4∞

17...♘xc5 18.♕xc5 ♗g4

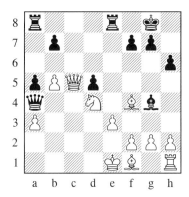

19.♗e2

19.f3 ♖ac8 20.♕xd5 g5 21.♗xg5 (21.fxg4
gxf4 22.♘f5 fxe3 23.♘xh6† ♔h8 24.♗xf7†
♔g7 25.♕g5† ♔f8 26.♗d3 ♖c1† 27.♔e2
♖xh1 28.♕h6† ♔xf7 29.♕h7†=) 21...♗e6
22.♕e5 ♖c1† 23.♔f2 ♕d1 24.♗g3 ♕e1†
25.♔f4 hxg5† 26.♕xg5† ♔f8∞

19...♖ac8 20.♗c7

20.♕xd5 ♖c1† 21.♔d2 ♖xh1 22.♗xg4
♕xa3∞

20...b6 21.♕xb6 ♗xe2 22.♔xe2 ♕c4† 23.♔f3
♖xc7 24.♕xa5±

b22) 16...♘f6 17.♘d4

17.♗d3 d4 18.♕xd4 ♕xa3 19.0–0 ♗e6∞

17...♘e4 18.♖c1 ♗d7 19.f3 ♘g5

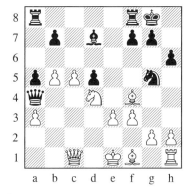

20.c6

20.♕b2 ♘e6 and now:

i) 21.♘f5 ♖fe8 22.♗d6 d4 23.e4 ♘xc5
24.♘xg7 ♖ec8 25.♘h5 ♘xe4 26.fxe4 ♖c2
27.♕a1 ♖ac8–+

ii) 21.♗e5 ♘xc5 22.♗xg7 ♖fe8 23.♔d2
♖xe3 24.♔xe3 ♕d1 25.♔f2 ♘a4 26.♕e2
♕xe2† 27.♗xe2 ♗xg7 28.♖c1 ♖c8 29.♖xc8
♗xc8 30.♗e3 ♔f6=

iii) 21.♘xe6 ♗xe6 22.♗d3 d4 23.exd4 ♗c4
24.♔d2±

20...♖ac8 21.♕c5

21.c7 ♘e6 (21...b6 22.♕b2 ♘e6 23.♘xe6
fxe6 24.♗d6 ♖f7 25.♗e2±) 22.♘xe6 fxe6
23.♕c5 ♖xf4 24.exf4 ♕xf4 25.b6 d4 26.♗e2
♕e3 27.♖f1±

21...bxc6 22.b6 ♘e6 23.♘xe6 fxe6 24.b7
♖ce8 25.♗a6 e5 26.♗g3±

We can see that in many cases White's dark-squared bishop is no worse than the black rook.

10.bxc3 0–0 11.♘d4 ♘e4 12.♗f4

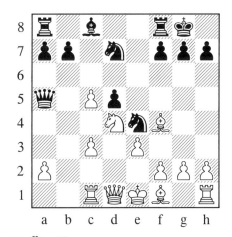

12...♕xa2!?

This is a risky move because White can take advantage of his lead in development.

12...♖e8 13.♗e2

13.f3?! ♘exc5 14.♗e2 ♘e5 15.♘b3 ♘xb3
16.axb3 ♘g6 17.♗g3 ♖xe3 18.0–0 ♗f5
19.♗f2 ♖e7∓ Giri – Kramnik, Monaco
(rapid) 2011.

13...♕xc5!?

13...♘dxc5 14.f3 ♘f6 (14...g5 15.fxe4 gxf4 16.0–0 ♖xe4 17.exf4± and the black king is somewhat weak) 15.♘b5 ♗e6 16.♗e5 ♘d7 17.♗g3 ♘b6 18.0–0 ♖d8 19.♘c7 ♘xc7 20.♗xc7 ♖d7 21.♗e5 ♘c4 22.♗d4± Cmilyte – Koneru, Moscow (rapid) 2011.

14.♘b5

14.0–0 ♘b6 15.♗d3 ♗d7 16.f3 ♘d6∞

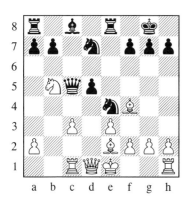

14...g5!

A typical idea for fighting against the bishop. 14...♘e5 15.♕d4 ♗d7 (15...a6 16.♕xc5 ♘xc5 17.♘c7 ♘ed3† 18.♗xd3 ♘xd3† 19.♔d2 ♘xc1 20.♘xe8 ♘d3 21.♘c7 ♘xf2 22.♘xa8 ♖xh1 23.♔e1+–) 16.♕xc5 ♘xc5 17.♖d1 ♗xb5 (17...♘ed3† 18.♖xd3 ♗xb5 19.♖xd5 ♗xe2 20.♔xe2±) 18.♗xb5 ♘c6 19.♖xd5 ♘e4 20.♖d7 ♘xc3 21.♖xb7 ♘a5 22.♗xe8 ♖xb7 23.♗c6 ♖d8 24.♗f3±

14...♘f8 15.♘c7 ♘e6 16.♘xe8 ♘xf4 17.♗f3±

15.♘c7 gxf4 16.♘xe8 ♔f8

16...fxe3 17.♕d4 exf2† 18.♔f1 ♔f8 19.♕xc5† ♘dxc5 20.♘c7 ♖b8 21.♘xd5 ♗e6∞

17.f3 ♘g5

17...♕xe3 18.fxe4 ♘e5 19.♘c7 (19.♕d2 ♘d3† 20.♕xd3 ♕c1† 21.♖d1 ♔xe8 22.exd5 ♗d7 23.0–0 ♕e3† 24.♕xe3† fxe3 25.♖e1 ♔e7 26.♖xe3† ♔d6⩲) 19...f3 20.♕d2 fxg2 21.♕xe3 gxh1=♕† 22.♔d2 ♘c4† 23.♗xc4 ♕xh2† 24.♔e2 ♕xc7

25.♕h6† ♔e7 26.♖f1→

18.exf4 ♘e6 19.f5 ♘d8

19...♘f4 20.♕d4 ♕xd4 21.cxd4 ♘xe2 22.♔xe2 ♔xe8 23.♖c7 ♔d8∞

20.c4 d4 21.♘c7 ♖xc7 22.♕xd4∞

12...♘dxc5 13.f3 ♘f6 14.♕d2 ♗d7 15.c4 ♕xd2† 16.♔xd2 ♖fc8 17.♗e5 dxc4 18.♗xc4 a6 19.e4± Le Quang Liem – Peralta, Mulhouse 2011.

13.♖c2

The alternative is 13.♗e2 and now:

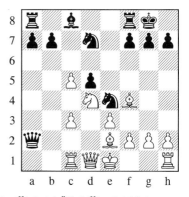

a) 13...♕a3 14.♘b5 ♕xc5 15.h3

Aimed against the ...g5 idea.

15.♘c7 g5 16.♘xa8 gxf4 17.♕d4 ♕d6 18.♖d1 ♕b8 19.♕xd5 ♘xc3 20.♕g5† ♔h8 21.♖xd7 ♗xd7 22.♕f6† ♔g8 23.♕xc3 ♗c6 24.0–0 ♕d6 25.exf4 ♖xa8∞

15...a5

15...♘df6 16.♘c7 ♖b8 17.♘a6 bxa6 18.♗xb8 ♘xf2 (18...♖xh3 19.♗e5±) 19.♔xf2 ♘e4† 20.♔g1 ♕xe3† 21.♔h2 ♗xh3 22.♕d3+–

16.♘c7 ♖a7 17.f3 ♘ef6 18.c4

18.♔f2!± is also strong.

18...♘h5 19.♗h2 ♕xe3 20.♘xd5 ♕e6 21.0–0

White has excellent compensation for the pawn.

b) 13...♕b2 14.♖c2

14.f3 ♘xc3 15.♕c2 ♕xc2 16.♖xc2 ♘e2 17.♔xe2 ♖d8 18.♖b1⩲

14...♕a3 15.0–0

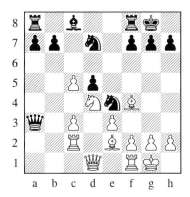

15...g5

15...♘dxc5 16.♘b5 ♕a5 17.♘c7 (17.f3
♗d7 18.fxe4 ♗xb5 19.exd5 b6∞) 17...♗d7
18.♘xa8 ♖xa8 19.♕xd5 ♘xc3 20.♕e5
♘xe2† 21.♖xe2±

15...♘df6 16.c4 ♗d7 17.cxd5 ♗a4 18.c6
bxc6 19.dxc6↑

16.♗g3 ♘xg3 17.hxg3 ♕xc5 18.c4 ♘f6
19.cxd5 ♕xd5 20.♕c1⩲

The black king is not very safe as a result of
the ...g5 move, and White has compensation.

c) 13...♕a5!

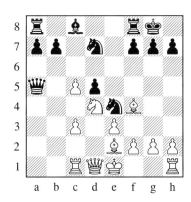

14.c6

14.0–0 ♘dxc5 15.c4 dxc4 16.♗xc4 ♗e6
17.♘xe6 ♘xe6 18.♗xe6 fxe6 19.♖c7 ♘d2
(19...♖ad8 20.♕g4 ♔f7 21.♖xf7 ♔xf7
22.♗h6 ♘e5 23.♗xg7 ♕f5∞) 20.♕g4 ♔f7
21.♕xe6 ♕f5 22.♕xf5 ♖xf5 23.♖fc1 b5∞

14...bxc6 15.f3
15.♘xc6 ♕a3 16.0–0 ♘xc3 17.♖xc3 ♕xc3
18.♕xd5 ♘b6 19.♕d6 ♗e6 20.♗e5 ♕b3
21.♗d4 ♔h8 22.♗d3 f6 23.♗e4 ♖ae8=

15...♘ef6 16.0–0 ♖e8
16...♗a6 17.♖a1 ♗xe2 18.♖xa5 ♗xd1
19.♖xd1⩲

17.c4 ♗a6
17...♘h5 18.♗d6↑

18.♖a1 ♕b6 19.♕d2 dxc4
19...♖xc4 20.♖fb1 ♕c5 21.♖a5 ♕f8 22.♗xc4
dxc4 23.♘f5↑

20.♖fb1 ♗b5 21.♗xc4 a6 22.♕a2 ♗xc4
23.♕xc4 ♕c5 24.♕xc5 ♘xc5 25.♘xc6 ♘d5
26.♗d6 ♖ec8 27.♗xc5 ♖xc6 28.♖a5=

13...♕a5

13...♕a4 14.f3± ♘exc5? 15.♗d6 ♖d8
16.♗e7 ♖e8 17.♗xc5 ♘xc5 18.♗b5+–

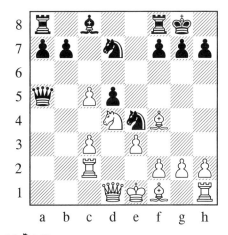

14.♘b5?

14.c6!N bxc6 (14...♘dc5 15.f3 ♘f6 16.cxb7
♗xb7 17.♗e2±) 15.♘xc6 ♕a3 and now:

a) 16.f3 ♘ef6
16...♘xc3 17.♕d2±

17.c4!?
17.♔f2 ♕c5 18.♘d4 ♘h5! Eliminating
the strong bishop. (18...♘b6 19.♕b1 ♗d7
20.♕b4±) 19.♗g3 (19.♗g5 h6 20.♗h4 ♘e5
21.g4 ♘g6 22.♗g3 ♘xg3 23.hxg3 ♗d7∞)

19...♘xg3 20.hxg3 ♘e5 21.c4 dxc4 22.♗xc4
♘xc4 23.♕d3 h6 24.♖xc4 ♕d5=

17...♖e8

17...♘h5 18.♗c7 (18.cxd5 ♘xf4 19.exf4
♖e8† 20.♗e2 ♗a6 21.0–0 ♗xe2 22.♖xe2
♕c5† 23.♔h1 ♘b6= and the d5-pawn will
fall) 18...♕xe3† 19.♕e2 ♕g5 (19...♕b3
20.cxd5 ♗a6 21.♕d2 ♗xf1 22.♖xf1 ♘hf6
23.♘e7† ♔h8 24.d6±) 20.cxd5 ♗b7 21.♔f2
♖fe8 22.♕d2±

17...dxc4 18.♕d2 ♖e8 19.♗xc4 ♘b6
20.0–0 ♘xc4 21.♖xc4 ♗d7 22.e4± It seems
likely that the a7-pawn will be weak rather
than strong, and so White has a symbolic
advantage in this position.

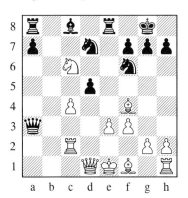

18.♕c1

18.cxd5 ♘b6 19.e4 (19.d6 ♘bd5 20.♘e7†
♘xe7 21.dxe7 ♕xe7=) 19...♘xe4 20.♖e2
♗g4 (20...♘f6 21.♖xe8† ♘xe8=) 21.♕c1
(21.fxg4? ♘xd5 22.♕xd5? ♕c3† 23.♔d1
♘f2† 24.♔xf2 ♖e1#) 21...♕xc1† 22.♗xc1
♘c3 23.fxg4 ♘bxd5 24.♖xe8† ♖xe8†
25.♔f2 ♖c8 26.♘e5 ♘d1† 27.♔e2 ♖xc1
28.♔xd2 ♘f2 29.♔xc1 ♘xh1=

18...♕xc1†

18...♕a4 19.♘d4 ♗a6 20.♔f2 dxc4 21.♗xc4
♖ac8 22.♗c7↑

19.♖xc1 dxc4 20.♗xc4 ♘b6 21.♔f2 ♘xc4
22.♖xc4 ♘d5=

b) 16.♕xd5 ♘df6 17.♕a5 ♕b3 18.♕a2 ♕xa2
19.♖xa2 ♘xc3 20.♖a5±

14...♘dxc5 15.f3 ♗d7! 16.♘c7

16...♗a4

Black could have obtained a large advantage
with:

16...♖ad8! 17.fxe4 dxe4 18.h4

18.♕b1 ♗a4 19.♕a1 (19.♕a2 g5 20.♗xg5
♘d3† 21.♗xd3 ♘xg5 22.♕xa4 exd3 23.♖d2
♕xe3† 24.♔d1 ♕c5 25.♘b5 a6∓)

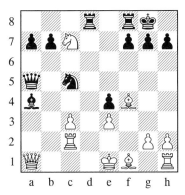

19...g5!−+ 20.♗g3 ♕b6 21.♖b2 ♘b3
22.♕xa4 ♕xe3† 23.♗e2 ♖d1† 24.♔xd1
♕c1#

18...♗b5 19.♕b1 ♗d3 20.♕a2 ♕b6 21.♖b2
♕c6 22.g3 ♗xf1 23.♔xf1 ♘d3 24.♘b5 ♘xb2
25.♕xb2 ♕b6∓

17.fxe4 ♗xc2 18.♕xc2 ♖ac8

18...♕a1† 19.♔f2 ♘xe4† 20.♔f3 (20.♔g1
♖ad8∞) 20...♖ad8 21.h4 (21.♘xd5 ♖fe8

22.♗d3 ♕xh1 23.♗xe4 ♕f1† 24.♔g3 ♕c4
25.♗xh7† ♔h8 26.♕f5 ♕xd5 27.♔h3 ♕d2
28.♗g6† ♔g8 29.♗h7† ♔f8 30.♕h8† ♔e7
31.♕xg7 ♕d5∓) 21...f5 22.g3 ♖f7 23.♔g2
♕xc3 24.♕xc3 ♘xc3 25.♘b5 ♘xb5 26.♗xb5
a6∞

19.♘xd5 ♖fe8 20.e5 ♖cd8

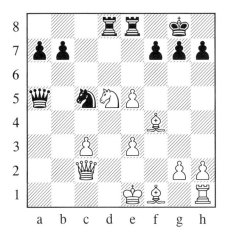

21.♗c4

White missed a chance to draw here, even
though the position looks as if it is bordering on
being lost: 21.e4! ♘xe4 22.♕xe4 ♖xd5 23.♔f2
♕c5† (23...♖d1 24.♗b5 ♖xh1 25.♗xe8 ♕xc3
26.♗xf7† ♔xf7 27.♕f5† ♔g8 28.♕e6† ♔f8
29.♕f5†=) 24.♗e3 ♖exe5 25.♗xc5 (25.♕xe5
♖d2† 26.♔e1 ♕xe5 27.♔xd2∞) 25...♖xe4
26.♗xa7 ♖f5† 27.♔g3 ♖e1 28.♗d3 Perhaps
White didn't see this move. 28...♖g5† 29.♔f4
♖xh1 30.♔xg5 ♖xh2 31.♗e4=

21...♕a1† 22.♕d1 ♕xd1† 23.♔xd1 b5 24.♗a2 ♖xd5† 25.♔xd5 ♖d8 26.♔c2 ♖xd5 27.♖b1 ♘e6 28.e4 ♖d8

28...♖c5 29.♗e3 ♖xe5 30.♗xa7 ♖xe4
31.♖xb5=

29.♗e3 a6

Black has the advantage thanks to his better
structure.

30.♖a1 ♖a8 31.♔b3

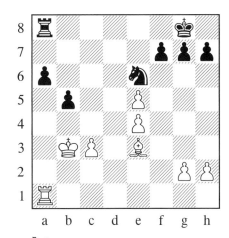

31...♘d8?!

There was no need for this move; simply
31...♔f8∓ was better. Black had no real reason
to worry about White playing ♔b4-a5-b6,
as at some point he can play ...♖c8 and keep
a solid advantage. Now White can put his
bishop to work, equalizing the position.

32.♗c5 ♘c6 33.♗d6 h5 34.c4 bxc4† 35.♔xc4

White's pieces are very active. The main idea
for Black is give up the a-pawn and use the
time to attack the pawns on g2 and h2.

35...♘d8 36.♔d5 ♘e6 37.g3 ♖c8 38.♖xa6 ♖c2 39.h4 ♖c3

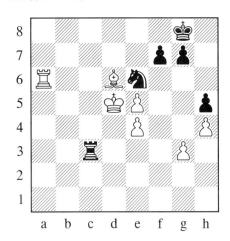

40.♖a3!

White's 40th move is a strong one! White is sacrificing the exchange, but he gets enough play to hold the draw.

40...♘c7† 41.♗xc7 ♖xa3 42.e6 fxe6† 43.♔xe6= ♖e3 44.♗f4 ♖e1

44...♖xe4† allows the white king to reach g6 and target the h5-pawn: 45.♔f5 ♖a4 46.♔g6 ♖a5 47.♗g5=

45.e5 ♔f8 46.♔f5 ♔f7 47.♔g5 g6 48.♔h6 ♖e2 49.♔h7 ♖e4 50.♔h6 ♖e2 51.♔h7 ½–½

GAME 26
▷ **P. Vallejo Pons (2716)**
▶ **V. Erdos (2608)**
Bundesliga, Muelheim
Round 1, 14.10.2011 **[D43]**
Annotated by Paco Vallejo Pons

In this game I managed to surprise my opponent with a dangerous novelty in 13.♘e5!?N. The game simplified into a major piece endgame in which White had an extra pawn and good winning chances, but I made a few subtle errors which enabled my opponent to hold the draw.

1.♘f3

I used this move during the Sao Paulo/Bilbao Grand Slam Final, and as this game was played just a few days later, I decided to keep playing with the same rhythm.

1...d5 2.d4 ♘f6 3.c4 c6 4.♘c3 e6

Back when I first started studying the Semi-Slav, I remember Dreev being its biggest supporter at the top level. Since then it has become even more popular, and nowadays virtually every top player in the world has incorporated it into his repertoire to some degree. If you want to fight for an advantage

with 1.d4 or 1.♘f3, you really need to have some ideas here! Of course the same applies to 1.e4 players against the Berlin Defence, amongst others...

5.♗g5 h6 6.♗xf6

This is the solid option. 6.♗h4 is the sharper move, but after 6...dxc4 7.e4 g5! (7...b5 transposes to the Botvinnik, another hugely complicated line) 8.♗g3 b5 practice has demonstrated that Black has enough resources. The position is highly unbalanced and plenty of wild chess is in store.

6...♕xf6 7.♕c2!?

An interesting sideline, keeping the options of e2-e4 and even long castling.

7.e3 is the main line. Here 7...g6!? is Black's latest approach to this position, trying to play ...♗g7 and ...0–0 as soon as possible. (The most frequent choice has been 7...♘d7, which has occurred in thousands of games.)

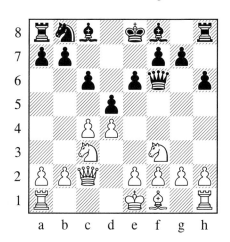

7...dxc4

This seems like the critical move to me, and has been the preferred choice of players such as Kramnik, Anand, Leko and Gelfand.

The other serious option is:
7...♘d7

But White has decent chances to fight for an advantage against this move.

8.e4 dxc4

8...dxe4 9.♕xe4 g6 10.♗d3 ♗g7 11.0–0 is more comfortable for White.

9.♗xc4

9.e5?! is premature, and after 9...♕f5 10.♕xf5 exf5 11.♗xc4 ♘b6⇄ Black is at least equal.

9...e5!

The only move that justifies this line for Black. If he played more modestly with 9...g6?! then he would find himself two tempos down on a known line where White plays ♗d3-xc4 and e3-e4.

10.0–0!

The most precise. Instead 10.d5 ♘b6 11.♗b3 ♗g4! is okay for Black.

10...♗d6

10...exd4? 11.e5! ♕g6 12.♗d3 ♕h5 13.♘xd4±

11.d5

White can play for the advantage with little risk.

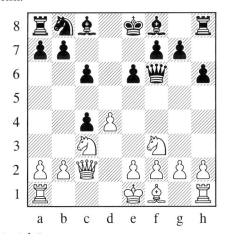

8.e3 b5

8...♕f5?! is a strange suggestion of Houdini. After the natural 9.e4 ♕g6 10.♘e5 ♕g5 11.♘xc4± White controls the centre and has a lead in development. (But note that 11.h4?! ♕d8! 12.0–0–0 b5 13.d5 ♕c7! would justify Black's unusual play.)

9.a4 ♗b7

Playing in Noteboom style with 9...♗b4? is ill-advised here: 10.axb5 cxb5 11.♕e4 ♕f5 12.♕xa8 ♕c2 13.♘d2 ♕xb2 14.♖a2! ♕c1† 15.♘d1 0–0 (15...c3? 16.♗xb5†) 16.♕xb8 a6 17.♗e2 c3 18.0–0+–

After the move played, the following sequence is more or less forced.

10.axb5 cxb5 11.♘xb5 ♗b4†□ 12.♘c3 0–0

Attempting to change the order of Black's development with 12...♘d7?! brings certain disadvantages: 13.♕a4 a5N (13...♗xc3† 14.bxc3 ♗xf3 15.gxf3 ♕xf3 16.♖g1 ♖b8 17.♖xg7 ♖b2 18.♖g2 ♕b7 19.♕xc4 ♖b1† 20.♖xb1 ♕xb1† 21.♔e2 ♕c2† 22.♔f3 ♕f5† 23.♔e2 ♕c2† 1–0 Komarov – Khenkin, Porto San Giorgio 1996.) 14.♘e5 ♖d8 15.♗xc4 ♔e7±

I prepared the following novelty for use in the Grand Slam Final, but it seems that the top players in the world have excellent intuition for avoiding preparation. My next move does not improve White's play in an objective sense, but it could well prove a highly effective surprise weapon against an unsuspecting opponent. That's modern chess!

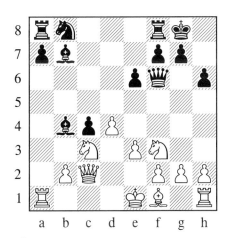

13.♘e5!?N

After the game finished, many players came to me to ask me why this natural move had never been tried before. Indeed, the fact that such a logical move was a novelty is really surprising, and says something about the lack of creativity of most players.

13.♗xc4!? led to success for White in one game, but Black did not react well: 13...♘d7? (the critical line is 13...♗xf3N 14.gxf3 ♕xf3 15.♖g1 ♘d7∞) 14.♗e2 e5 15.0–0 a5 16.♖ad1 ♖fc8 17.d5 a4 18.♕e4?! ♗xc3 19.bxc3 ♘c5?! (19...♖xc3) 20.♕xe5 ♕xe5 21.♘xe5 ♘e4 22.c4 ♘c3 23.♖d2 a3? 24.♗d3 ♘xd5 25.cxd5 a2 26.♖a1 ♗xd5 27.f4 ♖ab8 28.♔f2 1–0 Tischbierek – Luther, Austria 2002.

The previous position has occurred in close to 40 games, and 13.♗e2 has been White's choice in almost all of them. Still, but White has seldom managed to win a game with it at the top level. Here are a few relevant examples: 13...♘d7 14.0–0 ♖fc8 15.♖fc1 a5 16.♘d2 (16.♘a4 ♖ab8 17.♕d1 e5 18.♖xc4 ♖xc4 19.♗xc4 ♗xf3 20.♕xf3 ♕xf3 21.gxf3 exd4 22.exd4 ♘b6 23.♘xb6 ♖xb6 [the players agreed a draw here in Beliavsky – Kramnik, Dortmund 1998] 24.♖d1 ♔f8 25.b3 ♖g6† 26.♔f1 ♖g5 27.♖d3 ♖h5 28.♔g2 ♖g5† 29.♔f1 ♖h5 30.♔g2 ♖g5† ½–½ Kramnik – Leko, Miskolc 2007) 16...♘b6 17.♗f3 ♕e7 18.♗xb7 ♕xb7 19.h3 ♖c7 20.♕d1 ½–½ Aronian – Anand, Wijk aan Zee 2008.

13...♖c8!
The best reaction.

14.♗xc4 ♘c6
14...♗xg2!?
This move looks risky, but it is playable and may well be the critical continuation. Of course one can hardly blame Erdos for being reluctant to try it without any prior analysis.
15.♖g1 ♗b7

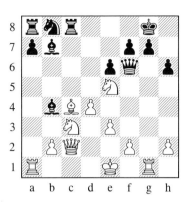

16.♔f1!?
16.♗d3 ♘c6 17.♗h7† ♔h8 18.♗e4 a5⇄
16.♕b3 a5 17.♖g4!? would be a nice idea, were it not for 17...♘c6! 18.♘xf7 a4!! when the complications work out in Black's favour.
16.♗g4!? ♕g5!? 17.h4! ♕e7 (17...♕xh4?! 18.♗xe6! fxe6 19.♕g6) Now 18.♘xh6†?! ♔h8 does not help White, but the superior 18.♗a2 keeps the game unclear.
16...♘c6 17.♘d7
17.♗g4? ♕h4 is good for Black.
17...♕e7 18.♘e4 ♔h8□

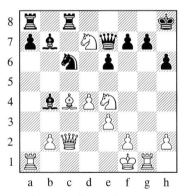

19.♖xg7! ♔xg7 20.♘ef6 ♕xf6!
20...♖h8? 21.♕e4 gives White a decisive attack.
21.♘xf6 ♔xf6 22.♕e4
The position is highly unclear, but I would estimate it to be roughly equal. Of course the whole line is rather messy, and practical testing will give a better idea as to what is really going on.

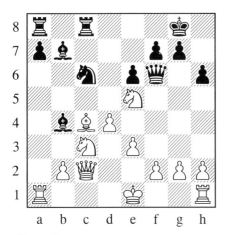

15.♘xc6 ♖xc6?!

Black would have done better to try 15...♗xc6 when he obtains decent compensation for the pawn. For instance: 16.♗a6 (16.f3 should be met by either 16...♕g5 or 16...e5!?, with decent compensation in either case.) 16...♕g5!! This subtle move would have been difficult to find over the board.

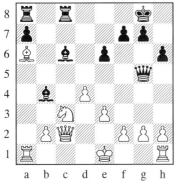

17.♖g1 (17.f4?! ♕xg2 18.♔xg2 ♗xg2 19.♖g1 ♖xc3! is an important tactical point) 17...♖c7∞

16.♗d3! ♖ac8 17.0–0 ♗xc3 18.bxc3 ♖xc3

Black has managed to regain his pawn, but this is by no means a guarantee of his safety.

19.♕b1! ♗d5! 20.♗h7†!

White should not destabilize his structure with 20.e4?! ♗b3.

Also 20.♖xa7? would be premature due to 20...♕g5 21.e4 ♖c1 22.♕b5 ♖xf1† 23.♗xf1 ♗xe4.

20...♔h8 21.♗e4

The opening is over and White's novelty has yielded pleasing results: a beautiful structure and virtually no risk of losing the game.

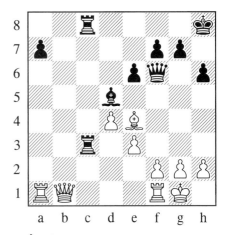

21...♗xe4

21...♖3c7? 22.♗xd5 exd5 23.♖a5 leaves Black with another weak pawn.

22.♕xe4 ♖3c7 23.g3

Another idea is 23.g4!? with the intention of preventing the typical ...g6/...h5 defensive formation. Still, I doubt that it is a real improvement over the game.

23...g6 24.♖a5

Stopping the possible ...♕f5 and preparing to double on the a-file.

24...♔g7 25.♔g2 ♖b8!

Trying to develop counterplay on the second rank.

26.♖a2

26.♖b1!? ♖xb1 27.♕xb1 ♕d8±

26...♖b5 27.♖fa1

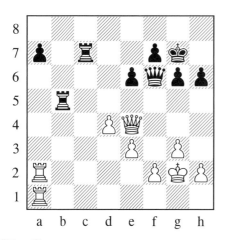

27...a5!

The best practical option, giving up the pawn in return for some activity.

28.Rxa5

After a long think I could find nothing better than going into the following endgame.

28...Rb2! 29.Wf3

After 29.Wf4?! Wxf4 30.gxf4 Rcc2 the change in the pawn structure does not improve White's chances compared with the game.

29...Rcc2 30.Rf1 h5

30...We7!? was possible.

31.h3!?

Preparing a small positional trap.

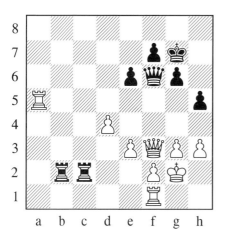

31...Rd2?!

The best way to hold the position was 31...Wxf3† 32.Kxf3 Kf6 (32...f5!?) when the pressure against f2 should be enough to ensure a successful defence. The only really important point is that after 33.g4 hxg4† 34.hxg4 Black must play 34...g5! when the draw is close.

32.g4! hxg4 33.hxg4 Wxf3†

33...g5?! would have been met by 34.Wg3! and with queens on the board Black will have to worry about his own king safety, for instance 34...Rdc2?! 35.Ra8±.

34.Kxf3 Rdc2 35.g5!±

Having achieved a bind on the kingside, White's advantage is quite serious.

35...Rd2 36.Kg3 Rdc2 37.Re5 Ra2 38.Rb5 Rd2 39.Rb3 Rdc2

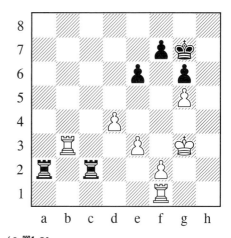

40.Rb8?

The last move of the time control, and the rook moves away from its ideal home. With the white pieces all on good squares, it was time to play 40.f4! with the following possible continuation: 40...Rg2† 41.Kf3 Rh2 42.Rc1 Rh3† 43.Ke4 Re2 44.Rcc3 Re1 45.Ke5 Re2 46.Kd6 Ra2 47.e4!?± Black faces an uphill struggle for a draw.

40...♖a5 41.f4 ♖a3! 42.♖e1 ♖d2 43.♖b4
♖c3 44.♔f3 ♖h2 45.♔e4 ♖h3 46.♖b2 ♖a3
47.♖d2

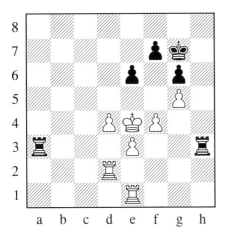

47...♖g3‼

An extremely deep move. Once I understood
it during the game, it discouraged me and I
began to have serious doubts as to whether I
could win.

48.d5?

This makes Black's defensive task easier.

48.♖d3 is the move White would like to
play, but it runs into the following defence:
48...♖xd3 49.♔xd3 f6! 50.gxf6† ♔xf6 51.♖f1

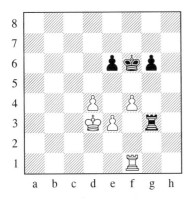

51...g5! 52.fxg5† ♔e7! Finally we see why it
was important for the rook to go to g3! (After
52...♔xg5 53.♔e4 ♔g6 White will certainly

not have an easy time winning, but Black
faces a treacherous defence with his king cut
off.) 53.♖a1 ♖xg5 54.e4 ♖g2 55.♖a7† ♔d6!
(55...♔f6? 56.e5†) 56.e5† ♔c6□ 57.♖e7 ♖g6
58.♔c4 ♖h6= White can make no further
progress.

48.♖f2! would have been the last real chance
to play for a win. Play may continue 48...f6
(48...♖h3 49.♖f3 ♖xf3 50.♔xf3 f6 51.gxf6†
♔xf6 reaches a similar endgame with one pair
of rooks removed) 49.gxf6† ♔xf6 when it is
hard to give a definite verdict, but Black would
clearly still have to work a lot longer to save
the game.

**48...exd5† 49.♖xd5 ♖h3 50.♖d8 ♖b3
51.♖e8 ♖a3 52.♖e2 ♖b3 53.♖a8 ♖h8**

This move was not necessary for the defence,
but nor does it harm it.

**54.♖xh8 ♔xh8 55.♖d2 ♔g7 56.♖d7 ♖a3
57.♔d4 ♖a4† 58.♔e5 ♖a5† 59.♖d5 ♖a3
60.e4 ♖a1 61.♖d7 ♖b1**

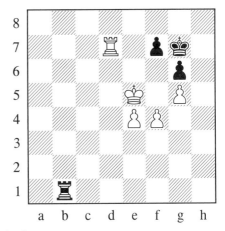

62.f5

The last try, but Erdos encountered the same
endgame against Navara not long before, so he
knew exactly what to do.

62.♖a7 ♖c1 63.♔d4 ♖f1 64.♔e3 ♖b1 65.e5
♔f8 66.♔e4 ♖b5 gives Black no trouble.

**62...gxf5 63.exf5 ♖e1†! 64.♔d6 ♖d1†
65.♔e7 ♖e1† 66.♔d6**

66.♔d8 ♖e5! is a dead draw.

**66...♖d1† 67.♔c7 ♖f1 68.♖d5 ♖g1 69.g6
fxg6 70.fxg6**

½–½

GAME 27
▷ **P. Eljanov (2683)**
▶ **A. Shirov (2713)**
Governor's Cup, Saratov
Round 7, 15.10.2011 **[D44]**
Annotated by Kamil Miton

The Botvinnik Semi-Slav still has some fans, Alexei Shirov being one of the most prominent of them. In this game Eljanov decided not to enter any sharp theoretical main lines, instead choosing 6.a4. Shirov answered with the interesting 6...b5!?, rather than the usual 6...♗b4. It turned out to be a good decision as Eljanov's reaction of 7.♗xf6 followed by 8.g3 was not the best. Black quickly assumed the initiative, although White's strong defensive play eventually brought him a draw in an endgame a pawn down.

**1.d4 d5 2.c4 c6 3.♘f3 ♘f6 4.♘c3 e6 5.♗g5
dxc4 6.a4**

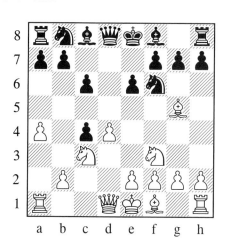

6...b5!?

The normal move is 6...♗b4, but Shirov had recently suffered an unpleasant defeat at the hands of Potkin in this line, so he decided to try an unusual and rather interesting alternative. (The Potkin – Shirov game is briefly referenced in the note to White's 11th move in Game 23 (Le Quang Liem – Dominguez Perez, D16, which began via a different move order).

7.♗xf6

A rare move, and probably not the best. Of the alternatives, it is worth paying attention to the natural 7.axb5 as well as the subtle 7.g3!?.

7.axb5 cxb5 8.♘xb5

Regaining the pawn is, unsurprisingly, White's most popular continuation.

8...♕b6

From this position both a) 9.♘c3 and b) 9.♘a3 deserve attention.

a) 9.♘c3 ♕xb2 10.♗d2

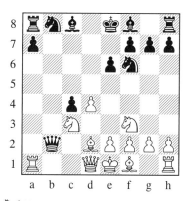

10...♘d5!

10...♗b4 11.♖b1 ♕a3 12.♘b5 ♗xd2†
13.♘xd2 ♕e7 14.e3 0–0 15.♗xc4±
10...♕b3 11.e3 ♘c6 12.♕c1 leaves Black's queen misplaced and the c4-pawn a target.
11.♘xd5

11.♖c1 should be met by the accurate
11...♘d7!, developing a piece and planning
...♘7b6 to guard the c-pawn. 12.e3 (White

should settle for a modest centre, as 12.e4 ♘xc3 13.♗xc3 ♗b4 14.♗xb4 ♕xb4† 15.♕d2 a5 16.♗xc4 0–0 gives Black promising counterplay against the pawns on e4 and d4.) 12...♘7b6 13.♘e5 ♗b4

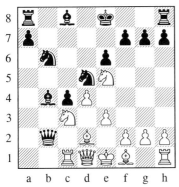

14.♖c2 (14.♖b1 ♕xd2†! 15.♔xd2 ♘xc3 16.♕h5 ♘xb1† 17.♔c1 g6 18.♕f3 0–0 19.♔xb1 ♖b8↑) 14...♘b3 15.♘e4 c3 16.♗b5† ♗d7 17.♘xd7 ♘xd7 18.0–0 ♖c8 19.♗xc3 ♘xc3 20.♘xc3 ♗xc3 (20...♖xc3 21.♖xc3 ♕xd1 22.♖xd1 ♗xc3 23.♖c1 ♔e7 24.♖xc3 ♖b8 25.♗d3=) 21.♕d3 ♔e7 22.♖fc1 ♘e5 23.dxe5 ♖hd8 24.♕e2∞

11...exd5 12.♖b1 ♕a3

Also possible is: 12...♕a2!? 13.e4 ♗d6 From here White can keep attacking the queen to force a draw, but if he tries to play more ambitiously then he risks suffering from some unpleasant tactics. For example: 14.♖b5 ♘c6

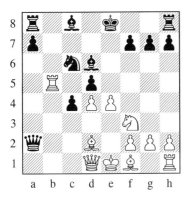

15.exd5 (15.♖xd5 ♖b8!–+) 15...♗a6! 16.♖b1 0–0 17.dxc6 ♖fe8† 18.♗e3 ♖ab8∓

13.e4

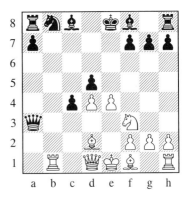

It looks like White has the makings of a promising initiative, but Black can equalize by returning his extra pawn.

13...♗d6

13...dxe4? is too risky: 14.♘e5 c3 15.♗c1 ♕a2 16.♗c4 c2 17.♗xa2 cxd1=♕† 18.♔xd1 ♗e6 19.♗xe6 fxe6 20.♖b7±

13...♘d7 14.exd5 c3 15.♗c1 ♕a2 16.♗d3 ♗d6 17.0–0 0–0 18.♖b3 ♗a6 19.♖xc3 ♗xd3 20.♕xd3 ♕xd5=

14.exd5 0–0 15.♗xc4 ♖e8† 16.♘e5 ♘d7 17.0–0

17.♖b3 ♕a4 18.♖e3 ♕xd1† 19.♔xd1 ♘xe5 20.♖he1 f6 21.dxe5 ♖xe5=

17...♘xe5 18.dxe5 ♖xe5 19.♗f4 ♖e4 20.♖a1 ♕c5 21.♗xd6 ♕xd6 22.♖e1 ♖xe1† 23.♕xe1 ♗d7=

b) 9.♘a3

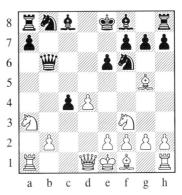

Now Black has a few possibilities, including an interesting untested one.

9...♖xa3!?N

9...♖xb2 10.♘xc4 ♗b4† 11.♗d2 ♗xd2†
12.♘cxd2 ♗a6 13.e3 ♗xf1 14.♔xf1 0–0
15.♘1d2 ♘bd7 16.0–0± Black is a bit worse as his a7-pawn could become weak.

9...♘e4 seems risky. In the following analysis I found no forced advantage for White, but still I would not entirely trust Black's play. 10.♘xc4 ♕b4† 11.♘cd2 ♘xg5 12.♘xg5 ♕xd4 13.e3

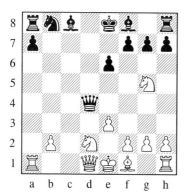

13...♕d7!? (13...♕xb2? 14.♖b1 ♕f6 15.♘ge4 ♕d8 16.♕f3+–; 13...♕d5 14.♗e2 ♗b7 15.♗f3 ♕d7 16.0–0 ♗e7 17.♘c4 ♕xd1 18.♖fxd1 ♗xf3 19.♘xf3 ♘c6 20.♘d6† ♗xd6 21.♖xd6±) 14.♕b3 ♗b7 15.♗b5 ♗c6 16.♗xc6 ♘xc6 17.0–0 ♗e7 18.♖fd1!? ♗xg5 19.♘e4 ♕c7 (19...♕e7 20.♘d6† ♔f8 21.♕a4↑) 20.♘xg5 h6 21.♘e4 0–0=

10.♕a4† ♘c6 11.♕xa3

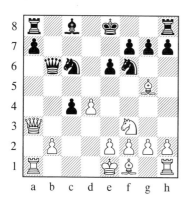

White seems to have the makings of a big advantage, as he has two bishops and the better pawn structure. Black needs to act quickly.

11...♘e4!

11...♕b4† 12.♗d2 ♕xa3 13.♖xa3±

11...♘xd4 12.♘xd4 ♕xd4 13.e3 ♕d5 14.h4!→ Black's king is vulnerable.

12.e3

After 12.♗f4 e5!? 13.♘xe5 ♘xd4 14.♕a4† ♔e7 15.♘xc4 ♘c2† 16.♔d1 ♕xf2 17.♔xc2 ♕xf4 neither king is particularly safe and the position is unclear.

12...f6

12...♕b4† 13.♕xb4 ♘xb4 14.♖c1 (14.♖a5!?) 14...♘d3† 15.♗xd3 cxd3 16.♗f4 g5! The d3-pawn is weak so Black must find some counterplay quickly. 17.♗c7 ♗b7 18.♘d2 g4 19.f3 gxf3 20.gxf3 ♘xd2 21.♔xd2 ♗xf3 22.♖hg1 ♔d7=

13.♗f4 ♘b4 14.♖c1 ♗a6

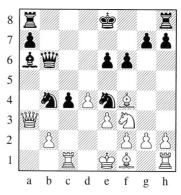

15.♗c7

15.♗e2 0–0 16.0–0 ♖fc8↑

15.♕a4† ♔e7 16.♗e2 ♖hc8 17.0–0 ♔f7∞

15.♗xc4 ♖c8 16.b3 (16.♕b3!?) 16...♘d3† 17.♗xd3 ♖xc1† 18.♕xc1 ♗xd3 19.♘d2 0–0 20.♘xe4 ♗xe4 21.0–0 ♕xb3=

15...♕xc7 16.♕xb4 ♖b8 17.♕a4†

17.♕a3 ♕e7 18.♕xa6 ♕b4† 19.♔d1 ♘xf2† 20.♔e2 ♕xb2† 21.♘d2 ♕xc1 22.♕xe6† ♔d8 23.♕d6† ♔c8=

17...♗b5 18.♕a3 ♕c6

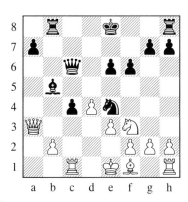

19.♗e2

　19.♘d2 ♘xd2 20.♔xd2 e5↑

19...c3 20.♗xb5 ♕xb5 21.bxc3 ♕d3 22.♕a2 0–0 23.♘d2 ♘xc3 24.♕xe6† ♖f7 25.♕c4 ♕xc4 26.♘xc4 ♖c7=

White's other interesting option on move 7 is: 7.g3!?

　Compared with the game continuation of 7.♗xf6 gxf6 8.g3, here it is less attractive for Black to advance his b-pawn.

7...♗b7

　7...b4?! does not work here, as after 8.♘e4 Black does not have the option of ...f6-f5.

8.♗g2

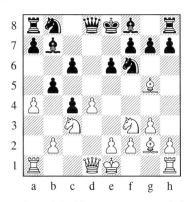

From here Black's two main candidates are a) 8...a6 and b) 8...♘bd7.

a) 8...a6 9.♘e5

　Opening the long diagonal and thus creating a threat of taking on b5.

9...♘bd7!?N

　An interesting new idea, returning the extra pawn to speed up Black's development.

　9...♕b6 has been played in several games.

　9...♕c8 10.0–0 transposes to a game which soon ended in a draw: 10...♘bd7 11.♘xd7 ♘xd7 (11...♕xd7 12.♗xf6 gxf6 13.axb5 cxb5 14.d5↑) 12.e4 h6 13.♗e3 ♗e7 14.e5 0–0 15.♕g4 ♔h8 ½–½ Romanishin – Movsesian, Solin 2006.

10.♘xc6

　Other moves are possible, but White does not seem to have an advantage anywhere:

10.0–0 ♘xe5 11.dxe5 ♕xd1 12.♖fxd1 ♘d5 13.axb5 cxb5 (13...axb5? 14.♖xa8† ♗xa8 15.♖a1 ♗b7 16.♖a7 ♗c8 17.♘e4±) 14.♘xd5 exd5 15.♗xd5 ♗xd5 16.♖xd5 ♗e7 17.♗e3 0–0 18.♖d7 ♖fe8 19.♔g2∞

10.♗xf6 ♘xf6 11.axb5 axb5 12.♗xc6† ♗xc6 13.♘xc6 ♕c8 14.♘e5 ♖xa1 15.♕xa1 ♕b7 16.0–0 ♗e7 17.♕a5 0–0 18.♕xb5 ♕xb5 19.♘xb5 ♖b8 20.♘c3 ♖xb2 21.♖a1 ♖c2 22.♖a8† ♗f8=

10...♕b6 11.d5

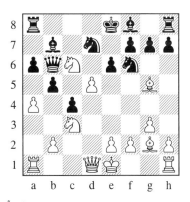

11...♗c5

　11...♘xd5 12.♘xd5 ♕xc6 13.♘f6† gxf6 14.♗xc6 ♗xc6 15.♗e3 ♗xh1 16.f3±

　11...b4 12.♗xf6 ♘xf6 13.a5 ♕c7 14.♘xb4 0–0–0∞

12.0–0 0–0 13.b4 cxb3 14.♕xb3 ♘xd5 15.♘xd5 exd5 16.♕xd5 ♖ac8 17.axb5 axb5 18.♕xd7 ♗xc6 19.♗xc6 ♕xc6 20.♕xc6 ♖xc6=

b) 8...♘bd7

Here is yet another line where Black returns the extra pawn to tame his opponent's initiative.

9.axb5

9.0–0 a6 10.♘e5 ♕b6 (10...♕c8) 11.♘xd7 ♘xd7 12.e4 e5 13.dxe5 ♘xe5 14.axb5 axb5 15.♖xa8† ♗xa8 16.♕h5 g6 17.♕h3 ♗e7 18.♗e3 ½–½ Wojtaszek – Smeets, Istanbul 2005.

9...cxb5 10.♘xb5 ♕b6 11.♘c3 ♕xb2 12.♗d2 12.♖b1 ♕xc3† 13.♗d2 ♕a3 14.♖xb7 ♖c8 15.0–0 ♕a6 16.♘e5 ♘xe5 17.dxe5 ♘d5 18.♕b1 ♗c5∓

12...♕b3 13.♕c1

White can also consider exchanging queens: 13.♕xb3 cxb3 14.0–0 ♗b4 15.♖fb1 a5 16.♖xb3 0–0 Ideally Black would prefer to put his king on e7, but here it might lead to tactical difficulties, for instance with a future bishop check on b4. 17.♘e1 ♗g2 18.♔xg2 ♖fc8 19.♘d3 ♗xc3 20.♗xc3 a4 21.♖ba3 ♘d5 22.♗e1 ♖c4 23.e3 ♖c2 24.♔f1 ♘5b6= Black keeps his a-pawn securely defended and it is tough for White to achieve anything.

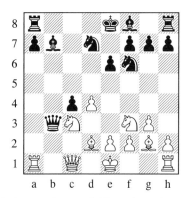

Black must be careful from here; he is behind in development, his queen is badly placed and the a7- and c4-pawns are weak.

13...♗c6 14.0–0 ♕b7 15.♖b1 ♘b6 16.♖e1 16.e4 ♘xe4 17.♘e5 ♘xc3 18.♗xc6† ♕xc6 19.♘xc6 ♘e2† 20.♔g2 ♘xc1 21.♖fxc1 ♗d6 22.♘xa7=

16...♖c8

16...♗e7 17.e4 0–0 18.♘e5 ♖ac8 19.♖a1↑ 17.♕c2 ♗e7 18.e4 0–0 19.♘e5 ♖fd8 20.♗e3 ♗e8∞

7...gxf6

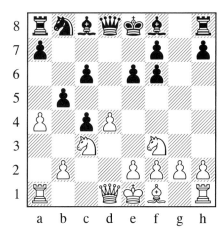

8.g3

After 8.e3 ♕b6 9.♘d2 ♗b7 10.♕h5 a6 11.♗e2 ♘d7 12.0–0 f5 White does not have enough compensation for the pawn.

8...b4

This move is often risky in such positions, as it weakens Black's structure on the queenside, especially the pawn on c4. But in this particular case, White does not have time to exploit this in a favourable way.

Another option was 8...♕b6!? 9.♗g2 ♗b7 10.0–0∞ with a complex position. White should go for a central break with e4 and d5, but Black's position should be quite reliable.

9.♘e4

The alternative was:

9.♘b1

This would have been a bit more challenging, although Black should be okay with correct play.

9...c5! 10.♗g2

10.♘bd2 c3 11.bxc3 bxc3 12.♘e4 ♗b7 13.♘xc5 ♗xc5 14.dxc5 ♘a6∓
10...♗b7 11.0–0

11.♕c2 cxd4 12.♕xc4 ♗d5 13.♕xd4 ♘c6 14.♕e3 f5 15.♘bd2 ♗g7 16.♖b1 ♕b6=
11...cxd4

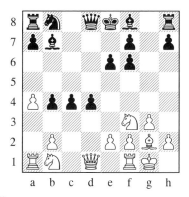

12.♕xd4

12.♕c2 d3 (12...c3 13.♖d1 cxb2 14.♕xb2 e5 15.e3⩲) 13.♕xc4 ♕d5 14.♕xd3 ♕xd3 15.exd3 If this pawn were back on e2, White would be better, especially if he could find time for the typical ♘e1-d3 manoeuvre. But here the pawn is unfavourably placed on d3, and this is enough to balance the chances.

12...♕xd4 13.♘xd4 ♗xg2 14.♔xg2 ♗c5 15.♘b5

After 15.♘f3 ♔e7 16.♘bd2 ♖c8 17.♖fc1 c3! Black exchanges his potential weakness, and 18.bxc3 ♘d7 is equal.

15...♔e7! 16.♘c7 ♖c8 17.♘xa8 ♗d4!

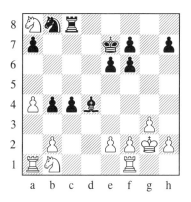

Black will soon round up the knight while keeping sufficient compensation for the exchange, for example:

18.a5 ♗xb2 19.♖a4 ♘c6 20.♘d2 ♖xa8 21.♘xc4 ♗c3⩲

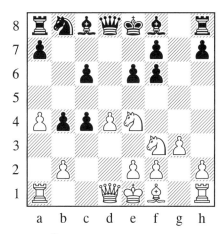

9...f5 10.♘c5

10.♘ed2 can be met by 10...c3 11.bxc3 bxc3 12.♘b3 ♗b4 or (12...♘d7 13.♗g2 ♖b8 14.0–0 ♕b6 15.♘c1 ♗a6) 13.♕c2 ♘d7 14.♗g2 0–0 15.0–0∞ when Black will soon play ...c5 with a decent position.

10...♕d5

10...♘a6 11.♘xa6 ♗xa6 12.♗g2 c5 13.♘e5 ♖c8∓

11.♖c1 ♗xc5 12.dxc5 ♘d7 13.♕d4 ♕xd4 14.♘xd4

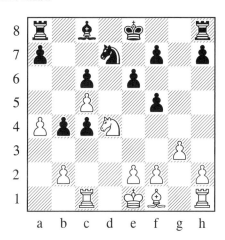

14...♘xc5

14...♗a6 is reasonable but gives Black no serious advantage: 15.e3 (15.♗g2 ♖c8 16.♗xc6 ♖xc6 17.♘xc6 ♗b7 18.♘xa7 ♗xh1 19.c6 ♘e5 20.c7 ♔d7 21.c8=♕† ♖xc8 22.♘xc8 ♔xc8 23.f4 ♘c6 24.♖xc4 ♗d5 White is worse, but he should be okay as long as he prevents the black king from coming to a5.) 15...♘xc5 16.♗c4 ♗xc4 17.♖xc4 ♘xa4 18.♖xb4 ♘b6 19.♖b3 Black keeps an extra pawn, but White's active pieces should be enough to draw.

15.♗g2 ♗d7 16.♖xc4 ♘xa4

White does not have full compensation for the missing pawn, although he should not be losing as Black has some pawn weaknesses and his pieces are not ideally coordinated.

17.♖xb4

17.♗xc6 ♖xc6 18.♘xc6 a5∓

17...c5 18.♖xa4 ♗xa4 19.♗xa8

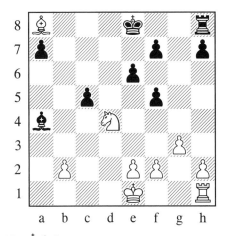

19...♔d7!?

After 19...cxd4 20.♔d2 ♗b5 21.♖a1 a6 22.♗b7 ♔e7 23.♖a3 ♖b8 24.♗xa6 ♗xa6 25.♖xa6 ♖xb2† 26.♔d3∓ White should draw.

20.♔d2 ♖xa8 21.♖a1!

A simple but important finesse.

21...♗c6 22.♘b3 c4 23.♘c5†?!

Instead of going for a blockade on the dark squares, White could have drawn more easily by attacking the c-pawn directly: 23.♘a5 ♗b5 (or 23...♗d5 24.♖a4 ♖c8 25.♔c3 followed by ♘xc4 and b3) 24.♔c3 ♖c8 25.♖d1† ♔e7 26.♖d4=

23...♔d6 24.♘a6 ♗b5 25.♔c3 ♔c6 26.♘b4† ♔c5 27.♘c2 a5 28.♘e3 a4 29.♘c2 ♖b8 30.♘b4 ♖d8 31.♘a2 h5!

If Black is to have any chance of winning the game, he must create a target on the kingside.

32.♔c2 h4 33.♘c3

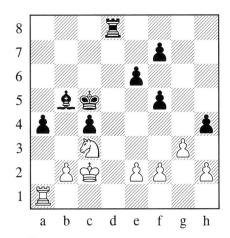

33...♖h8

Black's other possibility was to defend the a4-pawn and only then play ...♖h8 to go after the f2-pawn. But White can hold the draw here too with accurate defence: 33...♔b4 34.♖d1! (34.gxh4 ♖h8 35.♖h1 ♖xh4 36.h3 ♗c6 37.f3 f4∓; 34.♘a2† ♔a5 35.♖d1 ♖h8 36.♖d4 hxg3 37.hxg3 ♖h2 38.♖f4 ♗c6∓) 34...♖h8 35.♖d6 ♔c5 36.♘xb5 hxg3 37.hxg3 ♖h2 38.♖d7 ♔xb5 39.♖xf7 ♖xf2 40.♔d2 ♖g2 41.♖e7 ♖xg3 42.♖xe6 Not much material is left on the board, and White should have no problems drawing.

34.♘xa4† ♗xa4† 35.♖xa4 hxg3 36.hxg3 ♖h2 37.♔c3 ♖xf2 38.♖xc4† ♔d5 39.♖d4†! ♔e5 40.♖d2

The fast b-pawn will give White enough counterplay to draw.

40...♖g2 41.b4 ♖xg3† 42.♔c4 ♖g1 43.b5 ♖c1† 44.♔b4 f4 45.b6 ♖b1† 46.♔c5 f5

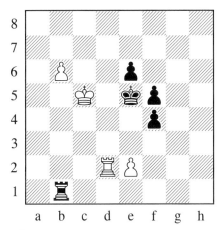

47.♔c6

47.♖c2 is also good enough: 47...♔e4 48.♖c4† (48.♖c3 e5 49.♔c6 ♖b2 50.b7 ♔d4 51.♖d3† ♔e4 52.♔c7 ♖c2† 53.♔d8 ♖b2=) 48...♔e3 49.♖b4 ♖c1† 50.♔d6 ♖c8 51.♖b2 f3 52.b7 ♖b8 53.exf3 ♔xf3 54.♔xe6 f4=

47...♔e4 48.♖d3 ♖b2 49.♔c5 ♖c2†

49...♖xe2?? 50.♖d4† followed by 51.b7 wins for White.

50.♔d6 ♖b2 51.♔c5

½–½

GAME 28
▷ **E. Bacrot (2705)**
▶ **S. Rublevsky (2681)**
12th Karpov International, Poikovsky
Round 8, 12.10.2011 **[D45]**
Annotated by Ivan Sokolov and Kamil Miton

Bacrot plays an interesting idea at an early stage in a well known line, and soon gets an edge. I would expect that Black's efforts will focus on looking at the alternative plans on move 10.

1.d4 d5 2.c4 c6 3.♘c3 ♘f6 4.e3 e6 5.♘f3 a6 6.b3 ♗b4 7.♗d2 ♘bd7 8.♗d3 0–0 9.0–0 ♗d6

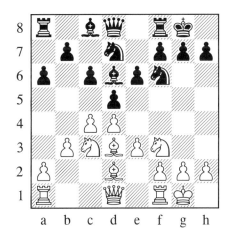

10.♖e1

This rare idea is interesting.

In practice White has often played 10.e4 dxc4 11.bxc4 e5 12.c5 ♗c7 13.♘a4 exd4 14.h3, with good compensation for the sacrificed pawn.

10...h6

This does not equalize and in future games Black is likely to look at different options:

a) 10...c5 11.cxd5 exd5 12.e4± dxe4 13.♘xe4 ♘xe4 14.♖xe4 ♘f6 15.♖h4→

b) 10...e5 11.cxd5 cxd5

11...exd4 12.exd4 ♘xd5 13.♘xd5 cxd5 and here both 14.♕c2 ♘f6 15.♘e5 and 14.♕e2 followed by ♘e5 are slightly better for White.

12.e4± exd4 13.♘xd5 ♘xd5 14.exd5 ♘f6 and now:

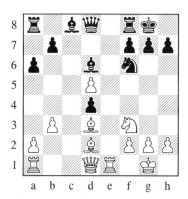

b1) 15.♗g5 h6 16.♗h4

After 16.♗xf6 ♕xf6, even if White wins the d4-pawn Black will have compensation thanks to the bishop pair, especially the strong d6-bishop.

16...♗b4 17.♖e5

17.♖e4 g5 and:

i) 18.♖xd4 ♗c3 19.♗g3 ♗xd4 20.♘xd4 ♘xd5∓

ii) 18.♗xg5 hxg5 19.♖xd4 ♗c3 (19...♗d6!?) 20.♕c1 ♗xd4 21.♕xg5† ♔h8 22.♕h6† ♔g8=

iii) 18.♘xg5 ♘xe4 19.♕h5 ♘xg5 20.♕xh6 ♕e7 21.♗xg5 f6 22.d6 ♕g7 23.♗c4† ♖f7∓

17...♗d6 18.♕d2 ♗xe5 19.♘xe5 ♕xd5 20.♗xf6 ♕d6 21.♗xg7 ♔xg7 22.♕f4 ♕f6 23.♕e4 ♗f5 24.♕xf5 ♕xf5 25.♘xf5 ♔f6 26.♘d7† ♔xf5 27.♘xf8 ♖xf8=

b2) 15.♕c2 ♗g4 16.♘xd4 ♖c8=

b3) 15.♘xd4 ♗g4

15...♘xd5 16.♘f5 ♘f4 (after 16...♗xf5 17.♗xf5 the bishop pair is much stronger

---

than the knight and bishop) 17.♗xf4 (17.♕g4!?±) 17...♗xf4 18.♘e7† ♔h8 19.♘xc8 ♖xc8 20.♕f3±

16.♘f3

16.♕b1 ♗c5=

16.f3 creates many weaknesses: 16...♗d7∞

16...♗c5

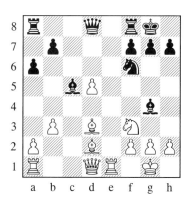

17.♗g5

17.h3 ♕xd5 18.♗xh7† ♔xh7 19.hxg4 ♖ac8∞

17...♕b6

17...h6 18.♗h4 g5 19.♗xg5 (19.♗g3 ♗b4 20.♔e3 ♘xd5 [20...♗c5!?] 21.♖e5 ♘c3 22.♕c2 ♖c8 23.♗f5 ♗xf5 24.♕xf5±) 19...hxg5 20.♕d2 ♘h5 21.♘xg5 ♕b6 (21...♗d6!?) 22.♘h7 ♖fd8 23.♕g5† ♔h8 24.♕xg4 ♗xf2† 25.♔h1 ♖xd5 26.♘g5 ♘g3† 27.hxg3 ♕h6† 28.♕h4 ♕xh4† 29.gxh4 ♗xe1 30.♗c4 ♗c3 31.♗xd5 ♗xa1 32.♘xf7† ♔g7=

18.♗h4 ♖ad8 19.h3

19.♗c4 ♗b4 20.♔e3 ♗c5∞

19...♘h5 20.g4 ♖xd5!

20...♗g6 21.♗xg6 fxg6 22.♖e5±

21.♖e5 ♖xe5 22.♘xe5 ♗d4 23.♗xf6

23.♘c4 ♕d8 24.♖c1 ♗g6 25.♗xg6 hxg6 26.♕f3 b5=

23...gxf6 24.gxh5 fxe5 25.♕g4† ♔h8 26.♕f5 ♕h6=

11.e4 dxc4 12.bxc4 e5 13.c5 ♗c7 14.♕c2 exd4

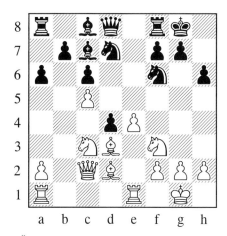

15.♘e2

This is the point behind White's play. White will recapture on d4 and in the resulting position with equal material, White will have the advantage because of his kingside pawn majority. Black will find it difficult to advance his queenside pawns or become active.

15...♘g4

15...♖e8 could be the best chance to try to equalize, even if White's position looks a touch better. We may well see it soon in practical games. 16.♘exd4 ♘e5 17.h3 ♕e7 and now:

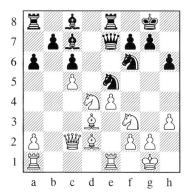

a) 18.♗f1 ♘xf3† 19.♘xf3 ♘xe4 20.♗d3 f5 21.♖ab1 ♕f7=

b) 18.♘xe5 ♕xe5 19.♘f3 ♕h5 20.e5
 20.♖e3 ♗f4 21.♖e2 ♗c7!= (21...♗xd2 22.♘xd2 ♗e6 23.f4±)

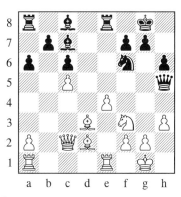

20...♗xe5

20...♗xh3 is also fine for Black: 21.exf6 (21.gxh3 ♕xf3 22.♖e3 ♕f4=) 21...♗xg2 22.♗h7† ♔h8 23.fxg7† ♔xg7 24.♗c3† ♔f8 25.♔xg2 ♕g4† 26.♔f1 ♕h3†=
21.♘xe5
 21.♖ac1 ♗c7 22.♖xe8† ♖xe8 23.♕b3 ♘f6 24.♗c4 ♘d5 25.♖e1 ♔f8∞
21...♖xe5 22.♖xe5 ♕xe5 23.♖e1 ♕d5 24.♖e3 ♗e6 25.♕b2 ♕xa2 26.♕xb7 ♖f8 27.♗c3 ♘d5 28.♖xe6 ♘xc3 29.♖xc6 ♘d1=

c) 18.♖ac1!? ♘xd3 19.♕xd3 ♘xe4 20.g4 ♗d7
 20...b6 21.♗b4±

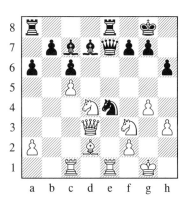

21.♖b1!

The reason for moving this rook away from c1 is illustrated by the line: 21.♖e2 ♘xc5 (21...♖ad8 22.♕c2↑) 22.♖xe7 ♘xd3 23.♖xd7 ♘xc1 24.♖xc7 ♘xa2 25.♖xb7 c5 26.♘f5∞
21...♖ab8 22.♖e2 g6

22...a5 23.罝be1 White does not need to hurry with this move, as Black is unable to free his position. 23...②xc5 24.罝xe7 ②xd3 25.罝xd7 ②xe1 26.罝xc7 ②xf3† 27.②xf3±
23.盦xh6 f5 24.②g5 豐xc5
24...②e5 25.②df3 豐d5 26.豐c2 ②xg5 27.②xg5 罝xe2 28.豐xe2 罝e8 29.豐c2 盦c8 (29...②e5 30.②f3 豐d5 31.豐c3 罝e7 32.豐f6 豐f7 33.盦g5 豐xf6 34.盦xf6 罝f7 35.g5↑) 30.罝d1 豐e5 31.豐b3† 罝e6 32.②f3 豐xc5 33.罝d3→
25.②xf5 盦xf5 26.gxf5 ②xg5 27.罝xe8† 罝xe8 28.盦xg5 豐xf5 29.豐xf5 gxf5 30.罝xb7 盦e5 31.罝b6 盦d4=
Black will play ...罝e2 next.

16.②exd4 ②de5

16...②ge5 17.盦f1 (17.盦e2 豐e7 18.罝ac1 罝d8 is similar) 17...豐e7 18.罝ac1 罝d8 19.h3±

17.h3 ②xd3

17...②h2 18.②xe5 豐xd4 19.②c4+– and the black knight is in trouble.

17...②xf3† 18.②xf3 ②e5 19.②xe5 盦xe5 20.罝ab1±

18.豐xd3 ②e5 19.②xe5 盦xe5

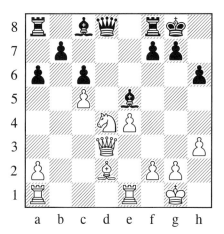

20.盦e3± 豐f6 21.罝ad1 罝d8 22.豐c4 盦c7
Black can try various other moves, but none of them equalize:

22...豐g6?? 23.②xc6!

22...盦e6 23.②xe6 豐xe6 24.豐xe6 fxe6 25.f4 盦c3 26.罝f1 ②f7 27.②f2±

22...盦xh3 23.gxh3 豐g6† 24.②f1 豐e4 25.盦xh6 (25.豐d3!? 豐h4 26.②g2 盦f6 27.f4 罝d5 28.豐e2±) 25...豐h1† 26.②e2 豐xh3 27.②f3 豐xh6 28.②xe5 豐h5† 29.②g4±

22...罝b8 23.②h1 盦c7 24.f4 盦xf4 25.罝f1 盦e6 25...罝xe3 26.罝xf6 gxf6 27.豐b3!±
26.豐c2
26.豐e2 g5 27.g3 罝xh3 28.罝f2 豐e5 29.gxf4 豐xe4† 30.②h2 g4 31.豐d3±
26...g5 27.g3 盦xh3 28.罝f2 盦g4
28...豐g6 29.gxf4 豐h5 and White must avoid 30.罝g1? 罝xd4! 31.盦xd4 罝d8 when he would have to return and all the sacrificed material, but instead 30.罝b1 leaves Black without sufficient compensation.
29.罝dd2
Black will not get enough compensation.

23.豐c2

23.②h1?! 豐h4 24.②f3 罝xd1 25.罝xd1 豐h5=

23...豐g6

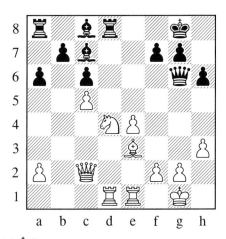

24.②f1

24.②f5 盦xf5 25.exf5 豐f6=

24.♔h1

This also looks better for White.

24...♖h5 25.f4 ♗g4

25...♖a5 26.♖g1! ♖e8 (26...♗xh3?? 27.gxh3 ♕xh3† 28.♕h2 ♕xe3 29.♖xg7†+– ♔f8 30.♖xf7†! ♔xf7 31.♕h5† ♔f8 32.♕xh6† ♔g8 [32...♔f7 33.♕h7† leads to mate] 33.♖g1†+–) 27.e5 f6 28.♕b3†±

26.♖d3 ♖e8 27.e5 ♖ad8 28.♔g1 ♗c8 29.♗f2±

24...♗d7 25.f4 ♕f6 26.f5!

Black's light-squared bishop will now remain passive.

26...b6

Black could just wait with 26...♗e8±, but he prefers to try to get some activity.

27.♘f3 bxc5 28.♗xc5

White is clearly dominating.

28...♗g3 29.♗d4 ♕e7 30.♗c5 ♕f6

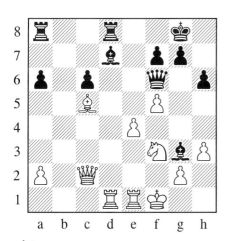

31.♗f2

The g3-bishop was annoying White, and so he decided to exchange it. This was not an easy choice to make, since White's bishop on c5 was also well placed.

31.♖e3 was an alternative.

31...♗xf2 32.♔xf2 ♕e7 33.e5 ♗e8

White has a great position; however, it is not so easy to increase his advantage into a decisive one

34.♕c3

34.g4 c5∞

34.♖xd8 ♖xd8 35.♖d1 ♖xd1 36.♕xd1 c5 37.♕d6 ♗a7±

34...c5 35.f6!

White has to go for a direct assault before Black activates his e8-bishop.

35...♕e6 36.♕xc5

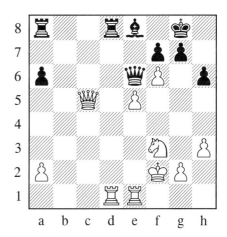

36...gxf6?!

36...♖xd1 37.♖xd1 ♖c8 38.♕a5 (38.♕e3 ♕xa2† 39.♔g1 ♗c6 40.fxg7 ♗xf3 41.♕xf3 ♕b2 42.♖f1 ♕b6† 43.♔h2 ♕e6=) 38...gxf6 39.♖d6 ♕c2† 40.♔g3 ♕xa2 41.♕xa2 ♖xa2 42.♖d8 ♔f8 43.exf6 ♖b2 44.♘d2 ♖b6 45.♘e4 ♖e6 46.♔f4↑

36...♖ac8 may be a more accurate defence: 38...♖dc8 37.♕a5 ♖c2† 38.♔g3 ♖dc8 39.♖d2 ♕f5 40.♖xc2 ♕g6† 41.♔f4 ♖xc2 (41...♖xc2 42.♕d8 ♖c4† 43.♗e3±) 42.♕xa6 ♖c6 43.♕a8 ♖c8 44.♕b7 ♖c7∞ 45.♕b3 ♕xg2 46.♖g1? g5†!

37.♖d6 ♖xd6

White gets a tremendous attack in the event of 37...♕xa2† 38.♖e2 ♖dc8! 39.♕e3 ♖c2 40.♘d2.

38.exd6 ♕xa2†

White has an obvious advantage. The white d-pawn is immensely strong, while the black kingside has been weakened. Still, accuracy is needed to bring this home.

39.♖e2 ♕a4

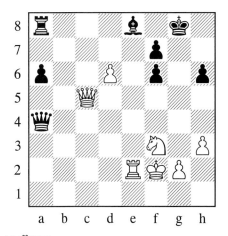

40.♕f5?!

It seems likely that White was in time pressure and missed Black's tactical resource on the 44th move.

40.♖e7, with ♘d4 to follow, looks strong for White, as does the immediate 40.♘d4.

40...♔g7 41.♖e7 ♖d8

White now makes a sensible decision to accept a forced drawing line.

42.d7

42.♕d3 would continue the fight, but after 42...♗b5 43.♖xf7† ♔xf7 44.♕h7† ♔e6 45.♕e7† ♔d5 46.♕xd8 ♕c2† the d6-pawn has become a weakness.

42...♗xd7 43.♕d5 ♕c2† 44.♔g1 ♕xg2† 45.♔xg2 ♗xh3† 46.♔xh3 ♖xd5=

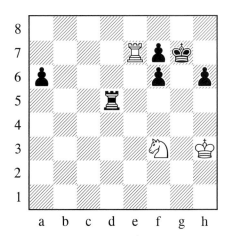

47.♖a7 ♖a5 48.♘d4 ♔g6 49.♘c6 ♖a3† 50.♔h4 ♖a4† 51.♔h3 h5
½–½

GAME 29
▷ **E. Tomashevsky (2710)**
▶ **Ni Hua (2670)**
Governor's Cup, Saratov
Round 3, 10.10.2011 **[D45]**
Annotated by Ivan Sokolov

In this topical line, Ni Hua opted for 16...♗g6, a move which was first played a few weeks earlier in Jakovenko – Sakaev, St Petersburg 2011. (Previously 16...♗f5 had occurred in Wojtaszek – I. Sokolov, Khanty-Mansiysk [ol] 2010.) Tomashevsky convincingly demonstrated the way to an advantage for White with the strong plan introduced by 18.♘a4!N.

1.d4 d5 2.c4 c6 3.♘c3 ♘f6 4.e3 a6 5.♕c2 e6 6.♘f3 c5 7.cxd5 exd5 8.♗e2 ♗e6 9.0–0

9.dxc5 ♗xc5 10.♘d4 0–0 has not proved to offer White much.

9...♘c6 10.♖d1 ♘b4 11.♕b1 ♕c8

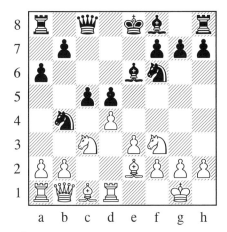

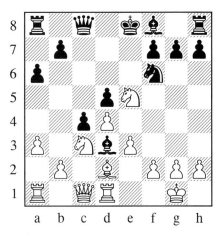

12.♗d2

With the black king still on e8, White can try opening up the centre with 12.e4. However, practice has shown that Black has enough resources and the game is approximately equal after 12...dxe4 13.♘xe4 ♗f5 14.♘fg5 ♘xe4 15.♘xe4 cxd4 16.♖xd4 ♗e7 17.♗g5 f6 18.♗d2 ♘c6 19.♖d5 ♗g6 20.♗d3 0–0, as in Mamedyarov – Grischuk, Baku 2008.

12...♗f5 13.♕c1 c4 14.a3

This idea for White was first played by Wojtaszek against me in the last Olympiad.

14.♘e1? ♗d6 15.b3 b5 16.bxc4 bxc4 17.♗f3 ♕e6 18.♘a4 a5 19.a3 ♘d3 20.♘xd3 ♗xd3 21.♘c5 ♗xc5 22.dxc5 0–0 23.♕b2 ♘e4 and Black was clearly better and went on to win in Krasenkow – I. Sokolov, Izmir 2004.

14.♘e5!? ♗d6 15.b3 b5 16.bxc4 bxc4 17.a3 ♘c6 18.♘xd5! The point behind White's play. 18...♘xe5 19.♕xc4 ♗e6 20.♘xf6† ♗xf6 21.d5 ♘e5 22.♕a2 ♗g4 23.f3 ♗d7 24.♖ac1 ♕b8 25.♗b4 With the black king stuck in the middle, White had strong compensation for the sacrificed piece and managed to win in Wang Yue – Rublevsky, Ningbo 2010.

14...♘d3 15.♗xd3 ♗xd3 16.♘e5

16...♗g6

This is the recent attempt for Black. In this position I opted for:

16...♗f5

The position looks dangerous for Black, however in the following game White did not manage to find a way to an advantage.

17.e4! dxe4 18.♗g5

It is important to note that the plan employed by Tomashevsky does not work here: 18.♘a4 ♕e6 19.♘xc4? With the c8-square covered by the f5-bishop, this blunders a pawn. 19...b5 20.♘cb6 ♖d8 21.d5 ♘xd5 22.♘xd5 ♖xd5 23.♘c3 ♖d3∓

18...♕e6! 19.♘e2 ♘d5 20.♘f4 ♘xf4 21.♗xf4 ♖c8! 22.d5 ♕f6 23.d6 ♗xd6 24.♖xd6 ♕xd6

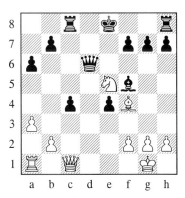

25.♘xf7 ♕e6 26.♘d6†

26.♘xh8 ♔f8= and the knight on h8 will be collected.

26...♔f8

26...♔e7? 27.♕c3

27.♕c3 ♖d8 28.♖d1?

A big mistake by White, which is difficult to explain.

28.♕a5 ♖xd6 29.♗xd6† ♔f7 30.♕c7† ♔g6 31.♗b4 ♕d5 32.♗c3 ♖g8 and a draw is the most likely result.

28...♔g8!∓ 29.♖d2 ♗g6 30.♗e5 ♖d7 31.♘xc4 h6 32.♘d6 ♔h7–+

Wojtaszek – I. Sokolov, Khanty-Mansiysk (ol) 2010.

17.e4 dxe4

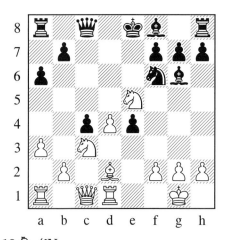

18.♘a4!N

Tomashevsky embarks on an interesting plan, showing the disadvantage of Black placing his bishop on g6 (instead of f5), and hence not controlling the c8-square!

Black is fine in the event of:

18.♗f4 b5 19.♘xg6 hxg6 20.♘xe4 ♘xe4 21.♕e3 ♕e6 22.d5 ♗c5

22...♕e7!? 23.d6 ♘xd6 24.♕b6 (24.♕c5 ♖c8) 24...♕b7 25.♖xd6 ♕xb6 26.♖e1† ♗e7 27.♖xb6 ♔f8∓

22...♕f5!? 23.♖d4 0–0–0 24.♖xe4 ♕xd5 25.♕b6 ♕b7∞

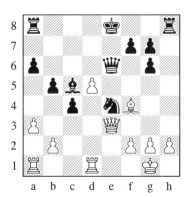

23.dxe6 ♗xe3 24.exf7† ♔xf7 25.♗xe3 ♖hd8 26.♗b6 ♖xd1† 27.♖xd1 ♖e8

This endgame was eventually drawn in Jakovenko – Sakaev, St Petersburg 2011.

18...♕e6 19.♘xc4!

19.♕xc4?? blunders a piece to 19...♕xc4 20.♘xc4 b5 21.♘cb6 ♖b8 22.♗f4 ♖b7 23.♖ac1 ♗f5.

19...♗e7

Black has a difficult task here, and other moves do not seem to equalize either:

19...♗h5?! 20.♖e1±

19...b5? is now bad for Black: 20.♘cb6 ♖d8 (20...♖b8? 21.d5+–) 21.d5! ♘xd5

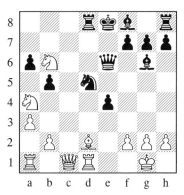

22.♗a5! bxa4 23.♘xd5 ♖xd5 24.♖xd5 ♕xd5 25.♕c8† ♔e7 26.♗b4† ♔f6 27.♗xf8+–

19...♘d5

Arguably Black's best alternative.

20.♘c3

White may also go for the more complicated 20.♘c5 ♗xc5 21.dxc5 0–0 22.♘d6 and now:

a) 22...♗h5 23.♖e1 f5 24.♘xb7 f4 (24...♕g6? 25.♕c4) 25.♘d6 e3 26.♕c4 ♔h8 27.fxe3 f3 28.♖f1 ♕g6 29.♖f2±

b) 22...f5 can be met by the safe 23.♗f4!± or the rather murky 23.♘xb7 f4 24.♘d6 e3 25.♗e1 e2 (25...f3 26.♕c4) 26.♖d4 f3 27.♕c4.

20...♖d8 21.♘xd5 ♖xd5 22.♗c3 f6 23.♘e3 ♖d8 24.d5±

20.♘c5

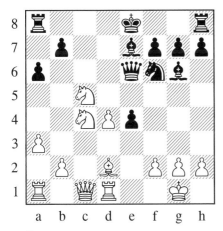

20...♕c6

20...♗xc5 21.dxc5 0–0 22.♘d6±

21.♘a5

The most direct, going for the b-pawn.

White could also play for a positional advantage: 21.♘e5 ♕d5 22.♘c4 ♕xc4 (After 22...b6 23.♕xd5 ♘xd5 24.♘xg6 hxg6 25.♘xe4± Black would have reasonable chances to hold, but he is a pawn down and would have to defend for a long time.) 23.♘xc4±

21...♕d5

This is the most natural square for the queen. After 21...♕b6 22.♘axb7 0–0 23.♘a5 White will gain a tempo with ♘c4.

22.♘axb7!

It is a good decision by White to take with the a5-knight. The other white knight remains on c5, controlling many squares! Should White take with the c5-knight (the move preferred by some computer engines), Black gets reasonable chances of counterplay:

22.♘cxb7 0–0 23.♕c7 ♖fe8 24.♖ac1

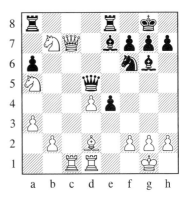

White's problem here is that his knights are not doing much, while Black obtains counterplay on the other side of the board.

24...♘g4

24...e3 does not seem to fully work for Black. Here is one interesting line: 25.♗xe3 (25.fxe3 ♗e4⩲) 25...♘g4 26.♖e1 ♘xe3 27.♖xe3 ♗g5 28.♖xe8† ♖xe8 29.♘d6 ♗f4! (29...♖f8 30.♕c5+−) 30.♕e7! ♖f8 31.♖c8 ♖xc8 32.♘xc8 h5 33.♕e1! ♗g5 (33...♖xd4 34.♘e7† ♔h7 35.♘xg6±) 34.♕e5 ♕a2 35.h3 ♗f6 36.♘e7† ♔h7 37.♕e3 ♗xe7 (37...♖xb2 38.♘ac6±) 38.♕xe7 ♕b1† 39.♔h2 ♕xb2 40.♕e3 ♕b6 41.♕c3 ♕b8† 42.♕g3 (42.g3? ♕b1 43.♘b3 ♗e4) 42...♕b5 43.♘b3 ♕d5 44.♔g1! ♗e4 45.♘c5 ♕xd4 46.♘xa6 f6 47.♘b4±

25.♕f4

25.♖e1? ♕xd4

25...♗h5

25...e3?! 26.fxe3

26.♖e1 ♕xd4

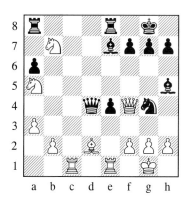

27.♗c3

27.♘c6?! ♕xb2 28.♖xe4 ♗f8 29.♕xe8 ♖xe8 30.♖xe8 and here the correct way to give the king some air is 30...h6∓. Instead 30...f6? would lead to an entertaining king chase: 31.♘e7† ♔f7 32.♘d6† ♔e6 33.♘g6†!+– ♔xd6 (33...♔d5 34.♘c4+–) 34.♖d8† ♔e6 35.♘xf8† ♔f5 (35...♔f7? 36.♖c7†) 36.♖d5† ♘e5 (36...♔e4? 37.♖xh5 ♕xd2 38.♖c4† ♔d3 39.♖d5†) 37.♖c4! ♕b1† 38.♗c1 ♗e2 (38...g5 39.h3+–) 39.f3! ♗xf3 (39...h5 40.♖f4† ♔g5 41.h4† ♔h6 42.♖xf6#) 40.gxf3+–

27...♕b6

Note that the white knights remain stranded on a5 and b7.

28.♖xe4 ♗h4 29.♖xe8† ♖xe8 30.♖f1

30.♗d4 ♗g5! 31.♖xg5 ♕xd4 32.♕c5 ♕xb2 is at least equal for Black.

30...♗xf2†!

Due to the badly placed white knights, Black can afford this tactical solution.

31.♖xf2 ♘xf2 32.♔xf2 ♕g6 33.♘c5 ♖e2 34.♕f1 ♕g5 35.♘ab3 ♕d5

Knights defending each other are generally not good – it is difficult for White to untangle, and Black has good compensation.

22...0–0

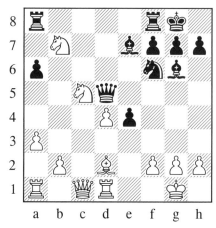

23.♕c3±

A difficult situation for Black. The white knights are simply controlling too many squares and no compensation for the lost pawn is to be found.

23...♖a7

Other ideas for Black do not work either. Some possible lines are:

23...♖ac8 24.♖ac1 ♖fe8 25.♕c4 ♕f5 26.h3 h5 (26...♘d5? 27.g4) 27.♕xa6 ♖a8 (27...♘d5? 28.♘d6) 28.♕c6 ♖ac8 29.♕b5 ♘d5 30.♕d7+–

23...♕f5 24.b4 ♘d5 25.♕b3 ♖fe8 (25...h5? 26.♖e1) 26.♖ac1 h5 27.♖e1 ♗f8 28.♘a5±

24.♘a5 ♗d6 25.♘c4 ♗b8 26.♘e5

The white knights are so strong that Black does not have even a glimmer of compensation.

26...♖e8

Black's problem here is that even if he manages to capture on e5 at a good moment and get his pawn back, White will still have a huge advantage due to his queenside pawn majority and the badly placed bishop on g6.

27.♖ac1 ♕d6 28.♕h3

White prepares a tactical solution.

28...♘d5

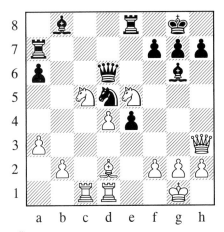

29.♘xg6!

Now Black has to choose between losing a second pawn or having his kingside pawn structure destroyed.

29...♛xg6 30.♘xe4 ♖ae7 31.♘c3 ♘f6 32.♛f3

Black's activity is of a rather temporary nature and is not even close to being compensation for the deficit of two pawns. Tomashevsky routinely brings his material advantage home.

32...♘g4 33.h3! ♘h2 34.♛d5 ♛d3

For Black's attack to work here, White would have to start seeing "ghosts".

35.♘b1 ♖e2 36.♗b4

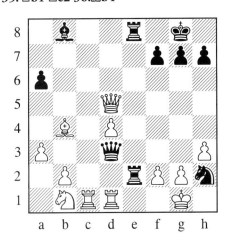

36...♖c2

36...♛g6 37.♖e1±

37.♗d6

White is completely winning.

37...♖xc1 38.♖xc1 ♘f3†

The only way for Black to prevent further material losses, but the game now becomes an endgame in which White is two pawns up.

39.♛xf3 ♛xf3 40.gxf3 ♗xd6 41.♔f1 a5 42.♖c6 ♗e7 43.♘c3 ♖b8 44.♘d5 ♗d8

Or 44...♗f8 45.♖b6 ♖d8 46.♖b5+–.

45.b4 ♔f8 46.♔e2

1–0

GAME 30

▷ **D. Jakovenko (2716)**
▶ **B. Gelfand (2746)**
European Club Cup, Rogaska Slatina
28.09.2011 **[D56]**
Annotated by Kamil Miton

In this game we witness an improvement to a game between Radjabov and Kramnik, with Jakovenko playing 37.h3!?N. However, it does not change the evaluation of the variation, because Black is still able to equalize. But it seems to me that Gelfand was quite surprised by this idea. He did not react properly at several points and was then faced with a difficult rook ending.

1.d4 ♘f6 2.c4 e6 3.♘f3 d5 4.♘c3 ♗e7 5.♗g5 h6 6.♗h4 0–0 7.e3 ♘e4 8.♗xe7 ♛xe7 9.♖c1 c6 10.♗d3

10.h4!? was the choice in Aronian – Harikrishna, Ningbo 2011 (see Game 31 in the previous issue of *Chess Evolution*).

10...♘xc3 11.♖xc3 dxc4 12.♗xc4 ♘d7

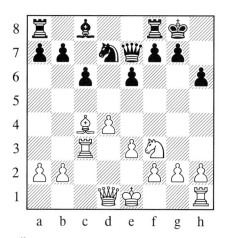

13.♕c2

13.0–0 is the main move.

13...b6

13...e5 is another plan for Black.

14.♗d3 ♘f6

14...♗b7 15.♗h7† ♔h8 16.♗e4±
The principal alternative is 14...c5 15.♗h7†
(15.dxc5 ♘xc5 16.♗h7† ♔h8 17.b4 ♘a6∓)
15...♔h8 16.♗e4 ♖b8 and now:

a) 17.b4 ♘f6⇄

b) 17.♗c6 cxd4
17...♗b7 18.♗xb7 (18.♗xd7?! ♕xd7 19.dxc5
bxc5 20.b3 One of White's idea is to get this
kind of position, but the final game of the
Topalov – Anand World Championship
match showed us that White does not have
enough time to take advantage of his better
structure, and that Black gains counterplay
thanks to his strong bishop. 20...♖fd8
[or 20...♕b5] 21.♖xc5 [21.0–0 ♗xf3
22.gxf3 e5 23.♔g2 ♖b6↑] 21...♗a6 22.♘e5
♕b7 23.♖c7 [23.f3∞] 23...♕xg2 24.♘xf7†
♔g8 25.♘xh6† ♔h8 26.♘f7†=) 18...♖xb7
19.0–0±
18.exd4
18.♘xd4 e5=

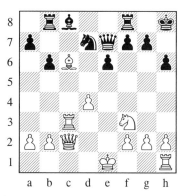

18...♗b7

18...♗a6!? 19.♕a4 e5 20.♖e3 (20.♕a3 ♖fe8
21.d5 ♘c5↑ 22.♗xe8 e4 23.♘d2 ♖xe8
24.♖xc5 ♕xc5 25.♕xc5 bxc5 26.♘b3 ♗c4
27.♘xc5 ♗xd5=) 20...♖bc8 21.♗xd7 ♖c1†
22.♔d2 ♖xh1 23.♘xe5 ♕h4 24.♕xa6
(24.g3 ♕xh2 25.♕xa6 ♕xf2† 26.♔e2
♕g1∞) 24...♕xd4† 25.♔c2 (25.♕d3 ♕xb2†
26.♕c2 ♕xc2† 27.♔xc2 ♖xh2 28.♗h3
♖h1∞) 25...♕d1† (25...♕b1 26.♘d3 ♖f1∞)
26.♔c3 ♕c1† 27.♔b3 ♕d1† The position
is very complicated, but it is clear that only
White can play for a win.
19.♗xb7 ♖xb7 20.0–0 ♘f6 21.♖c1 ♘d5
22.♖c4 ♔g8 23.♘e5

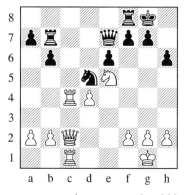

In my opinion, the position should be equal.
Black does not have any serious weaknesses and
has a strong knight on the d5-square. There is
not much that can be accomplished through
White's control of the c-file, and it is hard
to find a way to strengthen White's position.

Perhaps the moves a4 and b4-b5 could be employed in order to reinforce control of the c6-square, but Black should be fine.

c) 17.0–0

Compared with the main line after 13.0–0, the black king is on the inferior h8-square. This small difference means that king does not defend the f7-pawn and is further from centre. Maybe this is the reason why some players prefer to start with 13. ♕c2.

17...♘f6

17...♗a6 18.♖c1 ♖fc8 19.♕a4 ♗b7 20.♗xb7 ♖xb7 21.♕a6±

17...♗b7 18.♗xb7 ♖xb7 19.dxc5 ♘xc5 20.b4 ♘a6 (20...♘d7 21.♖c7±) 21.a3± and the a6-knight is poorly placed.

18.♘e5!?

18.dxc5 ♘xe4 19.♕xe4 bxc5 The same position, but with the black king on g8, occurred in the Topalov – Anand game that we have mentioned. 20.b3 ♗b7 21.♕f4 ♖fd8 22.♘e5 ♔g8 23.♖fc1 ♖bc8 24.♘d3±

18...♘xe4 19.♕xe4

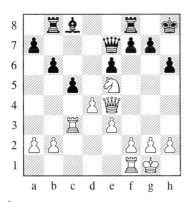

19...♗b7

19...cxd4 20.exd4 ♗b7 21.♕f4 ♖bc8 22.♖xc8 ♗xc8 23.♖c1 ♔g8=

20.♕f4 ♖bc8

20...♔g8 21.dxc5 bxc5 22.♖fc1±
20...cxd4 21.♖c7±

21.♖fc1

21.♖d1 cxd4 22.♖xc8 ♖xc8 23.♘xf7†

(23.♕xf7 ♕xf7 24.♘xf7† ♔g8 25.♘d6 ♖c7 26.♘xb7 dxe3 27.♘d6 e2 28.♖e1 ♖d7 29.♖xe2 ♖xd6=) 23...♔g8 24.♘d6 ♖c2 25.♘xb7 ♕xb7 26.♖xd4 ♕d5 27.♕xd5 exd5=

21...cxd4 22.♖xc8

22.♖c7?? ♖xc7 23.♖xc7 ♕xc7 24.♘g6† fxg6 25.♕xc7 ♖c8–+

22...♖xc8 23.♖xc8† ♗xc8 24.♘xf7† ♔g8 25.♘e5 dxe3 26.♕xe3 ♕b4=

Objectively White should have some advantage because queen and knight usually cooperate better than queen and bishop, and the pawn on e6 is badly situated, but for practical purposes the position is equal.

15.♖xc6

15.e4 ♗b7 16.0–0 ♖ac8 17.♖c1 ♖fd8= White's centre is good, but Black's position is very solid – his main plan is to prepare ...c5.

15.♘e5 ♘d5 16.♖b3 ♗b7 17.0–0 c5 18.dxc5 ♖ac8 19.c6 ♕d6 20.♕b1 ♗xc6 21.♘xc6 ♖xc6 22.♗h7† ♔h8 23.♗e4= Normally the bishop would be better than the knight, but here the queen on b1 and rook on b3 are uncoordinated.

15...♘d5

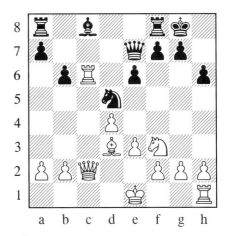

16.♕b3

16.a3 ♗d7 17.♖c4 ♗b5∓

16.♕d2 ♞b4
  16...♝b7 17.♖c4±

17.♖c3 ♞xd3†
  17...♞xa2 18.♖b3 a5 19.♖xb6 ♞b4 20.♝e2
♕a7 21.♖b5 ♝a6 22.♖xa5 ♕b6 23.♖a3 ♖fc8
24.♝xa6 ♞c2† 25.♔e2 ♖xa6 26.♖c3 ♖xc3
27.♕xc3 ♕b5† 28.♕d3 ♕xb2 29.♞d2 ♖a3
30.♖b1 ♕xb1 31.♞xb1 ♖xd3 32.♔xd3
♞e1†=

18.♕xd3 ♝b7

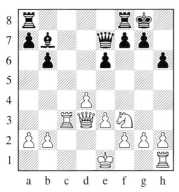

The strong bishop on b7, which may also
attack from the a6-square, compensates for
the loss of the pawn. The optimal solution
for White would be to position his pawns on
f3 and e4 in order to blunt the bishop and
place his king on the more secure f2-square.
However, White does not have enough time
to perform these actions.

19.♔e2
  19.e4 f5⇄
  19.0–0 ♝xf3 20.gxf3 ♕g5† 21.♔h1 ♕d5=

19...♕b4
  19...a5 20.♕c2 ♝a6† 21.♔d2∞

20.♖hc1 ♕xb2†
  20...♖fc8 21.♖xc8† ♖xc8 22.♖xc8† ♝xc8
23.b3 (23.♕b3 ♝a6† 24.♔d1 ♕a5 25.♞e5
♝f1 26.g4 ♕a6⇄) 23...♕a5 24.♕c2 ♝a6†
25.♔d1 ♝f1 26.♞e1 ♕h5† 27.♔c1 ♕xh2=

21.♖1c2 ♕b4
  21...♕b1 22.♖c7 ♖ab8 23.e4 ♖fd8 24.♔e3±

22.♖c7 ♖ab8 23.♞e5 ♕a5 24.♔d1 ♝a6
25.♕c3 ♕b5 26.♞d7 ♖bc8 27.♞xf8 ♖xc7

28.♕xc7 ♕f1† 29.♔d2 ♕xf2† 30.♔c1 ♕xe3†
31.♔b2 ♕xd4† 32.♔a3 ♝b5∞

16...♞b4 17.♖c1 ♞xd3† 18.♖xd3 ♝b7 19.0–0

After 19.♕b5 a6 20.♕xb6 ♝xf3 21.gxf3
♖ab8, none of White's options offer him any
advantage:

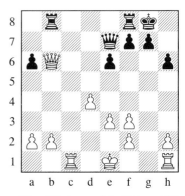

a) 22.♕c7 ♕b4† 23.♔f1 ♕d2 24.♕c2 ♖xb2
25.♕xd2 ♖xd2 26.a4 ♖b8=

b) 22.♕c5 ♕b7 23.♕c6 ♕xc6 24.♖xc6 ♖xb2
25.0–0 ♖xa2 26.♖b1 g5 27.♖b7 a5 28.♖cc7
♔g7 29.♖a7 ♖d2 30.♖xa5 ♖b8 31.♖aa7 ♖b1†
32.♔g2 ♖bb2 33.♖xf7† ♔g6∞

c) 22.♕xa6 ♕b4† 23.♔f1 ♕d2 24.♖b1 ♖c2
25.♔g2 ♕g6† 26.♔h3 ♕f5†=

19...♝xf3 20.gxf3 ♕g5† 21.♔h1 ♕d5 22.♕e4 ♕xa2

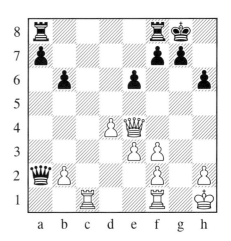

23.罝g1

White has the initiative thanks to his strong queen in the centre and his active rooks on the g- and c-files.

23.罝c7 營xb2 (23...罝ac8) 24.罝g1 罝ac8 25.營e5 g5=

23...罝fc8

23...罝ac8? 24.罝xg7†+–

23...營d5 24.營xd5 exd5 25.罝c7 罝fc8 26.罝gc1 罝xc7 27.罝xc7±

24.營b7 罝f8 25.營e4

25.罝xg7† 含xg7 26.罝g1† 含h8 27.營e7 罝g8 28.營f6† 含h7 29.營xf7† 含h8 30.營f6†=

25.罝g3 營d5 26.罝c7 (26.營e7 營d8=) 26...含h7 27.罝cg1 g6∞

25...罝fc8 26.營b7 罝f8 27.罝c7 營xb2 28.罝xf7 罝xf7 29.營xa8† 含h7 30.營e4† 含g8 31.營a8† 含h7 32.營e8 罝c7 33.營g6† 含h8 34.營e8† 含h7 35.營xe6 營xf2 36.營e4† 含g8

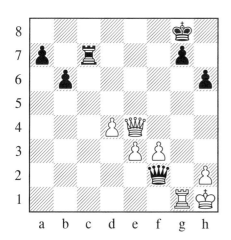

37.h3N

From this position, Radjabov – Kramnik, Kazan (1.3) 2011, ended in a perpetual check. The move in this game also leads to a draw. However, if Black's home preparation

is lacking, then he is presented with difficult practical problems to solve. We shall see several specific variations in which it turns out that the pressure along the g-file and the strong d-pawn are much more dangerous than the passed a- and b-pawns.

37.d5 罝e7= leads to perpetual check, and it is to avoid this that White plays 37.h3 before pushing the d-pawn.

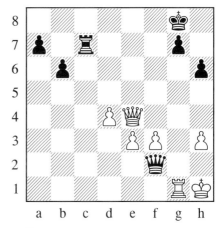

37...營c2

Black also faces difficulties after: 37...罝f7 38.營e8† (38.f4 營h4 39.營e6 營e7∞) 38...罝f8 39.營e6† 含f7 40.f4 b5 41.d5 a5 42.d6 營f3† 43.罝g2 營c6 44.含h2 含f8 45.罝d2 營d7 46.f5 b4 47.罝c2+–

Black would do better to play:
37...b5 38.d5
    38.罝g2 營f1† 39.含h2 b4 (39...營c4 40.營e5 b4 41.d5 營c5 42.營e6† 罝f7 43.d6 營f5 44.營e8† 含h7 45.營e4 含g8 46.營xb4 營e5† 47.f4 營xe3=) 40.d5 營b5 41.d6 罝d7 42.營e6† 含h7 43.f4 b3 44.f5 b2 45.營g6† 含h8 46.營e8†=
38...營b2
    With the idea of ...罝c2. In my opinion this is the simplest way for Black to make a draw. 38...罝f7 39.d6 罝xf3 40.營e6† 罝f7 41.d7 營f3† 42.含h2 營e2† 43.罝g2 營d1 44.營e8†

♖f8 45.♕e7 g5 46.h4 b4 47.e4 ♕f3 48.♕d6
♖d8 49.hxg5 h5 50.♖d2↑

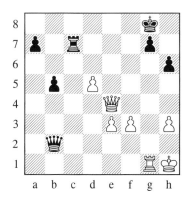

39.d6

39.♖g2 ♕f6 40.f4∞
39.♕e8† ♔h7 40.♕g6† ♔g8 41.♕xh6
♕e5∓
39...♖c2 40.♕e8†
40.♕f4 ♖c1=
40...♔h7 41.♕g6† ♔g8 42.♕g3 ♖c1
42...♖d2 43.e4 ♕d4 44.e5 g5∞
43.d7 ♖xg1† 44.♔xg1 ♕d2 45.♕g4 ♔f7=

38.♕e8† ♔h7 39.d5

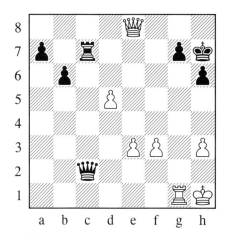

39...♕f5

White gains an initiative against the alternative:
39...♕c5 40.♕g6† ♔g8 41.d6 ♖f7 42.♕e6
42.♕d3 ♕h5 (42...♖d7 43.♖d1 b5 44.e4

♔f7 45.f4 ♕c4 46.e5 ♕xd3 47.♖xd3
♔e6∞) 43.♖g3 (43.♔h2 ♖xf3 44.♕c4† ♔f7
45.♕c8† ♔h7 46.d7 ♖f2† 47.♔g2 ♕f3=)
43...♖d7 44.f4 ♕c5 45.♕g6 b5 46.f5 ♕c4
47.♕xc4† bxc4 48.e4 c3 49.♖g3 ♖xd6
50.♖xc3=
42...♕c6
42...♕f5 43.♕xf5 ♖xf5 44.e4 ♖f8 45.e5 ♔f7
46.f4 g6 47.h4 h5 48.♔g2+−
43.♔h2

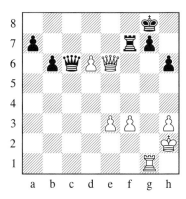

43...a5

43...♕xf3 44.d7 ♕e2† 45.♖g2 ♕d1 46.♕e8†
♖f8 47.♕e7 g5 48.h4→
43...b5 44.f4 b4 45.♖g2→
44.f4 a4 45.e4 a3 46.♖g2

46.f5 a2 47.f6 ♕c2† 48.♖g2 ♕xg2†
49.♔xg2 a1=♕ 50.♕e8† ♖f8 51.f7† ♔h7
52.♕xf8 ♕b2†=
46...b5 47.f5 b4 48.f6 ♔h7 49.fxg7 ♖xg7
50.♕f5† ♔g8 51.d7 ♖xg2† 52.♔xg2 ♕c2†
53.♔g3 ♕d3† 54.♔h4 a2 55.♕g6† ♔h8
56.♕xh6† ♔g8 57.♕g6† ♔h8 58.♕f6† ♔h7
59.d8=♕ ♕xd8 60.♕xd8 a1=♕ 61.♕e7† ♔g6
62.♕xb4 ♕f6† 63.♔g4 ♕g5† 64.♔f3 ♕h5†=

40.♕e4 ♕xe4

Black can opt for a slightly different rook ending with:
40...g6 41.♕xf5 gxf5 42.e4
42.♔h2!? is also possible.
42...fxe4 43.fxe4

Thanks to his further advanced pawns,

White holds the advantage. At this point, a lot will depend on which side can introduce his king into the game more effectively.

43...罝d7

43...罝e7 44.罝e1 含g6 45.e5 罝e8 46.e6 含f6 47.含g2+–

43...罝c3 44.罝d1 含g6 45.e5 罝c8 46.罝e1 罝e8 47.e6 含f6 48.含g2 含e7 49.含f3 含d6 50.含e4 罝c8 51.含f5 含xd5 52.罝d1†+–

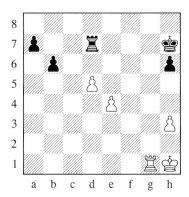

44.含h2

44.罝d1 含g6 45.e5 罝d8 46.e6 含f6 47.含g2 罝g8† 48.含f3 含e5=

44...a5

44...b5 45.罝b1 a5 (45...罝e7 46.罝e1 罝d7 47.含g3 b4 48.含f4 b3 49.罝b1 罝b7 50.d6 含g6 51.含e5 含f7 52.含d5+–) 46.含g3 (46.罝xb5 罝e7 47.d6 罝xe4 48.罝d5 罝e8=) 46...b4 47.含f4 罝b7 48.e5 a4 49.d6 a3 50.e6 a2 51.罝d1 b3 52.d7 b2 53.d8=豐 b1=豐 54.罝d7† 含xd7 55.豐xd7† 含h8=

45.罝b1 a4

45...罝e7 46.罝e1 罝d7 (46...含g6 47.含g3 a4 48.含f4 a3 49.d6 罝e8 50.e5 含f7 51.含f5+–) 47.含g3 a4 48.含f4 b5 (48...a3 49.罝a1 罝a7 50.d6 含g6 51.含e5 含f7 52.罝f1† 含e8 53.含e6 a2 54.罝g1+–) 49.含e5 b4 50.含d4 b3 51.e5 b2 52.e6 罝b7 53.e7 b1=豐 54.罝xb1 罝xe7 55.罝a1 罝a7 56.含c5+–

46.罝xb6 罝a7 47.含g3 a3 48.罝b1 a2 49.罝a1 含g6

The passive white rook allows Black to hold the draw.

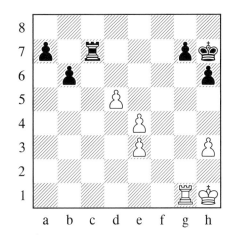

41.fxe4

41...含g8?

Black missed a surprising defence:

41...罝e7!

From the logical point of view, this move seems very difficult for a human to find, as White can now advance the d-pawn with tempo. However, it turns out that preventing e5-e6 was the more important task.

42.d6

42.含g2 含g6 43.e5 罝xe5 44.含f3† 含f6 45.e4 罝h5∞

42.含h2 罝xe4 43.含g3 罝xe3† 44.含f4 罝d3 45.含e5 罝xh3 46.d6 罝d3=

42...罝e8 43.罝f1

43.罝a1 含g6 44.罝xa7 含f6 45.罝b7 罝d8 46.罝xb6 含e5= A great idea – activity is often more important than material.

43...a5 44.罝b1 a4 45.罝xb6 罝a8 46.e5 a3 47.罝b1 含g6 48.e6 含f6 49.e7 含e6 50.罝a1 含xd6 51.罝xa3 罝e8=

42.e5+–

Black will not manage to stop the three passed pawns. In order to win the game White just needs to activate his king at the right moment.

42...含f7 43.罝f1†

43.♔g2 a5 44.♘f3 a4 45.♔e4 a3 46.♖f1†
♔e8 47.d6+–

43...♔e8 44.e6 ♔e7 45.e4 ♔d6

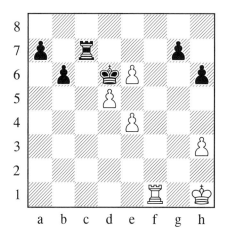

46.♖f8

46.♔g2 b5 47.♔f3 a5 48.♔e3 a4 49.♔d4
♖c4† 50.♔d3 ♖c7 51.♖f8 a3 52.♖a8 b4
53.♔d4 ♖b7 54.♖a6† ♔e7 55.♔e5+–

**46...♖b7 47.♖d8† ♔e7 48.♖c8 ♔d6 49.♔g2
b5 50.♔f3 b4 51.♔f4**

The white king has made his way to the
centre to support the advance of the pawns;
Black's position is hopeless.

**51...b3 52.♖c6† ♔e7 53.♔e5 b2 54.d6†
♔d8 55.e7† ♔d7 56.♖c8 ♖b5† 57.♔d4
♖b4† 58.♔c3 ♔xc8 59.e8=♕† ♔b7
60.♕d7† ♔a6 61.♕c8† ♔b7 62.♕c4† ♖b5
63.♕a2† ♔b6 64.d7**
1–0

GAME 31
▷ **E. Bacrot (2705)**
▶ **F. Caruana (2712)**
12th Karpov International, Poikovsky
Round 5, 08.10.2011 **[D86]**
Annotated by Kamil Miton

In one of the critical lines of the 7.♗c4
Grünfeld, Caruana played the interesting
16...♘b7!? instead of the better-known
16...♗b7 or 16...♕d6. In my opinion there
were two critical moments in the game. The
interesting 18...d3!? deserves attention, and
also 22...♖d7! looks like an improvement on
the game, when the plan of ...♖fd8, ...♕e7 and
...f6 should solve most of Black's problems.

**1.d4 ♘f6 2.c4 g6 3.♘c3 d5 4.cxd5 ♘xd5
5.e4 ♘xc3 6.bxc3 ♗g7 7.♗c4 c5 8.♘e2 ♘c6
9.♗e3 0–0 10.0–0 ♘a5 11.♗d3 b6 12.♕d2
e5 13.♗h6 exd4 14.♗xg7 ♔xg7 15.cxd4
cxd4**

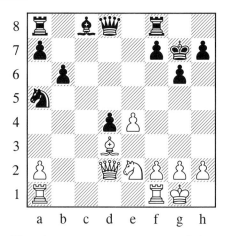

The players are contesting one of the most
topical modern lines of the Grünfeld. White
has given up a pawn in return for ongoing
compensation, based on Black's vulnerable
kingside and the wayward knight on a5.

16.♖ac1
The most common continuation has been:
16.f4 f6

And now it is worth considering a) 17.f5, b) 17.♖ac1 and c) 17.e5!?.

a) 17.f5 ♘c6 18.♗b5 ♘e5 19.♘xd4 gxf5 20.exf5 ♔h8 21.♖ad1 ♕e7∞

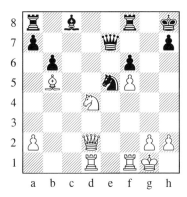

Black has returned the extra pawn but his knight now stands proudly in the centre. The position is balanced.

b) 17.♖ac1 ♗g4!
   The...♗g4-h5 manoeuvre is one of the main reasons why some experts prefer the 16.♖ac1 move order.
18.♘g3
   18.f5 ♗xe2 19.♕xe2 ♕d6 20.fxg6 hxg6 21.♕g4 ♘c6 22.♕xg6† ♔xg6 23.e5† f5 24.exd6 ♘e5 25.♗b1 ♖ad8 26.♖ce1 ♘c4 27.♖e6† ♔f7 28.♖e7† ♔g6=
18...♖c8
   Black does not care so much about the bishop, and instead focuses on improving his other pieces, especially the knight which can now come to c6.

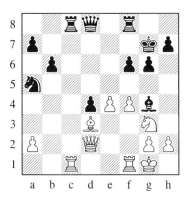

19.f5
   19.♖ce1 ♘c4 20.♗xc4 ♖xc4 21.f5 d3∓
19...♘c6 20.h3 ♗h5 21.♗b5
   21.♖f4 ♘e5∓
   21.♗a6 ♖c7 22.♗b7 ♘e5 23.♗d5 is met by 23...d3 intending ...♗e2.
21...♘e5 22.♖xc8 ♕xc8 23.♖c1 ♕d8 24.♗e2 ♗xe2 25.♘xe2 d3 26.♘f4 ♖e8 27.♘e6† ♖xe6 28.fxe6 ♕e7∞

   Black cannot be worse with such a strong knight and d-pawn.

c) 17.e5!?

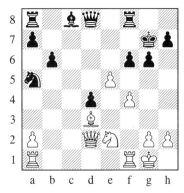

   As played by Topalov against Kamsky. The outcome of that game, along with the accompanying analysis, indicates that White has no advantage. Still, it is interesting to review the game and see what might happen if Black deviates. We will consider c1) 17...fxe5, c2) 17...♕d5 and the game continuation of c3) 17...♗d7!.

c1) 17...fxe5 18.fxe5 ♗b7 19.♖xf8 ♕xf8 20.♕g5 ♘c6 (20...♕d8 21.♕g3 ♕e7 22.♘f4→) 21.♘g3 ♕d8 22.♘h5† ♔h8 23.♘f6 ♕e7 24.♖e1 ♖f8 25.♘xh7 ♕xg5 (25...♕xh7 26.♗xg6 ♕g7 27.♖e4+−) 26.♘xg5 ♘b4 27.♗c4±

c2) 17...♕d5
   This fighting move is risky for Black.
18.exf6†

18.f5?! ♕xe5 19.fxg6 hxg6 20.♘f4 ♕e3†
21.♕xe3 dxe3 22.♘xg6 ♖d8 23.♗e4 ♗b7∓
18...♖xf6

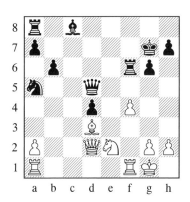

19.♖ac1!?

Preventing the knight from coming to c4.

19.♘g3 ♘c4 brings White no advantage:
20.♗xc4 (20.♕f2 ♘d6 21.♗e2 ♗b7 22.♗f3 ♕f7 23.♗xb7 ♕xb7 24.♕xd4 b5 25.♔h1 ♕b6) 20...♖xc4 21.♖ac1 (21.♘e4 ♖f8 22.♖ac1 ♕d5 23.♘c3 ♕d8 24.♘b5 ♗f5 25.♘xd4 ♖c8 26.♕b2 ♕f6=) 21...♕d5 22.f5 ♗xf5 23.♘xf5† ♖xf5 24.♗xf5 ♕xf5 25.♕xd4† ♔g8 26.♕c4† ♕f7=

19...♗d7

Black has a wide variety of alternatives:

19...♖c6? 20.♖xc6 ♘xc6 21.f5+−

19...♗e6?! 20.f5±

19...♗f5 20.♗xf5 ♖xf5 21.♘xd4 ♔g8 22.♕c3 ♖f6 23.f5 gxf5 24.♘e2→

19...♘c6 20.f5 ♗xf5 21.♕g5 h6 22.♕g3 ♗xd3 23.♖xf6 ♔xf6 24.♘f4 ♕d6 25.♘xd3 ♔e7 26.♕h4†±

19...♗b7 20.♘g3 ♖af8 (20...♖e8? 21.f5 ♖e3 22.♖c7† ♔g8 23.fxg6 ♖xf1† 24.♗xf1+−) 21.f5 ♗c6 22.♖f4 ♔h8 23.♕f2 gxf5 24.♘xf5 ♖g8 25.♖c2±

20.f5! ♕e5

20...♖af8 21.♕g5 h6 22.♕g3→

21.♖f3 ♖c8

21...♖af8 22.♖h3 gxf5 23.♕g5† ♔h8 24.♘f4 ♖g8 25.♕h4 ♖g7 26.♖e1 ♕d6 27.♘h5 ♖h6 28.♖g3 ♖xg3 29.hxg3 ♖g6 30.♖e7→

22.♖xc8 ♗xc8 23.♖h3 ♗xf5 24.♕h6† ♔f7 25.♕xh7† ♔e8 26.♕h8† ♔d7 27.♖h7† ♔c6 28.♗xf5 gxf5 29.♕c8† ♔b5∞

c3) 17...♗d7!

Kamsky's move is the strongest.

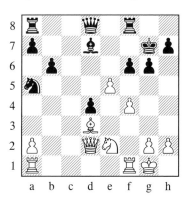

18.exf6†

18.♘xd4 ♘c6 19.♗e4 ♘xd4 20.♗xa8 ♗b5 21.♖f2 ♗e2† 22.♖xe2 ♖xe2 23.♕e3=

18.f5 fxe5 19.♘g3 ♗xf5 20.♗xf5 ♘c4 21.♕e2 ♘e3 22.♗d3 ♘xf1 23.♕xe5† ♕f6 24.♕xf6† ♖xf6 25.♘xf1 ♖c8∓

18.♖ac1!? fxe5 (18...♖c8 19.♘xd4) 19.fxe5 ♕e7 (19...♖xf1† 20.♖xf1 ♘c6 21.♘f4 ♘xe5 22.♗e4 ♖c8 23.♕xd4 ♕e7 24.♘d3 ♗b5 25.♘xe5 ♗xf1 26.♘c6† ♕f6 27.♕d7† ♕f7 28.♕xc8 ♗e2 29.♗f3 ♗xf3 30.gxf3 ♕xf3 31.♕d7† ♔h6 32.♕d2†±) 20.♘xd4 ♕xe5 21.♘f3 ♕d6 22.♕b2† ♔g8∞ The black king is not entirely safe. White has fair compensation for the pawn, but still no objective advantage.

18...♕xf6 19.♘g3 ♔h8 20.f5 gxf5 21.♗xf5 ♗xf5 22.♖xf5 ♕d6 23.♖af1 ♘c6 24.♘e4 ♕e7 25.♕h6 ♖xf5 26.♖xf5 ♘e5 27.h3 ♘g6 28.♖h5

28.♘g5 ♖c8∓

28...♖g8 29.♘f6 ♖g7 30.♘xh7 ♖xh7 31.♕xg6 ♕e3†=

Black forces a perpetual and the players agreed a draw in a few more moves, Topalov – Kamsky, Sofia 2009.

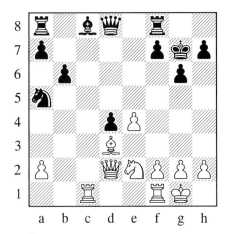

16...♘b7!?

Black hurries to improve his knight. Whether or not he succeeds in finding a good role for this piece will often be a key factor in determining the final outcome.

Two other moves also deserve attention.

16...♕d6?! 17.f4 f6 18.f5 ♕e5 19.♘f4 g5 20.♘h5† ♔g8 21.h4 h6 22.hxg5 hxg5 23.♖f3

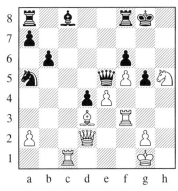

23...♔f7? (23...♗d7! was essential, although the whole line looks rather risky for Black in any case.) 24.♘xf6! ♗xf6 25.♖h3 ♖g8 26.♖h6† ♔f7 27.♖h7† ♔e8 28.♖cc7 ♔d8 29.♗b5 ♕xe4 30.♖xc8† 1–0 Topalov – Anand, Sofia (1) 2010.

16...♗b7

After this move White can develop a strong initiative on the kingside, although games such as Shirov – Vachier Lagrave show that both sides can play for win.

17.f4 ♖c8 18.f5 ♖xc1!

It is important to include this move in order to avoid a future sacrifice on c6. Here is a line to illustrate the point: 18...♘c6 19.f6† ♔h8 20.♕h6 ♖g8 21.♖f3 ♕f8 22.♖g5 ♖e8 (22...♘b4 23.♖h3 ♖xc1† 24.♘xc1 ♗c8 25.g4+–) 23.♖xc6! ♗xc6 24.♖h3 ♗d7 25.♖h4±

19.♕xc1 ♘c6

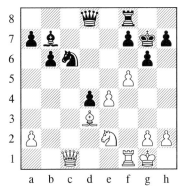

From this position it is worth considering a) 20.f6† as played by Shirov, and the possible improvement b) 20.♕f4!?.

a) 20.f6† ♔h8

Black has an extra pawn and is poised to take the e5-square under control. White needs to conduct the attack with vigour, otherwise he could easily find himself in a losing position. Obviously the position holds considerable danger for Black as well. Ultimately, after accurate play by both sides, my analysis indicates that the position is balanced.

21.♕g5

21.♘f4!? is playable but it is not a serious try for an advantage: 21...♘e5 (21...♕xf6 22.♘h5 ♕e7 23.♘f6 ♔g7 24.♕g5 h6 25.♘h5† ♔h7 26.♘f6† ♔g7=; 21...♕d6!?) 22.♘h3 ♖g8 23.♘g5 ♕d7 24.♕f4 (24.♗c4 ♖c8 25.♕f4 ♖xc4 26.♘xh7 ♘g4 27.♘f8 ♕e8 28.♘xg6† fxg6 29.f7 ♕f8 30.♕xg4

♔g7 31.♖g5 ♖c6 32.e5 d3 33.♖f6 ♕c5†
34.♖f2 ♕c1† 35.♖f1 ♕c5† 36.♔h1 ♕f8∞)

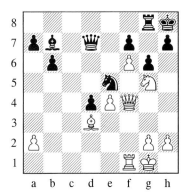

24...♘xd3 25.♕g4 (25.♖d6 ♕e8 26.♕g3
♗xe4 27.♕h4 h5 28.♕xe4 ♕xe4 29.♘xf7†
♔h7 30.♘g5† ♔h6 31.♖f7†=) 25...♕c7
26.♕h3!? (26.♕h4 h5 27.g4 ♘f4 28.♖xf4
♕xf4 29.♘xf7†=) 26...h5 27.♕xd3 ♖e8
28.♕xd4 ♔g8 29.♖d1∞

21...♕d6
21...♖e8 22.♘f4 ♕d6 23.♕h6 ♕f8
24.♘xg6†! fxg6 25.f7 ♖c8 26.♕f4 h6 27.e5
♘e7 28.h4→

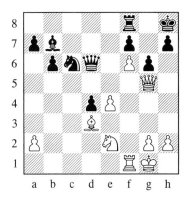

22.♖f4N
Transferring the rook to the h-file is a
standard procedure.
22.♘g3? ♖g8 23.♗c4 ♘e5 24.♗b3 d3
25.h3 ♗a6 26.♖f4 d2 27.♔h2 ♕c5 28.h4
♘d3 29.e5 ♘xf4 30.♘e4 ♘e6 31.♗xe6
♕c6 32.♗xf7 d1=♕ 0–1 Shirov – Vachier
Lagrave, Wijk aan Zee 2011.
22.♖f5!?N is another idea.

22...♖e8 23.♖h4 ♕f8
23...♔g8 24.♖g3 ♗c8 25.♖h5 ♕b4 26.h3
♕e1† 27.♔h2 ♘e5 28.♘f4 ♕f2 29.♗e2+–
23...♕b4!?
24.♘f4 ♘e5
24...♖e5? 25.♘xg6†! fxg6 26.♖xg6 ♕g8
27.♕xg8† ♔xg8 28.♗c4† ♔f8 29.♖xh7+–
25.♘h3
25.♗b5 d3⇄
25...♘d7 26.♖f4 ♔g8 27.♖g5 h5

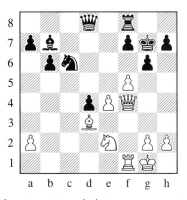

28.♖xh5!
28.g4? ♘e5 29.gxh5 ♘xd3 30.♕c7 ♖e5
31.♖g4 ♖xg5 32.♖xg5 ♗xe4–+
28...gxh5 29.♘h7 ♔xh7 30.♕f5† ♔h6
31.♕f4†=

b) 20.♕f4!?N

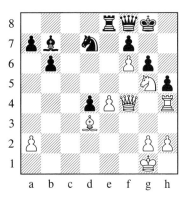

I also investigated this attempt to improve
Shirov's play. Once again the position should
be balanced, although the variations below

show that it would be easy for either side to lose the game. The first point to note is that 20...♕f6? 21.♕c7± is bad for Black. Apart from that unfortunate move, it is worth considering b1) 20...h6!?, b2) 20...f6, b3) 20...♕b8 and b4) 20...♘b4!.

b1) 20...h6!? leads to a murky endgame: 21.♘g3 (21.♕g3 ♕g5 22.♕d6 ♕d8=) 21...♘b4 22.♗c4 d3

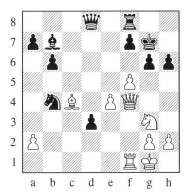

23.♕e5† f6 24.♕c3 b5 25.♗e6 ♘c6 26.fxg6 ♕d4† 27.♖xd4 ♘xd4 28.♗f5 ♘xf5 29.exf5 ♖d8 30.♘h5† ♔f8 31.♘xf6 d2 32.♖d1 ♖d4∞

b2) 20...f6
One of the most natural moves.
21.♕g3 ♘e5 22.♘f4 ♗c8

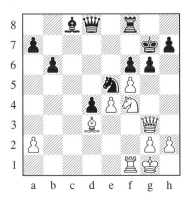

23.♘h5†
23.♗a6 can be met by 23...d3 or 23...♕d7 when Black is okay.
23...♔h8 24.♘xf6

24.fxg6 ♘xg6 25.e5 fxe5 26.♖xf8† ♕xf8 27.♗xg6 hxg6 28.♕xg6 ♗f5 29.♕g5 d3 30.♘g3 ♗h7 31.♕xe5† ♔g8∞
24...♕e7
24...gxf5 25.♕xe5 ♕xf6 26.♕xf6† ♖xf6 27.exf5±
25.♘d5 ♕d6

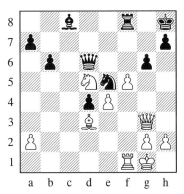

26.♖c1
26.f6 ♗e6 27.♘e7 ♕c5 28.h4 ♘g4 29.♘d5 h5∞
26...gxf5
26...♗b7 27.fxg6 ♖g8 28.♖c7 ♖xg6 29.♕h3 ♖h6 30.♕f5+−
26...♖d7!?
27.♖c7
27.♖c6 f4 28.♕xf4 ♖xf4 29.♖xd6 ♖f8=
27...♖g8 28.♕f4 ♕e6 29.♗c2
29.♖e7 ♘xd3 30.♕c7 ♕h6 31.♘f4 fxe4 32.♘xd3 ♖f8 33.♕e5† ♕f6 34.♕xf6† ♖xf6 35.♖xe4 ♗f5=
29...♗d7 30.♖xa7
30.♗b3 ♖g4 31.exf5 ♕xf5 32.♕xf5 ♗xf5 33.♖xa7=
30.h3!?
30...♖g4
30...d3? 31.♗b3 ♖g4 32.♖a8† ♔g7 33.exf5 ♕xf5 34.♕xf5 ♗xf5 35.♘e3 ♖g5 36.♖g8† ♔h6 37.♖b8 ♘f3† 38.♔f2 ♘xh2 39.♖xb6† ♔g7 40.♖b5±
31.♕f2 d3 32.♖a8† ♔g7 33.♗b3 ♖xe4 34.♘e3 ♕e7 35.♖g8† ♔h6 36.♕xf5 ♘g6 37.♗f7 ♗xf5 38.♘xf5† ♔g5 39.♘xe7 ♖xe7 40.♗xg6 hxg6 41.♖d8=

b3) 20...♕b8 21.♕h4

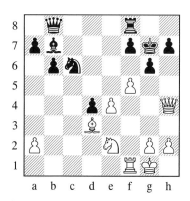

21...♕d6

The alternative is 21...♘e5 22.♘f4 with the following possibilities:

i) 22...♕d6 23.f6† ♔h8 24.♘h3 h5 25.♕f4 ♔h7 26.♘g5† ♔g8 27.g4 ♕a3 28.♕xe5 ♕xd3 29.♘xf7 ♕xe4 30.♘h6† ♔h7 31.♕xe4 ♗xe4 32.g5∞

ii) 22...♔g8 looks incredibly risky but the following computer line indicates that it is just playable: 23.f6 h5 24.♘xh5 ♖c8 25.♘f4 ♖c5 26.♗e2 ♕d6 27.♘h3 ♘d7 28.♘g5 ♘xf6 29.♘xf7 ♔xf7 30.♕h7† ♔e6

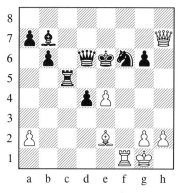

31.♗g4† ♘xg4 32.♕f7† ♔e5 33.♕f4† ♔e6 34.♕xg4† ♔e7 35.♕h4† ♔d7 36.♖f7† ♔e8 37.♖xb7 ♖c1† 38.♔f2 ♖c2† 39.♔g1=

iii) 22...♘xd3 23.♘xd3 ♕d6 24.f6† (24.e5?! ♕a3 25.f6† ♔h8 26.♕h6 ♖g8 27.e6 ♕xa2 28.♘f4 g5!)

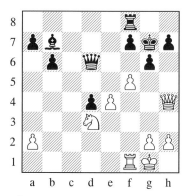

24...♔h8 25.♖f3 ♖e8 26.♖h3 h5 27.♘g5 ♕f8 28.g4 ♗c8 29.♘e5 ♖xe5 30.♕xe5 ♗g4 31.♖d3 ♕b4 32.♕e8† ♔h7 33.♕xf7† ♔h6=

22.♘f4 ♘e5

22...♕f6 23.♕g3→

23.f6† ♔h8 24.♘h3 h5

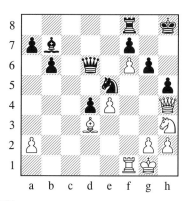

25.♖f5

25.♗e2 ♕a3 26.♘f4 ♕e3† 27.♔h1 ♕xe4 28.♗xh5 g5 29.♕xg5 ♖g8 30.♕h6† ♕h7 31.♕xh7† ♔xh7∓

25.♘f4 ♖c8 (25...♔h7!? 26.♘xh5 ♖h8 27.♘g7† [27.♕g3!?] 27...♔g8 28.♕g3 ♕c5 29.♘f5 ♖h5 30.♘e7† ♔h7 31.h3 ♖g5 32.♕h4† ♖h5 33.♕g3=) 26.♘xh5 ♔g8 27.♘f4 ♘xd3 28.♘e6!? (28.♘xg6 fxg6 29.♕h6 ♔f7 30.♕h7† ♔e6 31.♕h3† ♔f7=) 28...fxe6 29.f7† ♔g7 30.♕f6† ♔h7 31.♕h4† ♔g7=

25...♖e8

25...♖d8 26.♕g5 ♘g4 27.♘f4 ♗xe4 28.h3+−

26.♘f4

26.♗c4 ♖c8 27.♖xh5† gxh5 28.♕xh5† ♔g8
29.♕h6 ♕f8 30.♕g5† ♔h7 31.♕h5† ♔g8
32.♘g5 ♗xe4 33.♘xe4 ♖xc4 34.♕xe5∞

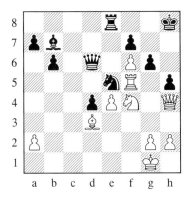

26...♕f8!=

26...♖c8 27.♕g5 ♖c1† 28.♗f1 ♘g4 29.h3
♖xf1† 30.♔xf1 ♕c7 31.♘d3 ♘e3† 32.♔g1
♔h7 33.♖f2±

b4) 20...♘b4!

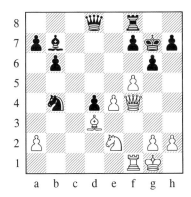

Although several of the other lines were
leading to equality, this is the most
straightforward. I must confess that initially
my intuition told me that this move could
not be good, as the knight moves away from
the crucial e5-square and from the kingside
in general. But now having analysed it, it
seems absolutely reliable.

21.♖f3

21.f6† ♔h8 22.♖f3 ♖g8 23.♖h3 g5 24.♕g4

♖g6 25.♗c4 ♕f8 26.♘xd4 ♗c8 27.♘f5
♕c5† 28.♔h1 ♗xf5 29.exf5 ♖xf6 30.♕xg5
♕xf5=

21.♗c4 d3 22.♘g3 d2 23.♗b3 ♕d4†
(23...♗a6 24.fxg6 fxg6 25.♘h5† gxh5
26.♕e5† ♔h6 27.♕e6†=) 24.♔h1 d1=♕
25.♖xd1 ♘d3 26.f6† ♔h8 27.♕d2 ♘f2†
28.♔g1 ♘h3† 29.♔h1=

21...f6 22.♖h3

22.♗c4 g5!

22.fxg6 hxg6 23.♖h3 ♖h8 24.♖xh8 ♕xh8
25.♕c7† ♔h6=

22...g5 23.♕g4 ♘xd3 24.♖xh7†!=

The game ends in a perpetual check.

Summing up, 16...♗b7 seems fully reliable.
Most variations are ending in perpetual
checks after accurate play by both sides, but
the positions are anything but peaceful and
hold great danger for all but the best-prepared
players.

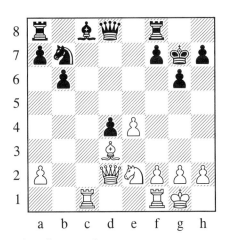

17.♗c4 ♘c5 18.♗d5 ♖b8

Black had an interesting alternative available:
18...d3!? 19.♘f4

19.♕b2† ♕f6 20.e5 ♕e7 21.♘d4 ♗b7
22.♗xb7 ♘xb7=

19.♗xa8 dxe2 20.♕xe2 ♗a6 21.♕b2† ♕f6
22.♕xf6† ♔xf6 23.♗d5 ♗xf1 24.♔xf1
♔e5↑

19...♖b8 20.♘xd3 ♘xd3 21.♕xd3 ♗e6

White's pieces are more active, but it will be hard for him to obtain anything real as Black has no weaknesses.

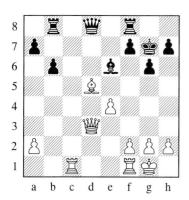

22.h4!?

Hoping to provoke some weakening of the black kingside.

22.罝c6 罝c8=

22.豐c3† 豐f6 23.盦xe6 豐xc3 24.罝xc3 fxe6=

22...h5

22...豐xh4? 23.盦xe6 fxe6 24.罝c7† is horrible for Black, as 24...堂f7? 25.豐c3†! wins immediately.

22...盦xd5 23.exd5 豐xh4 is not such a disaster, but after 24.d6∞̄ the d-pawn is extremely strong and Black faces a difficult defence.

23.罝fd1 罝c8!

23...豐xh4 is riskier: 24.盦xe6 fxe6 25.罝c7† 堂g8 26.豐e3 罝bd8 27.罝dc1 豐f4 28.豐xf4 罝xf4 29.罝xa7↑

24.罝xc8 豐xc8 25.豐d4† 堂g8 26.豐a4 罝d8 27.豐xa7 豐c2⇄

Black should have enough activity to hold the position a pawn down.

19.豐xd4† 豐f6

Trying to provoke an advance of the e-pawn.

20.豐e3!

20.e5 豐e7 leaves the bishop on d5 unstable, and after 21.e6† 豐f6 22.exf7 盦e6 the position is equal.

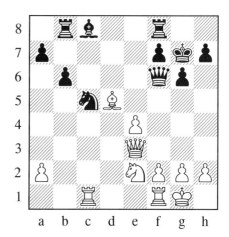

20...盦e6 21.公c3 罝bd8 22.罝fd1

White has a small edge thanks to his control over the d5-square.

22...罝fe8

I think Black's best idea would have been 22...罝d7! intending to fight for the d5-square. This would have given him good chances to equalize, for instance: 23.罝d4 罝fd8 24.罝cd1 豐e7 25.f4 (25.g3 f6=) 25...f6 26.h3 盦f7= Can White improve his position?

23.罝d4 豐e5 24.f4 豐f6 25.罝cd1 盦xd5

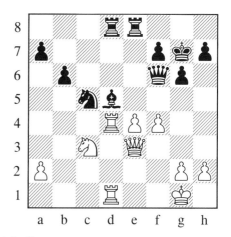

26.e5!

26.公xd5 would be inaccurate due to 26...罝xd5! 27.罝xd5 罝xe4=.

26...♕f5

The alternative was:

26...♘c6 27.♘xd5

27.f5 is premature and too optimistic: 27...♘e6 (27...f6!?) 28.fxe6 fxe6 29.♘e4 ♕c2 30.♖c1 ♕b2 31.♖xd5 ♖xd5 32.♘f6 ♖f8 (32...♖xe5 33.♘xe8† ♔f8=) 33.♖c7† ♖f7 34.♘h5† ♔g8 35.♖c8† ♖f8 36.♘f6† ♔g7=

27...♘e6 28.♖4d2 ♖f8

28...♕c5? is impossible due to 29.♕xc5 followed by ♘c7!.

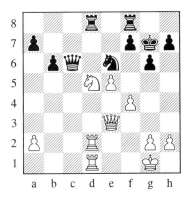

29.f5! ♕c5

29...gxf5 30.♕g3† ♔h8 31.♕h4 ♖g8 32.♕f6† ♖g7 33.h4!±

30.f6† ♔h8 31.♕xc5 bxc5

31...♘xc5 is met by 32.♘c7± intending ♘b5-d6.

32.♘c3 ♖d4 33.♖xd4 cxd4 34.♘e4 ♖b8 35.♔f1±

Black still has some problems: his d4- and f7-pawns are weak, and his king is cut off from play.

27.♘xd5 ♘e6 28.♖4d2

At first Black's position seems okay, but a closer inspection reveals two unpleasant threats in ♘c7 winning the exchange, and h3 preparing g4 to target the black queen.

28...h5

It was worth considering the straightforward

exchange sacrifice: 28...♖xd5!? 29.♖xd5 ♘xf4 30.♖5d4 g5 31.♖e1 ♖c8 32.♖d2±

28...♖c8 was playable, but White keeps the upper hand: 29.h3 h5 30.♕f3 h4 (30...♘c5? 31.♘f6 ♖h8 32.g4 hxg4 33.hxg4 ♕e6 34.♖d5 White is winning as f4-f5 is coming) 31.♕f2 g5 32.♘e3! ♕xf4 33.♘f5† ♔g6 34.♘d6± Once again White wins an exchange for insufficient compensation.

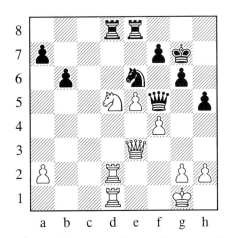

29.♘c7! ♘xc7 30.♖xd8 ♖xd8 31.♖xd8 ♕b1† 32.♔f2 ♘e6

32...♕xa2†? 33.♖d2 ♕a5 34.f5+−

33.♖d2±

White has a clear extra exchange, but winning the position is by no means easy, as his king is exposed and Black's queen and knight coordinate excellently. White's main plan will be to improve his position on the kingside, but this is far from easy as every pawn move will expose the king in some way. At the same time Bacrot is a world-class player and his technique is exemplary.

33...h4 34.h3 ♕f5

After 34...a5 35.♔f3! White simply intends to eat the h4-pawn with his king. 35...b5 36.♔g4 ♕b4 37.♔xh4 g5† 38.♔g4 gxf4 39.♕d3±

35.g4 hxg3†

35...♕xf4† 36.♕xf4 ♘xf4 37.♔e3 ♘xh3 38.♖d7±

36.♔xg3 b5

Black could have considered 36...♔h7!? intending to transfer the knight to f5, although he must ultimately be losing either way.

37.♖e2 a5 38.♕e4 ♕h5 39.♖f2 ♘c5 40.♕d5 ♘e6 41.♕e4 ♘c5 42.♕c2 ♘e6

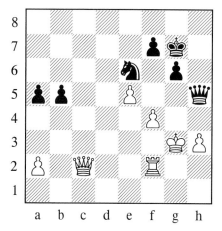

43.f5!?

43.♕e2 was simpler, for instance: 43...♕f5 (43...♕h6 44.♕g4±) 44.♕xb5 ♘d4 45.♕d5 ♕d3† 46.♔g2 ♕e3 47.e6 ♘xe6 48.♕e5†+−

43...♘d4 44.f6† ♔g8 45.♕e4 ♘e6 46.♖c2 ♕g5† 47.♔h2 b4 48.♖c8† ♔h7 49.♖c4 ♔g8

49...♕d2† 50.♔g3 ♕d7 51.h4±

50.♕a8† ♔h7 51.♕d5 ♔g8 52.♖g4 ♕h6 53.♕a8† ♔h7 54.♕e4 ♕d2† 55.♕g2 ♕h6 56.♕c2 ♕h5 57.♕e4 ♘g5 58.♕e3 ♘e6 59.♔g3 ♔g8 60.♔g2

It looks like Bacrot was just gaining some time on the clock before embarking on the final winning plan.

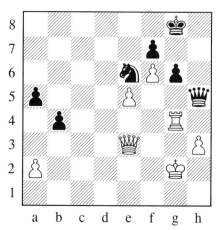

60...♔h7 61.♕e4 ♔g8 62.♕e3 ♕f5 63.♕e4 ♕h5 64.♕a8† ♔h7 65.♕a7 ♔g8 66.♕xa5+−

Finally the a-pawn falls. The b-pawn will shortly follow, and it will soon be time for Black to resign.

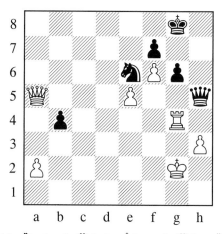

66...♘g5 67.♕d8† ♔h7 68.♕d3 ♘e6 69.♕e3 ♔g8 70.♖xb4 ♕d1 71.♖b2 ♕d5† 72.♔h2 g5 73.♖g2 ♔h7 74.♖d2 ♕a5 75.♕e4† ♔h6 76.♖c2 ♕a3 77.h4 ♔h5 78.♖g2

1–0

GAME 32

▷ **E. Bacrot (2705)**

▶ **S. Mamedyarov (2746)**

European Club Cup, Rogaska Slatina

01.10.2011 **[D86]**

Annotated by Borki Predojevic

The Classical 7.♗c4 variation against the Grünfeld is one of the most critical lines and in the last few months many strong players have started to play this line regularly. In this game Mamedyarov tried the line with 10...♕c7 and 11...b6. His idea was to play 12...♖d8 with quick pressure on the d4-pawn (an alternative was 12...♗b7). In my opinion this is not a natural line and even though Black played a novelty with 13...♕d6N, White found a clever way to gain the advantage. 18.f4! led to a strong attack for White and he won the game in fine style.

Bacrot has shown us how to play against the Grünfeld. We will see in the future if Black can find something else, perhaps in the line with 11...♖d8.

1.d4 ♘f6 2.c4 g6 3.♘c3 d5 4.cxd5 ♘xd5 5.e4 ♘xc3 6.bxc3 ♗g7 7.♗c4 c5 8.♘e2 ♘c6 9.♗e3 0–0 10.0–0 ♕c7

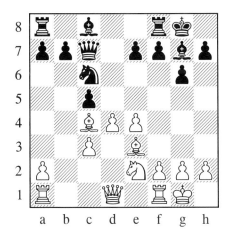

11.♖c1

The main line.

In the World Cup against Nepomniachtchi Kamsky chose instead 11.♖b1. After 11...a6 (11...cxd4 12.cxd4 ♘xd4 13.♗xf7† ♖xf7 14.♘xd4±) 12.♗f4 ♕a5 (12...e5 13.dxe5 ♘xe5 14.♗d5 ♖b8 15.♗g3 b5 16.f4↑) 13.♗d5 cxd4 14.cxd4 ♗g4 15.f3 ♗e6!? 16.♗d2 ♕c7 17.♗xe6 fxe6 18.♗c3 ♖ad8 19.♕b3 ♘xd4 20.♗xd4 ♗xd4† 21.♘xd4 ♖xd4 22.♕xe6† ♖f7± White had pressure and eventually won, Kamsky – Nepomniachtchi, Khanty-Mansiysk (m/1) 2011.

11...b6

Another option for Black is the more commonly played 11...♖d8 which was analysed in the September issue of *Chess Evolution*.

12.♕d2

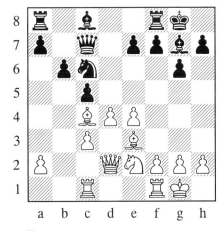

12...♖d8

I will briefly review some games in the alternative line:

12...♗b7 13.♗h6 ♖ad8 14.♗xg7 ♔xg7 15.♕e3 15.f4! was played in the game Vachier Lagrave – Morozevich, Biel 2011, and was analysed in the previous issue of *Chess Evolution*.

15...e5 16.♗d5 ♘a5 17.♗xb7 ♕xb7 18.f4N 18.♘g3 ♕e7= was analysed in the above mentioned game.

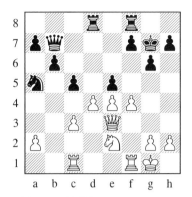

18...exd4 19.cxd4 ♖fe8 20.e5

Interesting was the concrete 20.d5 f5 21.♘c3 fxe4 22.f5 ♘c4! 23.f6† (23.♕g3 ♔h8 24.fxg6 ♕g7⇄) 23...♔g8 24.f7† ♕xf7 25.♕e2 ♕g7 26.♕xc4 ♕d4† 27.♖xd4 cxd4 28.♘b5 d3∞ with an unclear game.

20...cxd4 21.♘xd4 ♕d5 22.♘f3 ♘c4 23.♕f2 h6 24.♖fe1 ♖d7 25.h4 b5 26.h5 ♕e6 27.♖ed1 ♖ed8 28.♖xd7 ♖xd7 29.hxg6 ♕xg6!?⇄

Korobov – Nepomniachtchi, ECC 2011.

13.♗h6

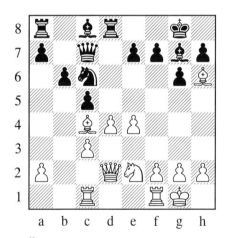

13...♕d6N

A novelty, but as we shall see, this move does not solve Black's problems.

13...♗b7?! makes less sense here since after 14.♗xg7 ♔xg7 15.f4!, compared to the line with 12...♗b7, Black has placed the other rook

on d8, which makes the black king's position weaker than in the normal line.

Black can avoid exchanges on g7 by playing 13...♗h8 but this is rather passive. The most logical way to continue is: 14.f4 ♘a5 15.♗d3

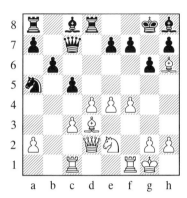

15...♕d7 (15...♗g4 16.d5 c4 17.♗b1 e5 18.♘g3 exf4 19.♗xf4± ↑ Svetushkin – Van Eijk, Budva 2009) 16.e5 White's position is promising. For example, after 16...♗b7 17.f5! ♗xe5 18.fxg6 hxg6 19.♕g5 ♕c6 20.dxe5 ♖xd3 21.♘f4 ♖e3 22.e6!± White was clearly better in Van der Sterren – Boll, Dieren 1980.

Reacting with 13...e6 would not affect White's typical plan; the normal 14.♗xg7 ♔xg7 15.f4↑ gives him better chances.

13...♘a5 looks imprecise after 14.♗d3 when Black has no pressure on the d4-pawn.

In 2009 Aronian played:
13...♖b8!?
    And he held the position against Ponomariov. The main idea of this move is to prepare a later ...b5 and also to leave the bishop on the c8-h3 diagonal to help with the defence. Ponomariov opted for the logical:
14.♗xg7 ♔xg7
    And now we have a split between a new move 15.f4 and the move Ponomariov played, 15.♕e3.

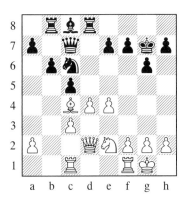

a) 15.f4N

This is best met by:

15...b5!

15...♗g4 16.♘g3 ♕d6 (16...♘a5 17.♗d3↑) 17.f5 cxd4 (17...♘e5? 18.♗d5!) 18.fxg6 dxc3 19.♕xc3† ♕d4† 20.♕xd4† ♘xd4 21.gxh7! (after 21.♖xf7† ♔xg6 22.♖xe7 ♖bc8 23.♗f7† ♔f6 24.♖xc8 ♖xc8 25.♖xa7 ♘c6 26.e5† ♔xe5 27.♖a3 ♘d4±/= Black has good chances of a draw) 21...♖bc8 22.♖xf7† ♔h8 23.♖ff1±/± White is a pawn up and has good winning chances.

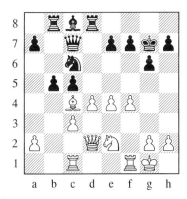

16.♗d5!

On 16.♗d3 cxd4 17.cxd4 ♕b6↑ White has problems with the pin on the g1-a7 diagonal.

16...e6 17.♗b3

Black gained a tempo with ...e7-e6, but on the other hand it weakened the dark squares around the king. Even so, Black looks okay after:

17...cxd4 18.cxd4 ♕b6 19.♖cd1 ♘a5 20.♖f2 ♖b7!∞

b) 15.♕e3 e5 16.♕g3! cxd4 17.cxd4 ♕d6 18.d5 ♘a5 19.♗d3

White's position looks preferable. The game continued:

19...♖b7!? 20.f4 exf4 21.♘xf4 ♔g8

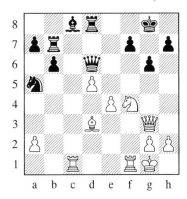

Here White should play:

22.♖f3!N

22.♕g5 f6 23.♕h4 ♖f7 led to a successful defence in Ponomariov – Aronian, Tal Memorial 2009.

Now it looks best for Black to play actively with:

22...b5

22...♕e5 23.♕h4 ♕e7 (23...f6 24.♗a6! ♖b8 25.♗xc8 ♖bxc8 26.♖e1±) 24.♕h6 ♕e5 (24...f6? 25.♗a6 ♖c7 26.♖xc7 ♕xc7 27.♘h5! gxh5 28.♗xc8 ♕c5† 29.♔h1 ♕f8 30.♗e6†+−) 25.♖g3 ♖c7 26.♖f1↑ White has an initiative and the better position.

The main problem with Black's active 22...b5 is that it creates weaknesses on the queenside. White has the following option:

23.♖f2!? a6 24.♖fc2 ♗d7 25.♘e2 ♕xg3 26.♘xg3±

White is better in the endgame; his plan is the simple ♔f2-e3-d4.

Finally, the inferior 13...e5?! leads to an advantage for White after 14.♗g5 ♖d7 15.d5 ♘a5 16.♗b5 ♖d6 17.f4±↑.

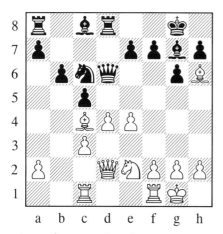

14.♗xg7 ♔xg7 15.♕e3 ♘a5

15...e5 is not good here. After 16.♗d5! ♖b8 (16...♗b7 17.dxe5 ♕xe5 18.f4±) 17.♗xc6 ♕xc6 18.d5 ♕d6 19.f4!?± and next c4 or f5, White has a stable advantage.

16.♗d3 cxd4 17.cxd4 e5

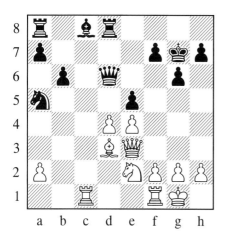

18.f4! exd4 19.♕g3⩱

After the pawn sacrifice White has created good attacking prospects; he will prepare a break with e5 or f5. Meanwhile Black's pieces are concentrated on the queenside, so he has to find a way to include them in the defence.

19...♔h8!

The only move; otherwise the direct e5 and f5 would give White a strong attack. For

example, after 19...♗b7? 20.e5 ♕e7 21.f5 ♔h8 22.e6! Black doesn't have anything better than 22...gxf5 23.exf7 ♕e3† (23...d5 24.♘f4 ♖d6 25.♗xf5+−) 24.♕xe3 dxe3 25.♖xf5+− and Black may have survived to an ending, but his position is hopeless.

20.♕h4 ♖g8

This move looks weird and passive, but it is hard to propose something better for Black.

One alternative was:
20...♗b7!?
    White would have another break:
21.f5!

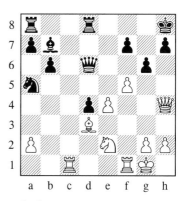

Now the best option is:
21...g5!
    21...♖g8 22.fxg6! fxg6 (22...♕xg6 23.g3±, with next ♖f6, is no better than the main line) 23.e5!

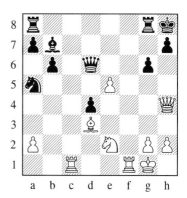

White's attack is developing by itself.
23...♕xe5 (23...♖d8 24.♖h6 ♖g7 25.♖f6+–)
24.♘f4 ♕e3† 25.♔h1 Black has huge
problems. After 25...♖g7 26.♕h6 ♕e8
(26...♖f7 27.♗xg6 ♖g7 28.♖ce1 ♕d2 29.♗e4
♗xe4 30.♖xe4 ♕xa2 31.♖e7+–) 27.♖ce1
♕g8 28.♖e6! ♗f8 (28...♕d8 29.♖xg6+–)
29.♖fe1+– Black can't hold the position.
Defending the 7th rank with 21...♖d7 is met
by 22.♘f4. Now the only move is 22...♘c6
to defend against the threats of fxg6 and e5.
Still after 23.♘d5! (planning ♘f6) Black
has to play 23...g5□ 24.♕xg5 f6 25.♕xf6†
♕xf6 26.♘xf6± when White has an extra
pawn *and* the better position.

22.♕xg5 ♘c6

Or 22...♖g8 23.♕h4 with the idea 23...♕d8?
24.f6+–.

With the text move Black takes control over
the e5-square, however White can reply
aggressively:

23.♖f3! ♘e5 24.♖h3

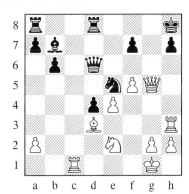

24...f6

24...♖g8 25.♕h4 h6 26.♕f4 ♔h7 27.♖c7!
♖g4 28.♖xf7† ♘xf7 29.♕xg4+–

25.♕h4 ♖d7 26.♘f4 ♖c8

26...♖g8 27.♘e6 ♖f7 (27...♕e7 28.♗b5!)
28.♗e2!± and next ♗h5 gives White the
better position.

27.♖xc8† ♗xc8 28.♘g6† ♘xg6 29.fxg6 ♖g7
30.♖f3 ♕e7 31.gxh7±

This leads to a simplified position where
White is much better.

21.e5!

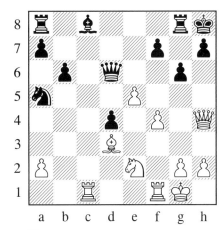

21...♕d8

Worse is: 21...♕d5 22.♖c7 ♗b7 (after
22...♗f5 23.♕f6† ♖g7 24.♗xf5 gxf5 25.♘g3
♖ag8 26.♖fc1! ♘b7 [26...♖e6 27.♘h5 ♕xf6
28.♘xf6+–] 27.♖c8 ♘d8 28.e6!+– Black has
no chance of surviving) 23.♕f6† ♖g7 24.♖f2
♖e8 25.♘g3 ♕d8 26.♖fc2± White is on top.

22.♕f2 ♕e7 23.♘xd4 ♖d8 24.♗e4 ♖b8

This is too slow. Better was:
24...♗a6!

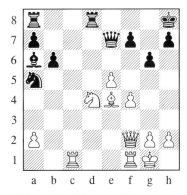

Here White should keep all the pieces on the
board by playing:
25.♖fe1

25.♗xa8 ♗xf1 26.♖xf1 ♖xa8± is also better
for White, but there is no concrete way to
attack the kingside and the position has
simplified.

25...罝ac8 26.罝cd1!

And now if Black plays:

26...♝b7

After the objectively more resistant 26...f5 27.♝f3± White's positional advantage is still clear.

27.♝xb7 ♞xb7 28.f5

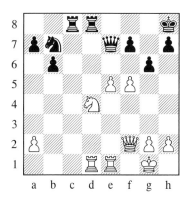

White has a strong attack. For example: 28...♞c5 29.♛e3 a6 30.罝f1 ♚g8 31.f6 ♛e8

31...♛f8 32.e6 ♞xe6 33.♞xe6 fxe6 34.f7†+– 32.罝de1!±

White has kept all the pieces on the board and next ♞f5 will increase the pressure on Black's position.

25.罝fe1 ♝b7?!

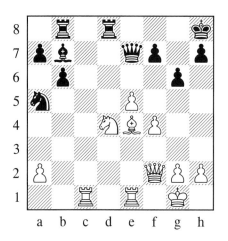

This helps White. Now after preliminary exchanges and then the f5-break, White's attack is decisive. Instead 25...♝a6 26.罝cd1!± would lead to a better version for White of the 24...♝a6 variation.

26.♝xb7 罝xb7

26...♞xb7? 27.♞c6+–

27.f5!+– gxf5

What else? 27...罝c7 28.f6 ♛d7 29.e6+–

28.♞xf5 ♛e6 29.♞d6 罝bd7 30.罝f1 罝f8 31.♛b2

More precise was 31.♛d4+– and next 罝f6 since Black cannot play ...f5. It matters little, as White is also winning after the move played in the game.

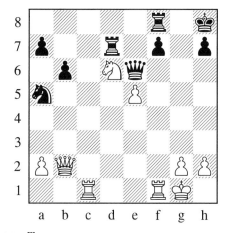

31...罝e7
1–0

Mamedyarov resigned before White could play 32.罝f6+–. For example: 32...♛xe5 33.♞xf7† 罝fxf7 34.♛xe5 罝xe5 35.罝xf7+–

More resistant was 31...f5, but after 32.罝xf5! 罝xf5 33.罝c8† ♚g7 34.♞xf5† ♚g6 35.♛b1!+– the king will not survive on g6.

GAME 33

▷ **G. Kamsky** (2741)

▶ **I. Nepomniachtchi** (2711)

FIDE World Cup, Khanty-Mansiysk
Round 3, Game 1, 03.09.2011 **[D87]**
Annotated by Kamil Miton

Here we have another ♗c4 Grünfeld. White went for 11.♖b1 instead of the more common 11.♖c1. Interestingly Kamsky has often faced the former move from the opposite side of the board, so could this sign of approval be taken as a recommendation for how White should play? Nepomniachtchi reacted with 11...a6, which is okay although in the notes we will also take a look at some other plans. The critical point came on the next move when Black erred with 12...♕a5?!, which allowed White to obtain some advantage. Instead the more promising 12...e5!? would have led to interesting play.

1.d4 ♘f6 2.c4 g6 3.♘c3 d5 4.cxd5 ♘xd5 5.e4 ♘xc3 6.bxc3 ♗g7 7.♗c4 c5 8.♘e2 ♘c6 9.♗e3 0–0 10.0–0 ♕c7

10...♗g4 is a big line which most famously occurred in several games between Kasparov and Karpov, but is nowadays considered rather worse for Black.

Another possibility is 10...♘a5 followed by ...b6.

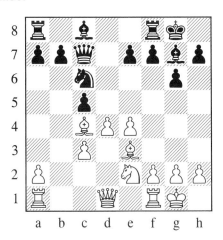

11.♖b1!?

More common is 11.♖c1, anticipating the opening of the c-file after an exchange on d4.

11...a6

The idea of this move is to prepare ...b5 and ...♗b7. Still, the move carries certain risks, as if Black fails to carry our his plan then the b6-square could become weak and White's pressure along the b-file more severe.

Several other moves can be considered.

11...e6 is directed against White's plan of putting a pawn or bishop on d5, but it has the drawback of weakening the f6-square. White's chances should be slightly higher after 12.♕c1! intending ♖d1 and ♗h6 to exchange the dark-squared bishops.

11...cxd4?!
This exchange is premature.
12.cxd4 ♘xd4 13.♗xf7† ♖xf7 14.♘xd4
White has a stable advantage, as his superior structure is more important than Black's bishop pair.
14...♕d7
14...♕c4?! 15.♕d2 e5 16.♖fc1 ♕a4 17.♘b5+−
14...♗d7 15.♕b3↑

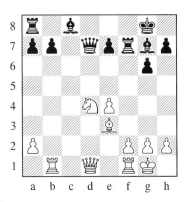

15.f3!

15.♘b5 is premature: 15...a6 16.♕xd7 ♗xd7 17.♘c7 ♖c8 18.♖xb7 ♗c6 19.♖a7

♗xe4 20.♘xa6 e6 21.♖xf7 ♔xf7= Black will soon regain the pawn.

15...b6 16.♘b5 e6 17.♕c2 ♗a6 18.♖fd1±

11...b6!?

This has not been the most popular, but it seems like a decent move.

12.♗f4

12.dxc5 Although there are exceptions, the general rule is that this exchange brings White nothing, as it compromises his centre and queenside. 12...♘e5 13.♗d5 ♖b8 14.cxb6 axb6∞ Black is fine, for instance: 15.f4 ♘g4 16.♗d4 ♗xd4† 17.cxd4 ♘e3 18.♕c1 ♘xd5 19.exd5 ♕d6=

12...e5

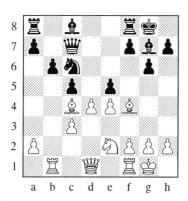

13.dxe5!?

13.♗g3 ♘a5 14.♗d5 (14.♗b5!?) 14...♗b7 15.dxe5 ♗xe5 16.♗xb7 ♘xb7 17.f4 ♗g7 18.f5 ♕e7 is more than okay for Black.

13...♘xe5 14.♗d5 ♗b7 15.c4 ♖ad8 16.♘c3∞

11...♖d8

This has been by far the most popular move.

12.♗f4

In this position 12...♕d7 13.dxc5!?± is a rare case where taking on c5 works well for White, due to Black's dubious coordination and the fact that the white rook stands much better on b1 than c1. For this reason Black's main candidates are a) 12...e5 and b) 12...♗e5, which we will analyse in turn.

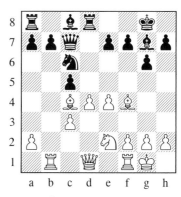

a) 12...e5 13.♗g5 ♖d6

From this position it is worth considering a1) 14.d5 and a2) 14.♗d5.

a1) 14.d5 ♘a5 15.♗d3 c4

Otherwise White will play c4 himself.

16.♗c2∞

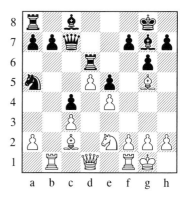

I will not analyse this position in detail, but will instead offer some general guidance on this structure, which quite often arises in the ♗c4 Grünfeld. A lot will be decided by which side succeeds in improving their pieces first. The black knight on a5 is out of play, and should be transferred via b7 to either c5 or, more commonly, d6. (In positions where the black bishop has gone to b7, this will mean spending an additional tempo on ...♗c8. Later Black may try to make progress on the queenside.

White's main plan of action will be to prepare f4. Then if Black plays ...exf4, White will obtain the d4-square for his knight and improved prospects for the c2-bishop. For this reason Black usually responds with ...f6 to maintain a pawn on e5. White will often employ the manoeuvring plan of ♔h1, ♘g1 and ♘f3. From f3 the knight eyes the e5-pawn and might eventually participate in a kingside attack after ♕e1 and ♕h4. Along the way White should protect the knight from being exchanged by ...♗g4.

a2) 14.♗d5

With this move White keeps more fluidity in the centre.

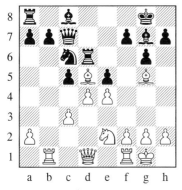

14...cxd4 15.cxd4 ♗g4 16.dxe5

Also quite promising is: 16.f3 ♗e6 17.♗xe6 fxe6 18.d5 a6 (18...exd5 19.♘c3!±) 19.♘c3 (19.♕c2 exd5 20.exd5 ♖xd5 21.♕c4 ♕d6 22.♖fd1 ♕c5† 23.♕xc5 ♖xc5 24.♖xb7 e4!?=) 19...b5 20.♔h1 b4 21.♘a4 exd5 22.exd5 ♘d4 23.♖xb4 ♖e8 24.♕d3 ♕a5 25.♖fb1 ♖xd5 26.♘c3 ♕e6 27.♘e4 ♖c6±
16...♘xe5

16...♗xe5 17.h3 ♗e6 18.♘f4±
17.h3!

17.♕d2 ♖xd5 18.exd5 ♘c4∞

17.♕c1 ♕a5 18.♗xb7 ♖b8 19.♗d5 ♖xb1 20.♕xb1 ♖xd5 21.exd5 ♗xe2 22.♕b8† ♗f8 23.♕xe5 ♗xf1 24.♔xf1 ♕xa2=
17...♗f3

17...♗xh3 is strongly met by 18.f4!.
18.♕c1 ♕xc1 19.♘xc1 ♖xd5 20.exd5 ♗xd5 21.♖d1±

b) 12...♗e5

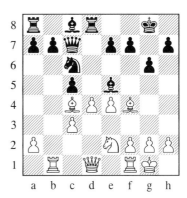

13.♗xe5 ♘xe5 14.♗b3 ♘g4

14...b6 15.f4 ♘g4 16.♕d3 ♗b7 17.♕h3 h5 18.f5→ ♗xe4 19.fxg6 ♗xg6 20.♘f4 c4 21.♗d1±
15.♘g3 ♕f4

Following the bishop exchange Black is trying to use his queen to protect his kingside, but the plan seems rather artificial.
16.h3

16.♕e1!? b6 17.f3 ♘e3 18.♖f2 ♗a6 19.♘e2 is interesting.
16...♘f6 17.e5

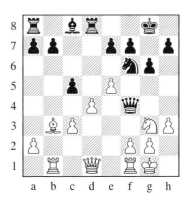

17...♘d5

17...♘e4 is well met by: 18.♘xe4 (18.♘e2 ♕h6∞) 18...♕xe4 19.♖e1 ♕f4

20.e6! Weakening the kingside even more. 20...f5 Trying to keep the kingside closed, but it is risky to leave the bishop buried on c8. (20...f6?! 21.♕d3 b6 22.d5 ♗b7 23.c4±;

Black's best chance is probably 20...♗xe6 21.♗xe6 fxe6 22.♖xb7 cxd4 23.♖xe6 dxc3 24.♕b3 ♔f8 25.♕xc3 ♖d1† 26.♔e1 ♖xe1† 27.♕xe1 ♕f6 28.♕e3±) 21.g3 (21.d5 b5!) 21...♗c7 (21...♖h6 22.♕f3 cxd4 23.cxd4 ♕xh3 24.♕f4+−) 22.♕f3 Black is in some danger, for instance: 22...cxd4 23.cxd4 ♖xd4 24.♖bc1 ♕d6 25.♖ed1+−

18.♘e2 ♕e4 19.♘g3 ♕f4 20.dxc5 ♗e6 21.♕d4 b6 22.♘e2

22.♗xd5 ♖xd4 23.cxd4 ♖xd5 24.cxb6 axb6 25.♖fd1 ♖a6 gives Black good drawing chances, for instance:

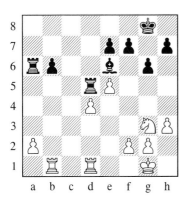

26.♘e2 (26.a3 ♖da5 27.♘e4 ♗f5 28.f3 ♖xa3 29.d5 ♗xe4 30.fxe4 ♔f8 31.d6 ♔e8 32.♖dc1 ♔d8 33.♖c7 ♖a7=) 26...♖d8 27.a4 (27.♘c3 ♗xa2 28.♘xa2 ♖xa2 29.♖xb6 ♖e2=) 27...♖xa4 28.♖xb6 ♗c4 29.♘c3 ♖a3 30.♘e4 ♖d3 31.♖xd3 ♗xd3 32.♘c5 ♖xd4 33.♖b7 ♗f5 34.♖xe7 ♖d5=
22...♕f5

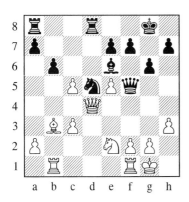

23.♖bd1!N
An improvement over 23.cxb6 ♘xb6 24.♕f4 (24.♘g3!?) 24...♖ac8 25.♕xf5 ♗xf5 26.♖bd1 ♗d3⮾ Ponomariov – Carlsen, Nice 2010.
23...♘c7
23...♖ac8 24.c6±
23...bxc5 24.♕xc5 ♖ac8 25.♕a5 ♕xe5 26.c4 ♕xe2 27.cxd5 ♕h5 28.♖fe1±
24.♕xd8† ♖xd8 25.♖xd8† ♔g7 26.♘d4 ♕xe5 27.c6 ♕c5 28.♗xe6 ♘xe6 29.♘xe6† fxe6 30.♖d7±

Summing up, the main line of 11...♖d8 12.♗f4 gives White good chances of an advantage if he plays accurately. However, the rare 11...b6!? may deserve more attention.

Let us now return to the game after **11...a6**.

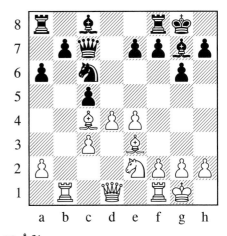

12.♗f4
This was Kamsky's novelty.

12.♕c1 has been White's usual choice, but after 12...b5 Black carries out his plan and should be okay.

12.a4!?± has only been played a few times, but looks sensible and should give White a slight edge.

12...♕a5?!

Nepomniachtchi immediately goes astray.

The critical move was obviously:
12...e5
   And now both a) 13.♗g3 and b) 13.dxe5 deserve attention.

a) 13.♗g3

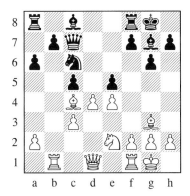

13...b5 14.♗d5 ♗b7 15.a4
   15.dxc5 ♘a5=
   15.dxe5 ♘xe5 16.♘f4 c4∞
   15.♗xc6 ♕xc6 16.d5 ♕d6= Black has more chances to gain the initiative through the light squares than White through the dark squares.
15...♘e7 16.♗xb7
   16.dxe5 ♘xd5 17.exd5 ♗xe5 18.d6 ♕c6∓
16...♕xb7

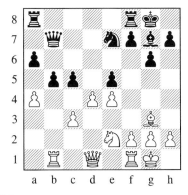

17.d5
   Usually this structure with a strong pawn on d5 is more appealing for White, but in this

particular case Black is well placed to put his knight on d6 and play for ...f5.
   17.axb5 axb5 18.♕d3 cxd4 19.cxd4 exd4 20.♖xb5 ♕a6=
A probably improvement is: 17.♗xe5! ♗xe5 18.dxe5 ♕xe4 19.axb5 axb5 20.♘g3 ♕xe5 21.♖e1 ♕c7 22.♖xb5↑ White has the initiative thanks to his active pieces, and he may go for an attack with ♘e4.
17...♘c8 18.f3 ♘d6 19.♗f2 ♕c7 20.♘c1
   White logically improves his pieces but Black remains okay.

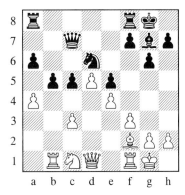

20...c4!
   Stopping the knight from coming to b3 or d3.
21.♕c2
   21.♘a2 f5 22.♕c2 fxe4 23.fxe4 ♖f4⇄ 24.♖fe1 ♖af8 25.♗g3 ♕c5† 26.♔h1 ♘xe4–+
21...f5 22.exf5 gxf5 23.♘e2 f4∞

b) 13.dxe5

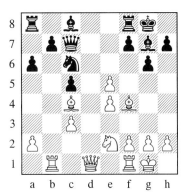

13...♘xe5

After 13...♗xe5 14.♗xe5 ♘xe5 the bishop exchange has weakened Black's kingside, and White has chances to start an attack. Still, in the following illustrative line Black turns out to be okay: 15.♘d5 ♖b8 16.f4 ♘g4 17.♕d2 b5 (17...♗e6 18.c4 b5 19.h3 ♘f6 20.e5 ♘d7 21.♘c3 bxc4 22.♗xe6 fxe6 23.♖xb8 ♖xb8 24.♘e4 ♘b6 25.♘f6† ♔g7 26.♖d1↑) 18.h3 ♘f6 19.f5 ♘xd5 20.exd5 ♗xf5 21.♖xf5 gxf5 22.♕g5† ♔h8 23.♕f6† ♔g8=

14.♗d5 ♖b8 15.♗g3!

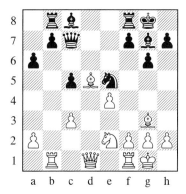

White's last move prepares f4-f5 with strong attacking prospects. Black can move his queen out of danger with b1) 15...♕e7, ignore the threat with b2) 15...b5 or continue developing with b3) 15...♗e6!.

b1) 15...♕e7 16.f4 ♘g4 17.f5 ♗e5 18.fxg6 hxg6 19.♘f4 ♔g7 20.♕f3→ Black must make some kind of concession here; the best chance seems to be giving up the exchange and trying to defend a worse endgame after: 20...b5 21.h3 ♘f6 22.♘e6† fxe6 23.♗xe5 exd5 24.♗xb8 ♘xe4 25.♗e5† ♔g8 26.♕xf8† ♕xf8 27.♖xf8† ♔xf8±

b2) 15...b5

This seems rather provocative.

16.f4 ♘g4 17.f5 ♕b6

17...♗e5 18.♕d2↑

18.♕d2 ♖b7

18...gxf5 19.h3 ♘f6 20.♗xb8 ♕xb8 21.exf5 ♕e5 22.♗c6 ♕c7 23.♗f3 ♗xf5 24.♖bd1±

19.♗xb7 ♗xb7 20.♖be1!?

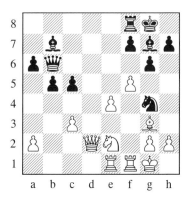

20...c4†

20...♗xe4 21.h3 ♘f6 22.♗e5 ♗xf5 23.♘g3 ♗c8 24.♕g5 ♘e8 25.♗xg7 ♘xg7 26.♘e4→

21.♘d4 b4 22.e5 bxc3 23.♕xc3 ♖d8 24.♖b1 ♕a7

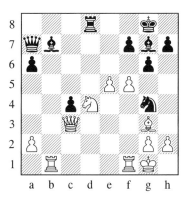

25.♔h1!

25.f6 is slightly premature: 25...♗h6 26.e6 ♗e3† 27.♔f2 ♗xf2† 28.♖xf2 ♖xd4 29.exf7† ♔xf7 30.♖xb7† ♕xb7 31.♕xd4 ♘f2 32.♕xc4† ♔xf6 33.♔xf2=

25...♗e4 26.♖bd1 ♕a8 27.♘f3 ♗xf5 28.♖d4±

Black does not have quite enough for the exchange, especially as the knight on g4 is uncomfortably placed.

b3) 15...♗e6!

The most accurate move. Black wastes

no time developing another piece and challenging the strong bishop on d5.

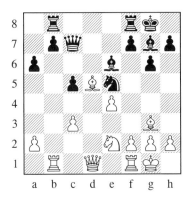

16.♘f4

Supporting d5 and hitting e6, but blocking the f-pawn.

16.c4!? is another idea.

16...♖fe8

16...♗d7 can be met by 17.h4!↑ when paradoxically, the heavily guarded g6-pawn may become the target of an attack.

17.♕b3

17.♘xe6 fxe6 18.f4 exd5 19.fxe5 ♖bd8 20.e6 ♕c6 21.♗h4 ♖d6 22.♕f3 ♖f8 23.exd5 ♖xd5 24.♕g4 ♖df5 25.♗xf5 gxf5 26.♕g3 ♕xe6 27.♖xb7 ♖f7=

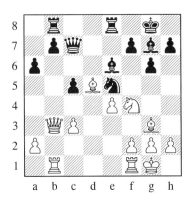

17...♗d7

17...c4?! 18.♕b6± ♕xb6 19.♖xb6 ♗xd5 20.♘xd5 ♘d7 21.♖b4 ♖bc8 22.♖xb7 ♘c5 23.♖a7 ♘xe4 24.♘e7† ♖xe7 25.♖xe7 ♘xg3 26.fxg3±

18.♖fd1

18.♕b6 ♕xb6 19.♖xb6 ♗b5∞

18...b5 19.♕a3 ♕b6∞

After a series of accurate moves Black has obtained a reasonable position.

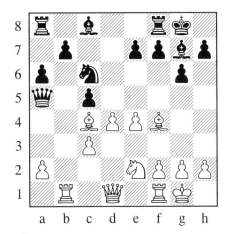

13.♗d5 cxd4

13...♖d8 14.♕b3! (14.♕c2 cxd4 [14...e6 15.♗xc6 bxc6 16.♘c1!] 15.cxd4 ♖xd5 16.exd5 ♕xd5 17.♕c5 ♗e6 18.♖xd5 ♗xd5 19.♖xb7 ♘xd4 20.♖xe7 ♘xe2† 21.♖xe2 ♗c4=) 14...e6 15.♗xc6 bxc6 16.♖fd1±

14.cxd4 ♗g4 15.f3

15.♖xb7 ♘xd4 16.f3 ♗e6 17.♘xd4 ♗xd5 18.exd5 ♕xd5=

15...♗e6

Black is willing to undertake doubled pawns in order to finish his development.

16.♗d2!

Before exchanging on e6, White drives the enemy queen to a worse position.

The immediate exchange gets nowhere: 16.♗xe6 fxe6 17.a4 (17.♖xb7 ♕xa2 18.♕d3 ♖fd8 19.♗e3 ♖ac8 20.f4 a5⇄) 17...♘xd4! (17...♖fd8 18.♗e3±) 18.♘xd4 ♖ad8 19.♗e3 ♕c3 20.♖b3 ♕c4 21.♕c1 (21.e5 ♗xe5 22.♖d3 ♗f4=) 21...♕xc1 22.♖xc1 ♗xd4 23.♔f2 b5 24.axb5 axb5 25.♖xb5 ♗xe3† 26.♔xe3=

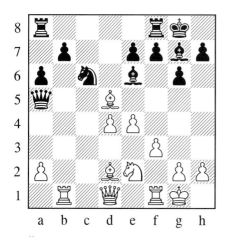

16...♕c7

After 16...♕a3 17.♗c1 ♕a5 (17...♕d6 18.♗xe6 fxe6 19.♗e3 b5 20.e5±) 18.♗xe6 fxe6 19.a4± b5 20.e5 ♕xa4 21.♕xa4 bxa4 22.♖a1 Black faces a difficult endgame.

17.♗xe6 fxe6 18.♗c3

18.♗e3!? was also reasonable.

18...♖ad8

Black must quickly obtain counterplay against d4, otherwise he will have no compensation for his dodgy structure, especially the weak e6-pawn.

19.♕b3

A possible improvement is:
19.♕a4!?

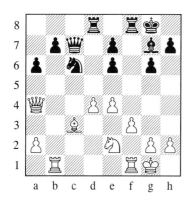

19...♘xd4

19...♖d6 20.e5! ♖d5 21.f4 ♕d7 22.♕c2± White is playing to shut the g7-bishop out of the game completely. Considerations such as giving up the d5-square are of little importance when you are virtually playing with an extra piece.

20.♗xd4

20.♘xd4 ♕c5 21.♖fd1 b5 22.♕xa6 ♖d6 23.♕xb5 ♕xc3 24.♘e2 ♕e3† 25.♔h1 ♖xd1† 26.♖xd1 ♔f7∞

20...♖xd4† 21.♘xd4 ♕c5 22.♖fd1 e5 23.♕b3† Also promising is: 23.♕c2 ♕a7 24.♕b3† ♖f7 25.♕xb7 ♕xb7 26.♖xb7 ♖xd4 27.♖xd4 exd4 28.e5±

23...♖f7 24.♕c2 ♕a7 25.♕c7 ♖xd4 26.♔f1±

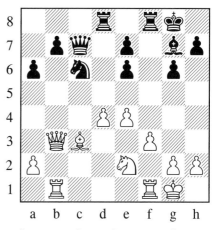

19...♘xd4 20.♗xd4 ♗xd4† 21.♘xd4 ♖xd4 22.♕xe6† ♖f7 23.♖bc1

23.♖fc1 leads to no advantage: 23...♕d6 (23...♕d7 24.♖c8† ♔g7 25.♕e5† ♔h6 26.♖c7 ♖d1† 27.♖xd1 ♕xd1† 28.♔f2 ♕d2† 29.♔g3 g5 30.h3 is a bit unpleasant for Black as his king is uncomfortable; 23...♕f4!?⇄ is interesting though.) 24.♕c8† ♔g7 25.♕xb7 ♖d2 26.♕b3 ♕d4† 27.♔h1 ♕f2 28.♕c3† ♔h6 29.♖g1 ♖xa2=

23...♕d6

23...♕a5!? was also playable: 24.♖c8† (24.♕c8† ♔g7 25.♕xb7 ♖d2=) 24...♔g7 25.♖h8 ♔xh8 26.♕xf7 ♕d8 27.h4↑

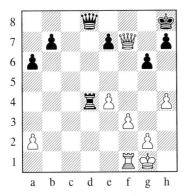

Maybe Black was apprehensive of this position. White's powerful queen paralyses the black pieces to some degree, but on the other hand it is not easy for White to include his rook in the attack.

24.♕c8† ♔g7 25.♕xb7 ♖d2 26.♕b3

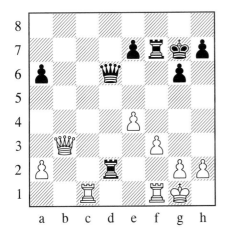

Black has just enough play for the pawn, as the presence of the white pawn on f3 instead of f2 weakens his kingside slightly.

26...e5?

The idea of activating the f7-rook was correct, but the execution was erroneous as Black has unnecessarily weakened his king.

More precise was: 26...♖f6! 27.♔h1 (27.♖cd1 ♕c5† 28.♔h1 ♖fd6 29.h3 a5∞; 27.♖fd1 ♕d4†

28.♔h1 ♖c6=) 27...♕b6 (27...♕e5!?) 28.♖fd1 ♕xb3 29.axb3 ♖b2=

27.♖cd1

Black's active rook must be exchanged.

27...♕d4†

27...♕c5† 28.♔h1 ♖fd7 29.♖xd2 ♖xd2 30.♕b7† ♔h6 31.♕xa6 ♕c2 32.♕e6 ♕xa2 33.♕g4±

The best chance was probably 27...♖c7 28.♔h1 a5 29.h3±.

28.♔h1 ♖d7

28...♖c7 29.♖xd2 ♕xd2 30.♕e6± also leaves Black in trouble as his king exposed and the e5-pawn is weak.

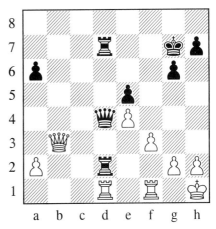

29.♖xd2 ♕xd2 30.♕e6 ♕d6 31.♕xd6 ♖xd6 32.h4 ♖d2 33.♖c1

Leading to a winning rook ending where White has two extra pawns on the kingside.

33...♖xa2 34.♖c7† ♔f6 35.♖xh7 a5 36.♖a7 a4 37.♔h2 a3 38.♔h3 ♔e6 39.♖a6† ♔f7 40.♔g3 ♔g7 41.♖e6 ♖e2 42.♖xe5 a2 43.♖a5 ♔f6 44.f4 ♖xe4 45.♖xa2 ♔g7 46.♔g4 ♖b4 47.♖a5

1–0

GAME 34

▷ **E. Bacrot (2710)**

▶ **A. Filippov (2606)**

FIDE World Cup, Khanty-Mansiysk
Round 2, Game 2, 01.09.2011 [**E07**]
Annotated by Kamil Miton

In the game below we may observe one of the structures from the Catalan Opening. White sacrificed the c4-pawn in exchange for a strong centre and the more active pieces. Black's position was very solid while White played for the initiative. The course of the game proved very interesting, though not devoid of mistakes on both sides. It turned out to be Black who made the final error.

1.♘f3 d5 2.d4 ♘f6 3.c4 e6 4.g3 ♗b4† 5.♗d2 ♗e7 6.♗g2 c6 7.0–0 0–0 8.♗f4 ♘bd7 9.♘c3 dxc4 10.e4 ♖e8

An interesting move. It allows the transfer of the knight to g6 (...♘f8-g6), and the rook may prove useful on e8 if Black plays a typical idea for these positions: ...e5, meeting dxe5 with ...♘g4.

The attempt to achieve a natural set-up with 10...b5 (followed by ...♗b7) results in unclear positions after 11.d5.

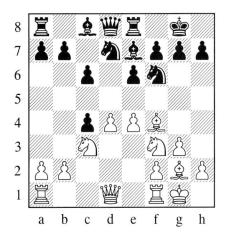

11.a4

The main alternative is:
11.♖e1 ♘f8
11...a5 12.d5↑
11...b5!? 12.d5 b4 (12...e5 13.♘xe5 ♘xe5 14.♗xe5 ♘g4 15.♗d4 c5 16.♗e3±) 13.dxc6 ♘c5 14.♘b5 ♕b6 15.♘c7 ♘d3 16.♖e3 (16.♘xe8 ♕xf2† 17.♔h1 ♘g4 18.♕d2 ♕c5∞) 16...♗a6 17.♘xe8 ♖xe8 18.♖xd3 cxd3 19.♘e5∞
12.a4
12.♕e2 b5 13.♘e5 ♗b7 14.♖ad1 ♘g6 15.♘xg6 hxg6 16.♗g5 ♘xe4∓
12...♘g6 13.♗g5 e5 14.dxe5 ♘g4
14...♘d7 15.e6 fxe6 16.♗xe7 ♕xe7

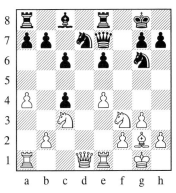

17.e5 (17.♕d4 ♕c5 18.♕xc5 ♘xc5 19.♗f1 e5 20.♗xc4† ♗e6=) 17...♘c5 18.♖e3 ♖d8 19.♕e2 b6 20.♕xc4 ♗a6 21.♕g4±
15.♕xd8 ♗xd8 16.♗xd8 ♖xd8 17.♖ed1 ♗e6
17...♖e8 18.h3 ♘4xe5 19.♘d2 ♖d8 20.f4 ♗xh3 21.fxe5 ♗g4 22.♘f3 ♗xf3 23.♗xf3 ♘xe5 24.♗e2∞
17...♖xd1† 18.♖xd1 ♗e6 19.♘e1 ♘6xe5 20.h3 ♘h6 21.f4 ♘d3 22.♘xd3 cxd3 23.♖xd3 f6 24.♔f2 ♘f7 25.a5 ♖d8 26.♖xd8† ♘xd8 27.♔e3±
18.♘e1 ♘6xe5 19.h3 ♘f6 20.f4 ♘d3 21.f5 ♘xe1 22.♖xe1 ♗d7 23.e5↑

11...a5

White's greater space and strong centre provide compensation for the pawn deficit. White may now play in either of two ways – to regain the c4-pawn (with ♕e2 and ♘d2) or to concentrate his efforts on the centre (with ♕c2 and ♖d1).

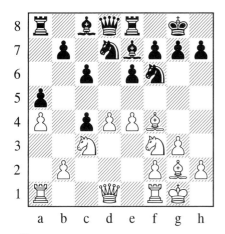

12.♕c2

12.♘d2 ♘b6 13.♕e2 (13.♗e3 e5 14.dxe5 ♘g4 15.♗xb6 ♕xb6 16.♘xc4 ♕c5∓) 13...♕xd4 14.♗e3 ♕d8 15.♖fd1 ♕c7 16.♗xb6 ♕xb6 17.e5 ♘d5 18.♘xc4 ♕b4 19.♘e4 b6∓

12.♕e2 b6 13.♘d2 ♗a6 14.♘xc4 By regaining the pawn, White has subjected himself to various motifs connected with the f1-a6 diagonal and the e-file. Black now has several options:

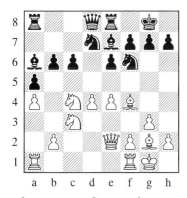

a) 14...♗b4 15.♖fd1 ♘d5 16.♗d2
16.exd5 exd5 17.♕c2 ♗xc4 18.b3 ♗a6 19.♘a2 ♗a3 20.♕xc6 ♘f6=
16...e5

16...♖c8!?
17.exd5 exd4 18.♕f1
18.♕h5 ♘f6 19.♕h4 dxc3 20.♗xc3 ♘xd5 21.♕xd8 ♖axd8 22.♗xd5 ♖xd5 23.♖xd5 cxd5 24.♘xb6=
18...dxc3
18...♘e5 19.♘b5±
19.♗xc3 cxd5 20.♗xd5 ♗xc3
20...♖a7 21.♖ac1↑
21.♗xa8 ♗xb2 22.♗c6 ♕c7 23.♖xd7 ♗xc4 24.♕g2±

b) 14...♖c8 15.♖fd1 ♘d5 16.♗d2 ♘b4 17.♖ac1 c5
17...e5 18.♗e3 ♕c7 (18...♗g5 19.f4 exf4 20.gxf4±) 19.♗h3 ♖cd8 20.♗xd7 ♕xd7 21.dxe5 ♘d3 22.♘d6 ♖xd6 23.exd6 ♕xd6 24.♗xb6 ♘xc1 25.♕xa6 ♖a8 26.♕c4 ♕b4 27.♕xc6 ♕xb2 28.♘d5 ♘d3 29.♕b5 ♕xb5 30.axb5∞
18.dxc5
18.♘b5 cxd4 19.♗xb4 ♗xb4 20.♖xd4 ♗xb5 21.axb5 ♕g5 22.♖cd1 ♕xb5 23.e5⯥
18.d5 exd5 19.♘xd5 ♘xd5 20.exd5 ♗f6 21.♗e3 ♗d4∞
18...♗xc4 19.♕xc4 ♘e5 20.♕e2 ♗xc5∞

c) 14...♗f8 15.♖fd1 (15.b3 b5∓) and now:

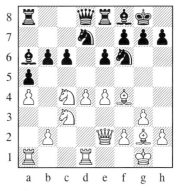

c1) 15...♕e7!?
Preparing both ...e5 and ...♕b4.
16.e5
16.b3 e5 17.dxe5 ♘xe5 18.♗xe5 ♕xe5

19.♘xe5 ♗xe2 20.♘xe2 ♖xe5 21.♖ac1 ♘xe4
(21...♗c5 22.♘f4±) 22.♖xc6 ♖b8 23.♘f4
♘f6=

16...♘d5

16...♕b4 17.exf6 ♗xc4 18.♕d2 ♘xf6
19.♗xc6 ♕b3 20.♗xa8 ♖xa8±

17.♗d2 f6

17...♖ac8!? 18.b3 c5 19.♘b5±

18.exf6 ♕xf6

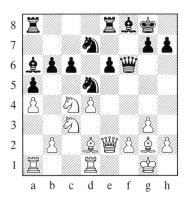

In most cases Black avoids this type of structure, because the e6-pawn is weaker than the one on d4 and the black king becomes a little exposed. However, in this particular position it will be difficult for White to prevent the move ...e5.

19.♘e4 ♕f5

19...♕xd4 20.b3 ♘e5 21.♕h5 ♗xc4 22.bxc4
g6 23.♗f4 gxh5 24.♖xd4 ♘xf4 25.♘f6†
♔h8 26.gxf4 ♗c5 27.♖dd1 ♘g6 28.♗xc6
♖f8 29.♘d7 ♖ad8 30.♘xf8 ♖xf8 31.♖a2±

20.♘g5

20.♕d3 e5 21.♕b3 exd4 22.♘cd6 ♗xd6
23.♘xd6 ♘c5 24.♗xd5† ♕xd5 25.♕xd5†
cxd5 26.♘xe8 ♖xe8⯑

20.f4 c5∞

20...h6 21.♘f3 e5 22.dxe5 ♗c5 23.♖e1 ♘xe5
24.♘fxe5 ♗xc4 25.♕xc4 ♖xe5 26.♖xe5 ♕xe5
27.♖e1 ♕xb2 28.♗xd5† ♔h8=

c2) 15...♘d5 16.♗d2 (16.♗c1 ♘xc3 17.bxc3
♘e5 18.dxe5 ♗xc4=) and Black has three options:

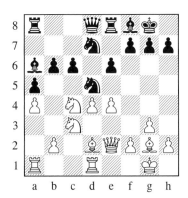

c21) 16...♘b4 17.e5 ♖c8 18.♘e4 c5 19.♗xb4
cxb4 20.b3±

c22) 16...e5!?N

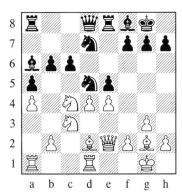

Black is worse in the centre and he should fight for it by employing either ...c5 or ...e5. It is crucial that Black makes these attempts before White solves the problems of the pin along the f1-a6 diagonal.

17.exd5 exd4 18.♕f1

18.♗e3 dxe3 19.fxe3 cxd5 20.♗xd5 ♖c8∞
21.♕f3 ♕f6 22.♗xf7† ♕xf7 23.♕xf7† ♔xf7
24.♖xd7† ♔e6 25.♘xb6 ♖c6 26.♘cd5 ♖xb6
27.♘xb6 ♖b8 28.♖d5 ♖xb6 29.♖xa5∞

18.♕g4 ♗xc4 19.♕xd4 (19.♗g5 ♘e5!)
19...cxd5 20.♘xd5 ♖c8 21.♗c3 ♗b3 22.♕g4
♗xd1 23.♖xd1 ♘e5 24.♕f5 ♖xc3 (24...♗d6
25.♗e4 g6 26.♘f6† ♔h8 27.♕xc8 ♕xc8
28.♘xe8 ♕xe8 29.♖xd6 ♔g8 30.♖xb6±)
25.bxc3 ♗c5=

18...♘e5

18...dxc3 19.♗xc3 cxd5 20.♗xd5 ♖c8
(20...♕c7 21.♕h3↑) 21.♗xf7†!? ♔xf7
22.♕h3 ♖e7 23.♘e5† ♔e8 24.♕xh7 ♘xe5
25.♖xd8† ♖xd8 26.♗xe5 ♖xe5 27.♕g6†
♔e7 28.♕xb6 ♖d6∞ The realization of
White's material advantage will not be
simple, because the activation of his pawns
may involve a considerable weakening of his
king.

19.b3

19.♘b5 cxb5 20.♘xe5 ♖xe5 21.axb5 ♗b7
22.♗f4 ♖xd5∓

19...♕f6

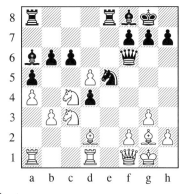

20.♘e4

20.♖ac1 ♘f3† 21.♗xf3 ♕xf3 22.♕g2 ♕xg2†
23.♔xg2 dxc3 24.♗xc3 ♗c5 25.♗d4 ♗xd4
26.♖xd4 cxd5 27.♘xb6 ♖ab8 28.♘d7 ♖xb3
29.♘c5 ♖b6 30.♖xd5 ♗c8=

20...♘f3† 21.♗xf3

21.♔h1 ♖xe4 22.♕d3 ♘xd2 23.♖xd2 ♖e5
24.dxc6 ♖ae8 25.h4 ♗b4∞

21...♕xf3 22.♘g5 ♕xb3 23.♖dc1 h6 24.♖ab1
♕a2 25.♘f3 cxd5 26.♖a1 ♕xc4 27.♖xc4
dxc4∞

c23) 16...♖c8 17.b3

17.♗e1 ♕c7 18.b3 ♗b4 19.♕b2 ♗xc4
20.bxc4 ♘xc3 21.♗xc3 ♗xc3 22.♕xc3
e5 23.♗h3 exd4 24.♖xd4 ♖cd8 25.♗xd7
♖xd7 26.♖xd7 ♕xd7 27.c5 ♕a7 28.♕c4
bxc5 29.♖c1 h6 30.♕xc5 ½–½ Gelfand –
Grischuk, Bursa 2010

17...c5

17...♘b4 18.e5 c5 (18...♘c2 19.♗g5 ♕xg5
20.♕xc2±) 19.♗f4 cxd4 20.♖xd4 ♕c7
21.♘e4↑ ♘c5 22.♘f6† gxf6 23.exf6 e5
24.♗h6+–

17...♕c7 18.♖ac1 ♗a3 19.exd5 cxd5 20.♖c2
dxc4 21.♘b5 ♗xb5 22.axb5 ♘f6 23.♖xc4
(23.bxc4 e5 24.dxe5 ♕xe5 25.♗xe5 ♖xe5
26.♗f4 ♖e7 27.♗e3 ♖xe3 28.fxe3 ♗c5⊗)
23...♕b8 24.♗c6 ♖ed8 25.♗g5±

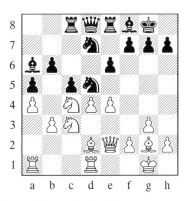

We now have a final split:

c231) 18.dxc5 ♘xc5 19.exd5 ♘xb3 20.dxe6
♖xe6 21.♗e3 ♕c7 22.♘b5 ♗xb5 23.axb5
♕xc4 24.♕xc4 ♖xc4 25.♗d5 ♖b4 26.♗xe6
♘xa1 27.♖xa1 fxe6 28.♗xb6 ♖xb5 29.♗xa5=

c232) 18.♘b5 cxd4

18...♗xb5 19.axb5 cxd4 20.♘xa5 bxa5
21.exd5 exd5 22.♕f3±

19.♘xd4 ♘c5 20.♘b5

20.♕f3 ♘f6 (20...♖xc4 21.bxc4 ♘b4
22.♗xb4 axb4 23.♘xe6 ♕e7 24.♘xf8 ♔xf8
25.♕e3±) 21.♗f4 ♗xc4 22.bxc4 ♘fxe4
23.♘xe6 ♕f6 (23...♕e7=) 24.♘c7 ♘d2
25.♕h5 ♖xc7 26.♗xc7 ♘ce4∞

20...♘xb3 21.exd5 ♘xa1

21...exd5 22.♕h5 g6 23.♕xd5 ♗xb5
24.♘xb6 ♘xa1 25.♘xc8 ♗e2 26.♖xa1 ♕xd5
27.♗xd5 ♖xc8=

22.dxe6 ♖xe6 23.♗e3 ♕e8 24.♖xa1 ♗xb5
25.axb5 ♕xb5 26.♗f1∞

c233) 18.exd5

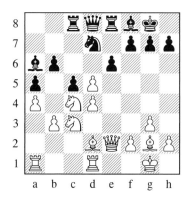

18...exd5

18...cxd4 19.d6 (19.♕f3 dxc3 20.♗xc3 ♗xc4 21.bxc4 ♖xc4 22.♗f1 ♕c7 23.d6 ♖c5 24.♗b5↑) 19...dxc3 20.♗xc3 ♘c5 and now:

i) 21.♖ab1 ♘xa4∞

ii) 21.♕h5 ♗xc4 (21...♘xb3? 22.♘e5±) 22.bxc4 ♗xd6=

iii) 21.♕e3 ♗xc4 (21...♘xb3 22.♘xb6 ♘xa1 23.♘xc8 ♗xc8 24.♗xa1±) 22.bxc4 ♗xd6 23.♗e5 ♗xe5 24.♖xd8 ♗xa1 25.♖xc8 ♖xc8

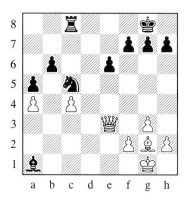

The black pieces will defend each other very well, making it difficult for White to improve his position. 26.♕f4 ♗c3 27.♕d6 ♗b4∞

19.♗e3 dxc4 20.♗h3 ♖c7

20...♕c7 21.bxc4 cxd4 22.♖xd4 ♘e5 23.♘d5 ♕c6 24.♕h5 ♗xc4 25.♖c1∞

21.bxc4

21.♘d5 cxd4 22.♖xd4 ♘e5 23.♘xc7 ♕xc7∞

21...cxd4 22.♖xd4 ♗c5 23.♖ad1 ♗xd4 24.♖xd4 ♗b7 25.♕d2 ♘e5 26.♖xd8 ♘f3† 27.♔f1 ♘xd2† 28.♖xd2 ♖xc4∞

12...b6

12...♘f8 13.♗e3 b6 14.♘e5 ♕c7 15.♘xc4 ♗a6 16.b3 ♗xc4 17.bxc4 e5 18.d5 ♘8d7∞

13.♖fd1

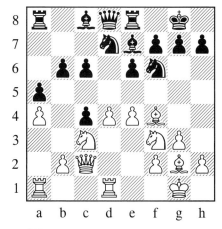

13...♗f8

Developing the other bishop comes into consideration:

13...♗b7 14.♘d2 ♗a6 15.d5 cxd5 16.exd5 e5 17.♗g5 ♖a7 (17...♗b4 18.d6±; 17...h6 18.d6 hxg5 19.dxe7 ♕xe7 20.♗xa8 ♖xa8 21.♘ce4±) 18.d6 ♗xd6 19.♘de4 ♗e7 20.♗xf6 ♗xf6 21.♖d5↑

13...♗a6 14.d5 cxd5 15.exd5 exd5 16.♘xd5 ♘xd5 17.♖xd5 ♗b7 18.♖d4 (18.♖ad1 ♗xd5 19.♖xd5 ♗f6 20.♕d2 ♖a7 21.♗h3 ♖e7 22.♗e5 ♕e8 23.♗xf6 gxf6 24.♕h6 ♕f8 25.♕f4∞) 18...♕c8 19.♘g5 g6 (19...♗xg5 20.♖xc4 ♘c5 21.♗xb7 ♕xb7 22.♗xg5±) 20.♖xc4 ♘c5 21.♘e4 ♕f5 (21...♗xe4 22.♗xe4 ♖a7 23.♗f3±) 22.♘xc5 ♕xc2 23.♖xc2 ♗xg2 24.♘d7 ♗f3 25.♘xb6 ♖a6⹀

14.d5

14.♘g5 h6 15.e5 hxg5 16.♗xg5 ♗b7
17.♘e4 ♗e7 18.exf6 ♘xf6 19.♘xf6† ♗xf6
20.♗xf6 ♕xf6 21.♕xc4 ♖ed8= and White's
greater space is balanced by the weakness of
the d4-pawn.

14...cxd5 15.e5

15.exd5 e5 16.♗e3 ♗b7 17.♘d2 ♖c8∞

15...♘e4

Black can improve here:
15...♘h5!N
This offers Black the better position, though
calculating all the resulting variations would
have been a very difficult task during the
game.
16.♘g5 g6 17.♘xd5 exd5 18.♗xd5 ♘xf4

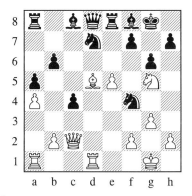

19.♗xf7†

19.♘xf7 ♕c7 20.gxf4 ♘c5 21.♘g5† ♗e6
22.♘xe6 ♘xe6 23.f5 gxf5 24.♕xf5 ♕f7
25.♕xf7† ♔xf7 26.♗xa8 ♖xa8∓
19.gxf4 ♘xe5 20.♗xa8 ♕f6∓
19...♔h8 20.gxf4 ♖xe5 21.♗xh7 ♖f5
21...♕h4 22.♘xf8 ♕g4† 23.♔f1 ♕h3†
24.♔g1=
22.♗e6 ♔xh7 23.♗xf5 ♕e8 24.♖e1 ♕f7∓

16.♘xe4 dxe4 17.♘g5 ♖a7

17...h6 18.♘xe4 ♗b7 19.♘f6† gxf6 20.♗xb7
♖a7 21.♗c6±

18.♕xe4 g6 19.♕xc4

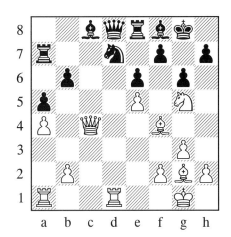

White has the more active pieces, and he
may try to take advantage of the weak d6- and
f6-squares and put pressure on the b6-pawn.
Black, on the other hand, should look for
opportunities to obtain counterplay against
the white pawn on e5.

19...♕c7 20.♕c6

20.♗c6 ♘b8 (20...♗c5 21.♗b5 ♖f8 22.♖ac1
♘xe5 23.♕e2 f6 24.♘e4 ♕e7 25.♘xc5 bxc5
26.♗xe5 fxe5 27.♕xe5±) 21.♘e4 ♗e7 22.♘d6
♗xd6 23.♖xd6 ♗a6 24.♕c3 ♘xc6 25.♖xc6±

**20...♗g7 21.♖ac1 ♕xc6 22.♗xc6 ♖f8 23.♘f3
♖c7 24.♖d6**

24.♗e3 ♗b7 25.♖xd7 ♖xd7 26.♗xd7 ♗xf3
27.♗c6 ♗xc6 28.♖xc6 ♗xe5 29.♖xb6 ♖d8
30.♖b5±

24...♘c5

24...♗b7 25.♖xd7 ♖xd7 26.♗xd7 ♗xf3
27.♗c6 ♗xc6 28.♖xc6 ♖b8 29.b3 ♔f8 30.♔g2
♔e8 31.♖c7 ♗f8 and Black intends ...♗e7-d8.

25.♗b5

25.♗e3 ♗a6 (25...♗b7 26.♗xb7 ♖xb7
27.♗xc5 bxc5 28.♖xc5 ♖xb2 29.♖xa5±)
26.♗xc5 bxc5 27.♖xc5 ♖fc8 28.♖xa5 ♗f8
29.♖xa6 ♗xd6 30.exd6 ♖xc6 31.d7 ♖c1†
32.♔g2 ♖d8 33.♘e5 ♖c5 (33...f6 34.♖xe6+−)
34.♖c6 ♖xc6 35.♘xc6 ♖xd7 36.b4±

25...♗b7 26.♘e1

26.♘d4 g5 27.♗e3 (27.♗xg5 ♖xe5 28.♗f4
♗xd6 29.♗xd6 ♖cc8 30.♗xf8 ♔xf8=)
27...♗xe5 28.♖xb6 ♗e4 (28...♗d5 29.♖xc5
♖xc5 30.♘c6 ♗d6 31.♘xa5±) 29.♘c6 ♗xc6
30.♖xc6 ♖xc6 31.♗xc6 ♘d3 32.♖c4±

26...♖cc8 27.♖xb6±

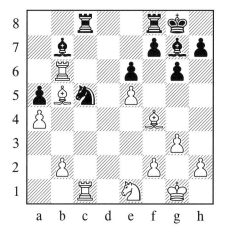

The realization of the pawn advantage will
require precision from White, as he has to get
his pieces coordinated while protecting the e5-
pawn.

**27...♗d5 28.♗e3 ♘b3 29.♖xc8 ♖xc8 30.♗a6
♖d8 31.♗b7 ♗c4 32.♖d6 ♖b8 33.♘f3 ♗f8
34.♖d7 h6**

Black could try:

34...♘c5 35.♗xc5 ♗xc5

An interesting way for Black to defend, he
wants to use his strong dark-squared bishop
to attack the b2-, e5- and f2-pawns.

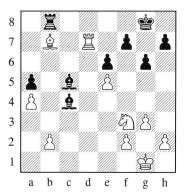

36.♖c7
　36.♘g5 ♗b3 37.♖c6 (37.♘xf7 ♗xa4
　38.♘h6† ♔h8 39.♖f7 ♗d4⇄) 37...♖c8
　38.♖b7 ♗b4 39.♘f3 ♖f8 40.h4 h6 41.♘e4
　♗xa4=
　36.♘d2 ♗a2 37.♘e4 ♗b6±

36...♗e2 37.♖xc5
　37.♘g5 ♗b6 38.♖d7 ♖d8 39.♖xd8† ♗xd8
　40.♘e4 ♗b6⇄
37...♖xb7 38.♘d4 ♗d1 39.b3 ♖b4 40.♖c8†
♔g7 41.♖d8 ♗xb3 42.♘xb3 ♖xb3 43.♖a8 g5
44.♖xa5±

**35.♘d2 ♘xd2 36.♗xd2 ♗b3 37.♗c6 ♖c8
38.♗b5 ♖c2 39.♖d8?!**

39.♗xa5 ♖xb2 40.♖c7! White prevents
...c5 and at the same time prepares to play
♗e8 next. 40...♖b1† 41.♔g2 ♗d5† 42.♔h3
♖b2 43.♗b6±

39...♔g7

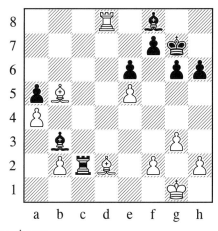

40.♔f1?!

The last two weak moves by White are
surely the effect of lack of time. He should not
have delayed eliminating the a5-pawn, and
he should have kept the rook on the seventh
rank, to maintain the additional possibility of
targeting the f7-pawn.

40.♗xa5 ♖xb2 41.♖d2

41.♖c8 ♗e7

41...♖b1† 42.♔g2 ♖a1

42...♗d5† 43.♔h3 ♗e7

43.♗d8 ♗xa4 44.♗xa4 ♖xa4 45.♗f6† ♔h7
46.♖d7 ♔g8 47.♖d8 ♖a7 48.h4

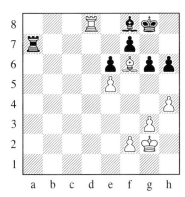

Black is forced to just move his rook along the seventh rank. The question is: does White have a winning plan?

48...♖b7 49.h5 ♖a7 50.f4 ♖b7 51.♔h3

Firstly, White needs to improve his king.

51.g4 gxh5 52.g5 (After 52.gxh5= White cannot make progress. For example, if the white king heads to the queenside to try to force the black rook off the 7th rank, then at the right moment Black can switch his rook to the first rank with the plan of checking from the rear.) 52...hxg5 53.♗xg5 f6 54.♗h6 fxe5 55.♖xf8† ♔h7 56.♖f6 exf4 57.♖xe6=

51...♖a7 52.♔h4 ♖b7 53.♖e8 ♖a7 54.g4+−

White will continue with g4-g5 and then penetrate to the h6-square with his bishop, finally capturing the black bishop.

40.♗xh6† ♔xh6 41.♖xf8 ♔g7 42.♖b8 ♖c1†
43.♔g2 ♗d5† 44.♔h3 ♖c2 45.f4 ♖xb2∞

40...♗e7 41.♖d3 ♗c5 42.♖c3

42.f4 ♖xb2 43.♗xa5 ♗d5 44.♖d2 ♖b1†
45.♔e2 ♖b3 and Black holds the position.

42...♖xd2 43.♖xc5 ♖d4 44.♔e2 ♖b4

44...♗xa4? 45.♗c4±

**45.♔d3 ♗xa4 46.♗xa4 ♖xa4 47.h4 ♖a1
48.♔c4 a4 49.♖a5**

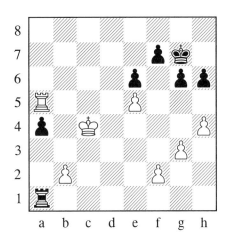

49...h5??

A terrible oversight. After this move, White gains a winning position and as a result Etienne levelled the match. Surely this mistake was not without its psychological influence on the course of the two play-off games which followed, as they also went to Bacrot.

49...♖b1 50.♔c3 ♖c1† 51.♔d3 ♖b1= is simply a draw. The more active white king cannot help to capture the a4-pawn because the black rook will always attack the b2-pawn.

50.b4+−

Now Black cannot stop the advance of the b-pawn.

**50...g5 51.hxg5 ♔g6 52.♔b5 a3 53.♔a6
♖b1 54.b5 ♖b2 55.b6 ♖xf2 56.b7 ♖b2
57.♖xa3 ♔xg5 58.♖a5**
1–0

GAME 35

▷ **Z. Almasi (2726)**
▶ **M.E. Parligras (2636)**
FIDE World Cup, Khanty-Mansiysk
Round 2, Game 2, 01.09.2011 **[E11]**
Annotated by Kamil Miton

In the Catalan Opening, Black has a number of solid variations against which it is difficult for White to gain an advantage. In the following game we will see one of them – 4...♗b4†. Almasi, who needed to win this game to stay in the World Cup, chose a rare plan with 10.♘bd2. Black's reaction with 10...♘h5 was very much appropriate. Only two subsequent inaccuracies resulted in White taking the initiative, which was later forfeited with the fatal mistake 21.♖e1.

1.d4 ♘f6 2.♘f3 e6 3.c4 d5 4.g3 ♗b4†

The idea of this move is based on inducing White's bishop to move to d2. If Black later chooses a set-up with ...b6 and ...c6 this will have considerable importance, because White will not have the opportunity of playing b2-b3 and ♗b2.

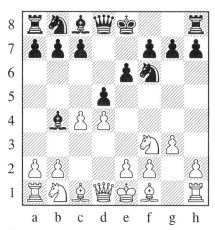

5.♗d2

As a general point, the move ♘d2 would be preferable if instead of ♘f3 White had played ♗g2, because after ...dxc4 White could win a piece after ♕a4.

5...♗e7 6.♗g2 0–0 7.0–0 c6 8.♕c2 ♘bd7 9.♗f4 b6 10.♘bd2

From d2 the knight controls the very important squares e4 and c4, however with the bishop on f4, White often prefers to develop the knight on c3, so that after a potential ...♘h5 the bishop could return to c1.

10.♖d1

White's main task is to fight for the centre and activate the g2-bishop by playing e2-e4. Black intends to move his queen's bishop, place the rook on c8 and then go ...c6-c5.

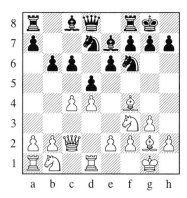

Black now has two main options: A) 10...♗b7 and B) 10...♗a6.

A) **10...♗b7 11.♘c3**

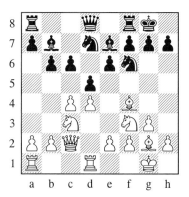

We need a further split: A1) 11...♖c8 and A2) 11...dxc4.

A1) 11...♖c8 12.♘e5

12.b3 c5 13.cxd5 (13.♘b5 cxd4 14.♘xa7 ♖c5∓) 13...cxd4! 14.♘xd4 (14.d6?! ♖xc3 15.dxe7 ♕xe7 16.♗d6 ♖xc2 17.♗xe7 ♗xf3 18.♗xf3 ♖e8 19.♗xf6 ♘xf6 20.♖xd4 e5∓) 14...♘xd5 15.♗xd5 ♗xd5 16.♘db5 a6 17.♘d6

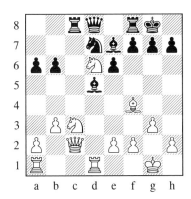

17...♗xd6 (17...♖xc3 18.♕xc3 g5 19.e4 gxf4 20.exd5 ♗xd6 21.dxe6 ♗e5 22.♕e1 fxe6 23.♖xd7 ♕xd7 24.♕xe5±) 18.♗xd6 ♖e8 19.♕d3 ♗b7 20.♖ac1 ♘f6 21.f3±

12...♘h5

12...♘xe5 13.dxe5 ♘d7 14.cxd5 cxd5 15.e4±

13.♗c1 ♘hf6 14.e4 ♘xe4

14...dxc4 15.♘xc4 b5 16.♘e3±

15.♘xe4 dxe4 16.♗xe4 f5 17.♘xd7 ♕xd7 18.♗f3 ♗f6 19.♗e3±

A2) 11...dxc4 12.♘d2 ♘d5 13.♘xc4 ♘xf4 14.gxf4 ♕c7 15.e3

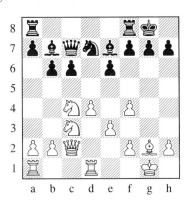

I had the opportunity to play this position against Movsesian. After the game, Sergey told me that even though White's position seems more pleasant, Black has the simple plan of ...c5 which should level the position with no difficulty. As an example, he provided the following game:

15...♖ad8 16.♖ac1

16.a4 ♗b4∞

16...c5 17.d5 exd5 18.♘xd5 ♗xd5 19.♖xd5 b5

Otherwise White would gain control over the light squares.

20.♘e5 ♘xe5 21.♖xe5 ♗d6 22.♖d5 ♗e7=

Sasikiran – Wojtaszek, Khanty-Mansiysk 2010.

B) 10...♗a6

Decidedly more active and aggressive than 10...♗b7. By pushing the bishop further, Black creates a problem on c4 straight away and White may be obliged to play the quite slow b2-b3. In most cases, after an exchange of pawns on d5 Black would be doing well because the g2-bishop remains weak. Then any attempt to introduce it into the game through playing e2-e4 would result in a position with an isolated pawn, where Black easily controls the important d5-square. While following ♘d2 Black always has ...♘h5 and the f4-bishop does not have a good escape square.

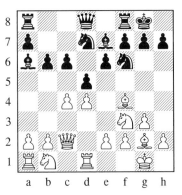

White has two main options: B1) 11.♘e5 and B2) 11.b3.

B1) 11.Ne5 Rc8

11...Nxe5 12.dxe5 Nd7 13.cxd5 cxd5 14.e4 d4 15.Rxd4 Bc5 16.Rd1 g5 17.Bc1 Qe7 18.Qa4 Bc8 19.b4 Bxb4 20.Bxg5 Qxg5 21.Qxb4 Nxe5 22.Nd2± White is targeting the king.

12.Nc3

12.Qa4 Nb8! 13.Nc3 b5∓

12...Bxc4 13.Nxc4 dxc4 14.e4 b5 15.a4 a6 16.axb5 axb5 17.d5

17.Ra6 Nb6 18.Ra7 Ra8 19.Rc7 Nh5 20.Rxc6 Nxf4 21.gxf4 b4 22.Ne2 Rc8 23.d5 exd5 24.exd5 Nf6 25.Ng3 b3∓ Caruana – Palac, Aix-les-Bains 2011.

17...cxd5 18.exd5 e5∞

B2) 11.b3 Rc8 12.Nc3

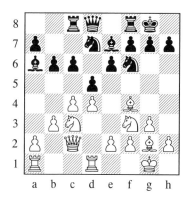

A key position in which Black has various possibilities: B21) 12...h6, B22) 12...dxc4 and B23) 12...Qe8.

B21) 12...h6 13.e4 dxc4 14.Nd2 b5 15.bxc4 bxc4 16.Bf1 Nb6

16...c5 17.d5 exd5 18.exd5 g5 19.d6 gxf4 20.Bxc4 Bxc4 21.Rxc4↑

16...Qa5 17.Nxc4 Bxc4 18.Bxc4 e5 19.dxe5 Nxe5 20.Be2±

17.a4 Bb4

17...c5 18.d5 exd5 19.a5↑

18.a5 Nbd7 19.Nxc4

19.Bxc4 Bxc4 (19...Bb5!∞) 20.Nxc4 Bxc3 21.Qxc3 Nxe4 22.Qc2 Nef6 (after

22...Ndf6 23.h4 White targets the e4-knight) 23.Bd6 Re8 24.Rab1↑

19...Bxc3

19...c5 20.Na2±

20.Qxc3 Nd5 21.Qd2 Nxf4 22.Qxf4 Bc4 23.Bxc4±

B22) 12...dxc4 13.Nd2

I don't know if this move is objectively best but Mikhail Gurevich said that he likes my game against Swiercz because it is a good example to show dynamic play in the Catalan.

Perhaps better is: 13.bxc4 Bxc4 14.Nd2 b5 (14...Bb5?! 15.Qb3 Nd5 16.Bxd5 exd5 17.Nxb5 cxb5 18.Qxb5±; 14...Ba6!? 15.Qa4 Bb7 16.Qxa7 Ra8 17.e4 c5 18.d5 exd5 19.exd5 Nh5 20.Be3 f5∞) 15.Nxc4 bxc4 16.Na4 Nd5 17.Nd2±

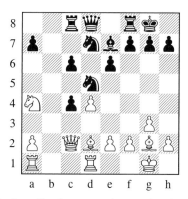

Black will play ...c5 but White's pair of bishops guarantee at least a symbolic advantage.

13...c5

13...b5 14.bxc4 bxc4 15.Qa4 Bb5 16.Qxa7 (16.Nxb5 Nb6) 16...g5 17.a4 (17.Bxg5 Ra8 18.Qb7 Rb8=) 17...Ra8 18.Qc7 gxf4 19.Qxd8 Rfxd8 20.axb5 Nd5!? 21.Rxa8 Rxa8 22.Nxd5 cxd5 23.Nxc4 Rb8 24.Nb2 fxg3 25.hxg3 Rxb5=

14.Nxc4

14.d5 exd5 15.Nxd5 Nxd5 16.Bxd5 Bf6∓
Better may be 14.dxc5 with the ideas

14...♗xc5 15.♘de4 ♘xe4 16.♘xe4 ♗e7
17.b4 ♗b7 18.♘c5 ♗xg2 19.♘xd7 ♗d5
20.♘xf8 ♕xf8 21.a3± or 14...♖xc5 15.b4.
14...cxd4

14...♗xc4 15.bxc4 cxd4 16.♖xd4 ♕e8∞
15.♖xd4 ♗c5 16.♖dd1 b5 17.♘d6

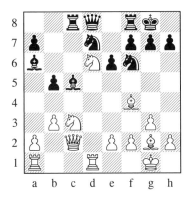

17...b4

17...♕b6?! 18.♘xc8 ♖xc8 19.♕d3 ♗xf2†
20.♔h1 b4 21.♘a4±
18.♘xc8 ♕xc8 19.♖ac1 bxc3 20.♕xc3 ♗e2
21.♖xd7 ♘xd7 22.b4 ♗xf2† 23.♔xf2 ♕a6

23...♕xc3 24.♖xc3 ♗b5 25.a4 ♗xa4 26.♖a3
♗b5 27.♖xa7 e5 28.♗e3 ♖b8 29.♗d5⩲
24.a4 e5 25.♗xe5

25.♗e3↑
25...♘xe5 26.♕xe5 ♗g4 27.♕d4

Miton – Swiercz, Czech Republic 2011, was
agreed drawn here.

B23) 12...♕e8

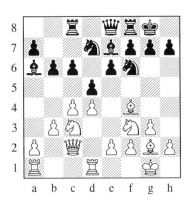

Black plans to capture the c4-pawn only
after the possible move e2-e4. Moreover, he
moves the queen away from the d-file, which
will be significant later on.

White's three important lines are B231)
13.e4, B232) 13.a4 and B233) 13.♖ac1!?N.

B231) 13.e4 dxc4

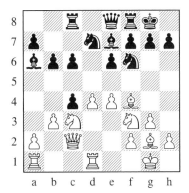

14.♘e2!?

14.♘d2 e5! That is why Black played
12...♕e8; in this variation the position is
equal.
14.bxc4 ♗xc4 15.♘d2 ♗a6 16.♕a4 ♗d3
17.♘b3 ♗c2 18.♖dc1 ♗d3 19.♖d1=
14...cxb3

14...b5 15.bxc4 bxc4 16.♘d2 c5 (16...♘b6
17.a4 c5 18.d5 exd5 19.a5±) 17.d5 exd5
18.exd5 ♘h5 19.♘e4 ♘xf4 20.♘xf4↑
15.axb3 ♗xe2 16.♕xe2 a5 17.♘d2

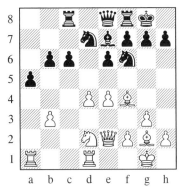

17...♗b4

17...c5 18.d5 exd5 19.e5 ♗d6 20.♖e1 ♘xe5
21.♗xe5 ♗xe5 22.♕xe5 ♕xe5 23.♖xe5±
18.♘c4 ♕e7 19.g4
  19.♗g5 h6∞
19...♖fd8
  19...b5 20.♘xa5 e5 21.dxe5 ♘xe5 22.g5
  ♘fd7 23.♗h3 ♖fe8∞
20.g5
  20.♗g3⇄
20...♘e8 21.e5 g6 22.♖ac1 b5 23.♘e3 ♘b6
24.♖xc6 ♖xc6 25.♗xc6 ♘c7 26.♘g4 a4∞

B232) 13.a4

This move forces the capture on c4 and is
also useful to potentially open the a-file and
then create pressure along it.
13...dxc4 14.bxc4 ♗xc4 15.♘d2
  15.♘e4 has also been tested.
15...♗d5!
  15...♗a6   16.a5   (16.♘de4!?↑)   16...b5
  17.♘ce4 ♕d8 18.♘d6 ♖c7 19.♘6e4 ♖c8
  20.♘b3⇄
16.e4 c5

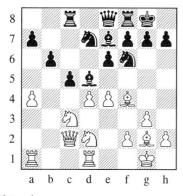

White has two ways to capture on d5:
B2321) 17.exd5 and B2322) 17.♘xd5.

B2321) 17.exd5 cxd4 18.d6 ♖xc3

Black should try: 18...♗d8 19.♘db1 dxc3
20.♘xc3 ♘d5 21.♗xd5 ♘f6 22.♖a3 exd5
23.♕d2 ♗xc3 24.♖xc3 ♖xc3 25.♕xc3 ♕e4∞
19.♕b2 ♗d8 20.♘b3 e5
  20...♖c8 21.♘xd4 ♘c5 22.a5 bxa5 23.♘b5
  ♕d7 24.♘c7 ♘d3 25.♖xd3 ♗xc7 26.♗e5

♗b6 27.♗xf6 gxf6 28.♕xf6 ♖c2 29.♕f3 ♕d8
30.♕h6→
21.♘xd4 ♖c4 22.♖e1
  22.♘f5!?
22...♖xd4 23.♗xe5 ♖e4 24.♗xe4 ♘xe5 25.♗g2
♘d3 26.♖xe8 ♘xb2 27.♖xf8† ♔xf8 28.♖c1
♘d3 29.♖c8 ♔e8 30.♗c6† ♘d7 31.♖c7
♘3e5 32.♗b5 a6 33.♗xa6 ♘c6 34.♖xc6 ♘b8
35.♗b5 ♘xc6 36.♗xc6† ♔f8 37.♔g2±

B2322) 17.♘xd5 exd5 18.exd5 ♘h5 19.d6
♗f6

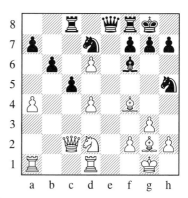

20.♗h3
  20.♖e1 ♕d8 21.♖ac1 (21.♗e5 cxd4 22.♗xf6
  ♘hxf6 23.♕d3 ♘c5 24.♕xd4 ♘e6 25.♕d3
  ♘c5=) 21...♘xf4 22.gxf4 ♗xd4 23.♖e7
  ♘f6 24.♘c4 a6 25.♕b3 ♖b8 26.♘e5 ♕xd6
  27.♖xf7 ♖xf7 28.♘xf7 ♗xf2† 29.♔f1 ♕xf4
  30.♘e5† ♔h8 31.♘f7†=
20...♘xf4 21.gxf4 ♗xd4 22.♖ab1 ♘f6? 23.♘b3
♖b8 24.♘xd4 cxd4 25.♖xd4 a6 26.♖bd1 b5
27.d7 ♕e7 28.a5±
  Miton – Yemelin, Czech Republic 2010.

B233) 13.♖ac1!?N

The moves ...♕e8 and ♖ac1 may be described
as mutual waiting moves before definite action
in the centre. Black does not rush to capture
on c4 and neither does White rush with
advancing e2-e4; nuances of this type, such
as between positioning the rook on c1 or a1,
can have great importance later in complex
variations. Let's check out the specific details.

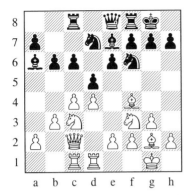

First there are four minor lines and then we can get to two major lines: B2331) 13...c5 and B2332) 13...h6:

13...♗b4 14.a3±

13...♘h5 14.♗g5± f6 15.♗d2 f5 16.a4↑

13...dxc4 14.bxc4 ♗xc4 15.♘d2 ♗d5 16.e4 c5 17.♘xd5 exd5 18.e5 ♘h5 19.♗e3 cxd4 20.♕xc8 ♕xc8 21.♖xc8 ♖xc8 22.♗xd4 ♗c5 23.♗a1±

13...♗a3 14.♖b1 ♗e7 (14...♕e7 15.e4 dxc4 16.bxc4 ♗xc4 17.♘d2 ♗b5 18.♘xb5 cxb5 19.♕b3 e5 [19...a6 20.e5±] 20.dxe5 ♘g4 21.♗h3±) 15.a4 dxc4 16.bxc4 ♗xc4 17.♘d2

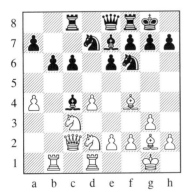

17...♗d5 (17...♗a6 18.♘de4 ♘xe4 19.♘xe4 ♕d8 20.♘d6 ♗xd6 21.♖xd6 ♖e8 22.e4 c5⇄) 18.e4 c5 19.♘xd5 exd5 20.exd5 ♘h5 21.d6 The rook is much better on b1 than on a1.

21...cxd4 22.♕f5 ♖c5 23.♕g4 ♗d8 24.♖e1 f5 25.♖xe8 fxg4 26.♖xf8† ♔xf8 27.♘b3↑

B2331) 13...c5

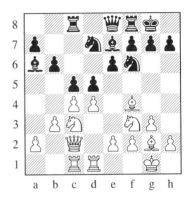

14.cxd5
    14.♘b5!? ♗xb5 15.cxb5±
14...cxd4 15.dxe6
    15.♘xd4 e5 16.♘c6 exf4 17.d6 ♗d8 18.gxf4∞
15...fxe6 16.♖xd4 ♗c5
    16...♘d5 17.♕b2 (17.♖xd5 exd5 18.♘d4 ♗a3 19.♗xd5† ♔h8 20.♖d1 ♗b4 21.♗c6 ♗c5 22.♗g2 ♘f6∞) 17...♖xc3 18.♖xc3 ♘xc3 19.♕xc3 ♗f6 20.♗d6 ♖f7 21.♕e3 ♗xd4 22.♘xd4⯹
17.♗d6
    17.♖a4 ♗b5 18.♖xa7 (18.♘xb5 ♗xf2† 19.♔xf2 ♖xc2 20.♖xc2 e5⇄) 18...♗xf2† 19.♔xf2 ♖xc3 20.♕b2 ♖xc1 21.♗xc1 ♕b8∞
17...♗xd4 18.♘xd4 ♖f7 19.♘c6

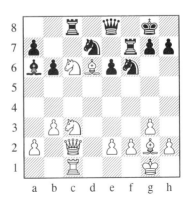

19...♘g4

19...♘f8 20.♘e5 ♘d5 21.♗xd5 exd5
22.♘xf7 d4 23.♗xf8 ♖xc3 24.♕b1 ♖xc1†
25.♕xc1 ♔xf7 26.♗d6 h6=
20.♘xa7 ♖xf2 21.♗f3 ♘de5 22.♗xg4 ♘xg4
23.♘xc8 ♕xc8 24.♕e4 h5 25.♗a3 ♗b7
26.♘d5 ♕d7 27.♘e7† ♔h8 28.♘g6† ♔g8
29.♘e7†=

B2332) 13...h6 14.e4

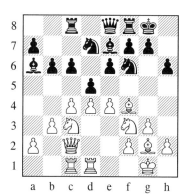

14...dxc4 15.bxc4 ♗xc4 16.♘d2 ♗a6
17.♕a4 ♗d3 18.♘b3 b5 19.♕a6 ♗c4
20.♘a5 e5

20...♘b6 21.a4 ♗b4 22.axb5 ♗xc3 23.♖xc3
cxb5 24.♕xa7 (24.♘xc4 ♘xc4 25.♖b3
♕c6 26.♕xc6 ♖xc6 27.♖xb5 ♖d8 28.d5±)
24...♕d8 25.♘xc4 ♘xc4 26.♖b3 e5 27.♗c1
exd4 28.♖xd4±

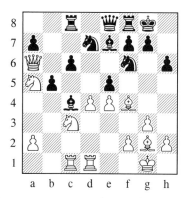

Now we must consider no fewer than four
alternatives:

21.dxe5 ♘c5 22.♕xa7 ♖a8 23.♕c7 ♖c8 leads
to a draw by repetition.

21.♗xe5 ♘xe5 22.dxe5 ♘g4 23.♘xc4 ♗c5
24.♘d6 ♕xe5 25.♘xc8 ♘xf2 26.♔f1 ♗xd1
27.♘xd1 ♕d4 28.♘e7† ♔h8

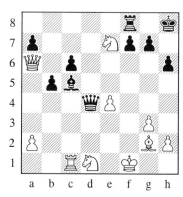

29.♔e2 (29.♘xc6 ♕g1† 30.♔e2 ♕xg2†
31.♔d3 f5 32.♖xc5 fxe4† 33.♔c3 ♕f3†
34.♔b4 ♕xd1∞) 29...♖d8 30.♘d5 cxd5
31.♕xb5 ♗b6 32.exd5 ♕e5† 33.♔f1 ♕d4
34.♔e2=

21.♘xc6 ♖xc6 22.♕xc6 exf4 23.♘xb5
23.e5 fxg3 24.hxg3 ♘b8 25.♕xe8 ♘xe8
26.♗d5 (26.d5 ♗a3⇄) 26...♘c7 27.♗xc4
bxc4 28.♘e4 ♘d5 29.♖xc4 ♘d7∞
23...♗e2 24.♖e1 f3 25.♗f1 ♗xf1
25...♗b4 26.♗xe2 ♗xe1 27.♗xf3↑
26.♖xf1 ♘b6 27.e5 ♘fd5 28.♕xe8 ♖xe8
29.♘xa7 ♖a8 30.♘c6 ♖xa2 31.♖a1∞

21.♘xc4 exf4 22.♘a5 ♘b8
22...♗a3 23.♘xc6 ♗xc1 24.♖xc1 ♘b6 25.d5
b4 26.♘b5 ♘xe4 27.♘bxa7±
23.♕xa7 ♕d8 24.e5
24.♘xb5 cxb5 25.♖xc8 ♕xc8 26.♕xe7 f3
27.♗f1 ♕c2 28.♖d3 ♕xa2=
24...♖c7 25.♕a8 ♕d7 26.exf6 ♗xf6 27.♖b1
♖a7 28.♗xc6 ♖xa8 29.♗xd7 fxg3 30.hxg3
♘xd7 31.♖xb5±

B24) 12...♘h5 13.♗c1

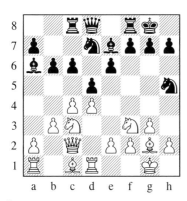

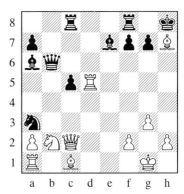

13...♘hf6!

Rather unambitious but probably Black's best option!

13...f5 One of Black's possible ideas is a transition to the so-called "stonewall" set-up, because the knight on c3 does not fight for the e5-square, which is important in these structures. In this situation, White has two plans: a4-a5 in order to open the a-file for the rook, although when White plays a4-a5, Black will respond with ...b5 and after a potential complete closure of the kingside, the position may have drawish tendencies. This is because, despite the space advantage, it may become difficult for White to win when play is on just one side. The other plan consists in taking control over the important e5-square, by employing a typical manoeuvre of the c3-knight: ♗b2, e2-e3 and ♘e2-♘f4-♘d3 or ♘c1-♘d3.

14.e4

14.♗b2 ♕c7 15.♖ac1 dxc4 16.bxc4 ♗xc4 17.♘e5 ♘xe5 18.dxe5 ♘d5 (18...♘d7 19.♘e4 ♗xa2 20.♘d6 ♘c5∓) 19.♘e4 b5 20.♘d6 ♗xd6 21.exd6 ♕d7 22.a4 f6 23.♗a3 ♘b6 24.a5 ♘a4 25.♖d4↑ Bacrot – Alekseev, Biel 2008.

14...dxc4 15.♗f4

15.♘d2 b5 16.bxc4 bxc4 17.♘a4 c5 18.d5 exd5 19.exd5 ♘e5 (19...♘g4!?) 20.♘b2 ♘xd5 21.♘dxc4 ♘xc4 22.♖xd5 ♕b6 23.♗e4 ♘a3 24.♗xh7† ♔h8

25.♕f5 (25.♕e4 ♗f6 26.♘a4 ♕b5 27.♗b2 ♖fe8∞) 25...♕e6 26.♘d3 ♕xf5 27.♗xf5 ♖cd8 28.♖xd8 ♖xd8 29.♗xa3 ♗xd3=)

15...♕e8 16.bxc4 ♗xc4 17.♘d2 ♗a6 18.♕a4 ♗d3 19.♘b3 ♗c2 20.♖d2 ♗xb3 21.axb3 a5 22.e5 ♘d5 23.♘xd5 cxd5 24.♗f1 ♘b8 25.♗b5 ♕d8⹂

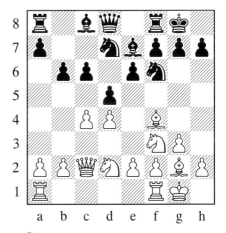

10...♘h5

Black has a couple of other options to consider:

10...♗a6 11.e4?! ♘xe4 12.♘xe4 dxe4 13.♘e5 ♘xe5 14.dxe5 ♕d3 15.♖ac1 ♕xc2 16.♖xc2 ♖ad8 17.♗e3 c5 18.♗xe4 f5=

10...♗b7 11.e4 dxe4 12.♘xe4 c5 13.♘xf6† 13.♘d6 ♗xf3 14.♗xf3 cxd4 15.♖ae1 e5 (15...♘c5 16.♘b7 ♕d7 17.♘xc5 bxc5 18.♗xa8 ♖xa8⹂) 16.♘f5 ♗b4 17.♖xe5

♘xe5 18.♗xe5 d3 19.♕b3 ♕d7 20.♘e3 ♗c5
21.♗xf6 ♖xe3 22.fxe3 gxf6 23.♗d5↑

13...♗xf6

13...♘xf6　14.♖ad1　♕c8　15.♘e5　♗xg2
16.♔xg2±

14.♘g5 ♗xg5 15.♗xb7 ♗xf4 16.♗xa8 ♕xa8
17.gxf4 cxd4 18.♖ad1 ♕f3 19.♕d3 ♕xf4
20.♕xd4 ♕f5 21.♖fe1±

11.cxd5

After 11.♗e3 ♘hf6= the bishop on e3 takes
away from White the sensible plan of playing
e2-e4.

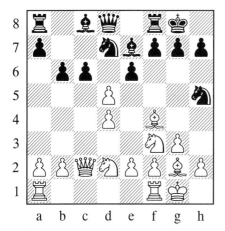

11...♘xf4

Another option is:

11...cxd5

As I have mentioned before, usually in this
type of position, following an exchange on
d5, Black should not face any problems. In
this specific example, White may rapidly
take the initiative because the black pieces,
in particular the knight on h5 and bishop on
c8, do not have good squares available.

12.♗c7 ♕e8 13.♖fc1 ♗b7

13...♘hf6　14.e4　dxe4　15.♘g5　♗b7
16.♘dxe4 ♘xe4 17.♘xe4 ♖c8 18.♕e2 ♗xe4
19.♗xe4 ♘c5 20.dxc5 ♖xc7 21.c6±

14.a4 ♖c8

14...♗b4 15.a5 bxa5 16.♘c4 ♖c8 17.♘xa5
♗a8 18.♕a4±

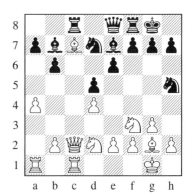

15.♕b3 ♗c5 16.dxc5 ♖xc7 17.cxb6 ♖xc1†
18.♖xc1 axb6 19.♖c7±

12.♕xc6

An interesting alternative is:

12.dxc6!? ♘xe2†

12...♘xg2　13.cxd7　♕xd7　14.♔xg2　♗b7
15.♔g1 ♖ac8∞

13.♔h1 ♗a6 14.cxd7 ♕xd7 15.♖fe1

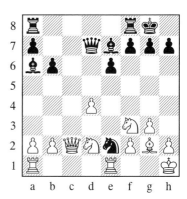

15...♘xd4

15...♖ac8 16.♕d1 (16.♕e4± exploits the
knight's location on e2) 16...♘xd4 17.♘b3
♗f6 18.♘fxd4 ♕a4 19.♖e4 ♖fd8 20.♕g4
♖c4 21.♘c2 h5 22.♖xc4 ♗xc4 23.♕xh5
g6 24.♕h6 ♗xb2 25.♖g1 ♕xa2 26.♕h4
♖c8∞

16.♘xd4 ♕xd4 17.♗xa8 ♖xa8 18.♕e4 ♕d8
19.♔g1∞

12...♘xe2† 13.♔h1

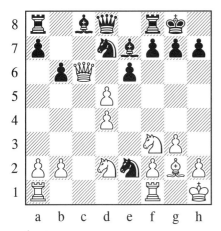

13...♗a6?!

With two possibilities to decide between, Black chose wrongly. A draw might have been earned after: 13...♖b8 14.dxe6 ♘xd4 15.♘xd4 ♘c5 16.exf7† ♖xf7 17.♕d5 ♗b7 18.♕xd8† (18.♕c4 b5↑) 18...♖xd8 19.♗xb7 ♗f6=

14.dxe6 fxe6

Another moment when Black might have played better. As proven by the analysis below, 14...♘f6 led to equality, although it is a much more complicated path than the one following 13...♖b8. Let's see:

14...♘f6 15.exf7† ♔h8

15...♖xf7 16.♘e5 ♖f8 17.♕e6† ♔h8 18.♘c6 ♘xd4 19.♘xd8 ♘xe6 20.♘xe6 ♗xf1 21.♗xa8 ♖xa8 22.♘xf1±

16.♕a4

16.♖fe1 ♘g4 17.♗f1 ♘xd4 18.♘xd4 ♖xd4 19.♗xa6 ♕xd2 20.♖xe7 ♘xf2†=

16...♕c8

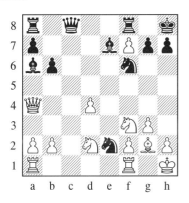

15.♕xe6† ♔h8 16.♖fe1 ♗f6

Two other possibilities are worth considering:

16...♖c8!? 17.♖xe2 (17.♗f1 ♘xd4 18.♘xd4 ♗b7† 19.♔g2 ♘c5 20.♕xe7 ♗xg2† 21.♔xg2 ♕xd4 22.♘f3 ♕xb2=) 17...♗xe2 18.♕xe2 ♖c2 19.♕b5 ♘f6 20.♔g1 ♕c7 (20...♘g4 21.♖f1 ♗f6 22.♕b3 ♖c7 23.♘e4↑ ♗xd4 24.h3± A white knight will soon head for e6.) 21.♖e1 ♖c1 22.♖xc1 ♕xc1† 23.♗f1∞

17.♖fe1

17.♖ae1 ♖xf7 18.♘e5 ♖f8 19.♗xa8 ♕xa8† 20.f3 ♕b7 21.♖f2 ♘xd4∓

17.♘e5 b5 18.♕d1 (18.♕a5 ♗d6 19.♘b3 ♗b7 20.♕xb5 ♗xg2† 21.♔xg2 ♘f4† 22.gxf4 ♗xe5 23.♕xe5 ♗g4† 24.♔h1 ♕f3† 25.♔g1=) 18...♘xd4 19.♘e4 ♕f5 20.♕xd4 ♖ad8 21.♕xa7 ♕xe5 22.f4 ♕e6 23.f5 ♖d7 24.fxe6 ♖xa7 25.♘xf6 gxf6∞

17...♘g4 18.♗f1 ♖xf7 19.♗xe2 ♘xf2†

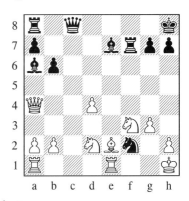

20.♔g2

20.♔g1 ♘h3† 21.♔g2 ♗b7 22.♖ac1 ♕g4 23.♖c7 ♘f4† 24.♔g1 ♘xe2† 25.♖xe2 ♖xf3 26.♖exe7 b5 27.♕xa7 ♕ff8 28.♕xb7 ♖xd4† 29.♔h1 ♕xd2 30.♖f7 ♕xb2 31.♖xf8† ♖xf8 32.♕c8=

20...♕h3† 21.♔g1 ♗b7 22.♗f1 ♕h5∞ 23.♖xe7 23.♘e5 ♖af8 24.♕d7 ♘d3↑

23...♖xe7 24.♕a3 ♖f7 25.♗xf2 ♗xf3 26.♘xf3 ♖af8 27.♗g2 ♖xf3† 28.♗xf3 ♕xh2† 29.♔e3 ♕h6†=

16...♗b4!? 17.♖xe2 ♗xe2 18.♕xe2 ♗xd2 19.♕xd2 ♕f6 20.♘g5 ♖ad8 21.f4∞

17.♖xe2 ♗xe2 18.♕xe2∞

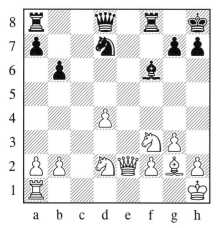

A very complex and intriguing position. In return for the exchange, White has two pawns and a strong initiative on the light squares. The weakened black king may also be in danger, as with White's pieces so well-coordinated it could easily become a target for attack. Black also has his trumps – a strong bishop on f6 and two rooks which will be very active on the open c- and e-files. Black's problem remains that the knight is badly out of play on d7.

18...♖e8 19.♘e4 ♖c8 20.♗h3 ♖c7

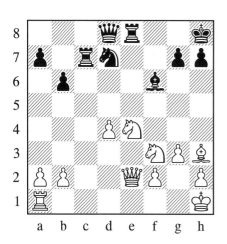

21.♖e1?

A mistake; after the correct move White could have gained a promising initiative. Let's see:

21.♖d1! b5

In order to improve the black knight's prospects by clearing b6.

21...g6 22.♔g1 ♕a8 23.d5 ♘c5 24.♘fd2 ♗xb2 25.d6↑

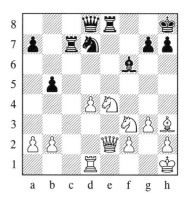

22.♔g1

22.d5 ♖c4 23.♗e6 ♘f8∞

22.♘e5 ♗xe5 23.dxe5 ♖xe5 24.♕d3 ♖e7 25.♘g5 ♕g8 26.♗xd7 ♖cxd7 27.♕xd7 ♖xd7 28.♖xd7 ♕a8† 29.♔g1 ♔g8 30.♘e6 ♕c6 31.♖xg7† ♔h8 32.♖e7=

22...♕a8 23.♖e1 ♘b6

23...♖e7!?

24.♘e5 ♗xe5 25.♘d6 ♖ee7 26.dxe5 ♘c4 27.♘xc4 ♖xc4 28.♖d1±

21...♗xd4∓ 22.♖d1

22.♘xd4 ♘c5 23.♗f5 g6∓; 22.♘fg5 ♘c5 23.♕h5 g6–+

22...♗f6 23.♗f5

Black is close to winning and probably only the knowledge that even a draw would guarantee qualification to the second phase of the competition stopped Parligras from collecting the full point, as he was satisfied with just a drawing continuation.

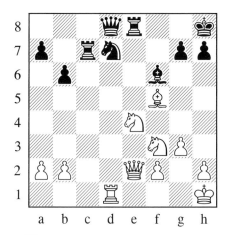

23...♕a8

23...g6 24.♗xd7 ♖xd7 25.♖xd7 ♕xd7
26.♘xf6 ♖xe2 27.♘xd7 ♖xf2 28.♘de5 ♖xb2
29.a4 ♖a2∓

**24.♘fd2 ♘c5 25.f3 ♖ce7 26.b4 ♘xe4
27.♘xe4 g6 28.♗h3 ♖xe4 29.fxe4 ♕xe4†
30.♕xe4 ♖xe4=**

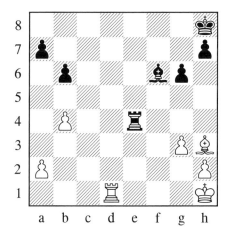

**31.b5 ♔g7 32.♗g2 ♖e7 33.♗c6 h5 34.♖d2
♗c3 35.♖d3 ♗b4 36.♖d7**

½–½

GAME 36

▷ **B. Gelfand (2746)**
▶ **E. Tomashevsky (2710)**

European Club Cup, Rogaska Slatina
Round 7, 01.10.2011 **[E11]**
Annotated by Borki Predojevic

Bogoljubow's defence is known as a solid but slightly passive option for Black. Many players choose to respond to 3....♗b4† with 4.♘bd2 in the hope of getting a more complicated game than after the more popular 4.♗d2. The next game showcases a new idea which will be of great interest to all players who are fans of the 4...0–0 5.a3 ♗e7 6.e4 d5 line. Tomashevsky played a strong idea with 11...f5! and 12...♗f6!N which I had also in my analysis. This new plan solves all Black's problems against the 7.♗d3 line, so White will have to find new ways to fight for the advantage.

**1.d4 ♘f6 2.c4 e6 3.♘f3 ♗b4† 4.♘bd2 0–0
5.a3 ♗e7 6.e4 d5 7.♗d3 c5 8.dxc5 dxe4
9.♘xe4 ♘xe4 10.♗xe4 ♕xd1† 11.♔xd1 f5!**

The best move, although it only really makes sense in conjunction with Black's next.

The main move is 11...♗xc5, but after 12.b4↑ White gets a pleasant and pretty much risk-free advantage.

Black has played 11...a5 in some high-level games, but White should keep an edge here too. His ideas include:

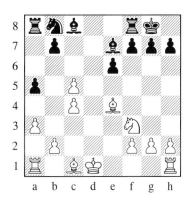

a) 12.♗f4 ♗xc5 13.♔e2 f5 14.♗c2 ♘c6 15.♖hd1 a4 Black went on to hold the draw in Gelfand – Ivanchuk, Biel 2009.

b) 12.♔e2! seems a bit more accurate: 12...f5 (12...♗xc5 13.♗e3±) 13.♗c2↑ White keeps some advantage. We can only guess how Gelfand was planning to improve on his game with Ivanchuk, but we can be sure he had a good idea of how to handle the position.

12.♗c2
Worse is 12.♗d3 ♘c6 13.♖e1 (13.b4 ♖d8 14.♗c2 e5!∓) 13...♗f6⯑ followed by ...e5 with some initiative.

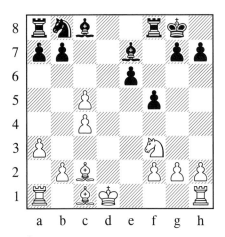

12...♗f6!N
An excellent novelty. I actually found this move in my home analysis a year before this game, and it was one of the main reasons why I started to play this line with Black. I was also playing at the same event, and happened to be walking around the playing hall when I saw this position at the table. I felt surprised and also rather sad when I saw that 'my' novelty had been revealed.

Black's idea is to adopt a true gambit strategy, activating his pieces and preparing to mobilize his central pawns without worrying about recapturing on c5.

Alternatives do not equalize, for instance:

12...♗xc5 is met by 13.b4 when, compared to the position after 11...♗c5 12.b4, Black has not benefitted from the inclusion of 11...f5 and 12.♗c2.

12...♘c6N
With this move Black goes for a similar strategy as in the game, but it is less accurate due to the strong answer:
13.♗a4!
13.♗e3? is a bad idea as Black will be able to gain a tempo with ...f4. After 13...e5 14.♔e1 a5! 15.♗a4 f4 16.♗d2 e4 17.♗xc6 bxc6 18.♘d4 ♗d7∓ Black is already better.
13.b4 is also not dangerous: 13...♗f6 14.♖b1 e5 15.b5! (15.♘d2 ♗e6 16.♗b2 e4 17.♔e1 ♘d4↑; 15.♗g5 e4 16.♗xf6 ♖xf6 17.♘d2 ♗e6 18.♗a4 ♘e5 19.♔c2 ♖d8! 20.♖bd1 ♘d3 21.♖hf1 ♗f7⯑ intending ...♖a6 with good play) 15...♘a5 16.♗b2 ♖d8† 17.♔e2 ♖e8 18.♘d2 ♗e6⇄ Black has a good game.

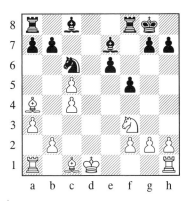

13...♗xc5
13...♗d7 14.♔e2 ♗xc5 15.♗e3 ♗e7 is playable, but White has a stable edge here. In the future he can exchange on c6 and take full control over the e5-square.
14.♗e3!
14.b4?! does not work, as after 14...♗xf2 15.♔e2 ♗b6 16.♗b2 e5!? Black has a nice game.

14.♔e2 is playable, but after 14...e5 15.♗xc6 bxc6 16.♘xe5 ♗d4 17.f4 ♗a6 18.♖d1 ♗xe5 19.fxe5 ♗xc4† 20.♔f2 ♗d5= Black has nothing to worry about.

14...♗d6

Black would like to advance with ...e5, but White has a good answer.

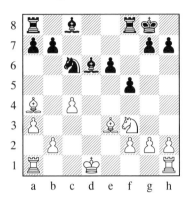

15.♔c2!

Calmly improving the pieces.

The more 'concrete' 15.b4 e5 16.c5 ♗c7 17.♗b3† ♔h8 leads to no advantage, for instance: 18.b5 (18.♗d2 e4 19.♘g5 ♘d4 20.♗c4 h6 21.h4 ♗d7 is okay for Black) 18...f4! 19.♗d2 e4 20.♘g5 ♗g4† (20...♘d4 21.♘f7† ♔g8 22.♘h6†□ ♔h8 23.♘f7† ♔g8= also leads to a draw) 21.♔c1 ♘d4 22.♘f7† ♔g8= with a draw by perpetual check.

15...e5 16.♖ad1 ♗c7 17.♗xc6!

17.b4 is possible but the text is stronger.

17...bxc6 18.♗c5 ♖f6 19.♖he1 e4 20.♘d4±

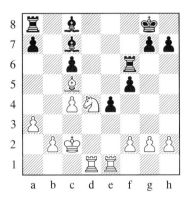

Black falls short of equality here, for instance: 20...a5 21.b3 ♗b7 22.g3 ♖e8 23.♘e2 ♗c8 24.h4 a4 25.b4 ♗a6 26.♔c3↑

White has a healthy positional plus and Black has no counterplay.

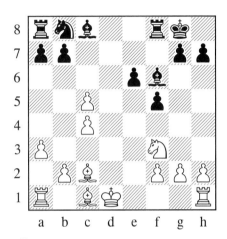

13.♖b1!

The critical continuation, and the only one that can possibly worry Black.

Returning the pawn with 13.♗f4? ♗xb2 14.♖a2 is dubious, as after 14... ♗f6∓ Black stands better. White may have restrained ...e5, but the c5-pawn will be next target for Black.

13.♔e2 e5 14.♖d1 ♘c6 is fine for Black, since 15.♗a4 is met by 15...♗e6!∓.

A bit more interesting is:
13.♖e1 ♖d8† 14.♔e2 e5 15.♗g5!?
15.♔f1 e4 16.♘d2 ♗e6∞ offers good compensation to Black.
15.♖d1 ♖xd1 16.♔xd1 e4 17.♘d2 ♗e6 18.♖b1 ♘c6∞
The text move sacrifices a piece, but Black has nothing to fear.
15...e4 16.♗xf6 exf3† 17.♔xf3 gxf6 18.♖ad1 ♖xd1 19.♖xd1 ♘c6 20.♔f4
White will pick up a third pawn for the knight, but he can hope for no more than equality.

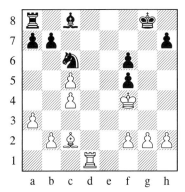

20...♔f7 21.♗xf5 ♗xf5 22.♔xf5 ♖e8 23.♖d7†
♖e7 24.♖xe7† ♔xe7=/∓

Only Black can play for a win here.

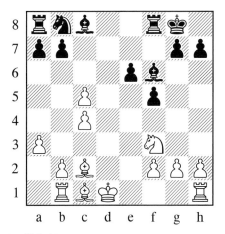

13...♖d8†!

The most precise move order.

13...♘c6

This natural move is not quite as good. It is
worth analysing both a) 14.♗g5 or b) 14.♗a4!.

14.♗g5 ♖d8† 15.♔e1 ♗xg5
  After 15...♘d4?! 16.♘xd4 ♗xg5 17.♘b5
  ♗e7 18.b4 a5 19.♘c7 ♖a7 20.♘b3± White
  is gradually neutralizing his opponent's
  activity while keeping his extra pawn.
16.♘xg5 ♘d4 17.♗d1 ♗d7!
  Black can recoup the sacrificed pawn with
  17...a5 18.♘f3 a4 19.♘xd4 ♖xd4 20.♗e2
  ♖a5, but after 21.♖d1 ♖xd1† 22.♔xd1 ♖xc5

23.♔d2± the a4-pawn is weak and White is
better.

17...b6 gives White the opportunity for
18.♗f3! ♘xf3† 19.♘xf3 bxc5 20.♘e5 ♖d4
21.f3, when he has returned the pawn in
order to secure a positional advantage. A
possible continuation is: 21...a5

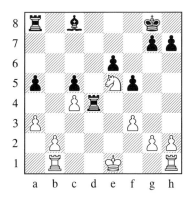

22.♖d1! ♖b8 23.♖xd4 cxd4 24.b4! axb4
25.axb4 ♖xb4 26.♔d2 ♖b2† 27.♔d3↑
Black faces a difficult defence, as 27...♖xg2?
28.♖b1+− wins immediately.

18.b4
  18.♘f3 ♗c6⇄

18...♗c6

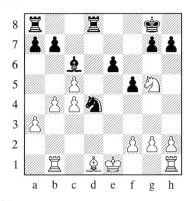

19.f3

19.♖g1 looks odd, and the straightforward
19...♖ac8 20.♖b2 h6 21.♘f3 ♗xf3 22.gxf3
(22.♗xf3 b6!) 22...e5⇄ offers Black good
compensation. His plan is to increase the
pressure on White's queenside pawns by
playing ...b6.

19...e5 20.♖b2

20.h4 can be met by 20...a5∞ intending to open the a-file.

20...a5 21.♔f2

21.b5 is positionally dubious, and after 21...♗e8 22.♔f2 h6 23.♘h3 ♘e6∓ Black has a great position.

21...h6 22.♘h3 ♔f7 23.♖e1 ♔f6∞

Black has excellent compensation for the small material investment of a mere pawn.

b) 14.♗a4!

This strong move leads to White's advantage after a forcing sequence.

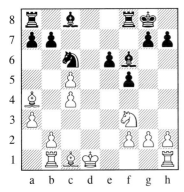

14...e5 15.♗xc6 bxc6 16.♗g5! e4

16...♗xg5 17.♘xg5 e4 18.f4! h6 19.♘h3 a5 20.a4!± gives White a definite positional advantage.

17.♗xf6 exf3 18.♗e5!

After 18.♗c3 f4! 19.gxf3 ♗f5 20.♖c1 ♖ad8† 21.♔d2 ♖d4 22.♖e1 ♖fd8 23.♖e2 ♔f7 Black is okay.

18.♗e7 fxg2 19.♖g1 ♖e8 20.♗d6 f4! 21.♖xg2 f3⇄ is also good for Black, whose ideas include ...♗f5 and/or ...♖e2.

18...♖e8 19.♖e1 fxg2 20.f4.

White is close to obtaining a serious bind over the position. Black can try to throw a spanner in the works, but he fails to equalize.

20...♗e6

Or 20...g5 21.♔e2 ♗e6 22.♖bc1 intending ♔f2 when White keeps the advantage.

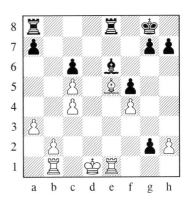

21.♖c1 ♖ad8† 22.♔e2 g5!

The best chance, but White can stay on top. 23.♖g1! ♗xc4†! 24.♖xc4 gxf4 25.♖xg2† ♔f8 26.♔f3 ♖xe5 27.♔xf4 ♖dd5 28.♖a4±

Black has solved some of his problems but White still keeps some pressure.

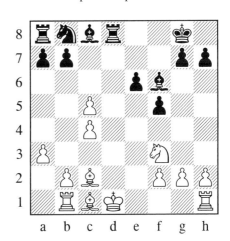

14.♔e2

Less natural is:

14.♔e1

This avoids a potential knight check on d4, but blocks the h1-rook.

14...♘c6

Black continues with his normal plan.

15.♗a4

In the present position this idea is not as strong as in some previous lines.

15.♗g5 ♗xg5 16.♘xg5 ♘d4 17.♗d1 ♗d7∞ transposes to variation 'a' after 13...♘c6 in the note to Black's 13th move, where White plays the imprecise 14.♗g5 instead of the stronger b) 14.♗a4!.

15...e5 16.♗xc6 bxc6 17.♗g5 ♗e6 18.♗xf6 gxf6 19.b3 ♖d3

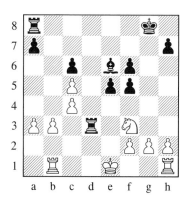

Black has promising play here, for instance:
20.♔e2

20.♘d2 ♖ad8 21.♖d1 ♖c3 22.g3 ♖c2 23.h4 ♖d3↑ is dangerous for White.

20...♖xb3 21.♖xb3 ♗xc4† 22.♖d3□ ♖d8 23.♖hd1 e4 24.♘e1 ♔f7 25.♔d2 ♗xd3 26.♔c3 ♖d5 27.♘xd3 exd3 28.♖xd3 ♖xc5†

Black is a pawn up, but the most likely result is a draw.

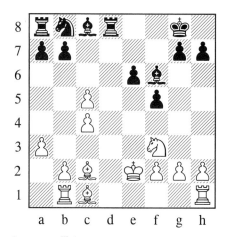

14...e5 15.♖d1

Alternatives are unconvincing, for instance:
15.♗e3?!

As we have said before, this does not seem natural as the bishop will be a target for Black's advancing central pawns.

15...e4 16.♘d2 ♘c6 17.f3

17.♖hd1 ♗e6 18.♗f1 ♘d4 19.♗a4 ♖ac8 20.b4 g5 21.g3 ♔g7∞ looks nice for Black.

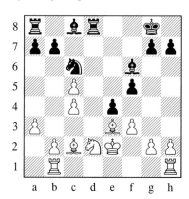

17...f4! 18.♗xf4 ♘d4† 19.♔d1 exf3→

Black has a strong attack, for instance:
20.gxf3 ♘xf3 21.♗e4

21.♗d6 ♗g4→

21...♗g4 22.♔c1 ♖d4 23.♗d5† ♔h8 24.♗e3 ♘xd2 25.♗xd2 ♗f5! 26.♗e3

26.♗c3?? ♗g5†–+

26.♖a1 ♖e8∓

26...♖h4→

Black keeps a promising initiative.

15...♖xd1 16.♔xd1

Also playable is:
16.♗xd1

Most players would reject this move and indeed it causes no real problems to Black, who should just continue with normal development.

16...♗e6 17.b3

17.♘d2 ♘c6 18.b4 ♘d4† 19.♔f1 ♖d8 20.♔g1 e4 21.h3 ♔f7∞ is at least equal for Black.

17...♘c6

Black can also regain his pawn with 17...♘d7 18.♘g5 ♘xc5 19.♗c2 ♗c8 20.♗e3 ♘e6 21.♗xe6 ♗xe6 22.♖d1 ♔f7 when the position is about equal.

18.♔f1

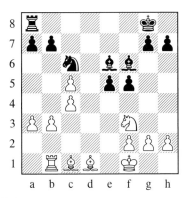

18...h6!

A nice positional move, planning to activate the king via f7.

19.♗b2 ♔f7 20.♗e2

20.♗c2 e4 21.♘xf6 ♔xf6 22.♘e1 ♘d4∓

20...e4 21.♘d2 ♖d8 22.♗xf6 ♔xf6 23.♖d1 ♖d7 24.♘e1 ♔e5!∓

Black's king dominates and his chances are higher.

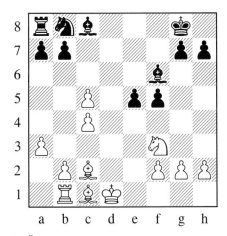

16...♘c6

This move is not bad, and Tomashevsky was probably still following the recipe prepared in his kitchen. There were two good alternatives, of which the second is especially interesting.

16...♗e6 17.b3 ♘c6 gives Black nice compensation, for example 18.♗g5 ♔f7 19.♗xf6 ♔xf6 20.♘d2 e4 21.♘g1 ♘d4 (or 21...♘e5!? 22.♘e2 ♖c8 23.♘c3 ♔e7 24.♘b5

a6 25.♘d4 ♖xc5∞ and Black should be okay) 22.♔c3 ♘xc2 23.♔xc2 ♖c8 with an equal game.

16...e4!

According to my analysis this ambitious move would have been even stronger.

17.♘d2 ♘c6 18.b4 ♗e6 19.g4 g6 20.♗b2

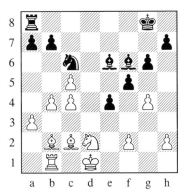

20...♔f7!∞

Black improves every one of his pieces. His rook is only one move from the d-file, and then his whole army will be perfectly coordinated. Here are some illustrative lines:

21.b5?!

A principled move, but Black is well placed to meet it.

21.♔e1 is more prudent, although after 21...♘d4 22.♗d1 ♖d8↑ Black has at least enough compensation.

21...♘d4!

21...♘e5 is less clear, as after 22.g5 ♗g7 23.c6 bxc6 24.bxc6 ♘xc6 25.♗xg7 ♔xg7 26.♖b7† ♔g8 27.c5 White also becomes active. A logical finish might be 27...♖c8 28.♗a4 ♘d4 29.♖b4 ♖d8 30.♔e1 a5 31.♖b6 ♗d5 32.♖a6 ♖c8 33.♖xa5 ♔f7 34.♖a7† ♔g8 35.♗d1 ♖xc5 36.a4 ♖c1 37.♖d7 ♘c2† 38.♔e2 ♘d4† 39.♔e1 ♘c2† with a draw.

22.c6 bxc6 23.g5 ♗e5 24.♗xd4 ♗xd4 25.bxc6 ♗xf2

Black has the better chances, for instance: 26.♖b7† ♔f8 27.♔e2 ♗c5 28.♖xh7 ♗f7∓

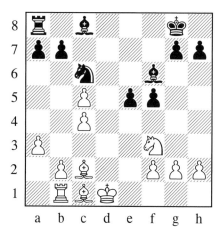

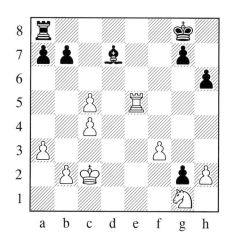

17.♗g5 ♗xg5 18.♘xg5 h6 19.♘h3

19.♘f3 is met by 19...e4 20.♘g1 ♗e6 21.b3 ♖d8† 22.♔e1 ♘d4 23.♖c1 ♖c8 24.♘e2 ♘xe2 25.♔xe2 ♖xc5=.

19...♘d4 20.♔d2 ♘xc2 21.♔xc2

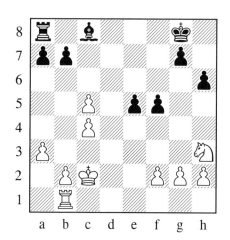

21...f4!

This strong move arrives just in time.

22.♖e1

White has no serious alternative.

22...f3 23.♖xe5 fxg2 24.♘g1 ♗d7 25.f3

Intending ♖e2.

25...♖c8!

This is definitely the best place for the rook.

26.b4

If White goes for the more reserved 26.b3 ♔f7 27.♔c3, keeping c4 defended, then Black has a nice idea: 27...♖e8! 28.♔d4 (The endgame after 28.♖xe8?! ♔xe8 29.♔d4 ♗f5 30.♔e3 ♔d7 31.♘e2 ♗c2 32.b4 ♗d1 33.♘g1 ♗b3 34.♔f2 ♔xc4 35.♔xg2 ♔c6↑ is dangerous for White.) 28...♖xe5 29.♔xe5 g5!⇄ Black is not worse.

26...b6 27.cxb6

White also gets no advantage with: 27.♖e7 ♖d8 28.cxb6 ♗f5† 29.♔c3 (29.♔b3? ♖d3† 30.♔a4 axb6 31.♖e2 ♗d7† 32.b5 ♖c3 is excellent for Black; 29.♔c1 axb6∞ is also fine for him, with ...♖c8 coming next.) 29...♖d3† 30.♔b2 ♖d2† 31.♔c3 ♖d3†=

27...axb6 28.♖e2
½–½

The players agreed a draw, which is logical enough. The continuation might have been 28...♖xc4† 29.♔b2 ♗f5 30.♖xg2 ♖d4∞ when Black is not worse as his active pieces provide full compensation for the missing pawn.

GAME 37

▷ **Le Quang Liem (2717)**
▶ **G. Meier (2648)**
5th SPICE Cup, Lubbock
Round 7, 22.10.2011 **[E11]**
Annotated by Arkadij Naiditsch

Le Quang Liem chose 8.♗f4, a line slightly less popular than it was a couple of years ago. Black reacted with 8...dxc4, choosing a very defensive line. I have to say that even if position is equal, it is very unpleasant to play for Black. He has no winning chances, but only the possibility of getting a worse endgame and suffering for many hours. The only plus is that the critical position, which I analyse in depth, might really be just a draw.

1.d4 e6 2.c4 ♘f6 3.♘f3 d5 4.g3 ♗b4† 5.♗d2 ♗e7 6.♗g2 0–0 7.0–0 c6 8.♗f4

8.♕c2 is the main line.

8...dxc4 9.♘e5 ♘d5 10.♘xc4

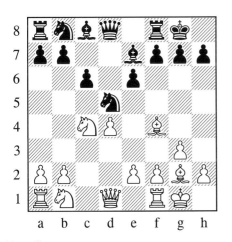

10...c5!

The key move of the line! Black exchanges the centre pawns and hopes to have enough time to complete his development, after which the position would be totally equal.

11.dxc5 ♘xf4 12.gxf4 ♕c7!

Hurrying to recapture the pawn is inaccurate:
12...♗xc5 13.e3

13.♘c3 ♕c7 14.e3 is just a transposition.
13...♕c7 14.♘c3
   14.♕b3 ♘c6 15.♘c3 ♗e7 16.♖fd1 ♘a5
   17.♘xa5 ♕xa5 18.♖ac1 ♖d8=
14...♘c6 15.♖c1
   15.♕h5 looks active, but it is not enough
   to get an advantage: 15...♗e7 16.♘b5
   ♕b8 17.♖fd1 g6 18.♕h6 e5! 19.♘bd6
   (19.fxe5 ♗e6 20.♕f4 ♗xc4 21.♕xc4 ♕xe5=)
   19...exf4 20.♕xf4 ♗e6 21.♗d5 ♗xd5
   22.♖xd5 ♕c7 23.♖ad1 ♖ad8=
15...♖d8 16.♕h5 ♗e7 17.♖fd1 ♖xd1† 18.♖xd1
g6 19.♕e2±

White is doing slightly better, since Black has not yet had time to play ...♗d7-e8.

13.e3

13.b4? ♗f6

13...♖d8

The critical moment of the game. If White wants to be better, then this must be the place to search for an advantage.

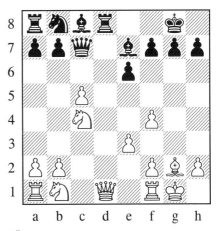

14.♘bd2

White may try the active:
14.♕h5!? ♘a6!

This development of the knight is quite untypical and it would be a hard move to find during the game.

Other moves allow White an edge:

a) 14...♕xc5 15.♖xc5 ♗xc5 16.♘bd2 ♘c6 17.♘b3 ♗e7 18.♗xc6 bxc6 19.♘e5± White has the better position, as the c6-pawn is weak and White is in time to set up a blockade on the c5-square. White's next moves may be ♖fd1, ♖ac1 and ♘c5 or ♘d4.

b) 14...♘d7 15.♘c3 g6 16.♕e2 ♘xc5 17.♘b5 ♕b8 18.♖fd1 ♗d7 19.♘a5 and Black is close to being equal, but it seems that White can keep an initiative:

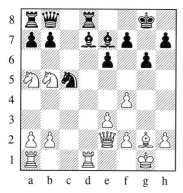

b1) 19...♗xb5 20.♕xb5 ♖xd1† 21.♖xd1 ♕e8 22.♕xe8† ♖xe8 23.♗xb7 ♖d8 24.♗f3 ♖xd1† 25.♗xd1 ♘d3 26.b3±

b2) 19...a6 20.♘d4 ♗e8 21.♖ac1±

b3) 19...♗e8 20.♘d4 e5 21.fxe5 ♕xe5 22.♘xb7 ♘xb7 23.♗xb7 ♖ab8 24.♗g2±

15.♘c3

15.c6 is a logical move, but it does not seem to give any advantage: 15...bxc6 16.♘e5 (16.♘c3 ♘b4 17.♖fd1 ♗a6=) 16...g6 17.♕h3 ♘b4 18.a3 (18.♘xf7 e5! 19.f5 ♖f8! 20.♘h6† ♔g7 21.♘c3 gxf5 22.♔h1 ♘f6 23.♖g1 ♖xh6 24.♗xc6† ♔f7 [24...♔h8 25.♗d5!+–] 25.♗d5† ♘xd5 26.♕xh6 ♘f6 27.♖g7† ♔e8 28.e4 ♕c4‡ and the position is very complicated, but Black seems to be better.) 18...♘d5 19.♘xf7 (19.♖c1 ♗b7∓) 19...♔xf7 20.♕xh7† ♔f8 21.♕h8† ♔f7 22.♕h7† ♔f8=

15...♗d7!?

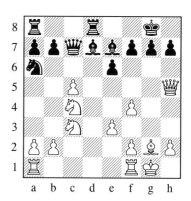

16.♕e5!

A great idea!

16...♕xc5 17.♘a5 f6

17...♕xe5 18.fxe5 ♖ab8 (18...♘c5 19.♘e4 ♘xe4 20.♗xe4±) 19.♖fd1 and White is slightly better.

18.♕xc5 ♗xc5 19.b4

19.♘e4 ♘xe4 20.♗xe4 ♗c8! A very cool and strong move! (20...♗b5 21.♗xb7 ♖ab8 22.♖fc1±) 21.♖ac1 ♖b8=

19...♘d3 20.♖ad1 ♘b2 21.♘xb7 ♘xd1 22.♖xd1 ♗xb4 23.♘xd8 ♖xd8 24.♘b5 a6 25.♘c7

25.♘c6 axb5 26.♗xd7 ♔f8 27.♖d3 ♔e7 28.♗xb5 ♖xd3 29.♗xd3 h6=

25...♔f7 26.♘xa6 ♗e7 27.♗f1 ♗c8 28.♖xd8 ♗xd8 29.♘c5 ♗e7 30.♘b3±

The position is probably a draw, but Black will still need to be accurate.

14...♗xc5 15.♖c1 ♘c6 16.♕h5

16.a3! was the last chance for White to try to be better, although the position may already be equal. 16...♗d7 17.b4 ♗e7 18.♘e5 a6 White has a symbolic advantage but I don't see any real winning chances. Black's next moves will be ...♗e8 and ...♖ac8, and with his development complete, Black should achieve a draw.

16...♗e7 17.♘e5 g6 18.♕e2 ♗d7 19.♖c2

19.♘xd7 ♕xd7 20.♖fd1 ♖ac8 21.♘b3 ♕e8 22.♕b5 ♖d7!=

19...♗e8 20.♖fc1

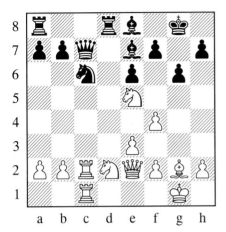

20...♕a5

20...♖ac8= was probably the most accurate move.

21.♘xc6

21.♗xc6!? would give White some chances: 21...bxc6 22.♘b3 ♕xa2 23.♘d4 c5 24.♘dc6 (24.b3 ♕a3) 24...♗xc6 25.♘xc6 ♖e8 26.b4 ♕d5 27.b5!±

21...bxc6 22.b3

22.♘b3 ♕xa2 23.♘d4 ♖ab8 24.♗xc6 ♖b6 25.♗xe8 ♖xe8 26.♘c6 ♗f6=

22...♖ac8 23.♘c4 ♕b5 24.♗f3 c5 25.♘e5

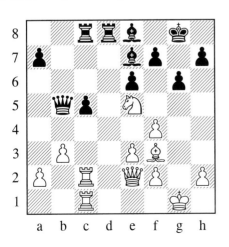

25...♕b6

Black has a clear plan, to exchange the light-squared bishop for the knight and then just sit there.

25...♕xe2 26.♗xe2 ♔g7 would probably also be enough to secure a draw.

26.♗e4 ♗b5 27.♕e1 a5 28.♘c4 ♗xc4!

Normally the side with the bishop pair does not want to exchange one of the bishops, but in this position it is the right idea! White has no winning ideas, as you can see during the following moves, and the players quickly agreed to a draw...

29.♖xc4 ♖c7 30.♖a4 ♖a7 31.♔g2 ♖dd7 32.♖c2 ♕d8 33.♗f3 ♖d3 34.♗e2 ♕a8† 35.♔g3 ♖dd7 36.♗f3 ♕d8 37.♔g2 ½–½

GAME 38
▷ **P. Eljanov (2683)**
▶ **D. Andreikin (2705)**
Governor's Cup, Saratov 2011
Round 9, 17.10.2011 [E15]
Annotated by Alexander Ipatov

A good fighting game, in which all three results seemed possible. White played the rare 11.cxd5, but even against the more popular 11.♗f4 it seems that Black can obtain good counterplay. Black didn't want to play passively, but quickly created counterplay on the queenside with ...b5. After a very complicated struggle White won the game, but I believe that Black had many chances to hold the position.

1.d4 ♘f6 2.c4 e6 3.♘f3 b6 4.g3 ♗b7

Another popular move is 4...♗a6, with a lot of theory lying ahead.

5.♗g2 c5

In former times this move was considered

dubious, but modern theory judges it to be playable.

A more solid set-up seems to be 5...♗e7 6.0–0 0–0, and in this tabiya of the 5...♗e7 subvariation White has many possible continuations, such as 7.♘c3, 7.♖e1 or 7.d5.

6.d5 exd5 7.♘h4 g6 8.♘c3 ♗g7 9.0–0

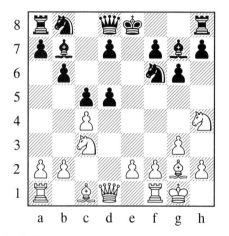

9...0–0
This is most popular, but Black has a couple of other options:

9...d6
This seems a fair alternative to me.
10.cxd5
Probably best. The idea of maintaining an outpost on d5 gives no advantage to White: 10.♗g5 ♕d7 11.♗xf6 ♗xf6 12.♗xd5 ♘c6 13.♘f3 ♗xc3 14.bxc3 0–0= White has got his outpost, but the weakness of his c-pawns kills any hopes of an advantage.
10.♘xd5 ♘xd5 11.♗xd5 ♘c6 12.♖b1 0–0 13.♘g2 ♕d7 14.b3 ♖fe8⇄ and the activity of Black's pieces fully compensates for the weak d5-square.
10...0–0 11.e4
We have a typical position for the Modern Benoni. White's plan is quite straightforward: to advance e4-e5 after some preparation,

while Black will think about the advance ...b5 and counterplay on the queenside.

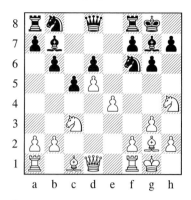

11...a6
11...♘a6!? 12.f4 ♘c7 13.a4 ♖b8 14.♗d2 a6 15.♔h1 ♘d7 16.♕c2 b5 17.♘d1∞ Conquest – Gallego Eraso, Bergara 2010.
12.a4 ♖e8 13.♕c2 ♘bd7 14.♘f3 c4 15.♘d4 ♘xd5 16.♘xd5 ♗xd4 17.♕xc4 ♗g7 18.♗e3± Dziuba – M. Popovic, Belgrade 2009.

9...♘a6
The idea behind this move is quite simple: to organize pressure on the d5-square, thereby preventing White from using it as an outpost.

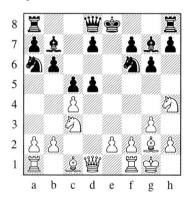

10.♗f4!
10.♘xd5?! ♘xd5 11.♗xd5 ♗xd5 12.♕xd5 0–0 13.♗g5 ♕e8 gives Black an ideal position. Although White has gained a space advantage, he cannot really maintain it with his pieces.

10.cxd5 d6 yields a pawn structure similar to a Modern Benoni, and is liable to transpose into Conquest – Gallego Eraso above. Black has easy play with ...0-0, ...♘c7, ...b5, while White's major plan is to advance f2-f4, e2-e4-e5, etc.

10.♗g5 ♘c7 11.cxd5 d6 (11...0-0?? 12.d6+−) 12.♕a4† ♕d7 13.♕xd7† ♘xd7= and the queen exchange seems to be in Black's favour.

10...0-0

10...d6? 11.♘b5±

11.♗d6 ♖e8 12.cxd5 b5 13.♘xb5 ♕b6 14.a4±

Black did not get sufficient compensation in Nyback – A. Mastrovasilis, Aix-les-Bains 2011.

10.♗g5

White's major idea is to get an outpost on d5 for his knight or bishop. In my opinion, this promises a little more for White than taking on d5 with a pawn and giving Black a good version of the Modern Benoni pawn structure.

10.cxd5 d6 transposes to 9...d6 10.cxd5 0-0 in the previous note.

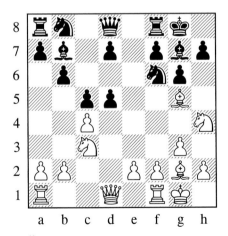

10...♕e8

The most popular choice nowadays. Black wants to escape the pin on the h4-d8 diagonal as soon as possible. Alternatives are:

10...♖e8 11.♕d2 a6 12.♘xd5 ♗xd5 13.♗xd5 ♘c6 14.♖ad1± and White was clearly better in Ki. Georgiev – Granda Zuniga, Bled (ol) 2002.

10...♕c7 11.♗f4 ♕c8 12.cxd5 ♘e8 13.♖c1 (better was 13.♕d2! d6 14.♗h6↑ with the same idea as in our main game) 13...d6 14.a3∞ Tal – Ljubojevic, Riga 1979.

11.cxd5

Worthy of consideration is:

11.♗f4!? ♕e7

11...♘e4?! 12.♘xd5 ♘a6 13.♕c2 f5 14.a3± gave White a clear positional advantage which he managed to convert into a full point in Zhao Jun – Zhou Jianchao, Manila 2010.

11...♕d8 and now:

a) 12.♗g5 ♕e8 13.♗f4 ♕d8 14.♗g5 ½-½ Ponomariov – Gashimov, Khanty-Mansiysk (5.1) 2011.

b) I believe that White could have fought for the advantage with 12.♗d6!? ♖e8 13.cxd5 ♗f8 (after 13...♘a6? 14.e4! ♗f8 15.♗xf8 ♔xf8 16.f4± White has a dangerous attack) 14.♗xf8 ♔xf8 15.e4 d6 16.f4 ♘bd7 17.a4± White's plan is simple: to play ♕c2 (or ♕d3), ♖ae1 and then push e4-e5 at the appropriate moment.

12.♗g5 ♕e8 13.♗f4 ♕e7 14.♘b5 ♘e8

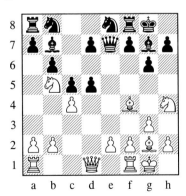

15.♖b1!

A useful move. White defends the b2-pawn

while waiting to see where Black is going to develop his queen's knight.

15.♗xd5?! is dubious, giving Black good chances in the resulting middlegame: 15...♗xd5 16.♕xd5 ♘c6 17.♕d2 ♕e6⇄ and Black had counterplay in Ponomariov – Andreikin, Saratov 2011.

15...♗c6

Forcing White to take on d5 with the bishop. 15...♘a6 16.♗xd5 ♗xd5 17.♕xd5 ♖d8 18.a3!± keeps the black knight on the edge of the board.

15...♘c6 16.cxd5 ♘a5 17.♕d3± is clearly better for White, as the black knight on a5 is out of play.

16.♗xd5 ♗xd5 17.♕xd5 ♘c6 18.e3!±

Compared with Ponomariov – Andreikin above, White doesn't need to worry about the b2-pawn as it is already defended by the rook. I think White has a clear advantage here due to Black's weak squares on the d-file.

11...d6

11...h6? has the obvious idea of preventing ♕d1-d2 and ♗g5-h6 to exchange the dark-squared bishops, but it is a grave mistake: 12.♗f4 Threatening to win an exchange by coming to d6. 12...g5 (12...♕d8 13.♗d6 ♖e8 14.e4±) 13.♗xb8 ♖xb8 14.♘f5± White has a crushing position.

12.♕d2

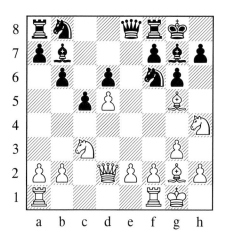

The first step in White's plan. He is going to exchange Black's active dark-squared bishop in order to weaken the kingside and then try to generate a direct attack on the king.

12...♘bd7N

12...♕e7 was played in Pontoppidan – Wochnik, corr. 2000.

13.♗h6 ♗xh6 14.♕xh6 a6

Black is playing in a principled way. His idea is simple: to create enough counterplay on the queenside to distract White from his kingside attack. Black first prepares ...b6-b5-b4 in order to decentralize White's knight.

15.a4

A prophylactic move. Also possible was the more aggressive:

15.♘f3!? ♕e7 16.♘g5 ♖fe8 17.♘ce4

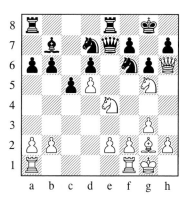

White tries to divert Black's pieces from the h7-square, but I do not think that a direct attack with just three pieces should succeed.

17...♘f8!

The h7-square is now well defended, so one may ask what White's pieces are doing on h6 and g5.

18.♘xf6† ♕xf6 19.♘e4

White has to change plan; his main idea will now be to advance his f- or g-pawn in order to weaken the pawn structure around the black king.

19...♕e5 20.♕h4 ♔g7 21.♖ad1 ♖ad8!

Black has to defend the d6-pawn in advance, so as to minimize the strength of White's f2-f4 move.

21...♗xd5? 22.f4 ♕e6 23.f5! gxf5 24.♘xd6 ♘g6 25.♕h5±

21...f5? 22.f4 ♕e7 23.♕xe7† ♖xe7 24.♘xd6±

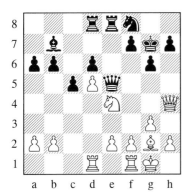

22.g4!

White prevents ...f5 by Black.

After 22.f4?! Black would exchange queens with 22...♕e7!∞ rather than win some dubious pawn on b2.

22...♕xb2

22...g5 23.♘xg5 h6 24.♘f3 ♕xe2 25.g5↑

22...♗xd5?? 23.f4 ♕e6 24.f5 gxf5 25.gxf5 ♕e5 26.♕g5† ♔h8 (26...♘g6 27.♖xd5!+−) 27.♘f6 ♕e3† 28.♕xe3 ♖xe3 29.♘d5+−

23.g5!

Fixing the weaknesses on h6 and f6.

23...♕xe2 24.♕f4!

Attacking the d6-pawn.

24...♖xe4

This seems to be the only move.

25.♗xe4 ♖e8 26.♖fe1 ♕c4 27.♕f6† ♔g8∞

The position is very unclear, but I slightly prefer White's chances.

15...b5!?

Black immediately looks for counterplay. The main idea of this move is to exchange as much material as possible in order to minimize White's attack on the kingside.

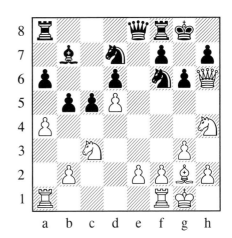

16.axb5 axb5 17.♘xb5 ♖xa1 18.♖xa1 ♕xe2 19.♘xd6 ♕xb2

19...♗xd5 would have led to a very pleasant endgame for White: 20.♘hf5 gxf5 21.♘xf5 ♕xf2†! A nice tactical trick. (21...♕g4?? 22.♗h3 ♕g6 23.♘e7†+−) 22.♔xf2 ♘g4† 23.♔g1 ♖xh6 24.♘xh6† ♔g7 25.♗xd5 ♔xh6 26.♖a7± This situation is highly unpleasant for Black. In open positions like this, rook and bishop are much better than rook and knight, and furthermore Black has two pawn weaknesses on f7 and c5. In view of this, it is understandable why Andreikin went for the more ambitious 19...♕xb2.

20.♖d1

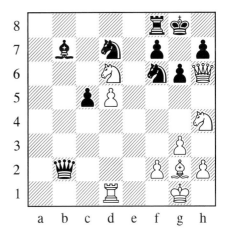

Play has followed a logical course since Black's 15th move. The position has changed a lot, although material is still equal. White retains a dangerous kingside attack which is unpleasant for Black to face over the board. On the other hand, Black has a passed pawn on the c-file which may create many problems for White if he doesn't succeed in making direct threats on the kingside as soon as possible.

20...c4

Black is happy to sacrifice this pawn in order to exchange queens and minimize White's attacking possibilities.

20...♗a8

Moving away the bishop from its "hanging" position makes ...♕xf2† into a threat.

21.h3

Preventing Black's idea.

21.♘hf5? gxf5 22.♘xf5 ♘e8 23.♗e4 ♔h8∓ and compared with the game, Black controls the important a1-h8 diagonal with his queen.

21...♕b6

After 21...♕c2 22.♖c1 ♕b2 23.♘c4 ♕d4 24.♘e3± White again consolidates his position.

22.♘c4

22.♘df5? gxf5 23.♘xf5 ♘e8! and everything is defended.

22...♕b3 23.♘e3±

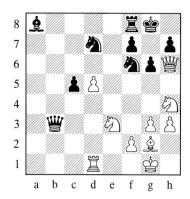

White has consolidated his position and has the better chances due to his good possibilities on the kingside.

20...♕b3!

A good idea. Black creates some small tactical tricks to stop White concentrating on his own attack.

21.♖c1 ♕b2

The best square for the queen, where it performs both defensive and attacking functions.

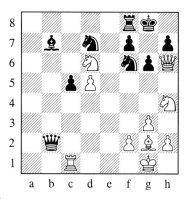

22.♘xb7

22.♖d1 ♕b3 23.♖c1 ♕b2 24.♖d1= with a repetition of moves would be a logical outcome.

22.♘c4? is not good without a pawn on h3, because of 22...♕xf2† 23.♔xf2 ♘g4† 24.♔g1 ♘xh6∓ and Black is a pawn up.

22.h3? loses the valuable d5-pawn: 22...♗xd5 23.♗xd5 (23.♘hf5? gxf5 24.♘xf5 ♘e4!∓) 23...♘xd5∓ with no real compensation for White.

22...♕xb7 23.d6 ♕b6 24.♕d2 ♖e8=

I don't see how White can improve his position, while the d6-pawn could be put in danger by ...♖e6 or ...♘e4.

21.h3

White is thinking only about attacking and does not want a slightly better endgame: 21.♘xc4 ♕xf2† 22.♔xf2 ♘g4† 23.♔g1 ♘xh6±

After the exchange of queens White's winning chances are greatly reduced. Nevertheless, White is still better in the endgame, although Black should not have huge problems making a draw.

21...c3

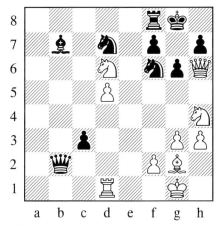

22.♘hf5!

The only move to fight for victory, now that Black's queen can't help on the a1-h8 diagonal.

22...gxf5 23.♘xf5 ♘e8 24.♗e4 ♔h8 25.♘g7! f5 26.♘xe8 ♖xe8?

Black had a stronger option: 26...c2!

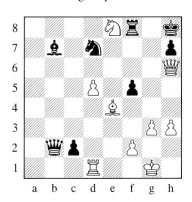

27.♗xc2 ♖xe8 28.♗xf5 ♘f6 29.d6 (29.♖b1?? fails to 29...♗xd5!∓, exploiting the weak back rank) 29...♕c3 (threatening ...♖e1†) 30.♔h2 ♖d8∞ White has compensation for the piece

but can't create immediate threats. I think the position is dynamically equal.

27.♗xf5 ♘f8??

In time trouble, Black plays a move that loses immediately.

The best defence was: 27...♖e7□ 28.♗xd7 ♖f7! 29.♕e3 c2 30.♖c1 ♗xd5 31.♗a4 ♖f3 (31...♗e4? 32.♗xc2! ♗xc2 33.♕d2+−) 32.♕e8† ♔g7 33.♕e7† ♗f7 34.♕g5† ♔g6 35.♗xc2±

28.♕f6†

28.♖d4! was winning more easily: 28...♕a1† (28...♖e1† 29.♔g2 ♗xd5† 30.♖xd5 ♕b8 31.♕f6† ♔g8 32.♗xh7† ♘xh7 33.♖d8† ♖xd8 34.♕xd8† ♔f7 35.♕c7†+−) 29.♔h2 ♕a6 30.d6 ♕e2 31.♕f6† ♔g8 32.♖f4! ♗f3 (32...c2 33.d7 c1=♕ 34.♗xh7† ♘xh7 35.♕f7† ♔h8 36.dxe8=♕†+−) 33.♖xf3□ ♕xf3 34.♗xh7† ♘xh7 35.♕xf3+−

28...♔g8

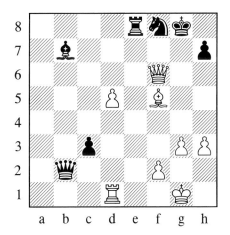

29.♖d4?

White was also short of time, and missed a second chance to win: 29.♗e6†! ♘xe6 30.dxe6 ♖f8 (30...♗c6 31.♕f7† ♔h8 32.e7 h6 33.♕f6† ♔h7 34.♕xc6 ♖xe7 35.♕f6!+−) 31.♕g5† ♔h8 32.♕c5!! ♔g7 33.e7 ♖e8 34.♕e5† ♔g8 35.♕e6† ♔g7 36.♕g4†

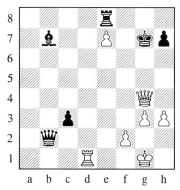

36...♔f6 (36...♔h8 37.♕d7+–) 37.♖d6† ♔f7
38.♕h5† ♔g7 39.♕h6† ♔g8 40.♖g6†!! hxg6
41.♕xg6† ♔h8 42.♕xe8† ♔g7 43.♕f8† ♔h7
44.♕f7† ♔h6 45.♕e6† ♔g7 46.♕e5† ♔h7
47.e8=♕ ♕c1† 48.♕e1+–

29...♕c1†??

Black had a final chance to hold the position:
29...♖e1† 30.♔g2 ♕e2!! 31.♗d3 ♕e6!!

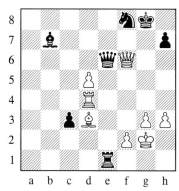

A computer defence; it's just impossible to
find such moves in time trouble. 32.♗xh7†
White has to try this. 32...♘xh7 33.♖g4†
♕xg4 34.♕d8† ♔f7 35.hxg4 ♖e7∞ A draw is
the most logical outcome here, but the onus is
on White to prove it.

30.♔h2 ♖e1

30...h5 doesn't help either: 31.♗g6 ♘xg6
32.♕xg6† ♔f8 33.♕f5† ♔g7 34.♕xh5+–

31.♗xh7†
1–0

GAME 39
▷ **I. Nyzhnyk (2561)**
▶ **S. Tiviakov (2647)**
  15th Unive Open, Hoogeveen
  20.10.2011 **[E17]**
  Annotated by Yannick Gozzoli

A very strange game from Tiviakov. He chose
the passive 7...♘e4?! in a 4.g3 Queen's Indian
and found himself in trouble after the opening.
11...c5!? would have been an interesting try
to free his pieces, but instead White seized
the initiative. He could have won easily after
Black blundered with 18...♗xc8?? but White's
hand became a little bit shaky and he couldn't
convert his huge advantage smoothly. The
ending reached later was still clearly in White's
favour and eventually he won.

Overall, this game wasn't good. Black found
himself in trouble because of his 7th move
which leads to a passive position. I think Black
should concentrate on 7...c5!? which is not
such an easy solution but it is totally playable.

**1.d4 ♘f6 2.c4 e6 3.♘f3 b6 4.g3 ♗b7 5.♗g2
♗e7 6.0–0 0–0 7.♖e1**

7.d5!? is a famous pawn sacrifice, leading to
obscure complications.

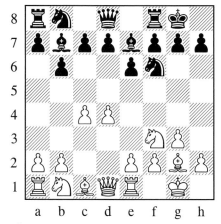

7...♘e4?!

In my opinion not the best move. Black has
a lot of alternatives:

7...♘a6

This was considered the main move but it's not easy for Black to equalize.

8.♘e5

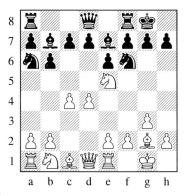

8...♗xg2

8...d5 9.cxd5 exd5 leads to a classical position from the Queen's Indian. Black will push ...c7-c5, followed by ...♘c7-e6. White will develop his play against Black's hanging pawns on c5 and d5. For instance: 10.b3 c5 11.♗b2 ♘c7 12.♘d2 ♖b8 13.dxc5 ♗xc5 14.♘d3 ♗d6 15.♘f3 ♘e6 16.♘d4 ♘xd4 17.♗xd4 ♖e8 18.♖c1 ♕e7 19.e3± Beliavsky – Brodsky, Kharkiv 2008.

9.♔xg2 c6

9...c5 10.d5 exd5 11.cxd5 ♕c7 12.♘f3 is also possible but gives White a good edge.

10.e4 ♕c7 11.♘c3 ♗b7 12.♘d3 d5 13.e5 ♘d7 14.cxd5 cxd5 15.h4±

White has a very pleasant edge and eventually won in Mamedyarov – Carlsen, Baku 2008.

7...a5 8.♗g5

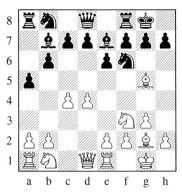

8...h6

8...d6 9.♕d3 ♗e4 10.♕e3 ♗b7 11.♘c3 h6 12.♗xf6 ♗xf6 13.♖ad1 ♘d7 14.♕d2 d5 15.cxd5 exd5 16.♕f4± Kasimdzhanov – Parligras, Konya 2011.

8...♘e4 9.♘fd2 f5 10.♘xe4 fxe4 11.♗f4 d5 12.♗h3 ♖f6 13.♘c3± Moiseenko – Parligras, Aix-les-Bains 2011.

8...c5 is the latest try in this variation but it weakens the queenside terribly. 9.♘c3 cxd4 10.♕xd4 h6 and here instead of 11.♗xf6 ♗xf6 12.♕d2 as in Vachier Lagrave – Polgar, Hoogeveen 2011, White could try 11.♗e3 ♗c5 12.♕d2 ♘a6 13.♖ed1 d5 14.cxd5± with a slight advantage due to the weakened queenside.

9.♗xf6 ♗xf6 10.♘c3 d6 11.♕d3 g6 12.h4 h5 13.♖ad1±

Rodshtein – Nikolov, Rogaska Slatina 2011.

7...♕c8 8.♗g5 h6 9.♗xf6 ♗xf6 10.e4 d6 11.♘c3

White has a good space advantage.

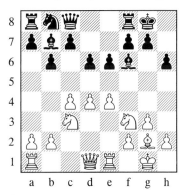

11...c5

11...♘d7 12.♕d2 c6 13.h4 a6 14.♖ad1 ♖d8 15.g4 c5 16.d5 ♘e5 17.g5 hxg5 (17...♘xc4 18.♕c1 hxg5 19.hxg5 ♗xc3 20.♕xc3 exd5 21.exd5 b5 22.g6 f6 23.b3 ♘b6 24.♕e3!+–) 18.hxg5± Akopian – Simantsev, Dubai 2011.

12.e5!? dxe5 13.d5 exd5 14.cxd5 ♘d7 15.♗h3 ♕c7 16.♘b5 ♕d8 17.♘d6∞

Akopian – Medvegy, Rijeka 2010.

7...c5!? 8.d5 exd5 9.♘h4

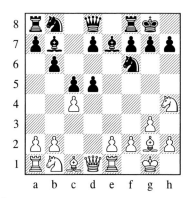

9...♘e4

In my opinion, this is the most ambitious way for Black to play.

10.cxd5 ♗xh4 11.♗xe4 ♗f6 12.♘c3 d6 13.♗f4

Although the position looks nice for White, Black has some Benoni-style counterplay. Despite this Black needs to be careful as his position is strategically worse and his light-squared bishop is misplaced on b7.

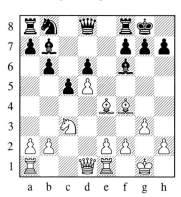

13...♕d7?!

13...♕e7 was better.

14.♕c2 g6 15.♗g2

And Black is already in deep trouble, as ♘e4 is threatened.

15...♘a6 16.♘e4 ♗e7 17.♗h6 ♖fe8 18.♕c3+– B. Socko – Abasov, Warsaw 2009.

8.♘fd2! d5

The only move to avoid a clearly worse position. 8...f5?! 9.d5! is clearly in White's favour, for example: 9...♘d6 10.♘c3 ♘a6 11.e4± Gozzoli – Roussel Roozmon, Nancy 2008.

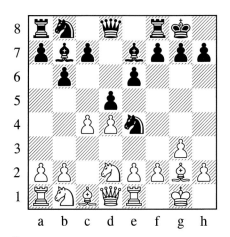

9.♘c3

This is technically not a novelty, but it was played only once 15 years ago!

9.♘xe4?! is not dangerous for Black. 9...dxe4 10.♘c3 f5 11.♗e3 ♗f6 12.♕d2 ♘c6 13.♖ad1 ♕e7 14.f3 ♖ad8 Black is fine, Tregubov – Terrieux, Aix-les-Bains 2011.

9.cxd5 exd5 10.♘xe4 dxe4 11.♘c3 f5 12.e3 (12.♗f4 is also possible. White has a pleasant advantage but Black's position remains very solid. He can try to develop an initiative along the c-file and/or break in the centre with f2-f3.) 12...♕d7 13.b4 ♔h8 14.♕b3 The position is more or less equal but looks easier to play for White, Rodshtein – Stella, Puerto Madryn 2009.

9...♘xd2

In the first game in this variation Black chose a logical continuation:

9...f5 10.♘dxe4
    10.cxd5   exd5   11.♘dxe4   (11.♕b3!?)
    11...fxe4 (11...dxe4 is the same position as

Rodshtein – Stella above) 12.♗f4± Followed by ♖c1, f2-f3, and b2-b4, ♕d1-b3 gives White a very nice position. 12.f3!? is also an interesting try.

10...dxe4 11.f3 ♗f6 12.♗e3 ♘c6

Black is fine, Gavrikov – Korchnoi, Switzerland 1996.

10.♗xd2± c6

Black has chosen a very passive but solid set-up, which gives White a space advantage and strong pressure in the centre. I really don't understand Tiviakov's opening choice, as it will turn out to be a long and hard struggle to equalize.

11.♕b3

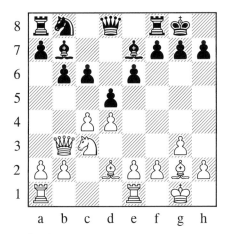

11...♘a6

11...c5!? is a good try to liberate his position and gain some fresh air for his pieces, but it's met by: 12.cxd5 cxd4 13.d6 (after 13.♘b5 ♗xd5 14.♗xd5 exd5 15.♘xd4± White has a very pleasant position but Black can hold) 13...♗xg2 14.dxe7 ♕xe7 15.♔xg2 dxc3 16.♗xc3 ♘d7 17.♖ac1 ♘c5 18.♕c4 ♖fd8 19.♖ed1 ♖ac8 20.♖xd8† ♖xd8 21.♗b4± White has the upper hand, but is far from winning.

12.♖ad1 ♘b4?!

The knight has nothing to do here and it gives White some extra tactical possibilities.

Instead 12...f5 was a good try to build a bind on the e4-square, but of course the knight has nothing to do on a6.

13.c5! ♘a6

We must also consider the following line: 13...bxc5 14.dxc5 a5 15.a3 ♘a6

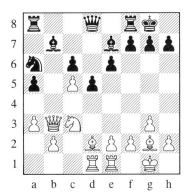

16.♘a4

16.♕xb7?! ♘xc5 17.♕xc6 ♖c8 18.♕b5 ♖b8=
16...♖b8 17.♕c3 f5

17...♗c8 18.e4 d4 (18...♗f6 19.♕c2±)
19.♕xa5 ♕xa5 20.♗xa5 e5 21.b4±
18.♖c1±

White will win the a5-pawn. Black will try to find some counterplay thanks to his strong pawn centre, but White should be able to deal with it.

14.♘a4

It was worth considering the immediate break with:
14.e4!?

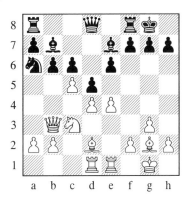

It's quite hard for Black to find a useful move!
14...♗c8 15.exd5

We must consider both pawn recaptures on
d5:

A) 15...cxd5 16.c6 ♘b4 17.♖c1 ♘xc6
18.♘xd5 exd5 19.♖xc6

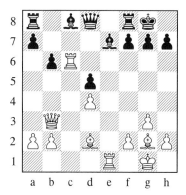

19...♗b7

19...♗e6?! 20.♖cxe6! fxe6 21.♖xe6± After
taking on d5, White will have two pawns
and a strong bishop pair for the exchange,
which is clearly more than enough.
19...♗d7 20.♖c3 ♗e6 21.♗f4± White has a
very pleasant advantage; his pieces are clearly
stronger than Black's and the d5-pawn and
c7-square are clear targets for the white
pieces.
20.♖cc1 ♗f6 21.♗b4 ♖e8 22.♖xe8† ♕xe8
23.♖c7 ♖b8 24.♗xd5 ♗xd5 25.♕xd5 ♖d8
26.♕b7 ♗xd4 27.♗e7 ♖b8
　　27...h6 28.b4 (28.♗xd8?! ♕e1† 29.♔g2
♕xf2† 30.♔h3 ♕f5† 31.♔g2 ♕f2†=)
28...b5 29.♔g2 ♖b8 30.♕d5 ♗b6 31.♖d7±
28.♕d5 ♗xb2 29.♖xa7±
White is of course better, but Black has good
drawing chances.

B) 15...exd5 16.♗f4 bxc5
　　16...♗e6 17.♕a4± This position cannot be
considered as a great success for Black. Also
17.♗f1 was possible.

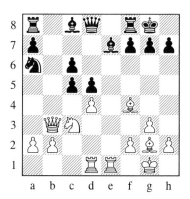

17.♘xd5 cxd5 18.♕xd5 ♖b8
　　18...♕xd5 19.♗xd5 ♗g4 20.♗xa8 ♖xa8
(20...♗xd1 21.♗b7+−) 21.f3! ♗xf3 22.♖d3±
19.♕xd8 ♗xd8 20.♗xb8 ♘xb8 21.dxc5±

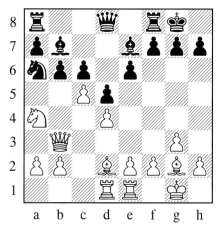

14...b5?!
　A very passive move which kills all Black's
dreams of counterplay.

14...♕d7!? was probably the best chance to
find some chances. 15.cxb6 c5 16.bxa7 ♖xa7
17.♘xc5 ♘xc5 18.dxc5 ♗xc5± White is a
pawn up but the open files on the queenside
give Black some counterplay. Of course it is
objectively still in White's favour, but over the
board it would not be so easy to deal with the
black pieces' activity.

15.e4!
　Logical and strong.

15...dxe4 16.♘c3

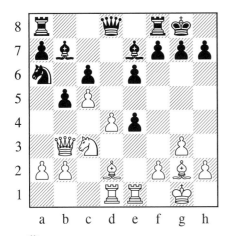

16...♕xd4?!

A mistake which gives White a huge advantage. 16...f5 17.♕xe6† ♔h8 18.♗f4 is also better for White but Black is still alive (18.♘e2!? is also possible). For instance: 18...♘c7 19.♕b3 (after 19.♕e5 ♘d5 20.♘xd5 cxd5± it would not be easy for White to break through) 19...a5 20.f3 a4 21.♕c2 exf3 22.♗xf3 ♕d7±

17.♗e3 ♕e5 18.♖d7?!

Not the best. Black now has a good opportunity to restore the balance and get back in the game.

18.♘xe4!

This was stronger with the idea of ♖d7. White has huge compensation for the pawn in every line.

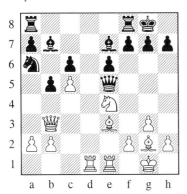

18...♕c7

18...♖fd8 19.♗f4 ♕h5 20.♗d6±

19.♗h3 ♖ad8 20.♖xd8 ♗xd8

20...♖xd8? 21.♗xe6! fxe6 22.♕xe6† ♔h8 (22...♔f8 23.♘g5+−) 23.♗g5 ♗c8 (23...♗xg5 24.♘xg5 g6 25.♕f6† ♔g8 26.♖e7+−) 24.♗xe7 ♕xe7 25.♗xe7+−

21.♖d1 ♗c8 22.a4↑

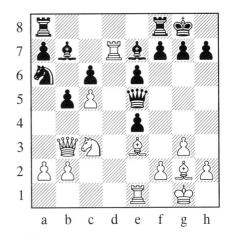

18...♗c8??

The decisive mistake. I don't see any way for White to claim an advantage after:

18...♗xc5! 19.♘xe4

19.♖xb7 is met by 19...♗xe3 20.♖xe3 ♘c5∓.

19...♗c8 20.♖dd1 ♗xe3 21.♖xe3 ♕c7 22.♕c3⇄

White has good compensation for the two pawns, thanks to the weakness of the black squares and his strong piece play, but it doesn't look enough for more than equality. For instance:

22...♗b7 23.♖ed3 ♖ad8 24.♘f6† gxf6 25.♕xf6 ♖xd3 26.♕g5† ♔h8 27.♕f6†

With a draw by perpetual check.

19.♗d4!+− ♕h5 20.♖xe7 ♕g5 21.♖xf7! ♖xf7 22.♘xe4 ♕h5 23.♘d6

White position is overwhelming. Black's knight is stuck on the rim, his a8-rook is passive and his queen is in danger.

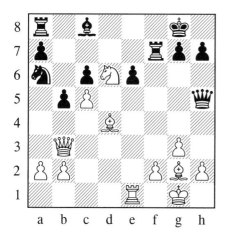

23...♗d7 24.♖e5 ♕g4 25.♖e4 ♕g6 26.♘xf7

This is good enough but 26.♕d1! threatening ♖g4 was even stronger.

26...♕xf7 27.♖f4 ♕e7 28.♖g4 g6 29.♖f4

29.h4! was better.

29...♖e8

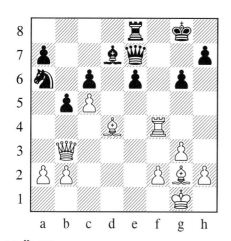

30.♕a3?!

White was not very precise in the last four or five moves and let Black stay in the game. More convincing was:

30.♗e5!

For example:

30...♕xc5

30...♘xc5 31.♕d1+–

31.♕d1! ♕xe5

31...♗c8 32.♗d6!

32.♕xd7 ♖f8

32...♖b8 33.♕f7† ♔h8 34.♕e7+–

33.♖xf8† ♔xf8 34.♕c8† ♔g7 35.♕xa6+–

30...e5!± 31.♖e4 ♕f6

More stubborn was: 31...♕f7! 32.♗c3 (32.♗xe5 ♕d5 33.♖e1 ♕xc5±) 32...b4 33.♕xa6 bxc3 34.bxc3 ♗c8 35.♕c4 ♕xc4 36.♖xc4 ♗d7±

32.♗c3 ♗c8 33.b4+–

White is winning again.

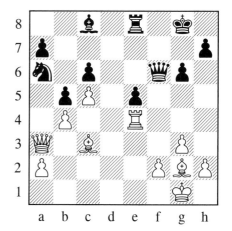

33...♕d8 34.♖e1 e4 35.♗xe4 ♘c7 36.♗xc6 ♖xe1† 37.♗xe1

Black is two pawn down and it looks as though he could resign, but the game suggests he was right to continue.

37...♗e6 38.♗f3

Why not 38.♕xa7 taking another pawn!

38...♕d4 39.♕c3?!

White chose to play an ending with a passed pawn and a pair of bishops against a knight and bishop (which is probably winning but requires some technique) instead of taking a third pawn – a very strange choice, perhaps influenced by time pressure. 39.♕xa7+– was very convincing.

39...♕xc3 40.♗xc3

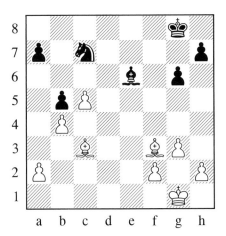

40...♗xa2±

The ending is *almost* winning, but now White has to win the game for a third time!

41.♗e5

A forced winning line was possible with: 41.c6! ♗e6

41...♗d5 42.♔g2 ♔f7 43.♗e5 ♗xf3† 44.♔xf3 ♘d5 45.♔e4 ♔e6 46.c7 ♘b6 47.♔d4 ♔d7 48.♔c5 ♘c4 49.♗f4 a6 50.h4 h5 51.f3 Zugzwang.

42.♗d4! ♔f7

42...♘a6 43.♗xa7 ♘xb4 44.c7 ♘a6 45.♗b6 ♗c8 46.h3 h5 47.h4 ♔f7 48.♗e4 b4 49.f4 ♔e6 50.♗xg6 ♔d6 51.♔f2 ♘xc7 52.♗xh5 ♗e6 53.♗xc7† ♔xc7 54.♔g6+–

42...a6 43.♗e5+– followed by c6-c7.

43.♗xa7 ♔d5 44.♗xd5† ♔xd5 45.♗c5 ♔e6 46.♔g2 ♘c7 47.♔f3 ♔d5 48.♗b6 ♔xc6 49.♗xc7 ♔xc7 50.♔e4+–

41...♘a6 42.c6 ♗e6 43.h3 h5 44.♗d6

The knight is dominated and White is back on the winning path.

44...♔f7 45.♗e2?!

The beginning of a risky plan. 45.h4 was easy; then just bring the king into the game and the win is straightforward.

45...♗c8 46.♗xb5 ♔e6 47.♗f8 ♔f7 48.♗xa6

48.♗h6 ♘xb4 49.♗d2 ♘d5± was the other option.

48...♗xa6 49.♗c5

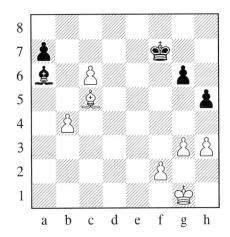

White increased Black's drawing chances by transposing to an opposite-coloured bishop ending with two extra pawns. Since he chose to do so, it probably means that it's winning, but who knows what can happen in such endings...

49...♗b5

49...♔e6 50.f3 ♔d5 51.c7 ♔c6 52.b5† ♔xb5 53.♗xa7 ♔c6 54.♗b8 ♗c8 55.g4 is probably winning.

50.c7 ♗d7 51.♔g2 a6 52.f3 ♔e6 53.g4 ♔d5 54.♗b6 ♔c4 55.♗a5 ♔d3 56.♔g3 ♔e2 57.f4 hxg4 58.hxg4 ♔e3 59.f5 gxf5 60.g5 f4† 61.♔h4 f3 62.♗b6† ♔e4 63.g6
1–0

GAME 40
▷ **D. Andreikin (2705)**
▶ **E. Tomashevsky (2710)**
Governor's Cup, Saratov
Round 2, 09.10.2011 **[E18]**
Annotated by Ivan Sokolov

In an old-fashioned Queen's Indian Tomashevsky played a strong novelty in 14...g5!, which equalized easily, and after a series of natural moves the players agreed a draw on move 32. If White wants to fight for an advantage he will have to deviate at an earlier stage, and you can find several interesting alternatives analysed in the notes.

1.d4 ♘f6 2.c4 e6 3.♘f3 b6 4.g3 ♗b7 5.♗g2 ♗e7 6.0–0 0–0 7.♘c3 ♘e4 8.♗d2

In this position Black has tried almost every legal move, and tons of theory have been developed over the years.

8...d5

Tomashevsky has played this move regularly in recent years, with solid results.

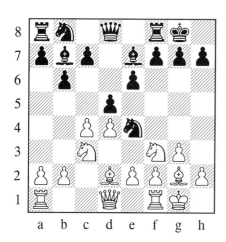

9.cxd5

This is White's usual choice.

After 9.♘e5 ♘d7 10.♘xe4 dxe4 11.♕c2 f5 12.♘xd7 ♕xd7 13.e3 c5 14.dxc5 ♗xc5 White

has an extra pawn on the queenside, but his light-squared bishop is passive and in the following game Black had no trouble holding the balance: 15.♗c3 ♖fd8 16.♖fd1 ♕e8 17.♗e5 ♗c6 18.♖xd8 ♖xd8 19.♖d1 ♖xd1† 20.♕xd1 ♕d7= Korchnoi – Kholmov, Tbilisi 1966.

9...exd5 10.♖c1

This natural move has been by far the most popular choice. However, it is also worth considering 10.♘e5, 10.♕c2 and 10.♗f4.

10.♘e5

This move never became really popular, despite having led to a big advantage against no less a player than Anatoly Karpov.

10...♘d7 11.♘d3 a5?!

Too optimistic. Black should prefer the thematic 11...c5, with the possible continuation: 12.♖c1 cxd4 13.♘b5 ♘dc5 (13...♗f6?! 14.♗b4) 14.♘xd4

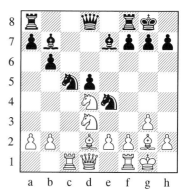

14...♘xd3 (14...♗f6!? 15.♗e3 ♖e8 is also possible, when Black has enough dynamic play) 15.exd3 ♘xd2 16.♕xd2 ♗f6 17.♘f5 ♖c8 (17...g6 18.♘h6† ♔g7 19.♘g4±) 18.d4 White keeps a minimal advantage but Black should not have any real trouble.

12.♖c1 ♘df6 13.♗f4 c6 14.♘e5 c5

Now Tal found a strong idea:

15.dxc5 ♘xc3 16.bxc3!

In order to batter the enemy centre with c4 later.

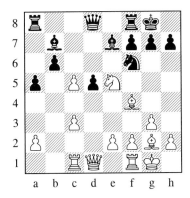

16...♗xc5 17.♗g5

Black has real problems now.

17...♖e8 18.♘g4 ♗e7 19.♗xf6 ♗xf6

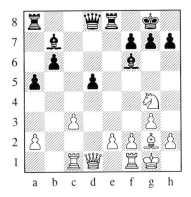

20.c4

20.♘xf6†! ♕xf6 21.c4± looks simple and strong.

20...♗e7 21.♘e3

If 21.cxd5 ♗c5 Black has some compensation.

21...♗g5

After 21...d4 22.♗xb7 dxe3 23.♗xa8 exf2† 24.♖xf2 ♕xa8 25.♖f3 Black does not have enough for an exchange.

22.♕d3

22.♕d4!?

22...d4 23.♗xb7 dxe3 24.♗xa8 exf2† 25.♔xf2 ♗e3† 26.♕xe3 ♖xe3 27.♔xe3 ♕xa8

Black was able to hold a draw in Tal – Karpov, Moscow 1971.

10.♕c2

This was used by Eljanov recently, but it

should not be dangerous for Black.

10...♘d7 11.♖fd1 c5 12.♗e3 ♘f6

Now White has to take a decision in the centre.

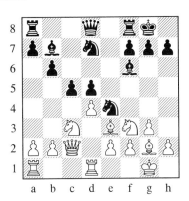

13.dxc5 ♘xc3 14.bxc3 ♘xc5

14...♖c8 15.cxb6 (15.♗h3!?) 15...♖xc3 16.♕d2 ♖xe3 17.♕xe3 ♗xa1 18.♖xa1 ♖e8 19.♕d2 ♘xb6 20.e3± The d5-pawn is weak.

15.♗xc5 bxc5 16.e4

This is the only way for White to exert any kind of pressure.

16...♕a5 17.exd5 ♖ad8 18.♖ab1 ♗xd5 19.♘g5 ♗xg5 20.♗xd5 ♗f6 21.c4 ♖b8 22.♔g2

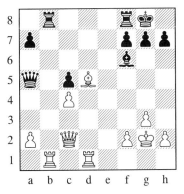

Obviously Black should not have any real problems here, although in Eljanov – Kryvoruchko, Kiev 2011, White incredibly managed to convert his microscopic advantage into a full point.

Finally, White can try activating his bishop:

10.♗f4 ♘d7

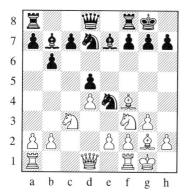

Now 11.♖c1 would transpose to the main game, but a) 11.♕c2 and b) 11.♕b3 are independent options.

a) 11.♕c2 ♘xc3 12.bxc3 c5 13.♖ad1 ♘f6 14.♗e5

Intending to provoke a weakening of Black's kingside, but the idea takes time.

14.♘e5 was a sensible alternative.

14...♕c8 15.♘g5 g6

Black has made a slight concession, but White is in no position to exploit it.

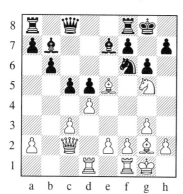

16.dxc5

This seems like the best attempt to make sense of White's position.

16.♕d2?! ♘h5! forces the white pieces back: 17.♘h3 ♕e6 18.♔h1 f6 19.♗f4 ♖ad8∓ Sakaev – Tomashevsky, Moscow 2007.

16...bxc5

16...♕xc5?! is less attractive as the white bishop will get an excellent square on d4.

17.♖b1 ♗c6

17...h6? 18.♗h3 ♕c6 19.♘e6! ♖fc8 20.♘f4 ♖d8 21.♘xg6+–

18.e4 dxe4 19.♘xe4 ♘xe4 20.♗xe4 ♕e6 21.♗xc6

21.♖fe1!? is possible although Black should be fine anyway.

21...♕xc6 22.c4 ♗f6=

The game should end in a draw.

b) 11.♕b3 ♘df6 12.♖ac1

12.♘e5!? is a sensible alternative, and 12...c5 13.♖ad1 looks a bit better for White.

12...c5 13.dxc5 ♗xc5 14.♘e5

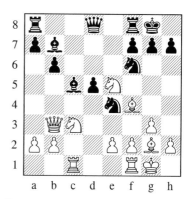

14...♘xf2!?N

14...♕e7 is also quite reliable, and enabled Black to equalize in the following game: 15.♘d3 d4 16.♘xe4 ♗xe4 17.♖fe1 ♗g2 18.♔xg2 ♘e4 19.♖c2 (19.f3 ♘g5 20.e4!± looks better for White) 19...♖ad8 20.f3 ♘g5 21.♗xg5 ♕xg5 White has his own weakness on e2 and the game was balanced in Potkin – Tomashevsky, Ulan Ude 2009.

15.♖xf2 g5 16.♗d2

16.♗xg5 ♗xf2† 17.♔xf2 ♘g4† 18.♘xg4 ♕xg5 19.♘xd5 ♗xd5 20.♗xd5 ♕xc1 21.♕f3 ♖ad8 22.♕f6 ♖xd5 23.♘h6† ♕xh6 24.♕xh6=

16...♗xf2† 17.♔xf2 ♕e7

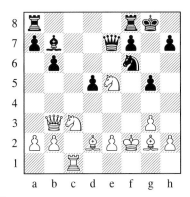

18.♘d3

18.♘f3 d4 19.♘xd4 ♘g4† 20.♔g1 ♕f6
21.♘f3 ♗xf3 22.♗xf3 ♕d4† 23.♔h1
♕xd2=

18...d4 19.♘d5 ♗xd5 20.♗xd5 ♖ae8

20...♘g4† 21.♔e1 ♖fe8 22.e4 dxe3 23.♗b4
♕d7 24.♗xa8 ♖xa8 25.h3 ♘h2 26.♘e5 ♕f5
27.♕xf7† ♔xf7 28.♗xf7 ♔xf7 29.♔e2±

21.♖e1 ♕d8 22.♗f3 ♘e4† 23.♗xe4 ♖xe4∞

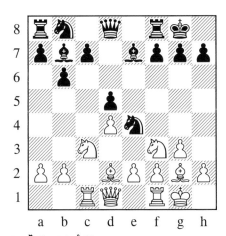

10...♘d7 11.♗f4

11.♘xe4 promises White nothing, as
shown after 11...dxe4 12.♘e5 ♘xe5 13.dxe5
c5 14.♗c3 ♕xd1 15.♖fxd1 ♖ad8 16.f3 exf3
17.exf3 f5 when Black was fine in Onischuk –
Alekseev, Foros 2008.

11.♕b3!?

This leads to interesting play.

11...♘df6

11...♘xd2 12.♘xd2 c6 (12...♘f6 13.♘f3±)
13.e4±

12.♖fd1 c5 13.dxc5 ♗xc5

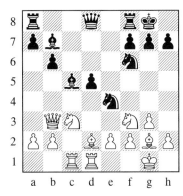

Here White should have gone for the tactical
sequence:

14.♘xe4!N

After 14.♘e1 ♕e7 15.e3 ♖ac8 16.♘b5 a5
17.♘bd4 ♗a6 18.♕a4 ♘g4 19.a3 ♖fe8
Black was at least equal in Smyslov – Tal,
Leningrad 1977.

14...dxe4 15.♗c3 ♗d5 16.♕c2

16.♗xf6 ♗xb3 17.♖xd8 ♖axd8 18.♗xd8 exf3
19.♗xf3 ♗xa2=

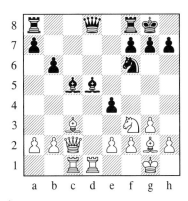

16...♗xf2†!

Other moves fail to solve Black's problems:

16...e3? 17.♗xf6 gxf6 18.♕f5+−
16...exf3 17.♗xf3 ♖c8 18.♗xd5! (18.e4 ♘xe4
19.♗xe4 ♖xe4 20.♕xe4 ♕g5=) 18...♗xf2†
19.♔xf2 ♘xd5 20.♕f5 ♖c5 21.♕f3± (21.e4?
♘xc3=) Black has problems with the pin on

the d-file, for example: 21...♕a8? 22.♗xg7! ♖xc1 23.♖xd5+–

Finally, 16...♖c8 17.♘d4 ♕d7 (17...♗b4? is refuted by 18.♗h3 ♖c4 19.♗xb4 ♖xc2 [19...♖xb4 20.♘c6+–] 20.♖xc2 ♖e8 21.♖c8+–) 18.e3 ♗b4 19.♘e2 leaves White with some advantage.

17.♔xf2 ♘g4† 18.♔g1 ♘e3 19.♕a4

19.♕b1 ♘xg2 20.♔xg2 exf3† 21.exf3 ♕d7=

19...exf3

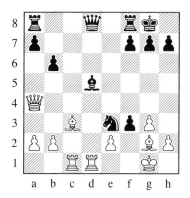

20.♗xf3

20.♕d4 ♕g5 21.exf3 ♘xd1 22.♖xd1 ♗xa2 23.f4 ♕c5 24.♕xc5 bxc5 25.♗xa8 ♖xa8=

20...♕g5 21.♗d2 ♕e5 22.♗c3 ♕g5

The position is equal, for instance: 23.♖d3 ♗xf3 24.exf3 ♖ad8 25.♖xd8 ♖xd8 26.♖e1 ♕c5 27.♔h1 h6=

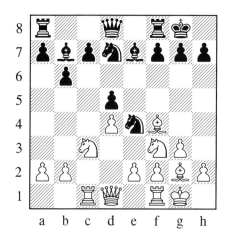

11...c5

Black is not worried about the possibility of an exchange on e4.

He can also make the exchange on c3 first.

11...♘xc3 12.♖xc3 c5

Optically White appears to be a bit better, but it is hard for him to achieve anything substantial.

13.dxc5 bxc5

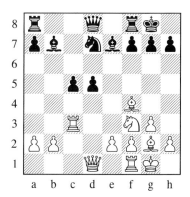

14.♘e5

14.b4?! looks principled, but in reality it is rather a dubious pawn sacrifice. 14...cxb4 15.♖c7 ♘c5 16.♘d4 ♖c8 17.♖xc8 ♕xc8 18.♕b1 a5 The players agreed a draw here in Carlsen – Alekseev, Foros 2008, although Black could have played on for a while as White can hardly aspire to any more than equality.

14...♘b6

14...g5!? is a thematic idea that could be considered here.

15.♕c2 ♕c8 16.♖d1 ♖d8

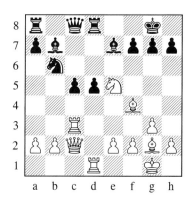

17.♗f3!

The most interesting continuation, preparing ♗g4.

17.b3 d4 should be fine for Black: 18.♗xb7 ♕xb7 19.♖f3 ♕d5 20.♘c4 ♕e6 21.♗c7 ♖d5 22.♗xb6 axb6 23.a4 ♖e8 24.e4 ♖d7∞

17...d4!

17...♕e6 is worse: 18.♗g4 (18.♖e3?! is met by 18...d4; 18.b4 ♗f6 [18...c4?! 19.♖e3↑] 19.bxc5 ♗xe5 20.♗xe5 ♕xe5 21.cxb6 axb6±)

18...♕f6 19.♗h5 g6 20.♘g4 ♕g7 21.♖e3↑

18.♗g4 ♗e4 19.♕xe4

19.♗xc8 ♗xc2 20.♖xc2 ♖axc8=

19...dxc3

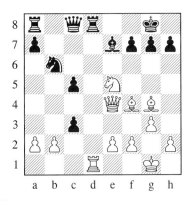

20.♖e1

20.♖b1 ♖d4 21.♕c2 ♕e8 22.bxc3 ♕a4 23.♕f5 ♖d1† 24.♔g2 ♖f8 25.♖xd1 ♕xd1∞

20...♖d4 21.♕c2 ♕e8 22.bxc3 ♖dd8 23.♗f3 ♖ac8

It looks like White should have promising compensation here, but he does not seem to have any real advantage. One possible continuation could be 24.♗g4 ♖a8 with an immediate draw. If White tries for more with 24.♗b7?!, then 24...♖c7 25.♗e4 ♗d6∓ could turn out in Black's favour.

12.♘xe4

12.♕a4!?

This is a reasonable alternative which deserves further investigations.

12...♘xc3 13.bxc3

It is worth considering 13.♖xc3!? with ♖d1 and dxc5 to follow.

13...a6 14.c4 dxc4 15.♕xc4 ♖c8 16.d5 b5 17.♕c2

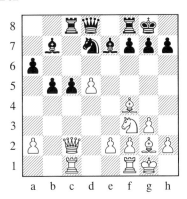

17...g5!?

17...♗xd5 18.♖fd1 ♗e6 19.♘e5 c4 20.♘c6 ♖xc6 21.♗xc6 ♕c8 is also far from clear.

18.d6

18.♗e3 ♗xd5 19.♖fd1 ♗e6 20.♘e5 ♘xe5 21.♖xd8 ♖fxd8 is fine for Black.

18...gxf4 19.dxe7 ♕xe7 20.♘g5 ♕xg5 21.♗xb7 ♖c7 22.♗xa6 c4

Black was not worse in Shulman – A. Ivanov, Philadelphia 2009.

12...dxe4 13.♘d2 f5 14.b4

14.♘c4 ♘f6 is safe enough for Black:

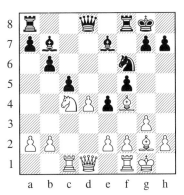

15.dxc5 ♗xc5 16.♖d6 ♗xd6 17.♘xd6 ♕d7 18.♘xb7 ♕xb7 19.♕b3† ♕d5 (19...♔h8 20.♖fd1 ♕e7 21.♕b5 g6 22.e3 ♖ad8=) 20.♕xd5† ♘xd5 21.♖fd1 ♖ad8 22.f3 ♘e3

23.♖xd8 ♖xd8 24.fxe4 ♘xg2 25.♔xg2 ♖d2 26.exf5 ♖xe2† 27.♔h3 ♖xb2=

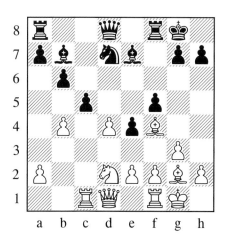

14...g5!

We have already encountered this move a few times in the notes. It is an idea that both sides should always consider in these positions, and in this case it secures Black easy equality.

14...♔h8 was played in a previous game in which Black failed to equalize: 15.bxc5 (15.dxc5 bxc5 16.♘c4 ♗a6 17.bxc5 ♘xc5 18.♗d6 ♖c8 19.♔h3 ♘e6 20.♗xe7 ♕xe7 21.♕a4 ♗xc4 22.♖xc4 g6 23.♖fc1 ♖xc4=) 15...bxc5 16.♘c4 cxd4 17.♖xd4 ♘b6 18.♕xd8 ♗xd8 19.♘d6 ♗d5 20.♖c2 ♗e7 21.♖fc1 ♖ad8 22.♘b5± Meier – Anisimov, Rijeka 2010.

15.dxc5

Inserting the moves 15.♕b3† ♔h8 would not change anything here.

15...gxf4 16.c6 ♗a6 17.b5

Alternatives also bring White no advantage:

17.♕b3† ♔h8 18.♖fd1 ♘f6 (18...♗e2 19.♘xe4 ♗xd1 20.♖xd1 fxe4 21.♖xd7 ♕e8 22.♗xe4 ♕f7 23.♕xf7 ♖xf7 24.c7 ♖af8 25.♗b7 fxg3 26.hxg3 ♖g7 27.a3 ♗c5 28.♖xg7 ♗xf2† 29.♔g2 ♔xg7 30.c8=♕ ♖xc8 31.♗xc8=) 19.♘xe4 ♕c7 20.♘xf6 ♗xf6 21.b5

♗c8 22.♕b4 ♗e7 23.♕d4† ♗f6 24.♕xf4 ♕xf4 25.gxf4 a6 26.c7 ♖a7 27.a4 axb5 28.axb5∞

17.cxd7?! ♕xd7 18.♕b3† Where should the black king go?

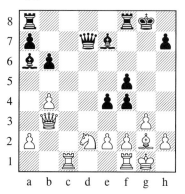

18...♔g7! (18...♔h8 is less accurate, although Black is still not worse after 19.♖fd1 ♕b5! [19...♗xe2?! 20.♘xe4! ♗xd1 21.♖xd1 ♕c7 22.♕b2† ♔g8 23.♘d6 ♖xd6 24.♗d5† ♖f7 25.♗xa8±] 20.a3 ♖ac8=) 19.♖fd1 ♗xe2! 20.♘xe4 ♗xd1 21.♖xd1 ♕c7 22.♕b2† ♔g6∓ This move shows why the king went to g7 instead of h8, and leaves White with insufficient compensation for the exchange.

17...♘c5 18.bxa6 fxg3 19.hxg3 ♕d6=

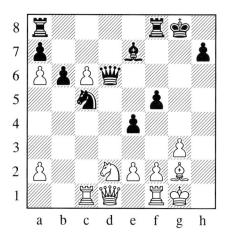

Tomashevsky's homework probably ended somewhere around here. His opening has been a success and the position is equal.

20.e3 ♖ad8 21.♘b3 ♕xc6 22.♕e2 ♕f6

The potential weakness of Black's f5-pawn is mostly academic here; besides, he has good chances to develop counterplay by pushing his h-pawn.

23.♘xc5 ♗xc5 24.♖fd1 ♔g7 25.a4 ♔g6! 26.a5 h5 27.axb6 ♗xb6 28.♕b5 ♖xd1† 29.♖xd1 ♖d8 30.♖xd8 ♕xd8 31.♗h3 ♕f6 32.♕c4

½–½

GAME 41

▷ **H. Melkumyan (2619)**

▶ **V. Gashimov (2756)**

Bundesliga, Muelheim
Round 3, 16.10.2011 **[E41]**
Annotated by Kamil Miton

In this game Black played a creative but highly questionable new idea in 9...e4?!. Perhaps feeling the effects of the opening surprise, White missed a chance to obtain a definite advantage with the simple 11.♕xd3!N. After White's error Black could have equalized the game, but he played some inaccurate moves and White got a winning position which he converted in the endgame.

1.d4 ♘f6 2.c4 e6 3.♘c3 ♗b4 4.e3 c5 5.♘f3 ♘c6 6.♗d3 d6 7.0-0 ♗xc3 8.bxc3 e5 9.d5

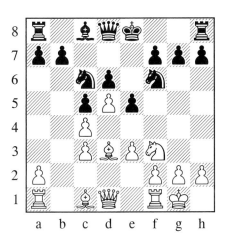

9...e4?!

Technically this was not a novelty, but it may as well have been, as it had only occurred in a single amateur game in which Black lost badly.

10.dxc6 exd3 11.cxb7

11.♕xd3!

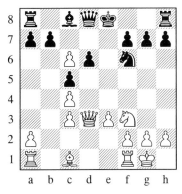

This simple move would have created significant problems for Black. We will consider the responses a) 11...0–0, b) 11...♕c7 and c) 11...bxc6.

a) 11...0–0 12.e4

White also has the option of 12.♖d1, when 12...bxc6 transposes to the note to Black's 12th move in line 'c' below.

12...bxc6 13.♗g5

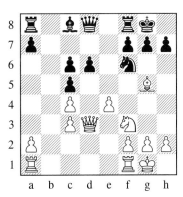

13...h6

13...♗g4 14.♖ad1 ♖e8 15.e5 ♗xf3 16.♗xf6 gxf6 17.♕xf3 fxe5 18.♕xc6 ♖e6 19.f4±

13...罝e8 14.罝fd1 奧g4 15.h3 奧h5 16.e5 dxe5
17.營xd8 罝axd8 18.罝xd8 罝xd8 19.公xe5
罝d6 20.g4 奧g6 21.奧e3 公d7 22.公xg6 hxg6
23.罝b1 罝d3 24.罝b7±

14.奧xf6

Attempting to force the play does not lead
to any advantage, so 14.奧h4 may well be an
improvement.

14...營xf6 15.罝fd1

15.罝ad1 奧e6 16.營xd6 奧xc4 17.營xf6 gxf6
18.罝fe1 奧xa2 is nothing much for White.

15...罝d8 16.e5 營e6 17.exd6 奧a6=

Black is okay as the c4- and d6-pawns are
weak.

b) 11...營c7

This runs into a strong reply.

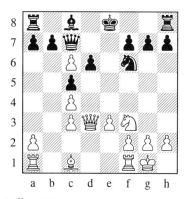

12.e4! 營xc6 13.e5

White can consider delaying this move
with 13.罝e1, although 13...奧e6 (13...0–0
14.奧g5±) 14.e5 dxe5 15.公xe5 營a6 16.奧g5
0–0 17.奧xf6 gxf6 is not completely clear.

13...dxe5 14.公xe5 營a6

14...營a4 15.營d6 奧e6 16.奧g5±

15.奧e3 0–0

15...b6 16.營d6+–

16.奧xc5 罝e8 17.罝fe1 奧e6 18.奧d4±

Black's main problem in not that he is a
pawn down, but rather that the white bishop
on d4 is incredibly strong. In the next few
moves White can put his queen on g3 and
play for an attack, which would also make

the opposite-coloured bishops into a positive
feature for him.

c) Finally, we come to Black's most obvious
move:

11...bxc6

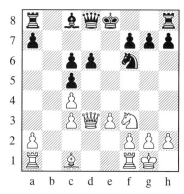

12.罝d1 奧a6

12...0–0 13.營xd6 營xd6 14.罝xd6 公e4
15.罝xc6 罝d8 16.奧a3 罝d7 17.公e5 罝e7 18.f3

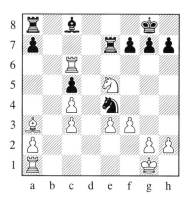

18...罝xe5 (18...奧b7 19.fxe4 奧xc6 20.公xc6
罝e6 21.公d4 [21.公a5!? 罝a6 22.奧b4 罝e8
23.罝d1 cxb4 24.cxb4↑] 21...cxd4 22.exd4
罝xe4 23.奧d6↑) 19.fxe4 罝xe4 20.罝xc5 罝xe3
21.罝d1 奧e6 22.奧b4 罝e2 23.a4±

13.奧a3!?

The simple 13.營xd6 營xd6 14.罝xd6 罝d8
15.罝xd8† 含xd8 16.公e5 罝e8 17.公xf7†
含d7 18.f4± leads to an endgame which is
obviously favourable for White, but it is
hard to say if it will be enough to win the
game.

13...♖c8

13...0–0 14.♕xd6 ♕xd6 15.♖xd6 leaves Black facing a tough endgame:

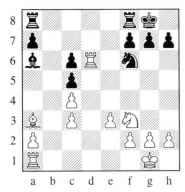

15...♘e4 (15...♖fc8 16.♘e5 ♘e4 17.♖xc6 ♖xc6 18.♘xc6 ♘xc3 [18...♖xc4? 19.♖c1 ♗xa2 20.f3+–] 19.♗xc5 ♖xc4 20.♘xa7±) 16.♖xc6 ♗xc4 17.♗xc5 ♗d5 18.♖c7 ♖ac8 19.♖xc8 ♖xc8 20.♗xa7 ♘xc3 21.a4 ♘xa4 22.♗d4±

14.♘h4!

A typical way of bringing the knight into the attack.

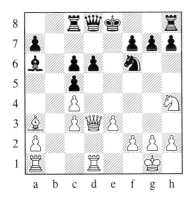

14...d5

14...0–0 15.♘f5±

14...g6 is strongly met by 15.f3! intending to take on d6 without allowing ...♘e4.

15.♘f5 ♗xc4 16.♘xg7† ♔f8 17.♕f5 h5!

17...♔xg7? 18.♕g5† ♔f8 19.♗xc5† ♔e8 20.♕e5† ♔d7 21.♖d4+–

18.♗xc5† ♔g7 19.♕g5† ♔h7 20.♗d4 ♖g8

21.♕xf6 ♕xf6 22.♗xf6±

White is a pawn up, although Black has fair chances to draw the rook and opposite-coloured bishop endgame.

11...♗xb7 12.♕xd3 0–0

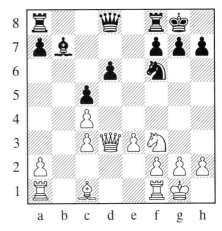

13.♘d2

White's problem piece is clearly his bishop. His last move prepares e3-e4 which will help to activate it, while conveniently stifling the power of Black's bishop on b7.

13...♘g4 14.e4 f5

Black must destroy the e4-pawn quickly, otherwise he will have nothing.

15.exf5 ♕f6

15...♕d7!? may have been better: 16.♖b1 ♗c6 17.♕h3 ♕xf5 (After 17...♖f6 18.♕xg4 ♖g6 19.♕h3 ♖xg2† 20.♔xg2 ♗xg2 21.♔xg2 ♕xf5∞ the position is quite unclear, although it is probably only White who can hope to play for an advantage.) 18.f3 ♘e5 19.♕xf5 ♖xf5 20.♖e1 ♖e8= Black obviously has sufficient counterplay for the missing pawn.

16.♘f3 ♖ae8

16...♕xf5 17.♕xf5 ♖xf5 18.h3 ♘f6 19.♘d2 ♖e8 20.♖b1 ♗c6 21.f3 ♖e2 22.♖b8† ♘e8 23.♘e4 ♖f8 24.♘g3 ♖xa2 25.♗g5↑

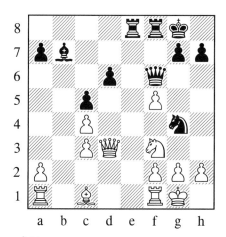

17.♗f4

17.h3 ♗e4 18.♕d1 ♕xf5 19.♘h4 (19.♕xd6 ♗xf3 20.hxg4 ♕xg4 21.♕g3 ♕h5 22.gxf3 ♖e6 23.♗g5 ♖g6 24.f4 h6 25.♕h2 ♕xh2† 26.♔xh2 hxg5 27.fxg5=) 19...♘xf2 20.♘xf5 ♘xd1 21.♖xd1 ♗xf5=

17...♗e4

It was worth considering 17...♕xf5 18.♕xf5 ♖xf5 19.♗xd6 ♗xf3 20.gxf3 ♘e5 21.♗xe5 ♖exe5 when White is a little better, but Black should be able to hold the rook endgame.

18.♕xd6 ♕xf5 19.♗g3 ♗xf3

19...♖f6 20.♘h4 ♕h5 21.♕d2 ♘e5 (21...g5 22.f3) 22.♗xe5 ♖xe5 23.f4 ♖ee6 24.♖ae1± ♕xh4 25.♖xe4 ♖xe4 26.♕d8† ♔f7 27.♕d5†±

20.gxf3 ♘f6?!

It looks like Gashimov was a bit too determined to keep the position complicated. He should have preferred:

20...♘e5

This allows a queen exchange, but Black has good chances to hold the ensuing endgame.

21.♕d5† ♔f7 22.f4

22.♖ab1 ♘xf3† (22...h5 23.♔g2 ♕xf3† 24.♕xf3 ♘xf3 25.♖b8 ♖xb8 26.♗xb8±) 23.♔g2 ♕g6 24.♖b7 ♖ef8 25.♔h1 h5

26.♗d6 ♖d8 27.♖xf7 ♕xf7 28.♕xf7† ♔xf7 29.♗xc5±

22...♘d3 23.♕xf5

23.♖ab1!?

23...♖xf5

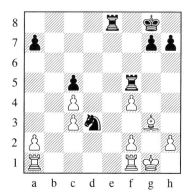

24.♖ab1

24.♖ad1 ♘xf4 25.♖d7 (25.♖fe1 ♘e2† 26.♔f1 ♘xg3† 27.hxg3 ♖xe1† 28.♖xe1 ♖f3 29.♖d5 ♖xc3 30.♖xc5 ♖a3) 25...♖f7 26.♖xf7 ♘e2† 27.♔g2 ♔xf7 28.♗d6 ♖e4 29.♔f3 (29.♗xc5 ♖xc4 30.♖xa7 ♘xc3 31.♖c1 ♖a4 32.♖xc3 ♖xa7) 29...♘xc3 30.♖c1 ♖xc4 31.♗e5 ♘e4=

24...♘xf4 25.♖fe1 ♖xe1† 26.♖xe1 ♔f7 27.♖b1 g5 28.♖b7† ♔g6 29.♖xa7 h5

White is better, but the most likely outcome is a draw.

21.♔g2 ♖e6 22.♕d2 ♘h5 23.♕d5 ♕g6 24.♔h1

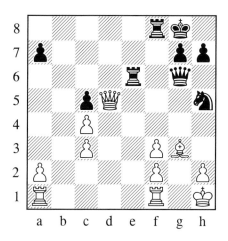

24...♔h8?

Losing valuable time. After the superior 24...♖f5 25.♕b7 ♕f7 26.♖ab1 ♖xf3 27.♕a8† ♖e8 28.♖b8 ♘xg3† 29.hxg3 ♖f8 30.♖xf8† ♕xf8 31.♕d5† ♕f7 32.♕xc5 h6± Black has good chances to save the game.

25.♖ae1 ♖ef6 26.♖g1 ♖f5 27.♖e5

27.♗e5±

27...h6

27...♘xg3† 28.♖xg3 ♕f6 29.♖xf5 ♕xf5 30.♔g2±

28.♕xc5 ♔h7 29.♖xf5 ♖xf5 30.♕e3 ♕c6 31.♔g2 ♕xc4 32.♕e4

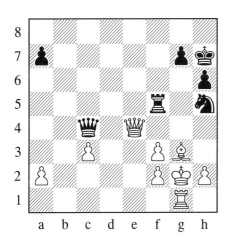

32...♕f7

32...♕xe4 33.fxe4 ♖c5 34.♖c1 ♖c4 35.f3+−

33.c4 ♕g6 34.♔h1 ♘f6 35.♕d3 ♕h5 36.♔g2 ♕g6 37.♖e1 ♘h5 38.♖e4 ♖a5 39.♕d2 ♖a3 40.♖d4 ♕b1

The time control has been reached. White has a winning position with two extra pawns, even if one of them is doubled.

41.♕e2

Intending to simplify. There is absolutely nothing wrong with this, although White could have won more quickly with the energetic

41.♖d6! ♖xa2 42.♕d5

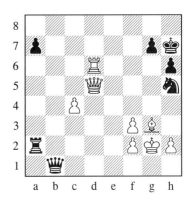

42...♘f6 (42...♖a1 43.♔h3+−) 43.♖xf6! gxf6 44.♕f7† ♔h8 45.♕xf6† ♔g8 46.♕e6†+−.

41...♖xa2 42.♕e4† ♕xe4 43.fxe4 ♘xg3 44.hxg3 a5 45.♔f3 a4 46.c5 ♖c2 47.♖xa4 ♖xc5 48.♔f4+−

Apparently not *all* rook endgames are drawn, and Melkumyan shows great technical skills to convert his advantage.

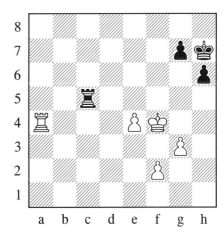

48...♔g6 49.e5 ♖c2 50.f3 ♖c3 51.g4 ♔f7 52.♖a7† ♔g6 53.♖a6† ♔f7 54.♔e4 ♖b3 55.f4 ♖b7 56.♔f5 ♖c7 57.♖d6 ♔e7 58.♖d4 ♖c6 59.♖a4 ♖b6 60.♖a7† ♔f8 61.♖d7 ♖a6 62.♖d6 ♖a4 63.♖b6 ♔e7 64.♖b7† ♔f8 65.e6 ♖a6 66.♖f7† ♔g8 67.g5 hxg5 68.fxg5 ♖b6 69.g6 ♖b5† 70.♔e4 ♖b4† 71.♔d5 ♖b5† 72.♔c6 ♖b8 73.e7 ♖a8

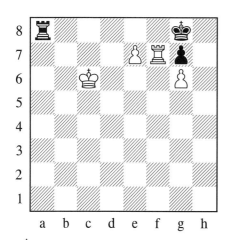

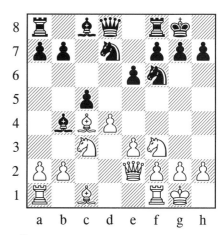

74.♔c7
1–0
Black resigned, as he is in zugzwang.

GAME 42
▷ **M. Roiz (2669)**
▶ **A. Naiditsch (2706)**
Serbian Team Championship, Valjevo
Round 7, 02.09.2011 **[E55]**
Annotated by Ivan Sokolov

In one of the most topical lines of the Nimzo-Indian, Naiditsch opted for the rarely played 9...♕e7 and later introduced the novelty 11...b6?!. After initially reacting well with 12.e4!, Roiz later made mistakes (actually a number of them!), and instead of achieving a winning advantage he found that his extra knight on b7 was destined to be a "dead" piece for quite some time. From the theoretical standpoint, 12.e4! seems to refute Naiditsch's idea. Given that the same move is suggested by most computer engines, it would be interesting to know what Arkadij had in mind – or was it over the board improvisation or bluff? I guess we will have to wait and see if Arkadij dares to repeat his experiment.

1.d4 ♘f6 2.c4 e6 3.♘c3 ♗b4 4.e3 0–0
5.♗d3 d5 6.♘f3 c5 7.0–0 dxc4 8.♗xc4
♘bd7 9.♕e2

9...♕e7
A rarely played continuation by Black – in my opinion, for good reason! The common moves are 9...cxd4, 9...a6 and 9...b6.

10.a3
The main move here.

Also possible for White is:
10.e4
We shall follow a practical example from more than sixty(!) years ago.
10...cxd4 11.♘xd4 ♘e5 12.♗b3 ♖d8 13.♖d1 ♗d7
The active 13...♗c5? is bad due to 14.♗e3, and if Black persists in playing actively he may find himself losing on the spot:
a) 14...♘fg4? 15.♘f5 exf5 16.♗xc5+−
b) 14...♘eg4? 15.e5 ♘xe5 16.♘f5 ♖xd1† 17.♖xd1 exf5 18.♗xc5 ♕e8 19.♖e1 ♘fg4 20.♗d6 and Black ends up a piece down.
14.♗f4 ♘g6 15.♗g3 ♗xc3 16.bxc3 ♖ac8 17.c4 ♕c5 18.e5 ♘e8 19.♕e3 ♕e7 20.f4
White was better and went on to win in Ilivitzki – Lisitsin, USSR (ch) 1948.

10...♗a5 11.♗d2 b6?!N
This does not improve on existing theory and I do not think it is likely to attract many followers.

Having said that, the previously played moves are not ideal either:

11...♗c7 12.dxc5 ♘xc5 13.e4 with advantage to White.

11...♗xc3 12.♗xc3 ♘e4 and now both 13.♖fc1 and 13.♗e1 are slightly better for White.

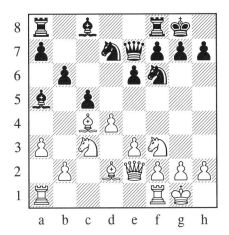

12.e4!

The most principled and also the best continuation.

12.dxc5 bxc5 leads to an approximately equal position; the black c-pawn is not an easy weakness to target, while Black has counterplay along the b-file.

12...♗b7

12...cxd4 13.♘xd4 ♗xc3 14.♗xc3 is clearly better for White.

13.e5

Black will soon run out of good moves.

13...♘g4

13...♘d5 is not good in view of: 14.♗g5 ♕e8 (14...♘xc3 15.♗xe7 ♘xe2† 16.♗xe2 ♖fe8 17.♗d6± ♖ac8? 18.b4+−) 15.♘e4 and White has a large advantage.

14.♗g5!±

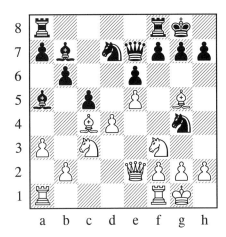

14...f6

Black goes in for a pawn sacrifice, perhaps prepared by Arkadij when opting for the 11...b6? idea. Though if this was indeed Black's aim, it looks a massive risk and Black would not be advised to repeat it. I would be interested to know whether Black has prepared something or was bluffing here!

White has a clear advantage in the event of 14...♗xf3 15.♗xe7 ♗xe2 16.♗xe2 ♖fe8 17.♗d6.

14...♕e8 15.♘e4 cxd4 16.♘d6 ♕b8 17.♘xb7 ♕xb7 18.h3 ♘h6 19.♗xh6 gxh6 20.b4 b5 21.♗d3 ♗c7 22.♗e4+−

15.exf6 ♘dxf6 16.♕xe6†

A good and logical move, though White had an even stronger option at his disposal: 16.♘e5!

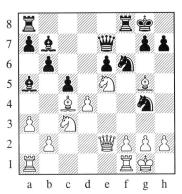

After this, it is difficult to find a way for Black to avoid landing in a lost position immediately!

16...♘h6

The tactical 16...♘xh2?? 17.♔xh2 cxd4 18.♘b5+– simply does not make any sense for Black.

And 16...cxd4? loses to 17.♘xg4 dxc3 18.b4.

17.♘d7!

If Black is lucky, he will end up "only" an exchange down.

16...♕xe6 17.♗xe6† ♔h8

White is a pawn up for no compensation and is clearly better. However, Black still has some motifs for counterplay, and matters are less trivial than White might have hoped.

18.♘b5

18.♖ad1± looks like a solid, sound position a pawn up.

18...♘h6 19.♗xh6

19.♘d6 leads to a large, perhaps winning, advantage for White: 19...♗xf3 (or 19...♗a6 20.♖fd1 ♗e2

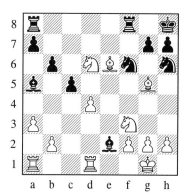

21.♘e5!+–♗xd1 22.♖xd1 ♖ad8 23.dxc5 bxc5 24.♗xh6 ♖xd6 25.♖xd6 ♗c7 26.♘f7† ♖xf7 27.♗xf7 ♖xd6 28.♗d2) 20.gxf3 ♖ad8 21.dxc5 bxc5 22.♘b7 ♖de8 23.♗c4 ♗b6 24.♘d6 ♖d8 25.♖ad1±

19...gxh6 20.♘e5 ♘h5

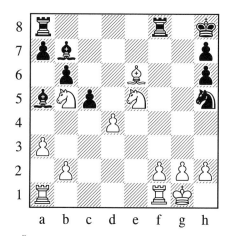

21.♘d6

Now White enters a tactical skirmish, but it seems to me that he had missed that his extra knight on b7 will be a "dead" piece.

21.g3 looks good and simple, especially because Black's tactical motifs do not work, for example: 21...♘f4 22.gxf4 ♖g8† 23.♔g4 h5 24.♘d6 ♗d5 25.dxc5 bxc5 26.♖fd1 and White wins.

21...♗xg2 22.♔xg2 ♘f4† 23.♔h1 ♘xe6 24.♖g1

24.d5 ♘f4 25.♖ad1± still leaves White with the advantage in a sound position.

24...♘g5 25.h4

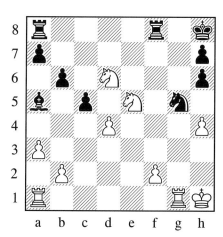

25...♖ad8!

Matters now start to get complicated.

26.♘b7 ♖xd4 27.hxg5 ♗d2! 28.g6

Better was 28.gxh6 ♖xf2 (28...♗xh6 29.♖ad1) 29.♖gf1=.

28...♖xf2=

Black is now out of the woods, and a draw would be the logical outcome.

29.♘f7†?!

White is still looking for a win, but it is no longer to be found. White should have surrendered himself to a draw.

29.♖g2 ♖f5 30.♘c6 ♖h4† 31.♖h2 ♖xh2† 32.♔xh2 ♗g5 33.♖d1 ♖f2† 34.♔g3 ♖xb2∓

29.♖g4 ♖xg4 30.♘xg4 ♖e2 31.gxh7 ♗g5= 32.♖f1 ♖xb2 33.♖f7 ♖e2 34.♘d6 ♖e7 35.♘f6 ♗xf6 36.♖xf6 ♔xh7 37.♘f5 ♖e1† 38.♔g2 ♖a1 39.♖xh6† ♔g8 40.♖h3 ♖a2† 41.♔f1 b5=

29...♔g7 30.♖g2 ♖h4†!

It seems likely that White had been counting on 30...♖xg2?! 31.gxh7!.

31.♔g1 ♖xg2† 32.♔xg2 hxg6 33.♖d1 ♗f4 34.♘fd8

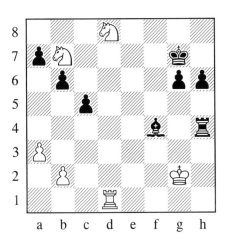

34...♔f6

There is material equality on the board at the moment, but the white pieces are very badly coordinated, the knights are locked out of play and the white queenside pawns are weak. Black is clearly better and the end comes quickly. White must have been rather shocked with the swift change of fortunes in this game!

35.♖d7 ♔f5 36.♘d6† ♔g4 37.♘e6 ♖h2† 38.♔g1 ♗xd6 39.♖xd6 ♖xb2 40.♘c7 ♔f5

0–1

GAME 43

▷ **V. Potkin (2682)**
▶ **A. Grischuk (2746)**
FIDE World Cup, Khanty-Mansiysk
Round 4, Game 1, 06.09.2011 **[E73]**
Annotated by Arkadij Naiditsch

It is quite popular to search for new opportunities in openings which are today a little forgotten. I think that Grischuk had an aggressive attitude in this game and truly wanted to win. This is demonstrated firstly by his choice of opening and then later by his selection of a rare continuation. However, in the end it turned out badly for him. The most critical line in this variation is 7...c6 8.♕d2 ♘c7 9.♗f3 d5! when I cannot find any advantage for White, although the position remains very complex. Also critical are 7...c6 8.♕d2 d5!? as played in the ensuing rapid game between Potkin and Grischuk, and the improvement 14...a4!? to the game Ivanchuk – Radjabov.

1.d4 ♘f6 2.c4 g6 3.♘c3 ♗g7 4.e4 d6 5.♗e2 0–0 6.♗g5

Averbakh's variation of the King's Indian Defence is not as popular today as it has been in the past. The idea of the variation is that

White does not rush with the move ♘f3, thereby gaining additional possibilities. One is the option to play f2-f4; and the second arises if the centre is closed (by ...e5, d4-d5) with the typical g2-g4 move, the aim of which is to gain space and hinder Black from carrying out the standard ...f5 break.

6...♘a6

The most popular plan is 6...c5.

7.f4

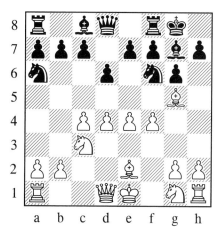

7...♕e8

The more common move is:

7...c6

After this, Black may try to develop his game in a several different ways: ...♘c7 and ...b5, seeking active opportunities on the queenside, or the manoeuvre ...♘c7-e6 aimed against the white bishop on g5, or thirdly the ...d5 break in the centre.

8.♕d2

8.♘f3 is the main alternative.

8...♘c7

8...d5!? 9.exd5 cxd5 10.♗xf6 exf6 (10...♗xf6 11.♘xd5 ♗g7 12.♘f3 ♗g4 13.♖d1±) 11.♘xd5 (11.c5 b6 12.cxb6 ♕xb6 13.♘xd5∞) and now Black may choose to aim for pressure down the e-file or to immediately undermine the knight

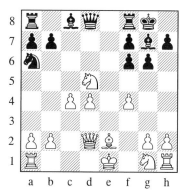

a) 11...♖e8 12.♘f3 (12.♘c3 ♕c7 13.♔f2 ♗e6 14.c5 ♘xc5 15.dxc5 ♖ad8↑) 12...♗e6 13.♘e3 ♕e7 14.♔f2 (14.0–0 seems to lose a tempo after 14...♗d7 15.♔f2 ♗c6 16.♖ae1 ♖ad8 17.d5 ♘c5 18.♗d3 ♕c7 19.g3 a5 20.♔g2 ♗d7 21.♘d1 f5 22.b3 b5⇄ Potkin – Grischuk, FIDE World Cup [4.4 – rapid], Khanty-Mansiysk 2011) 14...♖ad8 15.♖ad1 f5 16.♖he1 ♘c5 17.♔g1 ♘e4 18.♕a5 ♕d6 19.g3±

b) 11...b5 12.♘e3 bxc4 13.♗f3 (13.♘f3!?) 13...♖b8 14.♘e2 ♗e6 15.d5 ♘b4 16.0–0 f5 17.♖ad1 ♕b6 18.♔h1 ♖fd8 19.♘c3 ♕c7 20.a3 ♘d3 21.dxe6 fxe6 22.b4 ♘xf4 23.♕c1 ♘d3 24.♘cd5 ♕f7 25.♕xc4 ♘b2 26.♕c5 ♘xd1 27.♘e7† ♔h8 28.♖xd1 ♗f8 29.♕e5† ♗g7 30.♕c5=

9.♗f3

A new and interesting plan employed recently by Ivanchuk. Although White delays finishing his development, we will see that the set-up ♗f3, ♘ge2 can function very well. Black now has three options:

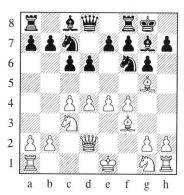

a) 9...♘d7!? 10.♘ge2 f5?! (After 10...f6!? 11.♗h4 e5 12.♗f2± White has more space, but Black may get some counterplay by taking on f4 and playing ...c5 to gain control of the e5-square. Weaker for White is 12.fxe5 dxe5 13.d5 cxd5 14.cxd5 ♘e8, and with the knight setting up a blockade on d6, the white pieces on f3 and e2 are not so well placed.) 11.exf5 gxf5 12.0–0 ♘f6 13.d5± e5? 14.fxe5 dxe5 15.♘g3± Miton – Socko, Bundesliga 2011.

b) 9...d5!

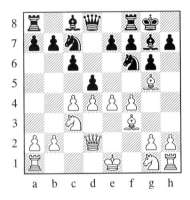

10.e5

10.cxd5 cxd5 11.e5 ♘e4 12.♘xe4 dxe4 13.♗xe4 f6 (13...♘e6 14.♘e2 ♘xg5 15.fxg5 f6⇄) 14.♗h4 was Hernandez Carmenates – Libiszewski, Montcada 2011, and now Black should play: 14...fxe5N 15.fxe5 ♗xe5 16.♘f3 ♗f4 17.♕d3 ♗f5 18.0–0 ♘d5=
10.♗xf6 exf6 11.exd5 cxd5 12.c5∞

10...♘e4 11.♘xe4 dxe4 12.♗xe4 ♘e6 13.♘f3
13.0–0–0 f6 14.exf6 exf6 15.♗h4 ♕xd4 16.♕xd4 ♘xd4 17.♖xd4!? f5 18.♗xc6 ♗xd4 19.♗d5† ♔g7 20.♘f3 ♗e3† 21.♔c2 ♗xf4 22.♖e1 ♗d6 23.♗f2↑
13.♗h4 ♕xd4 14.♕xd4 ♘xd4 15.♗xe7 ♖e8 16.♗d6 ♗f5 17.♗xf5 ♘xf5 18.c5 f6⇄

13...f6 14.♗h4 fxe5 15.fxe5 ♖f4 16.♕e3
16.♕d3 ♘xd4 17.0–0–0 ♗h6 18.♗g5 ♖xf3 19.gxf3 ♗xg5† 20.♔b1 c5 21.♖hg1 ♗f4 22.♗xg6 ♔h8 23.♗xh7 ♕f8↑

16...♕a5†

16...♗h6!? 17.♗g3 ♕a5† 18.♔f1 ♖xf3† 19.♕xf3 ♘g5 20.♕e2 ♘xe4 21.♕xe4 ♗e6 22.♕d3 ♖f8† 23.♔g1 b5 24.h3 ♗xc4 25.♕c3 ♖xc3 26.bxc3 ♗d2 27.♗e1 ♗e3† 28.♔h2 ♗f4†=

17.♔f1

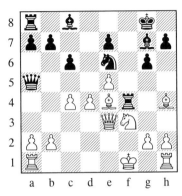

17...♕b6

17...♗h6 18.♗xe7 (18.♗f2!?) 18...♕b6 19.g3 ♕xb2 20.♖d1 (20.♖b1 ♖f7 21.♖xb2 [21.♕xh6 ♕xd4 22.♕h4 ♕xc4† 23.♔g1 ♘f4 24.gxf4 ♕xe4 25.♖d1 ♗e6 26.♘g5 ♕c2∓] 21...♗xe3 22.♗f6 ♘xd4=) 20...♖xf3† 21.♕xf3 ♘xd4 22.♕f2 ♗h3† 23.♗g2 ♘c2 24.♗xh3 ♘e3† 25.♔g1 ♘xd1 26.♕xb2 ♘xb2∞

18.♖d1 ♕xb2

18...♗e5?! 19.♗f2 ♗g7 20.b3 ♗d7 21.g3 ♖f7 22.♔g2±

19.g3 ♖f7

19...♖xf3† 20.♗xf3 g5 21.♖d2 ♕b1† 22.♔f2 ♕g6 23.d5 gxh4 24.dxe6 ♗xe6 25.♖hd1±

20.d5 ♗h6 21.♕xh6 ♘d4 22.♕e3

22.♖xd4 ♕xd4 23.e6 ♗xe6 24.dxe6 ♖ff8 25.♗xg6 ♕d1† 26.♔g2 ♕e2† 27.♔g1=

22...♗h3† 23.♔e1 ♘xf3† 24.♗xf3 ♖xf3 25.♕xf3 ♖f8 26.♗f6 exf6 27.e6∞

c) 9...♘e6 10.♗h4 c5 11.dxc5
11.d5 ♘d4 12.♘ge2 ♘xf3† 13.gxf3∞

11...♘xc5 12.♖d1
Otherwise after ...♗e6 White will not have b2-b3 because of ...♘xe4.

12...♗e6 13.b3 a5 14.♘ge2

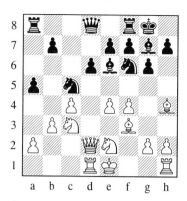

14...a4!?

The white king has not yet castled, so Black can try this active alternative.

14...♕c7 15.0–0± a4 16.f5 gxf5 17.exf5 ♗xf5 18.♗xf6 exf6 19.b4 ♘e6 20.♘b5 ♕b6† 21.♔h1 ♘g5 22.♗xb7± Ivanchuk – Radjabov, Medias 2011.

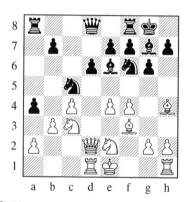

15.♘d4

15.b4 ♘cd7 16.♕d3 (16.c5 dxc5 17.e5 cxb4 18.♘b5 b3 19.exf6 ♘xf6∞) 16...♘b6 17.e5 (17.c5 ♘c4 18.e5 ♘b2 19.♕c2 ♘xd1 20.exf6 ♗xf6 21.♗xf6 exf6 22.♕xd1 dxc5 23.bxc5 ♕a5∞) 17...dxe5 18.c5 ♕xd3 19.♖xd3 ♘c4 20.♗xb7 ♖ab8 21.c6 ♗f5 22.fxe5 ♗xd3 23.exf6 exf6∞

15.e5 dxe5 16.fxe5 ♘g4 17.b4 ♘d7 (17...♕xd2† 18.♖xd2 ♘d7 19.♗xb7 ♖a7 20.♗f3 ♘dxe5∞) 18.♗xg4 ♗xg4 19.♘d5↑ ♖e8 20.h3 ♗e6 21.♘ef4 ♗xd5 (21...♗xe5

22.♘xe6 fxe6 23.♘xe7† ♖xe7 24.♗e2 ♔f7 25.♖hf1† ♔e8 26.c5 ♕c7 27.♗xe7 ♔xe7 28.♕g5† ♘f6 29.♖d6 ♗b2 30.♕e3±) 22.♘xd5 ♗xe5 23.0–0 f6 24.c5↑

15...axb3 16.axb3 ♕a5

16...♗g4 17.0–0 (17.♕c2 ♗xf3 18.♘xf3 ♘g4 19.♘d5 ♗f6 20.♗xf6 ♘xf6 21.♘xf6† exf6 22.0–0 ♕b6 23.♔h1 ♕xb3 24.♕xb3 ♘xb3 25.♖xd6=) 17...♗xf3 18.gxf3±

17.0–0

17.f5 ♗h6 18.♕xh6 ♕xc3† 19.♕d2 ♘fxe4 20.♕xc3 ♘xc3 21.fxe6 ♖xd1 22.♗xd1 ♖a2 23.♘c2 fxe6 24.♗xe7 ♖f4 25.♗xd6 ♖e4† 26.♔f2 ♘xb3 27.♔g3 ♖xc4∞

17...♕b6

Berczes – Spasov, Sibenik 2011, was agreed drawn here.

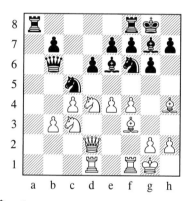

18.♘xe6

18.e5 dxe5 19.fxe5 ♘fd7 20.♘xe6 (20.♕f2 ♘xe5 21.♘xe6 fxe6 22.♗xe7 ♘xf3† 23.gxf3 ♖f5=) 20...♘xe6† 21.♗f2 ♕xb3 22.♕xd7 ♕xc3=

18.♗f2 ♕xb3 19.♕b2 ♗xc4 20.e5 ♘d7 21.♘e6 (21.♘d5 ♗xd5 22.♘f5 ♘d4 23.♘xe7† ♔h8 24.♗xd4 ♕xb2 25.♗xb2 ♗xf3 26.♖xf3 ♖fe8 27.♘d5 ♖ac8=) 21...♘bc5 22.♕xb6 ♘xb6 23.♘xf8 ♗xf1 24.♘xg6 hxg6 25.♔xf1 ♘c4∞

18...♘xb3†

18...♘xe6† 19.♔h1 ♕xb3 20.e5 dxe5 21.fxe5 ♖fd8 22.♕e1 ♖xd1 23.♗xd1 ♕xc4 24.exf6 ♗xf6 25.♗xf6 exf6 26.♖xf6±

19.♕f2 ♛xf2† 20.♖xf2 fxe6 21.e5 dxe5
22.fxe5 ♘e8 23.♗xe7
  23.♗xb7 ♖b8 24.♖xf8† ♔xf8 25.♖d7 ♗xe5
26.♗xe7† ♔g8 27.♘e4 ♘a5 28.♗a6 ♘c6
29.♗c5 ♘c7 30.♘f6† ♗xf6 31.♖xc7 ♘e5=
23...♖f7 24.♗xb7 ♖xf2 25.♔xf2 ♖a7 26.♖d7
♘a5 27.♖d5 ♖a6 28.♗b7 ♖a7= 29.♗c8 ♖xd7
30.♗xd7 ♔f7 31.♗d8 ♘xc4 32.♘e4 h6
33.♘c5 ♘xe5 34.♗xe6† ♔f8=

8.♘f3 e5

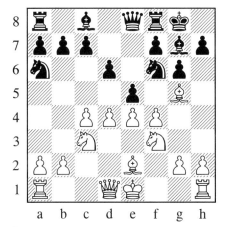

9.fxe5

Capturing the other way does not promise
White any advantage:
9.dxe5 dxe5 10.♘xe5 ♘c5 11.♗f3 h6
  11...♘e6 12.♗xf6 ♗xf6 13.♘d3 ♗xc3†
14.bxc3 ♕c6 15.f5 ♘g5 16.0–0∞ and the
position is somewhat unclear. However,
White may easily develop a strong initiative
because the dark squares are very weak and
the bishop on c8 is blocked in.
12.♗h4
  12.♗xf6 ♗xf6 13.♘d3 ♗xc3† 14.bxc3 ♘xe4
(14...♘xd3† 15.♕xd3 ♗e6 16.0–0 ♖d8
17.♕e3 ♗xc4 18.♖fd1 b6 19.f5↑) 15.0–0
♗f5 16.g4 ♘xc3 17.♕d2 ♗xd3 18.♕xd3
♘a4 19.♗d5 ♔g7 20.♕d4† f6 21.♗xb7 ♖d8
22.♕xa7∞
12...g5 13.♗g3
  13.♗f2 ♘fxe4 14.♘xe4 ♘xe4 15.♗xe4 gxf4
16.0–0 ♕xe5=

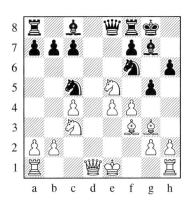

13...g4
  13...♘fxe4 14.♘xe4 ♘xe4 15.♗xe4 gxf4
16.♗xf4 ♗xe5 17.0–0 ♗xb2 18.♖b1 ♕xe4
19.♖xb2±
14.♗f2 ♕e7 15.♗xg4 ♗xg4
  15...♘xg4 16.♘d5 ♕d6 17.♘xg4 ♘xe4
18.0–0 ♗xg4 19.♕xg4 f5 20.♕h4 c6∓
16.♗xc5 ♕xc5 17.♘xg4 ♘xg4 18.♕xg4 ♖ad8
19.♕e2 ♖fe8↑
The black pieces are very active, and the
white king remains in the centre.

9...dxe5 10.d5

White rarely tries:
10.dxe5
This type of move is usually weak. White
spoils his strong centre and Black will gain
play on the dark squares. However, let us see
some specific variations.
10...♘g4
  10...♘d7 11.♘d5 c6 (11...♘xe5 transposes
to 10...♘g4) 12.♘f6† ♗xf6 13.exf6 ♕xe4
14.0–0±
11.♘d5 ♘xe5
  11...♗e6 12.0–0 ♘xe5 13.♘f6† ♗xf6
14.♗xf6 ♘g4 15.♗c3±
  11...c6 12.♘e7† ♔h8 13.♕d6 ♗e6 14.h3
♘xe5 15.♘xe5 ♖d8 16.♕xd8 ♕xd8
17.♘7xg6†±
12.♗f6
  12.♘f6† ♗xf6 13.♗xf6 ♘g4∓
  12.♗e7 c6 13.♗xf8 ♕xf8∓ The bishop on g7
is not worse than a white rook.

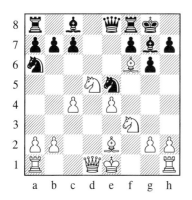

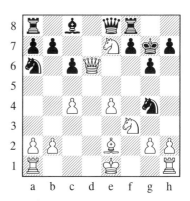

12...c6

Other moves are:

a) 12...♘xf3† 13.♗xf3 ♗e6 14.♘e7† ♔h8 15.♕d4 ♕xe7 16.♗xg7† ♔g8 17.♗xf8 ♖xf8 18.0–0±

b) 12...♘d7 13.e5 c6 14.♘e7† ♔h8 15.♕d4±

c) 12...♘g4 13.♗xg7 ♔xg7 14.♕d4† f6 15.h3 ♘e5 16.0–0 ♘xf3† 17.♗xf3 ♕e5 18.♕xe5 fxe5 19.♖xf8 ♔xf8 20.♖f1† ♔g7 21.c5 and now:

c1) 21...♘xc5 22.♘xc7 ♖b8 23.♗c4 b5 (23...♘xe4 24.♖f7† ♔h6 25.♖f8 ♘d6 26.♗e6 ♔g7 27.♖d8 ♔f6 28.♖xd6 ♔e7 29.♖d5 ♗xe6 30.♖xe5 ♔d6 31.♖xe6† ♔xc7 32.♖e7† ♔c6 33.♖xh7±) 24.♖f7† ♔h6 25.♘xb5 ♗e6 26.♖xe6 ♘xe6 27.♘d6 ♖xb2 28.♖xa7 ♔g5 29.♘c4 ♖c2 30.♘xe5 ♔f4⩲ One of the ways of defending inferior endings is to change the character of the game. Instead of passive defence, it is sometimes worth sacrificing material in order to gain activity.

c2) 21...c6 22.♗xa6 cxd5 23.♗e2 ♗e6 (23...dxe4 24.♗c4 e3 25.♖f7† ♔h6 26.♔f1±) 24.exd5 ♗xd5 25.♖d1 ♗c6 26.b4 ♖f8 Cutting off the white king. 27.b5 ♗e4 28.a4±

13.♘e7† ♔h8 14.♕d6

The most important factor is who can take control of the dark squares f6, e5, d4 etc.

14...♘g4 15.♗xg7† ♔xg7

White now chooses which side to castle:

a) **16.0–0 ♗e6**

16...♕d8!? 17.c5 ♕xd6 18.cxd6 ♘c5 19.♘g5 (19.e5 ♗e6 20.h3 ♘e3 21.♖fc1 ♘d7∞ Hoang Thanh Trang – Szuk, Hungary 1998) 19...♘e5 20.♖ac1 ♘e6 21.♘f3 ♘xf3† 22.♗xf3 ♗d7 The position is unclear. The knight on e7 and pawn on d6 hamper the actions of Black. However, if White is not careful, these pieces may prove to be a weakness.

17.♘g5 ♖d8 18.♕a3

18.♘xe6†?! fxe6 19.♕xe6 ♘c5 20.♕xg4 ♕xe7⩱

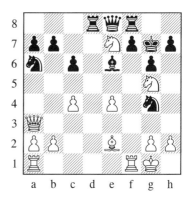

18...♗d7!?

18...♘e5 19.♘f5† ♗xf5 20.exf5 ♘d3 21.♘e6† (21.f6† ♔g8 22.♕e7 ♖d7 23.♕xe8 ♖xe8 24.♗xd3 ♖xd3 25.♖ad1 ♖xd1 26.♖xd1 h6 27.♘f3 ♘c5 28.b4 ♘e4 29.♖d7 ♖b8 30.♘e5 ♘xf6 31.♖c7 ♖e8 32.♘xf7 ♔g4 33.g3 ♖f8 34.♘d6 ♘e3=) 21...fxe6 22.♗xd3 ♕d7 (22...gxf5 23.♕c3† and White may continue with ♖f3 or g2-g4, with a strong attack) 23.fxg6 ♕d4† (23...hxg6 24.♖xf8 ♖xf8 25.♕c3† ♔f6 26.♖f1 ♕e7 27.♕xf6† ♕xf6 28.♖xf6 ♔xf6 29.♔f2 and White has the more pleasant ending because of the possibility of creating a outside passed h-pawn) 24.♔h1 ♘c5 25.gxh7 ♕xd3 26.♖xf8 ♖xf8 27.♕xc5 ♖f1† 28.♖xf1 ♕xf1† 29.♕g1 ♕xc4 30.b3±

19.♖f4

19.♖ad1 h6 20.♘h3 ♘f6 21.♖xf6 (21.♘f2 ♗e6 22.e5 ♘d7 23.♘xc6 bxc6 24.♕xa6 ♘xe5 25.♕xa7 ♗xc4 26.♖xd8 ♕xd8 27.♕e3 ♕g5=) 21...♔xf6 22.♘f4 ♔g7 23.♕c3† ♔h7 24.♕f6 ♘c5 25.♘h5 gxh5 26.♖d6 ♗e6 27.♘f5 ♗xf5 28.♕xf5† ♔g7 29.♖xh6 ♔xh6 30.♕xh5† ♔g7 31.♕g5†=

19...♘e5

19...h6 20.♘f3 b6 (20...g5 21.♘xg5 hxg5 22.♖xg4 ♗xg4 23.♗xg4 c5 24.♘f5† ♔g8 25.♖e1+−) 21.h3 ♘f6 22.♘xg6 fxg6 23.e5 ♘h5 24.♖xf8 ♕xf8 25.♕xa6 ♕c5† 26.♔h2 ♕f2⇄

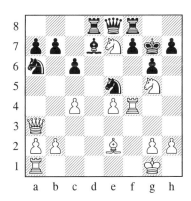

20.♖af1

20.♘f5† gxf5 21.exf5 f6 22.♘xh7 ♔xh7 23.♕g3 ♘g6 24.fxg6† ♔g7 25.♗d3∞

20...f6 21.h4 h5 22.g4

22.♖xf6 ♖xf6 23.♖xf6 ♗g4⇄

22...♗xg4 23.♗xg4 ♘xg4 24.♘e6† ♔f7 25.♘g5† ♔g7=

b) 16.0–0–0!?N f6

16...c5 17.♘g5→

16...♗e6 17.g5 ♖d8 18.♘xe6† fxe6 19.♕xd8 ♕xd8 20.♖xd8 ♖xd8 21.♗xg4 ♔f6 22.♘xc6±

17.h4!

17.e5 ♘f2 18.♖df1 ♘xh1 19.exf6† ♖xf6 20.♕e5 ♗e6 21.♘g5 ♕xe7 22.♖xf6 ♕xf6 23.♘xe6† ♔f7 24.♘g5†=

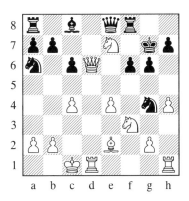

17...♖f7

17...♘f2 18.h5 ♘xd1 19.hxg6 hxg6 20.♗xd1 ♖h8 21.e5+−

17...h5 18.e5 ♖f7 (18...♘f2 19.♘hf1 ♘xd1 20.♘d4 f5 21.♗xd1+−) 19.♘xc8 ♖xc8 20.♘g5 ♘xe5 21.♘xf7 ♘xf7 22.♕d2±

18.♘xc8 ♕xc8

18...♖xc8 19.h5 ♕xe4 20.♘d4→

19.h5 ♕c7 20.♕d2

20.hxg6 ♕xd6 21.♖xd6 hxg6 22.♘d4 ♘e5 23.♘e6† ♔g8 24.c5 ♘c7 25.♘xc7 ♖xc7 26.♖xf6 ♖e7 White has an extra pawn, but making use of it will not be simple because of the strong knight.

20...gxh5 21.♘d4 ♔h8 22.♗xg4 hxg4 23.♘f5 ♘c5 24.♘d6 ♖e7 25.♕e3 b6 26.♔b1 White retains some initiative.

10...♘c5!?

10...h6 has usually been played here.

11.♘d2

11.♗xf6!? is interesting. At the cost of weakening his dark squares, White gains a large

space advantage on the queenside. 11...♗xf6
12.b4 ♘d7 (12...♘a6 13.a3 c5 14.♖b1±)
13.c5 ♗g7 14.0–0±

11...♘h5

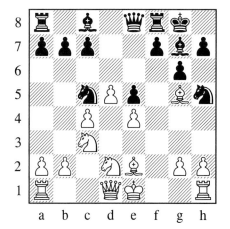

A typical idea in this type of structure.
Allowing the doubling of his h-pawns, Black
wants to carry out his main plan with ...f5 very
quickly, and moreover he gains the g-file for
his attack. An additional problem for White is
that conceding his light-squared bishop makes
it much more difficult to fight for the light
squares, especially the crucial e4-square. These
ideas can also be found in the Benoni Defence.

12.♗xh5

White could also consider:
12.b4 ♘f4
   12...♘a6±

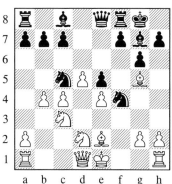

13.bxc5

  13.0–0 ♘a4 14.♘b5 c6 15.♘c7 ♕d7
16.♘xa8 ♘c3 17.♗g4 ♘fe2† 18.♕xe2
♘xe2† 19.♗xe2 b6 20.♗e3 ♗b7 21.♘xb6
axb6 22.♗xb6 cxd5 23.exd5 ♕a4∞

  13...♘xg2† 14.♔f2 ♘f4 15.♗f1
    15.♘b5?! ♘h3† 16.♔e1 ♘xg5 17.♘xc7
    ♕d8 18.♘xa8 ♕a5 19.♕c2 f5 (19...♗h6
    20.♔d1 ♗d7∞) 20.♖b1 fxe4 21.♖b5 ♕d8
    22.♕b3 ♘f3† 23.♗xf3 exf3 24.h4 ♗h6→
    15.♗xf4 exf4 16.♖c1 ♕e7 17.♘f3 ♕xc5†
    18.♔g2 ♖e8⯹
  15...f5 16.♔g1 h6 17.♗h4±

12...gxh5 13.♕xh5

  13.0–0 f5 14.♕c2 ♘xe4 15.♘dxe4 ♕g6
16.♗e7 ♖f7 17.♗c5 b6 18.♗a3 fxe4 19.♖xf7
♔xf7 20.♖f1† ♔g8 21.♘xe4 ♔h8 22.♗f8 ♗f5
23.♗xg7† ♔xg7 24.♖e1 ♖e8 25.♖e3 h4∞

13...♘d3† 14.♔e2 ♘f4†

  14...♘xb2 15.♖ab1 ♘a4 16.♘xa4 ♕xa4
17.♗h6 f6 18.♖b3→

15.♗xf4 exf4

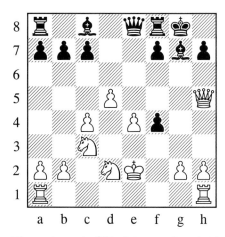

The main goal of Black is to seek an initiative
by opening the position (with ...f5, or ...c6 and
...b5). White needs to look out for his king in
the centre, because the black bishops could
become very dangerous.

16.♖hf1

White may also play:

16.g3!? f5

16...fxg3 17.hxg3 h6 18.g4→

16...f3† 17.♔xf3 a5 18.♔g2 ♖a6 19.♖he1
♖g6 20.♕e2±

17.♕xe8 ♖xe8 18.gxf4

18.♘b5 f3† 19.♔xf3 fxe4† 20.♘xe4 ♖e7
21.♖ae1 ♗h3 22.g4 ♗e5 23.♘g3 ♖f8†
24.♘f5 h5⇄

18...fxe4 19.♖hg1 ♔f7 20.♘e3

Black does not have enough compensation.

16...♗e5

16...♕e7 17.♖xf4 f5 18.♖af1 ♗d7 19.♔d1±

17.g3

Also good is:

17.♔d3 f5 18.♕xe8 fxe4† 19.♘cxe4

19.♘dxe4 ♖xe8 20.♖ae1 ♗f5 21.g4 ♗g6
22.♔d2 c6 23.♘c5 ♗d4 (23...♔f7 24.♘d3
♗xc3† 25.♔xc3 cxd5 26.c5±) 24.♘e6
(24.♘xb7 ♗e3† 25.♔e2 cxd5 26.♘xd5
♖ab8 27.♘f6† ♔g7 28.♘xe8† ♗xe8 29.♘d6
♖xb2† 30.♔f3 ♗c6† 31.♘e4 ♖c2 32.♖xe3
fxe3 33.♔xe3 ♗xe4 34.♔xe4 ♖xc4†=)
24...♗e3† 25.♖xe3 fxe3† 26.♔xe3 ♗f7
27.♘e4 ♗e7 28.♘4g5 cxd5 29.cxd5 ♖c8∞

19...♖xe8 20.♘f3 ♗xb2

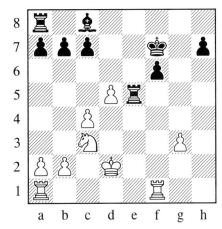

21.♘d4 ♗xa1 22.♘f6† ♔f7 23.♘xe8 ♔xe8
23...♗xd4 24.♘xc7 ♗e5 25.♘xa8 b6 26.a4
♗b7 27.♘xb6 axb6 28.♖b1+–
24.♖xa1±

17...fxg3 18.♘f3 ♗g7 19.e5 ♗xe5

19...a5 20.♖g1 ♖a6 21.♖xg3 ♖g6 22.♖ag1
♕e7 23.♔d3±

**20.♘xe5 f6 21.♕xe8 ♖xe8 22.hxg3 ♖xe5†
23.♔d2 ♔f7**

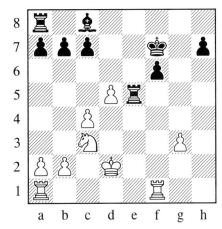

The ending which has resulted is
advantageous for White, because the pressure
on the f-pawn will force it to move to f5, which
will considerably weaken Black's dark squares
and seriously limit his bishop.

24.♖f4 ♖f5

Grischuk is a great technical player who
can defend inferior positions very well, and
he exchanged a pair of rooks in the belief that
by simplifying the material it would become
easier to seek drawing opportunities. But in
this position there are still many pieces on the
board and it might be more interesting from
a practical point of view to keep all the rooks
on, in the hope of gaining counterplay. As a
general principle, it is the stronger side who
should be aiming to exchange one pair of
rooks in order to avoid potential counterplay.

24...♗f5 25.♖af1 ♗g6 26.♘b5±

24...♗d7!? 25.♖af1

25.♘e4 ♗f5 26.♘c5 ♖ae8 27.♖af1 b6

28.♘a6 ♖e2† 29.♔d1 ♖xb2 30.♖xf5 ♖ee2
31.♖xf6† ♔g7 32.♘b4 ♖g2=

25...f5 26.g4 c6

26...♖g8 27.gxf5 White has captured the pawn, but as a result his rooks have suddenly lost their activity, unlike the black rooks. Black may play:

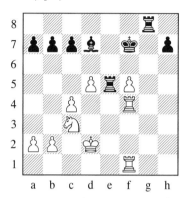

a) 27...♖g2† 28.♔d3 ♖xb2 29.♔d4 ♖e8
30.♘e4 ♖g2 31.♖h1 ♖h8 32.♘c5 ♗c8
33.♖h6 ♔g7 34.♘e6† ♗xe6 35.♖xe6 ♔f7
36.f6 ♖e8 37.♖xe8 ♔xe8 38.♖h4±
b) 27...h5 28.♘e4 (28.♔d3 ♖g4=) 28...c6
(28...♖g4 29.♖xg4 hxg4 30.♘g3 c6 31.♔d3
cxd5 32.♔d4±) 29.♖e1 cxd5 30.♘g5† ♔xg5
31.♖xe5 dxc4 32.♖d5 (32.♖xc4 ♔f6⇄)
32...♗c6 33.♖d6±

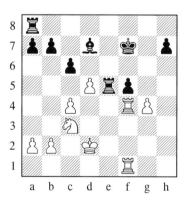

27.dxc6

27.gxf5 cxd5 28.cxd5 ♔f6 29.♘e4† ♔f7
30.♘g5† ♔g8 31.d6 h6 32.♘e6 ♗xe6
33.fxe6 ♖xe6 34.♖f6 ♖xf6 35.♖xf6 ♖e8
36.♖xh6 ♔g7=

27...bxc6 28.gxf5 ♖g8 29.♘e4 ♖g2† 30.♔c3
c5 31.♖h1
   31.f6 ♗c6 32.♘d6† ♔f8 33.♖1f2 ♖xf2
34.♖xf2 a5⇄
31...♗xf5 32.♖xf5† ♖xf5 33.♘d6† ♔e6
34.♘xf5 ♔xf5 35.♖xh7 ♖g3† 36.♔c2 ♔e4
37.♖d7 a5 38.a4±
   38.♖d5 a4⇄

25.♖af1 ♖xf4 26.♖xf4 ♗d7

26...a6 27.♘e4 (27.♔d3 ♔g6 28.♔d4 h5
29.♘e4 ♗f5⇄) 27...f5 28.♘c5±

26...♔g6 27.♘b5 c6 28.♘c7 ♖b8 29.d6±

27.♘e4 f5 28.♘c5 ♗c8 29.b4 b6 30.♘d3±

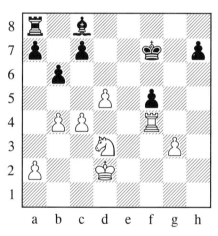

White has the better structure and pieces, as well as a simple plan to realize his advantage on the dark squares.

**30...♔f6 31.♖h4 ♔g7 32.♔c3 ♗d7 33.♘e5
♗e8 34.♔d4 h5 35.♘d3 ♗f7 36.♘f4 ♖e8
37.♘xh5† ♗xh5 38.♖xh5+− ♖e4† 39.♔d3
b5 40.c5!**

The final precise move.

**40...♖e5 41.d6 cxd6 42.c6 ♖e4 43.♖xf5
♖xb4 44.♖f2**
1–0

GAME 44

▷ E. Tomashevsky (2710)
▶ R. Ponomariov (2758)
European Club Cup, Rogaska Slatina
28.09.2011[E81]
Annotated by Borki Predojevic

This was part of a very important match in the 4th round of the 2011 European Club Cup. In his game against Tomashevsky, Ponomariov tried to reach a complicated position by choosing the King's Indian. Tomashevsky didn't deviate from his favourite Sämisch variation. Ponomariov went for the very popular line with 9...h5, where he has recent experience as White. I am sure that Pono had prepared an improvement after 12.♞d2, but sadly for him, he couldn't show it to us. Tomashevsky played the concrete 12.f4! and demonstrated brilliant high-level preparation. After White sacrificed an exchange for an attack, it was clear that Ponomariov's position was critical. Very soon Black was faced with serious problems and White won a very nice and easy game.

It seems that 12.f4! refutes the whole line with 9...h5. Since Black needs an alternative, I decided to also give some examples of the main line which arises after 9...e6.

1.d4 ♞f6 2.c4 g6 3.♞c3 ♝g7 4.e4 d6 5.f3 0–0 6.♝e3 c5 7.♞ge2 ♞c6 8.d5 ♞e5 9.♞g3

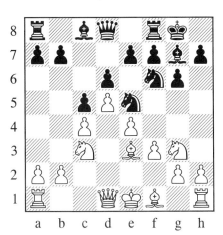

9...h5

This line recently became popular at the highest level; of course Black's main idea is to harass the g3-knight. In the old main line (see below) Black plays ...h5 later, when White has time to castle and so has the typical reaction ♞h1-f2.

The old main line, to which Black may need to return, is:
9...e6 10.♝e2 exd5 11.cxd5

And here Black has two plans. The first plan is connected with play on the queenside (...a6, ...♝d7 and ...b5) while the second plan involves the moves ...h7-h5-h4 and then playing on the kingside. We will check both of these plans.

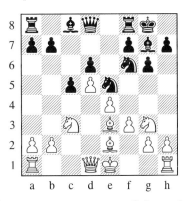

The two starting moves of these plans are A) 11...a6 and B) 11...h5.

A) 11...a6

We now need a further split between A1) 12.a4 and A2) 12.0–0!?.

A1) 12.a4 ♝d7
12...h5 would transpose to 11...h5 (line B). 13.0–0 b5 14.h3 ♞c4!
The best reply.
In the past the main move was 14...♜b8. After 15.axb5 for a long time the theory gave 15...♝xb5 as supposedly leading to easy equality. However, the following game shows that things are not so simple:

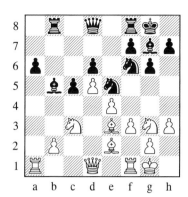

16.♘xb5! axb5 17.b3 ♖e8 (17...♕b6 is unnatural since after 18.♕c2± Black has to take care about the threat of b4) 18.♖a6 ♖e7 19.♕d2 ♘e8 20.♗g5! f6 (20...♘f6 21.♗xf6 ♘xf6 22.g5 ♘e8 23.f4 gives White good attacking chances) 21.♗e3 ♘c7 22.♖a7±↑ White was better in Wang Hao – Inarkiev, Poikovsky 2008.

15.♗xc4 bxc4 16.f4

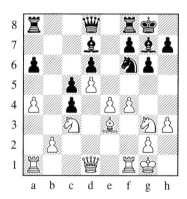

16...♖e8!

The most precise move.

After 16...♖b8 White can play 17.e5↑ and Black will have problems: 17...♘e8 (17...♖e8 18.♕d2 dxe5 19.fxe5 ♖xe5 20.♗f4 ♘e8 21.♗xe5 ♗xe5 22.♘ge4 ♗f5 23.♖ae1 ♘d6 24.♘xc5 ♗g7 25.♔h1± Khairullin – Yevseev, St Petersburg 2010) 18.♕d2 ♕c8 19.♖ae1↑ In this complicated position White has better chances, Tomashevsky – Inarkiev, Russia (ch) 2008.

In Kasimdzhanov – Bologan, Dresden (ol) 2008, White continued with:

17.♕f3 ♖b8 18.♖f2

But after:

18...♖b3 19.♖d1 h5 20.e5 dxe5 21.fxe5 ♖xe5 22.♗xc5 h4 23.♘f1 ♗xa4

White was fighting for equality.

A2) 12.0–0!?

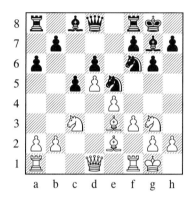

This calm move is very interesting; of course it lets Black play ...b5:

12...b5 13.h3

A typical move; White slowly prepares f4.

13...♖e8 14.♕d2 b4?!

This move looks suspicious.

14...♘c4 15.♗xc4 bxc4 16.♗h6 ♗h8 17.f4 ♖b8 18.♖ae1 ♘d7 19.e5 dxe5 20.f5= looks very nice for White.

14...♗b7 15.♖ae1↑

15.♘d1 h5

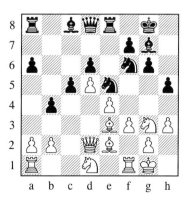

Here I suggest a novelty:

16.♗g5!?N

16.♗h6 has been played, but after 16...♗h8 17.♘e3 h4 18.♘h1 g5! 19.♘f5 ♘h7 20.f4 gxf4 21.♘f2 ♘g6∞ Black had a good position in Bu Xiangzhi – Zhao Jun, Danzhou 2010.

16...♕c7 17.♗h4

It seems White has the better chances. For example:

17...♘h7

White can reply with the typical:

18.f4 ♘d7 19.e5! dxe5 20.f5↑

With a strong initiative.

B) 11...h5 12.0–0

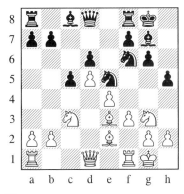

12...♘h7

A fresh example in this position is 12...a6 13.a4 ♕a5 which was played by a very original player, GM Boris Savchenko. However, the last move is not in the spirit of this position. After 14.h3 h4 15.f4! hxg3?! (better is 15...♘ed7 16.♘h1 ♖e8 17.♘f2±) 16.fxe5 dxe5 17.♗g5 ♘e8 18.d6! ♗e6 19.d7 f6 20.dxe8=♕ ♖axe8 21.♗h4± White was much better and won convincingly in Riazantsev – B. Savchenko, Rogaska Slatina 2011.

13.♕d2 h4 14.♘h1 f5

Another line is 14...g5 when I suggest the readers study the games Ivanchuk – Efimenko, Saint Vincent 2005, and Lautier

– Nataf, France (ch) 2004, as examples of how White should play in this variation.

15.♘f2 ♗d7∞

These moves are commonly played in this kind of set-up. Tomashevsky has played many games in this line and is a real expert, which of course is why I have quoted a few of his games as examples of how to treat this position with White.

10.♗e2 h4 11.♘f1 e6

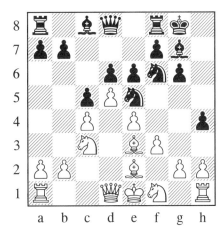

12.f4!

Tomashevsky plays the most concrete move. This very strong idea looks like a refutation of the 9...h5 line and the next few moves are forced.

First, we should consider a couple of other moves White has tried:

In the past White usually reacted with:

12.♘d2

Ponomariov has played this move twice.

12...exd5 13.cxd5 a6

Carlsen's choice here was 13...♗d7 14.0–0 b5, but after 15.♘xb5 ♗xb5 16.♗xb5 ♖b8 17.a4 ♘h5 18.f4! ♘d7 19.♕g4± but Black was worse in Ponomariov – Carlsen, Bazna 2010.

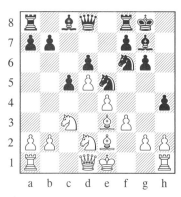

14.a4 ♗d7

14...♖b8?! 15.0–0 ♕e8 16.a5 ♗d7 17.h3!
♗b5 (17...♘h7? 18.f4 ♗h6 19.♕e1 ♕d8
20.♘d1 1–0 Edouard – Lanzani, Rijeka
2010) 18.f4 ♗xe2 19.♕xe2 ♘ed7 20.♗f2±
15.a5 b5 16.axb6 ♕xb6 17.♖a2 ♕b4 18.0–0
♗b5∞

The position was unclear in Ponomariov –
Grischuk, Wijk aan Zee 2011.

12.h3

This looks too slow.
12...exd5 13.cxd5 b5!

Black has the initiative.

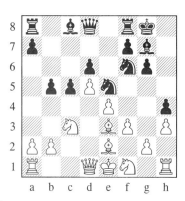

14.♘xb5

Worse is 14.f4?! ♘c4 15.♗xc4 bxc4 16.♘d2
♖e8 17.♕f3 ♖b8 18.0–0 ♖xb2∓ Oms Pallisse
– Damljanovic, Andorra (op) 2006.
14.♗xb5 ♖b8⯐
14...♖b8⯐

Black has excellent compensation.

12...♘eg4

12...♘ed7? is of course poor due to 13.dxe6±.

13.♗xg4

Worse is 13.♗g1? exd5 14.cxd5 b5! and
Black is already better. After 15.h3 b4 16.♘a4
♘h6 17.e5 dxe5 18.fxe5 ♘xd5∓ White had
serious problems in V. Gunina – O. Girya,
St Petersburg 2008.

13...♘xg4 14.♕xg4 exd5 15.f5

The natural move; instead 15.♕f3? d4↑ gives
Black a good game.

15...d4 16.♘d5

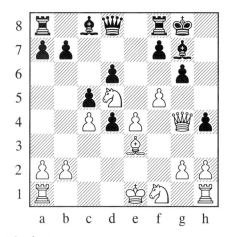

16...dxe3

Worse   is: 16...gxf5?   17.exf5   ♖e8
(17...dxe3   18.♘fxe3→)   18.0–0–0   dxe3
19.♘fxe3 ♔f8 20.♕f4 ♗e5 21.♕h6† ♗g7
22.♕f4 ♗e5 23.♕h6† ♗g7 24.♕h5± White
had a strong attack in Ward – Ye Jiangchuan
London 1997.

17.♘fxe3!

After 17.0–0–0 Black has the strong
intermediate move 17...e2! After 18.♕xe2
♖e8 (18...b5!? also looks promising) 19.fxg6
fxg6 20.♕d3 b5! 21.♘fe3 bxc4 22.♘xc4 ♗a6∓
White is faced with a hard task defending his
inferior position.

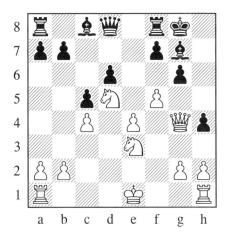

17...♗xb2N

This logical move is a novelty. It is easy to see that White is dominating the kingside thanks to the weakness on g6 – if the black pawn were on h7 the black king would be much safer.

Previously Black had played:
17...♕a5†?!
This looks extremely dubious.
18.b4!

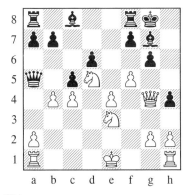

18...♕d8
18...cxb4 19.♘e7† ♔h7 20.fxg6† fxg6 21.♕xg6† ♔h8 22.♘3d5 b3† 23.♔e2+–
19.0–0 ♗d4
19...♗xa1 20.♖xa1= would lead to a similar position as in the game.
White now played logical moves:
20.♖ad1
20.♔h1!? was also possible.

20...♗d7 21.♔h1 ♖c8

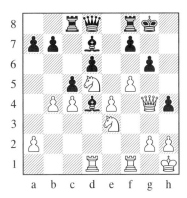

And here in the game Meessen – Ah, Leuven 1998, White missed a strong idea:
22.bxc5!N dxc5
22...♗xc5 23.♕f3±/+– and next ♘g4 gives White an almost decisive advantage.
23.e5!
The only way to stop ♘f6† is:
23...♗xe5
But then White wins with the simple:
24.♕e4 f6 25.fxg6+–

18.0–0 ♗xa1 19.♖xa1=

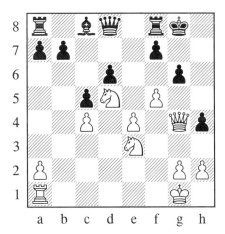

After a few more or less forced moves White gave up the exchange, but his attack looks very dangerous. It is not easy to suggest a defence for Black.

19...♔g7

The alternative 19...b6 does not make sense as the bishop cannot leave the h3-c8 diagonal. The simple 20.♖f1 ♖b8 21.f4! increases the pressure on Black's kingside; the idea is to play ♕h3 and ♖xh4. After 21...♔g7 22.♕f3 ♕g5 (22...f6 23.fxg6+–) 23.♕f2+– Black's position is hopeless.

After 19...♗d7 White would play 20.♕f4 g5 21.♕xd6 and if Black tries the confusing: 21...♗e6!? (21...♗c6 22.♕h6 f6 23.♕g6† ♔h8 24.e5+– also does not help Black) White has the simple: 22.♕e5! ♗xd5 23.f6 ♗xe4 24.♕xg5† ♗g6 25.♘d5+– In order to avoid mate Black needs to sacrifice his queen.

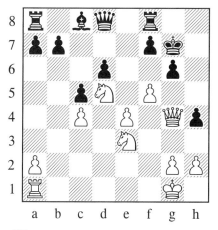

20.♖f1

Of course! White includes one more piece into the attack. A huge mistake would be 20.f6†? since after 20...♕xf6 21.♘xf6 ♗xg4 22.♘exg4 a6∞ Black has exchanged queens and has a good position.

20...♖h8

20...g5 is met by 21.♕h5. After 21...♖h8 22.f6† ♕xf6 23.♕xh8† ♔xh8 24.♖xf6+– White has a decisive advantage.

21.♕f4!

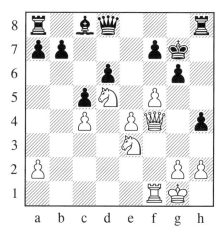

21...g5

This is the only way to fight against the deadly threat of fxg6.

After 21...gxf5 the black king would be in an even more dangerous situation. 22.exf5 ♔f8 23.♖e1! leaves Black with no chances of survival. 23...b5 is met by 24.cxb5 ♗b7 (24...h3 25.g3 doesn't help Black) 25.f6+– and next will be the decisive ♕g5.

22.♕f3 f6

It is very hard to recommend anything instead of the move played in the game.

22...♔f8 is met by: 23.♘g4!

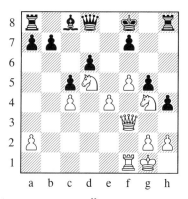

23...b6 (23...h3 24.♕c3 ♖h5 25.♖f3! hxg2 26.♖h3 ♖xh3 27.♕xh3 ♔g8 28.♕h6+–) 24.♕c3 ♖h7 (24...♖h5 25.♘gf6+–) 25.♘gf6

♖h6 26.♕e3 Black's position looks sad. After 26...♗b7 27.♕xg5 ♖h8 28.♘f4+– Black is completely crushed.

After 22...h3 White should continue with the aggressive: 23.♘g4! hxg2 24.♕c3† f6 25.♖d1 and Black is helpless.

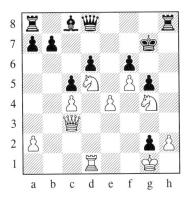

After the forced 25...♖f8 26.♕h3 ♖h8 27.♕xg2 ♖f8 (27...♔f7 28.♘dxf6+–) 28.♘gxf6 ♖xf6 29.♕xg5† ♔f7 30.♕h5† ♔g8 31.♖d3 ♖f7 32.♖g3† ♔g7 33.♖xg7† ♔xg7 34.♕g6† ♔f8 35.♘f6+– The black king is in a mating net.

22...b5 23.♘g4 (23.cxb5 ♗b7 24.f6† ♔f8 25.♕g4± also leads to an advantage, but the main move is more consistent) 23...b4 24.♕f2+– Again the white queen comes to the a1-h8 diagonal; Black's position is simply horrible.

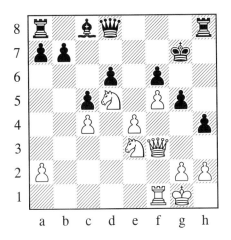

23.♘g4 ♖f8 24.♕e3!+–

The final touch; now White is ready to sacrifice one of his knights on f6.

24...♗d7

24...♔g8 also loses after: 25.♘gxf6† ♖xf6 26.♕xg5† ♔f7 27.♕h5† ♔g8 28.♕xh4 ♔f7 (28...♖f8 29.♕g4† ♔h8 30.♕h5† ♔g8 31.♖f3+–) 29.♕h5† ♔g8 30.♖f3+–

25.♘dxf6

25.♘gxf6 also wins after 25...♖xf6 26.♕xg5† ♔f7 27.♖f4+– and next ♖xh4.

25...♖xf6 26.♕xg5† ♔f7 27.e5 dxe5

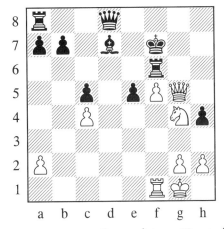

28.♖d1! ♖xf5 29.♘h6† ♔f8 30.♕g8† ♔e7 31.♕h7†

A very nice game by Tomashevsky!
1–0

GAME 45

▷ **A. Onischuk (2669)**
▶ **E. Bacrot Etienne (2705)**

12th Karpov International, Poikovsky
Round 2, 05.10.2011 **[E92]**
Annotated by Borki Predojevic

Bacrot is a very well prepared player who always tries to find new ideas in complicated positions. Recently he started to play the King's Indian against top-level grandmasters. In this game he faced Alexander Onischuk, a specialist in the Gligoric Variation with 7.♗e3. Bacrot responded with 7...exd4 and proved that he had done his homework, playing the interesting 13...♖e5!? followed by 14...♖c8!N which improved over a previous game where Onischuk had White. The American grandmaster achieved no advantage and soon lost a pawn. Fortunately for him, he was able to reduce the number of pawns on the board, and the Frenchman could not find a way to win the knight ending.

1.d4 ♘f6 2.c4 g6 3.♘c3 ♗g7 4.e4 d6 5.♘f3 0–0 6.♗e2 e5 7.♗e3

This is Onischuk's favourite line against the King's Indian, and in the last few years he has not played anything else.

7...exd4

The most direct approach. Exchanging these pawns is more natural here than after 7.0–0, as the dark-squared bishop could become a target for Black's play on the e-file.

8.♘xd4 ♖e8 9.f3 c6 10.♗f2

10.♕d2 d5 11.exd5 cxd5 12.c5 ♘c6 13.0–0 (13.♗f2 would resemble the main game, except White has put his queen on d2 instead of castling) 13...♖xe3!? is a famous sacrifice from the World Championship game Karpov – Kasparov, Lyon/New York (11) 1990.

10...d5 11.exd5 cxd5 12.0–0 ♘c6 13.c5

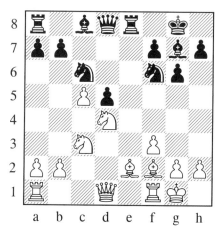

13...♖e5!?

This active move is a recent idea of Krishnan Sasikiran. Black intends to regroup with moves such as ...♕f8, ...♗d7 and ...♖ae8.

The main line is 13...♘h5 14.♕d2 ♗e5 15.g3 ♘g7∞, after which many open questions remain.

14.♗b5

Onischuk had previously used this move with success against Sasikiran, so Bacrot needed to be ready with a novelty. We will also check two other approaches for White.

14.♕a4 ♗d7 15.♖ad1 requires a calm reaction:

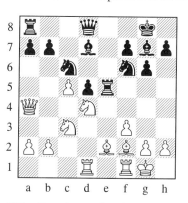

15...a6!N Guarding the b5-square. (After

15...♘h5 16.♗b5 ♕c8 17.f4! ♘xf4 18.♘xc6 bxc6 19.♕xf4 ♖f5 20.♕d2 ♗xc3 [20...cxb5 21.♘xd5±] 21.♕xc3 cxb5 22.♗d4± White was better in game Vazquez Igarza – Cabrera, Totana 2011.) 16.♖fe1 ♖c8 17.♕c2 ♕f8! Black should not have any problems.

White's most popular move has been: 14.♖e1

Here we will consider both a) 14...♕f8 and b) 14...♗d7.

a) 14...♕f8

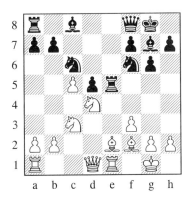

This was Sasikiran's choice in his first game with 13...♖e5. Black wants to regroup his pieces and hints at taking the c5-pawn, while also preparing to meet ♕d2 with ...♗h6. It is worth considering three replies: a1) 15.♗b5?!, a2) 15.f4 and finally the strongest a3) 15.a3!N.

a1) 15.♗b5?! can be dismissed easily, as the following forcing line favours Black: 15...♘g4! 16.fxg4 ♖xe1† 17.♕xe1 ♘xd4 18.♕d2 (18.♕d1 ♕xc5) 18...♗xb5 19.♘xb5 ♗xg4 20.♕xd5 ♖b8 21.♗d4 ♕e7 22.♗xg7 ♕e3† 23.♔h1 ♔xg7∓

a2) 15.f4

This leads to more complicated play, but ultimately Black has ever reason to be happy here too.

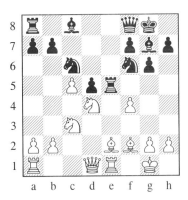

15...♖e8!N

The attractive 15...♘e4? 16.fxe5 ♘xf2 17.♔xf2 ♕xc5 is not working due to 18.♔f1! (18.♘cb5? ♗xe5∓) when Black is forced to simplify to a clearly worse endgame: 18...♕xd4 (18...♘xd4?? 19.♘a4+−) 19.♕xd4 ♘xd4 20.♘xd5±

A previous game continued: 15...♖e7 16.♗f3 (Better is 16.♘db5N ♗e6 17.♘d6 ♖d7 when the position remains unclear.) 16...♖xe1† 17.♕xe1 ♗g4 18.♕d1 ♗xf3 19.♕xf3 ♖e8↑

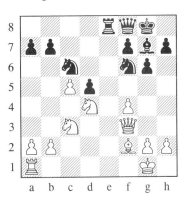

Black had the initiative and White was unable to solve his problems: 20.♘db5 ♘e4 21.♘d6? (Much better was 21.♘xe4! dxe4 22.♕e3 ♗xb2 23.♖d1 ♕e7 24.♘d6 ♖d8 25.♖b1 ♗d4 26.♕xe4 ♗xf2† 27.♔xf2 ♕xe4 28.♘xe4 f5 29.♘c3 [29.♘d6 b6!∓] 29...♖d7 when White should be able to hold the position.) 21...♘xd6 22.cxd6 ♕xd6 23.♘xd5 ♗xb2 24.♖d1 ♖d8 25.♘c3 ♕a3 26.♖xd8† ♘xd8 27.♕d5 ♕xc3 28.♕xd8†

⊜g7† Black has an extra pawn and a safer king, and he went on to win in Al Sayed – Sasikiran, Guangzhou 2010.

Although the above game turned out well for Black, the text move is even more precise. The point is revealed in the following line:

16.♘db5

Certainly the critical move.

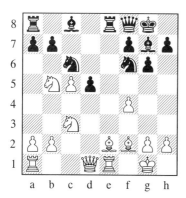

16...d4! 17.♘xd4

Risky is: 17.♘a4 ♗f5! (17...♖b8 is playable but the text is stronger) 18.♘c7 (18.♘d6 ♘e4 19.♘xe8 [19.♘xf5 ♘xf2 20.♔xf2 gxf5 21.♗d3 ♖e3!→] 19...♘xf2 20.♔xf2 ♖xe8⇄) 18...♖xe2 (18...♘e4 allows 19.♘xa8!) 19.♕xe2 ♖d8⇄ Black has superb compensation for the exchange. His d-pawn is free to advance and ...♘e4 could come at any moment. White has significant problems to solve.

17...♖d8 18.♕a4 ♘xd4 19.♗xd4 ♖xd4

19...♘e4!? 20.♗xg7 ♕xc5† 21.♗d4 ♖xd4 22.♕b5 ♖d2† 23.♕xc5 ♘xc5 24.b4∞

20.♕xd4 ♘g4

Now a forced sequence leads to a quick draw:

21.♕d6 ♕xd6 22.cxd6 ♗d4† 23.♔h1 ♘f2† 24.♔g1 ♘g4†=

Neither side can avoid the perpetual.

a3) 15.a3!N

This simple and strong move must be the reason why Sasikiran avoided 14...♕f8 in a subsequent game.

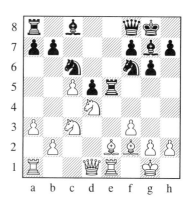

15...♗d7

Black can take pawn with 15...♕xc5, but after 16.♘f5 ♕f8 17.♘xg7 ♕xg7 (if 17...♔xg7 18.b4 a6 19.♘a4 Black's weak dark squares give White more than enough compensation) 18.b4 a6 (or 18...♗d7 19.b5 ♘e7 20.♕d2↑ followed by ♗d4 and White is better.) 19.♕a4 ♗d7 (19...♖b8?! 20.♗g3) 20.b5 ♘e7 21.♗d3 ♖e6 22.♕a5!?↑ White keeps the initiative and the advantage.

16.b4 ♖ae8 17.♘db5!

Creating unpleasant threats. Black's pieces are concentrated in the kingside, but can he do anything with them?

17...d4!?

17...♘h5 does not work: 18.♘d6 ♖g5 19.♗h4 ♖xg2† 20.♔xg2 ♗xc3 21.♘xe8 ♕xe8 22.♗b5±

18.♘xd4 ♘d5

Black seems to be developing some activity, but White can keep the position under control.

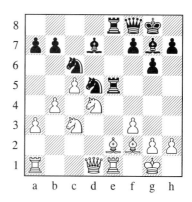

19.♘db5!

For the second time this move proves to be a strong one.

19...♘xc3 20.♘xc3 ♗f5 21.♖a2 a5 22.♕a4!?±

Black will find it hard to demonstrate full compensation for his material disadvantage.

To summarize, 14...♕f8 cannot be considered fully satisfactory for Black unless he can find an improvement in the above analysis.

b) 14...♗d7

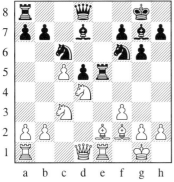

This seems more reliable than 14...♕f8. White may react with b1) 15.a3, b2) 15.♕b3 or b3) 15.♕d2.

b1) 15.a3

This does not work as well here as it did against 14...♕f8. In this position Black can play actively with:

15...♘h5! 16.g3 ♕g5

This could lead to sharp tactical play after the forcing:

17.h4!?N

In the game White collapsed with three weak moves: 17.♘xc6?! ♗xc6↑ 18.♕c1?! d4 19.♘b5?? ♕xc1 Now in El Debs – Sasikiran, Gibraltar 2011, White resigned without waiting for 20.♖axc1 ♖xe2 21.♖xe2 ♗xb5.

17...♕e7

17...♕d8?! 18.f4 leaves Black without the same tactical resource as in the main line below.

18.f4

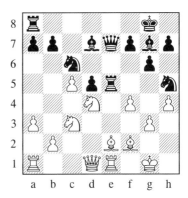

From here Black can justify his play with some lovely tactical shots.

18...♖e3! 19.♘xd5

19.♘xc6? bxc6∓

19.♗xh5?! ♗xd4 20.♗f3 ♖xe1† 21.♕xe1 ♕xc5 22.♘xd5 ♖d8↑ is better for Black.

19...♖xg3† 20.♗xg3 ♕xc5

Here an interesting idea is:

21.♘e7†!?

After the straightforward 21.♗xh5 ♗xd4† 22.♔h1 ♕xd5† 23.♗f3 ♕f5∞ Black has nice compensation, as White's pieces are disorganized and his king is unsafe.

21...♘xe7 22.♗f2 ♘xf4 23.♗f1

Now the most precise move is:

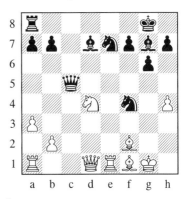

23...♕d6!

Another idea is 23...♘h3†!? 24.♗xh3 ♗xh3 25.♘e6 ♕c8 26.♖c1 (26.♘xg7?? ♕c6!) 26...♘c6 27.♘xg7 ♔xg7 28.♖c3 with unclear play.

24.♘b5 ♕xd1 25.♖axd1 ♗xb5 26.♗xb5
  26.♖xe7 ♗c6⩲

26...♘h3† 27.♔g2 ♘xf2 28.♔xf2 ♗f6 29.♖e4
♘f5 30.♗c4 ♗xb2 31.♖d7 ♖f8

The game remains roughly balanced and a
draw is the most likely outcome.

b2) White can also strive for an advantage
with:
15.♕b3

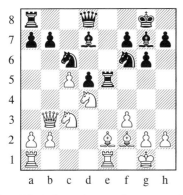

Here Black has plenty of options, but my
suggestion would be to follow the path of
GM Gallagher, a King's Indian expert:
15...♘h5

15...♘xd4 16.♗xd4 ♖e6 also looks reliable
enough. White has only slight pressure and
Black should be able to hold the position.

16.♕xb7 ♘xd4 17.♗xd4 ♖b8 18.♕xa7 ♖xb2
19.♖ab1 ♖exe2 20.♘xe2 ♖xe2

Here I checked a new approach for White:

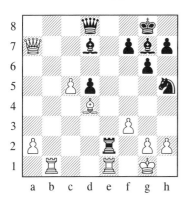

21.♖xe2!?N

21.♗xg7 ♖xe1† 22.♖xe1 ♔xg7 23.♕b6
♕h4 24.♖d1 ♕c4 25.♕b2† was unclear but
roughly equal in Volkov – Gallagher, Aix-
les-Bains 2011.

21...♖xd4† 22.♔h1 ♔g7 23.♖be1
Here Black can maintain the balance with a
beautiful sacrifice.

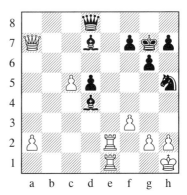

23...♗e6!! 24.♖xe6 ♕h4 25.♕c7 ♗f2 26.h3
  26.♕e5†? f6 27.♕c7† ♔h6†

26...♘g3† 27.♔h2 ♘f5 28.♕e5† f6 29.♕xf6†
♕xf6 30.♖xf6 ♔xf6 31.♖d1 ♔e6∞

The endgame is hard to assess, despite the
considerable simplifications.

b3) Finally, White can consider:
15.♕d2

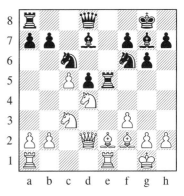

Arguably White's most logical move.
15...♕f8

15...♕a5 looks suspicious, and after 16.a3

♕xc5 17.♘e6! ♕e7 18.♘xg7 ♔xg7 19.b4⯹
White has more than enough compensation
for a pawn.

After the move played, the path divides
again. White can play b31) 16.♗f1, b32)
16.♘db5!?N or b33) 16.♖ad1N.

b31) 16.♗f1

This was White's choice in the one game in
which 15...♕f8 has been played thus far.
16...♗h6 17.f4

Here I found an improvement for Black.

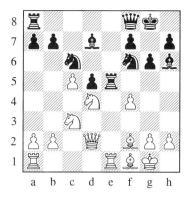

17...♖ae8!N

17...♖xe1 18.♖xe1 ♖d8 (18...♖e8 also
looks reasonable) 19.h3 ♗g7 20.♕d1 ♘e4
21.♘xe4 dxe4 22.♘xc6 ♗xc6↑ was also okay
for Black in Ulko – Sychev, Moscow 2011,
but the text move is the strongest. Now Black
threatens ...♘g4, as well as taking twice on
e1 when White would lose either the pawn
on f4 or the one on c5.
18.♖xe5 ♘xe5 19.h3

This is more or less forced.
19...♘c4 20.♕c1 ♘e4 21.♘xe4 ♖xe4 22.♗xc4
dxc4 23.♕xc4 ♕e8!↑

Black has a fine position.

b32) 16.♘db5!?

This could lead to extremely sharp play.
I suggest the following line:
16...a6! 17.♘d6 b6

Undermining the knight.

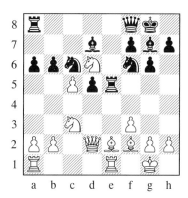

18.f4

18.♗g3? is bad, as after 18...bxc5 19.♗xe5
♘xe5 20.♘xd5 ♕xd6 21.♘xf6† ♕xf6 22.f4
there is a strong retort 22...♕h4! 23.fxe5
(23.g3 ♕h6–+) 23...♗xe5–+ when Black
wins.
18...♖e6 19.f5

19.♗f3?! is worse. 19...bxc5 20.♖xe6
♗xe6 21.♗xc5 ♖b8 22.♖e1 ♕d8 White
has problems with the knight on d6, for
example: 23.♔h1 ♕a5 24.♗a3 d4 25.♗xc6
dxc3 26.♕xc3 ♕xc3 27.bxc3 ♗f8!⩱
19...gxf5 20.♘xd5 bxc5 21.♘xf6† ♗xf6
22.♘xf5

22.♗xc5 is met by 22...♗d4†! 23.♗xd4 ♖xd6
24.♕g5† ♖g6 25.♕f4 ♘xd4 26.♕xd4 ♗c6
27.♗f1 ♖d8↑ with a good position for Black.
22...♖d8

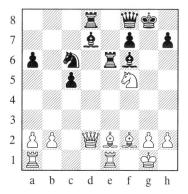

At first sight Black looks to be worse, as his
pawn structure is fractured and his king is
slightly exposed. However, his pieces are

nicely centralized and this should enable him to maintain the balance. I analysed the following lines:

23.♕f4

23.♖ac1 ♖e5 24.♘h6† ♔g7 25.♖c3 ♗e6 26.♖g3† (26.♕f4 ♕e7 27.♖g3† ♔h8) 26...♔h8∞

23...♗xb2 24.♖ad1 ♗f6 25.♖d5 ♗xf5 26.♖xf5 ♖xf5 27.♕xf5 ♖e8 28.♕g5† ♕g7 29.♕xc5 ♘d4 30.♔f1 ♘xe2 31.♖xe2 ♖xe2 32.♕c8† ♕f8 33.♕g4† ♔g7 34.♕xe2 ♕d6=

The game will almost certainly end in a draw.

b33) 16.♖ad1

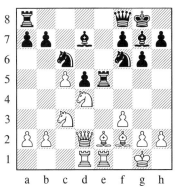

With this natural move White centralizes his last piece before taking direct action. But Black has a surprising possibility.

16...♕xc5!

Usually this capture is risky, but here Black can get away with it.

16...a6 and 16...♖d8 are both playable as well.

17.♘f5

17.♘db5 ♕f8 is good for Black.

17...♕a5 18.b4!?

The alternative is 18.♘xg7 ♔xg7. Usually in such positions White would have more than enough compensation for a pawn. The main difference here is that Black has the important move ...d4 to exchange White's strong dark-squared bishop. For example: 19.g4 (19.♗g3 ♖f5) 19...d4 20.♗xd4 ♘xd4

21.♕xd4 g5! 22.h4 h6 23.hxg5 hxg5 24.♗d3 ♖ae8 and Black is okay.

18...♕xb4 19.♖b1 ♕a5 20.♖b5 ♕d8

20...♗xf5? 21.♖xa5 ♘xa5 22.g4! is good for White.

21.♘xg7 ♔xg7

From this position, the following line looks like the most dangerous:

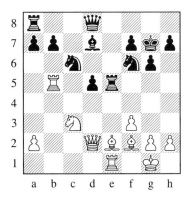

22.♖xb7

22.♗g3 ♖e6 23.♖xb7 (23.♘xd5 ♘d4!) 23...d4∞ leads to an unclear game.

22...d4 23.♘b5

But Black has a good reply:

23...♘a5! 24.♗xd4 ♖xe2 25.♗xf6† ♕xf6 26.♖xe2 ♘xb7 27.♕xd7 ♖d8! 28.♕xb7 ♖d1† 29.♔f2 ♕h4† 30.♔e3 ♕g5† 31.♔f2 ♕h4†=

The game ends in a draw.

14...♗d7 15.♕a4

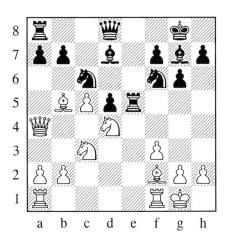

15...Rc8!N

A strong novelty by Etienne.

In a previous game Sasikiran played 15...Qc8, but after 16.Rfe1 a6 17.Bxc6 Bxc6 18.Qc2 Rh5 19.b4 Bd7 20.Rad1 Bh6 21.Bg3± White was better and gradually increased his advantage: 21...Bf8 22.a3 Bc6 23.Na4! Nd7 24.Nb6 Nxb6 25.cxb6 Bd7 26.Rc1 Qd8 27.Qc7 Bg7 28.Nb3 Ba4 29.Qxd8† Rxd8 30.Bc7 Rf8 31.g4 Rh6 32.Nc5 Bd4† 33.Kg2 Bxc5 34.Rxc5± White went on to win convincingly in Onischuk – Sasikiran, Ningbo 2011.

16.Rfe1

16.Nxc6 bxc6= is not helping White.

The alternative was:
16.Rad1
Now Black can play an interesting pawn sacrifice:
16...a6!?
On 16...Nh5 White has the strong 17.f4! Nxf4 18.Nxc6 bxc6 19.Qxf4 Rf5 20.Qd2 cxb5 21.Bd4 Rxf1† 22.Rxf1 Bxd4† 23.Qxd4 Bc6 24.b4 a5 25.a3 axb4 26.axb4 Qd7∞. According to the computer Black has no problem maintaining the balance here, but my human opinion is that his position is unpleasant.

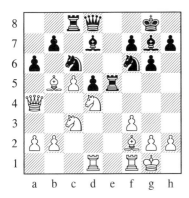

17.Bxc6 Bxc6

17...bxc6?! 18.Qxa6 Nh5 looks too optimistic. After 19.Na4! Ra8 20.Qb6 Qe8 21.Qb3 Nf4 22.Nb6± White is better.
18.Nxc6 bxc6 19.Qxa6 Nd7∞
At first Black's compensation seems questionable, but on closer inspection his position turns out to be okay, for instance:
20.Bd4
20.Qd3 Be6 21.b4 Ne5 22.Qc2 Nc4∞
20...Re6 21.Bxg7 Kxg7 22.Qd3 Qf6∞
All of Black's pieces are active and he intends ...Ne5-c4 next.

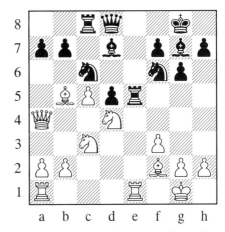

16...Rxe1† 17.Rxe1 Nxd4 18.Bxd4 Bc6=

Onischuk continued with same moves as in his game against Sasikiran, but there are clear differences. In the present game Black does not have any problems with his development, and his rook on c8 will be useful as the c5-pawn will soon be attacked.

19.Qd1 Qa5 20.Bf1 Re8 21.Rxe8† Nxe8 22.Qd2?

This natural move is a mistake which will cost White a whole pawn. Correct was 22.Nxd5 Bxd5 23.Bxg7 Bxf3 24.gxf3 Kxg7 (24...Nxg7 25.b4=) 25.Qd4† Nf6 26.a3 with an equal position.

22...Bxd4† 23.Qxd4

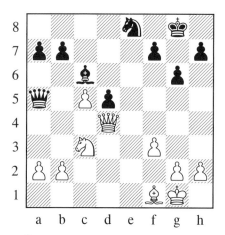

23...♘c7!

Perfect timing! The knight defends the d5-pawn while preparing to come to e6, seizing the initiative for Black.

24.b4

The only way to fight against Black's plan, but White still ends up a pawn down.

24...♘e6 25.bxa5 ♘xd4 26.a6 bxa6 27.♗xa6 ♘e6 28.♔f2 ♘xc5 29.♗c8 d4

Otherwise the king comes to d4.

30.♘e2 ♗d5!

30...d3? would have squandered Black's advantage: 31.♘c3 ♔f8 32.♔e3 ♔e7 33.♗h3! and White equalizes with g3 followed by ♗f1.

31.♘xd4 ♗xa2 32.♘c6 a6 33.♔e3 ♗e6□

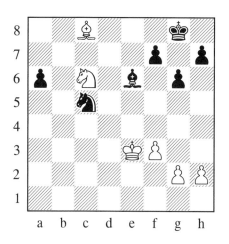

34.♗xe6 ♘xe6

After a few exchanges Black has retained an extra pawn, but converting it into a win will not be easy on account of White's active king and knight.

35.♔e4! ♔g7 36.♔e5 ♘c5 37.♔d4 ♘d7 38.♘b4

Finally it is time for White to fight against the a-pawn. The knight will come to d5 to restrict the black king, while White's king goes after the pawn. Black must look for a way to activate his pieces, but this is not easy.

38...a5 39.♘d5 g5!

Another interesting try was 39...♔h6!? intending to march the king with ...♔g5-f5-e5-d4. Here White has to respond with the careful 40.♘e3! (40.f4 ♔h5 41.♘e3 is strongly met by 41...♘f6! intending ...♘g4) 40...♔g5 41.g3 ♔f6 42.f4 h5 43.♔c4 ♘f8 44.♔b5 ♘e6 45.♔xa5 ♘d4 46.♔b4 ♘f3! 47.♔c4 ♘xh2 48.♔d4 ♘g4 49.♘c4∓ No doubt Bacrot would continue playing for a while, but objectively this endgame is a draw.

40.♔c4

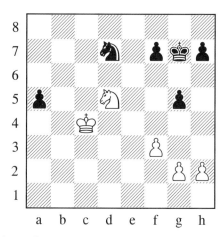

40...g4?

After this move Black has no real chance of winning the game.

40...♗g6!? would have been one simple improvement.

However, the best continuation of all was 40...♘e5†! 41.♔b5 ♘g6 42.♔xa5 ♘h4 43.♘e3 f5 when Black renews his one-pawn advantage. Play continues 44.♔b4 f4 45.♘c4 ♘xg2 46.♔c3 ♘e1 47.♘d2 ♔f6 (after 47...♔g6 48.♔d4 ♔h5 49.♔e5 ♔h4 50.♔f5 h5 51.h3∓ White should hold) 48.♔d4 ♔f5 49.♔d5∓ when White is in real danger although he may yet be able to survive.

41.fxg4 ♘e5† 42.♔b5 ♘xg4 43.♔xa5 ♘xh2 44.♔b4

White has enough time to get back with his king and the position is drawish.

44...♔g6 45.♔c3 ♔f5 46.♔d3 ♘g4 47.g3 ♔e5 48.♘f4 ♔f5 49.♘d5 ♘e5† 50.♔e3 ♔g4 51.♘f6† ♔f5

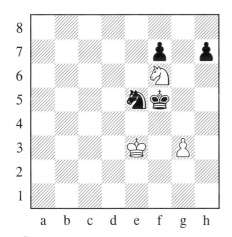

52.♘d5

Avoiding the final trap: 52.♘xh7?? ♘d7!–+ followed by ...♔g6 when the knight is trapped.

52...♔g4 53.♘f6† ♔xg3 54.♔e4! ♘d7 55.♘xd7 h5 56.♘f6 h4 57.♔f5 h3 58.♘g4 f6 59.♘e3 ♔f3

½–½

GAME 46
▷ **G. Meier (2648)**
▶ **S. Feller (2668)**
5th SPICE Cup, Lubbock
Round 5, 19.10.2011 **[E95]**
Annotated by Yannick Gozzoli

White chose the 8.♖e1 variation against the ...♘bd7 Classical King's Indian. The first important moment occurred on Black's 11th move, when Black had to choose between two important knight moves. My personal preference is for the dynamic 11...♘e5!?, but Feller's 11...♘c5 is totally playable. Then Meier avoided the usual 12.♖ad1 which has the reputation for being quite drawish, although the notes indicate that White has good chances for an advantage here. In the game Black could have got a nice position but he misplaced his pieces on the queenside, failed to find any counterplay and lost badly.

1.♘f3 ♘f6 2.c4 g6 3.♘c3 ♗g7 4.e4 d6 5.d4 0–0 6.♗e2 e5 7.0–0 ♘bd7 8.♖e1

In my opinion 8.♗e3 is the most challenging move, but that is another topic.

8...c6 9.♗f1

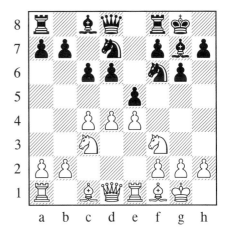

9...exd4

The main alternative is:
9...a5

Black hopes to improve his position before committing himself in the centre.

10.dxe5

After 10.♖b1 ♖e8 White lacks a useful move so he has to make a decision in the centre. 11.d5 ♘c5 12.b3 ♗d7 13.a3 cxd5 14.cxd5 b5 15.b4 axb4 16.axb4 ♘a4 17.♘xa4 ♖xa4 18.♗d3 ♕b6= Black was definitely not worse in Postny – Jovanovic, Sibenik 2011.

10...dxe5

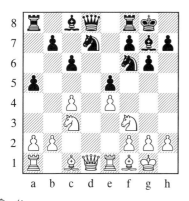

11.♘a4!

Highlighting the disadvantage of Black's 9th move.

11...♕e7 12.♕c2 ♘c5 13.♘xc5 ♕xc5 14.♗e3 ♕e7 15.h3±

Wojtaszek – Markus, Wroclaw 2010.

10.♘xd4 ♖e8 11.♗f4

White's other ideas include 11.♖b1, 11.♗g5 and 11.♘b3.

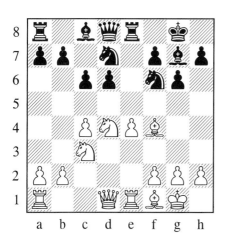

11...♘c5

This 'positional' approach is fine, but my personal preference is for the more dynamic knight move to e5.

11...d5? is premature: 12.cxd5 ♘xd5 (12...cxd5 13.♘db5±) 13.exd5 ♖xe1 14.♕xe1 ♗xd4 15.dxc6 (or 15.♖d1 c5 [15...♗g7 16.dxc6 bxc6 17.♗c4+− Gligoric – Pilnik, Amsterdam 1950] 16.d6±) 15...bxc6 16.♖d1+−

11...♘e5!?

This move is more aggressive than Feller's choice. Black is putting pressure on the c4-pawn, while shielding the d6-pawn from the enemy bishop. It should also not be forgotten that the knight is closer to the enemy king on e5 than c5. It is worth analysing the responses of a) 12.♕d2?! and b) 12.f3.

a) 12.♕d2?!

This mechanical move gives White nothing but troubles, and allows Black to exploit his dynamic potential.

12...♘h5! 13.♗g5 ♕b6 14.♖ad1?!

The lesser evil is 14.♘a4 although 14...♕xd4 15.♕xd4 ♘f3† 16.gxf3 ♗xd4 17.♖ad1 ♗e5= is of course pleasant for Black.

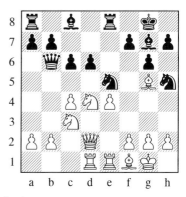

14...♗g4!

Now it will be hard for White to deal with the pressure against his centre.

15.♗e2

15.♖c1 ♘xc4 16.♗xc4 ♕xd4† wins a pawn for no compensation.

15...♘xc4

Also strong is 15...♗xe2 16.♕xe2 ♕b4† Gofshtein – Sutovsky, Tel Aviv 1994.

16.♗xc4 ♗xd1 17.♖xd1 ♕c5†

White faced an unavoidable loss of material in Antic – Vorobiov, Kavala 2010.

b) **12.f3**

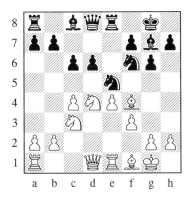

This is more solid, but Black can still obtain a good game.

12...a6 13.♔h1 c5 14.♘b3 ♘h5 15.♗e3

At this point Black could have reached a comfortable and promising position with:

15...♗e6!N

Instead of 15...♕h4? 16.♔g1 ♘c6 17.♕d2 ♗e5 18.g3 ♕f6 19.♘d5± Rakhmanov – Sutovsky, Moscow 2008.

16.♘d5 ♘f6 17.♕d2 ♘xd5 18.cxd5 ♗d7†

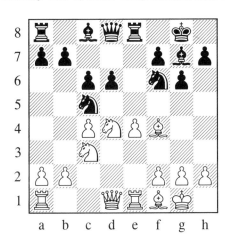

12.♕c2 ♘g4 13.♕d2

Moving the queen for the second time looks strange, but it has often been played since the early 1990s in order to avoid a forcing sequence that was considered drawish (at that time!).

13.♖ad1

This natural move was considered the main line until Black found an interesting way to deal with it:

13...♗xd4!?

13...♗e5 does not equalize: 14.♗g3 ♕f6 15.♕d2 h5 (15...♗xg3 16.hxg3 ♘d3 17.♗xd3 ♕xd4 18.♖f1 [18.♗c2 ♕e5 19.f3 ♕c5† 20.♕d4 ♘e5 21.♕xc5 dxc5 22.b3 f6 23.f4 ♘f7 is okay for Black] 18...♕e5 [18...♕c5 19.♗e2±] 19.♗e2 ♘f6 20.♕xd6 ♘xe4 21.♕xe5 ♖xe5 22.♖d8† ♔g7 23.♘xe4 ♖xe4 24.♗f3 ♖e5 25.g4± The ending is clearly in White's favour although the win is a long way off.) 16.f3 ♗xg3 17.hxg3 ♘e5 18.f4 ♘g4 19.♘f3 ♕d8 20.b4± White has a fine position, Averkin – Geller, Moscow 1969.

14.♖xd4 ♕f6 15.♘e2

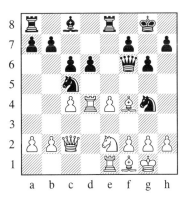

15...♘xf2!

The point of Black's play, although we will see that the evaluation is still far from clear.

16.♔xf2

16.♖xd6!? leads to complex play: 16...♕h4 (16...♕e7? 17.♘c3 ♘g4 18.♕d1!±) 17.♗g3 ♕xe4 18.♕d2 Intending ♘c3. 18...♘fd3

19.♘c3 (19.♖d1!?∞ Black has not completed his development so perhaps White can fight for an advantage here.) 19...♘xe1 20.♘xe4 ♘xe4 21.♕d4 ♘xd6∞ Black has a material advantage but his dark squares are weak and the knight on e1 is temporarily out of play.

16...g5 17.♖xd6 ♕e7 18.e5 gxf4 19.♘xf4

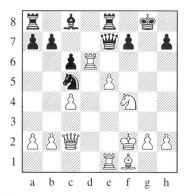

19...♕g5!

In a previous game Black went down quickly after 19...f5? 20.♗d3 ♘d7 21.♖e6 ♕c5† 22.♔f1+– Adamski – Mista, Trinec 1980.

The text move was a revolutionary novelty at the time, but it is not the end of the story as I also found a strong improvement for White.

20.♕d2!N

After 20.g3 the players agreed a draw in Burgess – Schlosser, Prestwick 1990, and indeed after 20...♗f5 21.♗d3 ♗xd3 22.♘xd3 ♘xd3† 23.♕xd3 ♖xe5 the position is equal.

20...♗f5

After 20...♖xe5? 21.♖d8† ♔g7 22.g3+– White's attack is irresistible.

20...f6 21.♖d8 ♗f5 22.♖xa8 ♖xa8 23.♕d4±

21.♕d4! ♖ad8 22.♘h5

22.♖xd8 ♖xd8 23.♕e3±

22...♖xd6 23.exd6 ♖xe1 24.♔xe1±

Black has nothing to show for the missing pawn.

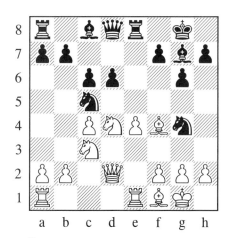

13...♘e5

Black can also play 13...a5 14.♖ad1 a4 15.h3 ♘e5 16.♗e3 ♕a5 17.♔h1 (17.f4 ♘ed7= Tukmakov – Vogt, Lenk 2000) 17...♕a6 18.♕c1 ♕a5 19.f3 a3N (19...f6?! led to an unpleasant position for Black in Zueger – Vogt, Switzerland 1997) 20.b3 ♘ed7⇄.

14.♖ad1 ♕b6 15.h3 a5 16.♗e3

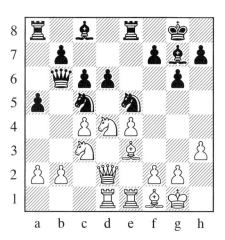

We have reached a typical-looking position for this opening variation. White has a strong position in the centre and will aim to break with e4-e5 or f4-f5. Black will try to develop his counterplay against the e4-pawn and on the queenside by harassing the c4- and b2-pawns. He may also consider pushing his a-pawn in order to soften the long diagonal and create new weaknesses on a2 and c3.

16...♘ed7

16...a4 17.f4 ♘ed7 18.♘f3± intending ♗d4 is slightly better for White.

17.♕c2 a4 18.f4 ♕b4?!

I don't like this square for the black queen.

18...a3!? 19.b3 ♕a5

This would have been a better idea for Black. Now White has some problems improving his position due to the pressure along the h8-a1 diagonal. Here are some illustrative lines:

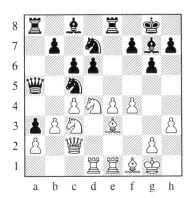

20.♘de2

Or 20.♗f2 ♘a6= intending ...♘dc5, ...♗d7 and ...♖ad8 with a good game for Black.
20...♘f6 21.♘g3

21.♗d2 ♕c7 22.♘g3 h5 Black is fine. White can try to complicate the game with 23.b4 ♘a6 24.e5!? but after 24...dxe5 25.fxe5 ♘h7∞ Black's chances are not worse.
21...♘g4 22.♗d4

22.hxg4 ♕xc3∓
22...♘e6 23.♗xg7

23.♘ge2 ♘xd4 24.♘xd4 ♘f6∓
23...♕c5† 24.♔h1 ♕f2!⇄

Maintaining a dynamic balance. It should be noted that winning material with 24...♘f2† 25.♔h2 ♘xd1 is risky in view of 26.♗f6!

♘xc3 27.♕xc3 ♕f2 (27...♘xf4 28.♕d2 ♘e6 29.♘f5→) 28.f5 ♘f8 29.♕c1→ (29.♗e2!?) when the black king is in danger.

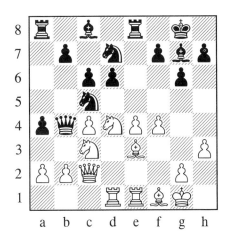

19.♗f2

Improving the scope of the rook on e1, while also preparing to deploy the bishop on g3 or h4 to support White's kingside play.

19...♘b6?!

The black knights are a bit shaky in the firing line of the bishop on f2. But aside from that, I simply don't understand Black's plan. White now has every chance to launch a successful attack, exploiting the fact that Black's pieces are so far away on the queenside.

Another idea was 19...a3 20.b3, but this underlines the bad position of the black queen, as b4 would be a better square for a black knight.

20.a3 ♕a5 21.g4 ♗d7?!

Black continues his faulty plan. There was still time to correct the strategy with 21...♘bd7±, when Black's position remains worse, but he would have reasonable chances to meet his opponent's initiative in the centre.

22.f5!

A powerful move, seizing the initiative in

the centre. The method is quite unusual as it weakens the e5-square. But in this particular position Black is unable to make much use of it, and it is clear that his pieces are misplaced on the queenside.

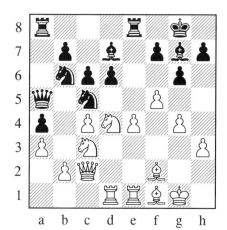

22...♖ad8 23.♗h4 ♖c8 24.♗f2 ♖cd8 25.♗h4 ♖c8 26.♘f3±

White has a huge advantage. Black has no counterplay and his knights are passive.

26...♘b3

The knight occupies an outpost, but it is completely out of play!

27.♕f2

Threatening to take on d6.

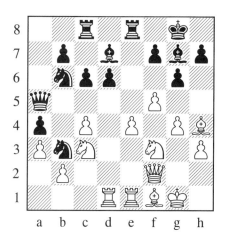

27...♗f8

27...♕c5 28.♕xc5 ♘xc5 29.♗f2 (29.♖xd6 ♗xc3 30.bxc3 ♖xe4 31.♖ed1 is also good for White) 29...♗f8 30.♗xc5 dxc5 31.♘xa4 ♘xa4 32.♖xd7±

28.♔h1!

A good prophylactic move against a possible ...c5.

28...♕c5 29.e5?

Giving Black a chance to get back into the game. Instead 29.♕g2!+– would have given White an overwhelming position, with absolutely no counterplay for Black.

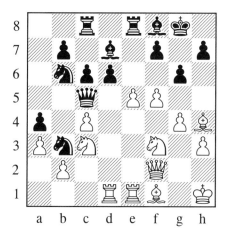

29...d5??

A blunder in time trouble.

29...♕xf2 30.♗xf2 c5! was the right continuation. White is still better, but his advantage is not that great. A possible continuation is: 31.♘d5 ♗c6 32.♘xb6 ♗xf3† 33.♗g2 ♗xd1 34.♘xc8 ♗xg4 35.hxg4 (after 35.♘xd6 ♗xd6 36.exd6 ♖xe1† 37.♗xe1 ♗xf5 38.♗xb7 ♗d7 Black has good drawing chances) 35...♖xc8±

In the game, after White's strong reply he is just winning.

30.♕c2!+−

Threatening e5-e6, destroying the enemy kingside.

30...♘xc4

30...♕a5 31.e6 fxe6 32.fxg6+− is easily winning.

31.♘xa4

Black could have resigned here, but in time trouble he played a few more moves in inertia.

31...♕b5 32.♗xc4 dxc4 33.♘c3 ♗xf5 34.gxf5 ♕a5 35.♘e4 ♗e7 36.♕xc4 ♗xh4 37.♘xh4
1–0

GAME 47
▷ **R. Kasimdzhanov (2678)**
▶ **L. D. Nisipeanu (2638)**
European Club Cup, Rogaska Slatina
Round 7, 01.10.2011 **[E97]**
Annotated by Sebastien Maze

In a Classical King's Indian with 9.♘d2, Kasimdzhanov played a good novelty with 19.♕e1. In my opinion this move enables White to count on some advantage. In the game Nisipeanu tried to set fire to the board with 20...♘f5?!, but after some precise defensive moves, most notably 29.♘c5!, White quickly obtained a winning position. According to my analysis 20...♘g8 is the right route to a playable position. The position remains slightly better for White, but Black can definitely hope for some counterplay on the kingside.

1.d4 ♘f6 2.c4 g6 3.♘c3 ♗g7 4.e4 d6 5.♘f3 0–0 6.♗e2 e5 7.0–0 ♘c6 8.d5 ♘e7 9.♘d2

The former FIDE World Champion has been playing this line quite often. 9.♘e1 and 9.b4 are the main moves.

9...a5 10.a3 ♘d7 11.♖b1 f5 12.b4 ♔h8

13.f3

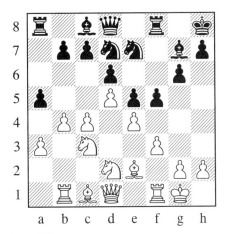

13...axb4

By far the most popular move has been 13...♘g8, which was especially popular in the 1990s as it was used many times by Kasparov. The main line continues 14.♕c2 ♘gf6 15.♗d3 f4 with an unclear position.

13...f4!? 14.♘b5 b6 15.♕c2 a4 16.♖d1 g5 17.g4! h5 (17...fxg3 18.hxg3 h5 19.♘f1 ♘g6 20.♗e3 h4 21.♕c1±) 18.h3 ♖f6 19.♗b2 occurred in the recent game Kramnik – Nakamura, Monte Carlo (rapid) 2011. Black eventually won this game, but at this stage White's position is preferable; he is solid on the kingside, and he has good chances to break open the centre with the timely c4-c5.

14.axb4 c6

Kasimdzhanov had already done well against the weaker 14...c5?! earlier in the year: 15.bxc5 ♘xc5 16.♘b3 b6 17.♘xc5 bxc5 18.♕b3 ♘g8 19.♕b6 ♗h6 20.♕xd8 ♖xd8 21.♖b6 White obtained an enduring advantage and won convincingly in the endgame, Kasimdzhanov – Mamedov, Konya 2011.

15.♔h1 ♘f6 16.♘b3

Both players continue to improve their positions. White wants to put a knight on a5 and Black wants to put a knight on h5!

16...cxd5 17.cxd5 f4 18.♞a5 ♞h5

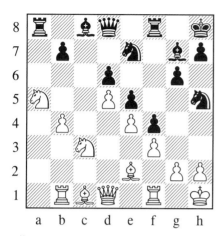

19.♕e1N

A strong novelty! The first idea is to prevent a quick ...♝f6-h4, and the second is to play ♞c4 followed by ♕f2-b6.

19.♔g1 ♝f6 20.♝d2 ♝h4 21.♝e1 ♞g3 22.♖f2 ♞xe2† 23.♖xe2 ♝xe1 24.♕xe1 g5 gave Black good chances in Lputian – Nataf, Warsaw 2005.

19...♝f6 20.♞c4

Now Black has to move his knight away from e7 in order to prepare ...♝h4. The problem is that the knight does not have a really good square available.

20...♞f5?

It looks like Black made a practical decision to complicate the game, but the sacrifice is objectively unsound.

Evidently the correct continuation was:
20...♞g8

Not an ideal square for the knight, but at least this piece will live to fight another day.
21.♕f2 ♖a6!

It is important to prevent the queen from coming to b6. Alternatives are worse:
21...♝h4? 22.♕b6 ♕g5 23.♕xd6 ♖e8

24.♝d3 ♞g3† 25.♔g1 ♞xf1 (25...♞h3 26.hxg3 ♝xg3 27.♖b2+−) 26.♝xf1+−
21...♞h6 22.♕b6 ♞f7 23.♕xd8 ♝xd8 24.♞b5 ♝e7 25.♝b2± Black faces an unpleasant endgame.

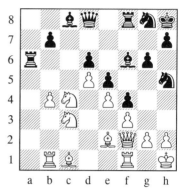

We have reached a position which is critical for the assessment of the whole opening line. White can choose between a) 22.♝d3?, b) 22.b5?!, c) 22.♝d1, d) 22.g4!? and finally e) 22.♖g1!.

a) 22.♝d3? ♝h4 23.♕c2 ♞g3† is a strong version of Black's thematic knight sacrifice. 24.♔g1 (24.hxg3 ♝xg3 25.♖f2 ♕h4† 26.♔g1 ♞f6 27.♝b2 ♞g4∓) 24...♞xf1 25.♔xf1 ♖a8 White has some compensation for the exchange but Black's position is better overall.

b) 22.b5?! is met by 22...♝h4 23.bxa6 ♝xf2 24.♖xf2 bxa6 25.♝a3 ♖f6 26.♖b6 ♞h6 with unclear play.

c) 22.♝d1!?
An interesting move. Compared with the weaker line 'a' above, the bishop controls the g4-square.
22...♝d7

22...♝h4 23.♕d2 ♞g3†? does not work here: 24.hxg3 ♝xg3 25.♖f2 ♕h4† 26.♔g1 ♕h2† 27.♔f1 ♕h1† 28.♝e2 ♝xf2 29.♔xf2 ♕h2 30.♝e2 ♞h6 31.b5 ♖a8 32.♝f1 ♖f6 33.♔e1+−

23.b5 ♗h4 24.♕d2 ♖a8 25.♘e2 ♘h6 26.♗a3

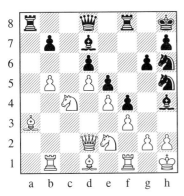

26...♘f7

It is important to give the d6-pawn some protection before focusing on the kingside attack.

26...♗g3?! is premature: 27.♗xd6 ♕h4 28.♘xg3 ♘xg3† 29.♔g1 ♕xh2† 30.♔xh2 ♘xf1† 31.♔g1 ♘xd2 32.♗xe5† ♔g8 33.♘xd2±

27.♖b3

27.♗c2? ♗g3 28.♘g1 (28.hxg3 fxg3∓) 28...♖xh2 29.♔xh2 ♕h4† 30.♘h3 ♗xh3 31.gxh3 ♖fc8∓

27...♗g3!

Black is setting a fire around the king!

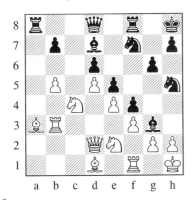

28.♘g1!

28.hxg3? fxg3 29.♔g1 ♕h4 30.♘xg3 ♘xg3 31.♖e1 ♘h6 gives Black a winning attack.

28...♗xh2 29.♔xh2 ♕h4† 30.♘h3 ♗xh3 31.gxh3 ♕g3† 32.♔h1 ♕xh3† 33.♔g1 ♘g3 34.♕g2 ♕xg2† 35.♔xg2 ♘xf1 36.♔xf1 ♖fd8

The endgame is complicated but roughly equal in my estimation.

d) 22.g4!?

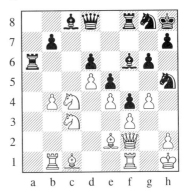

This move can occur in several lines of the Classical King's Indian. Here it may lead to great complications.

22...fxg3 23.hxg3 ♗g5

23...♗g7 is too timid and 24.♕h2 ♘h6 25.♗e3 ♘f7 26.♘a5 ♖a8 27.♖a1± favours White.

24.f4!?

An ambitious move, but also a risky one for White.

The following line illustrates the dangers in White's position: 24.b5 ♖a8 25.♗a3? (better is 25.♕h2 ♗xc1 26.♖bxc1 ♘gf6 27.♖b1 ♕e7∞ with mutual chances)

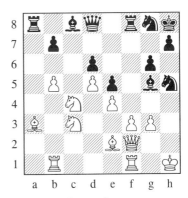

25...♖xa3! 26.♘xa3 ♘xg3† A super double sacrifice! 27.♕xg3 ♗f4 28.♕f2 ♕g5 White is in trouble as his king has no more protection.

24...♗h3 25.♖g1 ♘h6

25...exf4?! 26.♗xh5 gxh5 27.♗xf4 ♗e7 28.♕d4† ♗f6 29.♕d3±

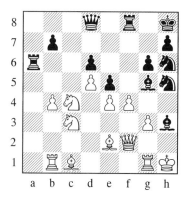

26.b5!?

Perhaps White could consider 26.♗xh5 gxh5 27.f5 ♘g4 28.♕e2 ♗h4 29.♘e3 ♖g8 30.♘xg4 ♗xg4 31.♕d3 ♗f6∞ although in terms of king safety, this position is also more dangerous for White.

26...♖a8 27.♕b6

Trying to exchange queens.

27...♘g4

After 27...exf4 the messy position may result in a draw: 28.♗xh5 gxh5 29.gxf4 (29.♕xd6 ♕c8 30.♘b6 ♕g4 31.♗b2 ♗f3† 32.♔h2 ♘g4† 33.♔xh3 ♘f2† 34.♔h2 ♘g4†= leads to a draw) 29...♗xf4 30.♕d4† ♕f6 31.♕xf6† ♖xf6 32.♗xf4 ♖xf4 33.♘xd6 ♖h4 34.♔h2 ♗f1† 35.♔g3 ♖g4† 36.♔h2 ♖h4†= with perpetual check.

28.♕xd8 ♗xd8 29.♘xd6 ♗b6 30.♘xb7

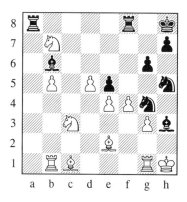

The position is completely crazy, but objectively, with the help of a computer we can say it should be at least equal for Black.

30...♗d4!

Worse is 30...♗xg1?! 31.♔xg1 ♘xg3 32.♗xg4 ♗xg4 33.♘d6 exf4 34.b6 f3 35.♗e3 ♘e2† 36.♔f2±.

Now the main line continues:

31.♗xg4 ♗xg4 32.♗d2 ♖a3 33.♖bc1 exf4 34.gxf4 ♗f3† 35.♔h2 ♘xf4 36.♖g3 ♘d3 37.♖f1 ♘e5 38.♘b1 ♖a1∓

e) So far Black has been holding his own everywhere, but White has a high-quality prophylactic move which should enable him to maintain the better chances:

22.♖g1!

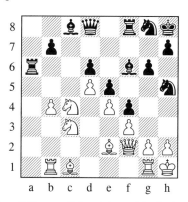

Now White will be able to block the attack on his queen.

22...♗h4

There is nothing better, for instance: 22...♘h6 23.b5 ♖a8 24.♗b2 ♘f7 (24...♗h4 25.♕b6 ♕g5 26.♖gc1 ♗g3 27.hxg3 fxg3 28.♔g1 ♕h4 29.♔f1+−) 25.♖a1±

23.g3 fxg3 24.hxg3 ♗g5 25.b5 ♖a8 26.♗a3!

It is interesting to compare this position with the note to White's 24th move in line 'd' above. Because of the position of the rook on g1 instead of f1, White no longer has to worry about the double sacrifice on a3 and g3. This is enough to swing the balance of the position in White's favour.

26.f4 is less promising. 26...exf4 27.♗xh5 gxh5 28.♗xf4 ♗g4 29.♕d4† ♗f6 30.♕d3 ♖c8 31.♘e2 ♗g5 32.♗xg5 ♕xg5 33.♘d4 The position remains quite complicated as White's king is weak.

26...♖f6

From here White can look to make something of his positional advantages. A sample line is:

27.♖a1 ♘h6 28.♕g2 ♘f7 29.♗b4 ♖xa1 30.♖xa1 ♗d7 31.♖a7 ♕b8 32.b6

White's chances are higher, although he will still have to be careful on the kingside.

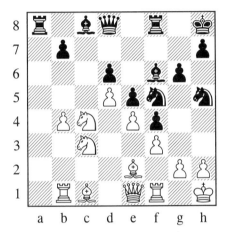

21.exf5 ♗h4 22.♕d1 ♘g3† 23.♔g1

But not 23.hxg3?? ♗xg3 when checkmate is coming!

23...♗xf5 24.♗d3

24.♖b3 is also good for White.

24...♖c8 25.♖b3 ♖xc4!?

Nisipeanu is doing his best to complicate the position.

25...♔g8 26.♖f2 e4 27.fxe4 ♘xe4 28.♘xe4 ♗xe4 29.♖f1 ♖xd5 30.♖xf4 ♖xf4 31.♗xf4 ♔h8 (31...♗xc4 32.♗xc4† ♖xc4 33.♕d5†+–) 32.♖c3 ♕f6 33.♕d2 b5 34.♗e3±

25...♗xd3 is the computer's top choice, but

a human player would have good reasons to reject it: 26.♖xd3 ♘xf1 27.♔xf1 ♕c7 28.♘d2 ♖a8 29.♖b1 ♖fc8 30.♘de4

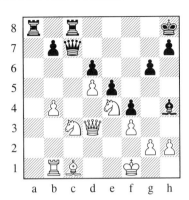

Black has a rook and pawn for two pieces, but strategically his position is completely lost. White's knights protect one another while blockading the e5-pawn. Black's bishop has no future, his rooks are not achieving anything on the open files, and White will easily improve his position.

26.♗xc4 ♕b6† 27.♖f2

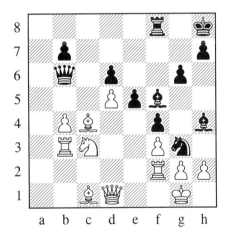

27...♖c8

27...♘h5 was another idea, but Black is losing here too: 28.♕d2 ♖c8 29.♗f1 ♘f6 Intending to play ...e4. 30.♕e2! (30.♗b2 g5 31.h3 h5 gives Black some counterplay) 30...♕d4 31.g3 fxg3 32.hxg3 ♗xg3 33.♗e3 ♕h4 34.♕d2 ♗xf2†

35.♖xf2 ♕xf2† 36.♔xf2+– The endgame is
hopeless for Black.

28.♘a4!

The key move (and also pretty much
the only good one in the position!), which
the Romanian grandmaster may well have
overlooked.

28...♕a7

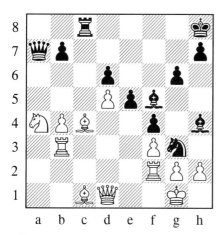

29.♘c5!

An excellent move. Now the black queen is
out of the game and the knight is a fantastic
blocker of all Black's play.

29...♘h5

29...dxc5? 30.hxg3 is winning.

30.♖d2 b5

After 30...dxc5 31.b5 White is the exchange
up with a strong passed d-pawn and no
counterplay for Black.

31.♖a3 ♕b8

31...♕c7 32.♗d3 dxc5 33.♗xf5 gxf5 34.♗b2
cxb4 35.♖a6±

32.♗d3

Forcing simplifications. The game is almost
over.

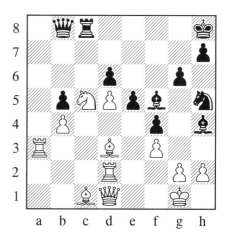

**32...dxc5 33.♗xf5 gxf5 34.bxc5 b4 35.♖a1
♖xc5 36.♗b2 ♗d8 37.♖a6 ♔g8 38.♕a4**

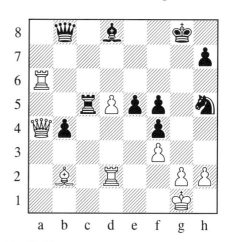

38...♖b5?

38...♘f6 would have prolonged the game
slightly, although 39.♖e6 ♔f7 40.♖xe5 ♖c1†
41.♖d1 ♖xd1† 42.♕xd1 ♕a7† 43.♔h1 is still
winning easily enough.

39.♖a8 ♕b6† 40.♔f1
1–0

GAME 48

▷ **V. Kramnik (2791)**
▶ **A. Giri (2722)**
Unive Crown, Hoogeveen
Round 1, 16.10.2011 **[E97]**
Annotated by Etienne Bacrot

In the Bayonet Attack against the King's Indian Defence, Vladimir Kramnik tried an unusual idea with 12.♗f3 (instead of the standard 12.f3). In such little explored territory, Black had decisions to make immediately on move 12. Giri's reaction looked sensible until he went wrong with 15...♘e8? after which White was clearly better. A few moves later a further slip from Black ensured that White would win.

Kramnik's 12.♗f3 is very interesting and should certainly be tested again.

1.♘f3 ♘f6 2.c4 g6 3.♘c3 ♗g7 4.e4 d6 5.d4 0–0 6.♗e2 e5 7.0–0 ♘c6 8.d5 ♘e7 9.b4 ♘h5

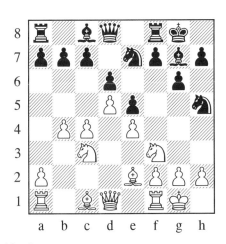

10.g3

A couple of months earlier, Vladimir tried the strange 10.c5 f5 11.a4 in Kramnik – Nakamura, Dortmund 2011, which was analysed in game 50 of the September 2011 issue of *Chess Evolution*.

10...f5 11.♘g5 ♘f6

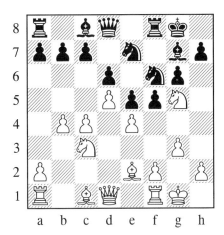

12.♗f3

An unusual try and an interesting one!

I cannot resist reminding the reader of a very exciting game of great theoretical importance for the previous main line, which was won by Black:
12.f3 f4 13.b5 fxg3 14.hxg3 h6 15.♘e6 ♗xe6 16.dxe6 ♕c8 17.♘d5 ♕xe6 18.♘xc7 ♕h3 19.♖f2 ♘xe4 20.fxe4 ♖xf2 21.♔xf2 ♖f8† 22.♔e3 ♕xg3† 23.♔d2 ♖f2 24.♘e8

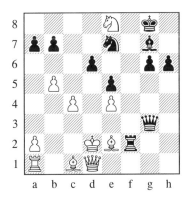

Van Wely, as White, was repeating a game he won in 2008 against *the* King's Indian expert, Teimour Radjabov (well, Kasparov has been retired for a long time!). But now came an unpleasant surprise:
24...♕f3!

White has no more than 0.00. Yes, it is the computer era in modern chess! White

followed up with normal human moves:
25.♘xd6 ♗f6 26.c5

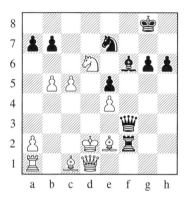

White is waiting for a perpetual such as
26...♗g5† 27.♔e1 ♖f1† 28.♔xf1 ♕g3†
29.♔e2 ♕g4† but instead:

26...♘d5!!

Simply giving up one of Black's remaining
pieces to avoid a nasty check on b3 and gain
the c3-square for a deadly check of his own.

27.exd5 e4 28.♔e1

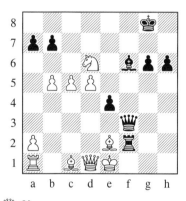

28...♕g2?

A pity; Black missed the completion of
his masterpiece: 28...♗c3†!! 29.♗d2 ♕g3!!
30.♗xc3 e3 And despite being +8 in material,
White cannot avoid mate in two.

29.♔d2 ♗xa1?

It was not too late to repeat the position with
29...♕f3!.

30.c6?

No, there is no time for queening! White

had a last chance to defend by repatriating
the knight with 30.♘c4!.

30...♕f3–+

Black is winning, and it would be unfair to
the gladiators not to show the final moves:
31.♘xe4 ♕xe4 32.c7 ♕f4† 33.♔e1 ♗c3†
34.♗d2 ♕g3 35.♗xc3 ♖f3† 36.♗d2 ♖xc3
37.d6 ♕e3† 38.♔e1 ♖c1 39.♕xc1 ♕xc1†
40.♔f2 ♕c5† 41.♔f3 ♔f7 42.♗f1 ♕f5†
43.♔g3 ♕e6 44.♔f2 h5 45.a4 ♔f6 46.♗g2
♕c8 47.♔g3 g5 0–1

Enough – a queen is quite strong, Van Wely
– Stellwagen, Amsterdam 2009.

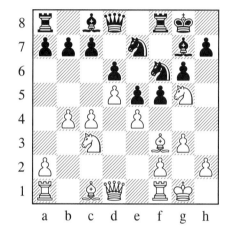

12...c6

This seems like the main move, but let's also
see some alternatives:

12...fxe4 13.♘cxe4 ♘f5 14.♗g2 Of course
White should play strategically: the strong
e4-square and the bad bishop on g7 are not
fully compensated by the knight invasion on
d4. (Direct play would not promise White an
advantage: 14.♘e6?! ♗xe6 15.dxe6 c6 16.b5
♘d4 17.bxc6 bxc6 18.♗e3 ♘xf3† 19.♕xf3
♘xe4 20.♕xe4 d5 21.e7 dxe4 22.exd8=♕
♖fxd8=) 14...♘d4 15.♗b2 White seems to be
better.

12...h6 13.♘e6 ♗xe6 14.dxe6 ♕c8 15.♘d5
looks bad for Black.

12...♔h8!? 13.b5 ♖b8 is a good direction in which to search if you do not want to repeat the game.

13.♗a3

Played quickly by Kramnik, so it makes little sense to search for an improvement for White!

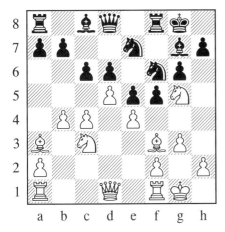

13...cxd5!

It is very important to try to open the c-file.

Let's also see another direct approach: 13...h6 14.♘e6 ♗xe6 15.dxe6 fxe4 16.♘xe4 ♘xe4 17.♗xe4 d5 18.♗g2

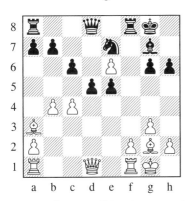

18...e4 (18...♕d6 19.♕b3 b5 20.cxd5 cxd5 21.♖ad1 ♖ad8 22.♗c1 This position can be considered, but it looks nasty for Black.) 19.b5! ♗xa1 20.♕xa1 White has huge compensation for the exchange.

14.exd5

The less usual way to recapture, but if instead: 14.cxd5 h6 15.♘e6 ♗xe6 16.dxe6 ♘xe4 17.♘xe4 (17.♗xe4 fxe4 18.♘xe4 d5 19.♘c5 ♕d6∞) 17...fxe4 18.♗xe4 d5 19.♗g2 e4 20.b5 ♗xa1 21.♕xa1 ♖c8!

Thanks to the open c-file, Black equalizes. 22.♕e5 ♖c2 23.♗b2 ♖xb2=

14...e4 15.♗e2

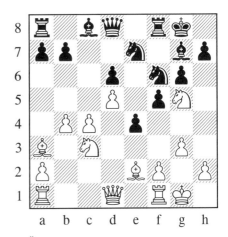

15...♘e8?

This passive move clearly gives the upper hand to White. Black had two ways to fight:

15...f4!? 16.♘gxe4!
   16.gxf4!? ♘f5 17.♖c1 ♖e8 is very messy, for example: 18.♖e1 e3 19.fxe3 (19.♗f3 exf2†
   20.♔xf2 ♘d4∞) 19...♖xe3 20.c5 a5∞
   16.c5 permits another typical break:
   16...fxg3 17.hxg3 e3 with good play.
16...♘xe4 17.♘xe4 ♗f5 18.♗f3 ♗xa1 19.♕xa1 ♗xe4 20.♗xe4 ♘f5

This position is not very appealing at first sight from Black's point of view. More in-depth analysis is required before it is ready to face an ex-world champion!

15...h6!?
Maybe this is the best choice.
16.♘e6 ♗xe6 17.dxe6 f4!

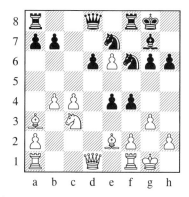

This position should be rechecked carefully, but for me now, the lines below are enough. Perhaps I will have to analyse it even more deeply for the next issue!

18.gxf4

18.♕d2 f3 19.♗d1 ♕c8 20.♖e1 ♕xe6 21.♗xf3 ♕xc4 White has compensation for the pawn but not enough to claim an advantage.

18...♘h5! 19.♗xh5
19.♘xe4 ♘xf4∞

19...♗xc3 20.♖c1 ♗g7 21.♗g4 ♖xf4
Black seems fine.

16.♖c1 h6 17.♘e6 ♗xe6 18.dxe6

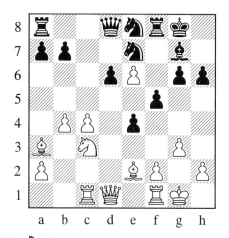

18...♘c7?

The decisive mistake; Black should instead have decided to take the e6-pawn with his queen:

18...♕c8 Now White has a choice of two more or less forcing lines, both of which secure a small but unambiguous advantage: 19.♘d5 ♕xe6 20.♘f4 ♕f7 21.b5 ♔h7 22.c5 d5 23.c6 bxc6 24.bxc6 ♘c7 25.♗xe7 ♕xe7 26.♘xd5 ♘xd5 27.♕xd5± or 19.c5 ♕xe6 20.cxd6 ♘xd6 21.♘b5 ♖fd8 22.♘c7 ♕xa2 23.♘xa8 ♕xa3 24.♗c4† ♔h7 25.♘c7 e3 26.♘e6 exf2† 27.♖xf2 ♖c8 28.♘xg7 ♘xc4 29.♕e1 ♘d5 30.♘e6 ♕xb4 31.♕xb4 ♘xb4 32.♖d2!±.

19.b5 ♗e5 20.♕b3 ♔g7 21.♖fd1 ♘xe6 22.c5+−

All White's pieces are on their ideal posts.

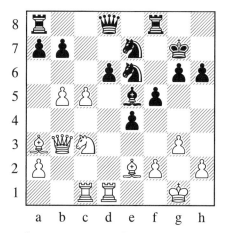

22...♘d4 23.♖xd4 ♗xd4 24.cxd6 ♘g8 25.♘d5 ♔h8 26.♖c7 ♗e5 27.♗b2

Of course White is still winning, but it was a shame to give up the d6-pawn; more logical was 27.♖e7 ♗xd6 28.♗b2† ♘f6 29.♖e6+−.

**27...♕xd6 28.♖xb7 g5 29.b6 a5 30.♗h5 ♖ab8 31.♖a7 ♗xb2 32.♕xb2† ♘f6 33.♗f7 ♔g7 34.♖d7 ♕c6 35.♗e6†
1–0**

24 Puzzles

by GM Jacob Aagaard

This is my second puzzle selection for *Chess Evolution* and this time it is a bit different from the previous version. Last time I had 12 easy to understand – play and win – puzzles. This time I have gone for a slightly different approach. The 24 positions I have chosen were selected from a list of 53 games supplied to me by Arkadij Naiditsch. Of these some were not really working as puzzles for various reasons, not least of all that the outcome was very uncertain once you analysed deeper! An example is the following:

Stojanovic – Kasimdzhanov, European Team Championship, 27.09.2011

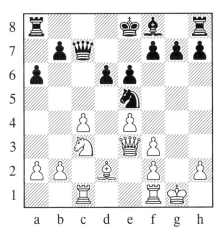

15.f4! ♘xc4?! 15...♘g4 16.♕g3 ♘f6 17.f5! is however also better for White. **16.♕e2 ♘xd2 17.♘d5 ♕d8 18.♘c7† ♔d7 19.♘xa8 ♘xf1 20.♖c7† ♕xc7 21.♘xc7 ♔xc7 22.♔xf1± ♗e7 23.♕h5 g6 24.♕a5† ♔d7 25.♕b4 ♖b8 26.♕a4† ♔c7 27.♕d4 ♖g8 28.a4 h5 29.b4 h4 30.b5 axb5 31.axb5 ♖c8 32.b6† ♔d7 33.♕a4† ♖c6 34.♕a7 ♖c1† 35.♔g2 ♔c6 36.♕a4† ♔xb6 37.♕e8 ♗f6 38.♕xf7 ♗d4 39.♕xe6 ♗c5 40.f5 gxf5 41.exf5 ♖c3 42.h3 ♖a3 43.f6 ♖a8 44.f7 1–0**

However the problem is that if Black plays 17...♕a5 18.♘c7† ♔e7 19.♘xa8 ♘xf1 20.♖c7† ♔f6 21.b4! ♕b5 22.e5† dxe5 23.fxe5† ♔g5 24.f4† ♔h6 25.♕g4 f6 26.♖c3, it looks bad, but things are not so clear:

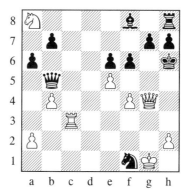

26...♘e3! 27.♖xe3 ♗c5 28.bxc5 ♕xc5 29.♕h3† ♔g6 30.♕g2† ♔f7 31.♕xb7† ♔g6 32.♕e4† f5
33.♕g2† ♔f7 34.♕b7† ♔g6 35.♕b3 ♔f7 36.♕b6 ♕c1† 37.♔g2 ♖c8 38.♕b7† ♔g8 39.♖e2 ♖c2
40.♖xc2 ♕xc2† 41.♔g3 h6⩲

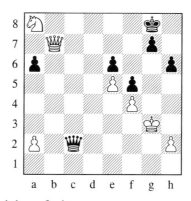

Maybe there is a win, but I did not find it.

In the end I decided to include a few positions that either led to a draw, gave only some advantage, or had two ways of winning the position. The ones leading to a draw are 6, 8 and 15. The ones leading to some advantage, but no guaranteed win are 10, 11, 17 and 20. Finally the ending in game 23 can be won prosaically as well as with a beautiful tactic.

1. Mamedyarov – Grandelius

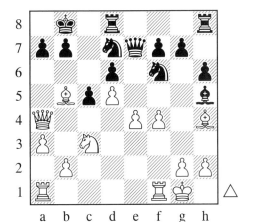

2. Nielsen – Volokitin

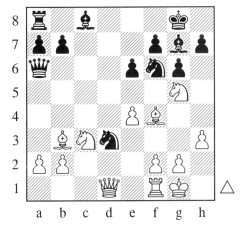

3. Korobov – Nepomniachtchi

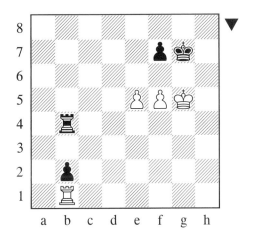

4. Tikkanen – Vitiugov

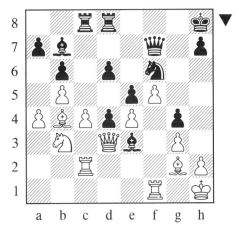

5. Movsesian – Naiditsch

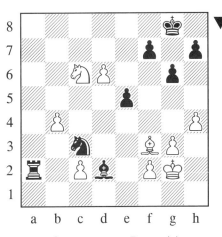

6. Pavasovic – Bauer (=)

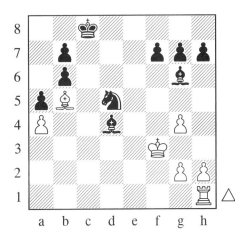

7. Areshchenko – Hracek

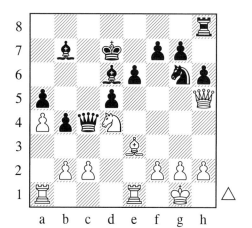

10. Thorfinnsson – Motylev (±)

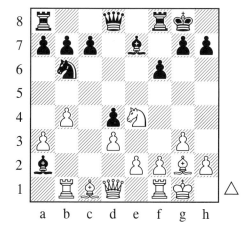

8. Bacrot – Melkumyan (=)

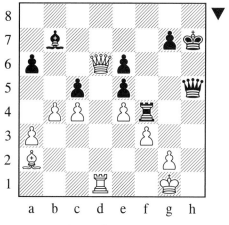

11. Nisipeanu – Najer (∓)

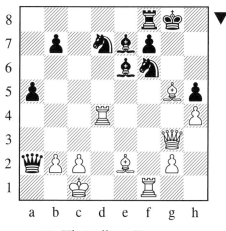

9. Deviatkin – Azarov

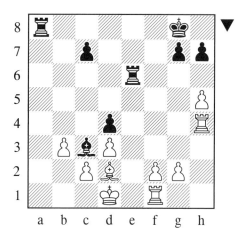

12. Khairullin – Kurnosov

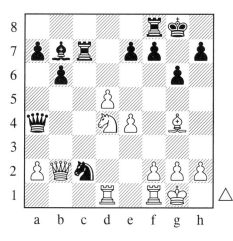

13. Popov – Khalifman

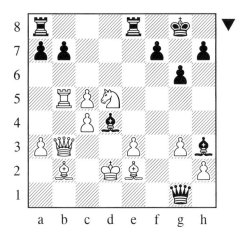

16. Kamsky – Svidler

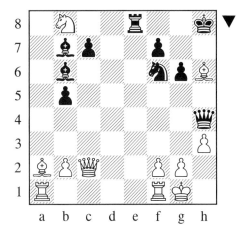

14. Bartel – Predojevic

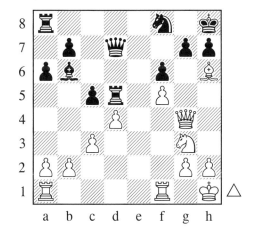

17. Rasulov – Khismatullin (∓)

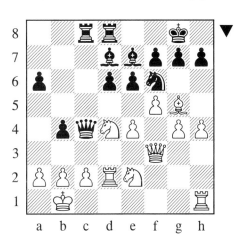

15. Heemskerk – Nisipeanu (=)

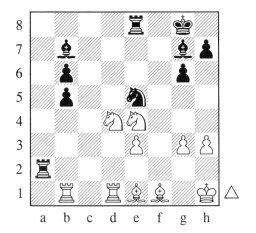

18. Ni Hua - Morozevich

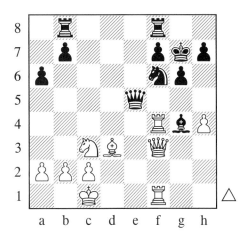

19. Le Quang Liem – Feller

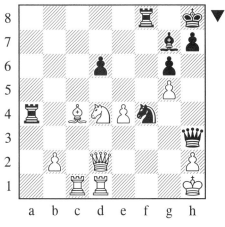

22. Predojevic – Mamedyarov

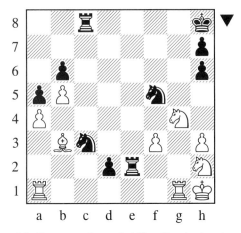

20. Predojevic – Mamedyarov (∓)

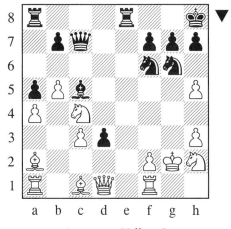

23. Ponomariov – Svidler (2 solutions)

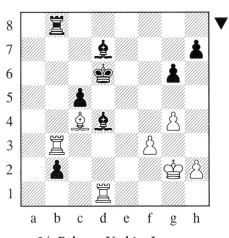

21. Aronian – Vallejo Pons

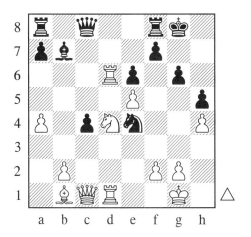

24. Polgar – Vachier Lagrave

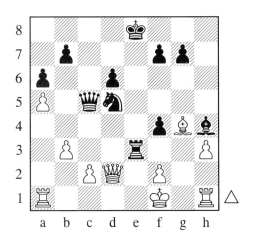

1. Mamedyarov – Grandelius, European Club Championship, 29.09.2011
17.e5! White wins a piece and quickly the game. **17...dxe5 18.fxe5 ♘xe5 19.♖ae1 ♗a8 20.♗g3 ♘fg4 21.h3 1–0**

2. Nielsen – Volokitin, European Club Championship, 01.10.2011
18.♗c2! Black resigned as **18...♘xf4 19.♕d8† ♗f8 20.♕xf6** leads to mate. **1–0**

3. Korobov – Nepomniachtchi, European Club Championship, 30.09.2011
44...f6†! This simple tactic decides the game. **45.♔h5** After 45.exf6† ♔f7 46.♔h6 ♔xf6 47.♔h5 ♔xf5 Black's king marches in. **45...fxe5 46.♔g5 ♔f7 47.f6 e4 0–1**

4. Tikkanen – Vitiugov, European Club Championship, 26.09.2011
White is too fragile on the long diagonal and his queen is overloaded. He is punished for this:
30...♘xe4!! 31.♗xe4 ♖xc4!! 32.♘d2 32.♗d2 ♖xc2 33.♕xc2 and now Black has many winning moves. The most pleasing to the eye is 33...♕c4!. **32...♖xb4 33.♖fc1 ♗xd2 34.♖c7 ♗xe4† 35.♕xe4 ♕f6 36.♕b7 ♖xc1 37.♖f7 ♕h6 38.♕e7 ♗g5 39.f6 ♖b1† 0–1**

5. Movsesian – Naiditsch, Croatian Team Championship, 04.10.2011
37...♗e3!! Just in time to stop the passed pawn. White must have missed this. 37...♔f8 38.d7 ♖a8= **38.fxe3** 38.d7 ♗b6–+ **38...♖xc2† 39.♔f1 ♖d2–+ 0–1, 70.**

6. Pavasovic – Bauer, European Club Championship, 26.09.2011
White saves a draw with a nice sacrifice. **27.♖d1! ♗e4† 28.♔xe4! ♘c3† 29.♔xd4 ♘xd1 30.h3!** The knight is in trouble. Black will not be able to make progress. **30...♔c7 31.♔d3 ♔d6 32.♔d2 ♘f2 33.♔e3 ♘d1† 34.♔d2 ½–½**

7. Areshchenko – Hracek, European Club Championship, 27.09.2011
White has a great position no matter what, but he can make it even better after: **23.♘xe6!!** 23.♖ad1+– **23...♔xe6 24.♗f4†! ♔d7 25.♕f5† ♔c6 26.♗xd6 d4!?** Hoping for a miracle. The point of the combination was of course 26...♔xd6 27.♕xf7 and White ends up with an extra exchange without facing counterplay. **27.♗g3 ♕d5 28.♕xd5† ♔xd5 29.♖ad1 ♖c8 30.♖d2 ♗a6 31.f3 b3 32.cxb3 d3 33.♖e3 ♖c1† 34.♔f2 ♔c6 35.♗e5 f6 36.♗c3 ♘f4 37.♗xa5 ♖h1 38.♖e1 ♖xh2 39.♔g3 ♖h5 40.♖c1† ♔d7 41.♖c7† 1–0**

8. Bacrot – Melkumyan, European Club Championship, 28.09.2011
Black missed a forced draw: **34...♗xe4!!** 34...♖h4 35.♗b1 (35.♗b3!± was correct here) 35...♖h1† 36.♔f2 ♕h4† 37.♔e2 ♖h2? (37...♕h2! would have held) 38.♖g1± 1–0, 83. **35.fxe4** 35.♖e1 ♕h4! is also okay for Black. White can play 36.♖f1 ♖xf3 37.♖xf3 ♗xf3 38.♕xe5 ♕g4 39.♗b1†, but after 39...g6 he has no serious prospects. A drawn queen ending is approaching fast. **35...♕e2! 36.♖d3□ ♕f2† 37.♔h2 ♖h4† 38.♖h3 ♕f4† 39.♔g1 ♖xh3 40.gxh3 ♕e3†=** Either Black has a perpetual, or after something like **41.♔f1 ♕xh3† 42.♔e2 ♕h2† 43.♔d1 ♕xa2=** he will draw by other means. For example a perpetual...

9. Deviatkin – Azarov, Chigorin Memorial, 22.10.2011

Black spotted a nice little mating combination: **27...♖a1† 28.♗c1 ♗b2 29.♔d2 ♖xc1! 30.♖hh1**
A bit strange. Resigns make more sense, or 30.♖xc1 ♗c3† 31.♔d1 ♖e1#. **30...♗xf1 31.♖xf1**
♗c3† 32.♔d1 ♗f7 33.f4 ♖e3 34.g4 h6 35.g5 c5 36.♖g1 ♔e6 37.♖h1 ♔f5 38.gxh6 gxh6 0–1

10. Bj. Thorfinnsson – Motylev, European Club Championship, 26.09.2011

White managed to take the initiative with a clever temporary rook sacrifice: **14.♘c5!! ♗xb1**
14...♖xc5 15.bxc5 ♗xb1 16.♕b3† ♔h8 17.cxb6± would leave White on the verge of winning.
15.♕b3† ♔h8 15...♖f7 16.♘xb7 ♕e8 17.♗b2± would leave White with excessive light-squared
compensation. **16.♘e6** 16.♘xb7 ♕d7 17.♘a5± was maybe even stronger. White is close to having
a clear advantage. **16...♕d7 17.♘xf8 ♖xf8 18.♗xb7 ♕a4?!** 18...c5 19.♗f3± was preferable, even
if White remains better. **19.♕xb1± c6 20.♕a2 ♗xb4 21.♕e6 ♗xa3 22.♗xc6 ♕b4 23.♗e4 f5**
24.♗xf5 ♘a4 25.♗f4 25.♗xa3 ♕xa3 26.♖b1 ♘c3 27.♖b7+– would have left Black with no real
chances. **25...♘c3 26.♗e5 ♕e7 27.♕xe7 ♗xe7 28.♗g4 ♗c5 29.♖a1 h5 30.♗f3 ♖e8 31.♗c7**
♖e7 32.♗b8 ♘xe2† 33.♗xe2? 33.♔g2 should still get the job done, but probably Thorfinnsson
was looking for clarity more than good moves? **33...♖xe2 34.♗xa7 ♗xa7 35.♖xa7 ♖d2** Black is
saving the draw. **36.♖a3 ♖d1† 37.♔g2 ♔h7 38.h3 g5 39.♔f3 ♖d2 40.h4 g4† 41.♔f4 ♖xf2†**
42.♔g5 ♖f3 43.♔xh5 ♖xg3 44.♖a7† ♔g8 45.♔g6 ♖f3 46.h5 g3 47.h6 ♖f8 48.♖g7† ½–½

11. Nisipeanu – Najer, European Club Championship, 29.09.2011

23...♔h8?? The only move was 23...♗g4!, when after 24.c3?! Black has: 24...♗a3!! (24...♘c5?!
allows White to get away with a draw: 25.♗xf6 ♗xf6 26.♖xg4†! hxg4 27.♖xf6 ♕a1† 28.♔c2
♕a4† 29.♔c1=; 24...♘e4 25.♖xe4 ♗xg5† 26.♔c2 ♘f6) 25.bxa3 ♖xe2∓ For this reason White
should play 24.♗xf6! ♘xf6 25.c3, although his prospects are dour after 25...♖d8. Still there
are reasonable drawing chances after: 26.♗xg4 ♘xg4 27.♖xd8† ♗xd8 28.♖f5 ♕a1† (28...♕e6
29.♖xh5 f5∓) 29.♔c2 ♕a4† 30.♔c1 ♗xh4! 31.♕f3 (31.♕xh4 ♕a1† 32.♔c2 ♘e3†) 31...♗f6∓
24.♖xf6?! 24.♗xf6†! ♘xf6 25.♕e5 won immediately. Why White did not play it is hard to guess.
24...♘xf6 25.♕e5 ♔g7 26.♗h6†? White could still have gained a clear advantage with: 26.♖f4!
♕a1† 27.♔d2 ♖d8† 28.♗d3 ♔f8 29.♖xf6± **26...♔xh6 27.♕g5† ♔h7 28.♗d3† ♔h8 29.♕h6†**
♔g8 30.♕g5† ♔h8 31.♕h6† ♔g8 ½–½

12. Khairullin – Kurnosov, European Club Championship, 29.09.2011

22.♘e6!! The computer points out a much more difficult win after 22.d6!? exd6 23.♘e6!! fxe6
24.♗xe6† ♔f7 25.♖xd6!, when Black's kingside cannot withstand the pressure. The main line is:
25...♕xe4 26.f3 ♕e3† 27.♔h1 ♕e2 28.♗xf7† ♖xf7 29.♖d8† ♖f8 30.♖xf8† ♔xf8 31.♖c1 and the
knight is just trapped. **22...fxe6 23.♗xe6† ♗f7 24.♕e5!** 24.d6 exd6 25.♖xd6 still won, but this is
hard to understand for a human. **24...♖c8 25.♕d3?!** White had a direct win with: 25.♗xf7† ♔xf7
26.♕e6† ♔f8 27.d6 exd6 28.♖xd6† and either ♕d7† on the next move, picking up the bishop,
or 28...♔g8 29.♕e6† ♔h8 30.♖d7 winning the queen or more. **25...♖cf8 26.♗xf7†** 26.♖c1!+–
26...♖xf7 27.♕b8† ♔g7 28.♕xb7± 1–0, 54.

13. Val. Popov – Khalifman, Chigorin Memorial, 16.10.2011

Clearly Black has the advantage, but he needs to exploit it before it disappears in the mist of
time. **27...♗xe3†! 28.♘xe3 ♖ad8†** The most natural, but Black could also prepare the check

with 28...♕f2!? based on 29.♕c3 f6 30.♕xf6 ♕xe3† 31.♔c2 ♗f5† with a mating attack. **29.♘d5 ♖xe2†!** Again the obvious move. The quaint 29...♗f1!? also wins, because of 30.♗d1 ♗xc4!! 31.♕xc4 ♕g2† 32.♔c1 ♖xd5 33.♗c3 ♕h1 34.♗d4 ♕e4 and Black wins material. **30.♔xe2 ♖e8† 31.♕e3** 31.♔d2 ♕e1† is mate in two. **31...♗g4† 32.♔d3 ♗f5† 33.♔e2 ♕xh2† 34.♔f3 ♗g4† 0–1**

14. Bartel – Predojevic, European Club Championship, 29.09.2011

30.♘h5!! The difficulty here is not so much to see the tactic, but to understand that after **30...gxh6 31.♘xf6 ♕f7 32.♘xd5 ♕xd5 33.♖ae1** Black is completely without any chances. **33...♕f7 34.f6 cxd4?!** Not the toughest defence, but 34...♘g6 loses to a computer line with 35.h4, or to the simpler 35.♕e6 ♕xe6 36.♖xe6 ♗c7 37.d5 ♖d8 38.d6!+–. **35.♖e7 ♕g6 36.♕f3 ♗d8 37.♕xb7 dxc3 38.♕xa8** 38.♖e8! would have been a nice trick shot, but taking everything also works. **1–0**

15. Heemskerk – Nisipeanu, European Club Championship, 25.09.2011

White missed an excellent defensive idea: **29.♗g2!** The game went: 29.♖xb5 ♗xe4†∓ 30.♔g1 ♔h8 31.♖xb6 ♗h6 32.♗f2 ♖f8 33.♗e2 ♗d3 34.♖e1 ♗c4 35.♖b4 ♘d3 36.♖xc4 ♘xe1 37.♗xe1 ♖xe3† 38.♔h1 ♗xd4 39.♗d3 ♖a1 40.♖xd4 ♖xe1† 41.♔g2 ♖d1 42.♖d5 ♖d2† 0–1 **29...♖xg2 30.♘d6!!** The fork leaves Black with instant material losses. His most dangerous continuation is not that dangerous. 30.♔xg2? ♗xe4†∓ **30...♖xg3†!?** 30...♖a8 31.♘xe8= **31.♔h2** 31.♘xb7 ♖xh3† 32.♔g2 ♖xe3 33.♘d6 is also equal. **31...♖g2† 32.♔h1 ♖a2† 33.♘xb7 ♘c4 34.♘xb5 ♖xe3 35.♖d8† ♗f8 36.♗b4** White is not worse.

16. Kamsky – Svidler, Khanty-Mansiysk (4.2), 07.09.2011

26...♖e2!! 26...♕g3 27.♘c6 ♖e2 28.♕c3 only leads to a draw: 28...♗xf2† 29.♔h1 ♕xc3 30.bxc3 ♗xc6 31.♖fd1! ♗c5 32.♖d2 ♗xg2† 33.♔h2 ♗d6† 34.♔g1 ♗c5† with perpetual check. This would of course have been okay for Svidler, as he would have progressed in the tournament, but the game move wins directly! **27.♕c3** 27.♕xe2 ♕g3 is mate in six. White can give up all his pieces except the f1-rook before he is inevitably mated. **27...♖xf2** White is mated. **28.♘c6 ♖xf1† 0–1**

17. Rasulov – Khismatullin, Chigorin Memorial, 20.10.2011

Black has a nice position in general, but this is not enough for Khismatullin, who plays a miraculous combination: **19...♘xe4!! 20.♕xe4 ♗g5 21.b3!** 21.hxg5 ♗c6–+ was the first point to see. **21...♗c6!!** Black has to have this, or otherwise the pin would disappear and White would win a piece. **22.♕xc6 ♕xc6 23.♘xc6 ♗xd2 24.♘e7†** 24.♘xd8 ♖xd8∓ **24...♔f8 25.♘xc8 ♖xc8?!∓** Here Black plays it safe. After 25...exf5! he could have obtained a significant advantage: 26.♘b6 ♖e8 27.♖h2 fxg4∓ The bishop will work very well with the four pawns. White will suffer badly. **26.♖d1 ♗e3 27.♖xd6** 27.fxe6 fxe6 28.♖xd6 ♔e7 29.♖d3∓ would have given White decent drawing chances. **27...exf5 28.gxf5 ♖e8! 29.c4 ♗f2!∓ 30.♘f4 ♗xh4 31.♖d1** 31.♖xa6 ♗g5 32.♘h5 g6 33.fxg6 fxg6! 34.♘f6 ♗xf6 35.♖xf6† ♔g7∓ and it looks like White should lose. **31...a5 32.♔c2 ♗g3 33.♘d5 h5 34.♖h1 h4 35.♔d3 g5 36.fxg6 fxg6 37.c5 ♔f7 38.♘e3 ♖e5 39.c6 ♖c5 40.♘c4 0–1**

18. Ni Hua - Morozevich, Governor's Cup, Saratov 11.10.2011

23.♕h1! This was the correct move, after which Black would have been in for a rough ride. The game continuation was: 23.♖xg4?! ♘xg4 24.♕xg4 ♖bd8± White of course has the advantage here, but the position is not entirely clear yet and actually Black managed to turn things around and won the game in 47 moves. 23.♕g2 ♕e3† 24.♔b1 ♗h3! 25.♕g5 ♘g4 leads to a mess and 23.♕f2 ♗h3! is also not clear. **23...♗f5 24.♗xf5 ♕e3† 25.♔b1 gxf5 26.♖xf5 ♘e8 27.♘e4** White is entirely winning. Here is a possible line: **27...f6 28.♘g5 ♔h8 29.♖e1 ♕d2 30.♖d5 ♕b4 31.♘xh7! ♖f7** Or 31...♔xh7 32.♖g1 f5 33.♖d7† ♔h8 34.♕f3 ♘f6 35.♕xf5 with mate. **32.♖e4 ♕b6 33.♘f8! ♖d8 34.♖g6† ♔h7 35.♘e7**

19. Le Quang Liem – Feller, Lubbock, 17.10.2011

32...♖xc4!! is a beautiful winning combination. Instead Black played: 32...♖aa8?= 33.♖g1 ♖ae8 34.♖g3 ♘h5 35.♘f3 ♘h3 36.♕g2 ♘f4 37.♕c2 ♖c8 38.b3 d5 39.exd5 ♘xd5 40.♕d3 ♘f4 41.♕f1 h6 42.b4 ♖f5 43.♖e1 ♖cf8 44.gxh6 ♕xh6 45.♕g1 ♘h3 46.♕g2 ♘f4 47.♕d2 g5 48.♘d4 ♕d6 49.♖d1 ♖e5 50.♘f3 and a draw was agreed. **33.♖xc4 ♗xd4 34.♕xd4† ♔g8** Surprisingly White cannot defend sufficiently against the threats on the light squares. **35.♕f2** The only move to cover both squares, but it has its own defects. **35...♘d3 36.♕g2** Forced. 36.♕e2 ♖f2–+ **36...♘f2† 37.♔g1 ♕xg2† 38.♔xg2 ♘xd1–+**

20. Predojevic – Mamedyarov, European Club Championship, 27.09.2011

21...♘h4†?! Black should have played: 21...♖e2!! 22.hxg6 Forced, otherwise Black takes on h5. (22.♕xd3 ♘xh5 23.♔h1 ♗xf2! is devastating. 24.♘d6 ♘e5 25.♕d1 ♘g3† 26.♔g2 ♗e1†–+) 22...♗xf2! 23.♔h1□ (23.♖xf2 ♖xf2† 24.♔xf2 ♕xh2†) 23...♗e3!! Preventing the bishop getting into the defence. Probably this is what Mamedyarov missed. 24.♕xe2□ (24.♘f3 ♕g3 25.♘xe3 ♕xh3† 26.♔g1 ♕g3† 27.♔h1 ♘g4 is hopeless.) 24...dxe2 25.♗xe3 exf1=♕† 26.♗xf1 fxg6∓ White has three pieces for his queen, but his position is in disarray and his king weak. **22.♔h1 ♕d7 23.♗e3 ♖ac8** The position around here appears sort of balanced (and deeply complicated). A funny line goes: 23...♕d5† 24.♘f3! ♕f5 (24...♘xf3 25.♘d2±) 25.♘g5 ♔g8!? (25...♕d5†=) 26.h6! gxh6 27.♖g1 ♖xe3 28.♘xe3 ♗xe3 29.♗xf7† ♔f8 30.♗e6 ♕g6 31.♗f7 ♕f5 32.♗e6= **24.h6! gxh6 25.♖g1 ♗xe3 26.♘xe3 b6 27.♘eg4!?** 27.♘d5 ♘e4 28.♕f1 ♕xh3 29.♘xb6± also favoured White, but is again very complicated. **27...♘e4 28.f3 ♘xc3 29.♕d2 ♖e2 30.♕f4! ♕f5 31.♕xf5??** A horrible move. Far stronger was 31.♕xh6! but White needs to stay clear of 31.♕g3?! ♘e4!! 32.♕xh4 ♕f4, e.g. 33.♖g2 ♖xg2 34.♔xg2 ♖c2† 35.♔g1 ♘g5∓ and Black keeps the initiative despite being two pieces down. **31...♘xf5 32.♗xf7?** 32.♗b1□ ♘xb1 33.♖axb1 d2∓ was not what White intended with his last move. **32...d2 33.♗b3** We have reached puzzle 22.

21. Aronian – Vallejo Pons, Grand Slam final, 26.09.2011

27.♕h6!! A very nice combination. **27...♘xd6** 27...♖e8 does not work. White regroups: 28.♘f3! ♘xd6 29.♘g5 ♕c6 30.♕h7† ♔f8 31.♗e4!+– **28.♗xg6!** This was obviously the idea. **28...fxg6 29.♕xg6† ♔h8 30.♕h6† ♔g8 31.♘xe6! ♘f5** 31...♖f7 32.♖xd6 ♕e8 33.♕xh5 is equally hopeless. **32.♕g6† ♔h8 33.♕xh5† ♔g8 34.♕g6† ♔h8 35.♘xf8 ♖xf8 36.♖d7** Winning back one of the sacrificed pieces, giving White four pawns for the piece on top of his positional advantage. **36...♕h6 37.♕xf5 ♖f8 38.♕g5!** The endgame holds no chances for Black. **38...♕xg5**

39.hxg5 ♗e4 40.♖xa7 ♖b8 41.f3 ♗f5 42.♖c7 ♗e6 43.♖c6 ♗g8 44.f4 ♖xb2 45.e6 ♖e2 46.f5 ♖e5 47.g4 ♖e4 48.♔f2 ♖xg4 49.e7 ♗f7 50.g6 ♔g7 51.gxf7 ♔xf7 52.♖e6 ♔e8 53.f6 1–0

22. Predojevic – Mamedyarov, European Club Championship, 27.09.2011

Black had to first chase the knight away with: **33...h5!** Instead Mamedyarov blundered with: 33...♘e4?? 34.fxe4+– ♘g3† 35.♖xg3 ♖e1† 36.♔g2 ♖xa1 37.♘xh6 ♗f8 38.♘f7† ♖xf7 39.♗xf7 ♖g1† 40.♔xg1 d1=♕† 41.♘f1 ♕d4† 42.♘e3 h5 43.♗d5 ♕xa4 44.♘f5 ♕a1† 45.♔f2 ♕b2† 46.♔f3 1–0. Also bad was 33...♘d4? 34.♘xh6†±. **34.♘f6** 34.♗c2 is refuted in almost any which way you like, but especially beautifully by 34...hxg4 35.♗xf5 g3! 36.♖xg3 (36.♘g4 ♖ce8 37.♗c2 h5 and Black will have an extra piece in a moment) 36...♘b1!! 37.♖xb1 ♖c1† 38.♖g1 ♖ee1–+ **34...♘d4** The simple way, but 34...h4 35.♘f1 ♘g3† 36.♘xg3 hxg3 37.♖xg3 ♖e1† 38.♖g1 ♘b1!! 39.♔h2 ♖xg1 40.♔xg1 ♖c3! also wins. The bishop is short of squares. **35.♗f7 d1=♕ 36.♖axd1 ♘xd1 37.♖xd1 ♖cc2 38.♘f1 ♘xf3** with impending mate on h2.

23. Ponomariov – Svidler, Khanty-Mansiysk (6.2), 13.09.2011

33...♖xb3!? The second best option, but still good enough. The pretty way was pointed out by the computer: 33...♗a4! 34.♖xb8 ♗xd1 35.♗d3 ♔c7!! The point; the rook is trapped. 36.♖b5 c4 37.♗xc4 ♗a4 38.♖b4 ♗c3–+ and Black wins a piece. **34.♗xb3 ♗b5?** Here it was much better to play 34...♗e6! 35.♗c2 ♔d5–+ and the win is elementary. **35.♗a2∓ ♔c6 36.♖d2 ♔b6 37.f4?** After 37.♗b1 or 37.♔g3 progress was not as simple. **37...♗c6† 38.♔g3 ♗e4!** Taking control of important squares and finishing the game. **39.♖d1 ♔b5 40.♖e1 ♗d3 41.♖e7 c4 42.♖d7 c3 43.♖d5† ♗c5 0–1**

24. Polgar – Vachier Lagrave, Hoogeveen, 20.10.2011

25.fxe3! 25.c4? was played in the game. Judit missed some tactical finesse (maybe her opponent's reply?) and lost all of her advantage. 25...♖d3! 26.♕e2† ♖e3 27.♕c2 (27.fxe3 ♘xe3† 28.♔g1 ♔f8 gives White time to get the bishop out of the way, but not to avoid the perpetual: 29.♗f3 ♘d1† 30.♔h2 ♗g3† 31.♔g2 ♘e3†) 27...♘b4 28.♕d2 ♗xf2? (28...♖xb3∓) 29.♕xf2 ♘d3 30.♕d2 f3? (30...♔d8±) 31.♖h2! ♕e5 32.♖d1 ♔f8 33.♗f2? (33.♗f5!+–) 33...♖xf2 34.♕xf2 ♕e4? (34...♖xb3±) 35.♕d2 ♔g8 36.♕xd6 g6 37.♕d8† ♔h7 38.♕f6? (38.♕d5 ♕f4 39.♖d3+–) 38...♖d3 39.♕xf7†?! (39.♕h4† ♔g7 40.♕e1±) 39...♔h6 40.♕f8† ♔h7 41.♖e1 ♖d1! 42.♕f7† ♔h6 43.♕f8† ♔h7 44.♕f7† ♔h6 and a draw was agreed. **25...fxe3** 25...♘xe3† 26.♔e2 leaves Black without a follow-up. **26.b4!!** This zwischenzug would have won the game quickly. 26.♖e1 ♔f8 27.♕d1 ♗xe1 28.♖xe1 ♕xc2 also looks insufficient for Black, although the position is not so simple. **26...♕c4†** Black is losing his coordination and at the same time his compensation. 26...♕c6 27.♕g2+–; 26...♘xb4 27.♕g2 d5 28.♖d1+– **27.♕d3 ♕f4† 28.♔e2 ♕f2† 29.♔d1 ♘f4 30.♕xd6 f5 31.♔c1 fxg4 32.hxg4 e2 33.♖b2 ♗f6† 34.♔a2+–** White's king is reasonably secure and her rooks will soon enter the attack with strong effect.

A Chess Evolution Adventure

by GM Etienne Bacrot

Having inspected the content carefully as the editor of the first two issues of your favourite periodical, I can honestly say that the chess work our team made was really useful in the study of the opening. We have all benefited from the work we have done, but this does not exclude the possibilities of some mistakes, which can later be spotted by really strong players. The worst one is probably the fact that I missed **13.♗d1!**, recently played in this position in Karjakin – Laznicka, Poikovsky 2011:

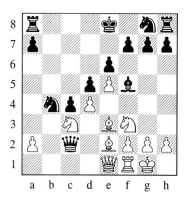

See game 7 for more detail. Please forgive us; chess is a complicated game!

Although we were very happy with the content, we had to react to the sales and the feedback from the readers. The project had to change or die. With the introduction of words in the annotations I decided to retreat and become a mere external help to *Chess Evolution*. I was very pleased to read the September issue with many interesting comments from the expanding team of grandmasters and the higher production level. I hope you were too.

Life, Puzzles & Endgames

From generalities to specifics. Let me share a few words about my past year. After showing strong play against the absolute top in October 2010 in Nanjing, I was hoping for further invitations, but had to accept that they never came. Thus I took the "clever" decision to play some opens – in Basel, Geneva and Neckar, all tournaments with double rounds – for which I was rewarded with a rating loss of 27 points throughout the year. A special mention goes to Neckar Open where I donated 20 rating points to the general well-being of my opponents.

While editing the May issue I also had the chance to be a part of Grischuk's team for the Candidates tournament and thus spend a month working on his preparation to face some of the top theoreticians in the world, Aronian, Kramnik and Gelfand. The latter of course ended up defeating Grischuk in the final and earning a match with Anand for the World Championship. This was very hard work, but at the same time a wonderful experience.

Back in France I delayed getting the necessary rest to first help Marseille to be French Club Champion.

After a small training session it was time for a new season with lots of challenging opponents. I performed above even my own expectations at the French Individual Championship, winning a nice game against Romain Edouard on the way (see game 22, page 167 of *Chess Evolution Sep 2011*), but missed a big opportunity in my game against Fressinet:

1. Fressinet – Bacrot, Caen 2011

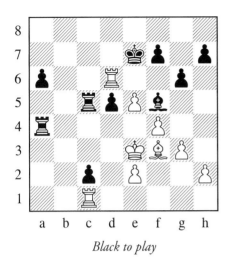

Black to play

I also missed a big chance in the decisive titanic clash:

2. Bacrot – Vachier Lagrave, Caen 2011

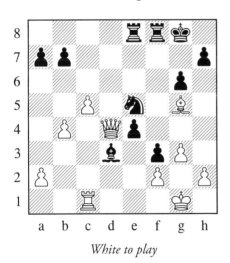

White to play

I played less well in the World Cup and only managed to progress to the third round by the help of Caissa (and maybe my opponents!).

3. Bacrot – Robson, Khanty-Mansiysk (1.3) 2011

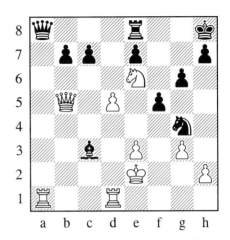

Black to play – find the best defence

4. Bacrot – Filippov, Khanty-Mansiysk (2.2) 2011

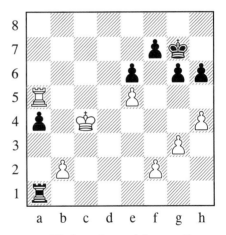

Black to play and draw easily

Finally my luck ran out in the third round and as I did not play well enough I went down.

5. Radjabov – Bacrot, Khanty-Mansiysk
(2.3) 2011

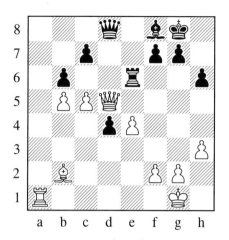

Improve on my play! Black to equalize

My final trip this autumn, leading up to this article, featured three tournaments back to back. As usual I excelled in a team competition, this time playing for Baden-Baden in the European Club Cup in Slovenia. Unfortunately we lost the last round when Adams lost on board one to Radjabov.

6. Bacrot – Wiersma, Rogaska Slatina 2011
(variation)

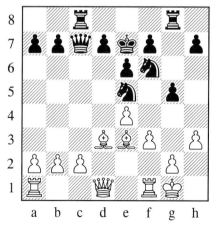

Black to play and draw

7. Postny – Bacrot, Rogaska Slatina 2011

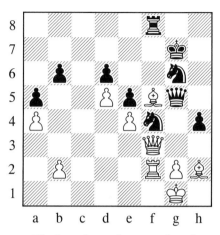

Black to play and secure a big edge

Right thereafter I travelled to Russia and won the Poikovsky tournament for the second time. Not in the convincing style of Morozevich, but on tie-break with a plus 2 score. Unfortunately I cannot compare to the Russian genius, still it is pleasant to win tournaments there!

In the penultimate round I missed a nice defensive tactic on move 40:

8. Bacrot – Rublevsky, Poikovsky 2011

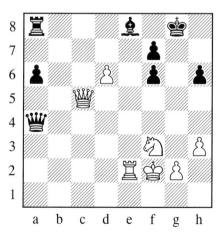

White to play and get a significant edge

However with a nice game in the last round it all ended as it should.

9. Efimenko – Bacrot, Poikovsky 2011

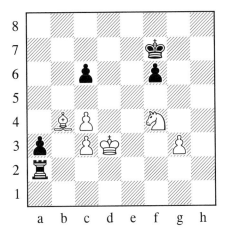

Black to play and win

After this I went to Germany to make a decent 2/3 in the Bundesliga, which is where I am at the moment, longing to get back to my family in Carqueiranne. But the Internet is like a big brother and Arkadij is skyping endless reminders to complete the material for the November issue, which brings us full circle back to the present.

Before I finish I want to show a few nice positions that caught my eye from recent events. The first is from my friend Sebastien Feller, who had a crazy game against Ray Robson, where he blundered in time trouble. I am sure you are eager to improve on his play?

10. Robson – Feller, SPICE Cup 2011

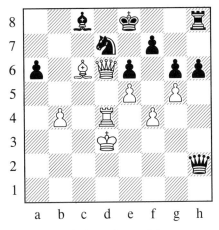

Black to play and draw

Endings

I have always been fascinated with endings and love analysing them. I came across a very interesting rook ending between Vachier Lagrave and Polgar. I analysed it for some hours to come up with the correct evaluation and found it quite fascinating.

I am offering you a few positions from my analysis as exercises. There are some tricky options available in this ending!

11. Black's 41st move

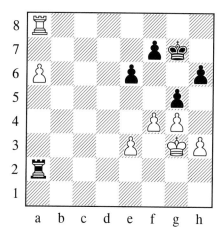

Black to play – what is the strongest move?

12. Note to Black's 43rd move

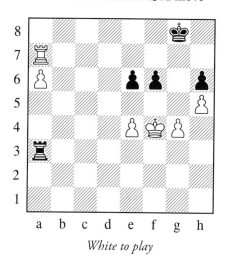

White to play

13. Note to Black's 46th move

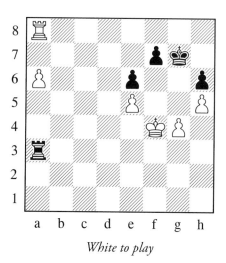

White to play

14. White's 48th move

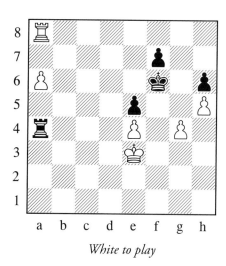

White to play

This has been quite a challenging essay for me to write. I hope it will be at least as challenging for the reader to solve these positions and not the least more enjoyable than it was to slave for Arkadij! Obviously I am just kidding. I will leave you with two final puzzles taken from my first round encounter in the World Cup with Ray Robson.

15. Bacrot – Robson, Khanty-Mansiysk (1.5)
2011 (variation)

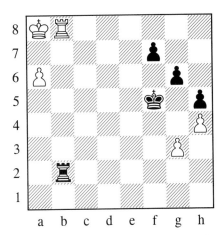

Black to play – calculate it accurately!

16. Bacrot – Robson, Khanty-Mansiysk (1.5)
2011

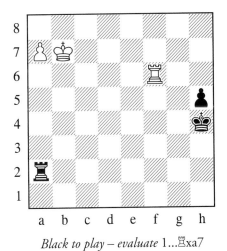

Black to play – evaluate 1...♖xa7

See you in January if I don't get fired!

Solutions

1. Fressinet – Bacrot, Caen 2011
1...♖b5! 2.♖c6 ♖a2 followed by ...♖b1 was winning. Instead I played 1...♗e6? after which the win became more difficult. In the end, of course, my opponent escaped a draw.

2. Bacrot – Vachier Lagrave, Caen 2011
Here I had the good feeling that opening the position would permit White to easily convert his extra material, but I chose to do it with the wrong break! **1.b5??** 1.c6! bxc6 2.♗f4 would have won the game and permitted me to win the championship. **1...♗xb5 2.♕xe4 ♘d3 3.♕d5† ♖f7 4.♖b1**

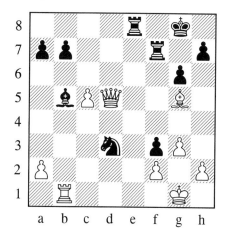

4...♘xf2! 5.♖xb5 ♘g4!! I missed this move completely when I played 1.b5??. **6.♖b1 ♖e2** Suddenly White should be happy that he can repeat the moves, despite being a queen up! **7.♕d8† ♖f8 8.♕d5†** A draw was agreed.

3. Bacrot – Robson, Khanty-Mansiysk (1.3) 2011
1...♗xa1!! A great move by my young American opponent. **2.♘xc7 ♕a2† 3.♖d2 ♖a8!!** The point. All other moves lose. **4.♖xa2 ♖xa2† 5.♔f1** The position is very unclear, with the most logical result being a draw. I was fortunate to win the game in a mutual time scramble.

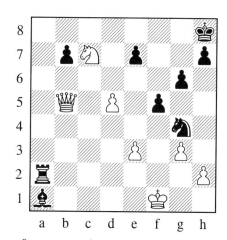

5...♘xh2†? 5...♔g7 was better to retain the choice of what knight move to make for the time being. **6.♔e1 ♔g7 7.♘e6† ♔f6 8.♕e8 ♘f3† 9.♔d1 ♖d2† 10.♔c1 ♖xd5 11.♘f4 ♖c5† 12.♔d1 ♗c3 13.♕f8† ♔g5 14.♕xe7† ♔g4 15.♕xc5 1-0**

4. Bacrot – Filippov, Khanty-Mansiysk (2.2) 2011
After winning the first game, my opponent could have drawn easily by three simple moves: 1...♖a2, 1...♖b1 and 1...♖c1. Instead he blundered horribly. **1...h5?? 2.b4!** An unpleasant surprise. Soon Black had to resign; the passed b-pawn supported by the king is too strong.

5. Radjabov – Bacrot, Khanty-Mansiysk (2.3) 2011
1...♕xd5?? Had I played 1...♕g5! the tie-breaks would only have been a few simple moves away. 2.c6 ♗c5 3.♖xd4 ♗xd4 4.♕xd4 ♕xb5= **2.exd5 ♖e5 3.d6 ♖xc5 4.♗xd4 ♗xd6** After 4...♖c4 5.dxc7 ♖xc7 6.♗xb6 ♖b7 7.♖a6 the white king will start his trip to c4, against which Black cannot defend. **5.♗xc5** This endgame is lost and no miracles allowed me to save it. Instead I had to go on a long journey back to France.

6. Bacrot – Wiersma, Rogaska Slatina 2011 (variation)

I luckily saw at last moment that I couldn't block the break with the otherwise obvious 1.f3?!, because of: **1...g4!** The following is forced for both sides: **2.fxg4 ♘fxg4 3.hxg4 ♘xg4 4.♗f4 ♕c5† 5.♔h1 ♕h5† 6.♔g1 ♕c5†** With a draw. Instead I played 1.♔h1 and won the game.

7. Postny – Bacrot, Rogaska Slatina 2011
1...♘xd5! 2.exd5 2.♕d1 ♘ge7∓ **2...♘e7 3.♕g4** 3.♗f4 gave more chances, but Black is better after: 3...♕xf4 4.♕xf4 exf4 5.♗e4 ♔h6∓ **3...♖xf5 4.♕xg5† ♖xg5** I soon won this endgame.

8. Bacrot – Rublevsky, Poikovsky 2011
1.♕f5? This obvious move fails to a nice trick. I could have obtained a big advantage with: 1.♖e7! ♗d7 (1...♔g7 2.d7 ♗xd7 3.♕d5 ♕c2† 4.♔g3 ♕g6† 5.♔h2 ♗xh3 6.♔xh3 should win) 2.♕c7 ♗b5 3.d7 ♕a2† 4.♔g1 ♕d5 5.♕c8† ♔g7 6.♖e8 and I think I should win this position. **1...♔g7!** This solves all of Black's problems. I even had to struggle a bit to make a draw. **2.♖e7** 2.♖e4 ♗d7! was the move I had missed. After this White cannot use the g4-square. **2...♖d8 3.d7 ♗xd7 4.♕d5 ♕c2† 5.♔g1 ♕xg2†** 5...♕b1† 6.♔f2 ♕b6† 7.♘d4 ♕b2† 8.♘e2 ♕b6† 9.♘d4= **6.♔xg2 ♗xh3† 7.♔xh3 ♖xd5 8.♖a7 ♖a5 9.♘d4 ♔g6 10.♘c6 ♖a3† 11.♔h4 ♖a4† 12.♔h3 h5** A draw was agreed in view of 13.♘b8 ♖a3† 14.♔h4 a5 15.♘c6 a4 16.♘e7†.

9. Efimenko – Bacrot, Poikovsky 2011
1...♖d2†! 2.♔xd2 a2 3.♗d6 a1=♕ 4.c5 ♕f1 and I soon won. White cannot establish a fortress.

10. Robson – Feller, SPICE Cup 2011
1...♕h3†! would have led to a draw. It is very important to keep control of the f3-square.

Instead Black played 1...hxg5? and lost after 2.♗xd7† ♗xd7 3.♕xd7† ♔f8 4.♕d8† ♔g7 5.♕f6† ♔h7 6.♕xf7† ♔h6 7.fxg5† ♔h5 8.♕f3†! ♔xg5 9.♕f6† 1-0. After **2.♔c2 hxg5 3.♗xd7† ♗xd7 4.♕xd7† ♔f8 5.♕d8† ♔g7 6.♕f6† ♔h7 7.♕xf7† ♔h6** Black is not worse.

11-14. Vachier Lagrave – Polgar, Hoogeveen 16.10.2011

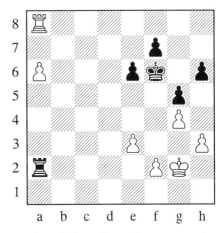

Rook and three kingside pawns each, with an extra a-pawn for the one side, but the rook in front of the pawn instead of behind it, is known to be a theoretical draw, but needs precise play from the defender, even if it is drawn by two tempos. Adding a pawn to the kingside clearly improves the advantageous side's possibilities. Still after thorough analysis, the conclusion is that Black should hold.

37.♖a7

A nice try. The rook is placed on the best square, preparing the manoeuvre ♖c7-a7 (after the sacrifice of a kingside pawn). If White was too impatient, he would have to play ♖c8-c6 instead in this case, as the pawn should not be pushed to a7 with the rook on a8 except for in rare circumstances where it just wins.

The king cannot come out immediately: 37.♔f1 ♖a1† 38.♔e2 ♖a2† 39.♔e1 (39.♔d3

♖xf2 40.♖c8 ♖a2 41.♖c6 ♔e5 42.♖c4 f5 easy draw) 39...♖a1† 40.♔d2 ♖a2† 41.♖c3 ♖xf2 42.♖c8 ♖a2 43.♖c6 ♔e5 44.♔b4 ♔e4 and the counter-play is strong enough to secure a draw.

37...♖a4?!

The immediate 37...♔g6, with the intention to meet 38.♔f1 with 38...h5 seems to be the most precise move order. White can also try 38.♔f3 h5 39.gxh5† ♔xh5 40.♔e4 ♔g6 41.f3 or play 38.♖a8 ♔f6, which leads back to the game.

38.♔f3

Why not give Black more problems by bringing the king out? The draw would look a bit more troubled after:
38.♔f1!? ♖a2!
    38...♔g6 39.♔e2 h5 40.♔d3 hxg4 41.hxg4 ♔f6 42.f3 looks very dangerous for Black.
    38...♖a1† 39.♔e2 ♖a2† 40.♔d3 ♖xf2 41.♖c7 ♖a2 42.a7 and White looks to be on top.
39.♔e1

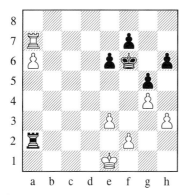

39...♔g6!
    This seems to be the only defence.
    39...♖a3 40.♔d2 ♖a2† 41.♔c3 ♖xf2 42.♖c7 ♖a2 43.a7 and White wins.
    39...♔e5? 40.♖xf7 ♖xa6 41.♔f1! and a second pawn is lost.
40.f3
Of course after Black has found the best

moves, White should play 40.♖a8! in order to try the same plan as in the game.
40...h5
Black seems to escape; for example:
41.♔d1 hxg4 42.hxg4 f5 43.gxf5†
    43.♖a8 fxg4 44.fxg4 ♔f6 45.a7 ♔e5=
43...exf5 44.♖a8 ♔g7 45.a7 ♖a1†
Black just gives checks and plays ...g4 at the appropriate moment.

38.f3 ♔g6 allows Black to draw in a similar fashion.

38...♖a2 39.♔g3

39.♔e4 also fails to win the game. The white king is not close enough to the a-pawn. 39...♔xf2 40.♖b7 (40.♖c7 ♖a2 41.a7 ♔g6 42.♔d4 f5=) 40...♖a2 41.a7 ♔g6 42.♔e5 f5 43.♔xe6 f4 44.e4 f3 45.♖b3 ♖xa7 46.♖xf3 ♖a6†=

39...♔g6 40.♖a8 ♔g7 41.f4

White tries what seems to be the best attempt.

41...♖a3?!

This is not losing yet, but it shows that Black has not found the (only!?) drawing plan. Optically 41...f5!! looks dubious, but with the white king blocked away, the pawn exchanges necessary to break him out would results in draw. Black just needs to be careful in the more tactical lines:

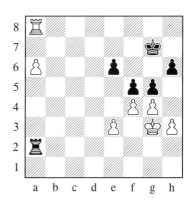

Now 42.♖a7† ♔g6 is no improvement for White, so we need to look at the following two options:

a) 42.a7 ♔h7

This is not the only way. For example: 42...♖a4 43.♔g2 ♖a2† 44.♔f1 ♔h7 45.♔e1 ♔g7 46.♔d1 ♔h7 47.♔c1 fxg4 48.hxg4 h5=

43.gxf5

43.fxg5 hxg5 44.h4 gxh4† 45.♔xh4 ♖a4 46.e4 fxg4 and White cannot recapture on g4 without losing the e-pawn – a draw.

43...exf5 44.h4

44.fxg5 hxg5 45.h4 f4†= (45...gxh4† also draws: 46.♔xh4 ♔g7=) 46.exf4 gxf4† 47.♔xf4 is a simple theoretical draw. This would also be the case if White is left with the g-pawn instead of the h-pawn.

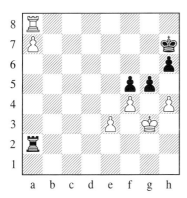

44...g4!

Black needs to be a bit careful. After 44...gxh4†? 45.♔xh4 ♖a3, White has a neat trick: 46.e4! fxe4 47.f5 e3 48.♔g3+–

45.♖f8 ♖xa7 46.♖xf5 ♖e7 47.♔xg4 ♖xe3 48.♖e5 ♖b3=

The defence of this pawn-down endgame is easy.

b) 42.♔f3 ♔g6 43.a7

Not the only move; let's look at some other white tries:

43.h4 gxh4 44.a7 ♔h7 45.♖e8 ♖xa7 46.♖xe6

h3 47.gxf5 ♖a2 48.♖e7† ♔g8 49.♖b7 h2 50.♖b1 ♔g7 51.e4 ♔f6 52.♖h1 h5 53.♔g3 ♖a3† 54.♔xh2 ♖e3=

43.gxf5† exf5=

43.fxg5 hxg5 44.♖a7 ♔f6 45.gxf5 exf5 46.♖a8 ♔g6 47.a7 ♔g7=

43...♔g7 44.♔g3 ♔h7 45.gxf5 exf5 46.e4

Other moves are analysed in the 42.a7 line above.

46...♖a3† 47.♔f2 ♖a2† 48.♔e1 ♖a1† 49.♔d2 ♖a2† 50.♔c3 g4!

After the white king has made it to the queenside, this pawn push equalizes.

42.♔f3

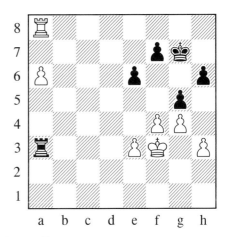

42...gxf4??

42...f5 would still have drawn the game in similar ways to the previous note. The line to check is 43.♔e2 gxf4 44.exf4 ♖xh3=.

43.♔xf4

The king now has easy access to the queenside.

43...♔f6

Black is lost, but should have made White's job more difficult with:

43...f6!!

An interesting subtle try, but now White changes his strategy and exploits that the 7th rank has been weakened.

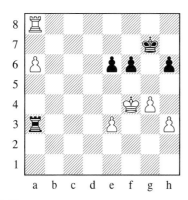

44.h4!!

This leads to a straightforward win. It is not clear if there are any other ways to win. The direct 44.a7 is probably a draw: 44...♖a5 45.♔e4 ♖a4† 46.♔d3 f5! 47.♔c3 h5! 48.♔b3 ♖a1 49.gxh5 e5 50.h6† ♔h7 51.♔c4 ♖a5 52.♔d3 f4 53.e4 ♖a2=

44...♔g6

44...♖a1 45.♖a7† ♔f8 46.g5+– and 44...♖a4† 45.e4! are no improvements.

45.h5†!

45.♖a7 ♖a4† 46.♔f3 f5=

45...♔g7 46.e4 ♔f7

46...♖a5 47.♖a7† ♔g8 48.♔e3 ♖a4 49.♔d3+–

47.♖a7† ♔g8

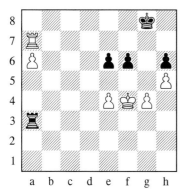

The white king seems to be blocked in, but...
48.g5!! fxg5† 49.♔e5 g4 50.♔f6 e5 51.♔g6 ♔f8 52.♖a8† ♔e7 53.a7 g3 54.♖g8 g2 55.♔f5 ♖xa7 56.♖xg2 ♖a3 57.♖g6+–

Black's pawns are doomed

44.h4 ♖a4† 45.e4

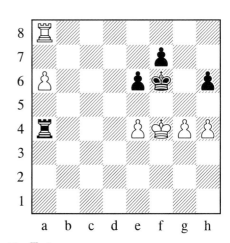

45...♖a5

45...♖a1 loses to the simple 46.e5† ♔g7 47.a7 and White takes the king to e7 and plays g5-g6, undermining the e6-pawn and eventually setting Black in zugzwang.

46.h5!

46.a7 e5†! resembles the game. White cannot exploit the fact that the pawn is still on h4: 47.♔e3 ♔g7 48.♔d3 ♖a1 49.♔c4 ♔f6 50.g5† hxg5 51.hxg5† ♔g7 52.♔d5 ♖a5† 53.♔d6 ♔h7 54.♔e7 ♔g7=

46...e5†

The best fighting chance was to cut off the enemy king:
46...♖a3! 47.e5†

Weaker is 47.g5†?! hxg5† 48.♔g4 ♔g7 49.♔xg5 f6†, when Black makes a draw: 50.♔f4 ♔h7 51.a7 (51.♖a7† ♔h6) 51...♖a5 52.♔e3 ♖a3† 53.♔d4 ♖a1 54.♔c5 ♖a6=
47...♔g7

Black looks solid, but White still has a winning plan here:

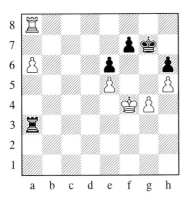

48.♖a7!!

Repeating the idea from move 37. White wants to give up a pawn on the kingside and put the rook on c7, in order to be able to push the pawn forward to a7 quickly.

48.a7 draws: 48...♖a4† 49.♔e3 ♔h7 50.♔d3 ♔g7 51.♔c3 ♔h7 52.♔b3 ♖a1 53.♔b4 ♔g7 54.♔c5 ♖a2 55.♔d6 ♖a3 56.♔e7 ♖a4 57.g5 hxg5 58.h6† ♔h7 59.♔xf7 g4=

48.♔e4 ♖a4† 49.♔d3 (or 49.♔f3 ♖a3† 50.♔f2 ♖a5 51.a7 with a draw) 49...♖xg4 50.♖c8 ♖a4 51.♖c6 ♔f8 52.♔c3 ♔e8 53.♔b3 ♖a1 54.♔b4 ♔d7=

48...♖a4† 49.♔e3 ♖a5

49...♔f8 50.♔d3+–

50.♔d4 ♖d5† 51.♔c4 ♖xe5 52.♔b4+–

Clearly Black's kingside counterplay will be too slow.

47.♔e3 ♖a4

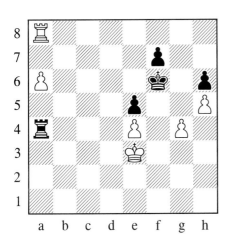

We have arrived at the most important point of the game – but only because Vachier Lagrave blundered horribly!

48.a7??

White must have made a horrible mix-up in his calculations. The win was easily achieved by activating the king:

48.♔d3! ♔g7

48...♖d4† 49.♔c3 ♖xe4 (49...♖a4 50.♔b3 ♖a1 51.♔c4 ♖a5 52.♔b4 ♖a1 53.♔b5 ♖b1† 54.♔c6 ♖a1 55.♔b6 ♖b1† 56.♔a7+–) 50.♖g8! ♖a4 51.g5† hxg5 52.h6 ♖xa6 53.h7 ♖a3† 54.♔b2 ♖h3 55.h8=♕† ♖xh8 56.♖xh8 Black is some tempos short of achieving a draw.

49.♔c3 ♖xe4 50.♔b3 ♖e1 51.♔b4 ♖a1 52.♔b5 ♖b1† 53.♔c5 ♖a1 54.♔b6 ♖b1† 55.♔a7 e4

White also wins after: 55...♖b4 56.♖b8 ♖xg4 57.♔b7 ♖b4† 58.♔a8 ♖a4 59.a7 f5 60.♔b7 ♔f6 61.a8=♕ ♖xa8 62.♖xa8+–

56.♖e8 ♖b4 57.♔a8 ♔f6 58.a7 ♔g5 59.♖b8 ♖a4 60.♔b7 e3 61.a8=♕ ♖xa8 62.♖xa8 ♔xg4 63.♔c6

And Black is too late.

48...♔g7 49.♔d3 ♖d4† 50.♔c3 ♖a4 51.♔b3 ♖a1 52.♔b4 ♖a2 53.♔c5 ♖a6 54.♔d5 ♖a5† 55.♔d6

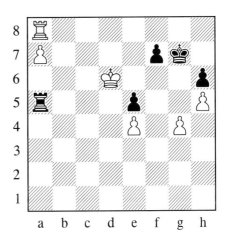

It is hard to guess what White believed when he went for this position. You could guess that it was a zugzwang, but now it is obvious that there is none.

55...♔h7 56.♔c6

56.♔e7 ♔g7 57.g5 hxg5 58.h6† ♔h7=

56...♖a1 57.♔b6

57.♖d8 ♖xa7 58.♖d7 ♖a4=

57...♖b1† 58.♔c5 ♖a1 59.♔d6 ♖a5 60.♖e8 ♖xa7 61.♖xe5 ♔g7 62.♖f5 ♖a6† 63.♔e5 f6† 64.♔f4

½–½

15. Bacrot – Robson, Khanty-Mansiysk (1.5) 2011 (variation)

I asked you to consider what would have happened had I played **1.♖b8!?.** Black draws like this: **1...♖a2 2.♖b5† ♔g4 3.♖g5† ♔f3 4.♔b7 ♖e2!** This rook shift decisively draws the game. After 4...♖b2† 5.♔c6 ♖a2 6.♔b6 ♖e2 7.a7 ♖e8 8.♖a5 White wins. **5.a7** Also after 5.♖a5 ♔xg3 is Black fast enough 6.a7 ♖e8 7.a8=♕ ♖xa8 8.♖xa8 ♔xh4 9.♔c6 ♔g3 10.♔d5 h4 11.♔e4 h3= **5...♖e7† 6.♔b6 ♖e8 7.♔c6 ♖e6† 8.♔b5 ♖e8=**

16. Bacrot – Robson, Khanty-Mansiysk (1.5) 2011

Instead I played: **1.a7 ♔g4 2.♖b8 ♖a2 3.♖b3 f6 4.♖b6 g5 5.♖xf6 gxh4 6.gxh4 ♔xh4 7.♔b7** Leading us to our final position. Black draws by a tempo if he knows his endgame theory (with these time controls it can at times be hard to find everything – or anything – over the board). Luckily Robson got it wrong at the absolutely last turn. **7...♖xa7† 8.♔xa7 ♔g3 9.♖g6†!** The standard trick, used to win a tempo. However it is not enough here. **9...♔f3 10.♖h6 ♔g4 11.♔b6 h4 12.♔c5 h3 13.♔d4 ♔g3 14.♔e3**

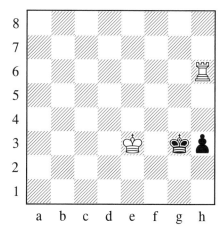

As ridiculous as it sounds, this position was reached five times in my database. Three players chose 14...♔g2! 15.♖g6† ♔f1, which draws easily. One player chose the equally strong option of agreeing an immediate draw! Only my poor opponent chose incorrectly and I was allowed to win the game after: **14...h2??** A famous mistake, often warned about in endgame theory. **15.♖g6† ♔h3 16.♔f2 h1=♘† 17.♔f3 ♔h2 18.♖g7 1–0**